W9-BJR-821

Language Files

Editors of Previous Editions

6th edition, 1994
Stefanie Jannedy
Robert Poletto
Tracey L. Weldon

5th edition, 1991
Monica Crabtree
Joyce Powers

4th edition, 1987
Carolyn McManis
Deborah Stollenwerk
Zhang Zheng-Sheng

3rd edition, 1985
Anette S. Bissantz
Keith A. Johnson

2nd edition, 1982
Carol Jean Godby
Rex Wallace
Catherine Jolley

1st compilations, 1977-79
Deborah B. Schaffer
John W. Perkins
F. Christian Latta
Sheila Graves Geoghegan

Language Files

Materials for an Introduction to Language & Linguistics

Seventh Edition

Editors

Nick Cipollone
Steven Hartman Keiser
Shravan Vasishth

Department of Linguistics
The Ohio State University

Ohio State University Press
Columbus

Library of Congress Cataloging-in-Publication Data

Language files : materials for an introduction to language & linguistics. — 7th ed. / editors, Nick Cipollone,
    Steven Hartman Keiser, Shravan Vasishth (Department of Linguistics, the Ohio State University)
        p.   cm.
    Rev. ed. of: Language files. 6th ed. / editors, Stefanie Jannedy, Robert Poletto, Tracey L. Weldon
(Department of Linguistics, the Ohio State University). © 1994.
    Includes indexes.
    ISBN 0-8142-5003-3 (pbk. : alk. paper)
    1. Linguistics. 2. Language and languages. I. Cipollone, Nick. II. Keiser, Steven Hartman. III. Vasishth,
Shravan, 1964-. IV. Ohio State University. Dept. of Linguistics.
P121.L3855   1998
410—dc21   97-51188
                                                                                        CIP

The paper used in this publication meets the minimum requirements of the American National Standard for Information Sciences — Permanence of Paper for Printed Library Materials. ANSI Z39.48-1992.

9   8   7   6   5   4   3   2   1

Contents

Contents

Preface to the Seventh Edition

The *Language Files* has grown from a collection of materials designed simply to supplement undergraduate linguistics courses into a full-fledged introductory textbook of remarkable breadth and depth. The comprehensive scope of the text makes it suitable for use in a wide range of courses, while its unique organization into instructor-friendly files allows for tremendous flexibility in course design.

The *Language Files* was originally the idea of Arnold Zwicky, who was among its first authors. Since the first edition, many editors have contributed to the development of the *Language Files*; the current edition is the result of this cumulative effort extending over twenty years.

As difficult as it may be to improve upon the work of the previous editors, in this seventh edition we have revised and updated several units and made extensive corrections throughout the text. We have completely rewritten the Semantics files and added two new files, Language and Gender (in the Language Variation unit) and Machine Translation (in the Language in a Wider Context unit). The introduction to the Language and Ethnicity file has been expanded to note the place of Ebonics in the larger discussion of AAVE. For those users of the *Language Files* for whom the International Phonetic Alphabet (IPA) is the norm, we have revised the Symbol Guide in Appendix C in order to provide a comparison of the symbols of the Americanist tradition with those of the IPA where the two differ.

A new *Language Files* home page has been created at http://ling.ohio-state.edu/files/files.html. This home page provides up-to-date links to language- and linguistics-related web sites, organized by topic. Finally, in order to facilitate feedback from users of the *Language Files*, we provide an electronic mail address, files@ling.ohio-state.edu, to which any suggestions, questions, and clarifications concerning this edition may be directed. Of course, any member of the Department of Linguistics at The Ohio State University can also be contacted in this connection by consulting the department's home page, http://ling.ohio-state.edu/.

Many people contributed to this edition. We are grateful to the students and faculty of the Department of Linguistics at The Ohio State University and to colleagues in other universities too numerous to mention here. In particular, we would like to thank the following people for their extensive comments and contributions to these files: David Dowty (Semantics), Bob Kasper (Machine Translation), and Norma Mendoza-Denton (Language and Gender). For invaluable help, comments, and suggestions, we are especially grateful to Allison Blodgett, Mike Cahill, Mike Calcagno, Kevin Cohen, Paul Fallon, Craig Hilts, Frans Hinskens, Tsan Huang, Martin Jansche, Stephanie Jannedy, Brian Joseph, Arlene Keeling, Matthew Makashay, Laurie Maynell, Claudia Morettini, Jennifer S. Muller, Jignesh Patel, Robert Poletto, Michelle Ramos-Pellicia, Craige Roberts, Elizabeth Strand, Jennifer Venditti, Pauline Welby, Don Winford, and Kiyoko Yoneyama.

Finally, we would like to thank the Ohio State University Press for their help, suggestions, and, above all, their patience. In particular, we are grateful to Ruth Melville for her careful and wide-ranging comments on our corrections and on the drafts of the new files.

Nick Cipollone
Steven Hartman Keiser
Shravan Vasishth

Department of Linguistics
The Ohio State University

Acknowledgments

The editors and publisher are grateful to the following sources for permission to reprint material appearing in:

File 2.2:
Adapted from Fromkin, Victoria, and Robert Rodman. 1978. "The Birds and the Bees." *An Introduction to Language.* 2nd Edition. New York: Holt, Rinehart and Winston: 41–45.

File 3.2:
Figure 1 from Lieberman, Philip, and Sheila E. Blumstein. 1990. *Speech Physiology, Speech Perception, and Acoustic Phonetics.* New York: Cambridge University Press.

File 3.9:
Figure 2 from Ladefoged, Peter. 1962. *Elements of Acoustic Phonetics.* Chicago: University of Chicago Press.

File 4.4:
Problems sets on Russian, Spanish, and Canadian French from Cowan, William, and Jaromira Rakusan. 1980. *Source Book for Linguistics.* Amsterdam: John Benjamins B.V.

Problem set on English from Akmajian, Adrian, David P. Demers, and Robert M. Harnish. 1984. *Linguistics: An Introduction to Language and Communication.* Cambridge, MA: MIT Press.

Problem set on Greek from Pearson, Bruce L. 1977. *Workbook in Linguistic Concepts.* New York: McGraw Hill, Inc. Reproduced with permission of McGraw Hill.

Excerpts of Tojolabal, Totonac, and Persian problem sets from *Descriptive Linguistics,* Workbook by Henry A. Gleason, Jr., copyright © 1955 and renewed 1983 by Holt, Rinehart and Winston, Inc., Orlando, FL, reprinted by permission of the publisher.

Problem set on Mokilese from O'Grady, William, and Michael Dobrovolsky. 1989. *Contemporary Linguistics: An Introduction.* New York: Saint Martin's Press, Inc.

Problem set on Sindhi from Ladefoged, Peter. 1971. *Preliminaries of Linguistic Phonetics.* Chicago: University of Chicago Press.

File 5.6:
Problem set on Cree from Cowan, William, and Jaromira Rakusan. 1980. *Source Book for Linguistics.* Amsterdam: John Benjamins B.V.

Problem sets on Isthmus Zapotec, Zoque, and Popoluca from Nida, Eugene A. 1949. *Morphology: The Descriptive Analysis of Words.* 2nd edition. Ann Arbor, MI: University of Michigan Press.

Problem set on Cebuano from Pearson, Bruce L. 1977. *Workbook in Linguistic Concepts.* New York: McGraw Hill, Inc. Reproduced with permission of McGraw Hill.

Problem set on Turkish from Akmajian, Adrian, David P. Demers, and Robert M. Harnish. 1984. *Linguistics: An Introduction to Language and Communication.* Cambridge, MA: MIT Press.

Excerpts of Swahili, Bontoc, and Hanunoo problem sets from *Descriptive Linguistics,* Workbook by Henry A. Gleason, Jr., copyright © 1955 and renewed 1983 by Holt, Rinehart and Winston, Inc., Orlando, FL, reprinted by permission of the publisher.

File 7.1:
Adapted from material by William Badecker and Thomas Ernst.

File 7.3:
Adapted from material by William Badecker and Thomas Ernst.

File 9.1:
Figure 1 by Carol Donner from "Specializations of the Human Brain" by Norman Geschwind. © September, 1979 by *Scientific American, Inc.* All rights reserved.

Figures in exercises 1.a–d adapted from illustration by Carol Donner from "Specializations of the Human Brain" by Norman Geschwind. © September, 1979 by *Scientific American, Inc.* All rights reserved.

File 9.2:
Adaptation of Lenneberg's characteristics from Aitchison, Jean. 1976. *The Articulate Mammal: An Introduction to Psycholinguistics.* London: Hutchison and Co.

File 9.8:
Chart adapted from Lenneberg, Eric H. 1967. *Biological Foundations of Language.* New York: John Wiley and Sons, Inc.

File 9.9:
Adapted from Clark, Herbert H., and Eve V. Clark. 1977. *Psychology and Language.* New York: Harcourt Brace Jovanovich, Inc.

File 10.2:
Figure 1 adapted from Jeffers, Robert J., and Ilse Lehiste. 1979. *Principles and Methods for Historical Linguistics.* Cambridge, MA: MIT Press.

File 10.5:
Excerpts of Proto-Tupi-Guarani and Proto-Western Turkic from Columbus, Frederick. 1974. *Introductory Workbook in Historical Phonology.* 5th edition. Cambridge, MA: Slavica.

File 12.4:
Figures 1–4 from Carver, Craig M. 1987. *American Regional Dialects.* Ann Arbor, MI: University of Michigan Press.

File 12.5:
Figures 1–3 from Burling, Robbins. 1973. *English in Black and White.* Orlando, FL: Holt, Rinehart and Winston, Inc. (Harcourt Brace Jovanovich).

File 12.6:
Adapted from sections of Zwicky, Ann D. "Styles." *Styles and Variables in English.* Timothy Shopen and Joseph M. Williams, eds. 1981. Cambridge, MA: Winthrop Publishers (Prentice-Hall).

Symbols

The following are some of the symbols used by linguists when studying language. Because linguistics is a diverse field of study, sometimes the same symbol is used in different ways, depending upon the language or topic being studied. Those different uses have been indicated here. For a comprehensive guide to the transcriptional or phonetic symbols used in the book, please see Appendix C.

→   In phonology "becomes"; in syntax, "dominates," or "is the mother of."

>   In historical linguistics "changes into."

[x]   'x' is a phone or allophone.

/x/   'x' is a phoneme.

*X   In synchronic linguistics, an asterisk marks an ungrammatical sentence; in diachronic linguistics (i.e., historical linguistics), it marks a reconstructed form.

X*   In syntax, any number of X's from zero to infinity.

X+   In syntax, any number of X's from one to infinity.

C   Any consonant.

V   Any vowel.

+   A plus sign marks the boundary between morphemes.

Ø   The null or empty set. Used in phonology to indicate the allophone or a phoneme that has been deleted. In semantics, this symbol may be used to indicate a set with no members (the set of all flowers that grow on Venus).

A number sign indicates a word boundary.

.   A period indicates a syllable boundary.

1

Introduction

Language fills every part of our lives; it gives words to our thoughts, voice to our ideas and expression to our feelings. It is a rich and varied human ability—one we can use without even a thought, that children seem to acquire automatically, and that linguists have discovered to be complex yet describable. This will be the object of our study.

File 1.1   Course Objectives

The thing we want you to draw from this course is a broad understanding of human language: what it is, what it's used for, and how it works. The purpose of this course is not to teach you to speak or write better, but the course should enable you to recognize an uninformed statement about language when you hear it. Five years after this course is over, after you may have forgotten all the definitions and phonetic symbols you will have learned in it, we hope the course will have left you with a sharper ear for language, a deeper understanding of its nature, and a livelier interest in all its manifestations.

The more immediate objectives of this course are:

1. To lead you to examine your own linguistic beliefs and attitudes.
2. To make you aware of both the diversity of language systems and their fundamental similarities.
3. To give you a reasonable taste of most of the subfields of linguistics: phonetics, phonology, morphology, semantics, syntax, pragmatics, historical linguistics, psycholinguistics, and sociolinguistics.
4. To equip you with some tools and techniques for linguistic analysis and to give you some practice in using these to discover the organizing principles of a language.
5. To acquaint you with the basic concepts necessary to further pursue linguistic studies, if you wish to.

General Conceptual Goals

Below is a list of some very general principles of human language that will be explained and illustrated throughout this course. Though the full significance of these characteristics won't be apparent to you at the beginning of the course, they are the underlying themes of many of the lectures you will hear and the assignments you will read.

1. Every language is enormously complex.
2. Despite this enormous complexity, every language is systematic, often in ways that are hidden and surprising. (General statements of the systematic relationships in a language are called rules.)
3. Not only is language systematic, but it is systematic on many levels, from the system of sounds to the organization of discourses.
4. This systematicity is sometimes hard to see, for at least two reasons:
   a. the very complexity of language obscures the patterns and regularities; and
   b. in actual speech, there are hesitations, errors, changes in midstream, interruptions, confusions, and misunderstandings.
5. Language varies systematically from person to person, area to area, situation to situation. There is variation at every level of structure. Speakers are not consciously aware of most of this variation.
6. Languages are diverse, often astonishingly so. There are surprising differences in the way individual languages are organized.
7. Despite this diversity, there are a great many universal properties of languages; that is, there are characteristics shared by all languages as well as characteristics no language can have.

8. Some properties of a language are arbitrary, in the sense that they cannot be predicted from other properties or from general principles.

9. It is not easy for speakers of a language to reflect on their speech; although a great many complex rules govern our speech, we are no more aware of them than we are of the principles that govern ball throwing or bicycle riding.

10. The attitudes that people hold about their language and other languages, or about their own speech and other people's, can be very different from the facts about them. These attitudes are often based on nonlinguistic factors and make an important field of study on their own.

11. Speech is the primary manifestation of language, and writing is only a secondary one.

12. Although children learn their first language, they cannot really be said to be taught it. They intuit the rules of their language from what they hear, guided by certain implicit assumptions about what language is like.

13. All languages change as time passes, whether speakers desire change or not; often they are not aware of it.

14. Linguists try to give accounts of the properties of a language that are both as precise and as complete as possible.

15. Linguists try to determine the ways in which all languages are alike and the ways in which they differ.

Therapeutic Goals

People have all sorts of beliefs about language, only some of which have been supported by the research of linguists. One of the incidental functions of this course is to correct misconceptions about particular languages and about language in general. Some of these misconceptions are harmless, while others are not; some of these beliefs could lead you to spend a great deal of time trying to change things that can't be changed or don't need fixing, and some can be used as instruments of prejudice against various groups. Here is a random list of misconceptions. Look over the list carefully. Some of the items you will readily perceive as misconceptions and will be able to explain why they're misconceptions. Others you may recognize as misconceptions without really being able to explain why. And still others you'll probably agree with. You may wish to refer to this list as the course progresses. At the end of this course, we hope you'll be able to look at this list and provide a cogent explanation of why these are misconceptions.

1. Writing is more perfect than speech.
2. Women generally speak better than men.
3. There are "primitive" languages with only a few hundred words.
4. French is a clearer and more logical language than English or German.
5. People from the East Coast talk nasally.
6. Homosexuals lisp.
7. People who say *Nobody ain't done nothin'* can't think logically.
8. Swearing degrades a language.
9. Kids need to study for years in school to learn to speak their language properly.
10. Some people can pick up a language in a couple of weeks.
11. It's easier to learn Chinese if your ancestry is Chinese.
12. Native Americans all speak dialects of the same language.
13. Some words, like *sapphire*, are naturally more beautiful than others, like *runt* or *stupid*.
14. The only reasonable way to arrange words in a sentence is to start with the subject and follow with the verb.
15. English is a simpler language than Latin or Greek.

16. Every language distinguishes singular nouns from plural nouns by adding an ending in the plural.
17. The only ways deaf people can communicate are by writing, by reading lips, and by spelling out English with their fingers.
18. People all over the world indicate "yes" or "no" by the same gestures of the head that we use.
19. Many animals have languages much like human languages.
20. You can almost always recognize Jews and Blacks by the way they talk.
21. Correct spelling preserves a language.
22. International relations would improve if everyone spoke the same language.
23. Japanese, Chinese, and Korean are dialects of the same language.
24. The more time parents spend teaching their children English, the better their children will speak.
25. There were once tribes of Native Americans that had no spoken language but relied solely on sign language.
26. Sloppy speech should be avoided whenever possible.
27. Eskimos don't have a general word for *snow*, therefore they can't think abstractly.
28. The more words you know in a language, the better you know the language.
29. Nouns refer to people, places, or things.
30. *It's me* is ungrammatical, bad English and ought to be avoided by educated speakers of English.

File 1.2 Major Subfields of Linguistics

Listed below are some of the major subfields of linguistics and the aspects of language with which each is especially concerned.

- **Anthropological Linguistics**. The study of the interrelationship between language and culture (particularly in the context of non-Western cultures and societies).

- **Applied Linguistics**. The application of the methods and results of linguistics to such areas as language teaching, national language policies, lexicography, translation, language in politics, advertising, classrooms, and courts, and the like.

- **Historical Linguistics**. The study of how languages change through time and the relationships among languages.

- **Morphology**. The study of the ways in which words are constructed out of smaller units that have a meaning or grammatical function.

- **Neurolinguistics**. The study of the brain and how it functions in the production, perception, and acquisition of language.

- **Phonetics**. The study of speech sounds; how they are produced in the vocal tract (articulatory phonetics), their physical properties (acoustic phonetics), and how they are perceived (auditory phonetics).

- **Phonology**. The study of the sound system of language; how the particular sounds used in each language form an integrated system for encoding information and how such systems differ from one language to another.

- **Pragmatics**. The study of how the meaning conveyed by a word or sentence depends on aspects of the context in which it is used (such as time, place, social relationship between speaker and hearer, and speaker's assumptions about hearer's beliefs).

- **Psycholinguistics**. The study of the interrelationship of language and cognitive structures; the acquisition of language.

- **Semantics**. The study of meaning; how words and sentences are related to the (real or imaginary) objects they refer to and the situations they describe.

- **Sociolinguistics**. The study of the interrelationships of language and social structure, of linguistic variation, and of attitudes toward language.

- **Syntax**. The study of the way in which sentences are constructed; how sentences are related to each other.

File 1.3   Speech and Writing

It is a very widely held misconception that writing is more perfect than speech. To many people, writing somehow seems more correct and more stable, whereas speech can be careless, corrupted (they believe), and susceptible to change. Some people even go so far as to identify language with writing and to regard speech as a secondary form of language used imperfectly to approximate the ideals of the written language.

One of the basic assumptions of modern linguistics, however, is that speech is primary and writing is secondary. The most immediate manifestation of language is speech and not writing. Writing is simply the representation of speech in another physical medium. Spoken language encodes thought into a physically transmittable form, while writing, in turn, encodes spoken language into a physically preservable form. Writing is a two-stage process. All units of writing, whether letters or characters, are based on units of speech, i.e., words, sounds, or syllables. When linguists study language, they take the spoken language as their best source of data and their object of description (except in instances of languages like Latin for which there are no longer any speakers). We will be concerned with spoken language throughout this course. Though ideally we would give our examples in audio form, for technical reasons we will instead use the conventional written or orthographic form, with the understanding that it is always the spoken form that is intended.

There are several reasons for maintaining that speech is primary and writing is secondary. The most important ones are the following:

1. Writing is a later historical development than spoken language. Current archeological evidence indicates that writing was first utilized in Sumer about 6,000 years ago. (What was once Sumer is in modern-day Iraq.) The Sumerians probably devised written characters for the purpose of maintaining inventories of livestock and merchandise. As far as physical and cultural anthropologists can tell, spoken language has probably been used by humans for hundreds of thousands of years.

2. Writing does not exist everywhere that spoken language exists. This seems hard to imagine in our highly literate society. But the fact is that there are still many communities in the world where a written form of language is not used, and even in those cultures using a writing system there are individuals who fail to learn the written form of their language. In fact, the majority of the earth's inhabitants are illiterate, though quite capable of spoken communication. However, no society uses only a written language with no spoken form.

3. Writing must be taught, whereas spoken language is acquired automatically. All children (except children with serious learning disabilities) naturally learn to speak the language of the community in which they are brought up. They acquire the basics of their native language before they enter school, and even if they never attend school they become fully competent speakers. Writing systems vary in complexity, but regardless of their level of sophistication, they must all be taught.

4. Neurolinguistic evidence demonstrates that the processing and production of written language is overlaid on the spoken language centers in the brain. Spoken language involves several distinct areas of the brain; writing uses these areas and others as well.

So what gives rise to the misconception that writing is more perfect than speech? There are several reasons:

1. The product of writing is usually more aptly worded and better organized, containing fewer errors, hesitations, and incomplete sentences than are found in speech. This "perfection of writing" can be explained by the fact that writing is the result of deliberation, correction, and revision while speech is the spontaneous and simultaneous formulation of ideas; writing is therefore less subject to the constraint of time than speech.

2. Writing is intimately associated with education and educated speech. Since the speech of the educated is more often than not set up as the "standard language," writing is associated indirectly with the varieties of language that people tend to view as "correct." However, the association of writing with the standard variety is not a necessary one, as evidenced by the attempts of writers to transcribe faithfully the speech of their characters. (Mark Twain's *Huckleberry Finn* and John Steinbeck's *Of Mice and Men* contain examples of this.)

3. Speech is ephemeral and transient, but because of its physical medium, writing lasts and can be preserved for a very long time. Spelling does not seem to vary from individual to individual or from place to place as easily as pronunciation does. Thus writing has the appearance of being more stable. Spelling does vary, however, as exemplified by the differences between the British and the American ways of spelling *gray* and words with the suffixes *-ize* and *-ization*. (The British spellings are *grey* and *-ise* and *-isation*.) Writing could also change if it were made to follow the changes of speech. The fact that people at various times try to carry out spelling reforms amply illustrates this possibility. (For instance, *through* is sometimes spelled *thru* to reflect its modern pronunciation more closely.)

File 1.4   What Do You Know When You Know a Language?

As a speaker of English, you know a great deal about your language, but suppose someone were to ask you to put all that knowledge down into a textbook to be used to teach English to others. You would soon find out that although you know perfectly well how to speak English, you are not consciously aware of most of that knowledge. Linguists are interested in this "hidden" knowledge, which they call linguistic **competence**. In this course we will be examining (among other things) the elements of linguistic competence—that is, what you know when you know a language.

But if linguistic competence isn't available to conscious thought, how can we find out what this competence is like? We can observe speakers' linguistic **performance** and draw conclusions about the knowledge that underlies it. You can think of linguistic competence as being a person's potential to speak a language, and his or her linguistic performance as the realization of that potential. Compare it with riding a bicycle. You can have the ability to ride a bike even when you're not using that ability and even though you probably aren't fully aware of all the complex motor tasks and feats of balance and timing that are involved. When you get on a bike and go, that's bicycling performance.

Now suppose you're riding along, and you hit a bump and fall off. That doesn't mean you're not a competent cyclist, even though your performance was impaired. Maybe you just weren't paying attention to where you were going, or a squirrel ran in front of your tire, or it was dark and you couldn't see well. Linguistic performance is quite similar; speech usually contains lots of mistakes and hesitations, but that doesn't mean that the competence underlying that speech is flawed. Since competence can't be observed directly, linguists use linguistic performance as a basis for drawing conclusions about what competence must be like. However, they try to disregard performance factors (the inevitable speech errors, incomplete utterances, and so on) and focus on consistent patterns in their study of linguistic competence.

So what are some of the things you know about your language? Here is a brief survey.

Phonetics

Part of your linguistic competence has to do with your knowledge of the sounds of your language. You know how to produce them though you may have never had to really think about the mechanics of doing so. Imagine, for instance, that you are trying to describe to someone else how the first sound in the word *the* is pronounced (*the*, by the way, contains only two sounds). Or suppose you had to explain the differences between the vowels in the words *bat, beat,* and *boot.* You have probably been producing these sounds for years without having to think twice about them. When you attempt to learn another language, you become acutely aware that other languages have sounds that English does not have—for example, French *r*, French or Spanish *p*, the German *ü* and *ö* vowels, the *ch* of German (which has more than a single pronunciation), or the clicks of some languages of Africa, such as Xhosa and Zulu.

Phonology

Not only can you produce and perceive the sounds of your language, you know how these sounds work together as a system. For instance, you know what sequences of sounds are possible in different positions. In words like *ptomaine* or *Ptolemy* English speakers usually omit the *p*, because *pt* is not a combination that can occur at the beginning of English words. There is nothing inherently difficult about this cluster, however; it occurs non-initially in many English words, such as *apt, captive,* and *lapped,* and some languages (such as Greek) do allow *pt* clusters to occur word-initially.

An even more dramatic demonstration of your inherent knowledge of possible sound sequences appears when you consider *Jumbles* and *Scrambles* from the newspapers. (These are actually concerned with unscrambling letters, not sounds, but the same principles apply.) For example, *gisnt* has five letters. There are 5! ($5 \times 4 \times 3 \times 2 \times 1 = 120$) possible arrangements of these letters. When you do a *Jumble*, however, you rarely consider many of the possibilities: you've probably already grouped *n* and *g* as *ng*, put the one vowel somewhere in the middle, and put *s* and *t* together in *st*. You don't even think of beginning words with *ng, gt,* or *gs* or ending them with *gnt* or *tn,* or even *gn* (this does occur, but it's rare and pronounced as *n*). Your inherent knowledge of what is a possible sequence of sounds in the English language enables you to eliminate these possibilities.

Your knowledge of phonology also allows you to make substitutions for unfamiliar sounds. Consider the sounds discussed earlier that are foreign to an English speaker. When we try to pronounce words containing such sounds, we usually replace them with sounds from our own language. For instance, English speakers often pronounce the German name *Bach* with a final *k* sound and replace the *ü* in German *grün* 'green' with the same vowel as in English *moon*. Or English speakers may ignore differences that are important in other languages but not in English, such as the tones in Thai and the Chinese languages.

Morphology

For the most part, speech consists of a continuous stream of sound with few pauses between words. Speakers, however, have little trouble breaking utterances down into the words that make them up. Thus an English speaker can easily analyze (a) as containing the sequence of words in (b), and a Welsh speaker can just as easily break (c) down into (d) (which means the same thing as (b)).

   (a)   Ihavetogohomeearlytoday.
   (b)   I have to go home early today.
   (c)   Rhaidimifyndadre'ngynnarheddiw.
   (d)   Rhaid i mi fynd adre'n gynnar heddiw.

You also know how to break individual words down into smaller parts that have a meaning or some other function, and you know how to create words by combining these smaller parts. For instance, how many parts are there to the words *desk, oranges,* and *unbelievability*? Can you produce an example of a word you've never heard or read before? You can certainly understand newly composed words—for example, *uncoffeelike*. As a speaker of some language, you know which such combinations are possible and which ones aren't. Compare *baker* with the nonword **erbake,* or *nicely* with **bookly* (the "***" is used to mark that something is ungrammatical—in this case, that it is not a possible word). What is wrong with these starred words?

Syntax

You can recognize well-formed—that is, grammatical—sentences:

    (a)   *You up pick at o'clock will eight.
    (b)   *I will picks you up at eight o'clock.
    (c)   I will pick you up at eight o'clock.
    (d)   At eight o'clock, I will pick you up.

Sentences (a) and (b) are ungrammatical; (a) is just nonsense and (b) violates the morphological condition imposed by modals that their verb complements appear in "bare" form. Sentences (c) and (d) are grammatical, and they are also syntactically related to each other. Why is (d) grammatical but (e) not?

    (e)   *You up at, I will pick eight o'clock.

       There is an important difference between the grammaticality of a sentence (whether it is structurally well-formed) and semantic acceptability (whether it makes sense). Below, (f) is structurally well-formed (compare it with the structurally parallel sentence in (g)), but semantically odd.

    (f)   Colorless green ideas sleep furiously.
    (g)   Contented little cats purr loudly.

Semantics

Part of your linguistic competence has to do with your ability to determine the meaning of sentences. Your competence also allows you to determine when a sentence has more than one meaning. Consider the following ambiguous sentences; what are the different meanings each one can have?

    (a)   I like chocolate cakes and pies.
    (b)   I'll meet you at the bank.
    (c)   Visiting relatives can be dreadful.
    (d)   I saw her duck.

You also know when different sentences mean the same thing.

    (e)   John is an unmarried male.
    (f)   John is a bachelor.
    (g)   The car bumped the truck.
    (h)   The truck was bumped by the car.

Above, (e) and (f) are synonymous sentences, as are (g) and (h). In addition, (g) and (h) are syntactically related (one is the **passive** of the other).

Pragmatics

Your understanding of the meaning of sentences and larger utterances also involves an understanding of how the **context** of those utterances influences their meaning. For instance, suppose you're a student in a classroom; there's a lot of noise out in the hall, and the instructor says to you, "Can you close the door?" Taken quite literally, this is an inquiry about your door-closing abilities, but you would probably not even think of taking the question in that way. Instead, you would understand it as a request that you close the door.

As a speaker of a language, you subscribe to unspoken conventions that enable you to use and interpret language correctly, though you may have never consciously become aware of these "rules." You also know how to use language to do things—to perform what are called *speech acts*. In the example above, your instructor performed the act of requesting you to close the door. Think about the many different ways you could use language to perform the act of, for example, finding out from someone what time it is, requesting information from someone, or giving someone a warning.

Styles of Speech

You also understand the contexts or situations in which different styles of language may be used. Suppose, for instance, you are explaining what it is you plan to do after college (a question most students are relentlessly subjected to). In what ways would your answer be different if you were talking to your roommate, to your parents, or to a prospective employer at a job interview? Speech styles can vary in pronunciation, vocabulary, and syntax, among other things. (Who are you more likely to use a sentence like this one with? *With whom is there a greater likelihood that one will employ a sentence of this genre?*)

You are also probably quite aware that not all speakers of your language talk in exactly the same way. Everyone speaks a dialect, and dialects can vary in subtle or striking ways. You can often draw conclusions about where a speaker is from, and you may make assumptions about their ethnic background or socioeconomic class based on the way they talk. Justified or not, most people have opinions about their own speech and that of others; though they may not realize it, these opinions are strongly influenced by nonlinguistic factors.

File 1.5

Prescriptive vs. Descriptive Rules of Grammar

To most people, the word *grammar* means the sort of thing they learned in English classes, when they were taught about subjects and predicates and parts of speech, and told not to dangle participles or strand prepositions. To a linguist, however, "grammar" means something rather different; it is the set of elements and rules that make up a language. Actually, linguists recognize three distinct things called "grammar."

The first kind of grammar is discussed in File 1.4. It is those aspects of a speaker's knowledge of language that allow him or her to produce grammatical utterances—that is, a speaker's linguistic **competence**. This kind of grammar is made up of knowledge of phonetics, phonology, morphology, syntax, and semantics. Everyone who speaks a language has a grammar of that language in his or her head, but details of this grammar will vary among dialect groups and even among speakers of the same dialect. Note that this grammar determines the structural well-formedness of utterances, not their appropriateness. You can imagine producing perfectly grammatical sentences that are pragmatically unacceptable or stylistically odd—for example, answering a question with a wholly irrelevant statement or using lots of slang on a graduate school application. Knowledge of pragmatics and language variation is not usually considered to be part of grammar proper, though it is an important part of your knowledge about language.

Linguists concern themselves with discovering what speakers know about a language and describing that knowledge objectively. They devise rules of **descriptive grammar**. For instance, a linguist describing English might formulate rules (i.e., descriptive generalizations) such as these:

1. Adjectives precede the nouns they modify.
2. To form the plural of a noun, add -*s*.
3. The vowel sound in the word *suit* is produced with rounded lips.

Descriptive grammar, then, is created by linguists as a model of speakers' linguistic competence.

When most people think of "grammatical rules," they think of what linguists call rules of **prescriptive grammar**. Prescriptive rules tell you how to speak or write, according to someone's idea of what is "good" or "bad." Of course, there is nothing inherently good or bad about any use of language; prescriptive rules serve only to mold your spoken and written English to some norm. Here are a few examples of prescriptive rules; you can probably think of others.

4. *Never end a sentence with a preposition.*
    NO: Where do you come from?
    YES: From where do you come?

5. *Never split an infinitive.*
    NO: . . . to boldly go where no one has gone before
    YES: . . . to go boldly where no one has gone before

6. ***Never use double negatives.***
   NO: I don't have nothing.
   YES: I don't have anything. I have nothing.

Notice that the prescriptive rules make a value judgment about the correctness of an utterance and try to enforce a usage that conforms with one formal norm. Descriptive rules, on the other hand, accept the patterns a speaker actually uses and try to account for them. Descriptive rules allow for different varieties of a language; they don't ignore a construction simply because some prescriptive grammarian doesn't like it.

So, if prescriptive rules are not based on actual use, how did they arise? Many of these rules were actually invented by someone. During the seventeenth and eighteenth centuries, scholars became preoccupied with the art, ideas, and language of ancient Greece and Rome. The classical period was regarded as a golden age and Latin as the perfect language. The notion that Latin was somehow better or purer than contemporary languages was strengthened by the fact that Latin was by then strictly a written language and had long ceased to undergo the changes natural to spoken language. John Dryden's preoccupation with Latin led him to write: "I am often put to a stand in considering whether what I write be the idiom of the tongue . . . and have no other way to clear my doubts but by translating my English into Latin." For many writers of the seventeenth and eighteenth centuries the rules of Latin became, whenever remotely feasible, the rules of English. The rules above are all results of this phenomenon.

Speakers of English have been freely ending sentences with prepositions since the beginning of the Middle English period (about 1100). There are even some instances of this construction in Old English. Speakers who attempt to avoid this often sound stilted and stuffy. The fact that ending sentences with prepositions is perfectly natural in English did not stop John Dryden from forbidding it because he found it to be non-Latin. His rule has been with us ever since.

Since the early Middle English period, English has had a two-word infinitive composed of *to* plus an uninflected verb (e.g., *to win*). English speakers have always been able to split this two-word infinitive by inserting words (usually adverbs) between the *to* and the verb (e.g., *to quickly hide*). There have been periods in English literary history when splitting infinitives was very fashionable. However, eighteenth-century grammarians noticed that Latin infinitives were never split. Of course, it was impossible to split a Latin infinitive because it was a single word (e.g., *describere* 'to write down'). But that fact did not prevent the early grammarians from formulating another prescriptive rule of English grammar.

The double negative rule has a different source. In Old and Middle English, double and triple negatives were common, and even quadruple negatives existed. The following sentence from Old English illustrates this; it contains two negative words and was entirely grammatical.

7. | ne | bið | ðær | nænig | ealo | gebrowen | mid | Estum |
   |----|-----|-----|-------|------|----------|-----|-------|
   | *not* | *is* | *there* | *not-any* | *ale* | *brewed* | *among* | *Estonians* |

   'No ale is brewed among the Estonians'.

By Shakespeare's time, however, the double negative was rarely used by educated speakers, although it was still common in many dialects. In 1762, Bishop Robert Lowth attempted to argue against the double negative by invoking rules of logic: "Two negatives in English destroy one another or are equivalent to an affirmative." Of course, language and formal logic are different systems, and there are many languages (e.g., Russian) in which multiple negation is required for grammaticality. Certainly no one misunderstands the English-speaking child or adult who says, "I don't want none." But Lowth ignored the fact that it is usage, not logic, that must determine the descriptive rules of a grammar.

It is somewhat surprising that rules that do not reflect actual language use should survive. There are several reasons, however, for the continued existence of prescriptive rules. First, they provide a standard form of a language that is accepted by most speakers of that language; adherence to prescriptive rules allows a speaker to be understood by the greatest possible number of individuals. This is especially important for a language such as German, which has dialects so different from one another that their speakers cannot always understand each other. Second, a set of standard rules is necessary for students learning English (or any other language) as a second language. Imagine the chaos if there were no guidelines for learning English (or Spanish, or German, or Russian, etc.). Thus they serve a very useful purpose for language teachers and learners as well. Finally, and most important, there are *social* reasons for their existence. Nonstandard dialects are still frowned upon by many groups and can inhibit one's progress in society. The existence of prescriptive rules allows a speaker of a nonstandard dialect to learn the rules of the standard dialect and employ them in appropriate social circumstances. Therefore, prescriptive rules are used as an aid in social mobility. This does *not* mean, however, that these judgments about dialects are *linguistically* valid. The idea that one dialect of a language is intrinsically better than another is simply false; from a linguistic point of view all dialects are equally good and equally valid. To look down on nonstandard dialects is to exercise a form of social and linguistic prejudice.

Exercises

1. Which of the following are prescriptive statements and which are descriptive?

   a. "It's me" is ungrammatical; "It's I" is the correct way to say this.
   b. People who say "ain't" may suffer some negative social consequences because many speakers of English associate "ain't" with the dialects of the working classes.
   c. In casual styles of speaking, English speakers frequently end sentences with prepositions; ending sentences with prepositions is avoided in formal styles.
   d. "Between you and me" is correct; "between you and I" is ungrammatical.

File 1.6   Arbitrariness in Language

It is generally recognized that the words of a language and the pieces that make up these words (all of which are discussed in some detail in later files) represent a connection between a group of sounds, which give the word or word piece its form, and a meaning. For example, the word for the inner core of a peach is represented in English by the sounds we spell as *p*, *i*, and *t*, occurring in that order to give the form pit. The combination of a form and a meaning connected in this way gives what may be called a **linguistic sign**.

An important fact about linguistic signs is that, in the typical instance in a language, the connection between form and meaning is **arbitrary**. The term *arbitrary* here refers to the fact that the meaning is not in any way predictable from the form, nor is the form dictated by the meaning. The opposite of **arbitrariness** in this sense is **nonarbitrariness**, and the most extreme examples of nonarbitrary form-meaning connections are said to be iconic. Iconic forms are directly representational of their meanings (for example, a deer-crossing sign). Moreover, the connection between form and meaning in such cases is not a matter of logic or reason, nor is it derivable from laws of nature.

Thus the fact that the inner core of a peach may be called a *stone* or even a *seed* as well as a *pit* points to arbitrariness in the above example, for if the connection between the form and the meaning here were nonarbitrary (because the form determined the meaning, or vice versa), there should only be one possible form to express this meaning. Also, there is nothing intrinsic in the combination of the sounds represented by *p*, *i*, and *t* that suggests the meaning 'inner core of a peach', for the same sounds combined in a different order have an entirely different meaning in the word spelled *t-i-p*.

Arbitrariness in language is shown by other considerations. For instance, it is usually the case that words with the same meaning have different forms in different languages and that similar forms express different meanings. Thus, what is *water* in English is *eau* in French, *Wasser* in German, *shui* in Mandarin Chinese, and so on. And the same form (pronounced like the English name *Lee*) means 'bed' in French (spelled "lit"), marks a question in Russian, and means 'meadow' or 'side sheltered from the wind' in English (spelled *l-e-a* and *l-e-e* respectively), as well as being an English proper name. If there were an inherent, nonarbitrary connection between form and meaning in all languages, with the meaning being determined by the form, then such cross-linguistic differences should not occur.

Similarly, the pronunciation of particular words can change over time (see File 10.3 on sound change). For instance, from a variety of evidence, including their spelling, we know that words such as *wrong*, *knight*, and *gnaw* must have had an initial *w*, *k*, and *g* respectively at some point in the history of English, and have thus undergone a change in their pronunciation, i.e., in their form. If we hold to the view that the form-meaning connection is determined and nonarbitrary, and if we further suppose that the original pronunciations of these words reflected this inherent and nonarbitrary relationship between form and meaning, then how can we maintain this inherent connection when the pronunciation changes without any accompanying changes in meaning? The relationship between the form and meaning of a word, therefore, has to be arbitrary in order to allow for the inevitable changes it may undergo.

It is clear, therefore, that arbitrariness is the norm in language, at least as far as the basic relationship between the form of a word and its meaning is concerned. At the same time, though, it turns out that there are many nonarbitrary aspects to language. Again, to focus just on vocabulary and the form-meaning connection (though nonarbitrariness can be found in other domains of language), notice that a small portion of the vocabulary of all languages consists of items whose forms are largely determined by their meanings. Most notable and obvious are the so-called **onomatopoetic** (or **onomatopoeic**) words, i.e., words that are imitative of natural sounds or have meanings that are associated with such sounds of nature.

Examples of onomatopoetic words in English include noise-words such as *bow-wow* for the noise a dog makes, *moo* for a cow's noise, *splat* for the sound of a rotten tomato hitting a wall, *swish* or *swoosh* for the sound of a basketball dropping cleanly through the hoop, *cockadoodle-doo* for the noise a rooster makes, and so on. Further examples include derivatives of noise-words, such as *cuckoo*, a bird name derived from the noise the bird makes; *babble*, a verb for the making of inarticulate noises derived from the perception of what such noises sound like; *burble*, a verb for the making of a rushing noise by running water derived from the sound itself, and so on. In all of these words, the matchup between the form of the word and the meaning of the word is very close: the meaning is very strongly suggested by the sound of the word itself.

Even in such onomatopoetic words, however, an argument for arbitrariness is to be found. While the form is largely determined by the meaning, the form is not an exact copy of the natural noise; roosters, for instance, do not actually say *cockadoodle-doo*—English speakers have just arbitrarily conventionalized this noise in that form. Moreover, when different languages imitate the same sound, they have to make use of their own linguistic resources. Different languages admit different sound combinations, so even the same natural sound may end up with a different form in different languages, though each of the forms is somewhat imitative. For example, a rooster says *cockadoodle-doo* in English but *kukuku* in Mandarin Chinese, even though (presumably) roosters sound the same in China as in America. If there were an inherent and determined connection between the meaning and the form of even onomatopoetic words, we would expect the same meaning to be represented by the same sounds in different languages. Thus, the strongest evidence for nonarbitrariness, namely, the existence of onomatopoetic words, is not quite so strong after all; in fact, comparison of such words in different languages can be used to argue *for* a degree of arbitrariness in linguistic signs. To make this point more clearly, we give below eleven natural sounds that are represented by onomatopoetic words in eight languages. The similarity among them is expected, owing both to the nature of the words and to the possibility of borrowing between geographically neighboring languages; still, the variation is also great.

Cross-linguistic Examples of Onomatopoeia

Sound	English	German	French	Spanish	Hebrew	Arabic	Chinese	Japanese
Dog barking	[bawwaw]	[vawvaw]	[wahwah]	[wawwaw]	[hawhaw]	[ʕawə]	[wãwwãw]	[wãwa]
Rooster crowing	[kakə-dudl̩du]	[kikəriki]	[kokoriko]	[kikriki] or [kokoroko]	[kikuriku]	[kikiki:s]	[kuku]	[koke-kokko]
Cat meowing	[miaw]	[miaw]	[miaw]	[miaw]	[miaw]	[maw-maw]	[meaw]	[niaw]
Cow lowing	[mu:]	[mu]	[mø:]	[mu]	[mu]	[ʕu:]	[mo]	[mo:mo:]
Sheep bleating	[ba:]	[mɛ:]	[be:]	[bɛ:]	[mɛ̃mɛ̃:]	[ma:ʔ]	[mɛ̃mɛ̃:]	[mɛ:mɛ:]
Bird chirping	[twit-twit]	[pip]	[kwikwi]	[pippip]	[tswits-tswits]	[zæg-zæg]	[čiči]	[čiči]
Bomb exploding	[bum]	[bum] or [vʀum]	[bʀum]	[bum]	[bum]	[bɔ̃m]	[bɔ̃ŋ]	[bãŋ]
Laughing	[haha]	[haha]	[haha]	[xaxa]	[haha]	[qahqah]	[haha]	[haha]
Sneezing	[ačuu]	[hači]	[ačum]	[ačuu]	[apči]	[ʕats]	[hačũ:]	[hakšɔ̃ŋ]
Something juicy hitting a hard surface	[splæt]	[pač]	[flæk]	---	[flox]	[ʔax]	[pyaʔ]	[gušaʔ]
Clock	[tɪktak]	[tɪktɪk]	[tɪktak]	[tɪktak]	[tɪktak]	[tɪktɪk]	[tiktɔk]	[čɪktakɯ]

In what may perhaps be considered a special subcase of onomatopoeia, it is often found that certain sounds occur in words not by virtue of being directly imitative of some sound but rather by simply being evocative of a particular meaning; that is, these words more abstractly suggest some physical characteristics by the way they sound. This phenomenon is known as **sound symbolism**. For instance, in many languages, words for 'small' and small objects or words that have smallness as part of their meaning often contain a vowel which is pronounced with the tongue high in the front part of the mouth (see File 3.3), which we will represent by the symbol [i]. This occurs in English *teeny* 'extra small', *petite* and *wee* 'small', and dialectal *leetle* for 'little', in Greek *mikros* 'small', in Spanish diminutive nouns (i.e., those with the meaning 'little X') such as *perrito* 'little dog,' where -*ito* is a suffix indicating 'little', and so on. Such universal sound symbolism—with [i] suggesting 'smallness'—seems to be motivated by several factors: first, the high, front vowel [i] uses a very small space in the front of the mouth, and second, [i] is a high-pitched vowel and thus more like the high-pitched sounds given off by small objects. Thus the use of [i] in 'small' words gives a situation where an aspect of the form, i.e., the occurrence of [i], is determined by an aspect of the meaning, i.e., 'smallness,' and where the form to a certain extent has an inherent connection with the meaning, even though not directly imitative in any way. We may thus characterize the appearance of [i] in such words as somewhat iconic—the "small" vowel [i] is an icon for the meaning 'small(ness)'.

In addition to such universal sound symbolism, there are also cases of language-particular sound symbolism, in which some sound or sequence of sounds can come to be associated in a suggestive way with some abstract and vague but often sensory-based meaning. For example, in English, words beginning with *fl-*, such as *fly, flee, flow, flimsy, flicker*, and *fluid*, are often suggestive of lightness and quickness. Also, there are many words in English that begin with *gl-* and refer to brightness (such as *gleam, glisten, glow, glint, glitter*, and *glimmer*), as well as a group of words signifying a violent or sudden action that all end in -*ash* (such as *bash, mash, crash*, and *flash*). In all such groups, an identifiable aspect of the form relates in a nonarbitrary way to the meaning.

Even in such cases, however, arbitrary aspects are again identifiable. Thus there are words which have the appropriate sequences of sounds but do not fit into the group semantically, such as *glove* and *glue* with respect to the *gl-* group, or *sash* and *cash* with respect to the -*ash* group. There are also words with appropriate meanings that do not fit in formally, such as *shine* or *hit*; note too that the English word *small* does not contain the "small" vowel [i], but instead a relatively "open" or "large" vowel (think about what a dentist or doctor might tell you to say in order to get your mouth open wide, and compare that to the vowel of *small*). Also, from a cross-linguistic perspective, it turns out that other languages do not (necessarily) have the same clustering of words with similar meanings and a similar form. For example, the Greek words for 'fly', 'flee', 'flow', and 'fluid' are *petó, févyo, troéxo, iyró* respectively, showing that the *fl-* sound symbol is an English-particular fact and so cannot be a matter of a necessary and inherent connection between form and meaning.

All in all, these examples show that nonarbitrariness and **iconicity** have at best a somewhat marginal place in language. At the same time, though, it cannot be denied that they do play a role in language and moreover that speakers are aware of their potential effects. Poets often manipulate onomatopoeia and sound symbolism in order to achieve the right phonic impression in their poetry; for example, Alfred Tennyson in his poem *The Princess* utilized nasal consonants to mimic the noise made by the bees he refers to:

> The *m*oan of doves in i*mm*e*m*orial el*m*s
> And *m*ur*m*uri*ng* of i*nn*u*m*erable bees   (v. 11.206–7)

Similarly, the successful creation of new words often plays on sound symbolic effects; for instance, the recently coined word *glitzy*, meaning (roughly) 'flashily and gaudily extravagant', fits in well with the group of English words discussed above with initial *gl-*. It seems, therefore, that even though arbitrariness is the norm in language and is an important distinguishing characteristic separating human language from other forms of communication (see File 2.1), an awareness of nonarbitrary aspects of language is part of the linguistic competence of all native speakers and thus is worthy of study by linguists.

Exercises

1. In what ways do compound words such as *blackboard* or *outfox* show a degree of nonarbitrariness in their form-meaning connection? Will this be true for all compound words? (Hint: think about the color of objects we call *blackboards*.)

2. In Chinese, expressions for moving from one city to another by way of yet another city must take the form 'from X pass-through Y to Z', and cannot be expressed as 'from X to Z pass-through Y'; this is illustrated in the examples below ('*' indicates that a sentence is unacceptable).

   a. *ta*   *cong*   *San Francisco*   *jinguo*   *Chicago* *dao*   *New York*
       he   from   pass-through   to
       'He went from San Francisco through Chicago to New York'

   b. **ta* *cong*   *San Francisco*   *dao*   *New York*   *jinguo*   *Chicago*
       he   from   to   pass-through

   How would you characterize the form-meaning relationship exhibited by these Chinese expressions?

3. Onomatopoetic words often show a resistance to change in their pronunciation over time; for example, in earlier stages of English the word *cuckoo* had roughly the same pronunciation as it has now, and failed to undergo a regular change in the pronunciation of vowels that would have made it sound roughly like *cowcow*; similarly, the word *babble* has had *b* sounds in it for over 2,000 years and did not undergo the sound shift characteristic of all the Germanic languages (see File 10.13) by which original *b* came to be pronounced as *p*. Can you suggest a reason for this resistance to change on the part of these (and similar) words?

4. One piece of evidence for sound symbolism is the often quite consistent responses that speakers of a language give to the judgment of the relative meanings of pairs of nonsense words, where the only clue to work from is the sound (i.e., the form) of the words. For example, speakers of English typically judge the nonsense word *feeg* to refer to something smaller than the nonsense word *foag*. Try the following experiment on a friend and then compare your friend's responses with your own and compare your results with those of others in your class.

   Pronounce the words below according to regular English spelling and decide for each pair of words which member of the pair could refer to something heavy and which to something light (you might want to ask if given a pair x and y, it is possible to say that "an x is a heavier y" or vice versa).

a.	lat—loat	e.	fleen—feen
b.	foon—feen	f.	seeg—sleeg
c.	mobe—meeb	g.	poas—poat
d.	toos—tace	h.	toos—tood

2

Animal Communication

The birds and animals are all friendly to each other, and there are no disputes about anything. They all talk, and they all talk to me, but it must be a foreign language, for I cannot make out a word they say.

MARK TWAIN, Eve's Diary

File 2.1   True Language?

Humans are not the only creatures that communicate. All varieties of birds make short calls and sing songs, cats meow to be fed or let outside, dogs bark to announce the arrival of strangers or growl and bare their teeth to indicate their intent to attack, and so on. The fact that other animals send and receive messages is in evidence all around us. One approach to determining the nature of language is to investigate the way other animals communicate and to explore the possibility that some species use a system that is fundamentally the same as human language. Most people assume that only humans use language—it is something that sets us apart from all other creatures. But is it possible that when we examine animal communication systems we will discover our assumption was wrong?

The task of comparing human language with various animal communication systems is not an easy one. First, we need a suitable working definition of "language" on which to base our comparisons. Unfortunately, no definition seems to adequately define language or be agreeable to everyone. One approach to getting around this problem, suggested by the linguist Charles Hockett, is that we identify some descriptive characteristics of language rather than attempt to define its fundamental nature. Then we can determine whether a particular animal communication system exhibits these characteristics as well. His list of characteristics, known as "design features," has been modified over the years, but a standard list is provided below. From what we now know about animal communication systems, we have found that none possesses *all* of these features, and thus we conclude that no nonhuman species uses language. Instead, they communicate with each other in systems called signal codes.

All communication systems have some features in common:

1. **A Mode of Communication**. This refers to the means by which the messages are transmitted. The mode of communication may be vocal-auditory, as in most human and most animal systems—the signals are transmitted by sound produced in the vocal tract and are received by the auditory system. The mode may be visual (e.g., apes' gestural signals), tactile (e.g., bees), or even chemical (e.g., moths).

2. **Semanticity**. The signals in any communication system have meaning.

3. **Pragmatic Function**. All systems of communication serve some useful purpose, from helping the species to stay alive to influencing others' behavior.

Some communication systems exhibit these features as well:

4. **Interchangeability**. This refers to the ability of individuals to both send and receive messages. Human language exhibits this feature because each individual human can both send messages (usually by speaking) and comprehend the messages of others (usually by listening). But not all animals can both send and receive messages. For example, the *Bombyx mori* (silkworm) moth uses a chemical communication system. When the female is ready to mate, she secretes a chemical that males can trace back to her. The males themselves cannot secrete this chemical; they can only be receivers.

5. **Cultural Transmission**. This is the need for some aspect of a communication system to be learned through communicative interaction with other users of the system. Human language exhibits this feature because humans must learn languages (even though the ability to learn those languages is innate). Thus a child of Russian parents will learn English if that is the language it is exposed to. In most organisms, the actual signal code itself is innate, or genetically programmed, so an individual can no more learn a code different from the one it is programmed for than it can grow an extra eye. However, in a few systems, including certain bird songs and chimpanzee signals, some of the signals seem to be genetically programmed or instinctive, while others are learned. Therefore these systems, too, exhibit cultural transmission. Humans, of course, must learn *all* the signals of their language.

6. **Arbitrariness**. This refers to the property of having signals for which the form of the signals is not logically related to its meaning (see File 1.6). The word *cat*, for example, does not sound like a cat or represent a cat in any logical way. We know what the word *cat* refers to because we learned the word as English speakers. If we were Spanish, the word would be *gato*, and if we were Russian it would be *koshka*. When the relationship between a signal and its meaning is arbitrary, then, there is nothing inherent in the form that designates its meaning. The meaning must be learned. Most animal systems use iconic signals that in some way directly represent their meaning, for instance, when a dog bares its teeth to indicate it is ready to attack.

7. **Discreteness**. This is the property of having complex messages that are built up out of smaller parts. Consider a sentence from a human language. It is composed of discrete units, independent words, which are in turn composed of even smaller discrete units, individual sounds. The messages in the animal communication systems with which we are familiar do not have this property. Each message is an indivisible unit. Even when some animals imitate human sounds so well, say parrots for example, these animals are merely memorizing a whole sequence that they reproduce, but they cannot break down the sequence into its discrete units. A parrot trained to say *Polly want a cracker* and *Don't go in there!* will never recombine the words of the sentence to say *Polly don't want a cracker* or recombine the sounds involved to say *Scram, rat!*

True language has, in addition to the above, the following characteristics:

8. **Displacement**. This refers to the ability to communicate about things that are not present in space or time. In human language, we can talk about the color red when we are not actually seeing it, or we can talk about a friend who lives in another state when he is not with us. We can talk about a class we had last year, or the class we will take next year. No animal communication system appears to display this feature.

9. **Productivity**. This refers to the ability to produce and understand any number of messages that have never been expressed before and that may express novel ideas. Human language is an "open-ended" system. However, in all animal communication systems, the number of signals is fixed. Even if some of the signals are complex (i.e., the system exhibits feature 7, discreteness), there is no mechanism for systematically combining discrete units to create new signals. These systems are thus called closed communication systems.

In the comparison of human language with animal communication systems, a debate has arisen about whether the two systems are *qualitatively* or *quantitatively* different. If there is merely a quantitative difference, then we would find an animal system that possessed *all* of these features, but some would not be present to the degree that they are found in human language. If, however, the two systems differ qualitatively, we would find no animal communication system that possessed each and every design feature. While this seems straightforward enough, there is still some disagreement on the application of this point.

Consider the feature of displacement, for example. It seems as if the bees' signal code exhibits this to a limited degree, since they communicate about food that is not visible while they are transmitting their message (see File 2.2). But note that we can "translate" the message of their behavior in a number of ways. We're in the habit of interpreting the bees' message as something like "there's a food source 40 feet from the hive at a 45° angle from the sun." In other words, our translation assumes they're relaying a message *about* a distant, invisible object. But the message can be represented differently—more simply, e.g., "perform this behavior now," that is, "fly 45° for 2 minutes." This is no different from most messages sent in animal systems. Think, for example, of a chimpanzee who adopts a grooming posture. This communicates the chimp's desire for another chimp to perform a particular behavior. The bees' messages are of this type—messages sent to alter the behavior of other individuals; their signals may not *represent* objects not present. Thus, some linguists claim the bees' system exhibits *limited* displacement, while others maintain it does not possess this feature in any degree.

At any rate, we say that a communication system must have *all* the design features to be considered qualitatively the same as human language, and no animal communication system has been identified to date that meets this criterion.

File 2.2 The Birds and the Bees

In File 2.1 it was claimed that no animal communication system is qualitatively the same as human language. No animal system with which we are familiar possesses all of the design features outlined in the previous file. In this file we will investigate two animal communication systems in detail, that of an Italian species of honeybee and that of the European robin, in order to support the claim that, although enormously complex, animal systems are quite different from human language.

Most animals possess some kind of "signaling" communication system. For example, among the spiders there is a complex system for courtship. The male spider, before he approaches his lady love, goes through elaborate gestures to inform her he is indeed a spider and not a crumb or a fly to be eaten. These gestures are invariant. One never finds a "creative" spider changing or adding to the particular courtship ritual of his species.

A similar kind of "gesture" language is found among the fiddler crabs. There are forty different varieties, and each species uses its own particular "claw-waving" movement to signal to another member of its "clan." The timing, movement, and posture of the body never change from one time to another or from one crab to another within the particular species. Whatever the signal means, it is fixed. Only one meaning can be conveyed. There is not an infinite set of fiddler crab "sentences." Nor can the signal be "broken down" into smaller elements, as is possible in any utterance of human language.

The "language" of the honeybees is far more complex than that of the spiders or fiddler crabs. When a forager bee returns to the hive, if it has located a source of food it does a dance that communicates certain information about that source to other members of the colony.

The dancing behavior may assume one of three possible patterns: *round, sickle*, and *tail-wagging*. The determining factor in the choice of dance pattern is the distance of the food source from the hive. The round dance indicates locations near the hive, within twenty feet or so. The sickle dance indicates locations at an intermediate distance from the hive, approximately twenty to sixty feet. The tail-wagging dance is for distances that exceed sixty feet or so.

In all the dances the bee alights on a wall of the hive and literally dances on its feet through the appropriate pattern. For the round dance, the bee describes a circle. The only other semantic information imparted by the round dance, besides approximate distance, is the quality of the food source. This is indicated by the number of repetitions of the basic pattern that the bee executes, and the vivacity with which it performs the dance. This feature is true of all three patterns.

To perform the sickle dance the bee traces out a sickle-shaped figure eight on the wall. The angle made by the direction of the open end of the sickle with the vertical is the same angle as the food source is from the sun. Thus the sickle dance imparts the information: approximate distance, direction, and quality (see Figure 1).

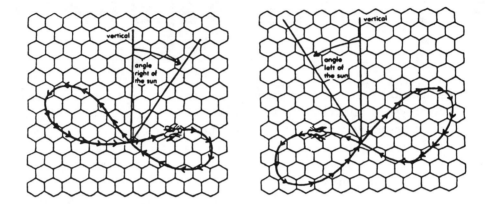

Figure 1.   The sickle dance. In this case the food source is twenty to sixty feet from the hive. Reprinted with permission from Fromkin and Rodman, *An Introduction to Language*, Second Edition (1978), p. 42.

The tail-wagging dance imparts all the information of the sickle dance with one important addition. The number of repetitions per minute of the basic pattern of the dance indicates the precise distance: the slower the repetition rate, the longer the distance (see Figure 2).

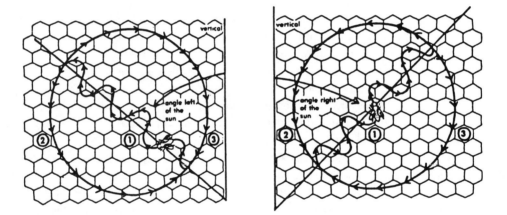

Figure 2.   The tail-wagging dance. The number of times per minute the bee dances a complete pattern (1-2-1-3) indicates the distance of the food source. Reprinted with permission from Fromkin and Rodman, *An Introduction to Language*, Second Edition (1978), p. 43.

The bees' dance is an effective system of communication, capable, in principle, of infinitely many different messages, and in this sense the bees' dance is infinitely variable, like human language. But unlike human language, the communication system of the bees is confined to a single subject. It is frozen and inflexible. For example, an experimenter forced a bee to walk to the food source. When the bee returned to the hive, it indicated a distance twenty-five times farther away than the food source actually was. The bee had no way of communicating the special circumstances or taking them into account in its message. This absence of *creativity* makes the bees' dance qualitatively different from human language.

The bees' dance does give us a chance to illustrate another very interesting property that every natural language of the world possesses, as previously discussed. We called this property the **arbitrariness** of the linguistic sign.

When we say that the linguistic sign is arbitrary, we mean that there is no connection between the linguistic form and its corresponding linguistic meaning (see Files 1.6 and 2.1). There is no connection between the sounds of the word *tree* and the concept "tree." Likewise there is no connection between a red light and the notion "stop—danger." The relationship in this case is a cultural matter. In all human languages the relationship between the sounds and meanings of the overwhelming majority of words is an arbitrary one.

What about the bees' dance? What are the forms of the sign, and to what meanings do they correspond? Are the relationships arbitrary or nonarbitrary? Consider the tail-wagging dance. One linguistic form is the vivacity of the dance, with a corresponding meaning "quality of food source." The relationship is clearly arbitrary, for there is nothing inherent about vivaciousness that indicates good or bad quality. In fact, we have been careful not to say whether more vivacity indicates a greater or lesser quality source of food. Because the relationship is arbitrary, there is no a priori way of telling.

What about distance? The question here is more complicated. Remember that the slower the repetition rate, the greater the distance. On the surface this relationship may seem arbitrary, but let's use a little physics to reword the relationship: the longer it takes to complete the basic pattern, the longer it will take a bee to fly to the source. Thus we see that this sign is in some sense nonarbitrary. Similarly, the direction-determining aspect of the dance is perfectly nonarbitrary.

It should be remembered, however, that there are many communication systems, other than language, which contain signs that are arbitrarily related to the meanings they stand for. "Arbitrariness" is not enough to make a system a language in the sense of human language.

We have talked about the "language" systems of spiders, crabs, and bees. What about the birds? It is known that the songs of certain species of birds have definite meanings. One song may mean "let's build a nest together," another song may mean "go get some worms for the babies," and so on. But the bird cannot make up a new song to cope with a new situation.

Two French scientists have studied the songs of the European robin. They found that the songs are very complicated indeed. But, interestingly, the complications have little effect on the "message" that is being conveyed. The song that was studied was that which signaled the robin's possession of a certain territory. The scientists found that the rival robins paid attention only to the alternation between high-pitched and low-pitched notes, and which came first didn't matter at all. The message varies only to the extent of expressing how strongly the robin feels about his possession and how much he is prepared to defend it and start a family in that territory. The different alternations therefore express "intensity" and nothing more. The robin is creative in his ability to sing the same thing in many different ways, but not creative in his ability to use the same "units" of the system to express many different "utterances," all of which have different meanings.

Bird songs, then, seem to be no more similar to human language than are the movements of the spider, the claw waving of the crab, or the dancing of the bees. All these systems are "fixed" in terms of the messages that can be conveyed. They lack the creative element of human language.

A study of higher animals also reveals no "language" systems that are creative in the way human language is. Wolves use many facial expressions, movements of their tails, and growls to express different degrees of threats, anxiety, depression, and submission. But that's all they can do. And the sounds and gestures produced by nonhuman primates, the monkeys and apes, show that their signals are highly stereotyped and limited in terms of the messages they convey. Most important, studies of such animal communication systems reveal that the basic "vocabularies" produced by either sounds or facial expressions occur primarily as emotional responses to particular situations. These animals have no way of expressing the anger they felt "yesterday."

The philosopher and mathematician René Descartes pointed out more than three hundred years ago that the communication systems of animals are qualitatively different from the language used by humans:

> It is a very remarkable fact that there are none so depraved and stupid, without even excepting idiots, that they cannot arrange different words together, forming of them a statement by which they make known their thoughts; while, on the other hand, there is no other animal, however perfect and fortunately circumstanced it may be, which can do the same. ("Discourse on Method")

Descartes goes on to state that one of the major differences between humans and animals is that human use of language is not just a response to external, or even internal, emotional stimuli, as are the grunts and gestures of animals. He warns against confusing human use of language with "natural movements which betray passions and may be . . . manifested by animals."

All the studies of animal communication systems provide evidence for Descartes's distinction between the fixed stimulus-bound messages of animals and the linguistic creative ability possessed by the human animal.

File 2.3 Primate Studies

Many species of animals have communication systems that are much more complex than one might imagine but that still appear to be very different from human language. The great apes (gorillas, chimpanzees, and orangutans), for example, communicate with facial expressions, gestures, and calls to express anger, dominance, fear, danger, acceptance in a group, and the like. But the precise meanings of the various expressions of a particular band of apes are by no means easy for the human outsider to decode. As complex as these systems are, they nevertheless lack displacement and productivity. Apes apparently do not communicate about things that are not physically present, nor can they combine their independent gestures or calls in novel ways to create new meanings.

The great apes are, however, very intelligent creatures and *Homo sapiens'* nearest relatives in the animal kingdom. Chimpanzees, for example, are said to share 99% of their genetic material with human beings. This biological similarity of ape and human, as well as the apes' intelligence, has prompted some scientists to wonder if language could be taught to apes, even though it does not occur naturally. Many such projects have been conducted, most in the past twenty years or so. The ape used most often has been the chimpanzee because it is considered by many to be the most intelligent of the great apes and the most social, and the easiest to procure and handle. An orangutan and a gorilla have also been used.

These experiments have generated both exuberance and disappointment and, since their inception, a debate about their results that continues to the present day. On the one hand, there are still some scientists who maintain that they have indeed taught an ape human language. On the other, there are many scientists who dispute this claim and have proposed alternative explanations for the behaviors some researchers assumed could only have been language use. We will return to this debate later.

Early Projects

The first such experiment conducted in the United States was in the 1930s. W. N. and L. A. Kellogg wanted to raise a baby chimpanzee in a human environment to determine if the chimp would acquire language on its own, just as a human child does, by virtue merely of being exposed to it. They therefore decided not to give training or "forcible teaching" to the chimp they acquired at 7 1/2 months and whom they named Gua, other than that which would be given a human infant. Gua was raised alongside the Kelloggs' newborn son, Donald, and the development of the chimp was compared to the boy's. W. Kellogg stated that his intent was to determine how much of human language ability derived from heredity and how much from education. He reasoned, a bit naively in retrospect, that what the chimp could not learn would be those aspects of language that a human inherently knows. Kellogg admitted one violation of this program when at one point he attempted to mold Gua's lips in an effort to teach her to say *papa*. This effort, lasting several months, proved unsuccessful. The duration of the Kelloggs' experiment was rather short (only nine months) in comparison to those that were to follow.

In the 1950s Keith and Cathy Hayes decided to raise Viki, a female chimp, also as much like a human child as possible, believing that with the proper upbringing a chimp could learn language. The Hayeses believed that they could teach Viki to speak, even though doubt was emerging among scientists at the time about whether the chimpanzee's vocal anatomy could even produce human speech sounds. The Hayes, however, believed that the vocal tract of the chimp was similar enough to a human's for it to be able to articulate human sounds. They had no aversion to "training," and their program included first teaching Viki to vocalize on demand (this alone took five weeks), and then shaping her lips with their hands into various configurations that yielded consonant sounds. After three years, Viki could "speak" three words: *cup, mama,* and *papa,* although they were accompanied by a "heavy chimp accent"; it sounded as if Viki were only whispering. The Hayeses reported that Viki could, however, "understand" many words, but they offered no experimental proof of this. The Kelloggs' and Hayeses' experiments were not viewed by scientists as successful attempts to teach language to apes.

Three words are not very many when one is trying to prove human language capability. Allen and Beatrice Gardner believed, contrary to the Hayeses, that chimps were not capable of producing human speech sounds, so trying to teach a chimp to speak was fruitless. But since chimps are manually dexterous and use gestures to communicate naturally, the Gardners decided to teach American Sign Language (ASL) to a chimp they named Washoe. Washoe was not raised as a human infant but was brought up with minimal confinement in a stimulating atmosphere. Spoken English was not allowed in her presence; the Gardners feared she would come to understand spoken language first and not be motivated to learn ASL. She also received deliberate training. Objects were presented to Washoe and the trainers molded Washoe's hands into the shapes for their signs. Eventually, in order to be rewarded, she had to produce the signs herself and with greater and greater accuracy. The experiment was considered at the time to be a great success. By the time Washoe was five years old, she had acquired 132 signs. More important, she had supposedly invented her own novel combinations, such as *dirty Roger,* where *dirty* was used as an expletive, and *water bird,* upon seeing a swan on a lake.

The Gardners' insight about the vocal limitations of the chimp has been noted by every researcher since them. Subsequent endeavors have all involved either ASL or invented languages that used visual signs such as plastic chips or "lexigrams," symbols composed of geometric shapes.

In 1972 Francine Patterson began to teach ASL to a gorilla named Koko. This project has been one of the longest of its kind, and Patterson has made some of the most dramatic claims for such a project's success. According to Patterson, Koko knows several hundred signs and has invented many of her own combinations, such as *finger bracelet* for 'ring'. In addition, she supposedly understands spoken English—so well, in fact, that Koko occasionally rhymes, putting together such signs as *bear* and *hair* even though the signs themselves have no visual similarity to each other. Koko also substitutes homonyms for words when she cannot think of the sign, such as *eye* for *I* or *know* for *no*. Koko also supposedly uses her signs to insult people and things she doesn't like. After being reprimanded one day, for example, Koko is said to have called Patterson a *dirty toilet devil*. Patterson's most astounding claim, however, is that "Koko is the first of her species to have acquired human language."

Anne and David Premack began in 1966 to work with a chimpanzee named Sarah. Their methods were quite a bit different from those discussed above. Rather than treat the chimp like a human child, David Premack decided to try to find and use the best possible training procedure. The "language" used was also atypical. Instead of ASL, Premack used differently shaped and colored plastic chips. With each chip he arbitrarily associated an English word. Communication between the trainers and Sarah involved placing these chips on the "language board." Sarah was taught how to do one type of "sentence" at a time. Typically, her task was to choose an appropriate chip from a choice of two or to carry out a task indicated on the language board. Premack intended to teach Sarah the names of objects as well as the names of categories of objects. He originally claimed to have taught her 130 signs, including category names such as *color* and concepts such as *same* and *different*.

Duane Rumbaugh wanted to design an ape language experiment with as much of the training taken out of the hands of human trainers as possible. He reasoned that if the training were automated, one could avoid cueing the animal and the training could be more efficient and constant and require fewer humans, thus leaving more time for experimental verification of claims. He and his associates designed a computer that could execute certain commands, such as dispensing food or displaying slides, in response to an operator lighting up the proper symbols. The symbols of this invented "language" were **lexigrams**—various combinations of nine different geometric figures, such as a big circle, a little circle, and a large X. The operator of the machine was, of course, a chimp; her name was Lana. Lana did learn to use her keyboard quite well, and Rumbaugh initially thought that he had succeeded in teaching a chimp some human language.

Criticisms of the Early Projects

The results and conclusions of these projects have been critically questioned on two fronts. In the late 1970s, Herbert Terrace began a project similar to that of the Gardners' with a chimpanzee he humorously named Nim Chimpsky (hoping that when Nim learned language, the joke would be on Noam Chomsky, the noted linguist who claimed such a thing was impossible). Terrace's concern was to prove that a chimp could acquire and display some use of grammar. Terrace believed, as did most researchers at this time, that evidence of human language capability was the use of grammar and not just the use of signs. (Current researchers are concentrating on the way signs are used by animals.) By the time Nim was four years old, he had acquired 125 signs, and Terrace felt Nim had indeed acquired human language abilities as well. This project was the first to videotape all interactions between chimp and trainer, however, and it was by reviewing these tapes that Terrace decided he must reverse his initial claim and instead acknowledge that the ape's use of signs was very different from human language. He noted that there were many dissimilarities between Nim's and a human child's acquisition of "language." Nim, for example, almost never initiated signing. Upon reviewing the tapes, Terrace found that only 12% of Nim's signs were spontaneous and a full 40% were mere repetitions of what the trainer had just signed. This subtle interaction was never noticed by the trainer at the time. In addition, Nim's signing was invariably a request for food or social reward; he never made unsolicited statements or asked questions. Quite unlike a human child, he never took turns and was more likely to interrupt his trainer's signing than not. There was also no evidence that Nim knew any grammar. His combinations had variable word order, and more importantly, Nim rarely went beyond two-word combinations; even when he did, the additional signs added no new information. For example, Nim's longest utterance was *give orange me give eat orange me eat orange give me eat orange give me you.*

Terrace called into question the results of all previous experiments. He reviewed tapes of Washoe and Koko that had been made for a PBS special and concluded that they too had been cued by their trainers. He and others leveled even more serious criticisms of the Premack project, arguing that the training procedure taught problem solving and not language, and that Premack's conclusions were not well founded, given his experimental design and his results. Consider Premack's claim that Sarah learned the word *insert*. As proof of this Premack offered that in one task, when Sarah saw *Sarah banana pail insert* on her language board, she correctly executed the task. When the word *insert* was tested against the word *give*, however, Sarah could not distinguish the two. Premack likewise claimed Sarah knew the prepositions *on* and *in* but never administered a test where Sarah would have to distinguish one from the other. Following instructions did not have to involve Sarah understanding a sentence on the language board, but rather recognizing, for example, a banana chip and a pail chip and imitating what she had been trained to do in the first stage of the test—in this case, insert the banana *in* the pail (a banana couldn't go *on* an upright pail.)

Current Projects

Terrace's revelations had a great effect on the field of animal language studies. Funding for projects was thereafter hard to come by, and many scientists responded with new cynicism to any and all claims of animal language researchers. Sue Savage-Rumbaugh maintains that both the initial easy acceptance of claims in this field and the post-Terrace cynicism are too extreme. She has begun another project with several chimpanzees and believes she has made the first real progress ever in teaching some human language skills to an ape. She has, however, leveled a different criticism against previous ape language studies. She believes that looking for evidence of grammatical capabilities in apes was far too premature. She has considered a more fundamental and critical question: when apes use a sign, do they know what it *means*?

This question is by no means easy to answer and it is ironic that the early researchers in this field took it for granted that when an ape produced a sign, it was using it in the same way humans do, as an arbitrary symbol to represent something. It is precisely this use of the symbol that Savage-Rumbaugh has considered and researched. Note that this approach represents a departure from the attempt to assess animal language capabilities in terms of descriptive "design features," such as productivity and displacement.

Human language does have these features that distinguish it from other communication systems, but a more fundamental difference is perhaps that of symbol use. Understanding the concept of *symbol* is difficult, partly because symbol use is innate to us. The use of a symbol involves a special relationship with at least three components. First, there is the physical, external substance of a word such as *tree*—either ink on a page in the shape of the letters *t–r–e–e* or a spoken word with a particular acoustic pattern. Second, it has a relationship to a real tree somewhere, which is sometimes known as the **referent** because the word *tree* refers to it. But, as you will see in File 7.1, not every word has a referent (e.g., *love, Martian, Godzilla*). The important relationship involved in a symbol is the mental representation we have for the word *tree*, an idea of *tree* that is called up when we hear, say, or see the word *tree*. Note that "mental representation" does not mean "image" or "picture"—not every word can have one of these either. Whereas one might be hard pressed to say what the referent or mental "image" of words such as "silly" or "love" is, we certainly possess some mental representation associated with them—an idea of what each means. Mental representations have an existence separate from their referents and can be manipulated independently of them. Thus we can think and talk about things that are not present; in fact, we can talk about things that don't even exist (e.g., unicorns).

No one disputes that humans use their words in this way. But how are we to know if an ape, when it uses a sign in the same way we might, really has a mental representation for it? Savage-Rumbaugh has suggested that in all previous experiments apes were not using their signs symbolically. Apes had merely learned to associate certain behaviors (making or seeing a particular sign) with certain consequences (e.g., getting something to eat)—similar to a dog, for example, which, upon hearing the word *walk*, knows it's going to get to go for a walk. This is an extremely subtle distinction for humans to perceive, since the use of symbols comes naturally to us. We interpret other creatures' signals to us in the same way we interpret those from each other, but that doesn't necessarily mean they're intended in the same way. For this reason Savage-Rumbaugh has pointed out the necessity of proper experiments that prove the ape has truly acquired a word in the same way a human has. She has criticized the claims of previous projects either because they were not based on testing with proper controls or because they had not been tested at all.

How is one to find evidence of a mental phenomenon? One must still find it in the behavior of the animal, or in the "processes of the exchange" with the trainer, but one must be more discriminating about what counts as evidence. In addition, Savage-Rumbaugh reasoned, apes had not learned to use symbols given the training techniques used previously, which had assumed the symbol aspect of sign use would come naturally to the ape; therefore, apes must specifically and intentionally be taught this first.

Savage-Rumbaugh and her colleagues have worked extensively with two male chimpanzees, Sherman and Austin, attempting to teach them language skills with the computer and the language of lexigrams used with Lana. They have found that the use of symbols by humans is not a single holistic phenomenon but is a complex of independent abilities and behaviors. For example, the ability to produce a symbol was found to be composed of at least three separate abilities. Using the association of a lexigram and an object to *request* the object is one of these (and a display of it does not prove the user has a mental representation for the symbol). *Naming* is another behavior that involves giving the lexigram associated with an object without expecting to consume or receive it. The third ability involved in production is called *comprehension* of the symbol. One might find it difficult to separate these three, but to the chimpanzee they all had to be taught separately, and the presence of one ability could not be assumed because of the presence of another. Savage-Rumbaugh points out the extreme importance of another aspect of symbol use and human communication that had previously been overlooked: that of the role of the receiver or listener. This in itself was also found to be a complex of skills and behaviors, each of which had to be taught separately to Sherman and Austin.

Savage-Rumbaugh claims to have been successful at teaching the chimps these skills as well as the links between them (the coordination of these occurs naturally in humans). She has conducted numerous experiments that indicate that the skills, as she has described them, have indeed been acquired. She has acknowledged Terrace's criticisms of other projects but maintains that Sherman and Austin do not evidence Nim's shortcomings. They take turns, their utterances are not imitations of their trainers, and supposedly they produce messages not only because they must, but because they wish to make statements.

This project certainly has made real progress both in clarifying what human language skills are and in teaching them to apes. Criticisms have been leveled, of course. Some suggest that, again, the apes have been skillfully trained and still do not comprehend what they are saying or use their signs symbolically. After all, it is perhaps impossible to know if another creature has a mental representation for a word; we couldn't see it even if we opened up its brain. Savage-Rumbaugh might respond that this criticism is a reflection of a cynical attitude rather than scientific considerations. However, given past experience and the tendency to overinterpret, there is a need to scrutinize the newest claims in this field.

Savage-Rumbaugh's most recently begun project must be mentioned. She has started to work with another species of chimpanzee, *Pan paniscus*, which she claims is more intelligent than *Pan troglodytes*, which has been used in all other projects. She claims that the new chimp she has been working with, Kanzi, has learned to comprehend spoken English just by being exposed to it and has spontaneously begun to use the keyboard with lexigrams to make requests and comment on his environment. Savage-Rumbaugh reports both anecdotal observations and the results of tests that might substantiate these astonishing claims. Again, these newest claims are difficult to accept without further confirmation and the demonstration of the kind of objective scrutiny and testing that was advocated at the inception of the Sherman and Austin project.

3

Phonetics

Phonetics is the study of speech sounds. This field, an experimental science, can be subdivided into three areas: the study of the production (articulatory phonetics), the perception (auditory phonetics), and the physical properties (acoustic phonetics) of speech sounds. Descriptions of the world's speech sounds are based on precise measurements of their physical or acoustic properties as well as on the movements of the various articulators.

File 3.1

The Sounds of Speech

Although languages can in principle use modes of communication other than sound (for instance, visual signals) to convey meaning, it is nevertheless true that most human languages are spoken. This may not be an accident: some theorists have claimed that using the vocal apparatus for language freed human hands to engage in other activities and thus had survival value in the evolution of the species. **Phonetics** is the study of speech sounds, which are known more technically as **phones**.

A whole chain of activities is involved in communicating meaning by sound. First of all, a speaker encodes meaning into sounds, which he or she produces using the tongue, lips, and other articulatory organs. These sounds are transmitted through the air to reach the hearer. Then the hearer perceives them through auditory processes, finally translating them back into meaning. There are therefore three aspects to the study of speech sounds: **articulatory phonetics**, the study of the production of speech sounds; **acoustic phonetics**, the study of the transmission and the physical properties of speech sounds (such as intensity, frequency, and duration); and **auditory phonetics**, the study of the perception of speech sounds.

The study of articulatory phonetics has had the longest history among the three subbranches of phonetics; it was already fairly developed by the nineteenth century. In the popular musical *My Fair Lady*, based on Bernard Shaw's play *Pygmalion*, the eccentric professor Higgins was actually modeled after the phonetician Henry Sweet. Acoustic phonetics, however, has mostly developed only in the past few decades. Acoustic phonetics has had to rely heavily on the use of sophisticated instruments that perform analyses of sound vibration. A particularly important instrument, the **spectrograph**, was invented only in the 1940s. Among the three branches of phonetics, auditory phonetics is the least understood, owing to gaps that remain in our understanding of human neurology and perception.

Articulatory phonetics involves the study of how phones are produced by speakers and the description and classification of those sounds according to their properties. Each of these aspects of articulatory phonetics will be considered in the files that follow, and the basic concepts of acoustic phonetics will be introduced. We will also be learning and using a system of phonetic symbols that linguists have developed for representing speech sounds. In a phonetic transcription one sound is represented by one symbol, and each symbol represents a single sound. Compare this system with English orthography (i.e., spelling), which is full of inconsistencies—for example:

- sometimes the same sound is spelled using different letters, as in sea, see, scene, receive, thief, amoeba, machine, and Aesop.
- sometimes the same letters can stand for different sounds, as in sign, pleasure, and resign, or charter and character, or father, all, about, apple, any, and age.
- sometimes a single sound is spelled by a combination of letters, as in lock, that, book, boast, shop, apple, or special.
- sometimes a single letter represents more than one sound, as in exit or use.
- sometimes letters stand for no sound at all, as in know, doubt, though, island, rhubarb, or moose.

Phonetic transcription, however, is consistent and unambiguous because there is always a one-to-one correspondence between sounds and symbols. This is even true across languages, so that the symbols you will be learning can be used to transcribe the sounds of any language. Phonetic symbols are written within square brackets, [ ], to distinguish them from letters or words written in ordinary orthography. It is important to remember that these symbols are not the same as letters, and that they represent the sounds of language, not letters of a writing system.

Phonetic Symbols for the Consonants of English

Symbol   *Sample Words*

[p]   pit, tip, spit, hiccough, appear

[b]   ball, globe, amble, brick, bubble

[t]   tag, pat, stick, pterodactyl, stuffed

[d]   dip, card, drop, loved, batted

[k]   kit, scoot, character, critique, exceed

[g]   guard, bag, longer, designate, Pittsburgh

[ʔ]   uh-oh, hatrack, Batman   (glottal stop)

[f]   foot, laugh, philosophy, coffee, carafe

[v]   vest, dove, gravel, anvil, average

[θ]   through, wrath, thistle, ether, teeth   (theta)

[ð]   the, their, mother, either, teethe   (eth [ɛð])

[s]   soap, psychology, packs, descent, peace

[z]   zip, roads, kisses, Xerox, design

[š]   shy, mission, nation, glacial, sure   (s-wedge, s-háček)

[ž]   measure, vision, azure, casualty, decision   (z-wedge, z-háček)

[h]   who, hat, rehash, hole, whole

[č]   choke, match, feature, righteous, constituent   (c-wedge, c-háček)

[ǰ]   judge, George, Jell-O, region, residual   (j-wedge, j-háček)

[m]   moose, lamb, smack, amnesty, ample

[n]   nap, design, snow, know, mnemonic

[ŋ]   sing, think, finger, singer, ankle   (engma)

[l]   leaf, feel, Lloyd, mild, applaud

[r]   reef, fear, Harris, prune, carp

[ɾ]   writer, butter, udder, clutter, cuter   (flap)

[w]   with, swim, mowing, queen, twilight

[y]   you, beautiful, feud, use, yell

[w̥]   which, where, what, whale,   (voiceless 'w')

           why (for those dialects in which *witch* and

           which do not sound the same)

Syllabic Consonants

[m̩]	possum, chasm, Adam, bottomless	(syllabic 'm')
[n̩]	button, chicken, lesson, kittenish	(syllabic 'n')
[l̩]	little, single, simple, stabilize	(syllabic 'l')
[r̩]	ladder, singer, burp, percent	(syllabic 'r')

Phonetic Symbols for the Vowels of English

Symbols	*Examples*	
[i]	beat, we, believe, people, money	('ee' as in *feel*)
[ɪ]	bit, consist, injury, malignant, business	(capital-'i')
[e]	bait, reign, great, they, gauge	('ay' as in *gray*)
[ɛ]	bet, reception, says, guest, bury	(epsilon, 'eh')
[æ]	bat, laugh, anger, comrade, rally	(ash, 'a' as in *apple*)
[u]	boot, who, sewer, duty, through	('u' as in *boot*)
[ʊ]	put, foot, butcher, could, boogie-woogie	(capital-'u')
[o]	boat, beau, grow, though, over	('o' as in *over*)
[ɔ]	bought, caught, wrong, stalk, core	(open 'o', 'au' as in *caught*)
[a]	pot, father, sergeant, honor, hospital	('a' as in *Say ahh.*)
[ʌ]	but, tough, another, oven	(wedge, stressed schwa)
[ə]	among, sofa	(schwa)

Diphthongs

Symbols	*Examples*
[ay]	bite, Stein, aisle, choir, island
[aw]	bout, brown, doubt, flower, loud
[oy]	boy, doily, rejoice, perestroika, annoy

See Appendix C, pp. 469–70, for a more comprehensive listing of phonetic symbols used in this book, including symbols used for languages other than English and a comparison of some International Phonetic Alphabet (IPA) conventions with the American tradition.

File 3.2 Articulation and Description of English Consonants

English speech sounds are formed by converting the stream of air that is forced out of the lungs through the oral or nasal cavities, or both, into soundwaves; sounds created in this way are said to be made by using a **pulmonic egressive airstream mechanism**. Other airstream mechanisms are possible but will not be discussed here.

Consonants, unlike vowels, are speech sounds produced with a narrowing somewhere in the **vocal tract**, which is usually sufficient to prevent them from functioning as **syllable nuclei** (the nucleus is the "heart" of the syllable, carrying stress, loudness, and pitch information; it usually consists of a vowel). When describing a consonant it is necessary to provide information about three different aspects of the articulation of the consonant:

1. Is the sound voiced or voiceless?
2. Where is the airstream constricted?
3. How is the airstream constricted?

Each of these will be discussed in turn. In the description of speech sounds, three *features* need to be specified: 1. Is the sound voiced or voiceless? 2. Where is its place of articulation? 3. What is the manner of articulation? Please note that in this file and elsewhere, whenever we say things like "[p] is a stop" or "the [p] in *pan*," what we *really* mean is the wordier "the sound represented by the symbol [p]." Remember that we are talking about sounds and sometimes about the phonetic symbols representing them, but not about letters.

Components of Human Speech Production

There are three basic components of human physiology important for the production of speech. (See Figure 1.) Only two of them will be discussed in detail. One is the **larynx**, which contains the **vocal folds** and the **glottis**; another is the **vocal tract** above the larynx, which is composed of the oral and nasal cavities. The third is the subglottal system, which is the part of the respiratory system located below the larynx. When air is inhaled, it is channeled through the nasal or oral cavity, or both, through the larynx into the lungs. Moving the stream of air out of the lungs and through the larynx and the vocal tract produces English speech sounds. The air passing through the larynx and glottis is the source of sound waves. These sound waves take on their characteristic shape as they are channeled through various possible vocal tract configurations in the oral or nasal cavities.

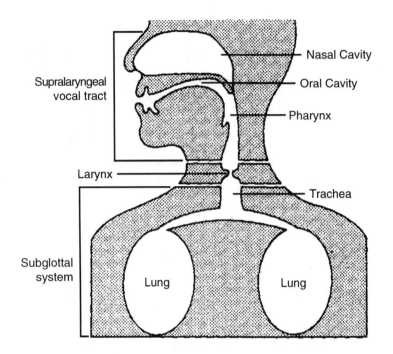

Figure 1.   The three components of speech production. From Lieberman and Blumstein, *Speech Physiology* (1990), p. 4. Copyright 1990 Cambridge University Press. All Rights Reserved. Reprinted with permission.

States of the Glottis

Humans have a larynx (sometimes called a voicebox) at the top of the **trachea** (or windpipe). Within the larynx are folds of muscle called vocal folds (these are popularly known as vocal cords, but they are not really cords). In Figure 2 the front of the throat is uppermost; compare this to the cross-section in Figure 1. A flap of tissue called the epiglottis attaches at the front of the larynx, and can fold down and back to cover and protect the vocal folds, which are stretched horizontally along the open center of the larynx. The opening between these folds is called the glottis. Both of the vocal folds are attached to cartilage at the front of the larynx but are separated at the back; by bringing the two free ends together, the vocal folds can be closed or approximated, allowing air to escape. When the folds are wide open the glottis has roughly the shape of a triangle, as can be seen in Figure 2.

The vocal folds can be relaxed so that the flow of air coming up from the lungs passes through freely. The folds may also be held close together so that they vibrate as air passes through. Try putting a hand lightly on your throat or putting your fingers in your ears, and then making a drawn out [s]. Your vocal folds are separated, so you should feel no vibration. But now make a [z] (again, draw it out), and you will feel a vibration or buzzing feeling. This is due to the vibration of the vocal folds. Sounds made with the vocal folds vibrating are called **voiced** sounds, and sounds made without such vibration are called **voiceless**. The italicized sounds in the following pairs of words differ only in that the sound is voiceless in the first word of each pair and voiced in the second. (It is important not to whisper when articulating these words, because whispering has the effect of eliminating vocal fold vibration.)

a.	[f] *f*at	b.	[θ] *th*igh	c.	[s] *s*ip	d.	[š] dilu*ti*on
	[v] *v*at		[ð] *th*y		[z] *z*ip		[ž] delu*si*on
e.	[č] ri*ch*	f.	[p] *p*at	g.	[t] *t*ab	h.	[k] *k*ill
	[ǰ] ri*dg*e		[b] *b*at		[d] *d*ab		[g] *g*ill

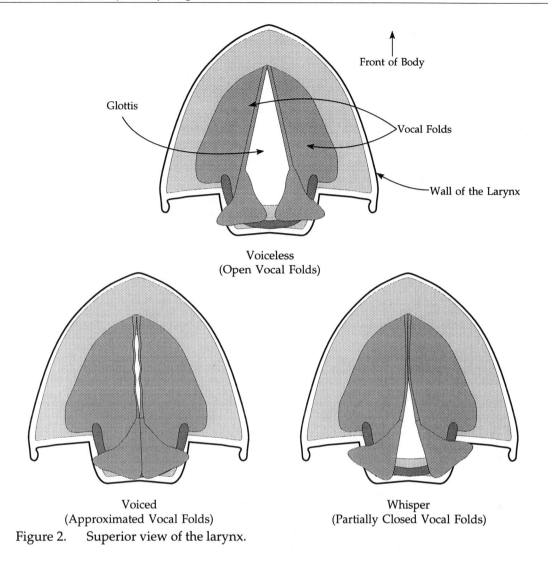

Figure 2.   Superior view of the larynx.

The first thing it is necessary to state about a sound when providing an articulatory description, then, is whether it is voiced (the vocal folds are vibrating) or voiceless (there is no vocal fold vibration).

Place of Articulation

In describing a consonant sound, it is also necessary to state where in the vocal tract a **constriction** is made—that is, where the vocal tract is made more narrow. This is referred to as the sound's **place of articulation**. When reading about each of the following points of articulation, refer to Figure 3 below.

- **Bilabial**—bilabial sounds are made by bringing both lips closer together. There are five such sounds in English: [p] *pat*, [b] *bat*, [m] *mat*, [w] *with*, and [ẉ] *where* (present only in some dialects).
- **Labiodental**—labiodental consonants are made with the lower lip against the upper front teeth. English has two labiodentals: [f] *fat* and [v] *vat*.
- **Interdental**—interdentals are made with the tip of the tongue between the front teeth. There are two interdental sounds in English: [θ] *thigh* and [ð] *thy*.
- **Alveolar**—just behind your upper front teeth there is a small ridge called the **alveolar ridge**. English makes seven sounds with the tongue tip at or near this ridge: [t] *tab*, [d] *dab*, [s] *sip*, [z] *zip*, [n] *noose*, [l] *loose*, and [r] *red*.

- **Palatal**—if you let your finger glide back along the roof of your mouth you will note that the anterior portion is hard and the posterior portion is soft. Sounds made with the tongue near the hard part of the roof of the mouth are called palatal sounds. English makes five sounds in the region of the hard palate: [š] *leash*, [ž] *measure*, [č] *church*, [ǰ] *judge*, [y] *yes*. (More precisely, [š, ž, č], and [ǰ] are **alveo-palatal** sounds, because they are made in the area between the alveolar ridge and the hard palate. We'll use the shorter term "palatal" to describe these sounds of English, however.)
- **Velar**—the soft part of the roof of the mouth behind the hard palate is called the **velum**. Sounds made with the tongue near the velum are said to be velar. There are three velar sounds in English: [k] *kill*, [g] *gill*, and [ŋ] *sing*.
- **Glottal**—the space between the vocal folds is the **glottis**. English has two sounds made at the glottis. One is easy to hear: [h], as in *high* and *history*. The other is called a **glottal stop** and is transcribed phonetically as [ʔ]. This sound occurs before each of the vowel sounds in *uh-oh*.

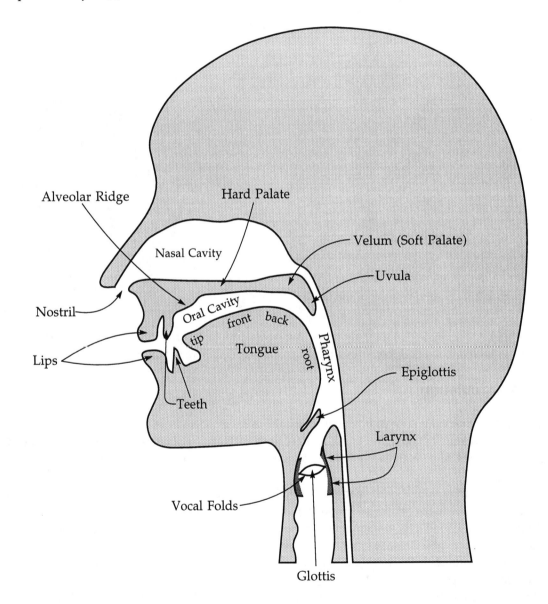

Figure 3.   Sagittal section of the vocal tract.

Manner of Articulation

Besides stating whether a sound is voiced or voiceless and giving the sound's point of articulation, it is necessary to describe its **manner of articulation**, that is, how the airstream is modified by the vocal tract to produce the sound. The manner of articulation of a sound depends on the degree of closure of the articulators (how close together or far apart they are).

   Stops—stops are made by obstructing the airstream completely in the oral cavity. Notice that when you say [p] and [b] your lips are closed together for a moment, stopping the airflow. [p] and [b] are *bilabial stops*. [b] is a *voiced bilabial stop*. [t], [d], [k], and [g] are also stops. What is the three-part description of each?

   The glottal stop, [ʔ], is made by momentarily closing the vocal folds. The expression *uh-oh* has a [ʔ] before each vowel. If you stop halfway through *uh-oh* and hold your articulators in position for the second half, you should be able to feel yourself making the glottal stop. (It will feel like a catch in your throat.) Nasal consonants are also stops in terms of their oral articulation; see below.

   Fricatives—fricatives are made by forming a nearly complete stoppage of the airstream. The opening through which the air escapes is so small that friction is produced (much as air escaping from a punctured tire makes a hissing noise). [š] is made by almost stopping the air with the tongue near the palate. It is a *voiceless palatal fricative*. How would you describe each of the following: [f], [v], [θ], [ð], [s], [z], and [ž]?

   Affricates—an affricate is made by briefly stopping the airstream completely and then releasing the articulators slightly so that friction is produced. (Affricates can be thought of as a combination of a stop and a fricative.) English has only two affricates, [č] and [ǰ]. [č] is a combination of [t] and [š], and so is sometimes transcribed as [tš]. It is a *voiceless palatal affricate*. [ǰ] is a combination of [d] and [ž], and is sometimes transcribed as [dž]. How would you describe [ǰ]?

   Nasals—notice that the velum can be raised or lowered. If it is *lowered*, as it is during normal breathing and during the production of nasal sounds, then the airstream can escape out through the nasal cavity as well as through the unobstructed oral cavity. When the velum is *raised* against the back of the throat (also called the **pharynx**), no air can escape through the nasal passages; sounds made with the velum raised are called **oral** sounds. The sounds [m], [n] and [ŋ] are produced with the velum lowered and a complete obstruction in the oral cavity. They are called **nasals** or nasal stops, since the oral cavity is completely obstructed, as it is during the production of oral stops. [m] is made with the velum lowered and a complete obstruction of the airstream at the lips. For [n], the velum is lowered and the tongue tip pressed against the alveolar ridge. [ŋ] is made with the velum lowered and the back of the tongue stopping the airstream in the velar region. In English, all nasals are voiced. Thus [m] is a *voiced bilabial nasal (stop)*; the only difference between [m] and [b] is that the velum is lowered for the articulation of [m], but raised for the articulation of [b]. How would you describe [n]? [ŋ]?

   Liquids—when a liquid is produced, there is an obstruction formed by the articulators, but it is not narrow enough to stop the airflow or to cause friction. The [l] in *leaf* is produced by resting the tongue on the alveolar ridge with the airstream escaping around the sides of the tongue. Thus it is called a lateral liquid. Liquids are usually voiced in English: [l] is a *voiced alveolar lateral liquid*. There is a great deal of variation in the ways speakers of English make *r*-sounds; most are voiced and articulated in the alveolar region, and a common type also involves curling the tip of the tongue back behind the alveolar ridge to make a **retroflex** sound. For our purposes [r] as in *red* may be considered a *voiced alveolar retroflex liquid*.

   Nasals and liquids are classified as consonants. However, they sometimes act like vowels in that they can function as syllable nuclei. Pronounce the following words out loud, and listen to the liquids and nasals in them: *prism*, *prison*, *table*, and *hiker*. In these words the nucleus of the second syllable consists only of a syllabic nasal or liquid; there is no vowel in these second syllables. In order to indicate the syllabic character of these nasals and liquids, a short vertical line is placed below the phonetic symbol. The final *n* of *prison* would be transcribed [n̩]; likewise [m̩], [l̩], and [r̩] in *prism*, *table*, and *hiker*.

Glides—glides are made with only a slight closure of the articulators. In fact, if the vocal tract were any more open, the result would be a vowel sound. [w] is made by raising the back of the tongue toward the velum while rounding the lips at the same time, so it is classified as a *voiced bilabial glide*. (Notice the similarity in the way you articulate the [w] and the vowel [u] in the word *woo*: the only change is that you open your lips a little more for [u].) [w̥] is produced just like [w], except that it is voiceless; not all speakers of English use this sound. [y] is made with a slight closure in the palatal region. It is a *voiced palatal glide*. (Notice the similarity between [y] and the vowel [i] in the word *yes*.)

The chart in Figure 4 of the consonants of English can be used for easy reference. To find the description of a sound, first locate the sound on the chart. You can find out the state of glottis by checking whether the sound is in the shaded part of the box or not—this will tell you whether the sound is voiced or voiceless. Then check the label at the top of the vertical column that the sound is in to see what its place of articulation is. Finally, check the manner of articulation label at the far left of the sound's horizontal row. Locate [ð], for example. It lies in a shaded region indicating that the state of the glottis during the production of this sound produces voicing. Now look above [ð]. It is in the vertical column marked interdental. Looking to the far left you see it is a fricative. [ð], then, is a *voiced interdental fricative*.

You can also use the chart to find a sound with a particular description by essentially reversing the above procedure. If you wanted to find the *voiced palatal fricative*, first look in the fricative row, then under the palatal column, and locate the symbol in the row marked "voiced": this is [ž].

The chart can also be used to find classes of sounds. For instance, to find all the alveolars, just read off all the sounds under the alveolar column. Or, to find all the stops, read off all the sounds in the stop row.

You should familiarize yourself with the chart so that you can easily recognize the phonetic symbols. The list of phonetic symbols for consonants, which was presented in File 3.1, should also help you remember which symbol represents which consonant. Remember that we are talking about *sounds* and not letters.

Manner of Articulation		Bilabial		Labiodental		Interdental		Alveolar		Palatal		Velar		Glottal	
Stop		p	b					t	d			k	g	ʔ	
Fricative				f	v	θ	ð	s	z	š	ž			h	
Affricate										č	ǰ				
Nasal			m						n				ŋ		
Lateral Liquid									l						
Retroflex Liquid									r						
Glide		w̥	w								y				

Place of Articulation

State of the Glottis: Voiceless Voiced

Figure 4.   The Consonants of English.

File 3.3   Articulation and Description of English Vowels

Vowels are the most sonorant, or intense, and the most audible sounds in speech. They usually function as syllable nuclei, and the consonants that surround them often depend on the vowel for their audibility. For example, in the word *pop*, neither [p] has much sound of its own; the [p]s are heard mainly because of the way they affect the beginning and end of the vowel sound.

We will need to describe vowels using different features than those we use for consonants. Vowels are sounds produced with a relatively open vocal tract, so they do not have a consonant-like point of articulation (place of constriction) or manner of articulation (type and degree of constriction), and they are almost always voiced.

Vocal fold vibration is the sound source for vowels. The vocal tract above the glottis acts as a resonator affecting the sound made by the vocal folds. The shape of this resonator determines the quality of the vowel—[i] vs. [u] vs. [a], for example.

There are several ways in which speakers can change the shape of the vocal tract and thus change vowel quality. They do this by

1. raising or lowering the body of the tongue
2. advancing or retracting the body of the tongue
3. rounding or not rounding the lips
4. making these movements with a tense or a lax gesture

Therefore, when describing a vowel, it is necessary to provide information about these four aspects of the articulation of the vowel. Refer to the chart in Figure 1 as each aspect is discussed.

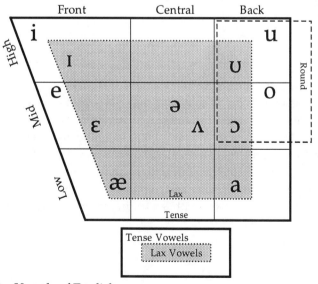

Figure 1.   The Vowels of English.

43

Tongue Height

If you repeat to yourself the vowel sounds of *seat, set, sat*—transcribed [i], [ε], [æ]—you will find that you open your mouth a little wider as you change from [i] to [ε], and then a little wider still as you change from [ε] to [æ]. These varying degrees of openness correspond to different degrees of tongue height: high for [i], mid for [ε], and low for [æ].

High vowels like [i] are made with the front of the mouth less open because the tongue body is raised, or high. The high vowels of English are [i, ɪ, u, ʊ], as in *leak, lick, Luke, look*. Conversely, low vowels like the [æ] in *sat* are pronounced with the front of the mouth open and the tongue lowered. [æ, a], as in *cat* and *cot*, are the low vowels of English. Mid vowels like the [ε] of *set* are produced with an intermediate tongue height; in English, these mid vowels are [e, ε, ʌ, ɔ, o] as in *bait, bet, but, bought, boat*. Note that the vowel [ə], as in the last syllable in *sofa*, is simply unstressed [ʌ].

In many American dialects, words like *caught* and *cot*, or *dawn* and *Don*, are pronounced differently, with an [ɔ] and [a], respectively. In other American dialects, these words are pronounced the same. If you pronounce these pairs the same, you probably use the unrounded vowel [a] in these words. For most speakers of English, however, the vowel [ɔ] appears in words such as *hall, ball*, and *tall*.

Tongue Advancement

Besides being held high or mid or low, the tongue can also be pushed forward or pulled back within the oral cavity. For example, in the high front vowel [i] as in *beat*, the body of the tongue is raised and pushed forward so it is just under the hard palate. The high back vowel [u] of *boot*, on the other hand, is made by raising the body of the tongue in the back of the mouth, toward the velum. The tongue is advanced or pushed forward for all the front vowels, [i, ɪ, e, ε, æ], as in *seek, sick, sake, sec, sack*, and retracted or pulled back for the back vowels, [u, ʊ, o, ɔ, a], as in *ooze, look, road, paw, dot*. The central vowels, [ʌ] as in *luck* or [ə] as the first vowel in the word *another*, require neither fronting nor retraction of the tongue.

Lip Rounding

Vowel quality also depends on lip position. When you say the [u] in *two*, your lips are rounded. For the [i] in *tea*, they are unrounded. English has four rounded vowels: [u, ʊ, o, ɔ], as in *loop, foot, soap, caught*. All other vowels in English are unrounded. In the vowel chart, the rounded vowels are enclosed in a dotted line forming a rectangle.

Tenseness

Vowels that are called **tense** have more extreme positions of the tongue or the lips than vowels that are **lax**. The production of tense vowels involves bigger changes from a mid central position in the mouth. On the vowel chart you can clearly see that the distance between the tense vowels [i] and [u] is bigger than the distance between the lax vowels [ɪ] and [ʊ]. For example, tense vowels are made with a more extreme tongue **gesture** to reach the outer peripherals of the **vowel space**. What this means is that the tongue position for the tense high front vowel [i] is higher and fronter than for the lax high front vowel [ɪ]. Lax vowels are not peripheral, on the outer edge of the possible vowel space. Compare tense [i] in *meet* with lax [ɪ] in *mitt*, or tense [u] in *boot* with lax [ʊ] in *put*. In the latter case you will find that the tense round vowel [u] is also produced with more and tighter lip rounding than the lax counterpart [ʊ]. Now we can consider some sample descriptions of English vowels:

- [i], as in *beat*, is high, front, unrounded, and tense.
- [ɔ], as in *caught*, is mid, back, rounded, and lax.
- [a], as in *cot*, is low, back, unrounded, and lax.
- [ʌ], as in *cut*, is mid, central, unrounded, and lax. (Note that "central" and "mid" refer to the same position in the vocal tract but on different dimensions)
- [e], as in *cake*, is mid, front, unrounded, and tense.

Diphthongs

At this point, we still have not described the vowel sounds of some English words such as *hide, loud,* and *coin.* Unlike the simple vowels described above, the vowels of these words are **diphthongs:** two-part vowel sounds consisting of a vowel and a glide in the same syllable. If you say the word *eye* slowly, concentrating on how you make this vowel sound, you should find that your tongue starts out in the position for [a] and moves toward the position for the vowel [i] or the corresponding palatal glide [y] (see Figure 2). (If you have a hard time perceiving this as two sounds, try laying a finger on your tongue and saying *eye.* This should help you feel the upward tongue movement.) This diphthong, which consists of two articulations and the two corresponding sounds, is written with two symbols: [ay], as in [hayd] *hide.* To produce the vowel in the word *loud,* the tongue and the lips start in the position for [a] and move toward the position for [u] or [w]; so this diphthong is written [aw], as in [lawd] *loud.* (For some speakers, the vowel part of this diphthong will be closer to [ɔ].) In the vowel of the word *coin,* the tongue moves from the [o] position toward the position for [i] or [y]; so the vowel of *coin* is written [oy], as in [koyn]. The charts below illustrate the tongue movements involved in the production of these diphthongs.

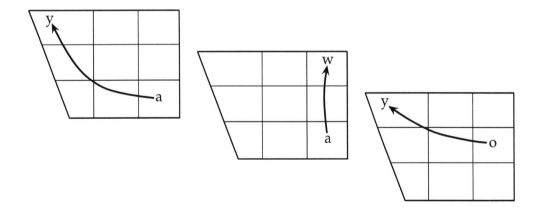

Figure 2.   The diphthongs of English.

The positions of the vocal organs for [y] and [w] are very close to the positions for [i] and [u], respectively. So diphthongs are often transcribed using the symbols for two vowels instead of a vowel symbol plus a glide symbol: [ay], [oy], and [aw] can be written [ai̯], [oi̯], and [au̯]. The mark under the symbol for the second vowel of a diphthong indicates that this vowel doesn't form a separate syllable, as a vowel usually would. ([au] would be the way to write *ah-ooh!* and [au̯] would be the way to write *ow!*)

vowel usually would. ([au] would be the way to write *ah-ooh!* and [au̯] would be the way to write *ow!*)

It is worth noting that although we will usually write just [e] or [o] for the vowel sounds of *stay* or *go*, these vowels are normally pronounced as diphthongs in English—that is, they are actually pronounced with a following glide, as [ey] and [ow] in [stey] and [gow]. The [ey] and [ow] of English are thus a bit different from the monophthongal [e] and [o] of some other languages, like French or Spanish, in which these vowels are produced without glides (e.g., French *été* [ete] 'summer' or *beau* [bo] 'beautiful'; Spanish *mesa* [mesa] 'table' or *boca* [boka] 'mouth'). When we try to speak those languages, we are inclined to use our English [ey] and [ow] instead of [e] and [o], and this sounds odd to native speakers—we have a foreign accent. Of course, the reverse occurs when they use plain [e] and [o] in English. This is one example of the many small details that contribute to what we call accents.

File 3.4

Sagittal Section Exercises

The following exercises are designed to help you become more familiar with the shapes of the vocal tract connected with the production of different consonant sounds. For each drawing presented below there is only one sound of English that could be produced by a vocal tract positioned as shown; you are to figure out which consonant sound is represented (either by referring to the descriptions of different sounds or by experimenting with your own vocal tract). Write the phonetic symbol for that sound between the brackets below the appropriate drawing. Note that voicing is shown by two wavy or "bumpy" lines where the larynx would be, while voiceless sounds are represented by two lines shaped as an ellipse, indicating an open glottis at that point. Take care also to note whether the air passage to the nasal cavity is open or closed (i.e., if the velum is raised or lowered). The first drawing is labeled to start you off.

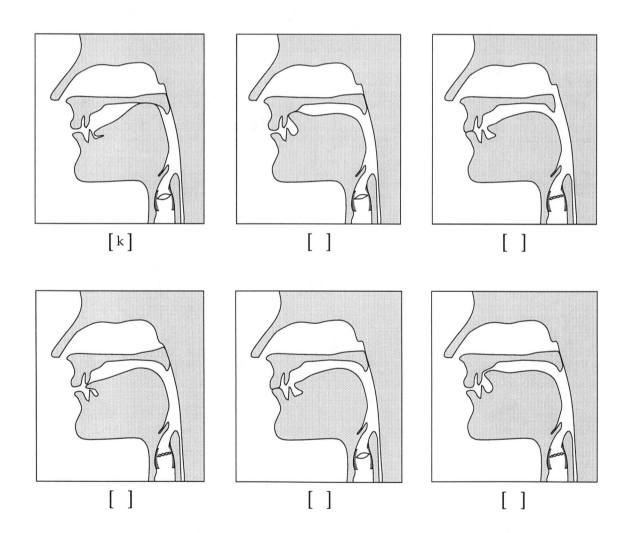

[k]   [ ]   [ ]

[ ]   [ ]   [ ]

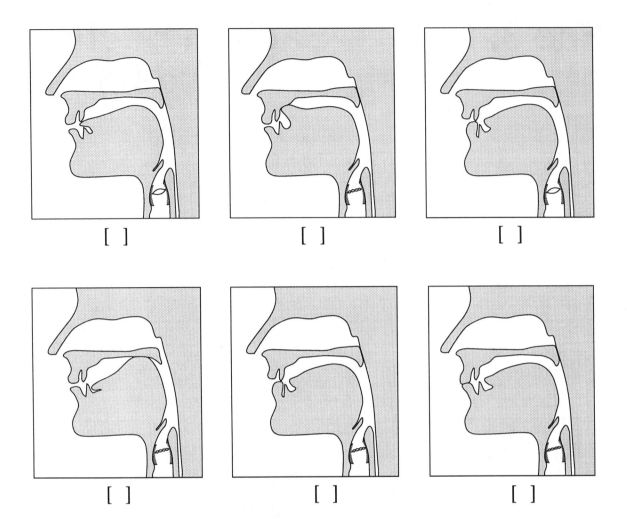

[　]   [　]   [　]

[　]   [　]   [　]

File 3.5

Exercises in Description and Transcription

1. Circle all the symbols below which represent voiced sounds:

   [s]　　[v]　　[h]　　[w]　　[r]　　[z]　　[k]　　[b]　　[t]　　[p]　　[ɪ]

   [o]　　[f]　　[š]　　[d]　　[g]　　[i]　　[m]　　[θ]　　[ʔ]　　[ð]　　[č]

2. Provide the phonetic symbol representing each of the following sounds (don't forget to use square brackets).

   a. high front tense unrounded vowel
   b. mid back lax rounded vowel
   c. low back lax unrounded vowel
   d. mid front lax unrounded vowel
   e. voiced labiodental fricative
   f. voiceless palatal affricate
   g. voiced velar nasal
   h. voiceless glottal fricative
   i. voiced interdental fricative
   j. voiced palatal fricative
   k. voiced alveolar lateral liquid

3. Provide the appropriate three-part articulatory descriptions for the consonant sounds represented by the following symbols:

   a. [z]
   b. [n]
   c. [č]
   d. [ŋ]
   e. [g]
   f. [f]
   g. [š]
   h. [r]

4. Provide the appropriate four-part articulatory descriptions for the vowel sounds represented by the following symbols:

   a. [ɪ]
   b. [o]

c. [ɛ]
d. [u]
e. [æ]
f. [ʊ]

5. Which of the following phonetic transcriptions represent actual English words? Write the real words in conventional spelling.

[swit]	[shut]	[čild]	[stuk]	[trad]
[sɪpd]	[θɛm]	[falw]	[strʌgl̩]	[left]

6. Give the conventional spelling for the following phonetically transcribed words. (Note that some may have more than one possible spelling.)

a.	[rič]	k.	[rat]	u.	[baks]	ee.	[ežə]
b.	[rɪč]	l.	[rut]	v.	[kloð]	ff.	[šak]
c.	[rɪǰ]	m.	[krɔld]	w.	[gres]	gg.	[pen]
d.	[rot]	n.	[sel]	x.	[byuɾi]	hh.	[lʊk]
e.	[krud]	o.	[slop]	y.	[θæŋk]	ii.	[kɔrl̩]
f.	[fʌǰ]	p.	[nešn̩]	z.	[sr̩čt]	jj.	[sr̩ve]
g.	[kayt]	q.	[krawd]	aa.	[poynt]	kk.	[prayd]
h.	[ækšn̩]	r.	[wɛnzde]	bb.	[šules]	ll.	[θawzn̩d]
i.	[pitsə]	s.	[ližr̩]	cc.	[ðo]	mm.	[kanšəs]
j.	[wɔrm]	t.	[fr̩m]	dd.	[bæŋ]	nn.	[sʌni]

7. Transcribe the following words.

a.	lose	p.	move	ee.	cookies	tt.	pure
b.	loose	q.	wove	ff.	bathtub	uu.	cane
c.	cough	r.	love	gg.	easy	vv.	sugar
d.	ghoul	s.	hour	hh.	icy	ww.	vision
e.	though	t.	rhythm	ii.	raspberry	xx.	child
f.	touch	u.	monkey	jj.	mother	yy.	lather
g.	huge	v.	torch	kk.	hoodlum	zz.	leather
h.	breath	w.	larynx	ll.	woman	aaa.	calves
i.	breathe	x.	said	mm.	women	bbb.	wrapped
j.	circus	y.	pushed	nn.	carrot	ccc.	punched
k.	brood	z.	Cairo	oo.	carton	ddd.	Godzilla
l.	stood	aa.	whale	pp.	slyly	eee.	January
m.	flood	bb.	mustache	qq.	union	fff.	February
n.	price	cc.	batch	rr.	cringe	ggg.	July
o.	prays	dd.	sewn	ss.	isn't	hhh.	August

8. Read the phonetically transcribed sentences below and write them out in ordinary orthography. These transcriptions represent the pronunciation of a particular speaker on a particular occasion and thus may differ from your own pronunciation of the same passages in certain minor details, but this should not cause you any difficulty. These passages are from Woody Allen's book *Without Feathers*.

a. [dʌbz æskt hɪz brʌðr̩ wʌt ɪt wʌz layk ɪn ði ʌðr̩ wr̩ld n̩d ɪz brʌðr̩ sɛd ɪt wʌz nat ənlayk klivln̩d] ([dʌbz] "Dubbs" is a proper name.)

b.   [itr̩n̩ nʌθɪŋnɛs ɪz oke æz lɔŋ æz yr̩ drɛst fr̩ ɪt]

c.   [ɪf yu ar sɪkstin ɔr ʌndr̩ tray nat tə go bɔld]

d.   [ænd sun ǰobz pæsčr̩z drayd ʌp n̩d ɪz tʌŋ klivd tu ðə ruf ʌv ɪz mawθ so hi kʊd nat prənawns ðə wr̩d fræŋkɪnsɛns wɪθawt gɛɾɪŋ bɪg læfs]
([ǰob] "Job" is a proper name)

e.   [mʌni ɪz nat ɛvriθɪŋ bʌt ɪt ɪz bɛɾr̩ ðæn hævɪŋ wʌnz hɛlθ]

f.   [ðə græshapr̩ pled ɔl sʌmr̩ wayl ði ænt wr̩kt n̩ sevd wɛn wɪntr̩ kem ðə græshapr̩ hæd nʌθɪŋ bʌt ði ænt kʌmplend əv čɛst penz]

g.   [ðə sæfayr̩ wʌz ərɪǰənəli ond bay ə sʌltn̩ hu dayd ʌndr̩ məstɪriəs sr̩kəmstænsəz wɛn ə hænd rɪčt awt ʌv ə bol əv sup hi wʌz itɪŋ n̩ stræŋgl̩d hɪm]

h.   [ðə gret ro ɪz ə mɪθək̩l bist wɪθ ðə hɛd əv ə layn̩ ænd ðə badi ʌv ə layn̩ bʌt nat ðə sem layn̩]
([ro] "roe" is a nonsense name)

File 3.6   Natural Classes

In studying phonetics we have noticed that sounds may be described by listing their articulatory features (voicing as well as place and manner of articulation for consonants; tongue height, tongue advancement, tenseness, and rounding for vowels). Thus, [t] is described as a voiceless alveolar stop consonant and [a] is described as a low, back, lax, unrounded vowel. This system of description lends itself quite handily to the description of natural classes of sounds.

Natural classes are groups of sounds in a language that share some articulatory or auditory feature(s). In order for a group of sounds to be a natural class it must include *all* of the sounds that share a particular feature or group of features, and not include any sounds that don't. Thus, when we refer to the natural class of voiced stops in English, we mean all of the sounds that are voiced stops in English (i.e., [b, d, g]) and no sounds that are not.

Describing sounds in terms of natural classes makes it possible to state generalizations concerning (1) the sound systems of human languages (e.g., the possible sequences of sounds that can occur together, and the possible modification of sounds when they occur next to other sounds), (2) dialect variation, (3) changes in the pronunciation of borrowed words, (4) the acquisition of language by children, (5) rules for rhyming in poetry, and (6) processes of sound change across the history of a language. All of these things are easier to understand when we understand what natural classes are.

What Is "Natural"?

What makes one group of sounds a natural class while another group of sounds (perhaps with the same number of members) is not a natural class? What is it that makes a natural class natural?

Consider two groups of sounds: [p, t, k] and [p, l, w]. The first of these two groups is a natural class, but the second isn't. Notice that [p, t, k] all share the feature of voicelessness and that they are all oral stops (as opposed to nasal stops [m, n, ŋ,] and glottal stop [ʔ]). In fact these three sounds are the set of all sounds in English that have both the features *voiceless* and *oral stop*. The sounds [p, l, w], on the other hand, have no feature in common (except that they are all consonants, and obviously [p, l, w] is not the set of all consonants in English). Thus, [p, t, k] is a natural class because it is the set of all sounds in English that are voiceless oral stops. The set [p, l, w], however, is not a natural class because the only feature these three sounds have in common is *consonant* which describes a much larger set of sounds. We might say that [p, l, w] is a subset of the natural class of consonants in English, but it is certainly not a natural class itself.

Features Used to Describe Natural Classes

All of the features used in Files 3.2 and 3.3 to describe individual sounds can also be used to describe natural classes. For example, in English the vowels [i, e, o, u] are all tense vowels, and there are no other tense vowels in English. Because these vowels share the feature *tense* they are members of the natural class of tense vowels in English. Likewise, the consonants [k, g, ŋ] are all described as velar consonants, and they are the only velar consonants used in English; thus they constitute the natural class of velar consonants in English.

In talking about groups of sounds, we must use a few features in addition to those used to describe the individual sounds. For example, if you look at the consonant chart in File 3.2 you will notice that the only labiodental consonants in English are the fricatives [f] and [v], while the bilabial fricative slots are left empty. In many situations it is advantageous to refer to [f] and [v] together with [p, b, m,

52

w] and [w̥] as belonging to the same natural class. For this purpose we use the feature *labial*. In other words, the fact that all of these sounds are produced with a lip **gesture** means that they all share the feature *labial*, and thus are grouped together in a natural class. This natural class is used by English speakers. For example, for most speakers of English the sound [w] does not occur after the consonants [m, b, p, f, v] (or [w]/[w̥]). As a result, **mwoast*, **pwell*, **bwint*, **fwallow*, and **vwoot* are not possible English words. If we had not noticed that [m, b, p, f, v, w, w̥] share the feature *labial* (and are thus members of the same natural class) we would have no simple way to account for the fact that speakers of English treat these sounds as if they were all the same in some way.

Some of the additional features used in describing natural classes focus on a similarity in sound quality. Up until now we have said that sounds are members of a natural class because they are similar in some aspect of their production. It is also the case that sounds may be grouped together by speakers because of a similarity in the way they sound. An example of a natural class based on an auditory feature is the class of **sibilant** consonants in English. Normally a noun is made plural in English by adding the suffix -*s*. This suffix is pronounced in three different ways depending on the last sound in the noun to which it is added. If the noun ends with a voiced sound, the phonetic form of the plural suffix is [z]. If the noun ends in a voiceless sound, the phonetic form of the plural suffix is [s]. Notice, however, that the form of the suffix indicating plural for words like *riches*, *bushes*, *kisses*, *garages*, *rouges*, and *mazes* is [əz] rather than [z] or [s]. The group of sounds that end these words are the consonants [č, š, s, ǰ, ž, z]. Note that these sounds differ with respect to voicing as well as place and manner of articulation. They do, however, have an auditory property in common: they all have a high-pitched hissing sound quality. These sounds form the natural class of sibilant consonants in English. It's important to realize that the feature *sibilant* refers to a real property that is shared by all of the sounds in this natural class. Using this feature makes it possible to state a generalization captured in the following two rules:

1. +plural → [əz] /after [č, ǰ, s, z, š, ž]
2. +plural → [əz] /after a sibilant consonant

In rule (1) we state that one phenomenon (plurality realized as [əz]) occurs in six different situations (after [č], after [š], and so on). In rule (2), on the other hand, we state that the one phenomenon occurs in one situation (after a sibilant consonant). The formulation in (1) makes no mention of any common property of the sounds involved and thus treats them as if they were a random collection of sounds with no relation to each other. By referring to natural classes, however, we can state generalizations, as in rule (2).

Another feature used to describe natural classes divides consonants into two groups, **obstruents** and **sonorants**. Obstruents are produced with an obstruction of the airflow. The sounds in this category are stops, fricatives, and affricates. Sonorants, on the other hand, are consonants produced with a relatively open passage for the airflow. Sonorant consonants include nasals, liquids, and glides. Thus, the class of labial obstruents in English is [p, f, b, v], while the class of labial consonants is [p, f, b, v, m, w, w̥]. As we will see in the phonology section of this book, being able to divide consonants into obstruents and sonorants is quite useful in stating phonological rules.

The simplest kind of natural class is one in which all of the members share *one* particular feature. For example, the natural class of velar consonants in English comprises all of those sounds in English that are produced with an obstruction of the vocal tract at the velum (i.e., [k, g, ŋ]). The natural class of high vowels contains all of those vowels described using the feature *high* ([i, ɪ, u, ʊ]). Another way that natural classes can be designated is by indicating more than one feature that all of the members of the class have. So, for instance, the high tense vowels of English are [i, u], the natural class of voiceless sibilants in English is [č, š, s], and so on. Notice that by adding to the number of features used to define the natural class we reduce the number of members in the class. In general it is true that a natural class defined by few features will be larger than one defined by many features.

voiceless sibilants in English is [č, š, s], and so on. Notice that by adding to the number of features used to define the natural class we reduce the number of members in the class. In general it is true that a natural class defined by few features will be larger than one defined by many features.

Conclusion

In this file we have shown that a natural class is a group of all the sounds in a language that share some articulatory or auditory feature(s). To describe natural classes we have used the features *consonant, vowel, labial, sibilant, obstruent,* and *sonorant,* as well as the features used to describe individual consonants and vowels.

Exercises

1. List the members of the following natural classes of English sounds.

    a. alveolar obstruent consonants
    b. voiced labial consonants
    c. velar oral stop consonants
    d. interdental fricative consonants
    e. high tense vowels
    f. low vowels
    g. palatal sonorant consonants
    h. voiced sibilant consonants

2. Describe the following natural classes of English sounds.

    a. [r, l]
    b. [f, s, š, h, θ]
    c. [w, y, w̥]
    d. [i, e, o, u]
    e. [p, b]
    f. [n, r, l]

3. Consider the following paragraphs and answer the questions about natural classes.

    a. The English indefinite article is *an* [æn] rather than *a* [ə] before words like *apple, onion, icicle, evening, eagle,* and *honor.* Members of what natural class of sounds begin the words of this list?

    b. Some American English speakers (largely in the Midwest and North) pronounce [ɪ] in words like *then, Kenny, pen, Bengals, gem, lengthen, Remington,* and *temperature* (where other speakers have [ɛ]). What natural class of sounds follows these vowels?

    c. Some midwestern American speakers in casual speech drop the unstressed vowel in the first syllable of words like *police, believe, parade, Columbus, pollution, terrific,* and *collision,* but do not drop it in words like *detective, dependent, majestic,* or *pedantic.* What natural class of sounds follows the unstressed vowel in the first syllable in this first group of words?

   d.   A speaker of German who is learning English might pronounce certain words as follows: *have* [hæf], *leg* [lɛk], *haze* [hes], *probe* [prop]. What natural class of sounds is being affected? What is happening to this natural class of sounds?

   e.   At some time during a child's language development, he or she might pronounce certain words as follows: *that* [dæt], *these* [diz], *this* [dɪs], and *three* [fri], *think* [fɪŋk], *bath* [bæf]. What natural class of sounds is being affected? Do the sounds used as replacements form a natural class?

   f.   During the history of the English language, a set of changes to the vowel system known as the Great Vowel Shift occurred. The Great Vowel Shift occurred during the transition from the Middle English (ME) to the Modern English (ModE) period. Before this change, ME had the following long vowels (the symbol [ː] after a vowel indicates that the vowel is long):

        ME: [iː, eː, ɛː, uː, oː, ɔː, aː]

One of the changes that occurred was the change of [iː] and [uː] to [ay] and [aw], respectively—so, for example, ME [miːs] became ModE [mays] and ME [muːs] became ModE [maws].

What natural class of ME long vowels was affected by this change (i.e., of [iː] to [ay] and [uː] to [aw])?

To what natural class do the ModE results belong? (Hint: they share a feature that was not discussed in this file, but that should be familiar to you by now.)

File 3.7 Suprasegmental Features

So far we have studied the characteristics of the segments (i.e., individual sounds) of speech: place and manner of articulation and voicing for consonants; tongue height and advancement, lip rounding, and tenseness for vowels. In this file we will consider other features that speech sounds may also have: length, intonation, tone, and stress. These features are called **suprasegmental features** because they are thought of as "riding on top of" other segmental features (*supra-* means 'over, above'). Suprasegmental features are different from the features we have studied so far in that not only may they belong to a single phonetic segment, they may (and often do) instead extend across numerous segments in an utterance.

Length

Not all speech sounds have the same duration. Some speech sounds are inherently longer than others; for example, all else being equal, high vowels are shorter than low vowels, and voiceless consonants are longer than voiced consonants. Voiceless fricatives are the longest consonants of all. The duration of a speech sound may also be influenced by the sounds around it. For example, say the words *beat* and *bead* aloud. In which word is the [i] longer? In English a vowel preceding a voiced consonant is about 1.5 times longer than the same vowel before a voiceless consonant. The place and manner of articulation of a following consonant can also affect vowel length. (Now try the word *bees*. How does it compare to *bead?*)

In some languages, differences in the duration of a segment are very important because substituting a long segment for an otherwise identical short segment (or vice versa) in a word can result in a different meaning—i.e., a different word. For example, consider the following data from Finnish. In Finnish both vowels and consonants may be long or short, and the difference in length can make a difference in the meaning of a word. (In the data below, long vowels and consonants are marked with a following [ː].)

1. a. [muta]   *mud*
    b. [muːta]   *some other*
    c. [mutːa]   *but*

2. a. [tapan]   *I kill*
    b. [tapaːn]   *I meet*

3. a. [tule]   *come!*
    b. [tuleː]   *comes*
    c. [tuːleː]   *is windy*

Intonation

Voiced speech sounds, particularly vowels, may be produced with different pitches (pitch is the psychological correlate of fundamental frequency, which depends on the rate of vibration of the vocal folds; see Files 3.9 and 3.10). Intonation is the pattern of rises and falls in pitch across a stretch of speech such as a sentence. The meaning of a sentence can depend in part on the sentence's intonation contour. For example, read the transcribed sentence below first with a falling pitch at the end, then with a rising pitch.

[yu gat ən e an ðə tɛst]

Which of the two intonation patterns makes the sentence sound like a question? Which makes it sound like a statement? Intonation also helps mark the boundaries of a syntactic unit. In the above example, the end of a sentence is marked by a rise or fall in pitch. Now imagine the same sentence as part of a larger one. For example read the following sentence out loud:

[yu gat ən e an ðə tɛst, ə si an ðə homwr̩k, n̩ ə bi an ðə kwɪz]

As you say this sentence aloud, you will see that the intonation pattern of the first part is not the same as when it formed a sentence by itself. Incompleteness is marked by a slightly rising or level pitch.

Tone

In many languages, the pitch at which the syllables in a word are pronounced can make a difference in the word's meaning. Such languages are called **tone languages** and include Thai; Mandarin and other "dialects" of Chinese (in fact, they are separate languages); Vietnamese; many of the Bantu languages of Africa such as Zulu, Luganda, and Shona; other African languages such as Yoruba and Igbo; and many North and South American Indian languages such as Apache, Navajo, Kiowa, and Mazotec. To see how the tone of a word can make a difference in meaning, consider the following words in Mandarin Chinese.

Segments	Tone Letter	Tone Pattern	Gloss
[ma]	˥	high level	*mother*
[ma]	˦	high rising	*hemp*
[ma]	˩	low falling rising	*horse*
[ma]	˥˩	high falling	*scold*

As you can see, the same segments in a word (in this case, the syllable [ma]) can be pronounced with different tones and as a result correspond to different meanings.

Tone languages fall into two categories, **register tone languages** and **contour tone languages**. The first kind of language contains only register, or level, tones such as high, mid, and low. Contour tone languages contain gliding tones as well as register tones. There is a difference in the tonal transcription system for register tone languages and for contour tone languages. Since contour lanuages can have four or even five distinct tones, the way tones are transcribed in these languages is more complex because more distinct tone levels need to be represented. Mandarin is a contour tone language that has four tones. As you can see from the examples above, it uses rising, falling, and level tones.

Many of the languages of sub-Saharan Africa are register tone languages and make use of tones to distinguish various words or to indicate grammatical distinctions. Even though these language usually only distinguish the level tones low and high, they can combine them to get rising and falling tones.

For example, in the Bantu languages Runyankore and Kikerewe, both spoken in Uganda, some words are distinguished by different tones. (The symbol ´ on a vowel indicates a high tone; ` indicates a low tone, and ˇ indicates a rising tone.)

Runyankore	*Tone Pattern*	*Gloss*
ènžù	low-low	*house*
ěnžù	rise-low	*gray hair*
àkèykò	low-low-low	*tiny wooden spoon*
àkéykò	low-high-low	*tiny trowel*

Kikerewe	*Tone Pattern*	*Gloss*
kùsàlà	low-low-low	*to be insane*
kùsálà	low-high-low	*to cut off meat*
kùsǐːngà	low-rise-low	*to defeat, win*
kùsìːngà	low-low-low	*to rub, apply ointment*
kùzúmà	low-high-low	*to insult, scold*
kùzùmà	low-low-low	*to rumble, be startled*

It is interesting and also important to note that the tones in a tone language are relative, not absolute. Thus the pitch of a high level tone spoken by a Mandarin speaker with a deep or low pitched voice will be considerably lower than the pitch of the same tone spoken by a female speaker or someone with a higher pitched voice. Note also that tone and intonation are not mutually exclusive: tone languages also use intonation.

Stress

Stress is a property of syllables, not individual segments. A stressed syllable is more prominent than an unstressed one. This prominence is due to a number of factors, including the fact that stressed syllables usually contain tense vowels, which are produced with more extreme positions of the tongue. This, in turn, leads to the perceptual impression that stressed vowels are produced with greater effort. Stressed syllables are also louder and longer. Unstressed syllables, on the other hand, often contain reduced vowels. A reduced vowel is one that is produced closer to the mid central position in the mouth, and that is more likely to be lax than its stressed, unreduced version. (For example, compare the second vowels in the words *photograph* and *photography*; how are they different?) English contains primary, secondary, and tertiary stress levels, as illustrated by a word like *photography*: in this word, the second syllable is most prominent (primary stress), the final syllable is next most prominent (secondary stress), and the other syllables are unstressed (tertiary stress).

In some languages the placement of stress on a word is predictable; for example, stress almost always falls on the first syllable of a word in Czech, on the next to last syllable of a word in Welsh, and on the last syllable of a phrase in French. In other languages such as Russian and English, stress placement is not predictable and must be learned for each word. In such languages the placement of stress can cause a difference in meaning. For example, what is the difference between a *bláckboard* and a *black bóard*? a *white hóuse* and the *White House*? Consider also the words *record*, *perfect*, and *subject*. How are their meanings different when stress falls on the first syllable as opposed to the second? Compare also the words *incite* and *insight*, which differ phonetically only in stress placement and which mean different things.

Much of our emphasis in the previous files has been on the transcription of speech sounds with a series of symbols. Suprasegmental features, on the other hand, prove to be difficult to transcribe this way because they are "superimposed" on the other features. For example, while the symbol [a] always represents the same speech sound whenever we write it, the symbol [:] has no meaning in isolation. Its meaning is a function of the meaning of the symbol (such as [a]) with which it is used, and even then it only indicates that a segment is long relative to the length of a similar sound transcribed without the [:]. Similarly, marking stress just indicates that the stressed syllable's segments are louder and longer than neighboring sounds. And you can change the intonational pattern of an English utterance radically without changing the segments on which the intonation rides. As you can see, our transcription system doesn't express these facts very well. Perhaps because of this, suprasegmental features are relatively poorly understood and remain an important topic in contemporary phonetic research.

File 3.8

Phonetic Detail and Narrow Transcription

So far we have been studying the inventory of phones (i.e., speech sounds) in English, and the properties or features of those phones—voicing, laxness, labiality, and so on. However, the descriptions of these sounds that we have developed so far show only a limited amount of phonetic detail. In fact, no sound is ever pronounced in exactly the same way twice. Its pronunciation varies among speakers, and even among different utterances by the same speaker. To some extent, however, variations in the way a phone is produced are predictable. The purpose of this file is to introduce some of the predictable phonetic variations of English, and to provide a system of **narrow phonetic transcription** that we can use to record those fine details of the articulation of phones. (Up until now we have been using **broad phonetic transcription**, which does not show much phonetic detail.)

Aspirated Stops

Not all voiceless stops are the same. Try pronouncing the words *pat* and *spat* while holding your hand (or a thin piece of paper, or a lighted match) in front of your mouth. You should notice a puff of air accompanying the [p] of *pat*, but not the [p] of *spat*. This puff of air is called **aspiration**; we transcribe it using a superscripted [ʰ], as in [pʰæt]. Aspiration occurs on all voiceless oral (i.e., nonglottal) stops occurring as the first sound in a stressed syllable in English:

pat	[pʰæt]	vs.	*spat*	[spæt]
kid	[kʰɪd]	vs.	*skid*	[skɪd]
top	[tʰap]	vs.	*stop*	[stap]
append	[əpʰɛnd]	vs.	*apple*	[æpl̩]

Unreleased Stops

Stop consonants, as you have learned, involve the complete blockage of the airflow in the oral tract. Ordinarily this stoppage is released before the next sound is produced, but it is also possible for an oral stop to be unreleased when it occurs before another stop. Try pronouncing the words *popcorn*, *kickback*, *labcoat*, *madman*, and *rugby* while making a conscious effort to release the stop at the end of the first syllable. You will find that this pronunciation is unnatural; instead, you probably pronounce these words as transcribed below (where [̚] following a stop indicates that it is unreleased).

popcorn	[pʰap̚kʰɔrn]
kickback	[kʰɪk̚bækʰ]
labcoat	[læb̚kʰotʰ]
madman	[mæd̚mæn]
rugby	[rʌg̚bi]

Note also that stops may be unreleased at the end of a word when that word is followed by a pause, or is utterance-final. For example, if you produced the sentence *She wore a labcoat*, you might pronounce the last word as [læb˺kʰot˺].

Flaps

Try pronouncing the pairs of words *ladder, latter* and *writer, rider*. Is there any difference between the medial consonants in these words? If you are a native speaker of American English, probably not. For such speakers each of these words contains a voiced alveolar **flap** instead of an alveolar stop in intervocalic (between vowel) position. The flap, transcribed [ɾ], is produced when the tongue tip hits the alveolar ridge at a high speed. Flaps replace voiced and voiceless oral alveolar stops after a stressed vowel and before an unstressed syllable, as in the following words:

catty	[kæɾi]
caddy	[kæɾi]
bitter	[bɪɾɾ̩]
bidder	[bɪɾɾ̩]
latter	[læɾɾ̩]
ladder	[læɾɾ̩]

Dental Consonants

Consonants that are ordinarily produced with the tongue at the alveolar ridge are articulated differently when followed by an interdental consonant (i.e., [θ] or [ð]). In this environment, they are pronounced with the tip of the tongue on the teeth rather than on the alveolar ridge; hence they are called dental consonants. For example:

health	[hɛl̪θ]
unthinkable	[ən̪θɪŋkəbl̩]
eighth	[et̪θ]
in this	[ɪn̪ ðɪs]

Velarized [ɫ]

In a broad phonetic transcription, the words *bowl* and *lobe* are represented as containing the same segments; only the order of segments differs. For many speakers, however, the [l]-sounds in these two words are not identical after all. Try pronouncing them, being careful to notice the difference. The [l] in *bowl* is velarized (or "dark"), while the [l] of *lobe* is "clear." Velarized [l]s are transcribed [ɫ] and are produced with the back of the tongue raised toward the velum. They occur following vowels, either at the end of a word or before a word-final consonant:

feel	[fiɫ]	vs.	*leaf*	[lif]
pill	[pɪɫ]	vs.	*lip*	[lɪp]
tall	[tɔɫ]			
golf	[gɔɫf]			

Voiceless Liquids and Glides

Liquids and glides in English are ordinarily voiced, but when they follow a voiceless obstruent in speech they are pronounced as voiceless consonants. This voicelessness is represented by putting a small open circle under the symbol for the liquid or glide (as a mnemonic, think of this circle as representing an open glottis). Note that a voiceless bilabial glide may appear in place of [w] following a voiceless obstruent and also (for some speakers) may appear without a preceding voiceless obstruent in words like *why* [w̥ay]. [l̥], [r̥], and [y̥], however, are restricted to appearing only after voiceless obstruents.

proof	[pr̥uf]
sleep	[sl̥ip]
quick	[kw̥ɪk]

Lengthened Vowels

As discussed in File 3.7, vowels in certain phonetic environments are *longer* than the same vowels in other environments. In particular, vowels which are followed by a voiced consonant are longer in duration than those followed by a voiceless consonant. In fact, the duration of the vowel is the discriminating factor in pairs of words like *bad* and *bat* if the final stop is unreleased. This extra length is transcribed using the symbol [:] following the vowel, as in the following examples.

peas	[pʰiːz]	vs.	*peace*	[pʰis]
had	[hæːd]	vs.	*hat*	[hæt]
road	[roːd]	vs.	*rote*	[rot]

Nasalized Vowels

Compare the words *green* and *greed*. To a native speaker of English these words will probably seem to contain identical vowels. On closer inspection, however, it turns out that these vowels are different in one respect: the vowel of *green* is nasalized as a result of the nasal consonant that follows it. The nasal consonant is produced with the velum lowered (that's what allows air to escape through the nasal passage); in producing a word like *green*, speakers lower their velum a little early and allow air to escape through the nasal as well as oral passages during the production of the vowel. We indicate nasalization by putting the symbol [˜] over the symbol for a vowel:

green	[grĩn]
tan	[tæ̃n]
sewn	[sõn]
lamb	[læ̃m]
tongs	[tã̃ŋz]

In English this nasalization of a vowel preceding a nasal consonant is entirely predictable, and speakers nasalize without being aware of doing so. But note that the same is not true of all languages, French being a well-known example. French contains both oral and nasal vowels, but the occurrence of one or the other can't be predicted on the basis of other sounds in a word. In fact, the choice between an oral and a nasal vowel can make a difference in the meaning of a word, as in the following examples:

beau	[bo]	'beautiful'	vs.	*bon*	[bõ]	'good'
laid	[lɛ]	'ugly'	vs.	*lin*	[lɛ̃]	'flax'
là	[la]	'there'	vs.	*lent*	[lã]	'slow'

File 3.9   Acoustic Phonetics Overview

Soun ys noght but eyr ybroken,
And every speche that ys spoken,
Lowd or pryvee, foul or fair,
In his substaunce ys but air.

Geoffrey Chaucer, *The House of Fame*

So far we have been concerned with articulatory phonetics, the study of how speech sounds are produced. In this file and the next we will examine speech sounds in terms of the physical aspects of the sound wave, i.e., the acoustic characteristics of the sounds.

One of the main difficulties in studying speech is that speech is fleeting; as soon as a sound is uttered, it's gone. One of the ways to capture it is to transcribe it using phonetic symbols, as we've seen in previous files. But transcription runs the risk of involving endless debate about what a speaker actually said (e.g., did she say short [a] or long [a:]?), even if the speech being transcribed has been recorded and can be played back again. However, modern technology has made it possible to conquer the fleeting nature of speech, at least to some degree, by making records of the acoustic properties of sounds.

Simple Sound Waves

Before we look at speech sounds, it is important to understand something of the nature of sound waves. Sound waves, unlike letters on a page, are not permanent things. They are disturbances in the air set off by a movement of some sort. One kind of movement that can set off a sound wave is vibration, such as that produced by violin strings, rubber bands, and tuning forks—or vocal folds. In this kind of sound wave a vibrating body sets the molecules of air surrounding it into vibration. In order to understand how this works, imagine that air molecules are like people in a crowded elevator trying to keep a comfortable distance from one another.

There are two physical phenomena resulting from this tendency toward equidistance that make it possible for sound waves to move through the atmosphere. These are **compression**, in which air molecules are more crowded together than usual, and **rarefaction**, in which air molecules are spread farther apart than usual. Because there is a tendency for air molecules to remain equidistant from one another, whenever they are placed in compression or rarefaction a certain instability is set up. Compressed molecules tend to move away from one another so that they are no longer compressed. Likewise, when air is rarefied there is a tendency for the molecules to move nearer together, as they were before rarefaction occurred.

When the string of a guitar is vibrating, it causes a sound wave in the following way: as the string moves away from its rest position, it pushes the adjacent air molecules closer to neighboring molecules, causing compression. The neighboring, compressed molecules move away from the first "uncomfortably close" molecules, toward others. Those other molecules in turn do the same, and the chain reaction continues.

As the vibrating guitar string moves in the other direction, back to its rest position and beyond, a rarefaction is created. This pulls the air molecules that had been pushed away back toward the string, which creates a rarefaction between them and the molecules on their other side, which pulls those molecules back, and so on. Note that the consequences of the movement (the crowding of the molecules) may be transmitted over a large distance while each individual molecule simply vibrates in place. This chain reaction, which is the consequence of the movement of the string, is the sound wave. When the string moves back and forth at a certain frequency, a group of air molecules which are at some distance from the string will alternately be compressed and rarefied at that frequency. If this chain reaction involving compression and rarefaction is repeated at a rate of 440 times a second, we will hear a musical tone known as "A above middle C." A sound wave such as this, which repeats at regular intervals, is called a **periodic wave**.

If we plot the energy with which the air molecules press against or pull away from one another in such a sound, the resulting plot looks like Figure 1. You can think of Figure 1 as a plot of the movement (vertical axis) of some air molecules across time (horizontal axis), or more accurately as being the amount of pressure exerted by the air molecules across time. When air molecules vibrate at rates from 20 to 20,000 times a second, the vibration is perceived as sound. It is interesting to note, however, that we don't really use this whole range for speech. In fact, the highest frequency that can be transmitted by a telephone is 3,500 cycles per second (hertz), and yet little essential information about the speech signal is lost by cutting off frequencies above this.

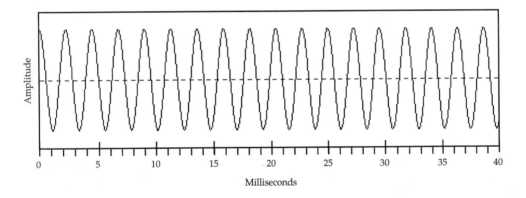

Figure 1.   440 hertz sine wave, the tone A.

Complex Sound Waves

Our discussion of sound waves up to this point has been very basic and somewhat simplified. In fact, simple sound waves such as those discussed in the previous section are not produced by guitar strings or human vocal folds. It's really not too difficult to understand why simple sound waves could not be produced by a guitar string. When we look at the vibration of the whole length of the string, it becomes clear that a simple wave cannot result. Figure 2 shows the vibrating string at two different points in time (solid and dashed lines); the amount of movement is exaggerated to make it easier to see.

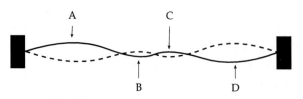

Figure 2.   Complex vibration of a string. Adapted with permission from Ladefoged, *Elements of Acoustic Phonetics* (1962), p. 24.

From this figure you can see that the string vibrates one way at A, another way at B, another way at C, and yet another way at D. The result of the parts of the string vibrating in different ways simultaneously is a complex wave, such as that in Figure 3c. Complex waves can be viewed as the combinations of a number of simple waves in the same way that the complex pattern of vibration in Figure 2 can be seen as the combination of several simpler patterns of vibration. Thus Figures 3a and 3b illustrate the simple wave components of the complex wave in Figure 3c.

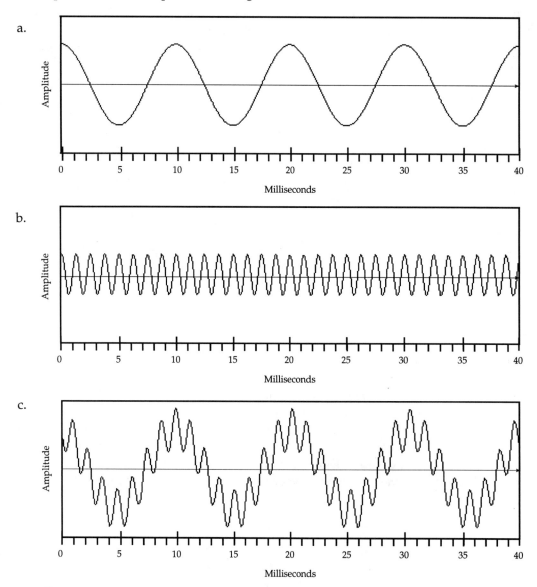

Figure 3.   Two simple waves combining to form a complex wave.

The sound wave that is produced by the vocal folds is a complex wave. This complex wave is composed of a fundamental wave which repeats itself at the frequency of the opening and closing of the vocal folds, and a set of **harmonic waves** which repeat at frequencies which are multiples of the fundamental. Thus, if the vocal folds open and close at a rate of 100 cycles per second, the fundamental frequency of the resulting sound wave is 100 hertz (cycles/second), the second harmonic is 200 Hz, the third harmonic is 300 Hz, and so on. Note that the first harmonic is the fundamental frequency.

The complex wave given off by the vocal folds is known as the *source wave*, because the vocal folds are the source of the sound wave; it is their movement which creates the wave. It can be represented in a histogram as in Figure 4a, where the horizontal axis stands for cycles per second, and the vertical axis represents the amplitude of the wave. Each line represents one component wave (or harmonic) in the complex vocal wave. Note that the relative amplitude of each wave gets progressively smaller at higher frequencies.

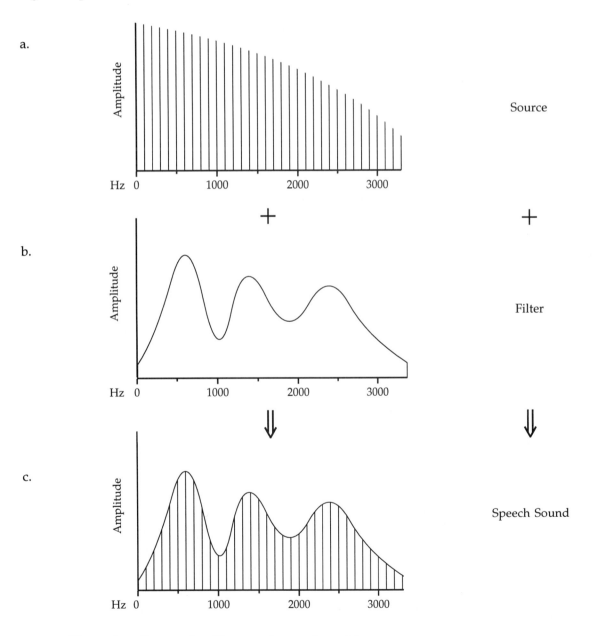

Figure 4.   Source plus filter equals speech sound.

As this sound wave passes through the vocal tract, the articulators shape it, or filter it, boosting the energy at some harmonic frequencies and damping the energy at others. This filter action is similar to the effect of room acoustics on a speaker's voice. Some rooms enhance the voice so that no amplification is needed, while others seem to absorb the voice, muffling the sound. In a similar way, the vocal tract acts as a filter on the source wave. In Figure 4, the vocal tract positioned for the vowel [a] has a filtering effect as in 4b, and harmonics at about 600 Hz, 1380 Hz, and 2500 Hz are enhanced, while harmonics at other positions are damped, yielding the output wave in Figure 4c.

Thus a speech sound (wave) is the result of two independent things: the source wave (the contribution of the vocal folds) and the filter (the contribution of the articulators and the vocal tract).

File 3.10

Acoustic Characteristics of Sound

In File 3.9 we looked at general characteristics of the speech sound wave. In this file we will examine the acoustic characteristics of various English speech sounds in more detail. We will be examining some of the acoustic properties of these phones that allow listeners to determine what sounds they are hearing. We will begin by discussing vowels, then we will briefly examine some of the acoustic characteristics of stops, fricatives, and nasals.

Vowels

In the production of vowels, the filtering effect of the vocal tract produces amplitude peaks at certain frequencies by enhancing the **harmonics** (which are the component waves of a complex wave form, produced by the vocal folds) at those frequencies while damping harmonics at other frequencies (see Figure 4 of previous file). These peaks in the filter function are called **formants** (resonant frequencies of the vocal tract). For example, as a trombone has particular resonant frequencies (determined by the length of the tube) that shape the sound produced by the vibration of the lips, in vowel sounds the vocal tract has resonant frequencies (determined by the length and configuration of the vocal tract) that shape the sound produced by vocal fold vibration. These resonant frequencies of the vocal tract are the vowel formants. Vowels have several formants, the first three of which are the most important for speech perception. The values of these formants differ from vowel to vowel. The following table lists typical formant frequencies for eight American English vowels.

Vowel	F1	F2	F3
[i]	280	2250	2890
[ɪ]	400	1920	2560
[ɛ]	550	1770	2490
[æ]	690	1660	2490
[u]	310	870	2250
[ʊ]	450	1030	2380
[ɔ]	590	880	2540
[a]	710	1100	2540

Frequencies in hertz (Hz) of the first, second, and third formants

We can plot these vowels by the frequencies of their first two formants, as in Figure 1. Note that the resulting diagram looks strikingly similar to the vowel chart in File 3.3. Thus we can see that the first formant corresponds inversely to the height dimension (high vowels have a low F1 and low vowels have a high F1) and the second formant corresponds to the advancement (front/back) dimension (front vowels have high F2 and back vowels have low F2).

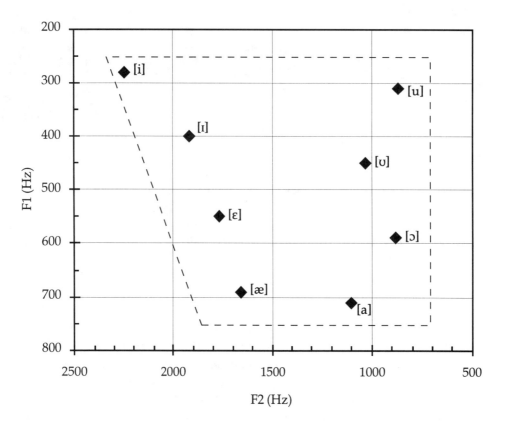

Figure 1.   Plot of the first formant (F1) against the second formant (F2) of some English
vowels.

A common method of representing acoustic properties of speech sounds is to use a **spectrogram**. Spectrograms are graphs that encode three acoustic dimensions: the vertical axis represents frequency and the horizontal axis represents time. A third dimension is represented by degree of darkness that indicates the amount of acoustic energy present at a certain time and at a certain frequency. Dark horizontal bands usually represent formants. Figure 2 shows spectrograms for the three vowels [i], [u], and [a]. The arrows point out only the first three vowel formants, termed F1, F2, and F3, although there are more formants visible in these spectrograms. The horizontal lines in each of these displays mark off frequency in hertz by the 1000s.

Frequency (Hz)

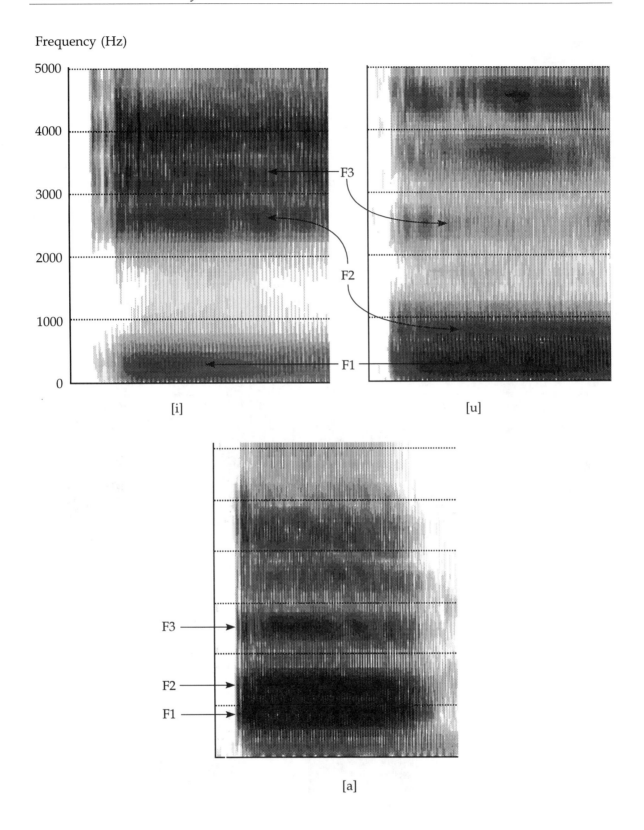

Figure 2.   Spectrograms of the vowels [i], [u], [a].

Stops

Stop consonants are easy to detect in wave forms because they are characterized by a lack of sound, or a gap in the spectrographic display, as illustrated in Figure 3 below. If the stop is voiced, the vocal folds vibrate during the closure. This is reflected by the voice bar that is clearly visible in all three cases. The acoustic characteristic of a stop reflects its manner of articulation: a stop involves a complete blockage of the air flow, and thus a complete damping of the sound emitted from the vocal tract.

The acoustic information corresponding to place of articulation for a stop is found mostly in the vowels around it. When we pronounce a sequence like [ada], the tongue can't move instantaneously from a low back tongue position to the alveolar ridge for the voiced alveolar stop and back to the vowel position. Rather, the tongue slides from one position to the next. Therefore, there are points in time when the tongue is in transition from the vowel to the consonant or the consonant to the vowel. Of course, this changing vocal tract shape affects the formants; as a result, during the early part of the second vowel the formants are also in transition toward their usual values. Figure 3 shows spectrograms of vowel-stop-vowel sequences in which we can see moving formants reflecting the moving articulator. (The horizontal lines in each of these displays mark off frequency in hertz by the 1000s.)

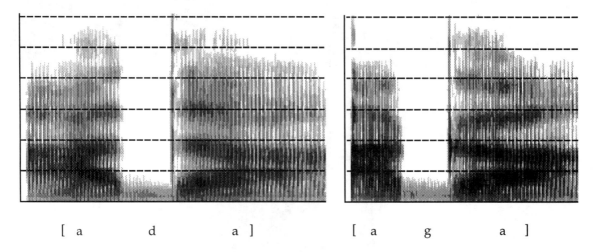

      [a   d   a]   [a   g   a]

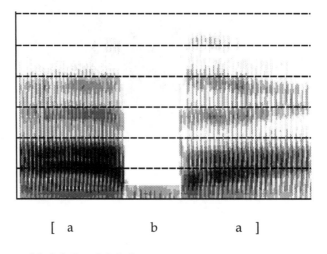

      [a   b   a]

Figure 3.   Spectrograms of [ada], [aga], [aba].

We can determine the place of articulation of the stop by examining the starting or ending points of the moving second formant. For alveolar stops the transition of the second formant starts at about 1700–1800 Hz. For bilabial stops the second formant starts relatively low and rises out of the stop closure and into the vowel. For velar stops it depends on what kind of vowel follows: before a front vowel the second formant starts high and falls, and before a back vowel the second formant starts lower, around 900 Hz or even less.

The main acoustic cues for voicing in English are complicated. When the stop consonant precedes a stressed vowel, the most important cue is the amount of time between the complete silence of the stop closure and the beginning of the vowel formants. This interval is called **voice onset time**, which is abbreviated as *VOT*. Following a voiceless stop, the onset of the vowel may be delayed while the vocal folds are held open for a brief while (about 50 milliseconds). This delays the vibration of the vocal

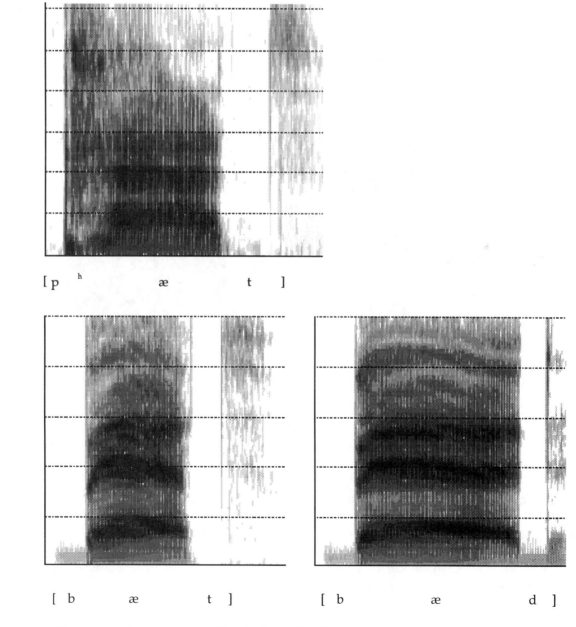

Figure 4.   Spectrograms of [pæt], [bæt], [bæd].

folds after the release of the stop closure and allows air to rush out. This delay produces the effect known as **aspiration**, as illustrated in the spectrogram of the word *pat* in Figure 4, above. In some languages, voicing starts before the voiced stop is released. Generally, after voiced stops there is very little or no delay in the onset of regular vocal fold vibration (i.e., voicing). When the stop in question follows a vowel, the main cue whether this stop is voiced or voiceless is the length of the vowel. In English, vowels are longer in duration before a voiced stop than before a voiceless one (cf. the vowels in [bæt] and [bæd]). (Note that the aspiration at the end of each of these three words was produced as the speaker exhaled, since these words were produced in isolation.)

Fricatives

Fricatives involve a new kind of sound that we have not dealt with up to this point. The difference between the noise found in vowels and in fricatives is that the sound in vowels has its source in the periodic vibration of the vocal folds, while the sound in fricatives comes from the aperiodic, or random, turbulence of the air rushing through a small opening. Note in Figure 5 that during the vowels there is a regular repetition (seen in the vertical stripes) while in the fricative portions there is no apparent pattern; it looks like static on a TV screen.

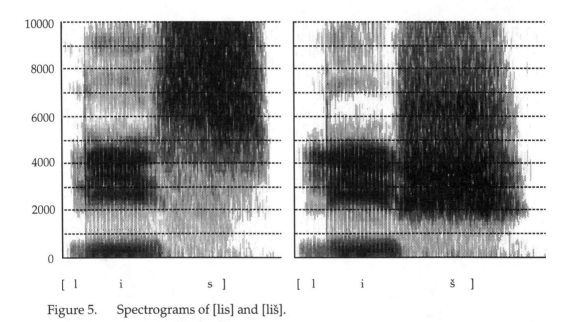

Figure 5.   Spectrograms of [lis] and [liš].

We find differences among English fricatives in the relative frequency of the noise (e.g., [s] has a higher frequency energy concentration in the frication noise than [š]), amplitude (e.g., [s] is louder than [f]), and duration (e.g., [s] is longer than [z]). As with stops, the formant transitions from the consonant into the vowel are also used by listeners to determine the place of articulation.

Voiced fricatives are interesting in that they combine periodic noise (the vocal folds are vibrating in a regular cycle) and aperiodic noise (there is turbulence from the air being forced through a small opening). Affricates are sequences of stop plus fricative both in their articulation and in their acoustic characteristics. A spectrogram of an affricate begins with a gap in the wave form, which is immediately followed by the aperiodicity of a fricative.

Nasals

In the production of nasal consonants, the oral cavity is closed as if for a stop, but air escapes past the lowered velum through the nasal cavity. In acoustic terms, the nasal passage serves as the filter for the vocal source, just as the oral cavity acts as a filter in vowels. All nasal consonants have quite similar formants (see Figure 6), reflecting the shape of the nasal passage, which enhances some harmonics and damps others; however, the transitions into the vowels are different. Nasal formants are somewhere around 250, 2500, and 3250 Hz. The place of articulation of nasal consonants, as you might expect, is best cued by the transitions into the vowel. Note that the F2 in the word [mi] is faintly visible at around 1750 Hz, whereas the F2 for [ni] is at around 1250 Hz. (The horizontal lines in each of these displays mark off frequency in Hz by the 1000s.)

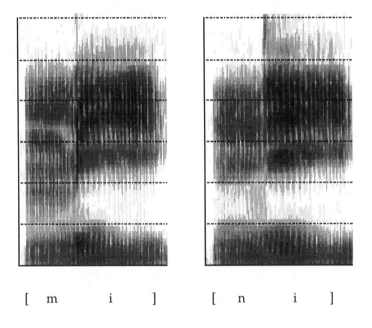

[m   i   ]   [n   i   ]

Figure 6.   Spectrogram of [mi] and [ni].

Exercise

A. On the next page you will find a spectrogram showing the formants of five vowels from a language called Mazotec. (Each vowel in the spectrogram is preceded by a fricative.) Mazotec has five vowels: [i], [e], [a], [o], and [u]. Your task is to measure the vowel space. Find the center value for the first and the second formants (in hertz). Be sure to take the value from the middle of the formant (both on the time axis and the frequency axis). Then plot the first formant values against the second formant values in the graph provided below. In other words, for each vowel, its first formant frequency will be the vertical (the "y") value and its second formant frequency will be the horizontal (the "x") value of a point. When you have finished, compare this chart with Figure 1.

Frequency (Hz)

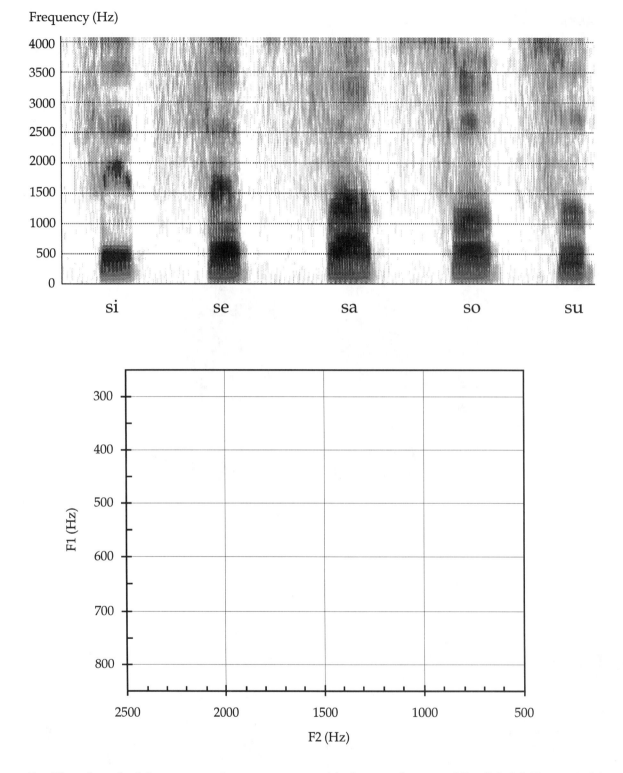

B. How does the Mazotec vowel space compare with the vowel space of English (cf. Figure 1, this file)? Are the vowels in the same place relative to each other, or are there differences in the way that English distributes its vowels compared to how Mazotec distributes its vowels?

File 3.11

Experimental Methods in Phonetics

This file describes several instruments and experimental methods that can be used to study speech sounds. By using these instruments and by doing these experiments, phoneticians have gained some insight into how speech sounds are produced and what their acoustic characteristics are. Consonants have been described in terms of voicing, place of articulation, and manner of articulation, while vowels have been described in terms of the height of the tongue, tongue advancement, lip rounding, and tenseness. The question arises, though, of how we can determine whether those descriptions are accurate and not merely based on speakers' intuitions. Try to figure out where your tongue is when you produce an [u] or what the back of your tongue does when you say [s] or the American English [r]. Even though most of us have a great deal of experience speaking, we do not know how we actually produce these sounds, we just do it. This section is concerned with some of the experimental methods and techniques that are used to answer questions such as whether or not a sound is voiced and where its place or manner of articulation is.

One important fact to keep in mind is that pronunciation is not static but happens over time. Aside from certain exclamations, like *Ah!* [a], *Sh!* [š] or *Oh!* [o], we usually speak in larger chunks than single static speech sounds. If you listen to your native language or to a language with which you are familiar, you can surely distinguish a [t] from a [d] (a difference in voicing); or a [t] from a [k] (a difference in the place of the stop closure); or a [t] from a [s] (a difference in manner). In some cases, it appears to be simple to distinguish between a voiced and a voiceless sound, for example, particularly when you are familiar with the language. However, while you can give an approximate description of someone's pronunciation of a sound or word, your perceptual system can easily fool you when it comes to details.

Voicing

Phoneticians use many different tools and measurement instruments, run experiments, and analyze vast amounts of data in order to come up with an accurate description of the sounds of speech. For example, in order to test whether a speech sound is voiced or voiceless, that is, whether the vocal folds vibrate or not, you can hold on to your larynx (voicebox) to feel the vibration. However, this is not a very precise and reliable method. To test more precisely whether a sound is voiced or voiceless, one can look at **spectrograms**, which are pictures of speech sounds that a computer calculates from the input of speech over a microphone or from a tape recording. Spectrograms are very reliable tools for a skilled and experienced phonetician because with some knowledge of what certain speech sounds typically look like and with a bit of experience one can practically begin to read the utterance from these displays. To address the question of whether or not a sound is voiced, look at the spectrograms below in Figure 1:

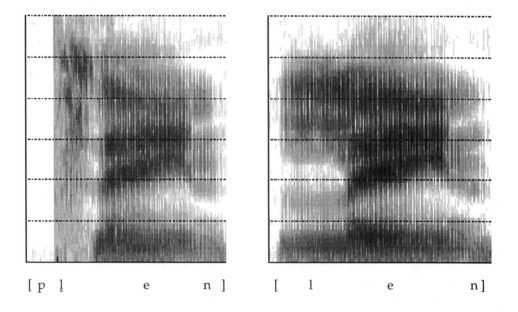

[p ḷ   e   n]   [l   e   n]

Figure 1.   Spectrograms of the words *plain* and *lane.*

Both spectrograms show words that contain the [l] sound. When you touch your larynx to discover whether this sound is voiced (if the vocal folds are vibrating) in each word, it is very unlikely that you will be able to feel a difference, because the time it takes to say the [l] is so short (10 or 20 milliseconds) and thus your intuition is not very reliable. Therefore, we need much finer grained methods of testing. Spectrograms are very useful in this respect. By reading and comparing the spectrograms, we know that the [l] on the left is voiceless and the [l] on the right is voiced. The [l] becomes voiceless since the onset of regular vocal fold vibration is delayed by the aspiration accompanying the release of the closure for the [p]. The **voice bar** at the very bottom of the spectrogram indicates that the [l] is voiceless here. The voice bar is an acoustic recording of the voicing of a speech sound. Each individual stripe in this bar indicates one *glottal pulse.* A glottal pulse is that short interval in time when the vocal folds open very briefly (letting air from the lungs escape) and then slam together again. The dark stripes indicate how often during a given interval the glottal folds are open. This slamming of the vocal folds generates the sound we perceive as voicing. To get a clearer picture of this process, try blowing some air through your approximated (lightly closed) lips and making them vibrate really fast. The rapid opening and closing of your lips is analogous to what happens at your glottis. Your lips are doing what the vocal folds do during voicing. The voice bar is a good indication of whether a sound is voiced or voiceless, because whenever the vocal folds are pushed open, energy is recorded on the spectrogram. This method is probably the fastest and easiest way to determine whether a sound is voiced or voiceless. However, there are many more methods that provide insight into articulatory mechanisms like voicing.

Another way of finding out whether a sound is voiced or not is to do an EGG (Electroglottograph) study. In an EGG study, electrodes are externally attached to the left and the right sides of a speaker's larynx. A very weak current flows from one electrode to the other, measuring the resistance that the current has to overcome by passing through the larynx. So if the vocal folds are open there will be a higher resistance than when the vocal folds are closed, since the current has to pass through air and is not transmitted through tissue. As the person speaks, a computer calculates from the recorded values for the resistance whenever the vocal folds make contact. However, this method does not tell us anything about how far apart, or how approximated, the vocal folds are (i.e., how wide the glottis is) or the shape of the vocal fold opening.

Some methods make it possible to look at vocal fold vibration directly. The most straightforward way is to make a high-speed video of the vocal folds as they vibrate during speech. Phoneticians, speech pathologists, and scientists in medical professions have learned much about the actual mechanisms of vocal fold vibration from this technique. A very thin fiberoptic line is inserted through the speaker's nostril and nasal cavity down into the upper part of the pharynx. This line conveys strong white light through the nasal cavity and the vocal tract so that the vocal folds are lit. A tiny camera lens, also connected to the fiberoptic line and hooked up to a computer or video recorder, tapes any movement of the vocal folds. As the subject speaks, the extremely fast vibrations of the vocal folds are filmed so that one can later look at and analyze these recordings frame by frame. By this method, scientists are able to observe the adjustments made by the vocal folds in the transition from voiced (approximated vocal folds) to unvoiced (open vocal folds). The advantage of this method is that the speaker is absolutely free to speak, since there are no obstacles inserted into his or her mouth, and yet we get a very clear picture of the mechanisms of voicing. However, this method is invasive and requires the presence of well-trained medical personnel.

Place of Articulation

In English [n] is described as having an alveolar place of articulation. This means that the tongue tip touches the alveolar ridge to form a complete obstruction of the airstream. Speakers of English are generally not aware that the place where the tongue tip touches the roof of the mouth for an /n/ can vary, depending on the sound that is produced after it. For example, say the word *in*, stop right on the [n], and sustain it. You will find that your tongue is up against the alveolar ridge, as is described for /n/ in the consonant chart. Then say the words *in this* and stop right on the [n]. Your tongue tip now is likely to be touching the back of your upper front teeth, and thus, the place of articulation has changed from *alveolar* to *dental*.

One experimental way to test where tongue contact is made is by **static palatography**. A mixture of olive oil and charcoal is applied to the tongue so that the whole tongue is blackened. Some lemon juice can be added to the mixture to make it taste a bit better. When the tongue now touches the roof of the mouth to form a closure for the [n], it leaves a visible trace of charcoal on the alveolar ridge or the teeth (depending on where the contact was made) and wherever else the tongue touched the hard palate to form the oral closure. If the hard palate is painted dark with the charcoal mixture and the tongue makes contact, the place where contact is made is shown as a dark trace on the tongue. This method only works, however, if the speaker produces single isolated sounds and the contact pattern is photographed or examined immediately.

In order to observe the interplay between articulations, that is, how one consonant's place of articulation affects another consonant's place of articulation, one uses **dynamic palatography** (also called EPG, which is the abbreviation for *electropalatography*). This method is similar to static palatography but more sophisticated because it allows the experimenter to record sequences of contacts that the tongue makes with the hard palate in the course of the production of an utterance. This method also is less messy than static palatography. The places where contact is made are directly recorded into a computer. Once the recordings are made, you can align a specific point in time of the waveform of the utterance with a specific EPG display. (A waveform is an acoustic display of the sound energy. This energy produces a periodic wave as the vocal folds are regularly vibrating when they are in the mode of "voicing.") This way you can measure exactly where, how much, and how long contact between the tongue and the roof of the mouth is produced at any given time in the utterance.

The speaker in such a study is required to use an artificial hard palate (like a retainer) that is custom made to fit exactly his or her hard palate shape. This artificial palate has many small embedded electrodes that record contact as soon as the tongue moves against them. So for any given moment in time during the recording the researcher knows exactly where the tongue contacts the roof of the mouth. Since the retainer only covers the hard palate, the exact amount of contact made in the soft palate region for velar consonants, such as /g/or /k/, is sometimes hard to see. Nevertheless, this method provides fairly exact data about where and at what point in time within an utterance the tongue touches the hard palate.

In Figure 2 you see a flattened version of the curved retainer. Every electrode on the retainer is represented by a little cross, and every electrode touched by the tongue is represented by a dark square. There are eleven rows of electrodes, counting down the middle of the display. The top row corresponds to electrodes that are located just behind the front teeth. The crosses in the second and third row correspond to the alveolar region. Rows 4 through 9 are located in the palatal region, and electrode rows 10 and 11 are in the back (velar area) of the oral cavity. (Note that in this particular retainer, on the right side, two electrodes were broken and did not record any contact.)

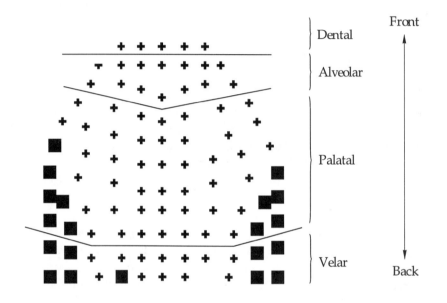

Figure 2.   Flattened version of the curved retainer that is used in EPG studies.

Apart from the information that we gather about the places of articulations of sounds by using dynamic palatography, we can also derive information about the temporal coordination of articulations. For example, when you make the transition between the words in the sequence *bad guy* very slowly, your tongue touches the alveolar ridge to form the stop closure for the [d], and then, immediately following the release of the [d], the back of the tongue rises to form the stop closure for the velar stop [g]. These individual movements of the articulators are termed **gestures**. Thus, the specific movement of the tongue (rising of the front of the tongue, contacting the alveolar ridge, lowering of the tongue) to produce the [d] is one gesture, and the specific movement of the tongue to produce the [g] is another gesture. However, when we speak at a normal rate or even a bit faster, we typically are not aware of how we coordinate these gestures that our articulators perform. That is, we are not really aware of when the gesture of [d] ends and the gesture for [g] begins, we just do it. This is like walking: in a sequence of two steps you don't really know when you lift one foot off the ground and put the other down, you just do it.

When we speak naturally, we do not produce individual sounds but rather whole strings of sounds, which form words. Dynamic palatographic pictures of a string of sounds as they occur in the phrase *bad guy* show us that the individual articulatory gestures are not truly single, isolated events, but instead that gestures overlap in time. The sequence of displays in Figure 3 illustrates that the gestures for the [d] and for the [g] in the phrase *bad guy* overlap in time. In other words, one gesture starts before the other is finished so that there is a period of time in which both gestures are active. In Figure 3 below, the individual tracings are numbered from left to right. Each of these tracings was recorded with a 10-millisecond interval.

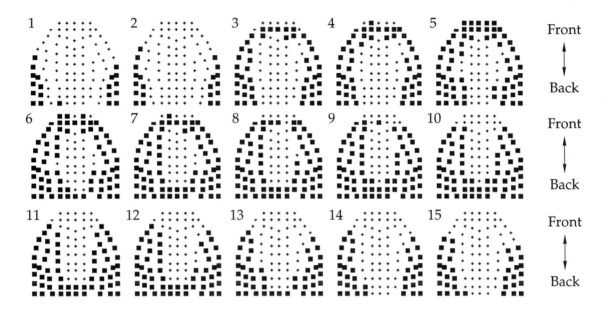

Figure 3.   Pattern recorded while a speaker pronounced the phrase *bad guy*, a reading taken every 10 milliseconds.

In displays 1 and 2 of the above figure, only the sides of the tongue touch the hard palate. In displays 3 through 5 you can see dark squares around the front of the palate. This shows that the tongue touched the retainer around the front part of the oral cavity to form the stop closure for a [d]. If you think about how we produce a [d] sound, you will remember that since this sound is a stop, the air is completely blocked for some time. Displays 6, 7, and 8 show that while the tongue is still forming the closure for the [d], there is some simultaneous contact reported by the electrodes in the last two or three rows, telling us that the back of the tongue contacted the velar region of the artificial palate. In other words, the [g] closure set on before the the closure for the [d] was released.

Displays 8 through 10 show that the [d] closure is slowly released and that the amount of contact between the front of the tongue and the retainer lessens as time passes (keep in mind, these are only milliseconds we are talking about). You can see this from the number of squares that have turned into crosses again. Displays 11 through 13 show that the contact on the sides and in the back lessens during those 20 milliseconds, and the closure for the [g] is totally released in displays 14 and 15, in which the articulators start to form the gesture for the first part of the diphthong [ay] in *guy*. Here, then, is convincing experimental evidence showing that certain sounds that we think of as being the same actually have different places of articulation. In addition, by using this method, we learn much about the temporal coordination of these articulatory gestures.

Using static or dynamic palatography, experimenters can only test sounds that are produced by the tongue contacting either the hard palate or the very front part of the soft palate. With the latter method, we can find out about the coordination of particular movements of our articulators as we speak, that is, we can see how long articulatory gestures overlap in fluent speech. It is, however, impossible with this kind of method to test sounds that are produced farther back in the oral cavity or that do not involve any contact between the tongue and the hard palate. In addition, dynamic palatography is a useful tool for speech therapy sessions in which the teacher and the learner wear such retainers as the learner attempts to produce and match the contact patterns that the teacher produces for a given sequence of sounds. The student thus practices sequences of gestures and their timing relative to each other.

There are places of articulation for certain consonants (such as pharyngeal consonants that occur, for example, in Arabic) that are produced so far back in the oral cavity that neither kind of palatography will tell us anything about the place of articulation. For cases in which the tongue does not make contact with any part of the oral cavity, as with vowels, this kind of experimental method also has limited value. To study those sounds and to look at place of articulation in such cases, phoneticians used to make X-ray movies of people talking. These X-ray films could be played over and over (like a video) to see tongue, lip, and jaw movements as they occur over time. The backward movement of the tongue in Arabic pharyngeal sounds can be seen quite clearly in these films. The midsaggital sections (see File 3.4) showing shapes of the vocal tract for the production of different sounds are based on these kind of studies. This methodology is not used anymore, though, since it turned out to be harmful for the speakers. There are now safer and much more accurate techniques that use highly advanced technology to investigate places of articulation.

Manner of Articulation

When talking of manners of articulation, we are essentially referring to the acoustic and aerodynamic properties of sounds. During the production of stop consonants, for example, the airstream coming from the lungs is completely blocked for a brief time. During that interval, there is no air escaping at all. The production of voiceless stop consonants involves the production of *silence*. Fricative speech sounds, on the other hand, involve the production of *turbulent airflow*, which is created when air is forced through a very small opening in the oral cavity, or blown against an obstacle like the front teeth. Yet another way of modifying the manner of articulation is to create *nonturbulent* airflow, as for example in nasals, liquids or glides. In these cases, the opening of the constriction in the vocal tract is not so small that turbulent airflow and therefore frication is created, but it is also not as big as in the production of vowels.

Some manners of articulation can be more easily tested than others; *nasality* is one of them. In fully nasal sounds, for example, the air escapes through the nasal cavity rather than the oral cavity. One way to observe this is to close off your nose (with your fingers) while trying to sustain a nasal sound like [m], [n] or [ŋ]. Even if you try hard, you cannot sustain the sound because the air cannot escape through the mouth or the nose. A more sophisticated method of observing how much air comes out of the nose during fluent speech is by measuring the amount of air exhaled. The speaker wears an airtight airflow mask that keeps the chambers for the mouth and nose distinct. The mask is equipped with airflow meters which are hooked up to a computer that then calculates the amount of air that escapes through the mouth and nose as the speaker says something.

French, for example, has vowels for which a difference in meaning can be created just by opening the nose (i.e., lowering the velum) when producing a vowel (i.e., nasalized vowels). For speakers of French, this difference is just as apparent as the difference between [i] and [a] for an English speaker. In contrast to French, in English or German whether or not the nose is open when producing vowels does not create a difference in meaning. In Figure 4 you can see nasal airflow as well as oral airflow tracings for the word *Anna*, produced by an American English speaker. In the upper panel the amount of air escaping through the mouth is displayed. On the lower panel the amount of air escaping through the nose is traced. One can see that already during the vowel [æ] that precedes the nasal [n], some air escapes through the nose, indicating that the nose is open. The straight line progressively elevates during the initial vowel and throughout the nasal: the steadily rising line indicates that the velum has already lowered during the initial vowel and that the speaker is getting ready to produce the nasal. The amount of air escaping through the nose decreases fairly abruptly as the velum closes again toward the end of the nasal for the production of the final vowel.

[æ   n   ə]

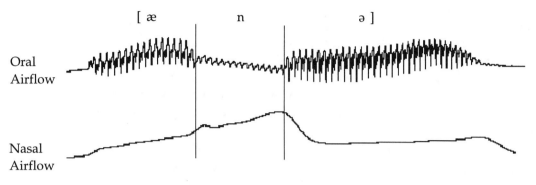

Oral
Airflow

Nasal
Airflow

Figure 4.   Oral and nasal airflow tracings of the word *Anna*.

Measuring the amount of air that escapes also helps to distinguish between stop consonants and fricative consonants, because during stops there is a total blockage of air and absolutely no air escapes. To test for fricatives, phoneticians usually use a spectrograph, which is a device designed to imitate the auditory response to sound. Fricatives are perhaps more apparent than other sounds because turbulent noise is generated during their production. These sounds are formed by approximating the articulators to such a degree that only a little opening is kept through which the air can escape. Fricatives are essentially just turbulent noise, produced when the air flows past an obstacle (e.g., a tooth) in the oral cavity. The pattern apparent in the spectrogram of [s] in [su] is characteristic of all fricatives. Depending on the place of articulation of the fricative, the energy concentration in the fricative will vary. Figure 5 shows a spectrogram of the fricative-vowel sequence [su].

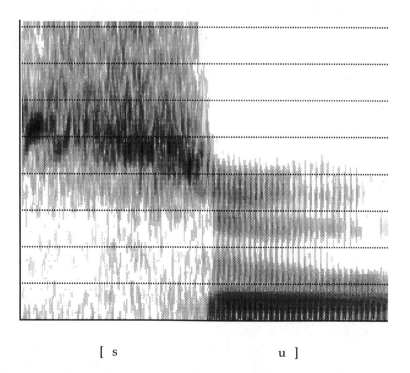

[s   u]

Figure 5.   Spectrogram of the fricative-vowel sequence [su].

We know a great deal about the manner of articulation of a sound from the acoustic properties of the airstream that is modified while passing through the oral or nasal cavity. Stop consonants are somewhat more complicated than fricatives because they involve a sequence of events rather than just a single acoustic or aerodynamic event. Every stop consonant has a phase during which the airstream is completely blocked. This is the *closure* phase and the first event in the sequence. During the closure, the vocal folds may or may not vibrate. The second event in the production of stop consonants is the *release* phase. There are several ways that stops can be released. For instance, in English, stop releases may coincide with voicing or there may be a period of aspiration during the release. In the example shown in Figure 6 you can see what such a noise looks like after the stop is released. The puff of air is termed **aspiration** and indicates that as the closure is released, there is a great deal of air escaping from the oral cavity. Aspiration delays the regular and periodic vibration of the vocal folds after the release of the stop closure.

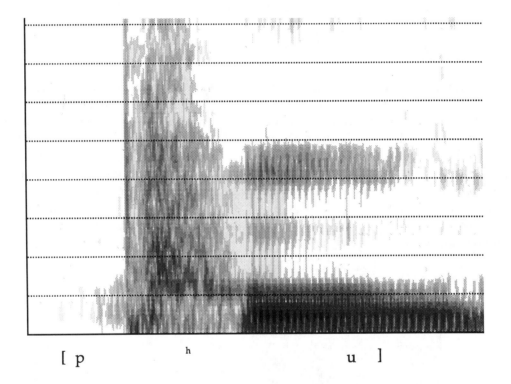

[p   ʰ   u   ]

Figure 6.   Spectrogram of the stop-vowel sequence [pʰu].

There are other ways of testing manners of articulation; however, the more common ones have been introduced here.

Experimental Methods

Experiments are necessary if you don't want to rely only on your intuitions. Very often these intuitions are different from the physical reality. Depending on what you want to know or what you would like to test, you have to select the appropriate tools and methods to apply. However, regardless of the experimental method employed, the more speakers you test, the more reliable your results. If you were to do an experiment with only one speaker of a given language, how would you know that the data that you had gathered were not just accidental observations and invalid for all the other speakers of that language? Well, unfortunately, you wouldn't. Therefore, you want to test more than one speaker of that language. If you repeat the same sound or string of sounds over and over again and record yourself, you will also be able to find differences in your pronunciations. No two words are pronounced exactly alike. In order to compensate and account for the variation in speech, more than one recording is necessary in which the speaker pronounces the words or phrases more than once.

Also, more than one speaker should be used so that you can examine the ranges of values possible and the kind of differences produced. In other words, you want to know how much variation is acceptable in the speech signal, that is, in the pronunciation of a particular word, so that listeners still analyze this item as that particular word. For example, if you make a recording of yourself saying the words *below, polite, support,* or *beret* very rapidly and play this tape to friends, some may perceive these words as *blow, plight, sport,* and *bray,* respectively. Therefore, in phonetics it is very important to use more than one speaker in the study and to make more than one recording of those pronunciations.

There are also other methods used to describe the physical properties and sounds of speech. Most of the methods and experiments employed in the field of phonetics use fairly advanced computer technology to measure and calculate precisely the speed of movements of the articulators, the places of articulations, the interplay between the articulators, the duration of some acoustic event, and so forth. Phoneticians collaborate with speech pathologists, electrical engineers, and artificial intelligence scientists, while others go out into the field and record speakers who are not readily available to them at the locations of their speech laboratories. Although some of the methods described may seem elaborate, there are many experimental tools available that fit into a suitcase so that field work can be done in the arctic regions of Alaska or the tropical forests of Brazil. This overview of experimental methods in phonetics is, of course, not exhaustive. There are many more ways to test and investigate the acoustic, aerodynamic, or auditory properties of speech sounds. However, this file demonstrates that there is a physical reality to the claims brought forward about the voicing of a sound, its place of articulation, and its manner.

Exercises

1. For which sounds of English can dynamic palatography be used to determine place of articulation?

2. The following displays show contact patterns extracted from a series of articulations that were recorded by means of dynamic palatography. The displays show contact patterns of the tongue with the roof of the mouth. What sounds are these articulations typical of?

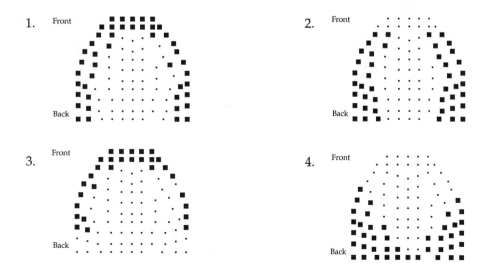

3. The following spectrograms show vowel-consonant-vowel sequences. Determine if the consonant is voiced or voiceless. How can you tell? One of the sounds displayed in the spectrograms is a fricative. Can you tell which?

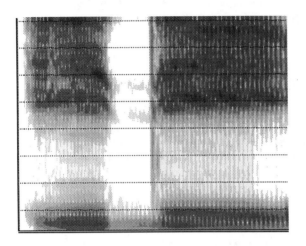

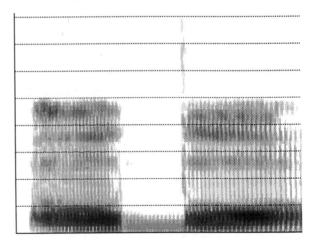

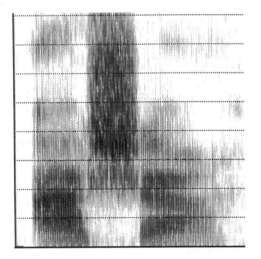

4

Phonology

Two languages can have all the same phones but may not sound the same. The explanation lies in each language's use of its inventory of sounds. Phonology studies the distribution of sounds in a language as well as the interaction between those different sounds.

File 4.1　The Value of Sounds: Phonemes

What Is Phonology?

Both phonetics and phonology can be generally described as the study of speech sounds. **Phonetics**, as we learned in the previous section, is more specifically the study of how speech sounds are produced, what their physical properties are, and how they are interpreted. **Phonology**, on the other hand, investigates the organization of speech sounds in a particular language. While we might find the same sounds in two or more languages, no two languages organize their sound inventories in the same way. An example will make this point more clearly.

In both Japanese and English we can hear the sounds [s] and [š]. The Japanese word [šimasu], *do*, contains both phones, as does the English word [slæš] *slash*. The difference between Japanese and English lies in the way the two sounds contribute to the meaning of a word. In English, the two phones can distinguish meaning, as shown by words like [šor] *shore* and [sor] *sore*, where alternating between [š] and [s] affects the meaning of the utterance. In this sense, phonologists say that the occurrence of these two sounds is **unpredictable**, since we cannot look at the rest of the word and guess which sound will occur. If we know that a word ends in [-ɪp], we cannot predict whether the word will start with [s] or [š] since both *sip* and *ship* are different, but possible, words.

In Japanese, however, these two sounds are predictable from their environment. Sounds are **predictable** when we expect to see one sound or the other based upon the sounds that precede or follow it. If we know that a Japanese word ends in [-in], we know that it can begin with [š] and cannot begin with [s], since the combination [si] does not occur in Japanese. However, in English we cannot make this prediction: the sound [s] does appear before the sound [i].

So while both Japanese and English contain the phones [s] and [š], the languages differ in that in Japanese we can predict the occurrence of one versus the other and in English we cannot. If someone learning Japanese were to use [s] before [i] the meaning of the word would not change. Instead, the speaker would sound funny or have an accent to a native speaker of Japanese. If a learner of English were to make the same substitution in English, on the other hand, then the meaning of the word is likely to change. Imagine confusing [s] and [š] and saying "I have to [šeyv] more money each month."

Phonologists ask these kinds of questions: Of all the sounds in a language, which are predictable? What is the phonetic context that allows us to predict the occurrence of these sounds? Which sounds affect the meaning of words? In the following files, we will learn how to answer these questions. We will examine English as well as other languages. You will develop the skill to look at languages and determine which sounds are predictable and which affect the meaning of a word.

Distinctive and Nondistinctive Sounds

In every language, certain sounds are considered to be the "same" sound, even though they may be phonetically distinct. For example, native speakers of English consider the [l] in *lay* to be the same sound as that in *play*, even though the former is voiced and the latter voiceless, as discussed in File 3.8. If you ask a native speaker of English how many different sounds are represented by the underlined letters in the words p̲in, b̲in, and sp̲in, they will probably say "two," grouping the aspirated [pʰ] of *pin* and unaspirated [p] of *spin* together. Though [pʰ] and [p] are phonetically different sounds, native English speakers overlook this difference.

In this file we will discuss the terms **allophone** and **phoneme**, which are the crux of phonological analysis, so it is important that these terms be clearly understood. Perhaps the best way to explain these terms is through examples. On a separate piece of paper, transcribe the following five words:

| top | stop | little | kitten | hunter |

It is likely that you transcribed all of these words with a [t]. And this is good, since it reflects something psychologically real to you. But in fact the physical reality (acoustic phonetic fact) is that the /t/ you transcribed in those five examples is pronounced slightly differently from one example to the next (the meaning of the slashes around 't' will be explained shortly). Pronounce the five words again. Concentrate on what the /t/ sounds like in each example, but be sure to say them as you normally would if you were talking to a friend.

| [tɔp] | [stɔp] | [lɪtl6] | [kɪtn̩] | [həntɹ̩] |

Did you notice any differences? Compare the /t/ of *top* to that of *stop*. You should be able to detect a burst or puff of air after the /t/ in *top* that is absent in *stop*. That puff of air is called **aspiration**, which we will discuss in more detail later; let's transcribe aspiration with a superscripted [ʰ]. So while one might transcribe *top* and *stop* with the same symbol, /t/, in fact they are two different sounds and could be transcribed differently, as in [tʰɔp] and [stɔp], respectively.

Say the words *little* and *kitten*. The /t/ in *little* sounds a lot "softer" than the one in *stop*, and is clearly voiced. For most speakers of American English (but not in England), the /t/ in words like *little* is pronounced as a flap, [ɾ], much like the *r* in Spanish in words like [paɾa] 'for' and [toɾo] 'bull.' *Kitten* is pronounced with the same sound we hear in the expression "uh-oh," a glottal stop [ʔ]. So we could transcribe *little* and *kitten* as [lɪɾl̩] and [kɪʔn̩], respectively.

For some speakers of American English, in casual speech words like *hunter* are pronounced with no /t/ at all, but rather as [hənɹ̩]. Try and say it this way and see if it sounds like something you've heard before. In any case, while you may have initially transcribed the five words above with a /t/, they may also be transcribed in a way that reflects the different pronunciations of that sound.

| [tʰɔp] | [stɔp] | [lɪɾl̩] | [kɪʔn̩] | [hənɹ̩] |

To a native speaker, all of the words above have a /t/ in them, at least at some psychological level. Proof of that lies in the fact that one may transcribe them all with a /t/, at least until trained in transcription. Someone who lacks linguistic training would probably not hesitate to state that all the above words have a /t/ and would need to be convinced that subtle differences, like aspiration, exist among them. In this sense, psychologically, the above words do have a /t/. On the other hand, we can observe that the /t/ is not always realized in the same way so that it may be pronounced several different ways.

Unlike a speaker of English, a native speaker of Hindi could not ignore the difference between aspirated and unaspirated sounds when speaking or hearing Hindi. To a speaker of Hindi, the aspirated sound [pʰ] is as different from unaspirated [p] as [p] is from [b] to our ears. The difference between aspirated and unaspirated stops must be noticed by Hindi speakers because their language contains many words that are pronounced in nearly the same way, except that one word will have an aspirated stop where the other has an unaspirated stop. The data below illustrate this.

Hindi	*gloss*
[kʰəl]	*wicked person*
[kəl]	*yesterday, tomorrow*
[kap]	*cup*
[kapʰ]	*phlegm*
[pʰəl]	*fruit*
[pəl]	*moment*
[bəl]	*strength*

A native speaker of English can overlook the difference between aspirated and unaspirated stops because aspiration will never make a difference in the meanings of English words. If we hear someone say [mæp] and [mæpʰ] we may recognize them as different pronunciations of the same word map, but not as different words. Because of the different ways in which [p], [pʰ], and [b] lead to meaning distinctions in English and Hindi, these sounds have different values in the phonological systems of the two languages.

So far, we have seen that there is *phonological* information (namely, information about which sounds are distinctive relative to which others) that cannot be extracted from a list of the sounds of a language. This information, however, is part of the "internal grammar" or linguistic competence that speakers have. In our example from English, we saw that the two phones [tʰ] and [t] are both present phonetically, but that speakers don't use these sounds to distinguish meanings of words. But in Hindi aspiration does make that difference: speakers of Hindi use aspiration to distinguish different words. Linguists attempt to characterize this information about the sound system of a language by grouping the sounds in the language's phonetic inventory into classes. Each class contains all of the sounds that a native speaker considers to be the "same" sound. For example, [t] and [tʰ] in English would be members of the same class. But [t] and [d] are members of different classes because they are distinctive. Speakers of Hindi would not classify [t] and [tʰ] as members of the same class because they perceive them as different. A class of speech sounds that are identified by a native speaker as the same sound is called a **phoneme**. The members of these classes, which are actual phonetic segments produced by a speaker, are called allophones—thus an **allophone** is a phone that has been classified as belonging to some class, or phoneme.

Phonologists say that the words *stop, top, little*, etc., do have a /t/ at a psychological level. They would say, then, that each contains the phoneme /t/. By saying that *stop* and *top* each have the phoneme /t/, we are saying that the sounds [t] and [tʰ] are related. The various ways that a phoneme is pronounced are called allophones.

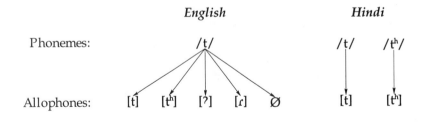

Figure 1.

In the above example, [t], [tʰ], [ɾ], [ʔ], and Ø (the symbol "Ø" indicates a deletion) are allophones of the same phoneme in English, which we can label /t/. However, in Hindi, these sounds are allophones of different phonemes. Note that symbols representing phonemes are written between slash brackets; this distinguishes them from symbols representing phones. Using these terms, we can say that the phoneme /t/ has the allophones [t] as in [stɔp], [tʰ] as in [tʰɔp], [ɾ] as in [lɪɾl], [ʔ] as in [kɪʔn̩], and Ø as in [hənṛ], where it is not pronounced at all. Figure 1 shows how the phoneme /t/ is related to its allophones and how the Hindi phonemes /t/ and /tʰ/ are related to their allophones. English /t/ has five different allophones, sounds that we actually hear but consider to be the same. On the other hand, the Hindi allophones [t] and [tʰ] are allophones of *different* phonemes.

By giving a description like this, linguists attempt to show that the phonological system of a language has two levels. The more concrete level involves the physical reality of phonetic segments, the allophones. Phonemes are something more abstract. Note that when linguists group sounds into phonemic classes, it is necessary to appeal to psychological notions like meaning. This is no accident, because phonemes are psychological units of linguistic structure.

To emphasize this point, linguists sometimes describe phonemes as the form in which we store sounds in our memory. It makes sense to remember words in terms of phonemes because it is much more efficient not to store information about phonetic details. As we will see, the details about the phonetic form of a word can be predicted from its phonemic form. For example, when we attempt to memorize a word like *path*, we notice that it begins with /p/, not /s/ or /ð/. But we need not learn as a particular fact about this word that the *p* must be aspirated; this is done automatically whenever the word is pronounced.

The first sound in a word like *path* is pronounced when the brain sends signals to the articulatory organs to produce a phonetic realization of the phoneme /p/—or, in everyday terms, to make the p-sound. [pʰ], an allophone of the phoneme /p/, is the product of these instructions. Since phonemes are psychological concepts, they are not directly observable in a stream of speech. Only allophones of phonemes are.

The phoneme is a unit of linguistic structure that is just as significant to the native speaker as the word or the sentence. Native speakers reveal their knowledge of phonemes in a number of ways. When an English speaker makes a slip of the tongue and says [či ken] for *key chain*, reversing [č] and [k], he or she has demonstrated that [č] functions mentally as a single unit, just as [k] does. Recall from File 3.2 that this is not the only way to conceptualize [č]: it is phonetically complex, consisting of [t] followed immediately by [š]. (Thus *key chain* can be transcribed as either [ki čen] or as [ki tšen].) Yet since [č] represents the pronunciation of a single phoneme /č/ in English, no native speaker would make an error that would involve splitting up its phonetic components; you will never hear [ti kšen] as a slip of the tongue.

Knowledge of phonemes is also revealed in spelling systems. For example, English does not have separate letters for [pʰ] and [p]; they are both spelled with the letter *p*. Examples like this show that the English spelling system ignores the differences in pronunciation that don't result in meaning distinctions. For the most part, the English spelling system attempts to provide symbols for phonemes, not phonetic segments. In general, alphabetic writing systems tend to be phonemic rather than phonetic, though they achieve this goal with varying degrees of success.

Distribution of Speech Sounds

The concepts of phoneme and allophone are related to another important concept in phonology: whether sounds are contrastive or not. If two sounds are separate phonemes, then the two speech sounds are contrastive. If the two phones are allophones of the same phoneme, then they are noncontrastive. Essentially, a pair of phones is **contrastive** if interchanging the two can change the meaning of a word. Conversely, two sounds are **noncontrastive** if the alternation of the phones does not result in a change of meaning.

Earlier we discussed the patterning of [š] and [s] in Japanese and English. Recall that we said that in English these two sounds could affect the meaning of a word based on examples like [šɪp] *ship* and [sɪp] *sip,* where the two meanings are distinguished by the occurrence of [s] or [š]. This means that the sounds [s] and [š] are contrastive in English.

Vowel length in English is noncontrastive. This means that while not all vowels are the same length (i.e., are pronounced for the same amount of time), changing the length of an English vowel will not change the meaning of the word. For example, the vowels of the words in the left column below are all short, while those on the right are long, and so are transcribed with the symbol [:].

[bit]	*beat*	[bi:d]	*bead*
[bɪt]	*bit*	[bɪːd]	*bid*
[hæt]	*hat*	[hæːd]	*had*
[kʰot]	*coat*	[kʰoːd]	*code*
[hak]	*hawk*	[haːg]	*hog*

Later we will discuss just how one can predict whether a vowel will be long or short depending upon its environment in English. If someone were to pronounce *bit* with a long vowel [bɪːt], this would not change the meaning of the word, nor would pronouncing *hog* with a short vowel as in [hɔg]. In Japanese, however, long and short vowels are contrastive. Changing the length of a vowel in Japanese can often change the meaning of the word. This is true in the pair [kuɾi] *buddhist temple kitchen,* and [kuːɾi] *empty theory.* A speaker of Japanese knows which meaning the speaker intends by the length of the vowel. This means that vowel length is predictable in English but important to word meaning in Japanese .

To find out which sounds are thought of by a native speaker as the same sound and which sounds are distinctive relative to one another, it is important to look at where these sounds occur in a language. In other words, linguists try to discover what the phonemes of a language are by examining the distribution of that language's phones. The **distribution** of a phone is the set of phonetic environments in which it occurs. For example, we saw in File 3.8 that nasalized vowels in English appear in the environment of a nasal consonant. More precisely, a linguist would describe the distribution of English [ĩ], [õ], and so on by stating that they occur immediately preceding a nasal consonant.

In general, speakers will attend to phonetic differences between two (or more) sounds only when the choice between the sounds can change the meaning of a word—that is, can cause a distinction in meaning. Such sounds are said to be **distinctive** with respect to one another. One way to determine whether two sounds in a language are distinctive is to identify a minimal pair. A **minimal pair** is defined as a pair of words with different meanings which are pronounced exactly the same way except for one sound that differs. When you find a minimal pair, you know that the sound that varies from one word to the other is contrastive. If you try, you can think of many minimal pairs in English, or any other language you know well. The minimal pair [ti:m] *team* and [di:m] *deem* shows that /t/ and /d/ are separate phonemes in English, since they can be used to contrast meaning. Similarly, the sounds /n/ and /m/ can be shown to be contrastive, since we can think of minimal pairs like [ti:m] *team* and [ti:n] *teen.* The words [pʰəl] *fruit* and [bəl] *strength* constitute a minimal pair in Hindi, contrasting [pʰ] and [b]; [pʰəl] *fruit* and [pəl] *moment* also form a minimal pair in Hindi. But notice that there are no English minimal pairs involving [pʰ] and [p]. These two sounds are never distinctive with respect to one another in English.

Consider another example in which two languages make different distinctions using the same set of sounds. In English it is possible to find minimal pairs in which [l] and [r] are contrasted; for example, *leaf* [lif], *reef* [rif]; *lack* [læk], *rack* [ræk]. However, [l] and [r] are never distinctive in Korean.

Consider the data below ([ɪ] represents a high central lax unrounded vowel).

Korean	gloss
[param]	*wind*
[irɪm]	*name*
[pal]	*foot*
[mal]	*horse*

As these examples illustrate, minimal pairs can never be found for [r] and [l] in Korean because these two sounds do not appear in the same positions in words: [r] appears only between two vowels, while [l] does not appear in this position. And this observation about the distribution of [r] and [l] is not merely a property of these isolated examples but true of all Korean words containing these sounds. Observations of this sort play an important role in determining which sounds are considered to be the "same" by a native speaker.

If you are presented with enough data from another language, you can find minimal pairs in them as well. Below are a few words from Spanish. The sound [ɣ] is a voiced, velar fricative, [ñ] is a palatal nasal, and [r̃] is a voiced, alveolar trill. For each minimal pair you find, you will know more about the phonemes of Spanish. For example, look at the words for *dog* and the conjunction *but*. They differ only in that *but* [peɾo] has a flap (as in English *atom* [æɾm̩]), and *dog* [per̃o] a trill. This minimal pair indicates that [r̃] and [ɾ] are contrastive in Spanish.

Spanish	gloss	Spanish	gloss
laɣo	*lake*	paɣo	*I pay*
kaða	*each*	kaɾa	*face*
pato	*duck*	gato	*cat*
kana	*cane*	kaña	*pipe*
peɾo	*but*	per̃o	*dog*

We now know that /ð/ and /ɾ/ are separate phonemes as well as /l/ and /p/ because the words *each* and *face* are a minimal pair, distinguished only by the sounds [ð] and [ɾ]. The minimal pair formed by the words for *cane* and *pipe* show that /n/ and /ñ/ are contrastive in Spanish also. What about the words for *duck* and *cat*; which two sounds do these demonstrate to be contrastive in Spanish?

We can also describe the distribution of one phone relative to that of another. Two speech sounds in a language will either be in overlapping distribution or complementary distribution with respect to one another. We will consider each of these distribution patterns in turn.

Two sounds are in **overlapping distribution** when the sets of phonetic environments in which they can occur are partially or completely identical. For example, consider a small selection of English words in which the sounds [b] and [d] appear. (Recall that "*" indicates that a word is unacceptable. *[dlit] is not a possible English word.)

bait	[bet]	*date*	[det]
lobe	[lob]	*load*	[lod]
knobs	[nabz]	*nods*	[nadz]
bleat	[blit]	—	*[dlit]

You can see that the set of environments of [b] is partially similar to that of [d]: both sounds occur word-initially before a vowel, and they both occur between [a] and [z]. (Of course, their actual distributions are much wider than this, but we are using a very limited set of data.) The distribution of these two sounds is not identical, however, because [b] can occur word-initially before [l], but [d] cannot. Nevertheless, their sets of possible phonetic environments overlap, and so we say that [b] and [d] are in overlapping distribution in English.

Some (but not all—see the paragraph below) sounds that are in overlapping distribution are contrastive with respect to one another, which is another way of saying that they are distinctive sounds. Remember that sounds are contrastive if interchanging the two can change the meaning of a word. Consider the [b] and [d] words above. *Bait* and *date* form a minimal pair, as do *lobe* and *load*, and *knobs* and *nods*. The choice between [b] and [d] in the environments [__et], [lo__], and [na__z] makes a difference in the meanings of these words. Because the difference between [b] and [d] can result in a contrast in meaning (*bait* vs. *date* and so on), we say that [b] and [d] are in **contrastive distribution**. As you know, two distinctive (or contrastive) phones are classified as being allophones of separate phonemes. Thus [b] is an allophone of the phoneme /b/, and [d] is an allophone of the phoneme /d/.

Complementary distribution is just the opposite of overlapping distribution. To understand this better, think about what the term complementary means: two complementary parts of something make up the whole. For example, the set of people in your class at any given moment can be divided into the set of people who are wearing glasses and the set of people who are not. These two sets of people complement each other. They are mutually exclusive, i.e., nonoverlapping, but together they make up the whole class. Therefore they are complementary sets.

Now let's consider a linguistic example. The sounds [p] and [pʰ] occur in English words such as the following.

spat	[spæt]	*pat*	[pʰæt]
spool	[spul]	*pool*	[pʰul]
speak	[spik]	*peek*	[pʰik]

As you can see, [p] and [pʰ] are not in overlapping distribution: they do not occur in the same phonetic environment. In fact, they are in complementary distribution. [p] occurs after [s] but not word-initially. [pʰ] occurs word-initially but not after [s]. There are no minimal pairs involving a [p]–[pʰ] contrast; since these sounds appear in different phonetic environments there can be no pair of words composed of identical strings of sounds except for [p] in one and [pʰ] in the other. Phones that are in complementary distribution are allophones of a single phoneme. In this case, [p] and [pʰ] are both allophones of the phoneme we can represent as /p/. The appearance of one allophone or the other is **predictable** when those allophones are in complementary distribution. Here we can predict that [pʰ] (but never [p]) will appear in word-initial position in words other than those listed above and that [p] (but never [pʰ]) will follow [s] in other words.

To summarize, a phone's distribution is the collection of phonetic environments in which the phone may appear; when linguists describe a phone's distribution they describe this collection. Relative to each other, two (or more) phones will be in overlapping or complementary distribution. If they are in overlapping distribution, they are either in contrastive distribution or in free variation. Phones in contrastive distribution may appear in minimal pairs and are allophones of different phonemes. Phones in free variation may appear in the same phonetic environments but never cause a contrast in meaning; they are allophones of the same phoneme. In either kind of overlapping distribution, given a particular phonetic environment (such as [be__] or [li__]), one cannot predict which of the phones will occur. If the two (or more) phones are in complementary distribution, their appearance in particular phonetic environments (such as [s__æt] or [__æt]) is predictable, they never appear in minimal pairs, and they are allophones of the same phonemes.

Free Variation

Other phones that are in overlapping distribution are in **free variation**. As an example, consider the following words containing [p] and [p˺] (recall from File 3.8 that [p˺] represents an unreleased voiceless bilabial stop).

leap	[lip]	*leap*	[lip˺]
soap	[sop]	*soap*	[sop˺]
troop	[trup]	*troop*	[trup˺]
happy	[hæpi]	—	*[hæp˺i]

It should be clear that these sounds are also in overlapping distribution because they share some of the same environments: they can both appear at the ends of words. Unlike the [b] vs. [d] examples, however, there are no minimal pairs in these data. Although there are pairs of words containing the same sounds but one, these words do not contrast in meaning. Thus the choice between [p] and [p˺] in *leap*, *soap*, and *troop* does not make a difference in meaning; rather, these sounds are interchangeable in word-final position. To a native speaker, sounds like [p] and [p˺] that are in free variation are perceived as being the "same" sound, and so we conclude that they are allophones of the same phoneme.

Exercise

1. Look at the following Ukrainian words containing the sounds [s], [s'], [š], and [š']. The sounds [s'] and [š'] are palatalized variants of [s] and [š]; palatalization sounds like a [y] sound right after (or on) the consonant; it is very close to the [y] sound in [byuɾi], *beauty*. You might want to review these definitions before you begin: *overlapping distribution, contrastive distribution, complementary distribution, distinctive,* and *minimal pair.* The words have been arranged to help you identify minimal pairs.

[s]		[s']		[š]		[š']	
1. lıs	*fox*	lıs'	*sheen*	lıš	*lest*		
2. mıska	*bowl*			mıška	*little mouse*	mıš'i	*mice*
3. sapka	*little hoe*			šapka	*hat*		
4. sıla	*strength*			šıla	*she sewed*	š'ist'	*six*
5. sum	*sadness*			šum	*rustling*		
6. sudı	*trials*	s'udı	*hither*			koš'i	*baskets*
7. sosna	*pine*	s'omıy	*seventh*	šostıy	*sixth*		
8. posadu	*job position* (acc.)	pos'adu	*I will occupy*				

a. What are the minimal pairs that you can find in these words?

b. Is there a minimal triplet (like a minimal pair, but involving three sounds and three words)? What is it?

c. Which three of these four sounds are in overlapping distribution? (Hint: those sounds are also contrastive. Remember what it means for sounds to be contrastive.)

d. One of these sounds occurs only before a particular vowel. What is this sound and what is the vowel? Which words indicate this?

e. What can you say about the distinctiveness of the sound you identified in (d)? Is it distinctive in Ukrainian, or not?

File 4.2   Phonological Rules

In File 4.1, we discussed the fact that phonemes and (allo)phones belong to different levels of structure in language—that is, phonemes are mental entities and phones are physical events. In this file we consider the connection between these two levels. The mapping between phonemic and phonetic elements is accomplished using **phonological rules** (recall that a rule of grammar expresses a pattern in a language). A speaker's knowledge of phonological rules allows him or her to "translate" phonemes into actual speech sounds; knowledge of these rules forms part of the speaker's linguistic competence. This change from the underlying phonemic form to the actual phonetic form of a word by means of phonological rules can be represented with a diagram:

phonemic form

⇓

rules

⇓

phonetic form

As an example, consider the English word *can* /kæn/. This word has a final /n/ sound in its phonemic form, and in fact it is frequently pronounced with a final [n]. If we listen carefully, however, we find that the final consonant of *can* (especially in casual speech) is often [m] or [ŋ]. The following examples illustrate this. (Here and throughout this file we use a fairly broad transcription style, recording phonetic detail only for the segments under discussion.)

I can ask	[ay kæn æsk]
I can see	[ay kæn si]
I can bake	[ay kæm bek]
I can play	[ay kæm ple]
I can go	[ay kæŋ go]
I can come	[ay kæŋ kʌm]

As these transcriptions show, /n/ is pronounced as [m] when it precedes a labial stop and as [ŋ] when it precedes a velar stop. We can state this fact about English as a descriptive rule:

/n/ is pronounced as   [m] before a labial stop
[ŋ] before a velar stop
[n] everywhere else.

(We will be adjusting this rule later on in this file.) Now consider how the phonetic forms of some of the above examples are derived from the phonemic forms:

phonemic form:	/kæn æsk/	/kæn bek/	/kæn go/
apply rule:	kæn æsk	kæm bek	kæŋ go
phonetic form:	[kæn æsk]	[kæm bek]	[kæŋ go]

This illustrates what happens in speaking. In listening, a hearer reverses this process: he or she perceives the phonetic form of an utterance, then sends it "backwards" through the phonological rules, finally obtaining a phonemic form that matches a form stored in memory.

Of course, more than one phonological rule may apply to a form. For example, consider the word *please*. A speaker will store this word in memory as the string of phonemes /pliz/, but when he or she utters the word it appears as the sequence of sounds [pʰl̥iːz]. What are the particular phonological rules required to derive [pʰl̥iːz] from /pliz/? Recall from File 3.8 our discussions of aspirated stops, voiceless liquids and glides, and lengthened vowels. Statements about where each of these kinds of phones occurs constitute phonological rules; thus, the rules involved in deriving [pʰl̥iːz] from /pliz/ are the following (in no particular order):

Aspiration: Voiceless stops become aspirated when they occur at the beginning of a stressed syllable.

Liquid and Glide Devoicing: Liquids and glides become voiceless when they occur following a voiceless obstruent.

Vowel Lengthening: Vowels become long when they occur preceding a voiced consonant.

Given these rules, we can describe the derivation of [pʰl̥iːz] from /pliz/ as follows:

phonemic form	/pliz/
rules:	
Aspiration	pʰliz
L-G Devoicing	pʰl̥iz
V Lengthening	pʰl̥iːz
phonetic form	[pʰl̥iːz]

Classification of Phonological Rules

Some phonological rules can be classified according to the kind of process that they involve. These processes are adjustments in the articulation of sounds. Four major kinds of processes, assimilation, dissimilation, insertion, and deletion, are discussed here, along with examples from the phonology of English.

1. Rules involving **assimilation** cause a sound to become more like a neighboring sound with respect to some feature. In other words, the segment affected by the rule assimilates or takes on a feature from a nearby (usually adjacent) sound. Rules of assimilation are very common in languages. The first rule we considered in this file falls into this category. We can call it **alveolar stop assimilation**, because it applies to all alveolar stops (/t/ and /d/, as well as the nasal stop /n/ in the examples above):

Alveolar stop assimilation: Alveolar stops assimilate in place of articulation to a following consonant.

Thus when a sound having the features alveolar and stop immediately precedes a labial consonant, this rule causes it to take on the feature labial (thereby replacing its original feature for place of articulation, alveolar). Similarly, this rule can apply to change the sound's place of articulation feature to dental when it precedes a dental consonant (recall examples such as *width* [wɪd̪θ] and *in this* [ɪn̪ ðɪs]), and so on for the other places of articulation.

Liquid and glide devoicing is another example of an English rule of assimilation. So is **vowel nasalization**; by now you should be able to provide a statement of these rules, based on the discussion in File 3.8. Some languages, such as Turkish, have rules of **vowel harmony**, which involve a kind of long-distance assimilation: they typically cause all the vowels in a word to agree in one or more features such as rounding or frontness.

2. Rules of **dissimilation** cause two neighboring sounds to become less alike with respect to some feature. These are much less common than assimilation rules, but an example of dissimilation in English (for some speakers) is the following:

Fricative dissimilation: /θ/ changes to [t] following another fricative.

For example, the word *fifth* is phonemically /fɪfθ/ but is often pronounced as [fɪft]; similarly, /sɪksθ/ [sɪkst], *sixth*. In these examples the fricative /θ/ becomes less like an adjacent fricative consonant; it does so through a change in its manner of articulation, thereby becoming a stop.

3. Phonological rules of **insertion** cause a segment not present at the phonemic level to be added to the phonetic form of a word. Examples from English of this kind of rule are:

Voiceless stop insertion: Between a nasal and a voiceless fricative, a voiceless stop with the same place of articulation as the nasal is inserted.

Glottal stop insertion: [ʔ] is optionally inserted before a stressed word-initial vowel.

Thus, for instance, the voiceless stop insertion rule may apply to the words *dance* /dæns/, *strength* /strɛŋθ/, and *hamster* /hæmstr̩/, causing them to be pronounced as [dænts], [strɛŋkθ], and [hæmpstr̩], respectively. And the glottal stop insertion rule can operate to realize the phonemic form of *That's awful!* /ðæts afl̩/ as [ðæts ʔafl̩], or *ouch!* /awč/ as [ʔawč].

4. **Deletion** rules eliminate a sound. Such rules apply more frequently to unstressed syllables and in casual speech. English examples include:

/h/-deletion: /h/ may be deleted in unstressed syllables.

Unstressed vowel deletion: A vowel that precedes a liquid consonant in an unstressed syllable may be deleted.

The /h/-deletion rule would apply to a sentence such as *He handed her his hat* /hi hændɛd hr̩ hɪz hæt/ to yield [hi hændɛd r̩ ɪz hæt]; the unstressed vowel deletion rule provides examples such as *police* /pəlis/ [plis] and *believe* /bəliv/ [bliv]. (This rule is not used by all English speakers.)

Notice that not all phonological rules fit neatly into one of these four categories. Examples of such hard-to-classify rules of English include **vowel lengthening, aspiration,** and **flapping:**

Flapping: Alveolar oral stops are realized as [ɾ] when they occur after a stressed vowel and before an unstressed syllable.

Writer /raytṛ/ → [rayɾṛ] and *rider* /raydṛ/ → [rayɾṛ] are examples of the application of this rule. Note that voicing assimilation is involved in the change of /t/ to [ɾ]: the /t/ takes on the "voicedness" of the vowels surrounding it.

Another common phonological process is **palatalization.** Palatalization refers to a special type of assimilation in which a consonant becomes like a neighboring sound. For example, when American English speakers say *Did you eat?* rapidly, they very often pronounce *Did you* as [dɪǰa]. The sound [d] has been turned into a **palatal** sound [ǰ] because of the influence of the following palatal glide [y]. Vowels also cause this change. The vowels most often responsible for it are [i] and [e]. For example, recall from File 4.1 that Japanese [s] never stands before the vowel [i]. Instead [s] must always become (if it isn't already) the sound [š]. This is a type of palatalization as well: /s/ becomes [š] when it stands before /i/. The most common types of palatalization occur when stops or fricatives made with the tongue (can you recall these?) appear before a front vowel. So, the following are all common types of palatalization: [t] → [č]; [d] → [ǰ]; [s] → [š]; [k] → [č]; [g] → [ǰ]. Notice that both alveolars (or dentals) and velars can be palatalized. There are variants on palatalization and other sounds can be palatalized, but the main things to look for are (1) a sound becoming a palatal and/or (2) a sound change conditioned by a front vowel or a high front vowel. Finally, don't confuse the process of palatalization with the secondary articulation known as palatalization. The secondary articulation refers to a [y] sound on the consonant (as in *beauty* [bʸuɾi]). Sometimes, the secondary articulation of palatalization occurs because of the phonological process of palatalization.

Notice also that phonological rules may be **obligatory** or **optional**. Obligatory English rules include aspiration, vowel nasalization, vowel lengthening, and liquid and glide devoicing. Such a rule always applies in the speech of all speakers of a language or dialect having the rule, regardless of style or rate of speaking. The effects of obligatory rules are often very subtle and difficult to notice, but they are an important part of a native accent. For instance, it may be difficult for us to tell that a vowel is nasalized in English, but the application of vowel nasalization makes us sound like native speakers of English. Optional phonological rules, on the other hand, may or may not apply in an individual's speech. Optional rules are responsible for variation in speech; for example, we can pronounce /kæn bi/ as either [kæm bi] or [kæn bi], depending on whether Alveolar Stop Assimilation is applied or not. The use of optional rules depends in part on rate and style of speech. Often rules involving assimilation or deletion are used more frequently in casual speech, including several of the rules discussed above.

Why Have Phonological Rules?

You may be wondering why languages use phonological rules at all. Wouldn't it be more efficient for each phoneme to have only one allophone, allowing phonemic and phonetic forms of words to be the same? There are two main reasons for the existence of phonological rules. First, some rules make sequences of sounds *easier to pronounce*. When we say [kæm bi] instead of [kæn bi], we produce two bilabial sounds in a row (using a single lip **gesture**) instead of making an alveolar [n] and then a bilabial [b] (using two different gestures). Vowel nasalization results from the fact that it is easier for speakers to begin lowering the velum (allowing air to escape through the nasal cavity) a little early, during a vowel, than it is to wait *exactly* until the beginning of the nasal consonant.

Second, some rules make sounds *easier to perceive*, as when voiceless stops are aspirated at the beginning of a stressed syllable. Insertions and dissimilations may contribute to ease of articulation, but they also function to preserve information and make sounds easier to perceive. While they may eliminate some phonetic difficulty, they do so by emphasizing a phonetic property of the sound being altered. In our examples of fricative dissimilation, when /θ/ becomes [t] it becomes more different from the adjacent fricative by acquiring a more extreme consonantal constriction, thus emphasizing the tongue-tip activity involved in /θ/-production. Voiceless stop insertion avoids the difficulty of going directly from a nasal articulation to a voiceless fricative articulation (which requires that the speaker release the stop closure of the nasal and raise the velum at precisely the same moment), but it does so by emphasizing the stop quality of the nasal consonant.

Exercises

1. Identify the phonological rule or rules operating in each of the following derivations.

    a. *little*   /lɪtl̩/   →   [lɪɾl̩]
    b. *galoshes*   /gəlašəz/   →   [glašəz]
    c. *haze*   /hez/   →   [heːz]
    d. *late bell*   /let bɛl/   →   [lep bɛːl]
    e. *rain*   /ren/   →   [rẽːn]
    f. *place*   /ples/   →   [pʰl̥es]
    g. *lance*   /læns/   →   [læ̃ːnts]

2. Examine the following sets of data, and for each set write a rule to describe the derivation of the phonetic forms from the phonemic ones. (To do so, determine what sound or natural class of sounds is being altered and what the environment of that alteration is.) Where possible, also explain what kind of process is involved in the rule.

    a. In the speech of some New Yorkers, examples like the following are found.

there	/ðɛr/	→	[ðɛ]		*marry*	/mæri/	→	[mæri]
court	/kɔrt/	→	[kɔt]		*Paris*	/pærɪs/	→	[pærɪs]
large	/larǰ/	→	[laǰ]		*for all*	/fɔr ɔl/	→	[fɔr ɔl]
stores	/stɔrz/	→	[stɔz]		*story*	/stɔri/	→	[stɔri]
cared	/kɛrd/	→	[kɛd]		*caring*	/kɛrɪŋ/	→	[kɛrɪŋ]

    b. Examples like the following are very common in English.

OSU	/oɛsyu/	[oɛšyu]
did you	/dɪd yu/	[dɪǰu]
capture	/kæptyr̩/	[kæpčr̩]
gracious	/gresyəs/	[grešəs]

c.   The following data are from German.

German	Gloss			
Bild	*picture*	/bɪld/	→	[bɪlt]
blieb	*remained*	/blib/	→	[blip]
Weg	*way*	/veg/	→	[vek]
fremd	*foreign*	/frɛmd/	→	[frɛmt]
gelb	*yellow*	/gɛlb/	→	[gɛlp]
Zug	*train*	/tsug/	→	[tsuk]
bleiben	*to remain*	/blaybn̩/	→	[blaybm̩]
Vogel	*bird*	/fogl̩/	→	[fogl̩]
Baum	*tree*	/bawm/	→	[bawm]
schnell	*fast*	/šnɛl/	→	[šnɛl]

File 4.3

How to Solve Phonology Problems

Because phonemes are important units of linguistic structure, linguists must have a general method for identifying them in all languages. But the task of determining what the phonemes of a language are and what allophones are assigned to them is not always straightforward. For one thing, the set of phonemes differs from language to language, and so a different analysis is required for each language. Moreover, phonemes are psychological units of linguistic structure and are not physically present in a stream of speech. As a result, it is not possible to identify the phonemes of a language simply by taking physical measurements on a sample of language. And it is not always easy to identify phonemes by investigating a native speaker's intuitions, since the minute phonetic details on which decisions about phonemes are made are often precisely those which speakers are not accustomed to noticing.

To get around these problems, linguists have developed an objective procedure by which the phonemes of a language can be discovered through examination of a set of words written in narrow phonetic transcription. This procedure is based on the following observations about patterns of sounds:

1. **Phonemes** *make distinctions in meaning.* If two sounds are members of separate phonemes, minimal pairs can almost always be found. For example, the minimal pair *led* and *red* is evidence that [l] and [r] are members of separate phonemes in English. But if two sounds are allophones of the same phoneme, minimal pairs differing only in those sounds will not exist. For example, [bʌʔn̩] and [bʌtʰn̩] are both possible pronunciations of the English word *button* (though [bʌtʰn̩] may sound a little stilted). This is because the sounds [ʔ] and [tʰ] are both allophones of the phoneme /t/. Thus the meaning doesn't change.

2. The **allophones** *of a phoneme are not a random collection of sounds but are a set of sounds that have the same psychological function.* Accordingly, allophones of the same phoneme are systematically related to one another:

    a. They share many phonetic properties.
    b. It is possible to predict which allophone will appear in a word on the basis of phonological rules.

Thus by analyzing the patterns of sounds that are *physically* present, it is possible to draw conclusions about the *psychological* organization of a language, which is not directly observable.

How to Do a Phonemic Analysis

Although a phonemic analysis can be performed successfully on any language, it is easiest to begin with a problem based on English, since we already know in effect what the solution is. Look over the data below, which are given in a fairly narrow phonetic transcription:

pray	[pʰɾ̥e]	*crab*	[kʰɾ̥æbˑ]
gray	[gre]	*fresh*	[fɾ̥ɛš]
crab	[kʰɾ̥æb]	*regain*	[rigen]
par	[pʰar]	*shriek*	[šɾ̥ik]
broker	[brokr̩]	*tar*	[tʰar]

Beginning with the sounds [r] and [ɾ̥], we attempt to answer the following question: are these sounds allophones of separate phonemes, or allophones of the same phoneme? (Of course, native speakers of English intuitively know that they are allophones of the same phoneme. However, the procedure for doing a phonemic analysis should produce the same answer without appealing to the intuitions of speakers.) In order to answer this question, it is necessary to examine scientifically the **distribution** of sounds within these data. That is, for each sound in question we need to determine the set of phonetic environments in which it can occur. But just what do we mean by "environment"? For the time being, we can define the **environment** of a sound as the sounds that immediately precede and follow it within a word. For example, in the word [gre], [r] is in the environment [g__e] (i.e., it is preceded by [g] and followed by [e]). Using the symbol "#" to represent a word boundary, we represent the environment of [g] as [#__r] and that of [e] as [r__#].

The best way to begin a phonemic analysis is to determine whether the sounds in question are in **overlapping distribution**. First, look for minimal pairs. Suppose for a moment we were interested in the sounds [pʰ] and [tʰ] in the data above. These sounds do appear in a minimal pair: [pʰar] and [tʰar] have different meanings, and differ phonetically only by a single sound in the same position. This tells us that [pʰ] and [tʰ] are in overlapping distribution—more specifically, they are in **contrastive distribution**, because the difference between them causes a difference in meaning. Therefore they are allophones of different phonemes. However, this minimal pair is irrelevant for the problem at hand, namely, determining the status of [r] and [ɾ̥]. There are no minimal pairs in the data that involve these two sounds.

In fact, in the list above there are no word-pairs that differ only by the sounds [r] and [ɾ̥]. But look at the words [kʰɾ̥æb] and [kʰɾ̥æbˑ]. These do not form a minimal pair because they mean the same thing. However, they differ phonetically only in their final consonant. This pair of words shows us that [b] and [bˑ] are in overlapping distribution (they both appear in the environment [kʰɾ̥æ__#]); more specifically, [b] and [bˑ] are in **free variation** (since the choice between them doesn't affect meaning). But once again, this discovery has no bearing on our analysis of [r] and [ɾ̥].

Since [r] and [ɾ̥] are not in overlapping distribution in our data, we can assume that they are in **complementary distribution**. However, we must prove that this is so by making a generalization about where [r] (but not [ɾ̥]) may appear, and vice versa. In order to do so we need to compare the phonetic environments of each of these sounds; the easiest way to do this is to make a list for each sound, as follows. (Recall that "#" indicates a word boundary.)

[r]	**[ɾ̥]**
[g__e]	[pʰ__e]
[a__#]	[kʰ__æ]
[b__o]	[f__ɛ]
[#__i]	[š__i]

Once you have collected the list of phonetic environments for each sound, it is necessary to proceed as follows:

1. *Look at the environments to find* **natural classes.** [r̥] is preceded by [pʰ], [kʰ], [f], and [š], all of which are voiceless consonants. This generalization permits us to simplify the description of the environment for [r̥]; instead of listing each sound separately, it is now possible to say simply:

[r̥] appears after voiceless consonants.

Now look at the environments in which [r] appears. Are there any natural classes? Yes and no. Certainly [b] and [g] are voiced consonants, and [a] is also voiced, but the set that includes [b], [g], [a], the beginnings of words, and the ends of words does not form a natural class. Thus the critical observation to make here is that there is no *single* natural class of environments in which [r] can be found. We have looked at the sounds preceding [r] and [r̥], but what about the sounds that follow them? As you can see, only [r] may occur word-finally, but either [r] or [r̥] can occur before a vowel. Thus the environments that condition the appearance of [r] or [r̥]—i.e., the **conditioning environments** of these particular allophones—are their immediately preceding sounds.

2. *Look for complementary gaps in the environments.* So far, we have shown that [r̥] appears after voiceless consonants, while [r] appears in an apparently random set of environments. Yet it is possible to make one more critical observation. [r] does not appear in the environments in which [r̥] appears, namely, after voiceless consonants. Moreover, [r̥] does not appear where [r] does; there is no [r̥] after voiced consonants or at the beginnings and ends of words. Since the environments of [r] and [r̥] have systematic and complementary gaps, we say that [r] and [r̥] are in complementary distribution. Therefore they are allophones of the same phoneme.

3. *State a generalization about the distribution of each of these sounds.* In other words, write a rule that will make predictions about where each of the sounds can occur. Actually, we've done the hard part of this already by observing that [r̥] occurs following voiceless consonants. How should we state the distribution of [r]? We could try formulating our rule as follows:

[r̥]   appears following voiceless consonants;
[r]   appears following voiced consonants or vowels, or at the beginning or end of a word.

However, that's not a very succinct formulation of the rule. To simplify it, recall that wherever [r̥] occurs, [r] can't, because their possible environments form complementary sets. Therefore we can revise our rule this way:

[r̥]   appears following voiceless consonants;
[r]   appears elsewhere.

4. *Determine the identity of the phoneme and its allophones.* This next step in writing the rule involves deciding what the phoneme to which these sounds belong should be. In order to do so, we need to decide which of the allophones is the **basic allophone** and which is the **restricted allophone**. We have determined that the conditioning environment for [r̥] consists of a single natural class of sounds. [r̥] is restricted to occurring only there, whereas [r] may appear anywhere else. Therefore we can identify [r̥] as the restricted allophone and [r] as the basic one. It makes sense to name the phoneme after the basic allophone, since it is the one that can show up in a wider variety of contexts. Furthermore, the basic allophone is assumed to be the closest approximation of the mental "sound" that speakers store in memory. In choosing a name for the phoneme, we have made the leap from observable phonetic reality to unobservable psychological reality. (It is not always possible to choose one allophone as basic, however. In that case the phonology problem's instructions will not tell you to do so,

and any of the allophones would serve equally well as the name of the phoneme.)

Now we can improve on our rule once more. The arrows in the rule below mean "is pronounced as." Recall that we use slash brackets around symbols representing phonemes and that the single slash indicates the beginning of the environment specification:

/r/ → [r̥] / after voiceless consonants;
/r/ → [r] / elsewhere.

Now that we have formulated the necessary phonological rule, we can see whether it involves a phonological process (cf. File 4.2). In this rule a voiced phoneme changes into a voiceless sound when it follows another voiceless sound. In other words, /r/ becomes more like a preceding sound with respect to the feature of voicelessness. Therefore we can conclude that the process of **assimilation** is involved in this phonological rule.

Some Potential Trouble Spots

The procedure outlined in the previous section will work for any language for which reliable phonetic transcriptions exist. However, beginners are often confused by certain questions.

For instance, if you discover that no minimal pairs exist for two sounds, isn't it possible to conclude automatically that they are allophones of the same phoneme? No. It is still necessary to show that the sounds are in complementary distribution, since allophones are **predictable** variant pronunciations of the same phoneme.

Consider what happens if you make a decision too soon. Using the data presented at the beginning of the previous section, suppose you wanted to know whether [g] and [š] are allophones of the same phoneme. Since there are no minimal pairs differentiated by these sounds, it might seem reasonable to conclude that they are. But a careful examination of the data reveals that this is the wrong conclusion. Listing the data and the relevant environments, you find:

[g] appears in *gray* [gre], *regain* [rigen]
     generalization: [g] appears between vowels or at the beginnings of a word;

[š] appears in *fresh* [fr̥eš], *shriek* [šr̥ik]
     generalization: [š] appears at the beginning or end of a word.

But there are no generalizations to make about where [g] and [š] occur. In fact, their distributions overlap: either may occur at the beginning of a word. (Of course, a speaker of English should have no trouble thinking of a minimal pair involving these two sounds. However, the data you will be given in phonology problems will be sufficient for you to solve those problems.)

Since there is no single natural class in the environments for either [g] or [š], no phonological rule can be responsible for their distribution. And they are not in complementary distribution because both can appear at the beginnings of words. In general, when *no generalization* can be made about where a group of sounds can occur, it is possible to conclude that they are members of separate phonemes. A conclusion based on such a demonstration is just as valid as showing that minimal pairs exist. This alternative way of showing that sounds are members of separate phonemes is useful because it's not always possible to find minimal pairs for all distinctive sounds. For example, there are no minimal pairs involving [ŋ] and [h] in English. But they belong to separate phonemes because they share few phonetic properties, and no phonological rule determines where they can occur.

The range of tests for identifying phonemes can be broadened somewhat by the use of **near-minimal pairs**. Recall that a minimal pair is a pair of words differing in meaning but phonetically identical except for one sound in the same position in each word. The definition of near-minimal pairs is the same, except that the words are *almost* identical except for the one sound. For example, *heard* [hr̩d] and *Bert* [br̩t] form a near-minimal pair involving [h] and [b]. We are justified in saying that [h] and [b] are allophones of separate phonemes because no conceivable phonological rule would permit only [h] at the beginnings of words ending in [d], and only [b] at the beginnings of words ending in [t].

One final point about minimal pairs: notice that we have *not* defined them as pairs of words that rhyme. It is not necessary for two words to rhyme in order to form a minimal pair—consider English *state* [stet] and *steak* [stek], for example, or *boat* [bot] and *beat* [bit]. Nor is rhyming sufficient to qualify a pair of words as a minimal pair: *gray* [gre] and *pray* [pʰre] from the list of data above rhyme, but differ in *two* sounds. And to take another example, *glitter* and *litter* rhyme but do not form a minimal pair because they do not contain the same number of sounds.

Another question that often troubles beginners is this: when describing the environment in which a sound appears, how do you know where to look? In the problem we solved in the previous section, we considered only the sounds that *preceded* [r] and [r̩]. This is certainly not the only possibility. In fact, identifying conditioning environments is the most challenging part of doing a phonemic analysis.

Recall that in the previous section we temporarily defined the environment of a sound as the sounds immediately surrounding it. Occasionally, however, it is necessary to look beyond the sound's immediate environment. For instance, if you are examining the distribution of a vowel allophone, you may need to look at the vowels that appear in adjacent syllables, even though consonants may intervene. It may also be necessary to consider preceding or following sounds even when they belong to another word that is adjacent in the stream of speech. However, it is best to examine the immediate environment of an allophone first when you are trying to determine what its conditioning environment is.

Since there are many logically possible environments to consider, the task is made easier by eliminating all of those except the most plausible. This can be accomplished by using strategies like the following:

a. *Formulate hypotheses about the allophones.* Investigation of the world's languages has revealed that some sounds are more common than others. For example:

- Voiced nasals and liquids are more common than voiceless ones.
- Oral vowels are more common than nasal vowels.
- Consonants of normal duration are more common than long consonants.
- "Plain" consonants are more common than those with secondary articulations like velarization, palatalization, and labialization.

On the basis of these generalizations, it is possible to speculate that if an uncommon sound appears in a language, it is probably a restricted allophone. But these tendencies should be used only as a guide for forming hypotheses, not as a basis for jumping to conclusions, since some languages exhibit exceptions. For example, French has both nasal and oral vowel phonemes.

b. *Keep in mind that allophonic variation results from the application of phonological rules.* Also remember that rules often involve some phonological process, such as assimilation or deletion. Once you have a hunch about which allophone is the restricted one, check the environment in which it appears for evidence that a phonological process has operated. This may involve looking in more than one place until you have discovered a reasonable candidate. In the problem in the previous section, we were guided by the knowledge that voicing differences in consonants are often caused by voicing assimilation, and that voicing assimilation frequently occurs in consonant clusters. Since /r/ is the second member of all of the clusters given, we concluded that the consonant preceding it constituted the conditioning environment. Even if it is not obvious that a phonological process has been at work, you should be able to write a phonological rule—i.e., state a generalization about—where the allophones of the phoneme occur.

The flowchart on the next page should help you to identify the type of distribution two (or more) sounds in a language have. The rectangular boxes ask you to do something or give you some information that your working through the flowchart has revealed. The diamond-shaped boxes pose a question. Try reading through the flowchart before you attempt to analyze the languages in the next file; it may help you to understand the relationship between the different types of distributions of sounds in a language.

Flowchart for Discovering the Distribution of Sounds

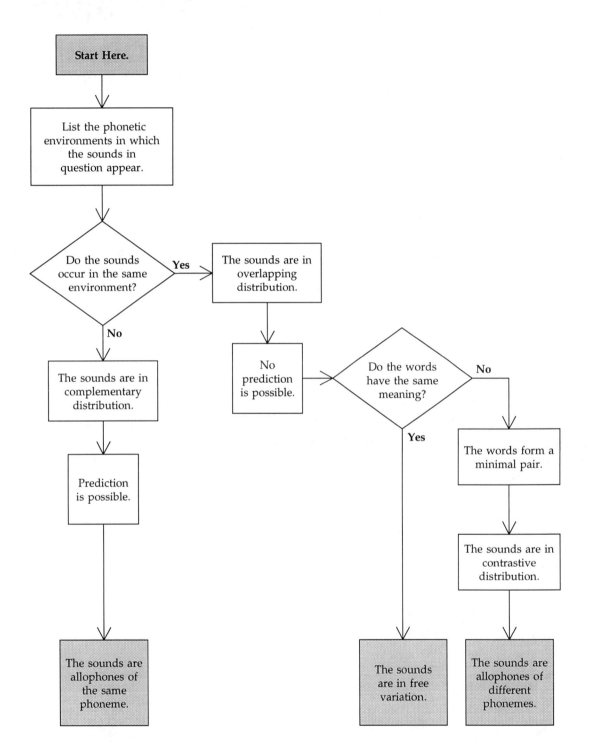

Use this flowchart to learn the distribution of a pair of sounds. Work through each step, giving the requested information, answering the question posed, or taking note of the conclusions provided. Steps in a diamond shape involve answering a "yes-no" question. Steps in a rectangle indicate what you can conclude about the sounds in question.

File 4.4 Phonological Analysis Problems

This file is designed to give you practice in doing phonemic analysis at the beginning, intermediate, and more advanced levels. The instructions to each problem are somewhat different in each case, so read them carefully before proceeding. However, each problem requires that you follow the step-by-step procedure for doing a phonemic analysis outlined in the previous file. The problems are designed to introduce you to problems involving minimal pairs, complementary distribution, and free variation. (A linguist making a phonemic analysis of an unknown language would of course examine hundreds of words in order to be sure to have enough data to find the relevant minimal pairs, complementary distributions, etc. But to save you time, the data in the problems below have been carefully selected to give you all the relevant information you will need in a very small set of words. The same applies to all the phonology problems you will be asked to solve in this course.)

0. Sample Problem

0.0 *Mokilese*

(Answers to all zero problems can be found in Appendix A)

Mokilese is a language spoken in Micronesia. Examine the pairs [i, i̥] and [u, u̥]. For each pair, determine whether they are allophones of different phonemes or allophones of the same phoneme. Provide evidence for your answer. If they are allophones of one phoneme, state the contexts in which each sound occurs and decide which sound is the basic sound. Can any generalizations be made? (Hint: refer to natural classes.)

1.	[pi̥san]	*full of leaves*	7.	[uduk]	*flesh*
2.	[dupu̥kda]	*bought*	8.	[kaskas]	*to throw*
3.	[pu̥ko]	*basket*	9.	[poki]	*to strike something*
4.	[ki̥sa]	*we two*	10.	[pil]	*water*
5.	[su̥pwo]	*firewood*	11.	[apid]	*outrigger support*
6.	[kamwɔki̥ti]	*to move*	12.	[luǰuk]	*to tackle*

1.   Beginning Problems

1.1   Sindhi

The following data are from Sindhi, an Indo-European language spoken in India and Pakistan. Examine the phones [p], [pʰ], and [b]. Determine if the three are allophones of separate phonemes or allophones of the same phoneme. What is your evidence? Is the relationship among the sounds the same as in English? Why or why not?

1.	[pənu]	*leaf*	7.	[təru]	*bottom*
2.	[vəǰu]	*opportunity*	8.	[kʰəto]	*sour*
3.	[šeki]	*suspicious*	9.	[bəǰu]	*run*
4.	[gədo]	*dull*	10.	[bənu]	*forest*
5.	[dəru]	*door*	11.	[bəču]	*be safe*
6.	[pʰənu]	*snake hood*	12.	[ǰəǰu]	*judge*

1.2   Italian

Consider the following data from Italian. Answer the questions that follow.

1.	[tinta]	*dye*	7.	[tiŋgo]	*I dye*
2.	[tɛnda]	*tent*	8.	[tɛŋgo]	*I keep*
3.	[dansa]	*dance*	9.	[fuŋgo]	*mushroom*
4.	[nero]	*black*	10.	[byaŋka]	*white*
5.	[ǰɛnte]	*people*	11.	[aŋke]	*also*
6.	[sapone]	*soap*	12.	[faŋgo]	*mud*

1. Are there any minimal pairs? If so, what are they and what can you conclude to be true of Italian from those minimal pairs?

2. State the phonetic environments in which the sounds [n] and [ŋ] appear. Identify any natural classes of sounds that appear in the environments you've provided.

3. Given what you know about the distribution of sounds and the environments you listed in (2), are [n] and [ŋ] in complementary or overlapping distribution? Please explain your answer.

1.3 Spanish

Examine the phones [d] and [ð]. Determine whether they are allophones of one phoneme or of separate phonemes. If they are allophones of one phoneme, identify the type of distribution. If they are in complementary distribution, state a rule that describes the distribution. If [d] and [ð] are allophones of separate phonemes, give minimal pairs that prove this.

1.	[drama]	*drama*	7.	[komiða]	*food*
2.	[dolor]	*pain*	8.	[anda]	*scram*
3.	[dime]	*tell me*	9.	[sueldo]	*compensation*
4.	[kaða]	*each*	10.	[durar]	*to last*
5.	[laðo]	*side*	11.	[toldo]	*curtain*
6.	[oðio]	*hatred*	12.	[falda]	*skirt*

1.4 Russian

Determine from the following Russian data whether [a] and [ɑ] ([ɑ] is a backed version of [a]) are allophones of the same phoneme or whether they are in contrast as allophones of separate phonemes. If they are allophones of separate phonemes, provide evidence for your claim. If they are in complementary distribution, pick one allophone as the basic sound and give the conditioning phonetic contexts for its allophones. ([ł] represents a velarized [l], [s'] a palatalized alveolar fricative, and [m'] a palatalized voiced bilabial nasal.)

1.	[atəm]	*atom*	6.	[pɑł]	*he fell*
2.	[dva]	*two*	7.	[dɑł]	*he gave*
3.	[dar]	*gift*	8.	[pɑːłə]	*stick*
4.	[mas]	*ointment*	9.	[ukrɑłə]	*she stole*
5.	[matə]	*mint*	10.	[brɑł]	*he took*

1.5   Burmese

The following Burmese data contain both voiced and voiceless nasals. The latter are indicated by a small circle placed under the symbol. Are [m] and [m̥] allophones of the same phoneme, or are they different phonemes? What about [n] and [n̥]? Is the same also true for [ŋ] and [ŋ̊]? Give evidence for your answer. If there is a phonological process involved, state what it is and give the conditioning environment and the conditioning property of the environment. Note: Burmese is a tone language, where [´] indicates a high toned vowel, [`] a low toned vowel, [^] a falling toned vowel, and nothing a mid toned vowel. The sequence of sounds [ey] is a diphthong.

1.	[mî]	*fire*	14.	[nyè]	*fine, small*
2.	[mwêy]	*to give birth*	15.	[nwâ]	*cow*
3.	[myiʔ]	*river*	16.	[ŋâ]	*five*
4.	[myâwn]	*ditch*	17.	[ŋouʔ]	*stump (of tree)*
5.	[myín]	*to see*	18.	[mîn]	*old* (people)
6.	[nê]	*small*	19.	[hm̥í]	*to lean against*
7.	[nyiʔ]	*dirty*	20.	[hm̥wêy]	*fragrant*
8.	[nwè]	*to bend flexibly*	21.	[hm̥yayʔ]	*to cure* (meat)
9.	[hm̥yawʔ]	*to multiply*	22.	[hm̥òwn]	*flour, powder*
10.	[hn̥êy]	*slow*	23.	[hn̥yiʔ]	*to wring, squeeze*
11.	[hn̥wêy]	*to heat*	24.	[hn̥yeyʔ]	*to nod the head*
12.	[hn̥yaʔ]	*to cut off* (hair)	25.	[hŋ̊â]	*to lend property, borrow*
13.	[hŋ̊eʔ]	*bird*	26.	[hîn]	*curry*

1.6   Korean

In the following Korean words, you will find the sounds [s] and [š]. Determine whether the sounds [š] and [s] are allophones of the same phoneme or separate phonemes. If the sounds are allophones of the same phoneme, give the basic and derived allophones and the environment in which the derived allophone occurs.

1.	[ši]	*poem*	11.	[sal]	*flesh*
2.	[mišin]	*superstition*	12.	[časal]	*suicide*
3.	[šinmun]	*newspaper*	13.	[kasu]	*singer*
4.	[tʰaksaŋšikye]	*table clock*	14.	[sanmun]	*prose*
5.	[šilsu]	*mistake*	15.	[kasəl]	*hypothesis*
6.	[ošip]	*fifty*	16.	[čəŋsonyən]	*adolescents*
7.	[čašin]	*self*	17.	[miso]	*smile*
8.	[paŋšik]	*method*	18.	[susek]	*search*
9.	[kanšik]	*snack*	19.	[tapsa]	*exploration*
10.	[kaši]	*thorn*	20.	[so]	*cow*

1.7   Same

Examine the data from Same (also known as Lappish) below. First consider [tʸ] and [kʸ] ([ʸ] indicates that the sounds are palatalized). Are they allophones of the same phoneme or do they belong to separate phonemes? Identify the type of distribution. Give evidence for your claim. Second, consider the sonorants. Are the voiced and voiceless sonorants in contrastive or complementary distribution? Give evidence for your claim. Finally, consider the phone [ʔ]. Is it an allophone of /t/ or an allophone of a separate phoneme? Give evidence for your claim.

1.	[pa:tʸtʸi]	*smithy*	8.	[fana:s]	*boat*
2.	[la:kʸkʸu]	*meadow*	9.	[vahn̥emaht]	*parents*
3.	[pa:tni]	*tooth*	10.	[tsabma]	*she/he whips*
4.	[kihlʸi:ht]	*engagement*	11.	[la:itas]	*unpleasant*
5.	[liehm̥u]	*mild*	12.	[la:tʸtʸu]	*meadow*
6.	[pa:kʸkʸi]	*smithy*	13.	[nama:ht]	*names*
7.	[miha:]	*a lot*	14.	[pa:ʔni]	*tooth*

1.8 English

In the following dialect of English there is a predictable variant [əy] of the diphthong [ay]. What phonetic segments condition this change? What feature(s) characterize the class of conditioning segments?

1.	[bəyt]	*bite*	6.	[fəyt]	*fight*	11.	[taym]	*time*
2.	[tay]	*tie*	7.	[bay]	*buy*	12.	[təyp]	*type*
3.	[rayd]	*ride*	8.	[rəys]	*rice*	13.	[naynθ]	*ninth*
4.	[rayz]	*rise*	9.	[fayl]	*file*	14.	[fayr]	*fire*
5.	[rəyt]	*write*	10.	[ləyf]	*life*	15.	[bəyk]	*bike*

1.9 Totonac

Examine the classes of voiced versus voiceless vowels in Totonac, a language spoken in Mexico. Are voiced and voiceless vowels in Totonac in contrast, in free variation, or in complementary distribution? If the sounds are in complementary distribution, pick one sound as the basic sound and give the phonetic contexts for its allophones. (Note that [c] represents a voiceless alveolar affricate and [ɬ] a velarized [l].)

1.	[capsḁ]	*he stacks*	7.	[snapapḁ]	*white*
2.	[cilinksḁ]	*it resounded*	8.	[stapu̥]	*beans*
3.	[kasitti̥]	*cut it*	9.	[šumpi̥]	*porcupine*
4.	[kuku̥]	*uncle*	10.	[ta:qhu̥]	*you plunged*
5.	[ɬkakḁ]	*peppery*	11.	[tihašɬi̥]	*he rested*
6.	[miki̥]	*snow*	12.	[tukšɬi̥]	*it broke*

1.10 Japanese

Examine the pairs of phones [s]–[š] and [h]–[f] in the Japanese data below. Are [s] and [š] allophones of separate phonemes or the same phoneme? What about [h] and [f]? If either of these pairs is in complementary distribution, identify the basic allophone and the conditioning environments of the other allophone. Then give a rule that describes this distribution. Finally, name the process that is at work here.

1.	[higaši]	*east*	8.	[honto]	*really*
2.	[heya]	*room*	9.	[fuɾui]	*old*
3.	[hyaku]	*one hundred*	10.	[futatsu]	*two units*
4.	[gohan]	*cooked rice*	11.	[šimasu]	*do*
5.	[haha]	*mother*	12.	[ofuɾo]	*bath*
6.	[šiɾoi]	*white*	13.	[sensei]	*teacher*
7.	[san]	*three*	14.	[soɾa]	*sky*

2. Intermediate

2.1 Tojolabal

Tojolabal is a language spoken in Mexico. Determine whether plain [k] and glottalized [k'] are allophones of a single phoneme, in free variation, or in contrast. Support your answer with specific examples. (Hint: Don't forget that near-minimal pairs can be as convincing as minimal pairs.)

1.	[kisim]	*my beard*	7.	[sak]	*white*
2.	[cak'a]	*chop it down*	8.	[k'išin]	*warm*
3.	[koktit]	*our feet*	9.	[skuču]	*he is carrying it*
4.	[k'ak]	*flea*	10.	[k'uutes]	*to dress*
5.	[p'akan]	*hanging*	11.	[snika]	*he stirred it*
6.	[k'aʔem]	*sugar cane*	12.	[ʔak']	*read*

2.2 Spanish

Examine the following data from Spanish and answer the questions which follow. Note that [β] represents a voiced bilabial fricative, and [ɣ] a voiced velar fricative.

1.	[bino]	*he came*	8.	[uβa]	*grape*
2.	[diβino]	*divine*	9.	[golpe]	*a hit*
3.	[kaβo]	*end*	10.	[gato]	*cat*
4.	[suβteraneo]	*subterranean*	11.	[aɣo]	*I do*
5.	[brotar]	*to sprout*	12.	[iɣaðo]	*liver*
6.	[imbierno]	*winter*	13.	[teŋgo]	*I have*
7.	[diɣno]	*worthy*	14.	[leɣal]	*legal*

   a. The allophones [b] and [β] are in complementary distribution, as are [g] and [ɣ]. Determine the conditioning environments for each pair and state a rule that describes the distribution of the allophones.

   b. Refer to problem 1.3. and the rule for the distribution of the allophones [d] and [ð]. Describe the distribution of [b], [d], [g] and [β], [ð], [ɣ] in the most general terms possible, assuming each pair of allophones follows the same pattern.

2.3 Kenyang

Examine the following data from Kenyang, a language spoken in Cameroon. Are the phones [k] and [q] in contrastive or complementary distribution or in free variation? If they are in complementary distribution, state a rule that describes their distribution. If they are in contrastive distribution or free variation, give evidence for your claim. Finally, what does this type of distribution prove about the sounds [k] and [q] in Kenyang? ([q] represents a voiceless uvular stop.)

1.	[enɔq]	*tree*	7.	[enoq]	*drum*
2.	[eket]	*house*	8.	[nčiku]	*I am buying*
3.	[nek]	*rope*	9.	[ekaq]	*leg*
4.	[ngaq]	*knife*	10.	[naq]	*brother-in-law*
5.	[etɔq]	*town*	11.	[pɔbrik]	*work project*
6.	[ayuk]	*(person's name)*	12.	[ndek]	*European*

2.4 Canadian French

Consider the distribution of [t] and [c] (a voiceless alveolar affricate) in the data below. State their distribution and determine if they are allophones of one phoneme or of separate phonemes. [ü] and [ʊ̈] are high, front, rounded vowels, tense and lax, respectively.

1.	[tu]	*all*	7.	[telegram]	*telegram*
2.	[abuci]	*ended*	8.	[trɛ]	*very*
3.	[tɛl]	*such*	9.	[külcür]	*culture*
4.	[tab]	*stamp*	10.	[minʊ̈t]	*minute*
5.	[cimɪd]	*timid*	11.	[cü]	*you*
6.	[cɪt]	*title*	12.	[cüb]	*tube*

2.5 German

Examine the voiceless velar fricative represented by [x] and the voiceless palatal fricative represented by [ç] in the German data below. Are the two sounds in complementary distribution or are they in contrast? If the sounds are allophones in complementary distribution, state the phonetic contexts for each allophone.

1.	[axt]	*eight*	7.	[ɪç]	*I*
2.	[bu:x]	*book*	8.	[ɛçt]	*real*
3.	[lɔx]	*hole*	9.	[špre:çə]	*he/she/it would speak*
4.	[ho:x]	*high*	10.	[lɛçəln]	*to smile*
5.	[flʊxt]	*flight*	11.	[ri:çən]	*to smell*
6.	[laxən]	*to laugh*	12.	[fɛçtən]	*to fence*

2.6   Old English

In Old English, [f] and [v], [h] and [x], and [n] and [ŋ] were in complementary distribution. Based on the following data, what is the distribution? The symbol [x] represents a voiceless velar fricative.

1.	[briŋgan]	*to bring*	11.	[lʊvʊ]	*love*
2.	[driŋkan]	*to drink*	12.	[mannes]	*man's*
3.	[fæst]	*fast*	13.	[moːna]	*moon*
4.	[fiːfta]	*fifth*	14.	[niːxsta]	*next*
5.	[fɔlk]	*folk*	15.	[noːn]	*noon*
6.	[fɔnt]	*font*	16.	[ɔffrian]	*to offer*
7.	[haːt]	*hot*	17.	[ɔvnas]	*ovens*
8.	[hloːθ]	*troop*	18.	[ruːx]	*rough*
9.	[hlüxxan]	*to laugh*	19.	[ləŋgan]	*to lengthen*
10.	[θʊŋgɛn]	*full grown*	20.	[hrævn̩]	*raven*
			21.	[nixt]	*night*

2.7   Persian

Persian (or Farsi) is an Indo-European language which is the most widely spoken language in Iran. In the following data, do [r̄], [r̥] and [ɾ] belong to one, two or three different phonemes? If they belong to different phonemes, give the pairs of forms which show this. If they are allophones of one (or two) phonemes, state the rule for their distribution. Which one would you choose to represent the phonemic form, and why?

[r̄] voiced trill			[r̥] voiceless trill			[ɾ] voiced flap		
1.	[ær̄teš]	*army*	7.	[ahar̥]	*starch*	13.	[ahaɾi]	*starched*
2.	[far̄si]	*Persian*	8.	[behtær̥]	*better*	14.	[bæɾadær̥]	*brother*
3.	[qædr̄i]	*a little bit*	9.	[hær̄towr̥]	*however*	15.	[beɾid]	*go*
4.	[r̄ah]	*road*	10.	[čar̥]	*four*	16.	[biɾæŋg]	*pale*
5.	[r̄is]	*beard*	11.	[čejur̥]	*what kind*	17.	[čeɾa]	*why*
6.	[r̄uz]	*day*	12.	[šir̥]	*lion*	18.	[daɾid]	*you have*

2.8 Bukusu

Bukusu is a Bantu language spoken in Kenya. The nasal prefix [n-] indicates that the verb is in the first person ('I eat, go, sing', etc.). If the verb is in the first person, the nasal [n] has to be a prefix of the phonemic structure of the word. Two different processes occur when [n] stands before another consonant. Look at these words and think about what is happening. The symbols [β], [ñ], and [x] represent, respectively, a voiced bilabial fricative, a palatal nasal, and a voiceless velar fricative.

1.	[ndiila]	*I hold*	10.	[ñǰina]	*I scream*
2.	[seenda]	*I move*	11.	[suna]	*I jump*
3.	[ñǰuuŋga]	*I watch*	12.	[xala]	*I cut*
4.	[ŋgaβa]	*I divide*	13.	[ŋgeta]	*I pour*
5.	[mbiima]	*I weigh*	14.	[ndasa]	*I add*
6.	[xola]	*I do*	15.	[mbula]	*I roam*
7.	[mbuka]	*I perish*	16.	[ndula]	*I trample*
8.	[fuka]	*I cook*	17.	[fwaara]	*I dress*
9.	[funa]	*I break*	18.	[mbala]	*I count*

a. How does the behavior of a nasal differ when it stands before the different types of obstruents (remember the natural class *obstruent*)?

b. There are two phonological processes at work here. What are they?

c. Write a phonological rule or rules to capture the facts about the nasal prefix [n-] in Bukusu.

3. Advanced

3.1 Greek

Examine the sounds [x], [k], [ç], and [c] in the following data. [x] represents a voiceless velar fricative, [ç] a voiceless palatal fricative, and [c] a voiceless palatal stop. Which of these sounds are in contrastive and which are in complementary distribution? State the distribution of the allophones.

1.	[kano]	*do*	10.	[kori]	*daughter*
2.	[xano]	*lose*	11.	[xori]	*dances*
3.	[çino]	*pour*	12.	[xrima]	*money*
4.	[cino]	*move*	13.	[krima]	*shame*
5.	[kali]	*charms*	14.	[xufta]	*handful*
6.	[xali]	*plight*	15.	[kufeta]	*bonbons*
7.	[çeli]	*eel*	16.	[oçi]	*no*
8.	[ceri]	*candle*	17.	[oci]	*2.82 pounds*
9.	[çeri]	*hand*			

3.2 Igbirra

Examine the sounds [e] and [a] in the following data from Igbirra, a language spoken in Nigeria. Do they appear to be allophones of separate phonemes or allophones of the same phoneme? If the two sounds are in complementary distribution, state the conditioning environments for the allophones.

1.	[mezi]	*I expect*	5.	[mazɪ]	*I am in pain*
2.	[meze]	*I am well*	6.	[mazɛ]	*I agree*
3.	[meto]	*I arrange*	7.	[matɔ]	*I pick*
4.	[metu]	*I beat*	8.	[matʊ]	*I send*

3.3   Ukrainian

Ukrainian is a slavic language spoken in Ukraine, a country that was part of the former Soviet Union. Compare the masculine nominative singular forms of nouns with the vocative forms (nominative is used for the subject of a sentence and vocative is used when calling to or addressing someone, as in "Hey, Robin."). There is a phonological change between the nominative and the vocative, which adds the ending [-e] to the nominative form. Three pairs of sounds are in allophonic variation. What are these pairs of sounds? What sort of phonological process is at work here (there is a special name for it; see File 4.2)? What do you think is conditioning this alternation? (The symbols [ɦ] and [x] stand for a voiced glottal fricative and a voiceless velar fricative).

	Nominative	Vocative	Gloss
1.	[rak]	[rače]	*lobster*
2.	[yunak]	[yunače]	*young man*
3.	[žuk]	[žuče]	*beetle*
4.	[pastux]	[pastuše]	*shepherd*
5.	[ptax]	[ptaše]	*bird*
6.	[boɦ]	[bože]	*God*
7.	[pluɦ]	[pluže]	*plough*

3.4   Maltese

Maltese is a Semitic language spoken on the island of Malta, in the Mediterranean. Look at the following words and answer the questions that follow them. Compare how the indefinite (*a, some*) and the definite (*the*) are formed. Maltese forms the definite of a noun by attaching either /il-/ or /l-/ to it. Examine the data below remembering this. The symbol [ħ] represents a voiceless pharyngeal fricative.

A.

Indefinite		Definite	
[fellus]	*chicken*	[ilfellus]	*the chicken*
[arya]	*air*	[larya]	*the air*
[mara]	*woman*	[ilmara]	*the woman*
[omm]	*mother*	[lomm]	*the mother*
[kelb]	*dog*	[ilkelb]	*the dog*
[ʔattus]	*cat*	[ilʔattus]	*the cat*
[ħitan]	*walls*	[ilħitan]	*the walls*
[abt]	*armpit*	[labt]	*the armpit*
[ispanyol]	*Spanish*	[lispanyol]	*the Spanish (language)*

1. How can you predict the form of the definite marker?

2. What natural classes of sounds are involved?

Now look at these nouns in the indefinite and the definite:

B.   *Indefinite*   *Definite*

[tiin]	*fig*	[ittiin]	*the fig*
[dawl]	*light*	[iddawl]	*the light*
[sħab]	*clouds*	[issħab]	*the clouds*
[natura]	*nature*	[innatura]	*the nature*

4. The definite marker has the same phonemic form in these words as it had above, but a phonological process has changed its phonetic form.

     a. What type of process is responsible for the change? How did it affect the definite marker?

     b. What natural class of sounds causes the change from the phonemic form to the various phonetic forms in part B?

5. Give the definite form of the following nouns:

Indefinite		*Definite*	
[daar]	*house*	_____	*the house*
[zift]	*pitch*	_____	*the pitch*
[azzar]	*steel*	_____	*the steel*
[ingliz]	*English*	_____	*the English (language)*
[belt]	*city*	_____	*the city*

File 4.5   Sound Substitution and Phonotactic Constraints

Sound Substitutions

Not all sound systems are the same, as we discovered in conducting phonemic analyses of different languages. Some languages have fewer or more phonemes or allophones than English does, and we can detect this when we hear non-native speakers of English pronounce English. For instance, French speakers often pronounce English *this* [ðɪs] as [zɪs] and *thin* [θɪn] as [sɪn]. The reason for this mispronunciation is that the phonemic inventory of French does not contain /ð/ or /θ/, so French speakers substitute the nearest equivalent sounds, the fricatives /z/ and /s/, available in their phonemic inventory.

This is known as **sound substitution**, a process whereby sounds that already exist in a language are used to replace sounds that do not exist in the language when borrowing or trying to pronounce a foreign word. Another familiar example comes from German, a language that has a voiceless velar fricative phoneme, represented by the symbol /x/. English, of course, lacks this sound, though we do have a voiceless velar stop /k/. Most speakers of English substitute /k/ for /x/ in a German word like *Bach* /bax/, producing [bak]. Another example of the same substitution is the way Americans often pronounce the German word *Lebkuchen* /lebkuxən/ 'Christmas cookie' as [lebkukən]. Some English speakers, striving for a more "Germanlike" pronunciation, will pronounce it instead as [lebkuhən]. Why do you suppose an English speaker might substitute /h/ for /x/?

Phonotactic Constraints

In every language there are restrictions on the kinds of sounds and sound sequences possible in different positions in words (particularly at the beginning and end). These restrictions can be formulated in terms of rules stating which sound sequences are possible in a language and which are not. Restrictions on possible combinations of sounds are known as **phonotactic constraints**. Languages generally prefer a consonant (C) first, vowel (V) second syllable structure, but some languages allow a syllable to begin with more than one consonant. For instance, English allows up to three consonants to start a word, provided the first is /s/, the second /p/, /t/, or /k/, and the third /l/, /r/, /y/, or /w/ (see below). There is a wide variety of syllable types in English:

V	oh	CV	no	CCV	flew	CCCV	spree
VC	at	CVC	not	CCVC	flute	CCCVC	spleen
VCC	ask	CVCC	ramp	CCVCC	flutes	CCCVCC	strength
VCCC	asked	CVCCC	ramps	CCVCCC	crafts	CCCVCCC	strengths

Other languages, however, do not have such a large number of syllable structures, as the following lists illustrate. (N represents a nasal stop. Hebrew CVCC syllables are allowed only at the end of a word.)

Hebrew	Japanese	Hawaiian	Indonesian
CV	V	V	V
CVC	CV	CV	VC
CVCC	CVN		CV
			CVC

Notice that this means that Hebrew does not have any initial consonant clusters and that Indonesian has clusters only in the middle of words; that is, there are no clusters initially or finally. Hawaiian does not permit clusters in any position. We can investigate examples of restrictions on consonant sequences in more detail by considering some in a language we know very well—English. To start with, any consonant of English may occur initially (at the beginning) in words except for two: [ž] and [ŋ]. While some speakers *do* pronounce these sounds in borrowed words such as *Jacques* and *Nguyen*, no native English word begins with them. A large number of two consonant combinations also occur, with a stop or fricative being followed by a liquid or glide:

[br]	*bring*	[gl]	*glean*	[my]	*music*	[kw]	*quick*
[θr]	*three*	[fl]	*fly*	[hy]	*humor*	[sw]	*sweet*

In addition, [s] can also be followed by voiceless and nasal stops (as in *stay, small*) and by [f] and [v] in a small number of borrowed words (*sphere, svelte,* etc.). [š] can be followed by a nasal stop or a liquid, but only [šr] is a cluster native to English (e.g., *shrink*). The others are present only in borrowings from Yiddish and German (*Schlemiel* 'clumsy person', *schnook,* 'fool', *Schwinn*).

Borrowing and Accents

If a language has severe restrictions on its phonotactics, the restrictions will apply to every word in the language, native or not. Therefore, just as languages substitute familiar sounds for unfamiliar ones, languages also seek to overcome problems of borrowing a foreign word that violates their phonotactics. For instance, in English, two stops cannot come at the beginning of words, nor can stop plus nasal combinations. So, in order to more easily pronounce the foreign words *Ptolemy* and *gnostic*, English speakers simply drop the first consonant and pronounce the words [taləmi] and [nɔstɪk], respectively.

There are different ways of handling phonotactic problems. Japanese and Finnish provide us with instructive examples. Japanese and Finnish only allow the CV-type syllable, with a few exceptions. When borrowing a foreign word that violates the CV structure, the two languages must force it somehow to fit. CCV, CVC, and other non-CV syllables must be forced into a CV framework. There are two ways to do this. One is to drop or delete the extra consonant(s); the other is to insert vowels to separate the consonants. Finnish opts for deletion. In loanwords, Finnish drops the first of a series of consonants that do not conform to its phonotactics. Thus Germanic *Strand* (CCCVNC) ends up as *ranta* 'beach' (CVNCV) in Finnish, and *glass* becomes *lasi*. Note also the addition of a final vowel to avoid a consonant in syllable final position.

The other way to break up consonant clusters is used in Japanese. Japanese inserts vowels into the cluster, so that (for example) a CCC sequence will end up as CVCVCV. The insertions are rule-governed, meaning that the insertion always works the same way. Thus we can predict the shape of new words in Japanese (e.g., recent English loanwords in the language). The vowel /u/ is inserted, except after /t/ and /d/. Notice the substitutions made by Japanese for English sounds:

/l/	→	/r/	/e/	→	/e/	/ə/	→	/a/
/v/	→	/b/	/ɪ/	→	/i/	/æ/	→	/(y)a/
/θ/	→	/s/	/ɔ/	→	/o/	/Vr/	→	/V:/
/ð/	→	/z/	/ʊ/	→	/u/			

Furthermore, the nasals [m] and [n] are allowed syllable-finally. So, for example, when the English term *birth control* was borrowed into Japanese, it became [ba:su kontoro:ru].

/bərθ/	→	/ba:su/
/kəntrol/	→	/kontoro:ru/

The /u/ in [ba:su] and the last /u/ in [kontoro:ru] are inserted to keep the word-final syllables from ending in a consonant. The second [o] in [kontoro:ru] is inserted to prevent [t] and [r] from forming a cluster.

We can conclude by observing that substitutions by non-native speakers and strategies for handling phonotactic constraints both result in foreign accents, as well as changes in words that have been borrowed into another language. A Spanish speaker does not pronounce *student* as [ɛstudɛnt] because he or she doesn't know any better, but because the consonant clusters /st/, /sk/, and /sp/ never occur at the beginning of a word in Spanish without being preceded by a vowel—for example, in the words *estudiante* 'student', *escuela* 'school', and *espalda* 'shoulder'. The Spanish speaker who says [ɛstudɛnt] is simply applying the phonological rules of Spanish when speaking English words.

File 4.6   Implicational Laws

In studying phonetics, you saw that human languages use a wide variety of sounds. In spite of this variety some sounds are more common than others. Thus while it is true that almost all human languages use the stop consonants [p] and [t] and the vowel [a], relatively few languages use pharyngeal fricatives ([ħ] and [ʕ], the "throaty" sounds used in Arabic), voiceless vowels (like in whispered speech), and clicks (*tsk, tsk!* and horse calling sounds are American examples). So [p], [t], and [a] are very *common* in languages while pharyngeal fricatives, voiceless vowels, and clicks are very *uncommon* speech sounds. The purpose of this file is to explain why some sounds are more common than others. Before attempting an explanation, however, we will make four observations concerning common and uncommon speech sounds.

Sound Inventories

The first observation concerning common and uncommon speech sounds has to do with the inventories of sounds in languages. The observation is basically this: if a language uses an uncommon sound, one of its more common counterparts will also be used. Two parts of this statement need clarification. First, when we say that a language *uses* a sound we mean that that sound is in the inventory of phonemes in the language. In other words, that sound is distinctive relative to other sounds in the language.

The second part of the statement that needs clarification is the phrase "one of its more common counterparts." This phrase refers to the fact that there tends to be a common sound associated with each uncommon sound which is just like the uncommon sound except for one or two phonetic features. For instance, the common counterpart of a voiceless vowel is a voiced vowel of the same tongue height, tongue advancement, and lip rounding. Likewise, the common counterpart of a voiceless pharyngeal fricative is a voiceless velar fricative.

In the following chart we present some (relatively) uncommon sounds and their (relatively) more common counterparts.

Uncommon	*Common*
[ã]	[a]
[ḁ]	[u]
[x]	[k] or [s]
[s]	[t]
[θ]	[t] or [s]
[ð]	[d] or [z]

So, uncommon sounds differ from their common counterparts in only one or two features. Notice that [x] (voiceless velar fricative) has two counterparts, [k] and [s]. [k] is a voiceless velar stop, so it differs from [x] by only one feature; [s] is a voiceless alveolar fricative, so it too differs from [x] by only one feature. [θ] and [ð] are in a similar relation. [θ] differs from [s] in its place of articulation (interdental versus alveolar), and it differs from [t] in its manner of articulation (fricative versus stop) as well as its place of articulation.

One other thing to notice about this chart is that [s] appears both as a common sound (as opposed to [x] and [θ]) and as an uncommon sound (as opposed to [t]). This illustrates the fact that by using the terms "common" and "uncommon" to designate the sounds in an implicational law, we are not referring to an absolute standard. Rather, "common" and "uncommon" are used in a *relative* way. In other words, [s] is uncommon in relation to [t], and common in relation to [θ]. In terms of an absolute sense of commonness, [s] would surely count as a common sound because it is used in many (if not most) of the world's languages, but [s] is relatively less common than [t] and therefore is uncommon in relation to it.

Now, we have said that if a language uses an uncommon sound, one of its more common counterparts will also be included in that language's inventory of distinct sounds. In terms of the chart presented above, this means that any language that uses [ã] will also use [a], any language that uses [ą] will also use [a], any language that uses [x] will also use [k], and so on. This type of observation is called an **implicational law** because the presence of the uncommon sound *implies* that the common sound will also be used in the language. Of course the implication cannot be reversed. In other words, the fact that English uses the sound [k] does not imply that we also use [x].

Implicational laws can be stated for natural classes of sounds rather than just for individual pairs of sounds. For instance, the class of voiceless consonants is relatively more common than the class of voiced consonants. In other words, if a language makes use of voiced stops it will also make use of voiceless ones, but the reverse is not true. There are some languages that have only voiceless stops. Thus the presence of voiced stops implies the presence of their voiceless counterparts, while the presence of voiceless stops does not imply the presence of voiced ones.

Another implicational law that can be stated in terms of a natural class of sounds is that the presence of fricatives in a language implies the presence of homorganic stops (stops with the same place of articulation) in that language. Thus, if a language uses an [s], then it also uses a [t].

Frequency and Distribution

The second observation concerning implicational laws is that they are not only generalizations concerning inventories of sounds; they are also related to the *degree* to which sounds will be used in a particular language and the *range of distribution* of the sounds in the words of the language. Thus, even if a language makes use of a pharyngeal fricative, this uncommon sound will be used in fewer words than will the more common alveolar fricative. In other words, the pharyngeal fricative will have limited usage compared with the velar fricative. Common sounds also have a *wider distribution* within a language—i.e., they are used in more phonetic environments than uncommon sounds. So, for instance, Cantonese Chinese has both stops and fricatives in its inventory of sounds, but fricatives may occur in only one spot in the syllable, as the first sound. Stops have wider distribution: they occur both syllable-initially and syllable-finally in Cantonese.

An English example of the limited usage and limited distribution of uncommon sounds has to do with the sound [ð]. The sound [ð] can be classified as uncommon because it is relatively rare in the languages of the world, and anywhere [ð] occurs in English, [z] can also occur. If you try to think of words that contain [ð], you will probably find that your list is limited to "grammatical" words like *this, that, those, them,* and *they,* and a few other words like *either* and *lathe.* Furthermore, [ð] occurs as the last sound in English words less often than [z] does. Compared with the number of words that contain [z], it is obvious that [ð] has limited use in English.

Acquisition of Sounds

A third type of observation related to the implicational laws has to do with the order of the *acquisition* of sounds: children learning a language acquire the use of common sounds before they acquire the use of uncommon ones. As a result, children who have not yet mastered the complete sound inventory of their native language will substitute common sounds when trying to say uncommon sounds. When a little girl says [dis wən] for *this one*, she is replacing the relatively uncommon [ð] with [d], a much more common sound. This is an indication that the child has not yet acquired the use of [ð], although [d] is readily available for use. When the language development of a child is followed from babbling through maturity, a characteristic order of acquisition appears. This order in the acquisition of sounds is relatively constant for children around the world, no matter what language they are learning. Once again the implicational laws capture a generalization about language; namely, that the acquisition of a relatively uncommon sound implies that its more common counterpart has already been acquired.

Sound Change

The fourth and last type of observation that is related to implicational laws involves *language change*. This observation is that uncommon sounds tend to be less stable than common ones. Thus, in the course of language change, if any sound is going to be lost, it will be an uncommon one rather than its more common counterpart. An illustration of this can be drawn from the history of English. In the Old English pronunciation of the word *knight* there was a voiceless velar fricative [x] between the vowel and the [t]. As you can see, the letters *gh* indicate where this consonant used to be. During the development of English, this velar fricative was lost (so *knight* now rhymes with *quite*). In fact, all instances of the velar fricative sound (as in *height, sight, fight, might,* and so on) were lost. English speakers just stopped using velar fricatives altogether, so now we find it hard to learn how to say them when we are trying to learn a language like German. This observation fits in with the implicational law that says that fricatives are less common than stops. Therefore the fricative [x] is less stable and more likely to be lost than the corresponding stop consonant [k].

Explanation

At this point we can summarize what we have observed about common and uncommon speech sounds:

1. the presence of an uncommon sound in a language implies that its more common counterpart will also be present;
2. uncommon sounds have limited usage and distribution in the languages that do make use of them, as compared with common sounds;
3. the use of common sounds is acquired before the use of uncommon ones;
4. uncommon sounds tend to be less stable than common ones and are thus more likely to be lost or changed over time.

We might be tempted to say that the implicational laws are themselves the explanations of the observations in 1–4. Thus, we might say that [x] is more likely to be lost in language change than is [k] because [k] is more common than [x]. Or we might want to say that [k] is acquired by children before [x] because [k] is more common than [x]. This type of explanation is, however, circular. The circularity stems from the fact that we distinguished between common and uncommon sounds by making the observations in 1–4.

Ease of Production

The alternative to this circular form of explanation is to explain the observations in 1–4 (and thus the implicational laws) in terms of the communicative nature of language. It is important to realize that when people use language, their goal (generally speaking) is to communicate—that is, to successfully transmit a message from a speaker to a hearer. Focusing on the function of language leads us to ask what sounds are most useful for transmitting a message from speaker to hearer. First of all, notice that if a sound is difficult to produce, speakers will be somewhat inconsistent in pronouncing it, and this inconsistency will result in confusion on the part of the hearer. To avoid being misunderstood, speakers may avoid words with difficult sounds (resulting in limited usage), and if enough speakers avoid a difficult sound it may disappear from the language entirely (language change). Of course, sounds that are difficult to produce (such as fricatives, whose production involves delicate control of muscles) are not likely to be mastered by children before easier sounds are. As you can see, there are at least some instances where the observation that sound X is more common than sound Y is directly tied to the fact that sound X is easier to produce than sound Y. Thus, [k] is more common than [x] because stops are easier to produce than are fricatives. Alveolar fricatives are more common than pharyngeal fricatives because the tip of tongue is more agile than the back of the tongue, hence alveolar consonants are easier to produce than are pharyngeal ones. Thus ease of production is an explanation of at least some of the implicational laws.

Ease of Perception

Another way to answer the question of what sounds are most useful for transmitting a message from speaker to hearer focuses on the hearer's point of view. It is reasonable to suppose that if a sound blends into the surrounding sounds too much, its distinctive qualities may become difficult to hear. So, for example, if Morse code were made up of long dashes and no-so-long dashes, or dots and somewhat shorter dots, rather than dots and dashes, it would be difficult to use. In the same way, the consonants and vowels which make up syllables are most usable when they are quite different from each other. So, the kind of syllable which is most useful in transmitting messages in language is composed of *maximally distinct* consonants and vowels. By this we mean that the consonants have very few qualities in common with the vowels, and the vowels are likewise very different from the consonants. The value of maximally distinct carriers of information is obvious when we think about Morse code. If you can't tell the difference between dots and dashes, then little communication can take place. In the same way, if you can't tell the difference between consonants and vowels, then communication using language is likely to be very inefficient also.

Perhaps a couple of examples of the ways that consonants can be more vowel-like, or vowels can be more consonant-like, are in order. One implicational law that we noticed is that the use of voiced consonants in a language implies the use of voiceless ones (thus voiceless consonants are more common than voiced ones). The natural explanation for this implicational law is that voiceless consonants have fewer qualities in common with vowels than do voiced consonants; thus, in syllables containing consonants and vowels, voiceless consonants are perceptually more salient (or noticeable) than voiced ones. A way that vowels can be less consonant-like is to be pronounced with the mouth wide open, as in the vowel [a]. Because consonants are made by obstructing the vocal tract in some way, a vowel that is pronounced with the mouth wide open will be more distinct from surrounding consonants than will be a vowel like [i] or [u] which is pronounced with the mouth somewhat closed. It just so happens that there is an implicational law corresponding to this distinction between [i], [u], and [a]. The presence of a closed vowel ([i], [u]) implies the presence of an open vowel ([a]). Thus, syllables with maximally distinct consonants and vowels are easier to perceive than syllables with consonants and vowels that resemble each other, and therefore some implicational laws exist for the sake of the listener, to make language easier to perceive.

Conclusion

In this file we have seen that although there is a great variety in the sounds which can be employed in language, there are universal tendencies, namely to restrict the inventory of sounds to certain common sounds, to restrict the degree of utilization and distribution of uncommon sounds in languages that do use them, to acquire common sounds earlier than uncommon ones, and for uncommon sounds to be unstable in the face of language change. We have also shown that these observations concerning common and uncommon sounds are related to the ease of production and ease of perception of those sounds, that the implicational laws can be explained by assuming that people are using language in order to communicate, and that this produces a need for efficiency which leads to the use of easily produced and perceived sounds.

5

Morphology

Morphology is the study of the building blocks of meaning in language. How do languages build words and indicate grammatical relationships between words? Very often, the answer lies in their morphology.

File 5.1　The Minimal Units of Meaning: Morphemes

A continuous stream of speech can be broken up by the listener (or linguist) into smaller, meaningful parts. A conversation, for example, can be divided into the sentences of the conversation, which can be divided up further into the words that make up each of the sentences. It is obvious to most people that a sentence has a meaning, and that each of the words in it has a meaning as well. Can we go further and divide words into smaller units that still have meanings? Many people think not; their immediate intuition is that words are the basic meaningful elements of a language. This is not the case, however. Many words can be broken down into still smaller units. Think, for example, of words such as *unlucky*, *unhappy*, and *unsatisfied*. The *un-* in each of these words has the same meaning, loosely, that of *not*, but *un* is not a word by itself. Thus, we have identified units—parts smaller than the word—that have meanings. These are called **morphemes**. Now consider the words *look*, *looks*, and *looked*. What about the *-s* in *looks* and the *-ed* in *looked*? These segments can be separated from the meaningful unit *look*, and although they do not really have an identifiable meaning themselves, each does have a particular function. The *-s* is required for agreement with certain subjects (*she looks*, but not *she look), and the *-ed* signifies that the action of the verb *look* has already taken place. Segments such as these are also considered morphemes. Thus, a *morpheme* is the smallest linguistic unit that has a meaning or grammatical function.

Some words, of course, are not composed of other morphemes. *Car*, *spider*, and *race*, for example, are words, but they are also morphemes, since they cannot be broken down into smaller meaningful parts. Morphemes that are also words are called **free morphemes** since they can stand alone. **Bound morphemes**, on the other hand, never exist as words themselves, but are always attached to some other morpheme. Some examples of bound morphemes in English are *un-*, *-ed*, and *-s*.

When we identify the number and types of morphemes a given word consists of, we are looking at what is referred to as the **structure** of the word. Morphology is the study of how words are structured and how they are put together from smaller parts. Morphologists not only identify the different classes of morphemes but also study the patterns that occur in the combination of morphemes in a given language. For example, consider the words *rewrite*, *retake*, and *relive*. Notice that *re-* is a bound morpheme that attaches only to verbs and, furthermore, attaches to the beginning of the verb, not the end. Every speaker of English knows you can't say *write-re* or *take-re* (where *re-* is connected to the end of the free morpheme), nor can you say *rechoice* or *repretty* (where *re-* is connected to a morpheme that is not a verb). In other words, part of a speaker's linguistic competence is knowing, not only the meaning of the morphemes of a language but also the ways in which the morphemes are allowed to combine with other morphemes.

Morphemes can be classified as either bound or free, as we have seen. There are three additional ways of characterizing morphemes. The first is to label *bound* morphemes according to whether they attach to the beginning or end of a word. You are most likely familiar with these terms. A **prefix** attaches to the beginning and a **suffix** attaches to the end of a word. The general term for prefixes and suffixes is **affix**, so bound morphemes are also referred to as affixes. The second way of characterizing morphemes is to classify *bound* morphemes according to their function in the complex words of which they are a part. When some morphemes attach to words, they create, or *derive*, new words, either by changing the meaning of the word or by changing its part of speech. For example, *un-* in *unhappy* creates a new word with the opposite meaning of *happy*. Notice that both *unhappy* and *happy* are adjectives. The suffix *-ness* in *quickness*, however, changes the part of speech of *quick*, an adjective, into a noun, *quickness*. Morphemes that change the meaning or part of speech of a word they attach to are called **derivational** morphemes. Other morphemes do not alter words in this way but only refine and give extra grammatical information about the word's already existing meaning. For example, *cat* and *cats* are both nouns that have basically the same meaning (i.e., they refer to the same sort of thing), but *cats*, with the plural morpheme *-s*, contains only the additional information that more than one of these things are being referred to. The morphemes that serve a purely grammatical function, never creating a new word but only a different *form* of the same word, are called **inflectional** morphemes.

In every word we find that there is at least one free morpheme. In a morphologically complex word, i.e., one composed of a free morpheme and any number of bound affixes, the free morpheme is referred to as the **stem, root,** or **base**. However, if there is more than one affix in a word, we cannot say that all of the affixes attach to the stem. Consider the word *happenings*, for example. When *-ing* is added to *happen*, we note that a new word is derived; it is morphologically complex, but it is a word. The plural morpheme *-s* is added onto the word *happening*, not the suffix *-ing*.

In English the derivational morphemes are either prefixes or suffixes, but by chance, the inflectional morphemes are all suffixes. Of course, this is not the same in other languages. There are only eight inflectional morphemes in English. They are listed below, along with an example of the type of stem each can attach to.

The Inflectional Suffixes of English

Stem	*Suffix*	*Function*	*Example*
wait	-s	3rd per. sg. present	She wait*s* there at noon.
wait	-ed	past tense	She wait*ed* there yesterday.
wait	-ing	progressive	She is wait*ing* there now.
eat	-en	past participle	Jack has eat*en* the Oreos.
chair	-s	plural	The chair*s* are in the room.
chair	-'s	possessive	The chair*'s* leg is broken.
fast	-er	comparative	Jill runs fast*er* than Joe.
fast	-est	superlative	Tim runs fast*est* of all.

The difference between inflectional and derivational morphemes is sometimes difficult to see at first. Some characteristics of each are listed below to help make the distinction clearer.

Derivational Morphemes

1. Change the part of speech or the meaning of a word, e.g., *-ment* added to a verb forms a noun, *judg-ment*, and *re-activate* means 'activate again'.

2. Are not required by syntax. They typically indicate semantic relations *within* a word, but no syntactic relations outside the word (compare this with #2 below, under inflectional morphemes), e.g., *un-kind* relates *un-* 'not' to *kind* but has no particular syntactic connections outside the word; note that the same word can be used in *he is unkind* and *they are unkind*.

3. Are usually not very productive—derivational morphemes generally are selective about what they'll combine with, e.g., the suffix *-hood* occurs with just a few nouns such as *brother, neighbor,* and *knight*, but not with most others, e.g., *friend, daughter,* or *candle*.

4. Typically occur before inflectional suffixes, e.g., *govern-ment-s*: *-ment*, a derivational suffix, precedes *-s*, an inflectional suffix.

5. May be prefixes or suffixes (in English), e.g., *pre-arrange, arrange-ment.*

Inflectional Morphemes

1. Do not change meaning or part of speech, e.g., *big, bigg-er, bigg-est* are all adjectives.

2. Are required by the syntax. They typically indicate syntactic or semantic relations <u>between</u> different words in a sentence, e.g., *Nim love-s bananas*: *-s* marks the 3rd person singular present form of the verb, relating it to the 3rd singular subject *Nim*.

3. Are very productive. They typically occur with all members of some large class of morphemes, e.g., the plural morpheme *-s* occurs with almost all nouns.

4. Occur at the margin of a word, after any derivational morphemes, e.g., *ration-al-iz-ation-s* : *-s* is inflectional, and appears at the very end of the word.

5. Are suffixes only (in English).

It is useful to make one final distinction between types of morphemes. Some morphemes have semantic content. That is, they either have some kind of independent, identifiable meaning or indicate a change in meaning when added to a word. Others serve only to provide information about grammatical function by relating certain words in a sentence to each other (see #2 under inflectional morphemes, above). The former are called **content** morphemes, and the latter are called **function** morphemes. This distinction might at first appear to be the same as the inflectional and derivational distinction. They do overlap, but not completely. All derivational morphemes are content morphemes, and all inflectional morphemes are function morphemes, as you might have surmised. However, some words can be merely function morphemes. Examples in English of such free morphemes that are also function morphemes are prepositions, articles, pronouns, and conjunctions.

In this file, we have been using conventional spelling to represent morphemes. But it is important to realize that morphemes are pairings of *sounds* with meanings, not spellings with meanings, and representing morphemes phonetically reveals some interesting facts. We find that just as different free morphemes can have the same phonetic representations, as in *ear* (for hearing) and *ear* (of corn), the same is true of bound morphemes. For example, the plural, possessive, and third person singular suffixes can all sound identical in English (e.g., *cats* [kæts], *Frank's* [fræŋks], and *walks* [waks]). These three suffixes are completely different morphemes, they just happen to be homophonous, or sound alike, in English. Similarly, there are two morphemes in English which sound like [ɪn]. One means 'not' as in *inoperable* or *intolerable*, and the other means 'in' as in *intake* or *inside*.

One of the more interesting things revealed by transcribing morphemes phonetically is the interaction of phonological and morphological processes. For example, some morphemes have more than one phonetic representation depending on which sounds precede or follow them, but since each of the pronunciations serves the same function or has the same meaning, it is considered to be the same morpheme. In other words, the same morpheme can be pronounced differently depending upon the sounds that follow or precede it. Of course, these different pronunciations will be patterned. For example, the phonetic representation of the plural morpheme is either [s] as in *cats*, [z] as in *dogs*, or [əz] as in *churches*. Each of these three pronunciations is said to be an **allomorph** of the *same* morpheme because [s], [z], and [əz] all have the same function (making some word plural) and because they are similar phonetically. Note that this same phonological process, which causes the plural morpheme /s/ to be pronounced as [s] after voiceless sounds, [z] after voiced sounds, and [əz] after sibilants, also applies to the possessive morpheme /s/ and the 3rd person singular morpheme /s/. Consider the morpheme /ɪn-/, which means 'not' in the words *inoperable, incongruent,* and *impossible.* What are the allomorphs of this morpheme?

We now call your attention to a few pitfalls of identifying morphemes. First, don't confuse morphemes with syllables. A few examples will show that the number of morphemes and syllables in a word are independent of each other. Consider the word *coats.* It is a one-syllable word composed of two morphemes. *Coat* happens to be one morpheme and consists of a single syllable, but *-s* is not even a syllable, although it is a morpheme. Note that *syllable* is a three-syllable word composed of only one morpheme.

Second, note that a given morpheme has a particular sound or sound sequence associated with it, but not every instance of that sound sequence in the language represents that morpheme. For example, take the plural morpheme /s/. When you hear the word [karts] in isolation, you can't determine if the [s] is an instance of this plural morpheme (*the carts are back in the store*), or of the possessive morpheme (*the cart's wheels turn funny*), or of the 3rd person singular morpheme (*he carts those books around everyday*). That sound sequence may not even be a morpheme at all. The [s] in [sun], for example, is not a morpheme. Likewise, the [ɪn] of *inexcusable* is the morpheme that means 'not', but the [ɪn] of *print* is not a morpheme.

Third, remember to analyze the phonetic representations of morphemes and not their spellings. A morpheme can have one or more allomorphs, and these allomorphs might be represented by the same or different spellings. The *-er* in *writer* is the same morpheme as the *-or* in *editor* and the *-ar* in *liar,* since all three mean 'one who', but they do not represent separate allomorphs since their pronunciations are identical, namely, [ɹ]. On the other hand, the *-s* in *Mark's, John's,* and *Charles's* are the same morpheme but represent three different allomorphs, since each is pronounced differently.

We include below a summary list of criteria that might help you to identify the different types of morphemes.

Given a morpheme,

1. Can it stand alone as a word?

    YES →   it's a *free* morpheme (e.g., *bubble, orange*)
    NO   →   it's a *bound* morpheme (e.g., *-er* in *beater, -s* in *oranges*)

2. Does it have the principal meaning of the word it's in?

    YES →   it's the *stem* (e.g., *happy* in *unhappiness*)
    NO   →   it's an *affix* (e.g., *-or* in *contributor, pre-* in *preview*)

3. Does it create a new word by changing the meaning or part of speech or both?

    YES →   it's a *derivational* affix (e.g., *re-* in *rewind, -ist* in *artist*)
    NO   →   it's an *inflectional* affix (e.g., *-est* in *smartest*)

4. Does it have a meaning or cause a change in meaning when added to a word?

    YES →   it's a *content* morpheme (e.g., *un-* in *untrue*)
    NO   →   it's a *function* morpheme (e.g., *-s* in *books*)

File 5.2   Exercises in Isolating Morphemes

1. The following words are made up of either one or two morphemes. Isolate them and decide for each if it is free or bound, what kind of affix is involved, and (where applicable) if it is inflectional or derivational.

   a. cats
   b. unhappy
   c. rejoin
   d. catsup
   e. milder
   f. hateful
   g. succotash
   h. bicycle
   i. greedy
   j. entrust
   k. signpost
   l. spacious

2. Divide the words below into their component morphemes and give the information about the morphemes as you did in 1. Note: words may consist of one, two, or more than two morphemes.

   a. comfortable
   b. Massachusetts
   c. environmentally
   d. reconditioned
   e. unidirectional
   f. senseless
   g. thickeners
   h. rationalization
   i. unspeakably

3. In each group of words below, two words have a different morphological structure than the others; one has a different type of suffix, and one has no suffix at all. Identify the word that has no suffix and the word whose suffix is different from the others. Isolate the suffix that the remaining two words share and give its type (as in 1) and function.

   a. rider
      colder
      silver
      actor
   b. tresses
      melodies
      Bess's
      guess
   c. running
      foundling
      handling
      fling
   d. tables
      lens
      witches
      calculates

4. In each group of words that follows, identify the parts of speech of the stems and the parts of speech of the whole words.

   a. government
      speaker
      contemplation
   b. fictional
      childish
      colorful
   c. calmest
      lovelier
      sillier

5. Isolate the bound affixes in the following groups of words. Then name the part of speech of the stem and say whether the affix changes the part of speech, and if so, to what.

   a. spiteful
      healthful
      truthful
   b. unsure
      untrue
      unhappy
   c. retake
      review
      relive
   d. stoppable
      fixable
      laughable

6. From the examples given for each of the following suffixes, determine: (i) the part of speech of the expression with which the suffix combines, and (ii) the part of speech of the expressions formed by the addition of the suffix.

    a. -ify: solidify, intensify, purify, clarify, rarefy
    b. -ity: rigidity, stupidity, hostility, intensity, responsibility
    c. -ize: unionize, terrorize, hospitalize, crystallize, magnetize
    d. -ive: repressive, active, disruptive, abusive, explosive
    e. -ion: invention, injection, narration, expression, pollution
    f. -less: nameless, penniless, useless, heartless, mindless

7. Write the following word pairs phonetically and identify any allomorphs that are uncovered.

    a. autumn/autumnal
    b. hymn/hymnal
    c. damn/damnation
    d. condemn/condemnation
    e. divide/divisible
    f. profane/profanity
    g. serene/serenity
    h. receive/receptive

File 5.3
The Hierarchical Structure of Words

When we examine words composed of only two morphemes, we implicitly know two facts about the ways in which affixes join with their stems. First, the stems with which a given affix may combine normally belong to the same part of speech. For example, the suffix *-able* attaches freely to verbs, but not to adjectives or nouns; thus, we can add this suffix to the verbs *adjust, break, compare,* and *debate,* but not to the adjectives *asleep, lovely, happy,* and *strong,* nor to the nouns *anger, morning, student,* or *success.* Second, the words formed by the addition of a given affix to some word or morpheme also normally belong to the same part of speech. For example, the expressions resulting from the addition of *-able* to a verb are always adjectives; thus *adjustable, breakable, comparable,* and *debatable* are all adjectives.

These two facts have an important consequence for determining the way in which words with more than one affix must be formed. What it means is that words are formed in steps, with one affix attaching to a complete word, which can be a free morpheme or a morphologically complex word. Words with more than one affix are not formed in one single step, with the affixes and stem just strung together. For example, consider the word *unusable,* which is composed of a prefix *un-,* a stem *use,* and a suffix *-able.* One possible way this morphologically complex word might be formed is all at once, as in: *un + use + able,* where the prefix and the suffix attach at the same time to the verb stem *use.* However, this cannot be the case knowing what we know about how affixes attach only to certain parts of speech and create words of certain parts of speech. The prefix *un-,* meaning 'not', attaches only to adjectives and creates new words that are also adjectives. (Compare with *unkind, unwise,* and *unhappy.*) The suffix *-able,* on the other hand, attaches to verbs and forms words that are adjectives. (Compare with *stoppable, doable,* and *washable.*) Therefore, *un-* cannot attach to *use,* since *use* is a verb and not an adjective. However, if *-able* attaches *first* to the stem *use,* then it creates an adjective, *usable,* and the prefix *un-* is allowed to combine with it. Thus, the formation of the word *unusable* is a two-step process whereby *use* and *-able* attach first, then *un-* attaches to the word *usable.*

Recall that what we are analyzing is the internal structure of words. Words, since they are formed by steps, have a special type of structure characterized as **hierarchical**. This hierarchical structure can be schematically represented by means of a *tree* that indicates the steps involved in the formation of the word, i.e., which morphemes joined together first and so on. The tree for *unusable* is:

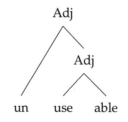

Now consider the word *reusable.* Both the prefix *re-* and the suffix *-able* attach to verbs, but we have already shown that one must attach first. Which is it? Notice that *reusable* cannot be regarded as the result of adding the prefix *re-* to the word *usable,* since *re-* attaches only to verbs (compare with *redo, relive,* and *refuel*) and *usable* is an adjective. However, *-able* can attach to the verb *reuse,* since *-able*

attaches to verbs. Thus, our understanding of how the affixes *re-* and *-able* combine with other morphemes allows us to conclude that the verb *reuse,* but not the adjective *usable,* is a step in the formation of the adjective *reusable.*

Interestingly, some words are ambiguous in that they have more than one meaning. When we examine their internal structure, we find an explanation for this: their structure may be analyzed in more than one way. Consider, for example, the word *unlockable.* This could mean either 'not able to be locked' or 'able to be unlocked'. If we made a list to determine the parts of speech the affix *un-* attaches to, we would discover that there are not one but two prefixes that sound like *un-.* The first combines with adjectives to form new adjectives and means 'not'. (Compare with *unaware, unintelligent,* or *unwise.*) The second prefix *un-* combines with verbs to form new verbs and means 'do the reverse of'. (Compare with *untie, undo,* or *undress.*)

Remember from Files 5.1 and 5.2 that even though these prefixes sound alike, they are entirely different morphemes. Because of these two different sorts of un- in English, *unlockable* may be analyzed in two different ways. First, the suffix *-able* may join with the verb *lock* to form the adjective *lockable; un-* may then join with this adjective to form the new adjective *unlockable,* with the meaning 'not able to be locked'. This way of forming *unlockable* is schematized in the following tree:

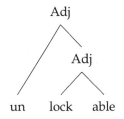

The second way of forming *unlockable* is as follows. The prefix *un-* joins with the verb *lock* to form the verb *unlock.* The suffix *-able* then joins with this verb to form the adjective *unlockable,* with the meaning of 'able to be unlocked'. This manner of forming *unlockable* is represented by the following tree:

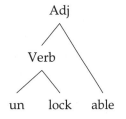

Morphemic Association to Multiple Parts of Speech

There are a few prefixes that do not attach exclusively to one part of speech. For example, consider the prefix *pre-. Pre-* attaches to verbs and does not change the part of speech, as the following examples show:

preexist   *predecide*
predetermine   *predefine*
premeditate

However, there are examples of words with the prefix *pre-* that do not follow the same pattern as those cited above:

preseason	*predawn*
prewar	*pregame*

In these words *pre-* attaches to a noun and forms an adjective (*the preseason game, the prewar propaganda, the pregame warm-up*). However, the "meaning" of the prefix is the same as in *preexist, predecide,* etc. (although its function is different). In addition, there are sets such as:

prefrontal	*predental*
preinvasive	*prehistoric*

In these words, *pre-* is attaching to an adjective, forming adjectives, and has the same "meaning" as in *preexist, predecide,* etc. So this is a bit problematic. We don't want to throw out the idea that a given affix attaches only to one part of speech, since the overwhelming majority of affixes adhere to this pattern. Apparently, some morphemes become so productive that their combinatorial possibilities can be extended. Such must be the case with *pre-*. Note, however, that its combinations are nevertheless rule-governed. When *pre-* attaches to verbs, it forms only verbs. When it attaches to nouns, it forms only adjectives, and when it attaches to adjectives, it forms only adjectives. So, it is advisable to consider many examples when attempting to determine the rules by which a given affix combines.

Exercises

0. Draw a tree diagram for the word *disappearance*. (Answers to all zero problems appear in Appendix A.)

1. Draw tree diagrams for each of the following words:

a.	reconstruction	j.	international	s.	unmistakable
b.	unaffordable	k.	misunderstandable	t.	insincerity
c.	un-American	l.	dehumidifier	u.	dysfunctional
d.	manliness	m.	unrespectable	v.	inconclusive
e.	impersonal	n.	nonrefundable	w.	premeditatedly
f.	irreplaceability	o.	mismanagement	x.	overgeneralization
g.	oversimplification	p.	underspecification	y.	reformer
h.	unhappiness	q.	restatement	z.	infertility
i.	impotency	r.	inflammability	aa.	dishonesty

2. We said that polar opposite ('not') *un-* attaches only to adjectives, but two exceptions to this rule are *Uncola* and *Uncar*. Why are these exceptions? Why would someone have made them up in the first place when the words fail to follow the rule?

File 5.4   Word Formation Processes

In the previous files of this section on morphology, we have been looking at how words are put together out of smaller parts. We have seen that English makes use of derivational morphemes to create more words than would exist with only free morphemes. Of course, English is not the only language that enlarges its vocabulary in this way. When linguists observe a language which uses the combining of bound and free morphemes to form additional words, they note that the occurring combinations are systematic, i.e., rule-governed, as we have certainly seen is the case in English. To illustrate, recall that the prefix *un-*, meaning 'not', attaches only to adjectives, the prefix *re-* attaches only to verbs, and the suffix *-ful* attaches only to nouns. Because these combinations are rule-governed, we can say that a *process* is at work, namely, a **word formation process**, since new words are being formed. What we will consider in this file are the ways in which languages create new words from bound and free morphemes. There are other ways in which new words come into use in a language, but they will be discussed in Files 10.6 and 10.7, under Historical Linguistics.

     Before describing some of the word formation processes found in the world's languages, we must first address the question, in what sense is it meant that new words are being "formed"? Do we mean that every time a speaker uses a morphologically complex word that the brain reconstructs it? Some linguists would maintain that this is the case. They would claim that in a speaker's mental dictionary, called the **lexicon**, each morpheme is listed individually, along with other information such as its meaning, its part of speech (if a free morpheme), and possibly a rule naming what it can combine with, if it is a bound morpheme. Thus, each time a word is used, it is re-formed from the separate entries in the lexicon. However, there is evidence that indicates this is not actually the case; even morphologically complex words apparently have a separate entry in the adult lexicon. There are other reasons, though, to consider *derivation* a process of word formation. A linguist analyzing a language uses the term *formation* to mean that the lexicon of a language includes many items that are systematically related to one another. Speakers of a given language, however, are also often aware of these relationships. We see evidence of this when new words are formed based on patterns that exist in the lexicon. For example, a speaker of English may never have heard words such as *unsmelly, smellness,* or *smellful* before, but he or she would certainly understand what they mean. The word *stick-to-it-ive-ness* causes some prescriptivists to wail; why create this new word when a perfectly good word, *perseverance,* already exists? This word illustrates that speakers of a language have no problem accessing the patterns in their lexicons and applying them for new creations. Thus, the term *formation* is applicable. Rules that speakers actually apply to form words that are not currently in use in a language are termed **productive**. English has examples of nonproductive morphemes as well; for example, the suffix *-tion* is not used by speakers to form new nouns, whereas the suffix *-ness* is.

Affixation

Words formed by the combination of bound affixes and free morphemes are the result of the process of **affixation**. Although English uses only prefixes and suffixes, many other languages use **infixes** as well. Infixes are inserted within the root morpheme. Note that English really has no infixes. At first glance, some students think that *-ful* in a word like *doubtfully* is an infix because it occurs in the middle of a word. Recall from File 5.3, however, that *doubtfully* has a hierarchical structure that indicates that the

143

-ly suffix attaches not to the affix *-ful* but rather to a complete word, *doubtful*. Thus *-ful* attaches to the word *doubt* as a suffix and does not break up the morpheme *doubt*. Tagalog, one of the major languages of the Philippines, uses infixes quite extensively. For example, the infix *-um-* is used to form the infinitive form of verbs:

Verb Stem		*Infinitive*	
[sulat]	*write*	[sumulat]	*to write*
[bili]	*buy*	[bumili]	*to buy*
[kuha]	*take, get*	[kumuha]	*to take, to get*

Compounding

Compounding is a process that forms new words not from bound affixes but from two or more independent words. The words that are the parts of the compound can be free morphemes, words derived by affixation, or even words formed by compounding themselves. Examples in English of these three types include:

girlfriend	air conditioner	lifeguard chair
blackbird	looking glass	aircraft carrier
textbook	watch maker	life insurance salesman

Notice that in English compound words are not represented consistently in the orthography. Sometimes they are written together, sometimes they are written with a hyphen, and sometimes they are written separately. We know, however, that compounding forms *words* and not just syntactic phrases, regardless of how the compound is spelled, because the stress patterns are different for compounds. Think about how you would say the words *red neck* in each of the two following sentences:

1. The wool sweater gave the man a red neck.
2. If you want to make Tim really angry, call him a redneck.

Compounds that have words in the same order as phrases have primary stress on the first word only, while individual words in phrases have independent primary stress. Some other examples are listed below. (Primary stress is indicated by ´ on the vowel.)

Compounds	*Phrases*
bláckbird	bláck bírd
mákeup	máke úp

Other compounds can have phrasal stress patterns, but only if they can't possibly be phrases. These same compounds might also have stress on the first word only, like other compounds. For example:

eásy-góing	eásy-going
mán-máde	mán-made
hómemáde	hómemade

German is one of the many languages that also use compounding to form new words. Some examples of the numerous compounds in German are:

Muttersprache	'native language'	< 'mother tongue'
Schreibtisch	'desk'	< 'writing table'
stehenbleiben	'stand (still)'	< 'stay remain'
Wunderkind	'child prodigy'	< 'miracle child'
Geschwindigkeitsbegrenzung	'speed limit'	< 'speed limit'

Reduplication

Reduplication is a process of forming new words either by doubling an entire free morpheme (**total reduplication**) or part of it (**partial reduplication**). English makes use of reduplication very sporadically. Some English examples are *higglety-pigglety*, *hoity-toity*, and *hocus-pocus*. However, note that these partial reduplications are not a single morpheme. Other languages, however, do make use of reduplication more extensively. Indonesian uses total reduplication to form the plurals of nouns:

Singular		*Plural*	
[rumah]	*house*	[rumahrumah]	*houses*
[ibu]	*mother*	[ibuibu]	*mothers*
[lalat]	*fly*	[lalatlalat]	*flies*

Tagalog uses partial reduplication to indicate the future tense:

Verb Stem		*Future Tense*	
[bili]	*buy*	[bibili]	*will buy*
[kain]	*eat*	[kakain]	*will eat*
[pasok]	*enter*	[papasok]	*will enter*

In conjunction with the prefix -*maŋ* (which often changes the initial consonant of a following morpheme to a nasal with the same place of articulation as the original initial consonant), Tagalog uses reduplication to derive words for occupations:

[mamimili]	*a buyer*	< /maŋ +bi+bili/	(cf. [bili] *buy*)
[manunulat]	*a writer*	< /maŋ +su+sulat/	(cf. [sulat] *write*)
[maŋʔiʔisda]	*a fisherman*	< /maŋ +ʔi+ʔisda/	(cf. [ʔisda] *fish*)

Morpheme-internal Changes

Besides adding an affix to a morpheme or copying all or part of the morpheme to make new words or make morphological distinctions, it is also possible to make morpheme-internal modifications. There are a few examples of this in English.

1. Although the usual pattern of plural formation is to add an inflectional morpheme, some English plurals make an internal modification:

man	men
woman	women
goose	geese
foot	feet

2. The usual pattern of past and past participle formation is to add an affix, but some verbs also show an internal change:

ring	rang	rung
sing	sang	sung
swim	swam	swum

   Some verbs show both an internal change and the addition of an affix to one form:

break	broke	broken
bite	bit	bitten

3. Some word class changes are also indicated only via internal changes:

strife	strive
teeth	teethe
breath	breathe
life	live (V)
life	live (adj.)

Suppletion

Languages that employ morphological processes to form words will usually have a regular, productive way of doing so according to one or more of the processes discussed above. They might also have some smaller classes of words that are irregular because they mark the same morphological distinction by another of these processes. Sometimes, however, the same distinction can be represented by two different words that don't have any systematic difference in form—they are exceptions to all of the processes. This completely irregular situation is called **suppletion** and usually occurs only in a few words of a language.

In English, for example, the regular past tense is formed by the ending realized by the allomorphs [t], [d], or [əd]. Most English verbs, and any newly made-up words such as *scroosh* or *blat*, will have this past tense form:

[wak]	*walk*	[wakt]	*walked*
[skruš]	*scroosh*	[skrušt]	*scrooshed*
[blæt]	*blat*	[blætəd]	*blatted*

There are also some smaller classes of very common words that form the past tense by an internal vowel change:

[sɪŋ]	*sing*	[sæŋ]	*sang*
[rʌn]	*run*	[ræn]	*ran*

But a small number of individual verbs have **suppletive** past tenses:

[æm]	*am*	[wʌz]	*was*
[go]	*go*	[wɛnt]	*went*

Note that there is no systematic similarity between the past and present tense forms of these verbs.

Classical Arabic provides another example of suppletion (as could most languages). The normal plural form for nouns ending in [at] in Arabic involves the lengthening of the vowel of this ending (a morpheme internal change):

[dira:sat]	*(a) study*	[dira:sa:t]	*studies*
[harakat]	*movement*	[haraka:t]	*movements*

There are also some irregular plurals of nouns ending in [at] that involve other internal changes:

[ǰumlat]	*sentence*	[ǰumal]	*sentences*
[fikrat]	*thought*	[fikar]	*thoughts*

However, the plurals of other forms are clearly cases of suppletion, for example:

[marʔat]	*woman*	[nisa:ʔ]	*women*

Exercises

1. Imagine for a moment that *-ful* is an infix in English. How would it attach to a morpheme like *hope*? What would the entire word look like? (Note that there are two possibilities.)

2. Think up other examples of suppletion in English. (Hint: start with some common adjectives.)

File 5.5

How to Solve Morphology Problems

When a linguist comes in contact with a new language, one of his or her major tasks is to discover the meaningful units out of which the language is composed. Just as with discovering phonemes and allophones, it is important that the linguist have procedures for discovering these minimal units, since it is impossible to isolate morphemes by intuition.

For example, the Classical Greek word [grapʰɔ:] means 'I write', but if the word is considered in isolation the linguist has no way of knowing what sound or sequence of sounds corresponds to 'I' and which sequence corresponds to 'write'. It is only by comparing [grapʰɔ:] with another form, for instance, [grapʰe:] 'he writes', that one is able to determine what the morphemes of these Greek words are.

Comparison, then, is the best way to begin morphological analysis. But of course you will not want to compare just any forms. Comparing a Greek word like [pʰɛ:mi] 'to speak' with [grapʰɔ:] will not provide us with much information, since the forms are so dissimilar and seem to have no single morpheme in common. What must be compared are partially similar forms in which it is possible to recognize recurring units. In this way we can identify the morphemes of which words are composed.

Now let us consider our Classical Greek example once more. If we compare [grapʰɔ:] with [grapʰe:] 'he writes', we note similarities between the forms. The sequence [grapʰ-] appears in both forms [grapʰ-e:] and [grapʰ-ɔ:], and if we compare these to the English correspondences we find the meaning 'write' appears in both 'he writes' and 'I write'. From this, we are justified in concluding that [grapʰ-] means *write*, since [grapʰ-] and *write* are constants in both the English and Greek. Furthermore, since the final vowels in both Greek forms contrast—and since this contrast is accompanied by a difference in meaning in our English correspondence—we can safely assume the difference between vowels in Classical Greek corresponds to differences in meaning in our English translation. Therefore we assign the meaning 'I' to [-ɔ:] and 'he' to [-e:]. In sum, then, the initial step in doing morphological analysis is to *compare and contrast* partially similar forms.

To give yourself practice, identify and translate the morphemes in the Hungarian data below. ([j] is a voiced palatal stop.)

[hɔz]	*house*
[ɛjhɔz]	*a house*
[hɔzɔ]	*his/her house*
[boɾ]	*wine*
[ɛjboɾ]	*a wine*
[boɾɔ]	*his/her wine*

But, sometimes just comparing and contrasting partially similar forms is not enough to allow a complete morphological analysis. Consider the following examples.

1. Compare the following English words:

    work – worker   fast – faster,

We notice the morpheme spelled *-er* and pronounced [ɹ̩] for both [fæstɹ̩] and [wɹ̩kɹ̩]. However, if we think about it for a minute, it is apparent that *-er* has two different meanings even though phonetically it looks like the same morpheme. The *-er* in *worker* is the same *-er* that shows up in words like *painter, killer, lover,* and *actor.* In each of these cases, *-er* attaches to verbs to form a noun and means something like 'one who paints', 'one who kills', 'one who loves', etc. The suffix *-er* in these cases is known as the *agentive* morpheme.

The *-er* in *faster,* on the other hand, is the same *-er* that shows up in words like *wider, longer, colder, prettier,* etc. In each of these cases, *-er* attaches to adjectives to form a new adjective, with the extra meaning 'more'. The suffix *-er* in these cases is known as the *comparative* morpheme.

We will want to argue, then, that [ɹ̩] represents two separate morphemes—[ɹ̩] as an agent marker, and [ɹ̩] as a comparative marker—even though they are the same phonetically, i.e., *homophonous* morphemes. The [ɹ̩] that is added to verbs to yield nouns and the [ɹ̩] that is added to adjectives to yield new adjectives clearly have *distinct* meanings.

2. Compare the following set of words in (a), (b), and (c). We notice that each word has a prefix that means 'not'.

    a. *imbalance*   [ɪmbæləns]
    b. *inability*   [ɪnəbɪləɾi]
    c. *incomplete*   [ɪŋkəmplit]

The problem here is the inverse of the problem in example (1). Whereas in example (1) we had the same phonetic forms representing two different meanings, in example (2) we have three different phonetic forms with the *same* meaning. Since the phonetic forms of the morpheme meaning 'not' can be predicted on the basis of phonetic environment, i.e.,

> [ɪm] before labials—[p], [b], [m]
> [ɪŋ] before velars—[k] ,[g]
> [ɪn] elsewhere (before vowels and other consonants),

we conclude that even though the forms differ phonetically, they belong to the *same* morpheme since they have the same meaning. Recall that we call [ɪm], [ɪŋ], and [ɪn] **allomorphs** of the same morpheme. Another example of allomorphy in English is the plural morpheme, which is realized as either [s], [z] or [əz], depending on the form of the root to which it attaches. (See File 5.1.)

Procedure for Doing Morphological Analysis

Goal:

Given a set of data in phonetic representation, perform a morphological analysis of the forms in the data, identifying each morpheme, its meaning and type. You should also be able to tell where a morpheme appears with respect to other morphemes in the word. Is it a prefix, suffix, or base? Does it attach directly to the root or does it attach after or before another morpheme?

Procedure (Keys to Analysis):

1. Isolate and compare forms that are partially similar, as we did for Classical Greek [graph-e:] and [graph-ɔ:].
2. If a single phonetic form has *two distinctive meanings*, it must be analyzed as representing two different morphemes (as in example 1).
3. If the *same meaning* is associated with different phonetic forms, these different forms all represent the same morpheme (i.e., they are allomorphs of the morpheme), and the choice of form in each case should be predictable on the basis of the phonetic environment (as in example 2).

Some Cautionary Notes

People frequently assume that languages are pretty much the same in terms of what each language marks morphologically. For example, English speakers often assume that all languages mark the plurals of nouns with an ending, or that the subject and the verb agree in person and number in other languages. This is simply not the case. For example, Tagalog does not usually mark the plural of nouns (in most cases, the number is clear from the context). When it is necessary to be specific, a separate word, *mga*, is used to indicate plural.

| [aŋ bata?] | *the child* |
| [aŋ mga bata?] | *the children* |

When a number is specifically mentioned, no plural marker appears in Tagalog, although the plural marker is obligatory in English (**three dog* is ungrammatical).

| [dalawa] | *two* | [dalawaŋ bata?] | *two children* |
| [lima] | *five* | [limaŋ bata?] | *five children* |

([-ŋ] is a "linker" that links numerals and adjectives to the nouns they modify; English does not use this type of device.)

English marks subject-verb agreement (e.g., *I eat* vs. *he eats*), but Tagalog does not. In Tagalog, the same form of the verb is used with all subjects.

| [kumakain ako] | *eat I* | = | *I eat* |
| [kumakain siy] | *eat he* | = | *he eats* |

Other languages also make distinctions that we don't. While English distinguishes only singular and plural verbs, some languages have a dual verb form for when just two persons are involved. Consider Sanskrit *juhomi* 'I sacrifice', *juhuvas* 'we (two) sacrifice', and *juhumas* 'we (pl.) sacrifice'.

Some languages also have two kinds of first person plural pronouns where English has only *we*. Notice that English *we* in *we are going*, for example, may include everyone in the group the hearer is addressing (i.e., *we* = every one of us), or it may include only some hearers (i.e., *we* = 'I and (s)he', but not 'you'). Many languages distinguish these two *we*'s: Tagalog has *tayo* (inclusive, i.e., 'you and I') in addition to *kami* (exclusive, i.e., 'he and I').

Comanche, a Native American language of the Uto-Aztecan family, makes a number of distinctions that English doesn't. In addition to a singular/dual/plural distinction and an inclusive/exclusive distinction, Comanche also makes a distinction between visible/not visible and near/far. Thus, if you are referring to a thing that is within your view, you use a different form than if the thing is not visible to you. Likewise, a nearby object is designated with a pronoun different from the one used for an object that is far away. Consider the following subject forms:

singular/dual/plural distinction		*inclusive/exclusive distinction*	
ini	'you (singular)'	taa	'we (inclusive)'
nikwɨ	'you (two)'	ninɨ	'we (exclusive)'
mɨɨ	'you (plural)'		

visible/not visible		*near/far distinction*	
ma?	'it (visible)'	?i?	'it (proximate)'
?u?	'it (invisible)'	?o?	'it (remote)'

The lesson to be learned here is that you cannot assume that another language will make distinctions in the same way that English does. For example, while every language has some method of indicating number, not all languages do so in the same way or under the same circumstances. As we've seen, English uses an affix, Tagalog uses a separate word, and Indonesian reduplicates the word to show plurality (see File 5.4). Nor can you assume that the distinctions English makes are the only ones worth making. Languages must be examined carefully on the grounds of their own internal structures.

File 5.6   Morphology Problems

The following problems are provided to give you practice in doing morphemic analysis at the beginning, intermediate, and advanced levels. Be sure to read the directions to each problem carefully. As with the phonology problems, there are enough critical data from each language to enable you to discover the correct generalizations.

0.   Sample Problem

0.0   *Isthmus Zapotec*

(Answers to all zero problems appear in Appendix A.)

Examine the following data from Isthmus Zapotec, a language spoken in Mexico. Answer the questions which follow.

1.	[palu]	*stick*	7.	[spalube]	*his stick*	13.	[spalulu]	*your stick*
2.	[ku:ba]	*dough*	8.	[sku:babe]	*his dough*	14.	[sku:balu]	*your dough*
3.	[tapa]	*four*	9.	[stapabe]	*his four*	15.	[stapalu]	*your four*
4.	[geta]	*tortilla*	10.	[sketabe]	*his tortilla*	16.	[sketalu]	*your tortilla*
5.	[bere]	*chicken*	11.	[sperebe]	*his chicken*	17.	[sperelu]	*your chicken*
6.	[doʔo]	*rope*	12.	[stoʔobe]	*his rope*	18.	[stoʔolu]	*your rope*

a.   Isolate the morphemes that correspond to the following English translations:

_____ possession (genitive)
_____ 3rd person singular
_____ 2nd person plural

b.   List the allomorphs for the following translations:

_____ _____ *tortilla*   _____ _____ *rope*
_____ _____ *chicken*

c.   What phonological process conditions for these allomorphs?

1.   Beginning

1.1   *Turkish*

Examine the following data from Turkish and answer the questions that follow.

1. [deniz]	*an ocean*	9. [elim]	*my hand*
2. [denize]	*to an ocean*	10. [eller]	*hands*
3. [denizin]	*of an ocean*	11. [dišler]	*teeth*
4. [eve]	*to a house*	12. [dišimizin]	*of our tooth*
5. [evden]	*from a house*	13. [dišlerimizin]	*of our teeth*
6. [evǰıkden]	*from a little house*	14. [elǰike]	*to a little hand*
7. [denizǰıkde]	*in a little ocean*	15. [denizlerimizde]	*in our oceans*
8. [elde]	*in a hand*	16. [evǰıklerimizde]	*in our little houses*

     a.   Give the Turkish morpheme that corresponds to each of the following translations:

_____	*ocean*	_____	*in*	_____	*my*
_____	*house*	_____	*to*	_____	*of*
_____	*hand*	_____	*from*	_____	*our*
_____	*tooth*	_____	*(plural marker)*		
_____	*little*				

     b.   What is the order of morphemes in a Turkish word (in terms of noun, plural marker, etc.)?

     c.   How would one say 'of our little hands' in Turkish?

1.2   *Bontoc*

Bontoc is a language spoken in the Philippine Islands. Examine the data from Bontoc below and answer the questions that follow.

1. [fikas]	*strong*	5. [fumikas]	*he is becoming strong*
2. [kilad]	*red*	6. [kumilad]	*he is becoming red*
3. [bato]	*stone*	7. [bumato]	*he is becoming stone*
4. [fusul]	*enemy*	8. [fumusul]	*he is becoming an enemy*

     a.   What word formation process is used to form the verbs?

     b.   What type of affix is used to form the verbs? Describe its form and relationship to the rest of the word.

     c.   Given [pusi] 'poor', what would be the most likely meaning of [pumusi]?

     d.   Given [ŋitad] 'dark', what would be the most likely form meaning 'he is becoming dark'?

     e.   Given [pumukaw] 'he is becoming white', what is the most likely form meaning 'white'?

1.3   Luiseño

Examine the following data from Luiseño, a Uto-Aztecan language of Southern California, and answer the questions that follow.

1.	[nokaamay]	*my son*	13.	[pokaamay]	*his son*
2.	[ʔoki]	*your house*	14.	[poki]	*his house*
3.	[potaana]	*his blanket*	15.	[notaana]	*my blanket*
4.	[ʔohuukapi]	*your pipe*	16.	[pohuukapi]	*his pipe*
5.	[ʔotaana]	*your blanket*	17.	[nohuukapi]	*my pipe*
6.	[noki]	*my house*	18.	[ʔokaamay]	*your son*
7.	[ʔomkim]	*your (pl.) houses*	19.	[pompeewum]	*their wives*
8.	[nokaamayum]	*my sons*	20.	[pomki]	*their house*
9.	[popeew]	*his wife*	21.	[čampeewum]	*our wives*
10.	[ʔopeew]	*your wife*	22.	[čamhuukapim]	*our pipes*
11.	[ʔomtaana]	*your (pl.) blanket*	23.	[ʔomtaanam]	*your (pl.) blankets*
12.	[čamhuukapi]	*our pipe*	24.	[pomkaamay]	*their son*

a.   Give the Luiseño morpheme that corresponds to each English translation. Note that the plural marker has two allomorphs; list them both.

_____ *son*	_____ *my*	_____ *their*
_____ *house*	_____ *his*	_____ *(plural marker)*
_____ *blanket*	_____ *your (sg.)*	_____ *pipe*
_____ *wife*	_____ *your (pl.)*	_____ *our*

b.   Are the allomorphs of the plural marker phonologically conditioned?

c.   If so, what are the conditioning environments?

1.4   Quiché

Some sentences from Quiché, a Native American language spoken in Guatemala, Central America, are given with their English translation. Analyze the morphemes in these sentences and then fill in the exercises that follow the language data. Note that [x] is a voiceless velar fricative.

Quiché	*English*
1. [kiŋsikíx le líbr]	*I read (present tense) the book*
2. [kusikíx le líbr]	*He reads the book*
3. [kiŋwetamáx le kém]	*I learn the (art of) weaving*
4. [kataxín kiŋwetamáx le kém]	*I continually learn the (art of) weaving*
5. [kataxín kawetamáx le kém]	*You continually learn the (art of) weaving*
6. [šiŋwetamáx]	*I learned (it)*
7. [šuwetamáx le kém]	*He learned the (art of) weaving*
8. [šasikíx le líbr iwír]	*You read the book yesterday*

a. Fill in the blanks with the corresponding Quiché morphemes:

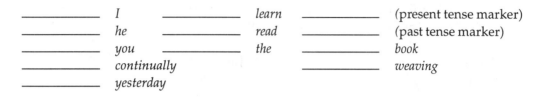

_____	*I*	_____	*learn*	_____	(present tense marker)
_____	*he*	_____	*read*	_____	(past tense marker)
_____	*you*	_____	*the*	_____	*book*
_____	*continually*			_____	*weaving*
_____	*yesterday*				

b. What is the order of Quiché morphemes (in terms of subject, verb, object, and tense marker)?

1.5 Michoacan Aztec

Examine the following words from Michoacan Aztec, a language of Mexico, and answer the questions that follow.

1.	[nokali]	*my house*	6.	[mopelo]	*your dog*
2.	[nokalimes]	*my houses*	7.	[mopelomes]	*your dogs*
3.	[mokali]	*your house*	8.	[ikwahmili]	*his cornfield*
4.	[ikali]	*his house*	9.	[nokwahmili]	*my cornfield*
5.	[nopelo]	*my dog*	10.	[mokwahmili]	*your cornfield*

a. Fill in the blanks with the corresponding Michoacan morphemes:

_____	*house*	_____	*my*
_____	*dog*	_____	*your*
_____	*cornfield*	_____	*his*
_____	(plural marker)		

b. What is the English translation for the Michoacan word [ipelo]?

c. How would you say 'his cornfields' in Michoacan?

1.6 Cebuano

The following nouns are from Cebuano, a language of the Philippine Islands. Examine them and answer the questions that follow.

1.	[bisaya]	*a Visayan*	6.	[binisaya]	*the Visayan language*
2.	[inglis]	*an Englishman*	7.	[ininglis]	*the English language*
3.	[tagalog]	*a Tagalog person*	8.	[tinagalog]	*the Tagalog language*
4.	[ilokano]	*an Ilocano*	9.	[inilokano]	*the Ilocano language*
5.	[sibwano]	*a Cebuano*	10.	[sinibwano]	*the Cebuano language*

a. State the rule (in words, precisely) for deriving language names from the names of ethnic groups.

b. What type of affixation is this?

1.7 Isleta

Consider the following data from Isleta, a dialect of Southern Tiwa, a Native American language spoken in New Mexico, and answer the questions that follow.

1.	[temiban]	*I went*	4.	[mimiay]	*he was going*
2.	[amiban]	*you went*	5.	[tewanban]	*I came*
3.	[temiwe]	*I am going*	6.	[tewanhi]	*I will come*

    a.   List the morphemes corresponding to the following English translations.

        _____ *I*   _____ *go*   _____ (present progressive)

        _____ *you*   _____ *come*   _____ (past progressive)

        _____ *he*   _____ (past)   _____ (future)

    b.   What sort of affixes are the subject morphemes?

    c.   What sort of affixes are the tense morphemes?

    d.   What is the order of morphemes in Isleta?

    e.   How would you say each of the following in Isleta?

        1.   *He went.*
        2.   *I will go.*
        3.   *You were coming.*

1.8 German

Isolate the morphemes and word formation processes used to mark the plural in German. Don't worry about trying to describe which plural morpheme goes with which type of word. Just list the morphemes. (Note that the vowels [ü] and [ö] are front rounded vowels and that 'äu' is pronounced [oy].)

	singular	plural	gloss
1.	Bild	Bilder	*picture*
2.	Büro	Büros	*office*
3.	Tüte	Tüten	*bag*
4.	Loch	Löcher	*hole*
5.	Uhr	Uhren	*watch*
6.	Rind	Rinder	*bull/cow*
7.	Wagen	Wagen	*vehicle*
8.	Stift	Stifte	*pen*
9.	Haus	Häuser	*house*
10.	Laus	Läuse	*louse*
11.	Hut	Hüte	*hat*
12.	Hütte	Hütten	*hut*
13.	Buch	Bücher	*book*
14.	Dach	Dächer	*roof*
15.	Kind	Kinder	*child*

2.   Intermediate

2.1   *Swahili*

Examine the following data from Swahili, a language spoken in East Africa, and answer the questions that follow.

1. [atanipenda]	*s/he will like me*	15. [atanipiga]	*s/he will beat me*
2. [atakupenda]	*s/he will like you*	16. [atakupiga]	*s/he will beat you*
3. [atampenda]	*s/he will like him/her*	17. [atampiga]	*s/he will beat him/her*
4. [atatupenda]	*s/he will like us*	18. [ananipiga]	*s/he is beating me*
5. [atawapenda]	*s/he will like them*	19. [anakupiga]	*s/he is beating you*
6. [nitakupenda]	*I will like you*	20. [anampiga]	*s/he is beating him/her*
7. [nitampenda]	*I will like him/her*	21. [amekupiga]	*s/he has beaten you*
8. [nitawapenda]	*I will like them*	22. [amenipiga]	*s/he has beaten me*
9. [utanipenda]	*you will like me*	23. [amempiga]	*s/he has beaten him/her*
10. [utampenda]	*you will like him/her*	24. [alinipiga]	*s/he beat me*
11. [tutampenda]	*we will like him/her*	25. [alikupiga]	*s/he beat you*
12. [watampenda]	*they will like him/her*	26. [alimpiga]	*s/he beat him/her*
13. [atakusumbua]	*s/he will annoy you*	27. [wametulipa]	*they have paid us*
14. [unamsumbua]	*you are annoying him/her*	28. [tulikulipa]	*we paid you*

a.   Give the Swahili morphemes for the following English translations:

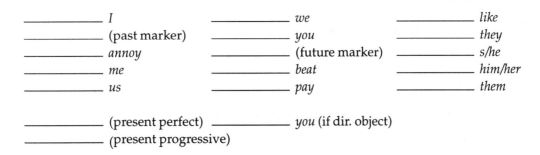

_____ *I*	_____ *we*	_____ *like*
_____ (past marker)	_____ *you*	_____ *they*
_____ *annoy*	_____ (future marker)	_____ *s/he*
_____ *me*	_____ *beat*	_____ *him/her*
_____ *us*	_____ *pay*	_____ *them*

_____ (present perfect)   _____ *you* (if dir. object)
_____ (present progressive)

b.   What is the order of morphemes in Swahili (in terms of subject, object, verb, and tense)?

c.   Give the Swahili word for the following English translations:

1. *I have beaten them.*   4. *You have beaten us.*
2. *They are beating me.*   5. *We beat them.*
3. *They have annoyed me.*   6. *I am paying him/her.*

d.   Give the English translation for the following Swahili words.

1. [atanilipa]   2. [utawapiga]
3. [walikupenda]   4. [nimemsumbua]

2.2   Cree

Examine the following data from Cree, an Algonquian language spoken in Canada, and answer the questions that follow.

1.	[či:ma:n]	*canoe*	12.	[nitospwa:kan]	*my pipe*
2.	[niči:ma:n]	*my canoe*	13.	[akimew]	*s/he counts*
3.	[so:niya]	*money*	14.	[nitakimen]	*I count*
4.	[niso:niya]	*my money*	15.	[apiw]	*s/he sits*
5.	[wiya:š]	*meat*	16.	[nitapin]	*I sit*
6.	[niwiya:š]	*my meat*	17.	[ispelohkew]	*s/he rests*
7.	[e:mihkwa:n]	*spoon*	18.	[nitispelohken]	*I rest*
8.	[nite:mihkwa:n]	*my spoon*	19.	[kaakimew]	*s/he will count*
9.	[astotin]	*hat*	20.	[nikaakimen]	*I will count*
10.	[nitastotin]	*my hat*	21.	[kaapiw]	*s/he will sit*
11.	[ospwa:kan]	*pipe*	22.	[nikaapin]	*I will sit*

a.   What are the Cree morphemes for the following?

_____ *I* _____ *my* _____ *s/he* _____ (future tense)

b.   What are the allomorphs for 'I' and 'my'?

c.   What are the conditioning environments?

d.   How does the morpheme 'I' differ from the morpheme 'my'?

2.3   Zoque

Examine the following data from Zoque, a language spoken in Mexico, and answer the subsequent questions.

1.	[kenu]	*he looked*	7.	[kenpa]	*he looks*
2.	[sihku]	*he laughed*	8.	[sikpa]	*he laughs*
3.	[wihtu]	*he walked*	9.	[witpa]	*he walks*
4.	[ka?u]	*he died*	10.	[ka?pa]	*he dies*
5.	[cihcu]	*it tore*	11.	[cicpa]	*it tears*
6.	[sohsu]	*it cooked*	12.	[sospa]	*it cooks*

a.   What is the Zoque morpheme indicating the past tense?

b.   What is the Zoque morpheme meaning 'he' or 'it'?

c.   List the allomorphs of each of the verb stem morphemes, along with their meanings.

d.   What conditions the appearance of these allomorphs? What phonological process is involved?

2.4   Swedish

Swedish is a Germanic language with morphological marking of nouns similar to that of English, but with some significant differences. Consider the following forms of nouns and answer the questions.

1.	en lampa	*a lamp*	12.	en bil	*a car*
2.	stolen	*the chair*	13.	bilar	*cars*
3.	en tidning	*a newspaper*	14.	kattarna	*the cats*
4.	lampan	*the lamp*	15.	en katt	*a cat*
5.	bilen	*the car*	16.	soffor	*sofas*
6.	en stol	*a chair*	17.	tidningarna	*the newspapers*
7.	sofforna	*the sofas*	18.	bilarna	*the cars*
8.	katten	*the cat*	19.	lamporna	*the lamps*
9.	tidningen	*the newspaper*	20.	stolarna	*the chairs*
10.	kattar	*cats*	21.	en soffa	*a sofa*
11.	tidningar	*newspapers*	22.	soffan	*the sofa*
			23.	lampor	*lamps*

a.   What Swedish word corresponds to the English indefinite article ('a(n)')?

b.   What are the allomorphs of the definite morpheme? Where do they appear?

c.   How is the indefinite plural formed? The definite plural?

d.   How would you say the forms of the following words?

		Definite	Plural	Definite Plural
en flicka	*a girl*	_____	_____	_____
en klänning	*a dress*	_____	_____	_____
en blomma	*a flower*	_____	_____	_____
en buss	*a bus*	_____	_____	_____

2.5   Hanunoo

Hanunoo is a language spoken in the Philippine Islands. Examine the data from this language below and answer the questions which follow.

1.	[ʔusa]	*one*	8.	[kasʔa]	*once*	15.	[ʔusahi]	*make it one*
2.	[duwa]	*two*	9.	[kadwa]	*twice*	16.	[duwahi]	*make it two*
3.	[tulu]	*three*	10.	[katlu]	*three times*	17.	[tuluhi]	*make it three*
4.	[ʔupat]	*four*	11.	[kapʔat]	*four times*	18.	[ʔupati]	*make it four*
5.	[lima]	*five*	12.	[kalima]	*five times*	19.	[limahi]	*make it five*
6.	[ʔunum]	*six*	13.	[kanʔum]	*six times*	20.	[ʔunumi]	*make it six*
7.	[pitu]	*seven*	14.	[kapitu]	*seven times*	21.	[pituhi]	*make it seven*

a.   Two affixes are illustrated in these data. Identify each of them, state what kind of affix each one is, and tell what information each one provides.

b.   What phonological processes are evidenced in the two morphophonemic changes in the roots?

3.   Advanced

3.1   Hungarian

Examine the Hungarian data below and answer the questions that follow. Note that [ü] represents a high front rounded vowel.

		Singular	Plural
1.	*table*	[ɔstɔl]	[ɔstɔlok]
2.	*worker*	[munka:š]	[munka:šok]
3.	*man*	[ɛmbɛr]	[ɛmbɛrɛk]
4.	*white*	[fɛhe:r]	[fɛhe:rɛk]
5.	*this*	[ɛz]	[ɛzɛk]
6.	*line*	[šoɾ]	[šoɾok]
7.	*eyeglasses*	[sɛmüvɛg]	[sɛmüvɛgɛk]
8.	*shirt*	[iŋ]	[iŋek]
9.	*head*	[fɛy]	[fɛyɛk]
10.	*box*	[doboz]	[dobozok]
11.	*drum*	[dob]	[dobok]
12.	*age*	[kor]	[korok]
13.	*coat*	[kɔba:t]	[kɔba:tok]
14.	*flower*	[vira:g]	[vira:gok]

a.   What are the allomorphs of the Hungarian plural?

b.   State the conditioning environment.

3.2　Popoluca

Examine the following data from Popoluca, a language spoken in Mexico, and answer the questions that follow.

1. [ʔiŋkuʔtpa]　　*you (sg.) eat it*
2. [ʔanhokspa]　　*I hoe it*
3. [ʔikuʔt]　　　*he ate it*
4. [ʔimoːya]　　*his flower*
5. [moːya]　　　*flower*
6. [ʔampetpa]　*I sweep it*
7. [ʔimpet]　　　*you swept it*
8. [ʔantɛk]　　　*my house*
9. [ʔinhokspa]　*you hoe it*
10. [noːmi]　　　*boss*
11. [ʔanoːmi]　　*my boss*
12. [ʔikaːma]　　*his cornfield*
13. [ʔiŋkaːma]　*your (sg.) cornfield*
14. [ʔamoːya]　　*my flower*
15. [ʔinoːmi]　　*your (sg.) boss*

　　a.　List all of the Popoluca allomorphs corresponding to the following translations.

_____ *cornfield*	_____ (past tense)
_____ *flower*	_____ (present tense)
_____ *boss*	_____ *I/my*
_____ *house*	_____ *you/your* (sg.)
_____ *eat*	_____ *he/his*
_____ *sweep*	_____ *hoe*

　　b.　State the phonetic environments that condition the occurrence of allomorphs when one morpheme has more than one allomorph.

3.3.   Mongolian

Examine the following Mongolian data. Note that [ü] represents a high front rounded vowel, [ö] represents a mid front rounded vowel, and [x] represents a voiceless velar fricative.

		Stem	*Future Imperative*
1.	*enter*	[or-]	[oro:roy]
2.	*go*	[yav]	[yava:ray]
3.	*sit*	[su:-]	[su:ga:ray]
4.	*come*	[ir-]	[ire:rey]
5.	*do*	[xi:-]	[xi:ge:rey]
6.	*come out*	[gar-]	[gara:ray]
7.	*take*	[av-]	[ava:ray]
8.	*study*	[sur-]	[sura:ray]
9.	*finish*	[büte:-]	[büte:ge:rey]
10.	*drink*	[ü:-]	[ü:gö:röy]
11.	*find out*	[ol-]	[olo:roy]
12.	*conquer*	[yal-]	[yala:ray]
13.	*ask*	[asu:-]	[asu:ga:ray]
14.	*finish*	[tögsg-]	[tögsgö:röy]
15.	*beat*	[dev-]	[deve:rey]
16.	*give*	[ög-]	[ögö:röy]
17.	*say*	[xel-]	[xele:rey]
18.	*meet*	[u:lz-]	[u:lza:ray]
19.	*become*	[bol-]	[bolo:roy]
20.	*write*	[bič-]	[biče:rey]
21.	*develop*	[xögž-]	[xögžö:röy]

a.   List all of the allomorphs of the Mongolian future imperative marker.

b.   What environments condition their appearance?

3.4. *Japanese*

Consider the following data of verbal inflections in Japanese and answer the questions that follow. (Note: remember that Japanese is an example of a primarily CV language—morphemes will follow this.) Words in parentheses are not expressed in the Japanese data but are implied—i.e., don't try to figure out how to say 'she' or 'them', etc.

1.	[tabeta]	*(She) ate (it).*
2.	[aketa]	*(She) opened (them).*
3.	[tabesaseta]	*(She) made (him) eat (it).*
4.	[akesaseta]	*(She) made (him) open (them).*
5.	[taberareta]	*(It) was eaten.*
6.	[akerareta]	*(They) were opened.*
7.	[tabesaserareta]	*(He) was made to eat (it).*
8.	[akesaserareta]	*(He) was made to open (them).*
9.	[tabesasenai]	*(She) doesn't/will not make (him) eat (it).*
10.	[tabenai]	*(She) doesn't/won't eat (it).*
11.	[tabesaserareru]	*(He) is/will be made to eat (it).*

a. Give the Japanese morphemes for the following English translations:

　　　＿＿＿＿ *open*
　　　＿＿＿＿ *eat*
　　　＿＿＿＿ passive marker ('…was/were … VERB,' e.g., 'They were eaten')
　　　＿＿＿＿ causative marker ('…make…,' e.g., 'Robin made Tracey laugh', 'caused Tracey to laugh')
　　　＿＿＿＿ non-past marker (present or future)
　　　＿＿＿＿ perfect marker (past)
　　　＿＿＿＿ negative marker

b. Indicate the order in which the following morphemes may occur in a Japanese verb form. Note that the root will be the morpheme you indicated in part (a) as 'open' or 'eat'.

　　1. passive, root, perfect, causative
　　2. causative, non-past, root
　　3. root, negative, causative

c. Give the Japanese word for the following English translations. Remember that you won't need to worry about words like *she, him,* and *them.*

　　1. 'She will make him open them.'
　　2. 'He will be made to open them.'

d. Considering the fact that [uketa] means '(She) took (a test),' how would you say the following in Japanese? Again, don't try to translate the pronouns.

　　1. 'She was made to take (a test.)'
　　2. 'She makes him take (a test.)'
　　3. 'She will not take (a test.)'

File 5.7 Morphological Types of Languages

Languages are often classified according to the way in which they put morphemes together to form words. There are two basic morphological types of language structure, analytic and synthetic, and several subtypes.

Analytic Languages

Analytic or isolating languages are so called because they are made up of sequences of free morphemes—each word consists of a single morpheme, used by itself with meaning intact. Purely analytic languages do not use prefixes or suffixes to compose words. Semantic and grammatical concepts, which are often expressed in other languages (like English) through the use of suffixes, are thus expressed in isolating languages by the use of separate words.

Mandarin Chinese is an example of a language that has a highly analytical structure. In the example sentences below, for instance, the concept of plurality and the concept of a completed action in the past are communicated in Mandarin through the use of invariant morphemes rather than the use of a change of form (cf. English, *I* to *we* to indicate plurality) or the use of a variable affix (cf. English *-ed* for past tense).

(1)   [wɔ mən tan tɕin]
        I   plural play piano
        'We are playing the piano'

(2)   [wɔ mən tan tɕin lə]
        I   plural play piano past
        'We played the piano'

Note that the form of 'we' (I-plural) that is used in the subject position is [wɔ mən] and that the pronoun has the same form when it is used as the object, placed after the verb:

(3)   [ta da wɔ mən]
        s/he hit(s) I plural
        'S/he hits us'

Only the position of a word in a sentence shows its function. English is unlike Mandarin in this respect, since the personal pronoun *we* is changed in form to *us* when it is used as the object of a verb. But English is like Mandarin in that word order is used to show the functions of nouns in a sentence, and in that nouns (unlike pronouns) are not marked by affixes to show their functions. (For example, in the sentence *Tracy likes cats* the noun *Tracy* functions as the subject and the noun *cats* as the direct object, but just the opposite is true of *Cats like Tracy*; these differences in function are signaled only by the order of words in the sentence.)

Synthetic Languages

In synthetic languages, affixes or bound morphemes are attached to other morphemes, so that a word may be made up of several meaningful elements. The bound morphemes may add another element of meaning to the stem by indicating the grammatical function of the stem in a sentence. The term *stem* refers to that part of the word to which affixes are added. It may consist of one or more morphemes: for instance, in *reruns, -s* is added to the stem *rerun*, which is itself made up of two morphemes.

Hungarian is a synthetic language. In the examples below, bound morphemes show the grammatical functions of nouns in their sentences:

(4)   ɔz   ɛmber laːtjɔ ɔ   kucaːt
       the   man   sees   the dog-(object)
       'The man sees the dog'

(5)   ɔ   kucɔ laːtjɔ ɔz   ɛmbɛɾt
       the dog   sees   the   man-(object)
       'The dog sees the man'

As mentioned above, in English it is the position in the sentence of the noun phrase *the man* or *the dog* that tells one whether the phrase is the subject or object of the verb, but in Hungarian a noun or noun phrase may appear either before or after the verb in a sentence and be recognized as the subject or object in either position because it is marked with a bound morpheme (the suffix [t]) if it is the direct object. (Other synthetic languages behave similarly.) So both examples below mean the same thing, even though the position of the noun phrase meaning 'the man' is different with respect to the verb meaning 'sees'.

(6)   ɔ   kucɔ laːtjɔ ɔz   ɛmbɛɾt
       the dog   sees   the   man-(object)
       'The dog sees the man'

(7)   ɔz   ɛmbɛɾt   laːtjɔ ɔ   kucɔ
       the   man-(object) sees   the dog
       'The dog sees the man'

Synthetic languages like Hungarian also use bound morphemes to indicate some concepts that English signals by means of free morphemes. For example, Hungarian indicates personal possession and location by the use of suffixes attached to the stem (*haːz,* 'house'), whereas in English these concepts are expressed by the use of free morphemes. For example,

(8)   ɔ   haːzunk zöld
       the house-our green
       'Our house is green'

(9)   ɔ   haːzɔd   fɛheːr
       the house-your white
       'Your house is white'

(10)   ɔ   se:kɛd   ɔ   ha:zunkbɔn   vɔn
           the chair-your the house-our-in is
           'Your chair is in our house'

Agglutinating Languages

The kind of synthesis (putting together) of morphemes we find in Hungarian is known as **agglutination**. In agglutinating languages, like Hungarian, the morphemes are joined together relatively "loosely." That is, it is usually easy to determine where the boundaries between morphemes are, e.g.,

ha:z-unk-bɔn
house-our-in
'in our house'

ha:z-ɔd
house-your
'your house', etc.

Swahili is another example of an agglutinating language. Swahili verb stems take prefixes to indicate the person of the subject of the verb (first, second, or third) and also to indicate the tense of the verb, as in the following list of forms for the verb 'read'.

ni-na-soma	*I-present-read*	'I am reading'
u-na-soma	*you-present-read*	'You are reading'
a-na-soma	*s/he-present-read*	'S/he is reading'
ni-li-soma	*I-past-read*	'I was reading'
u-li-soma	*you-past-read*	'You were reading'
a-li-soma	*s/he-past-read*	'S/he was reading'
ni-ta-soma	*I-future-read*	'I will read'
u-ta-soma	*you-future-read*	'You will read'
a-ta-soma	*s/he-future-read*	'S/he will read'

A second characteristic feature of agglutinating languages is that each bound morpheme carries (ordinarily) only one meaning: *ni* = 'I', *u* = 'you', *a* = 's/he', *na* = 'present', etc.

Fusional Languages

In **fusional** languages, another subtype of synthetic language, words are formed by adding bound morphemes to stems, just as in agglutinating languages, but in fusional languages the affixes may not be easy to separate from the stem. It is often rather hard to tell where one morpheme ends and the next begins; the affixes are characteristically fused with the stem.

Spanish is a fusional language that has suffixes attached to the verb stem to indicate the person (*I/you/he/she/it*) and number (singular/plural) of the subject of the verb. It is often difficult to analyze a verb form into its stem and suffix, however, because there is often a fusion of the two morphemes. For example, in the forms:

(11)	hablo	'I am speaking'
(12)	habla	'S/he is speaking'
(13)	hablé	'I spoke'

these morphemes can be isolated:

[-o]	first person singular present tense
[-a]	third person singular present tense
[-é]	first person singular past tense

However, it is difficult to separate out a stem that means 'speak'. The form *habl-* never appears in isolation in Spanish. In the following forms:

(14)	hablamos	'We are speaking'
(15)	hablan	'They are speaking'

where these morphemes can be isolated:

[-mos]	first person plural present tense
[-n]	third person plural present tense

it seems possible to say that the verb stem is *habla-*, to which the suffixes [-mos] and [-n] are added. But in the case of examples (11), (12), and (13) above, it is apparent that if there is a stem *habla-*, it has been fused together with the suffixes [-o], [-a], and [-é].

Fusional languages often differ from agglutinating languages in another way as well: agglutinating languages usually have only one meaning indicated by each affix, as noted above, but in fusional languages a single affix may convey several meanings simultaneously. Russian is a fusional language in which bound morphemes attached to verb stems indicate both the person and number of the subject of the verb and the tense of the verb at one and the same time. For example, in the verb form:

(16)	[čitayɛt]	's/he is reading'

the bound form [-yɛt] signifies third person as well as singular and present tense. In the form:

(17)	[čital]	'he was reading'

the suffix [-l] means singular, masculine, and past tense, simultaneously. (Compare the Swahili examples above, where person and tense are signaled by separate affixes.)

Polysynthetic Languages

In some synthetic languages, highly complex words may be formed by combining several stems and affixes; this is usually a matter of making nouns (subjects, objects, etc.) into parts of the verb forms. Sora, a language spoken in India, allows such incorporation of objects (subjects, instruments, etc.) into verbs:

(18)	anin	ñam -	yɔ -	te -	n
	he	*catch*	*fish*	*non-past*	*do*
	'He is fish-catching'				
	i.e., 'He is catching fish'				

(19)   ñam - kɪd - te - n - ai
        catch tiger non-past do first person agent
        'I will tiger-catch'
        i.e., 'I will catch a tiger'

Such verbs are roughly comparable to an English construction like *baby-sit*, but the polysynthetic constructions may be more complex, including several nouns as well as a variety of other affixes:

(20)   pɔ - poŋ - kon - t   -   am
        stab belly knife non-past thee
        '(Someone) will stab you with a knife in (your) belly'

(21)   ñɛn - əǰ - ǰa - dar - si - əm
        I   not receive cooked rice hand thee
        'I will not receive cooked rice from your hands'

The *incorporated* or "built-in" form of the noun is not necessarily identical to its free form. In Sora, the free form of 'tiger' is [kina], that of 'hand' is [siʔi], that of 'knife' is [kondi].

Summary

From the discussion, we can extract the following statements about language types:

1. *Analytic* languages build up the meanings of sentences through the use of isolated morphemes. They do not use affixes (prefixes or suffixes).

2. *Synthetic* languages build up the meanings of sentences by combining free and bound morphemes to make up words.

   a. *Agglutinating* languages are languages in which the affixes can easily be separated from the stems to which they are attached and in which each affix generally conveys only one meaning.

   b. *Fusional* languages are languages in which the affixes and the base to which they are attached are fused together in pronunciation as a result of phonological processes or change, and therefore they are not easily separated from one another. In addition, there is generally a fusion of meanings that is represented by the affixes in such languages.

   c. *Polysynthetic* languages are languages in which several stem forms may be combined (along with affixes) into a single word. Such a word is usually a verb with its associated nouns "built-in" or *incorporated*, so that the verb alone expresses what seems to us to be about the equivalent of a whole sentence.

It is important to note that languages are rarely "pure" types; they usually combine elements of a variety of types.

6

Syntax

Words in a sentence are more than a simple concatenation of items—there are patterns and regularities that can be discovered. Syntax studies the organization of words into phrases and phrases into sentences.

File 6.1

Linear Order, Hierarchical Structure, and Ambiguity

While a dictionary of all the words in any human language (at a given time) can be made, it is impossible to compile a dictionary of all the sentences of a language; unlike words, sentences are not finite in number, and therefore sentences, unlike words, are not learned individually. However, native speakers of a language seem to get along amazingly well without such a dictionary for sentences—they can use and understand sentences in their language that they have not previously encountered. Why is it that we cannot always properly use or understand a word in our language that we have not heard before but can spontaneously produce and understand new sentences? If what we learn is not the sentences themselves, what *do* we learn that enables us to produce and understand an infinite number of sentences? This is the question we will be concerned with as we consider syntax, the study of the structure of phrases and sentences.

Though we use sentences all the time, we don't normally think about how they are structured. However, a little consideration reveals that the principles by which words are organized into sentences are, in fact, quite complex. In this file, we will consider two basic principles of sentence organization: linear order and hierarchical structure.

Linear Order

The most obvious principle of sentence organization is linear order; the words in a sentence must occur in a particular sequence if the sentence is to convey the desired meaning. Consider, for example, the following sentence of English.

   (1) John glanced at Mary.

If we rearrange the words in this sentence, we come up either with nonsense, as in (2) (the * denotes an ungrammatical expression):

   (2) *Mary John at glanced.

or with a sentence whose meaning is distinctly different from that of (1):

   (3) Mary glanced at John.

Clearly, the ordering of the words in sentences determines, in part, whether a sentence is grammatical or not and what the sentence means.

170

One of the many rules of English requires that the grammatical subject of a sentence normally precedes the main verb, which in turn normally precedes its direct object; thus, *she resembles him* is English (where *she* is the subject and *him* is the object), but *resembles she him* and *she him resembles* are not. However, an important fact about rules of word order is that they are language-specific—that is, languages vary in the ways in which they order words. (See File 6.7.)

Hierarchical Structure

Although linear order is an important principle of sentence organization, sentences are more than just ordered sequences of words; they have internal hierarchical structure as well. That is, the individual words in a sentence are organized into natural, semantically coherent groupings, which are themselves organized into larger groupings, the largest grouping of all being the sentence itself (and the smallest of all being individual words). These groupings within a sentence are called **constituents** of that sentence. The relationships between constituents in a sentence form the **constituent structure** of the sentence.

For example, consider the sentence in (4).

(4) Many executives eat at really fancy restaurants.

We can easily distinguish a number of meaningful groups of words in this sentence: *many executives* and *eat at really fancy restaurants*, for instance, clearly have meanings of their own, and each makes a coherent contribution to the meaning of (4) as a whole. For these reasons, they are constituents of this sentence. On the other hand, some groups of words in sentence (4) do not naturally form meaningful units; *executives eat at* and *eat at really*, for example, don't clearly have meanings of their own. Thus, these groups of words are *not* constituents of (4).

Constituent Tests

If a constituent is a semantically coherent group, then, of course, sentences are always constituents, as are the individual words within a sentence. In sentence (4), for instance, the largest constituent is the sentence itself; the smallest constituents are the individual words *many, executives, eat, at, really, fancy,* and *restaurants*. Other constituents within a sentence are not always so easy to identify. However, there are a number of useful tests for distinguishing constituents, which are syntactic units, from mere strings of words, which aren't constituents and therefore do not behave as a single unit.

Ability to Stand Alone

Constituents can often be sensibly used alone, for example as exclamations or as answers to questions:

(5) What do many executives do?
     Eat at really fancy restaurants.

This isn't true of nonconstituents: if we were asked "Do fancy restaurants do much business?" we couldn't sensibly answer *"(Well), executives eat at."

Substitution by a Pro-form

It is often possible to replace a constituent with a single word having the same meaning as that constituent. For example, if someone asked "What do many executives do?" we could answer either with sentence (4) or with sentence (6), in which the constituent *many executives* is replaced with the single word *they* (which in this context would mean the same thing as *many executives*). Note that it is a certain category of word which is used for the substitution test, namely, a **pro-word** (or **pro-form**). Pronouns are one type of pro-form (e.g., *he, she, it, they, us, her,* and *that*). There are pro-verbs such as *do, be,* and *have*, pro-adverbs such as *there* and *then*, as well as a pro-adjective, *such*. You may use these pro-forms when attempting to determine constituency.

   (6) *They* eat at really fancy restaurants.

Similarly, if someone asked "Who eats at really fancy restaurants?" we could answer either with (4) or with (7), in which the constituent *eat at really fancy restaurants* is replaced with the single word *do* (which would mean the same thing in this context).

   (7) Many executives *do*.

But there is no word that could possibly replace the nonconstituent *eat at really* in (4) and mean the same thing, no matter what question was asked.

Movement

If some part of a sentence can be moved around—usually to the beginning or end of the sentence—it is a constituent. For example, one could say:

   (8) At really fancy restaurants, many executives eat.

It may sound a bit stilted, but it sounds grammatical to many English speakers in the right context. Thus, *at really fancy restaurants* must be a constituent because it can be moved to the front of the sentence. Compare this with:

   (9) *fancy restaurants many executives eat at really.

This is not grammatical; according to the movement test, *fancy restaurants* is not a constituent in this sentence, since it cannot be moved.

One thing to keep in mind when you apply these tests is that they are not an absolute indicator of constituency. A group of words in a sentence may past two tests and fail one and still be a constituent. For example, in the above sentence, the phrase *eat at fancy restaurants* is taken to be a constituent because it passed the Ability to Stand Alone test. But, most English speakers do not think that one can say *Eat at fancy restaurants many executives*. Thus, this constituent fails the Movement test. However, it does pass the Substitution by Pro-form test: *Many executives do*. Second, some tests are better indicators of constituency than others—if a group of words passes Substitution by Pro-form and Ability to Stand Alone, you probably will want to consider it a constituent, even if it fails the Movement test. The key here is not to apply the tests blindly but to consider how convincing each test is and to develop some intuitions about English constituents.

Other Issues Concerning Constituents

Two points must be kept in mind regarding constituents. First, given a group of words, we cannot say once and for all whether or not it is a constituent; rather, we can only say whether or not it is a constituent relative to a particular sentence. To illustrate this, consider sentences (10) and (11).

(10) Pat and Leslie raised llamas.
(11) Robin raised Pat and Leslie adopted Chris.

In (10), *Pat and Leslie* is a constituent: it functions as a coherent, meaningful unit within the sentence, in particular, as its subject. In (11), however, the very same sequence of words is *not* a constituent: because *Pat* is the direct object of the first clause and *Leslie* is the subject of the second clause, the sequence *Pat and Leslie* does not make a coherent contribution to the meaning of this sentence. We can apply the constituent tests to verify this claim. For example, although *Pat and Leslie* can be replaced with *they* in (10), this isn't possible in sentence (11). Thus, we can properly say that a string of words is a constituent only with respect to a particular sentence.

　　The second thing that must be kept in mind is that constituent structure is *hierarchical*—that is, one constituent may be part of another. What this means, in turn, is that sentences are composed of parts that have been grouped together before they are grouped into the sentence. Consider sentence (4) again.

(4) Many executives eat at really fancy restaurants.

Among the constituents in this sentence is the sequence *really fancy*. To see this, note that *really fancy* can be used by itself:

(12) How fancy was it?
　　　Really fancy.

and that it can be replaced with the single word *such*:

(13) Who eats at really fancy restaurants?
　　　Many executives eat at such restaurants.

But *really fancy* is also part of a larger constituent, namely, *really fancy restaurants;* this in turn is part of a larger constituent, *at really fancy restaurants*, which is itself part of the still larger constituent *eat at really fancy restaurants* and ultimately of the largest constituent in the sentence, namely, the sentence itself. If we underline each of the constituents in (4), the hierarchical nature of its constituent structure is easier to see:

(14) <u>Many　executives　eat　at　<u><u>really　fancy</u>　restaurants</u>.</u>

　　Underlining is, as in (14), one way of representing the hierarchical nature of constituent structure. Another way is with **tree diagrams**: branching structures in which each constituent forms a "branch." For example, the tree diagram for sentence (4) is in (15):

(15)

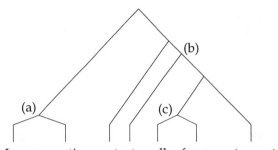

Many executives eat at really fancy restaurants.

In this diagram, each of the constituents of sentence (4) forms a branch: for example, *many executives* corresponds to the branch labeled (a); *at really fancy restaurants*, to the branch labeled (b); and *really fancy*, to the branch labeled (c). Observe, in addition, that groups of words that are not constituents of sentence (4) do *not* form branches in this tree diagram; *executives *eat at* and **eat at really*, for instance, clearly aren't constituents according to the diagram in (15). In principle, underlining is just as good as tree diagrams for representing constituent structure, but because tree diagrams are somewhat easier to read, they are usually preferred.

Ambiguity

In every human language we can find individual expressions that have two or more distinct meanings. For example, the italicized portions of the following sentences of English can be interpreted in more than one way:

(16)   a.   Larry raises *miniature badgers and raccoons*.
       b.   We need *more intelligent leaders*.
       c.   The *cranes* were transported by boat to Minneapolis.

In (16a), *miniature badgers and raccoons* can mean either 'miniature badgers and miniature raccoons' or 'miniature badgers and raccoons (of any size)'; in (16b), *more intelligent leaders* can mean either 'a greater quantity of intelligent leaders' or 'leaders who are more intelligent'. This property of having two or more distinct meanings is called **ambiguity;** an expression with two or more distinct meanings is ambiguous.

Often, an expression is ambiguous because it has more than one possible constituent structure. Consider, for example, the expression *miniature badgers and raccoons* in sentence (16a): it can have either of the following constituent structures.

(17)

miniature badgers and raccoons

(18)

miniature badgers and raccoons

In (17), *badgers and raccoons* forms a constituent; (17) therefore represents the interpretation in which the adjective *miniature* applies to both the badgers and the raccoons. In (18), on the other hand, *miniature badgers* forms a constituent; (18) therefore represents the interpretation in which only the badgers are miniature. An expression that is ambiguous because it has more than one possible constituent structure is said to be **structurally ambiguous**.

The italicized portion of sentence (16b) is also structurally ambiguous: it can have either of the following constituent structures.

(19)

more   intelligent   leaders

(20)

more   intelligent   leaders

In (19), *intelligent leaders* is a constituent; for this reason, (19) represents the interpretation 'a greater quantity of intelligent leaders'. In (20), however, *more intelligent* forms a constituent; (20) therefore represents the meaning 'leaders who are more intelligent'.

Although structural ambiguity is a very common kind of ambiguity, it is not the only kind. Individual *words* are sometimes ambiguous; for example, *crane* can refer either to a kind of bird or to a large construction device. Because words like *crane* have no internal constituent structure, sentences containing such words clearly can't be structurally ambiguous. Instead, a sentence containing a word with more than one meaning is said to be **lexically ambiguous**. Thus, both meanings for (16c) are represented with the same constituent structure.

Exercises

0. Apply the constituent tests to determine if the underlined expressions in the following sentence are constituents. (Answers to all zero problems can be found in Appendix A.)

    a.   <u>Many retired workers</u> spend their time on relaxing hobbies.
    b.   Many retired workers spend their time <u>on relaxing hobbies</u>.
    c.   Many retired workers <u>spend their time</u> on relaxing hobbies.

1. Which of the underlined expressions in the following sentences are constituents? Which are not? Why? (Use the constituency tests mentioned above to determine which are constituents in each case.)

    a. Chris ate <u>the stale candy</u>.
    b. Chris <u>ate the stale candy</u>.
    c. My little <u>brother snores</u>.
    d. My <u>little brother</u> snores.

2. Apply each of the constituency tests to the underlined expressions and determine whether they are constituents. Remember that a constituent does not necessarily have to pass *all* the constituency tests.

    a. The clouds rolled <u>across the sky</u>.
    b. My aunt crashed <u>our new car</u>.
    c. Mattingly hit the ball <u>over the fence</u>.
    d. Some <u>students hate</u> computers.
    e. <u>The ancient ruins of the temple</u> were covered by earth.
    f. The <u>women wept</u>.
    g. Too many <u>noisy birds are</u> nesting on campus.
    h. Joggers like to run <u>along the river</u>.
    i. The bride and groom ran out of <u>the church</u>.
    j. The thieves <u>opened the door with</u> a credit card.
    k. <u>The tired teachers</u> had a party.
    l. <u>She paid</u> the woman with a twenty dollar bill.
    m. A rabid dog <u>on the street</u> scared everyone inside.
    n. <u>We drank too much</u> coffee last night.
    o. The children ate their dinner <u>quickly</u>.
    p. Michael suspects <u>his wife had an affair</u>.

3. Find all of the constituents in the following sentence and list them.

    The science books on the table fell suddenly to the floor.

4. Discuss the ambiguity of the following sentences. Which are lexically ambiguous? Which are structurally ambiguous?

    a. John sat on Jumbo's trunk.
    b. The little girl hit the child with the toy.
    c. Chocolate cakes and pies are my favorite desserts.
    d. We used to meet near the bank every afternoon.

File 6.2   Lexical Categories

One aspect of our syntactic competence is our understanding of the similarities and differences in the behavior of the words in our language. Though all human languages have numerous words, each word in a given language is not entirely different in its behavior from all the other words in that language. Instead, a large number of words often exhibit the same properties, which suggests that a language's enormous inventory of words can be grouped into a relatively small number of word classes based on their morphological and syntactic properties. We will call these word classes **lexical categories**, because the **lexicon** is the list of all the words in a language (plus various kinds of information about those words). For example, one of the morphological properties of the word *book* is that it has a plural form, *books*. But this is by no means a unique property of the word *book*. Thousands of other words in English have a plural form—e.g., *box, song, child, rock*. All these words can occur in the following context:

    (1) _____+ plural morpheme

      That is, *book* and words like it appear in the **morphological frame** given in (1). A morphological frame is the position of a word with respect to the bound morphemes that can attach to it within a word. Thus the word *book* combines with plural /-z/ to form the word *books*. (In English /-z/ is the usual plural morpheme, though there are irregular plural forms such as *children* and *oxen*, which do not contain /-z/.)

      Now, is the fact that *book* and certain other words have plural forms a significant one, or is it merely an accidental feature of all these English words? After all, thousands of words could share some feature without there being any interesting reason to group them together. For instance, a large number of English words have the sound [k] in them—*take, chemistry, tacky*, and so on—but this fact does not contribute to our understanding of the syntax of English (nor would similar facts in any language be relevant to the syntax of that language). Is the singular-plural distinction that numerous English words share such an accidental, unrevealing property, or is it a significant criterion for grouping all such words together? It turns out that it *is* a significant property, since all the words that show this property also behave similarly in other respects, thus indicating that they do act as a group, all having something in common. For instance, the words that occur in the morphological frame in (1) can also occur in the **syntactic frames** in (2) and (3). A syntactic frame is a position in which a word occurs relative to other classes of words in the same phrase. In other words, it is the syntactic context of a word. Example (2) shows that this group of words can combine with determiners (abbreviated DET: words such as *a, the, some, many, several, few*), and (3) shows that this group of words can occur after DET and adjective (ADJ) combinations; adjectives are words such as *small, unexpected, bright, friendly*.

    (2) DET _____

    (3) DET ADJ _____

      We group all the words that share this cluster of properties into the lexical category of *nouns*. A lexical category is a class of words that all share morphological and syntactic properties—that is, words that may appear in the same morphological and syntactic frames. In this case, *noun* is a lexical category whose members all share the morphological property of having a plural form (they occur in the morphological frame in [1]) and the syntactic properties of combining with determiners (frame [2]) or with both determiners and adjectives (frame [3]). (We shall soon discuss determiners and adjectives, which are also lexical categories in English.)

Each lexical category has a unique set of morphological frames and syntactic frames, and so the morphological and syntactic frames of a given word can be used as diagnostic tests for deciding which lexical category that word belongs to. That is, the morphological and syntactic frames of a word act as clues to the lexical category of that word. Given below are the patterns of some more lexical categories in English. Even though there are some universal tendencies across languages in the area of lexical categories, and the strategies we lay out here are valid tools in the investigation of other languages, it is important to note that what follows is a description of English lexical categories, and the details are not the same in other languages.

Verbs

Members of the lexical category of verbs (V) have the morphological property of having tense distinctions, such as *present* and *past* (e.g., *sing – sang; walk – walked; drive – drove; is – was*); this is shown in the morphological frame in (4):

(4) _____+ tense morpheme

(In English /-d/ is in general the past tense marker, even though a large number of English verbs have a past tense form other than /-d/; for example, *sang* and *drove*.)

Another morphological property of English verbs is that they sometimes show a contrast in number and person. Compare *he walks* with *I walk, they walk*, and so on. Thus the suffix /-z/, which denotes third person singular agreement, can be used as a morphological frame for verbs in English. This is given in (5):

(5) _____+ third person singular morpheme

Verbs may also be suffixed with *-ing*, which is attached when the verb is used in the progressive (e.g., *I am walking*). This morphological frame for verbs is shown in (6):

(6) _____+ progressive morpheme

One of the syntactic properties of verbs is that they combine with auxiliary verbs (abbreviated AUX), such as *may, might*, and *will*, to form, for example, *may go, might be, will drive*. (See section on closed categories for more on AUX.) This syntactic frame is given in (7):

(7) AUX _____

Another syntactic frame for verbs is given in (8), which shows that verbs can occur in the beginning (or optionally after *please*) in orders or requests (e.g., *(Please) leave!, Shut up!, Listen to me!, Please take a seat*).

(8) (please) _____ . . . !

Adjectives

Adjectives (ADJ) have the property of having comparative and superlative forms (e.g., *tall, taller, tallest; affectionate, more affectionate, most affectionate*). Note that with some adjectives (such as *tall*) this property is reflected as a morphological frame as given in (9); with some others (such as *affectionate*) it is reflected as a syntactic frame, given in (10):

(9)   _____ + er/est

(10)   more/most + _____

Adjectives can also occur in the syntactic frame in (11), which shows that they can occur before a noun (N), which they *modify* (i.e., describe or give more information about), and after a determiner—e.g., *a true story, the unexpected guests.*

(11)   DET _____ N

Another syntactic frame for adjectives is given in (12), which shows that if a word can occur after a *linking verb*, such as *is, seems,* or *looks*: e.g., *is sunny, seems angry, looks ready,* then it is an adjective.

(12)   LINKING VERB _____

Adjectives can also be modified by adverbs (ADV), such as *very* in *very rude*, *highly* in *highly qualified*, or *amazingly* in *amazingly perceptive*. Example (13) is this syntactic frame:

(13)   ADV _____

Adverbs

It is hard to come up with hard-and-fast tests for identifying adverbs (ADV), since their morphological and syntactic frames (if any) do not always rule out other possibilities. One somewhat useful characteristic is that a large number of adverbs are formed by adding *-ly* to adjectives. So, if a word ends in *-ly*, and if the part without the *-ly* is an adjective, then the word is an adverb—for example, *happily, unexpectedly, skillfully, eagerly*. We can represent this as in (14), but notice that this is not the same kind of "fill-in-the-blank" notation that we've used for other frames. Instead, it's a description of the internal structure of many adverbs.

(14) $[\text{ADJ} + \text{ly}]_{\text{ADV}}$

While (14) tells us that all adjective + *-ly* combinations are adverbs, it does not cover ***all*** adverbs, since there are other adverbs that are not formed from adjectives, including *well, westward, agewise*, and so on. Note also that not all words ending in *-ly* are adverbs; for example, *likely, lovely,* and *friendly* are all adjectives (of course, *like, love,* and *friend* are not adjectives).

Adverbs usually modify adjectives, verbs, and other adverbs; thus you find them in phrases like *unusually nice, quite big, quietly entered the room,* and *moved carefully*. The syntactic frame that illustrates this is given in (15):

(15) _____ ADJ
     _____ VERB or VERB PHRASE
     _____ ADV

Adverbs may also be difficult to identify using a syntactic frame because they often have the option of occurring in several positions in a sentence, as can be seen in (16):

(16) a. Anxiously, the bride went to her wedding.
     b. The bride anxiously went to her wedding.
     c. The bride went anxiously to her wedding.
     d. The bride went to her wedding anxiously.

Like adjectives, many adverbs can fit in frame (10) as well, for example, *more unexpectedly, more skillfully*, etc. , but by no means do all, e.g., **more very*.

Closed Lexical Categories

Closed classes are sometimes known as **function words**. The members of closed classes, unlike the lexical categories discussed above, have little meaning outside of their grammatical purpose and are used to relate phrases of various types to other phrases. These classes are called "closed" because the addition of a new member to a closed category rarely occurs. This contrasts with open classes, such as N, V, ADJ, and ADV, to which new members can be added easily. Consider the fairly recent additions to nouns—*geek, sputnik, yuppie*, and so on. The closed classes include determiners, auxiliary verbs, prepositions, and conjunctions.

(Note that in the discussion that follows, reference is made to **phrases**, for example, verb phrases and noun phrases (abbreviated VP and NP, respectively). These are technical terms and will be explained further in File 6.3.)

Determiners (DET) often signal that a noun or adjective + noun is following, as in *the book, many blue pencils*. This class includes words like *a, the, many, several, few, some, all*, and *which*. It also includes possessive words and phrases, for example, *my, her, your*, and *our*. The syntactic frame for determiners is given in (17). (The parentheses around ADJ indicate that the adjective is optional—it may or may not be there.)

(17) _____ (ADJ) N

Auxiliary verbs (AUX) often indicate tense and aspect. Examples of auxiliaries are *may, might, can, should, will*, and *must*, and forms of *do, have*, and *be* that are used with another verb. They often precede verb phrases (VPs), and in questions they precede noun phrases (NPs); for example, auxiliary verbs occur in the sentences *I might go, I have gone, Did I go?* and *I am going*. AUXs may also be followed by *not*, as in *will not* and *should not*. Note that non-auxiliary verbs do not follow this pattern, **went not, *ate not*, and that *not* doesn't precede the AUX, **not will, *not did*. The syntactic frames in (18), (19), and (20) illustrate these facts:

(18) NP _____ VP

(19) _____ NP VP ?

(20) _____ not

Prepositions (P) combine with noun phrases (NPs) to form prepositional phrases (PPs), which modify nouns or verbs as in *the man with the beard* or *ran to the store*. One syntactic frame for prepositions is given in (21):

(21) _____ NP

Another syntactic frame for prepositions shows that they may sometimes be preceded by *right*, as in *right into the store, right on campus, right over the bleachers*, etc.

(22) right _____ NP

Conjunctions (CONJ) join words and phrases of the same category. Examples of conjunctions are *and, but, or*; some sample syntactic frames are given in (23):

(23) N _____ N
      ADJ _____ ADJ
      NP _____ NP
      ADJ P _____ ADJ P
      S _____ S (where S = sentence)

Pronouns (PRO) include *he, she, we, they, I*, and *you*, which are used as subjects; *him, her, us, them*, and *me*, which are used as objects; and *it* and *you*, used for both subjects and objects. Note that the so-called possessive pronouns are not pronouns (e.g., *her, my, his, our*, and *their*). They are determiners, since they fit in frame (17), the syntactic frame for DET.

Some Suggestions

1. It is important to keep in mind several factors when determining the lexical category of a word. As you might have noticed, the classification of words into lexical categories is somewhat similar to the traditional notion introduced in primary school as *parts of speech*. You are encouraged to compare the two notions if you understand the high school introduction to parts of speech well, but it has to be stressed that there are important differences. While parts-of-speech classification relies heavily on meaning-based definitions (e.g., "a noun is a person, place, or thing"), classification into lexical categories relies solely on the morphological and syntactic properties of a word; for the purposes of understanding and working with the concepts in the syntax files in this book, you are better off following the criteria given in the above section in identifying the lexical category of words.

2. Sometimes the same word belongs to more than one category, with roughly the same meaning, because of the word-formation process of functional shift (see File 10.7). For example, words like *walk* and *promise* can be used as nouns or as verbs—e.g., *I took a long walk* vs. *I walked*. It is generally accepted that such words have two separate entries in the lexicon, and, of course, any given instance of such a word in a sentence is a member of only one category.

3. Words with completely different meanings and/or category membership sometimes sound identical; these are **homophones** ("sound-alike" words). For example, there is a verb *rock*, as in *I rocked the baby till it fell asleep*, and a noun *rock*, as in *She threw a rock into the pond*. These two words are not related by any word-formation processes, nor do they have similar meanings; that the words are pronounced alike is simply coincidental.

4. Use *all* the tests for a given lexical category before you decide that a word belongs to that category. For example, if you use the syntactic frame given in (11) alone, you might decide that *army* is an adjective since you sometimes seem to find the word in that syntactic frame (*the army uniform, an army officer*), but the word does not meet the other criteria for being an adjective: for example, there is no *armier, *armiest* or *more army, *most army,* or *very army*. (In the examples *army uniform* and *army officer, army* is the first member of a compound noun, not an adjective.)

5. In some cases, the information about the subcategories within a lexical category (File 6.4) will be useful in addition to the criteria already discussed in this section.

Exercises

1. Identify the lexical category of the underlined word in each of the following sentences.

    a. I collect antique <u>glassware</u>.
    b. There was a <u>large</u> piano wedged in the doorway.
    c. You <u>must</u> be there on time.
    d. Susan <u>bought</u> a new car last week.
    e. The squirrel scrambled <u>up</u> the tree.
    f. Chris plays volleyball <u>and</u> swims.
    g. The river is <u>very</u> full now.
    h. <u>Every</u> good boy deserves favor.
    i. <u>Give</u> me something unusual.
    j. <u>Would</u> you hand me that wrench?

2. In each of the following pairs of sentences, the underlined word in the (i) sentence belongs to a different lexical category than the underlined word in the (ii) sentence. Identify the lexical category of the underlined word in each of the sentences.

    a. i. It was a <u>cold</u> and dreary day.
        ii. I can't seem to get rid of my <u>cold</u>.
    b. i. You must <u>dry</u> cilantro leaves before storing.
        ii. The <u>dry</u> heat of the desert proved to be deadly.
    c. i. There has been some improvement in the <u>past</u> week.
        ii. In the <u>past</u>, there has not been much improvement.
    d. i. That's a <u>promise</u>.
        ii. I <u>promise</u> to take you to the zoo tomorrow.

3. Examine the following sentences and answer the questions that follow.

    Leslie is working, and so is Nancy.
    Philip went bankrupt, and so did Max.
    Lucy had seen the dog, and so had her mother and her neighbors.
    Robin will avoid the construction, and so will Pat.

a. Think up several more sentences that have the *and so* construction.

b. Now consider the syntactic frame:

    and so ____ NP

    What kind of lexical category fills this pattern?

4. Explain how the differences in the category and meaning of the homophonous words *fly* and *fly*, and *like* and *like*, are exploited in the following saying:

    Time flies like an arrow;
    Fruit flies like a banana.

    Do the same for the following sentence by identifying the lexical category of each occurrence of *can*:

    Can he can me for kicking the can?

File 6.3 Phrasal Categories

Phrasal Categories

So far we have discussed only lexical categories, that is, classes to which individual words belong. However, there is another kind of syntactic category, namely the **phrasal category**. Recall that we determine a word's category by finding characteristics it shares with other words. That is, we find words that behave the same, or have the same distribution, as other words, and these sets of words we group into a category and give it a name, such as *noun* or *verb*. Then recall that words can combine with other words to form semantically coherent groupings, or **constituents**. A phrasal category is a set of constituents that behave the same, or share the same functions and distribution.

For instance, consider the following sentence:

(1) The joggers ran through the park.

One constituent of this sentence consists of the words *the joggers*, as can be demonstrated by applying the constituent tests discussed in File 6.1. Upon examining the lexical categories involved, we see that this constituent is formed by the combination of a determiner and a noun. Now consider each of the words or groups of words below. Note that each of them could be substituted for the phrase *the joggers* in sentence (1), and a grammatical sentence would result:

(2) a. Susan
     b. students
     c. you
     d. most dogs
     e. some children
     f. a huge, lovable bear
     g. my friend from Brazil
     h. the people that we interviewed

Each of the examples in (2) could likewise be shown to be a constituent in this sentence if it occurred in place of *the joggers* . Note, however, that some have different structures than the DET + N constituent in *the joggers*. Examples (a) and (b) are single Ns, (f) is composed of DET + ADJ + N, (g) is composed of DET + N + PREP + N, and (h) is different from all of these. Note that other sets of words that are constituents cannot be substituted for *the joggers*, for example, *in the tree* or *made a cake*. What we have discovered is that constituents with different structures can have the same functions because they can be used in the same position in a sentence. This means that they belong to the same *category*, and since some constituents may involve combinations of more than one word, these categories are called *phrasal* categories. In the category discussed above, a noun alone or a noun plus other words forms a **noun phrase** (NP). Sometimes, a single word can count as an NP all by itself, but not always. For example, the word *dog* cannot be substituted for the NP slot in (3):

(3) _____ ran through the park.

Thus, in the sentence *The dog ran through the park*, *dog* is an N, but not an NP (whereas *dogs*, and other nouns in the plural, would count as both if placed alone in the slot). So we observe from (2) and (3) that proper nouns, pronouns, and plural nouns can be used individually as NPs, but some types of singular Ns cannot be.

An NP can be used as the subject of a sentence, as in (4); as the direct object, as in (5); as the indirect object, as in (6); and in many other ways as well. These are descriptions of the *functions* that NPs can perform.

(4) *Some children* like ice cream.
(5) Harold likes *some children.*
(6) The teacher gave *some children* a scolding this morning.

Now consider the sentence in (7):

(7) The mothers visited their children.

Constituency tests demonstrate that *visited their children* is a constituent. It is composed of V + NP. Note that this particular structure does not share the same properties as the structures grouped into the category of NP because we could not insert *visited their children* in the slot in (3). Other structures could be substituted for *visited their children*. For example:

(8) a. snored
b. love music
c. walked the dog through the park
d. believe that dogs are smart
e. wanted to leave
f. will sleep soundly
g. can lift 100 pounds
h. are wearing sunglasses
i. go home and have a beauty rest

All of these structures behave the same and thus can be grouped into another phrasal category, namely, that of **verb phrase** (VP). Note that VPs can consist of a single V or a V plus other words; for example, (f) is V + ADV and (c) is V + NP + PP.

A VP can be used as the predicate of a sentence—i.e., it combines with a subject NP to form a whole S, as shown in (9):

(9) a. Pat *loves music.*
b. Henry *wanted to leave.*

Another phrasal category is that of **adjective phrases** (ADJPs), such as those in (10):

(10) a. smart
b. very expensive
c. as tall as his father
d. smarter than the average bear
e. certain to win

Note that each of the words or phrases in (10) could be inserted into the syntactic frame in (11):

(11) John is ————

ADJPs are often used to modify nouns and thus often appear as elements of noun phrases; for instance, *a very expensive watch; anyone as tall as his father*.

Adverbial phrases (ADVPs), such as those in (12), are often used to modify verbs and adjectives and adverbs, and thus appear as constituents of VPs and ADJPs, as in (13).

(12) a. soundly
      b. fiercely
      c. as fluently as a native
      d. almost certainly

(13) a. speak Russian as fluently as a native (VP)
      b. fiercely loyal (ADJP)
      c. sleep soundly (VP)

Another phrasal syntactic category is that of **prepositional phrases** (PPs). PPs always consist of a preposition plus an NP:

(14) a. from Uganda
      b. with Howard and his dog
      c. for nothing
      d. to the head honcho

A PP can be a constituent of a wide range of phrases:

(15) a. go to the movies (VP)
      b. my friend from Uganda (NP)
      c. angry with Howard and his dog (ADJP)
      d. separately from the others (ADVP)

Sentences (Ss) also form a phrasal syntactic category. Sentences are, of course, often used by themselves:

(16) a. It is raining.
      b. Robin likes apples.

But a sentence may also appear as a element of another expression; for example, each of the following expressions contains a sentence.

(17) a. the fact that *it is raining* (NP)
      b. a student who met Leslie last Thursday (NP)
      c. discover that *it is raining* (VP)
      d. glad that *it is raining* (ADJP)

Note that any expression resulting from the combination of two or more smaller expressions by a **conjunction** belongs to the same category as the smaller ones do. Thus, both *Howard* and *his dog* are each separate NPs, and in (14b) and (15c) *Howard and his dog* is also an NP. Likewise, *faster than a speeding bullet and more powerful than a locomotive* is a larger ADJP containing two conjoined ADJPs; and similarly the sentence *It is raining, but it may sleet* contains two conjoined Ss.

Tree Diagrams

Tree diagrams are one way of graphically representing the structure of a sentence. In File 6.1 we saw that tree diagrams could represent which words grouped together to form constituents, and which, in turn, formed larger constituents. Now we see that each constituent in a sentence belongs either to some lexical or phrasal category. This can also be represented in the tree diagram by labeling each of the **nodes**, or points that indicate a constituent, with the name of the syntactic category to which the lexical or phrasal constituent belongs. For example, consider the sentence in (18):

(18) My mother likes her cats.

We can determine (with constituent tests) that the phrasal constituents of this sentence are the following:

     (a) my mother (NP)
     (b) likes her cats (VP)
     (c) her cats (NP)
     (d) my mother likes her cats (S)

We know that each word is a constituent as well, and we can determine each lexical category. A tree diagram representing the structure of this sentence looks like:

(19)

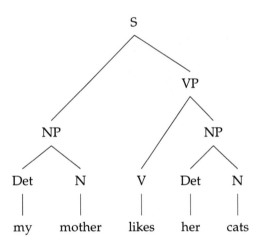

Note that the tree diagram represents many aspects of the structure of a sentence. First of all, the linear order is represented because the words appear in some specific order (in the above case, they are in the proper order). Second, the categories to which words and phrases belong are indicated; for example, the noun *mother* is labeled as being an N, and the phrase *my mother* is labeled as an NP. Furthermore, the hierarchical structure is represented by the lines, which indicate which words group to form constituents, and, in turn, which constituents join to form larger constituents. For example, the line from the DET above *her* and the line from the N above *cats* join at a node to indicate that the DET + N form a constituent. This constituent joins with the V above *likes* to form another constituent, as indicated by the lines above NP and V, which join at a node labeled VP.

Exercises

0. Draw a tree for the following sentence. (Answers to all zero problems can be found in Appendix A.)

    Many retired workers spend their time on relaxing hobbies.

1. Identify the phrasal category of the underlined constituent in the following sentences:

    a. We were in Holland <u>at that time</u>.
    b. <u>Our loud neighbors</u> will be away this weekend.
    c. The guests ate too much <u>at the reception</u>.
    d. Me and my friends play <u>basketball</u> every Saturday.
    e. <u>Over the holidays</u> I will be traveling to France.
    f. She painted a portrait of <u>her niece from Boston</u>.
    g. The experienced chefs complained about the <u>excessively sweet</u> sauce on the duck.
    h. The newborn babies <u>cried</u>.
    i. The building <u>across the street</u> is Oxley Hall.
    j. <u>Stars</u> can be seen best during the winter.
    k. <u>Which of these contradictory suggestions</u> should the conscientious health nut follow?
    l. <u>The twins and their mother</u> got sick from eating the egg salad.
    m. <u>Tom's</u> sister is a lawyer.
    n. <u>Alex tried all his tricks</u> but nothing worked.
    o. The cat on the couch <u>thinks you are crazy</u>.
    p. You have an <u>extremely efficient</u> secretary.
    q. The fact that <u>you can whistle better</u> doesn't impress me.
    r. I <u>strongly refuse to be involved in this</u>.
    s. <u>No one except Larry</u> can come up with such strange excuses.
    t. <u>Drinking and driving</u> should not be mixed.
    u. The lifeguard found <u>my cousin from Alabama's</u> ring in the pool.
    v. He joined us <u>silently but unwillingly</u>.

2. Draw tree diagrams for the following sentences.

    a. My father is an artist.
    b. The relatives of my husband live in Chicago.
    c. Robin drove her car into a tree.
    d. Chefs from many countries competed in a difficult contest.
    e. The teacher threw a book out the window.
    f. That dentist charged too much money for the dentures.
    g. The walk through the park was very pleasant.
    h. The birds sang.
    i. Tonika's favorite show is about a rich family from California.
    j. Some people like cats and dogs, but many people hate snakes.

File 6.4

Subcategories

Subcategories within Lexical Categories

According to our characterization of the lexical category of verbs given in File 6.2, *sleep, assume,* and *buy* belong to this category, since they all share the morphological and syntactic frames for verbs given there. However, if we look more closely at the syntactic frames in which these verbs appear, we can see that, although they behave enough alike to be grouped together as verbs, they behave differently from one another in other ways. Consider the fact that *sleep,* but not *think* or *buy,* can occur in the syntactic frame in (1) (which gives us examples like *I left, he slept, the children played*); *think,* but not *sleep* or *buy,* can occur in (2) (which gives us examples like *everyone knows the earth is round* and *Lucy thinks it's raining*); *buy,* but not *sleep* or *think,* can occur in (3) (e.g., *we bought a new one, my brother ate two hamburgers*); and *give,* but not *sleep* or *think,* can occur in (4) (e.g., *Sarah gave her daughter a new toy*).

(1) NP____
(2) NP____ S
(3) NP____ NP
(4) NP____ NP NP

Just as not all verbs share exactly the same syntactic frames, so are there differences among adjectives. For example, although *asleep* and *utter* are both adjectives, *asleep* cannot occur in the syntactic frame for adjectives repeated below as (5), and *utter* cannot appear in the syntactic frame repeated below as (6), although *asleep* can fit in (6) (*the baby is asleep*) and *utter* can fit in (5) (*that utter fool*):

(5) DET _____ N   but not * *an asleep baby*
(6) LINKING VERB _____   but not **that fool is utter*

In other words, many adjectives can fit into both frames (5) and (6), but not all adjectives can. What this suggests is that the classification of words into lexical categories, even though it does capture many generalizations about the behavior of words, is not sufficient when we are dealing with differences *within* a lexical category. We need to make finer distinctions than can be made using the lexical categories we have already discussed. We will further subdivide lexical categories into groups of words, or **subcategories**, that share common properties within a lexical category. Some of the common subcategories within various lexical categories are discussed below.

Verbs

Intransitive Verbs (V_i): Verbs that can occur in the syntactic frame in (1) above will be called intransitive verbs. Intransitive verbs do not take an object NP, which is why nothing follows the verb slot in (1). Examples of this subcategory of verbs include *run, walk, sleep, sigh,* and *sneeze.*

Transitive Verbs (V_t): Verbs that occur in the syntactic frame in (3) are called transitive verbs because they take an NP object, which follows the verb in (3). Examples of this subcategory of verbs are *buy, meet, kill, throw,* and *see.*

Ditransitive Verbs (V_{dt}): Ditransitive verbs take two NPs as their object, as the syntactic frame in (4) shows. Examples of this subcategory are *give, sell*, and *tell*.

Verbs with Sentential Complements (V_s): These are verbs that take a following whole sentence, as (2) shows. Some of them require a **complementizer** (COMP) plus a sentence; the words *that, if*, and *whether* are complementizers. (Complementizers form another closed class of lexical items.) Some verbs requiring sentence complements may *optionally* take the complementizer *that*. The examples below contain verbs of this subcategory.

(7) The ancients *believed* (that) the earth was flat.
(8) The doctor *asked* if she felt any pain.
(9) The witnesses *say* (that) the light was red.

Other examples of this subcategory of verb are *assert, claim, think*, and *deny*.

Linking Verbs (V_l): This small subcategory contains verbs such as *seem, appear, be, look*, and *become*. The characteristic peculiar to this class is the ability to occur with phrases of different kinds following them—ADJPs, NPs, and PPs:

(10) You look marvelous.
        My sister became a doctor.
        This book is from the library.

Adjectives

As mentioned above, most, but not all, adjectives can occur in both the syntactic frames given in (5) and (6). Adjectives like *long, boring*, and *clean* can occur in both; others, such as *utter* and *total*, can occur only in (5) (between a DET and an N); and still others, such as *ajar* and *asleep*, can occur only in (6) (following a linking verb). We will assign no particular names to these subcategories.

There is also a difference between what are called **stative** and **nonstative** adjectives. Semantically, stative adjectives (including *tall, blue*, and *wooden*) denote more permanent qualities, whereas nonstative ones (including *impatient, kind*, and *naughty*) denote more or less temporary or changeable qualities. There are syntactic differences between these two subcategories of adjectives as well; this can be seen in the following patterns. Stative adjectives cannot occur in (11) (i.e., they cannot occur in the progressive aspect). However, nonstative adjectives can occur in both (11) and (12).

(11) You are being very _____ (e.g., You are being very kind/*You are being very tall)
(12) You are very _____ (e.g., You are very kind/You are very tall)

Nouns

Two important subcategories within the category of nouns are **count** and **mass** nouns. Count nouns, as the name suggests, denote objects that are discrete, countable units (e.g., *table, song, computer*), whereas mass nouns usually refer to things that cannot be counted (*water, wheat, furniture*). Another class of nouns is **abstract** nouns (*honesty, peace*), which generally behave more like mass nouns than count nouns. The difference in the syntactic behavior of these subcategories can be illustrated by the fact that count nouns, but not mass or abstract nouns, can combine with determiners that make reference to numbers. Hence only count nouns occur in the syntactic frame in (13) (cf., for example, *a table* with **a furniture*). In contrast, singular abstract and mass nouns can occur without any determiner at all, as in (14), but singular count nouns cannot (compare *water is a liquid* with **computer is a machine*).

(13) A/two/every/few _____

(14) _____ VP

Notice that count nouns, if they are in the plural form, can occur without a determiner and can fill the slot in (14) (e.g., *Computers are a must, *computer is a must, I sell computers, *I sell computer*).

Some Suggestions

1. The above discussion on subcategories is not exhaustive; however, it should be an adequate introduction to the idea that words of a lexical category, while sharing enough properties to be classified as members of the same lexical category, might still show enough differences to warrant further subclassifications. You should expect to find more instances of subcategories than have been discussed here.

2. The same word can be used in more than one way, and therefore can belong to more than one subcategory of a lexical category (just as a word like *walk* can belong to more than one lexical category). For instance, the verb *eat* can be used either as a transitive verb (i.e., with a noun phrase object) or as an intransitive verb (without an object), as the examples below show:

    (15) I ate an apple.
          I ate.

3. Sometimes speakers leave out information that was given earlier in the sentence or in the conversation. For instance, one could say *She asked me to follow her, and I followed*, meaning 'She asked me to follow her and I followed her'. Could one conclude that the verb *follow* is intransitive, since the second instance of that verb in the actual utterance has no object noun phrase after it? No, because the verb cannot be used without an object except where the information about the object can be retrieved from previous parts of the conversation. Notice that it would be strange to say *I followed* without any relevant information available from previous conversation. True intransitive verbs do not need any such carried-over information about their objects because they do not *have* objects. Notice also that true intransitive verbs can never have an object noun phrase, whereas *follow* can. Compare *I followed her* with **I sneezed her*, and *Who did you follow?* with **Who did you sneeze?* Thus it is necessary to separate out conversational factors from the properties of a word that are inherent to it.

File 6.5 Phrase Structure Rules

Part of every language user's knowledge of his or her language is the knowledge of how constituents are put together and categorized in that language. This special sort of knowledge can be represented as a set of rules called **phrase structure rules (PS rules)**. In this file, we consider the nature of such rules and discuss several important properties that make them useful for describing the syntactic competence of language users.

Phrase Structure Grammar

Before we discuss phrase structure rules as tools for studying the syntax of human languages, let us look at the nature of grammatical descriptions that use PS rules. PS rules can be understood as simple instructions for building larger constituents from smaller ones, and they also give information about the order in which the constituents appear, and their categories. Thus, the PS rule in (1a) gives the instructions in (1b) and (1c):

(1) a. S → NP VP

     b. To build a constituent of the category S, take a constituent of the category NP and combine it with another constituent of the category VP.

     c. In building an S constituent in this manner, put the NP constituent first and the VP constituent after it.

Thus (1a) merely says a sentence is made up of an NP and a VP in that order. As part of the descriptive devices available in a phrase structure syntax, we have tree structures (already discussed in File 6.3). There is a direct connection between PS rules and tree structures. For instance, the rule in (1a) allows you to construct a tree structure as in (2a), but the ones in (2b) and (2c) (among numerous other trees) are not allowed by (1a):

(2)

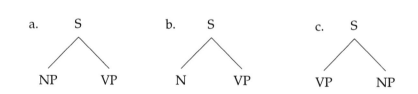

To gain a precise understanding of the instruction-giving aspect of PS rules, let us for a moment take examples of PS rules that do not describe English or any other human language. Let us create what linguists call a "toy grammar" for a "language" whose lexical categories consist of *a, b, c,* and *d.* Its phrasal categories are *X* and *Y,* in addition to *S* (for *sentence*), which is also a phrasal category. The instructions (i.e., PS rules) for building sentences in this language are given in (3):

(3) a. S → X Y
    b. X → ab
    c. X → a
    d. Y → bcd
    e. Y → cd Y
    f. Y → cd

Now what "sentences" are acceptable (i.e., grammatical, able to be produced with this set of rules) and what sentences are ungrammatical (i.e., cannot be produced using this system of rules)? The shortest sentence produced by this system is *acd*, the derivation of which is given in (4) using tree structures:

(4)

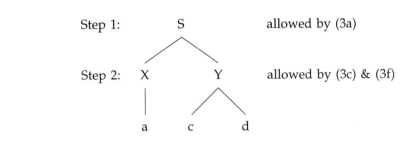

At this point, no further instructions can be carried out, and the sequence *acd* has been successfully derived in accordance with the rules. On the other hand, the sequences **abd* or **abc* cannot be derived using the instructions in (3). The sequences *abcd, abbcd, acdcd, abcdcdcd,* and *abcdcdcdcd* are all grammatical in this language, however. Can you work out which rules must apply to derive each of these?

The simple rule system in (3), far from being a grammar for human languages, still is not as simple as it looks. The "language" it produces has some of the salient properties of the syntax of human languages that we wish to focus on. To be specific, it has the properties of **generativity, ambiguity, hierarchical structure,** and **infinite recursion** (i.e., productivity). We will now see how the grammar in (3) shows these characteristics.

First, it is **generative** because it does not *list* the grammatical sentences in the language; instead, it gives a schematic strategy for getting the *infinite* set of grammatical sentences using a *finite* set of rules. Recall that languages that have productivity (i.e., infinite output) cannot be described by listing. Thus, this toy grammar has one of the desirable properties that we would want in a grammar for human languages.

Second, human languages contain some structurally **ambiguous** sentences, and a grammar for a human language should reflect this property. The grammar in (3) has the power to produce structurally ambiguous sentences. Consider the sentence *abcd* in this language. It could be derived in two different ways, each resulting in a different constituent structure, i.e., a different way of grouping words together. The two different derivations are given in (5):

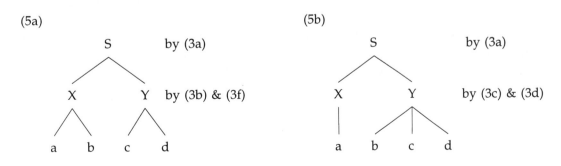

Example (5a) shows a structure where *ab* is a constituent and *cd* is another, since by using (3b) one could combine *a* and *b* to form *X*; and by using (3f), *c* and *d* can be combined to form Y. The grouping is [*ab*] [*cd*] in (5a). In (5b), on the other hand, the grouping is [*a*] [*bcd*], using (3c) and (3d). If (3b), (3c), or (3d) were to be removed from (3), the grammar in (3) would lose the power to represent structural ambiguity, since it is the presence of *all* these rules that allow *b* to be part of either X or Y.

Third, the language produced by (3) contains infinitely many sentences, just as human languages do. Rule (3e) can be used *ad infinitum* to keep generating longer sentences (i.e., *cd* can be added any number of times), and no matter how many sentences have already been generated, there are always more sentences that the grammar can generate. Rule (3e) is an example of a **recursive** rule. Example (6) shows how this works:

(6)

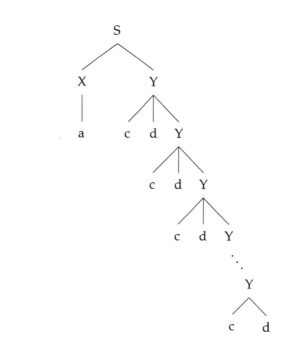

Finally, the grammar produces sentences with **hierarchical structure**, not just linear order. It has phrasal categories X and Y, which have internal complexity of their own.

With the properties of PS rules that (3) illustrates in the background, let us now look at a PS grammar for human languages, focusing on English.

Phrase Structure Rules for English

As a speaker of English, you know how to put together constituents of each syntactic category of English. (This knowledge is, of course, largely unconscious: you may not be able to explain how to form complex constituents in English, but your linguistic behavior still shows that you know how to do it.) You know, for example, that a sentence (S) of English can be formed by joining a noun phrase (NP) with a verb phrase (VP), as in (7). You also know that, as shown in (8), an NP may be formed by joining a determiner (DET) with a constituent containing a noun (N). And you know that a VP may consist of a (transitive) verb followed by a direct object NP, as in (9).

(7) S =	NP	+	VP
	John		snored.
	Everyone		fled the volcano.
	The mayor		smoked a cigar.
	A book		lay on the table.

(8) NP =	Det	+	N
	the		mayor
	a		book
	every		student
	my		python

(9) VP =	V	+	NP
	fled		the volcano
	smoked		a cigar
	imitated		a flamingo
	squeezed		some fresh orange juice

We can represent these three pieces of information in a succinct way with the following three PS rules.

(10)	S	→	NP VP
(11)	NP	→	Det N
(12)	VP	→	V NP

The arrow in these rules can be read as "may consist of." Thus rule (10) is just a concise way of saying "a sentence may consist of a noun phrase followed by a verb phrase"; similarly, rule (11) just says "a noun phrase may consist of a determiner followed by a noun." Now, what does rule (12) say?

Recall from File 6.3 that a syntactic category is a group of constituents with different structures that share certain properties. NPs, for example, could be composed of DET + N, as in (8) above, but they may also have the following structures:

(13) My uncle from France

A rule for this NP would look like:

(14) NP   →   NP PP

Rules (10), (11), (12), and (14) specify five ways in which constituents can be combined to form larger, more complex constituents. Some constituents, however, do not result from the combination of smaller constituents; instead, they consist of a single word. For example, a noun phrase may just consist of a proper name (e.g., *John, Paris*), a plural noun (e.g., *elephants, leaves*), or a noun referring to a substance (e.g., *clay, gasoline*); similarly, a verb phrase may just consist of an intransitive verb, such as *sneeze, die, vanish,* or *elapse*. These sorts of knowledge can also be represented with PS rules:

(15) NP → N
(16) VP → V

The set of rules for NPs, so far (11), (14), (15), and (16), express the generalization that all of these structures belong to one category by the name of NP. However, given the PS rules we have developed so far, the grammar (i.e., the collection of all the rules) will generate ungrammatical as well as grammatical sentences. For example, using the entire set of rules given above, the following tree structure can be generated:

(17)

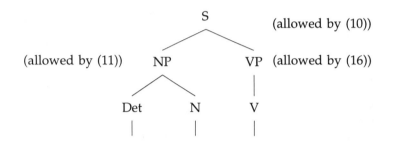

Now, words from the lexicon must be selected from the appropriate lexical categories and inserted below the lexical category nodes in this tree. But any word that belongs to the category V may be inserted, including intransitive verbs. Inserting such a word would generate a sentence such as *The children chased*, which of course is not grammatical. Therefore, information about subcategories must be included in the PS rules. Thus, (16) would be written:

(18) VP → V_i,

where the subscript (i) indicates that this V must be chosen from the subcategory of intransitive verbs. Transitive verbs (verbs that must take NP objects) will also be called for in other PS rules. What would the PS rule for VPs containing transitive verbs look like?

A similar situation exists for NPs. Leaving (15) as it is would generate a sentence such as *boy woke up in the middle of night*. How might rule (15) be rewritten to prevent this?

It is very important to understand that PS rules express generalizations over many individual sentences. The term **rule** is used because a rule describes a pattern found in a language. Many sentences can have the structure in (19):

(19)

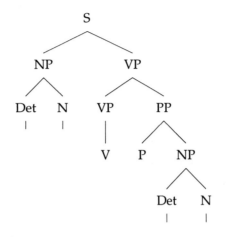

For example, *The dog ran through the woods, The woman jumped on the bug, Some students read during the night, Our books fell to the floor,* and *The rain fell from the sky* all have this structure, and this pattern is reflected in the fact that the same PS rules generate each of these sentences.

However, once you understand the structure of a particular sentence, you can determine what PS rules must be involved in deriving that structure. For example, using constituency tests and our knowledge of lexical and phrasal categories, we can determine that the structure of the sentence *The man in the kitchen drives a truck* is as follows:

(20)

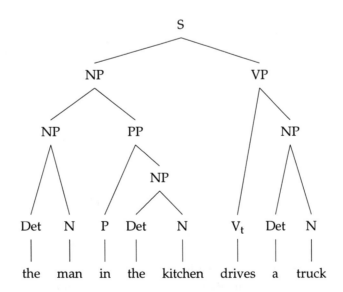

Starting at the S node, we can formulate the PS rules that generate this structure. The S is composed of an NP and a VP (as usual), so a rule that expresses this fact would be written as (10) above: S → NP VP. The highest NP is composed of an NP and a PP. A rule that expresses this fact would be written as NP → NP PP, and so on.

Infinity and Recursion

One of the things linguists attempt to do is to analyze the structure of sentences in a given language and construct a set of rules that can generate the grammatical sentences of that language but that does not allow the generation of ungrammatical sentences. In addition, the set of rules must be able to generate an infinite number of sentences. One of the ways this can be accomplished is by using recursive rules, as discussed above. One example of recursion in English involves the pair of rules in (21) and (22) below.

(21) NP   →   NP PP
(22) PP   →   P NP

Together these rules generate phrases such as *the man with the dog, the painter from California, some preachers in their pulpits, a large ant in my drink*, and so on. But notice that when one rule is applied in succession, the pair is recursive; note that since NP occurs on the left of the arrow in (21) and on the right in (22), it would be possible to continue to use them over and over to form a tree such as that in (23):

(23)

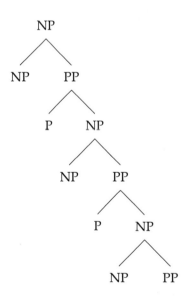

Of course, every sentence terminates at some point. However, there always exists the possibility that given a sentence of a certain length, another one that was longer could be created. Thus, an infinite number of structures could be generated from just these two rules alone.

The property of infinity is the result of other phenomena as well. Consider:

(24) He's a big dog.
      He's a big, furry dog.
      He's a big, furry, shy dog.
      He's a big, furry, shy, energetic dog.

It seems English allows any number of adjectives to be inserted into the NP. We can represent this fact in the PS rules with some extra notation. An asterisk on a constituent in a PS rule means "use any number from 0 to infinity." Thus the rule:

(25) NP   →   DET ADJ* N

is the way to express "an NP may consist of a DET, any number of ADJs from 0 to infinity, and an N."

A similar phenomenon exists for constituents involving conjunctions (CONJ). Consider the following sentence:

(26) Mary walked to Zeke's house.

We can add on to this sentence in a number of ways to form an infinite number of new sentences. One way to add on to sentence (26) is to add more NPs with conjunctions, e.g.:

(27) John and Mary walked to Zeke's house.
      Bill, John, and Mary walked to Zeke's house.
      Jane, Bill, John, and Mary walked to Zeke's house.

In principle, there is no limit to the number of new NPs that we could connect to the subject of (26) in this way. Similarly, we can use *and* to connect one or more new VPs to the predicate of (26):

(28) Mary walked to Zeke's house and delivered the letter.
      Mary walked to Zeke's house, delivered the letter, and ran home.
      Mary walked to Zeke's house, delivered the letter, ran home, and made dinner.

No matter how many new VPs we connect to the predicate of (26), we will never reach a point at which another one cannot be added. Likewise, we can connect any number of new prepositional phrases to *to Zeke's house* in (26):

(29) Mary walked to Zeke's house, to the post office, to the bookstore, and to the new Burger King.

And we can connect any number of new sentences to (26) itself:

(30) Mary walked to Zeke's house, John drove to the post office, Bill stopped by the bookstore, and Jane checked out the new Burger Chef.

Thus, another reason why there are an infinite number of English sentences is that it is possible to use conjunctions such as *and* and *or* to connect an indefinitely large number of expressions of any given syntactic category.

Again, with some new notation, we can write PS rules that will generate all of the sentences above. Let us illustrate how this is done for the NP phrases discussed so far, and leave it as an exercise for the reader to develop PS rules for the other constituents. If we examine the structures of the sentences in (27), we note that the addition of new NPs within the subject NP follows a pattern. When two

NPs make up the subject NP, the conjuction separates them, e.g., *Mary and John*. When a third NP is added, the conjunction still precedes the final NP, and when a fourth is added this pattern remains. Thus, an NP may consist of any number of NPs, the conjunction, and another NP. We can't use the asterisk above that means "from 0 to infinity" since we don't want to allow the sentence *and the man went to the store* (where *and* is joining NPs and not Ss), so we'll make use of the symbol $^+$, which means "any number from 1 to infinity." Thus, we can express the pattern of conjoined NPs with the rule in (31):

(31) NP → NP$^+$ CONJ NP

The three smallest trees that (31) generates are those in (32)

(32)

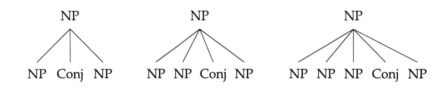

Some Phrase Structure Rules for English

Below is a list of some PS rules for English, some of which have been introduced above. This list is a convenient reference, but it is by no means exhaustive.

i.	S	→	NP VP
ii.	NP	→	DET ADJP* N
iii.	NP	→	PRO
iv.	NP	→	N_{pr}
v.	NP	→	(DET) ADJP* N_{pl}
vi.	NP	→	(DET) ADJP* N_m
vii.	NP	→	NP PP
viii.	VP	→	AUX VP
ix.	VP	→	V_i
x.	VP	→	V_t NP
xi.	VP	→	V_{dt} NP NP
xii.	VP	→	VP PP

xiii.	ADJP	$\rightarrow$	ADV* ADJ
xiv.	PP	$\rightarrow$	P NP
xv.	NP	$\rightarrow$	NP^+ CONJ NP
xvi.	S	$\rightarrow$	S^+ CONJ S

Note that the subscripts stand for the following subcategories: $(_{pl})$ for plural nouns, $(_{pr})$ for proper nouns, $(_c)$ for count nouns, and $(_m)$ for mass nouns; $(_i)$ for intransitive verbs, $(_t)$ for transitive verbs, and $(_{dt})$ for ditransitives. Parentheses indicate an *optional* element.

Summary

In this file we have discussed phrase structure rules, which are linguists' models of a language user's knowledge of how constituents are put together and categorized in his or her language. PS rules may be regarded as generating a certain set of tree diagrams—or, in a related sense, as generating a certain set of sentence structures; a set of PS rules that generates sentence structures in some language, as opposed to just listing them, is thus a generative set of rules. Although there is an infinite number of possible sentences in English or in any human language, it is possible to write a finite set of rules that generates them all. This is because of two special properties of PS rules: on the one hand, a single PS rule may allow an expression to consist of an indefinitely large number of constituents; and on the other, a finite set of PS rules may be recursive—that is, may be used over and over again to generate a tree of indefinite length.

Exercises

1. Examine the following set of rules and answer the following questions *based only on these rules.*

S	$\rightarrow$	NP VP		DET	=	the, some
NP	$\rightarrow$	DET N		N	=	elephants, raccoons, tigers, bears,
VP	$\rightarrow$	V_t NP				grain, peanuts, mice
VP	$\rightarrow$	V_i		V_t	=	eat, scare
VP	$\rightarrow$	VP^+ CONJ VP		V_i	=	gallop, swim
				CONJ	=	and

    a. For each of the following sentences, circle *yes* if these rules generate it; circle *no* if it is not generated by these rules.

i.	The elephants and the mice eat peanuts.	yes no
ii.	Elephants eat peanuts.	yes no
iii.	The tigers scare the grain.	yes no
iv.	The raccoons eat the grain, scare the mice, and swim.	yes no
v.	The tigers gallop.	yes no
vi.	The tigers eat some grain and scare the mice.	yes no

    b. Draw the trees for two of the sentences for which you circled *yes.*

c.   What changes can be made for this set of rules so that it will generate the sentences for which you circled *no*? *Be explicit.*

d.   Does this set of rules generate an infinite number of sentences? Why or why not?

2.   a.   Write a set of phrase structure rules that generates all of the following sentences. (Hint: draw the tree diagrams for each sentence first.)

i.   John strummed his guitar.
ii.   Janet played the trumpet.
iii. Marilyn sang.
iv. Larry danced.

b.   Give a sentence that your set of rules does not generate.

c.   Write a single rule that, when added to your set of rules, allows it to generate both of the following sentences:

v.   John sang and danced.
vi. John sang, danced, and played the trumpet.

d.   Give two other sentences that your revised set of rules now generates.

3.   In File 6.4 on subcategories, the following type of sentence was introduced:

i.   Sally claimed Bill bought the car.
ii.   Robert said he plays the piano.
iii. Cathy denied her mother lives in Reno.

a.   In prose, say what the structure of the verb phrases in these sentences is.

b.   Write a single rule that, in conjunction with the other rules on pages 200–201, generates all of the verb phrases in (i)–(iii).

c.   List the other phrase structure rules that are needed to generate all of the sentences in (i)–(iii).

d.   Show how the rule you have written for the verb phrases results in recursion in conjunction with (an)other rule(s). (Draw a tree diagram and explain how the rules are recursive.)

4.   Look back at the list of phrase structure rules on pages 200–201. Examine (xii) carefully.

a.   Think of at least two sentences that would have the structures generated by (xii) in conjunction with (ix) and then two generated by (xii) and (x).

5.   Look back at the list of phrase structure rules on pages 200–201. You may have noticed that the PS rules for NPs with an ADJ constituent and the ADJP were modified somewhat from what had been presented in the text. For ease of reference one such NP rule and the ADJP rule are rewritten below:

NP   →   DET ADJP* N$_C$
ADJP   →   ADV* ADJ

Determine why the ADJP* was added to the NP rule, replacing just an ADJ* (i.e., why an adjective *phrase*, and not just an adjective is needed in the NP rule), by thinking up sentences in English that have a structure that would necessitate the modified rule. (Hint: consider adverbs such as *very* and *quite*.)

File 6.6   Transformations

File 6.5 demonstrates how syntactic patterns of a language can be described by phrase structure rules. But not all sentence patterns can be described efficiently by such rules alone. For example, the sentences in (1) are examples of English sentences that cannot be generated by the PS rules for building sentences:

(1) a. What can Mary accomplish?
      b. What should John give Bill?
      c. Who will Sheila call?

The sentences in (1), all of which are questions, are best analyzed as systematic variations of the ordinary (non-question, declarative) sentences in (2), which our PS rules *can* generate; thus, questions are systematically related to the ordinary sentences:

(2) a. Mary can accomplish a great deal.
      b. John should give Bill his address.
      c. Sheila will call my aunt.

This is somewhat similar to the systematic relationship between, say, singular *book* and plural *books*. That is, given the singular form of nouns, and a systematic way of deriving the plural forms from singular nouns, the plural forms need not be stated individually in the lexicon (except in irregular cases, which are relatively few).

We can similarly derive questions from declarative sentences. One way to do it is to have ordinary PS rules generate the declarative sentences, then change them into questions by using a new kind of rule called a **transformation**. Transformations express changes that may be made in the structure of sentences generated by PS rules. For example, consider the "echo questions" in (3):

(3) a. Mary can accomplish what?
      b. John should give Bill what?
      c. Sheila will call who?

Like the sentences in (2), the sentences in (3) are generated with PS rules alone—in fact, largely the same PS rules used to generate the sentences in (2). (A new PS rule for the wh-pronouns (PRO$_{wh}$) *what* and *who* will be needed: NP → PRO$_{wh}$.) The sentences in (3) may either be left as is or may undergo a transformation that moves the elements of these sentences around and forms the sentences in (1). Unlike PS rules, we will express transformations in words rather than in formal notation. Nevertheless, they are rules in the sense that they express patterns in language. The transformation that forms questions can be expressed as follows:

Wh-Question Transformation

    (i)   Place the first auxiliary of the sentence to the left of the subject NP (the first NP in the sentence).
    (ii) Move the PRO$_{wh}$ (e.g., *what, who, where,* and *how*) to the beginning of the sentence.

In general, transformations change sentences created by PS rules into sentences with equivalent meanings, but different structures. As such they give an account for why some sentences seem to be related to other sentences. These changes are accomplished by adding or deleting words, or by rearranging word order.

Part (i) of the Wh-Question Transformation tells us that (3a), *Mary can accomplish what?*, can be converted into *Can Mary accomplish what?* Part (ii) of the transformation further converts this into *What can Mary accomplish?*, which is (1a). Stop at this point to see that this transformation correctly converts (3b) into (1b), and converts (3c) into (1c). What is the result of applying this transformation to the sentence *I must put the beer where?* In other words, the syntactic structure of a sentence such as *What can Mary accomplish?* is described in two steps: the PS rules of English form the basic sentence *Mary can accomplish what?*, then the Wh-Question Transformation forms the question from this. Linguists refer to the form of a sentence produced by PS rules alone as the **Deep Structure** of a sentence, and the form that the sentence has after one or more transformations has been applied as the **Surface Structure** of the sentence. For example, the sentence which has the Surface Structure (1a) has the Deep Structure (3a); the same goes for (1b) and (3b), and (1c) and (3c). Of course, the sentence (3a) is also a grammatical English sentence as it stands, and if we are describing (3a) by itself, we might say that its Deep Structure is the same as its Surface Structure, even though no transformation was used to form it.

Why do linguists adopt this complicated two-step analysis of the sentences like those in (1)? That is, why couldn't we just as well describe such sentences directly by PS rules alone, without making use of transformations at all? The answer is that no set of PS rules (as they are defined) will allow us to generate all the sentences in (1) *and no ungrammatical sentences*. Let's attempt to alter the PS rules we have to illustrate why this approach is not workable.

First, we will need to make use of the PS rule in (4), which was mentioned earlier in the file. This rule is not part of the problem—it's needed to generate even the sentences in (3) where no transformation applies.

(4)　NP　　→　　PRO$_{wh}$

To generate the sentences in (1) with only PS rules, we will need to add another rule to our set of PS rules:

(5)　S　　→　　PRO$_{wh}$ AUX S

It may appear that the addition of this rule alone is sufficient. For instance, when added to the PS rules we have already, it allows the set to generate the following tree structure for sentence (1a):

(6)

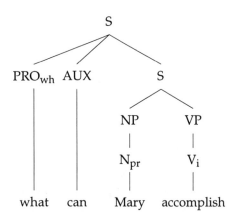

The problem with the tree structure in (6) is that *accomplish* is a transitive verb (V_t), and therefore, it can't be inserted under a V_i node. The only rule in our set that introduces a V_t node is:

(7) VP   → V_t NP

But using this rule to generate (1a) creates a different problem. Consider the tree that uses (7):

(8)

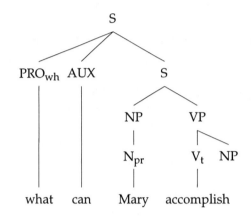

Now we have an "empty" NP node (no lexical item has been inserted), which is not allowed. Inserting something under the node results in ungrammatical sentences, as in (9):

(9) *What can Mary accomplish a great deal?

Perhaps our dilemma can be resolved by adding another PS rule to our set:

(10) VP   → V_t

Now we can generate a tree structure for (1a) that allows us to insert a transitive verb under a transitive verb node and doesn't leave an empty NP node:

(11)

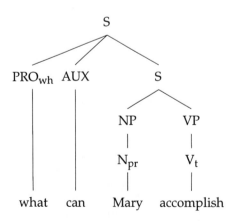

But now that the rule in (10) is in our set, we can combine it with other rules. Unfortunately, nothing prevents the following ungrammatical sentence from being generated:

(12)

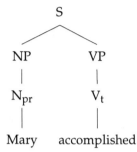

It should be clear that no set of PS rules can do the job. Thus we need the Wh-Question Transformation.

To summarize this discussion, we have, in effect, observed that a set of questions in English beginning with *what, who*, etc., lacks exactly one NP to the right of the verb that would be present in the corresponding declarative sentence. The Wh-Question Transformation analysis of such sentences describes the situation correctly, since it stipulates that an NP is moved to the beginning of the sentence as the sentence is transformed. This kind of fact about syntax is just what cannot easily be described by PS rules alone.

Having discussed one transformation in detail, we now present two additional examples of transformations in English. We will not explain the reasons for proposing these transformations as we did for Wh-Question Transformation because, in some cases, these reasons are more complicated to describe.

The Passive

(a) John ate an apple.   (Deep Structure, before transformation)

(b) An apple was eaten by John.   (Surface Structure, after transformation)

Passive Transformation: Move the subject NP (the NP that begins the sentence) to the end of the sentence, insert the preposition *by* just before it, and move the object NP (the NP just after the main verb) to the beginning of the sentence. Then, change the verb to the past participle form and insert the appropriate form of the AUX *be* after the subject NP.

Verb-Particle Shift

(a) The surgeon sewed up the wound.   (Deep Structure, before transformation)

(b) The surgeon sewed the wound up.   (Surface Structure, after transformation)

Verb-Particle Transformation: Move the particle (the preposition-like word immediately to the right of the verb) after the first NP following the verb.

Exercises

1. Examples (a) and (b) are definitely not grammatical questions in English:

   (a) *What has an hour elapsed?
   (b) *What will John disappear?

   This fact is related to another fact about the verbs *elapse* and *disappear*, namely, that these verbs cannot be followed by an NP in declarative sentences; a comparison of (c), (d), with (e), (f) confirms this:

   (c) An hour has elapsed.
   (d) John will disappear.
   (e) *An hour has elapsed the clock.
   (f) *John will disappear the rabbit.

   Think about the Wh-Question Transformation. Why would this rule not apply to a sentence that used a verb such as *elapse* or *disappear*?

2. Assume that each set of sentences in **A** and **B** below are related by a transformation. **A** represents the deep structure, and **B** represents the surface structure. Describe the kind of transformation needed to "convert" the **A** sentences into the **B** sentences.

	A	**B**
i.	a. Ralph gave Flo the apple.	a. Ralph gave the apple to Flo.
	b. The pitcher threw the catcher the ball.	b. The pitcher threw the ball to the catcher.
	c. The salesman sold the manager a car.	c. The salesman sold a car to the manager.
ii.	a. Jack will marry a German, and Bill will marry a German, too.	a. Jack will marry a German, and Bill will, too.
	b. Susan has eaten lobster, and her mother has eaten lobster, too.	b. Susan has eaten lobster, and her mother has, too.
	c. Jo is wearing a sweater, and Bob is wearing a sweater, too.	c. Jo is wearing a sweater, and Bob is, too.
iii.	a. Larry ran up the stairs.	a. Up the stairs ran Larry.
	b. Three soldiers walked into the room.	b. Into the room walked three soldiers.
	c. The boss stormed out the door.	c. Out the door stormed the boss.

3. For each deep structure below, determine which transformations mentioned in the text and in Exercise 2 can be applied. In some cases, more than one transformation can be applied to the same sentence.

   a. The boy can eat the beans.
   b. The black cat walked up the street.
   c. The millionaire gave the money to the young woman.
   d. The teacher looked up the word.
   e. Everyone will see the show.

File 6.7   Word Order Typology

In a declarative sentence in English, the subject precedes the verb and the object follows it, e.g., [*the cat*] [*chased*] [*the mouse*]. English is referred to as an SVO language (where S refers to *subject*, V to *verb*, and O to *object*). Only 35% of the world's languages display this same word order, however. Some place the verb at the beginning of the sentence, followed by the subject, then the object and are thus labeled VSO languages. Irish, Arabic, and Welsh are among the 19% of the world's languages that have this word order. VOS languages, which place the verb first, followed by the object then the subject, also exist, although they are quite rare. (Only 2% of all languages are VOS types.) The most prevalent type of word order is SOV, where the subject precedes the object, but the verb is placed at the end of the sentence. Forty-four percent of the world's languages are SOV types, including Russian and Turkish. In addition, there are languages (such as Dyirbal, an Australian aboriginal language) in which the normal order of subject, verb, and object is remarkably free. Clearly, there is no set of word order rules that is valid for all languages.

An interesting fact about word order typology is that within phrasal categories languages tend to place the head of the phrase either consistently before its modifiers and complements or after its modifiers and complements. The **head** of a phrase is the central, *obligatory* member of the phrase (e.g., an NP always has an N). Phrasal categories are typically named after their heads; so, the head of an NP is N, the head of a PP is P, the head of an ADJP is ADJ, etc. (But note that although V is usually the head of VP, when AUX occurs in a VP, it is the head of the VP, which isn't contradictory, since AUXs are also a subtype of verb.) The other constituents in phrases are either modifiers, which serve to modify the meaning of the head, or complements, which are other constituents that typically occur with the head. Languages can be roughly classified as either **head-initial** or **head-final**. Some head-non-head ordering combinations are given below.

	Type of Phrase	Head-Initial Languages		Head-Final Languages	
		Head	Non-head	Non-head	Head
a.	VP	V_t	(object) NP	(object) NP	V_t
b.	VP	AUX	VP	VP	AUX
c.	PP	P	NP	NP	P
d.	NP	NP	relative clause	relative clause	NP
e.	NP	N	possessive NP	possessive NP	N
f.	NP	N	ADJP	ADJP	N

There is a special term for a "preposition" that appears in a head-final language: "postposition." They usually serve the same function as a preposition but appear after the noun phrase. So in (c) above, the capital *P* can stand for either "preposition" or "postposition." In a language such as Japanese, which is generally SOV (i.e., head final), the grammatical relationship between words is often expressed using postpositions. See the exercises below for some examples of postpositions in Hindi and Japanese.

It is important to note that a particular language does not necessarily display the ordering relations of one of these types exclusively, even though the majority of the world's languages do exhibit consistent ordering relations across phrasal categories. English, for example, has mostly head-initial characteristics, but it also has some head-final characteristics. Specifically, English has the head-initial characteristics a–e above, but also possesses the head-final characteristics e and f. For example,

Head-Initial Features	***Head-Final Features***
a. eat apples	
b. may go	
c. at home	
d. man who left	
e. cover of the book	e. the book's cover
	f. good food

A language is classified as head-initial or head-final according to the majority of its ordering relations with phrases. Once again, the distinction between head-initial and head-final languages is a significant one because most languages tend to lean strongly one way or the other.

Exercises

1. Following are some example phrases from Hindi (a language spoken in northern India), French, and Japanese. First analyze the constituent structure of each sentence or phrase: what are the constituents of each sentence; what are the constituents of each phrase? How are the relationships between the words in a phrase indicated: by word order alone, or by pre- or postpostions? Then determine whether the language is SVO, VSO, VOS, or SOV. Then, based on the sentences given, classify the three languages into the two language types, head-initial or head-final, with respect to each of the ordering relationships of a–f.

   a.   Hindi

   i.   Ram-ne   seb   kʰaːya
          Ram   *apple*   *ate*
          'Ram ate an apple.'

   ii.   Ram   Angrezi   bol   səkta   hɛ
          Ram   *English*   *speak*   *able*   *is*
          'Ram can speak English.'

   iii.   larke-ne   čari-se   kutte-ko   maːra
          boy   *stick-with*   *dog*   *hit*
          'The boy hit the dog with a stick.'

   iv.   ǰis   larke-ne   kutte-ko   maːra   vo   mera   bhai   hɛ
          which   *boy*   *dog*   *hit*   *he*   *my*   *brother*   *is*
          'The boy who hit the dog is my brother.'

   v.   Ram-ki   bahin
          Ram's   *sister*
          'Ram's sister'

vi. safed   pʰul
    white   *flower*

b. French

  i. Jean   a   mangé une   pomme.
    žã   a   mãže   ün   pom
    Jean   *has*   *eaten*   *an*   *apple*
    'Jean ate an apple.'

  ii. Jean   peut   parler anglais.
    žã   pö   paʀle   ãŋgle
    Jean   *can*   *speak*   *English*
    'Jean can speak English.'

  iii. Le   garçon a   frappé le   chien   avec   un   baton.
     lə   gaʀsõ   a   fʀape   lə   šyɛ̃   avɛk   ə̃   batõ
     the   *boy*   *has*   *hit*   *the*   *dog*   *with*   *a*   *stick*
     'The boy hit the dog with a stick.'

  iv. Le   garçon qui   a   frappé le   chien   est   mon   frère.
    lə   gaʀsõ   ki   a   fʀape   lə   šyɛ̃   e   mõ   fʀeʀ
    the   *boy*   *who*   *has*   *hit*   *the*   *dog*   *is*   *my*   *brother*
    'The boy who hit the dog is my brother.'

  v. la   soeur   de   Jean
    la   söʀ   də   ẑã
    the   *sister*   *of*   *Jean*
    'Jean's sister'

  vi. une   fleur   blanche
    ün   flöʀ   blãš
    a   *flower* *white*
    'a white flower'

c. Japanese

  i. Taroo-ga   ringo-o   tabeta
    Taroo   *apple*   *ate*
    'Taroo ate an apple.'

  ii. Taroo-wa   Eigo-ga   hanaseru
    Taroo   *English*   *speak can*
    'Taroo can speak English.'

  iii. sono   otokonoko-wa boo-de   inu-o   butta
     that   *boy*   *stick–with*   *dog*   *hit*
     'That boy hit the dog with a stick.'

iv. inu-o   butta   otokonoko-wa   wataši-no   otooto-da
     dog   *hit*   *boy*   *my*   *brother-is*
     'The boy who hit the dog is my brother.'

v.   Taroo-no   imooto
     Taroo's   *sister*

vi. široi   hana
     white   *flower*

2. a. A word-by-word translation of English PPs, such as *on the tree, from the mountain*, etc., into Tamil, a language spoken in southern India, would be:

   the tree on
   the mountain from

   i. If you had to guess the word order typology of this language using this fact, would you think it is head-final or head-initial?

   ii. Modify the PS rule for English PPs so as to generate Tamil PPs.

   b. The translation of English VPs such as *think that he is a fool* and *know that the earth is round* into Tamil would read:

   he is a fool that think
   the earth is round that know

   i. Do these phrases show a head-final or head-initial pattern? Is it the same as what you found in a.i. or is it different?

   ii. Modify the PS rule that generates these English VPs so that they will generate the corresponding Tamil VPs.

   c. Based on what you know about Tamil from the previous two problems, give a word-by-word translation of the English phrases *people from Boston* and *the mouse in the barn*.

7

Semantics

So far we have considered language from a structural perspective, with relatively little concern for meaning. But words, phrases, and sentences mean something. Why does a certain set of words mean one thing and a similar set mean something very different? When do two different sentences mean the same thing? How can one sentence mean more than one thing? What is meaning? Semantics addresses and attempts to answer these questions.

File 7.1

The Goal of Semantics

Semantics as a subfield of linguistics is the study of meaning in language. Semantics deals with the meanings of words, and how the meanings of sentences are derived from them.

In order to understand what meaning in language is, it is important to realize that it is a multi-faceted phenomenon; different aspects of meaning need to be explained in different ways, so they are studied differently and are governed by different theories. In this file, these various aspects of meaning are introduced.

First, language meaning communicates information about the world around us: we can refer to persons, places, and (abstract and concrete) things, and then assert that these things have certain properties or stand in certain relationships to one another (such as the property "is asleep" or the relations "is a brother of," "is located at," and "strongly dislikes"). By using sentences of a common language, one person can expand another person's knowledge of the world—from simple facts, like who is sitting in the next chair, to obscure facts in astrophysics. A language is thus fundamentally a system of symbols, and symbols are things that stand for other things. Theories of the **information content** of language take as basic the relationship between a word and what it refers to, or a sentence and the fact or situation it correctly describes (see File 7.4). Of course, language can be used to talk about imaginary situations and things, like unicorns or Santa Claus, as well as actual ones. This would seem to be a problem for theories that describe meaning in terms of the potential for reference, but see File 7.2.

Second, meanings are also things that are grasped and produced in the mind of the speaker/hearer as she uses language; meanings are therefore a cognitive and psychological phenomenon. When we ask whether the meaning of a noun like *bird* is more like a dictionary definition, a mental image, or the concept of the typical bird, we are asking about the cognitive aspect of meaning, not its reference (the reference of *bird* is an actual bird or birds, not something in the mind). The cognitive process of language comprehension can be studied through laboratory experiments with human subjects as they hear or speak words and sentences, in much the same way as other problems in cognitive psychology are studied, although some linguists have attempted to construct theories of the **mental representations** of meanings from examining the language itself. Another window into the cognitive processes of language understanding is to study exactly what children understand words and sentences to mean at various stages of the language acquisition process, and how meaning develops from one stage to the next. Note that semantic theories of the information content of language do not, in themselves, say anything about the mental processing of linguistic meaning, or how it is acquired.

Third, language meaning is a social phenomenon, in that relationships between the speaker and hearer come into play in all sorts of ways in determining what our utterances mean. Language doesn't just present information independent of the **context of an utterance.** For example, think about the relationship between the sentence *John is asleep* and *Is John asleep?* These two sentences are in a sense about the same state of affairs (John being asleep), but when the first is used, the speaker already knows a certain fact and aims at increasing the knowledge of the hearer by adding this fact to it; whereas with the second sentence, the speaker does not know whether this possible state of affairs is a fact and makes a request to be informed whether it is a fact or not. Commands (and suggestions, warnings, promises, etc.) involve yet other kinds of interaction using meaning. Even in assertions, meaning depends in many ways on the context of the assertion: the things referred to by words like *I, you, they, here, now, there,* and *the* depend on when, where, by whom, and to whom they are uttered.

But meaning depends on context in much more subtle ways. For example, compare the information in *The door opened and two men went in* with *The door opened and two men came in.* (Where is the speaker with respect to the door?) This third facet of meaning—the appropriateness of meaning in a situation—is known as **pragmatics,** but pragmatics and semantics interact so much that they can't really be separated in all cases.

Fourth, meanings of words and sentences have a variety of important relationships among themselves, which can be studied independently of both information content (i.e., how language relates to what it's about) and hypotheses about cognition. An example of this that you're probably already familiar with is classifying pairs of words as synonyms, antonyms, and homonyms, but there are more significant relationships of this kind (see File 7.3).

It is important to realize that information content, cognitive meaning, and social (pragmatic) meaning are complementary aspects of the general phenomenon of meaning (semantics): the ability to learn and use a language would not be such a remarkably useful characteristic of our species if we could not use language to talk about all the things in the world, but by the same token, language would also not be possible without the mental capacity to process and produce the mental counterparts of this information and integrate it with our other thoughts and perceptions. The same goes for principles of language use and context-dependence. We will not have fully understood the phenomenon of meaning until *all* these aspects are understood.

Another way to study meaning, relatively new but increasingly important, is by constructing a computational system for processing language—-for example, in a question-answer system that allows users to get information from a computer database by "asking" the computer questions in ordinary English, receiving answers in English, and engaging in further dialog in English with the computer. Obviously, the meanings of the words and sentences involved must be analyzed and treated computationally in some way in order to construct such a system.

A major division in semantics, which cuts across the distinctions drawn above, is between **lexical semantics,** the meanings of words, and **compositional semantics,** the way that the meanings of whole sentences are determined from the meanings of the words in them by the syntactic structure of the sentence. It's obvious from two simple sentences like *Dog bites man* and *Man bites dog*, which have the same words but not the same meaning, that syntactic structure plays a role in determining sentence meaning. We don't grasp the meaning of a sentence by just putting together the meanings of the individual words involved in any old way. But how do we know that systematic principles are involved?

When we think of meaning in its nonlinguistic sense, we almost always think of word meanings. After all, we are all familiar with looking up words in dictionaries or asking someone about the meaning of a word we haven't seen before, and with discussing (or even arguing about) exactly what a certain word means. But we don't do this as often with the meanings of sentences. (Notice there are no dictionaries of the meanings of sentences!) Every person hears and uses new sentences every day that she or he has never heard or used before, sentences that may never have been uttered before by anyone; as an example, consider the nightly television news. We understand the meanings of new sentences, and all speakers of English understand a novel sentence in the same way (that is, its linguistic meaning, though they may differ in the further interpretation and consequences of that meaning). In fact, this would be true of the meaning of any grammatical and semantically well-formed sentence you could make up. (This is why there could never be a "dictionary of all sentences.") Thus, we know that systematic principles exist that determine the meaning of any sentence from its syntactic structure along with the meanings of the individual words in it, and that furthermore these principles apply recursively (can be applied again to their own output, over and over again) to produce meanings for new sentences and for ever longer, more complex sentences. (Note that this conclusion exactly parallels the one we drew about the principles of syntax; see File 6.5.) These semantic principles are called **rules of compositional semantics.** The ways that these principles work can be remarkably varied as well as systematic; see File 7.4. We can also see the effects of compositional semantic rules in the fact that ambiguity in syntactic structure produces a corresponding ambiguity in meaning (File 7.4).

Lexical semantics and compositional semantics are fundamentally different because the number of words in a language is finite, while the number of sentences is not. We tend to notice it when we hear a new word for the first time, and we may or may not be able to guess what it means, even if it is formed by a semantically regular suffix (like *-er*). But we generally never notice whether a sentence and its meaning happen to be new to us or not. This is because we learn word meanings individually, one at a time, each independently of the others, but we don't "learn" individual sentence meanings—we simply compute them mentally and unconsciously by compositional rules.

File 7.2

Theories of Meaning

In this file, we consider what it means to say that a given word or phrase has a certain meaning. We will look at several different answers to this question, but let's begin with the most obvious one: taking a word's meaning to be its dictionary definition.

Dictionary Definitions

Before we can talk about word meanings as dictionary definitions, a clarification about the use of dictionaries is necessary. In our culture, where the use of dictionaries is widespread, many people may have the impression that a word's meaning is simply its dictionary definition. A little thought should show, however, that there must be more to meaning than this. It is true that when someone wants to find out what a word means, an easy and practical way to do it is to look the word up in a dictionary. Most people in our culture accept dictionaries as providing unquestionably authoritative accounts of the meanings of the words they define. This role of dictionaries as authorities on meaning leads many people to feel that the dictionary definition of a word more accurately represents the word's meaning than does an individual speaker's understanding of the word. Keep in mind, however, that the people who write dictionaries arrive at their definitions by studying the ways speakers of the language use different words. There simply is no higher authority than the general community of native speakers of the language. A word's meaning is determined by the people who use that word, not by a dictionary.

To return to the idea that a dictionary definition is all there is to a word's meaning, this view poses a serious problem when one considers that in order to understand the dictionary definition of a word, one must know the meanings of the words used in that definition. For example, if the word *ectomere* is defined as "a blastomere that develops into ectoderm," one must know the meanings of the words *blastomere* and *ectoderm* in order to understand the definition. Not only that, but one must also understand the words *a, that, develops,* and *into* (as well as the principles for interpretation of English syntactic constructions). One may take this ability for granted, but it is necessary for understanding definitions nonetheless.

If a word's meaning is its dictionary definition, then understanding this meaning involves understanding the meanings of the words used in the definitions. But understanding the meanings of these words must involve understanding the meanings of the words in *their* definitions. And understanding these definitions must involve understanding the words they use, which of course would have to involve understanding even more definitions. The process is never ending.

Sometimes the circularity of a set of dictionary definitions is apparent by looking up just a few words. For instance, one English dictionary defines *divine* as "being or having the nature of a deity," but defines *deity* as "divinity." Another defines *pride* as "the quality of state of being proud," but defines *proud* as "feeling or showing pride." Examples like these are especially graphic, but essentially the same problem holds for any dictionary-style definition. Dictionaries are written to be of practical aid to people who already speak the language, not to make theoretical claims about the nature of meaning. People can and do learn the meanings of some words through dictionary definitions, so it would be unfair to say that such definitions are completely unable to characterize the meanings of words, but it should be clear that dictionary definitions can't be all there is to the meanings of all the words in a language.

A dictionary entry doesn't really explain the meaning of a word or phrase in terms of something more basic, it just gives paraphrases (gives you one lexical item for another), and even if this could somehow be done without circularity, there's no real explanation of what meaning is in a dictionary entry.

Mental Images

If a word's dictionary definition is not all there is to meaning, what else is there? One possibility is that a word's meaning is a **mental image.** This is an attractive idea in many ways because words often do seem to conjure up particular mental images. Reading the words *Mona Lisa*, for example, may well cause an image of Leonardo Da Vinci's painting to appear in your mind.

However, a mental image can't be all there is to a word's meaning, any more than a dictionary definition can be. One reason is that different people's mental images may be very different from each other, without the words really seeming to vary much in meaning from individual to individual. For a student, the word *lecture* will probably be associated with an image of one person standing in front of a blackboard and talking, and may also include things like the backs of the heads of one's fellow students. The image associated with the word *lecture* in the mind of a teacher, however, is more likely to consist of an audience of students sitting in rows facing forward, and may include things like the feel of chalk in one's hand, and so on. A lecture as seen from a teacher's perspective is actually quite a bit different from a lecture as seen from a student's perspective. Even so, both the student and the teacher understand the word lecture as meaning more or less the same thing, despite the difference in mental images. It's hard to see how a word like this could mean essentially the same thing for different people if meanings were just mental images.

Another problem with the idea that meaning is just a mental image is that the image associated with a word tends to be of a typical or ideal example of the kind of thing the word represents. Any word, however, can be used to represent a wide range of things, any one of which may or may not be typical of its kind. For example, try forming a mental image of a bird, and make sure it's clear in your mind before reading on. If you are like most people, your mental image was not one of an ostrich or a penguin. Yet ostriches and penguins are birds, and any analysis of the meaning of the word *bird* must take this into account. It may be that such an analysis should also provide some indication of what the typical bird is like, but clearly some provision must be made for atypical birds.

The idea that a word's meaning is just a mental image has an even more serious problem than the fact that mental images exclude atypical exemplars of the word. Many words, perhaps even most, simply have no clear mental images attached to them. What mental image is associated in your mind, for example, with the word *forget*? How about the word *the* or the word *aspect*? Only certain words seem to have definite images, but no one would want to say that only these words have meanings.

Meaning and Reference

What else might be involved in a word's meaning, besides a definition and a mental image? As already mentioned in File 7.1, language is used to talk about things in the outside world, and many words seem to stand for (or refer to) actual objects or relations in the world. It seems reasonable, then, to consider the actual thing a word refers to—that is, its **referent**—as one aspect of the word's meaning.

But once again, it would be a mistake to think of **reference** as all there is to meaning. To do so would tie meaning too tightly to the real world. If meaning were defined as the actual thing an expression refers to, what would we do about words for things that don't exist? There is simply no actual thing that the words *Santa Claus* refer to, yet obviously these words are not meaningless. (Note that this would not cause a problem for a theory of mental images, since almost everyone has a clear mental image of Santa Claus.) Language can be used to talk about fiction, fantasy, or speculation in addition to the real world, and any complete explanation of meaning must take account of this fact.

But even some sentences about the real world appear to present problems for the idea that an expression's meaning is just its referent. If meaning is the same as reference, then if two expressions refer to the same thing, they must mean the same thing. It follows that you should be able to substitute one for the other in a sentence without changing the meaning of the sentence as a whole. For instance, since the name *Bill Clinton* and the phrase *the winner of the 1996 U.S. presidential election* both refer to the same individual, the following two sentences should mean the same thing:

> *Bill Clinton is married to Hillary Rodham Clinton.*
> *The winner of the 1996 U.S. presidential election is married to Hillary Rodham Clinton.*

And these two sentences do indeed seem to describe the same fact. But look now at a sentence like the following:

> *Robin wanted to know if Bill Clinton was the winner of the 1996 U.S. presidential election.*

Try substituting *Bill Clinton* for *the winner of the 1996 U.S. presidential election.* What you get is: *Robin wanted to know if Bill Clinton was Bill Clinton.* But these sentences don't mean the same thing at all. They don't even describe the same fact.

If the idea of meaning as reference is going to work, it has to provide some explanation for why this sort of substitution doesn't work. A further problem for the theory of reference is that prepositions, abstract nouns, and words such as *forget* and *the* still have no clear meaning—what real-world entities could these words possibly refer to?

Meaning, Truth Conditions, and Truth Value

No complete account of meaning can ignore the phenomenon of reference, yet it is clear that the meaning of an expression is not just its real-world referent. Despite problems with this idea of meaning as reference, however, it is probably not necessary to give up the key insight it provides: that meaning involves a relation between language and the world. To see how the problems with this characterization can be avoided, consider for a moment how a sentence relates to the world, rather than just how individual words relate to the world.

Sentence meaning, even more than word meaning, may seem like a difficult concept to define; but perhaps it can be understood more clearly if instead of asking, "What is sentence meaning?" we take an indirect approach and ask, "What do you know when you know what a sentence means?" Stop and think about this for a moment, using a particular example, for instance, *Bill Clinton is asleep.*

Obviously, to know what this sentence means is not the same as to know that Bill Clinton is asleep, since any English-speaking person knows what the sentence means, but relatively few people know at any given time whether Bill Clinton is asleep or not. However, anyone who does understand the sentence knows what the world would have to be like in order for the sentence to be true.

That is, anyone who knows a sentence's meaning knows the conditions under which it would be true; they know its **truth conditions.** You know, for example, that in order for the sentence *Bill Clinton is asleep* to be true, the individual designated by the words *Bill Clinton* must be in the condition designated by the words *is asleep.* If, in addition to the truth conditions, you in fact know whether or not the sentence really is true, then you also know another facet of the sentence's meaning, its **truth value.** (This is always either "true" or "false.")

Note that the truth conditions and truth value of a sentence relate it to the world but in a somewhat different way than ordinary reference relates particular words or expressions to the world. Sentences about Santa Claus, for instance, do have truth conditions, even though the words *Santa Claus* have no real-world referent. Everyone knows what Santa Claus would have to be like if he were real, so it is not hard to describe the conditions under which a sentence containing these words would be true. Interestingly, it is less clear that sentences about Santa Claus have truth value: is the sentence *Santa Claus is asleep right now* true or false? Many people have the intuition that asking such a question is inappropriate; the sentence is neither true nor false, since we know that Santa Claus doesn't exist, and giving either answer would seem to imply that he does exist. (An entire subfield of semantics, the study of **presupposition,** is devoted to researching phenomena such as this.)

Going back to our previous example, since the conditions under which something qualifies as "Bill Clinton" are different from the conditions under which something qualifies as "the winner of the 1996 U.S. presidential election," an explanation of meaning that includes the notion of truth conditions is also able to explain why the phrases *Bill Clinton* and *the winner of the 1996 U.S. presidential election* cannot be freely substituted for one another, even though they refer to the same individual. Reference to the same individual is not enough to guarantee that two words or phrases have identical meanings; it matters how one arrives at that individual. The name *Bill Clinton* directly picks out the individual Bill Clinton, once and for all. But *the winner of the 1996 U.S. presidential election* picks out whoever won in 1996; if the election had gone differently, it would pick out Bob Dole; if Ross Perot had run and been successful, it would pick out Perot, and so on.

Possible Worlds

Can we unite the theory that names and other noun phrases (NPs) always have reference with the theory that a sentence's meaning is captured by having truth conditions? One way to do this is to describe meaning in terms of "possible situations," or alternatively "possible scenarios." We need such a concept anyway to describe the semantics of counterfactual sentences: that is, *If I had an apple, I would eat it right now* is analyzed as saying that in possible scenarios similar to the situation I am actually in except that the statement *I have an apple* is true, then *I will eat it right now* is true in those scenarios as well. In this case, the possible scenarios are implied to be incompatible with what is actually true (hence the term "counterfactual"), but in indicative conditionals like *If John gives me an apple, I will eat it right now,* one of the possible scenarios involved could eventually turn out to be the actual course of events. With this idea, we can define the meaning (information content) of a sentence, i.e., its truth conditions, to be the collection (set) of all those possible scenarios in which the sentence is true. Thus the meaning (information content) of the sentence *Bill Clinton is in Columbus* is conceived of in this theory as the set of all the possible scenarios which this sentence describes truthfully. What this boils down to in terms of a speaker/hearer's knowledge is the idea that a person understands the meaning (information content) of *Bill Clinton is in Columbus* if and only if the person knows how to distinguish possible scenarios where Clinton is in Columbus from scenarios in which he is not—given an opportunity to make the relevant observations of things in each scenario. Thus in this theory the meaning of a sentence, a linguistic object, is explained in terms of nonlinguistic objects (scenarios). The information content of the sentence, when uttered, amounts to letting the hearer know that the actual world fits one or another of these scenarios. (We will get an idea of how this set of possible scenarios is determined from the words and syntax of the sentence in File 7.4 below.)

Since what we are calling "possible scenarios" or "possible situations" can potentially involve rather large chunks of the universe and not just local situations, they are officially known in the semantics literature as **possible worlds,** hence the term **possible worlds semantics.** Unfortunately, that term suggests science fiction, time travel, parallel universes, and the like, and this makes some people suspicious of the theory. But such "worlds" are not really relevant to the reasoning people do with language: if Mary says, upon leaving her house in the morning, *I wonder whether it will rain today?*, the kinds of scenarios that she is talking about are ones in which she takes her umbrella and rain falls, ones in which she takes her umbrella but no rain falls, one in which she leaves her umbrella at home and rain falls, etc.—but not ones in which rain falls and a flying saucer lands on her lawn, even though such a scenario is technically part of the meaning (set of possible scenarios) of *it rains*.

Another way in which possible scenarios can help us is by augmenting the theory of reference in such a way that imaginary items and individuals can receive referents. We simply allow referents to be in non-actual scenarios. So the name *Santa Claus* can in fact be given a referent, namely, the large man in the red suit who lives at the North Pole. The only difference is that this man exists only in non-actual scenarios. We can similarly give referents to such words as *unicorn, centaur,* and *one-eyed, one-horned flying purple people eater.* While the availability of extra referents does not help for words such as *the* and *forget,* it does represent an improvement over the case where the notion of possible scenarios was not available and a word like *unicorn* had no reference.

Meaning and Language Use

Specifying truth conditions effectively characterizes many important aspects of literal meaning, especially for ordinary declarative sentences. But how can you determine the conditions under which a question is true? Or an order or a wish? In fact, many types of sentences do not even seem to be true or false at all. It should be clear, then, that truth conditions are just one aspect of sentence meaning.

In addition to the conditions under which a sentence is true, meaning is probably also determined in part by the conditions under which a sentence may be used. Questions are used differently from assertions, orders are used differently from wishes, and so on. By specifying the kind of practical situation that must exist in order for a speaker to use a particular type of utterance (or speech act), many facts about the meaning associated with that particular speech act type may be made explicit. This is the goal of pragmatics (discussed in Files 8.1–8.5).

By examining general conventions on language use, or **Gricean maxims** (see glossary and File 8.3), it is also possible to explain how utterances can imply things above and beyond their literal meaning.

Summary

Although there is much more to be said about the nature of meaning, a few things should be clear: (1) Meaning (like any other aspect of language) is provided by a community of native speakers, not by some special authority like a dictionary or grammar book. (2) The meaning of an expression is not just a definition composed of more words in the same language, since ultimately the meaning of some words would have to be known in order to understand the definitions. (3) The meaning of an expression is not just a mental image, since mental images seem to vary from person to person more than meaning does, since mental images tend to be only of typical or ideal examples of the things they symbolize, and since not all words have corresponding mental images. (4) The meaning of a word involves more than just the actual thing the word refers to, since not all expressions have real-world referents, and substituting expressions with identical referents for each other in a sentence can change the meaning of the sentence as a whole. (5) Knowing the meaning of a sentence involves knowing the conditions under which it would be true, so explaining the meaning of a sentence can be done in part by explaining its truth conditions. (6) One way to look at the meaning of a sentence is to equate it with the set of all possible worlds or scenarios in which the sentence is true. (7) Knowing the meaning of an utterance also involves knowing how to use it, so conditions on language use also form an important aspect of meaning.

File 7.3

Lexical Semantics

Lexical semantics deals with a language's **lexicon,** or the collection of words in a language. It is distinguished from **compositional semantics** (File 7.4) in that the former is concerned exclusively with individual words, while the latter is concerned exclusively with the meanings of phrases and sentences. Of the many ways that lexical semantics can be studied, we will discuss two in this file: (1) classifying the semantic relationships that word meanings hold to each other in general terms, and (2) componential analysis, which is one way of analyzing word meanings into smaller parts. Both of these involve meanings and meaning relationships in isolation, that is, without attention to their contribution to reference and truth conditions, or to the way they are stored and used mentally.

Meaning Relationships

There are many ways for two words to be related. We have already seen a number of ways: they may be morphologically related (e.g., *lift/lifted,* which both share the same stem), they may be syntactically related (e.g., *write/paint,* which are both transitive verbs), or they may be phonologically related (e.g., *night/knight,* which share the same pronunciation). There is another way two words can be related, however, and that is semantically. For instance, the word *pot* is intuitively more closely related semantically to the word *pan* than it is to the word *floor.* The reason, clearly, is that both *pot* and *pan* have meanings that involve the act of cooking, while *floor* does not in any obvious way.

What kind of semantic relationships are there? Before we answer that question, let's decide on how we are going to talk about meanings. We'll talk first about nouns. Nouns can be given a fairly straightforward denotation using the formalism of **sets.** A set is simply a collection of items of any sort. The items that belong to a particular set are called that set's **elements** or **members.** Some examples of sets are the set of red bicycles in North America, the set of whole numbers from 1 to 5, and the set consisting of the *Queen Elizabeth II* and the remains of the *Titanic.*

Getting back to nouns, given a particular noun N, we will say that the meaning of N is the set of entities in the world which N describes. So the meaning of *dog* determines the set of dogs in the world. For an adjective A we can similarly take A's meaning to be the set of entities of which A is true. So the meaning of *red* determines the set of things which are red.

The first kind of semantic relation we can talk about is **hyponymy.** This is the most commonly seen type of relationship. We can say that word X is a hyponym of word Y if in all possible scenarios, X's set is always contained in (is always a subset of) Y's set. For example, let us consider the words *poodle* and *dog.* Suppose that the current set of poodles includes Froofroo, Princess, and Sophie. The current set of dogs will then include at least these three dogs, and possibly others as well (such as Fido the retriever).

The set of poodles is then contained in the set of dogs. It's clear from our knowledge of the meaning of these words that the same will be the case regardless of what particular dogs there are in the world. Hence we conclude that the word *poodle* is a hyponym of the word *dog.*

Hyponymy can be viewed as "the loss of specificity." It involves moving from something specific to something more general. Imagine a biologist's taxonomy: if you know an organism's species (the most specific category), then you automatically know its kingdom (the most general category), since every species belongs to one and only one kingdom. However, you cannot go the other way—

just knowing an organism's kingdom ("animal," for instance) is certainly not enough information to allow you to infer the species to which it belongs.

A second kind of semantic relation, perhaps a more familiar one, is **synonymy.** Two words are synonymous if they have the same meaning; in the case of nouns and adjectives, if the sets of entities they pick out are always equivalent. While it is difficult and perhaps impossible to find pairs of words that are truly 100% interchangeable, pairs such as *couch/sofa, dog/canine, groundhog/woodchuck,* and *quick/rapid* come close. There is no entity that one would call a canine but not a dog, and vice versa. Similarly, for most people every couch is also a sofa and every sofa is also a couch.

A third kind of semantic relation is **antonymy.** The basic meaning of antonymy is of being "opposite" in some sense, but there turn out to be several ways a pair of words can be opposites. The most straightforward are **complementary** or **contradictory** pairs. Given two words X and Y, if every entity in the world is either in X's set or in Y's set but not in both, then X and Y form a complementary pair. Pairs such as *married/unmarried* and *visible/invisible* are complementary; everything is one or the other, but nothing is both. **Relational opposites** or **contraries** are another sort of antonym. Given two words X and Y, we say that X and Y are relational opposites if everything in the world is either in X's set, in Y's set, or in neither, but not in both sets. (In other words, the sets do not have any common elements, nor do they necessarily include every entity in the world.) Pairs such as *over/under, alive/dead,* and *married/bachelor* are examples: an object may be over or under another object, but not both. Yet it could also be next to that object, meaning it is neither over nor under.

A last sort of "opposite" relationship is very similar to relational opposites, but it includes the concept of a scale between two endpoints. If the two words X and Y under consideration fulfill the criteria for being relational opposites but in addition can be seen as endpoints on some scale (of temperature, size, height, age, etc.), then X and Y are called **scalar antonyms** or **gradable pairs.** *Good/bad, hot/cold,* and *strong/weak* are examples. Something can be hot or cold or neither (lukewarm), but it cannot be hot and cold at the same time. (Let's disregard situations in which part of an object is hot and part is cold.) Words that qualify as potential members of gradable pairs can usually be modified with *quite: This apple is quite good/bad, He is quite strong/weak.* Contrast these with **The bug is quite under/over the rock* and **He has been quite married/a bachelor for the last twenty years.*

Semantic Features

Another way of analyzing lexical meaning is to try to decompose word meanings into more basic parts. The process is called **lexical decomposition** or **componential analysis.** The idea is that most words have meanings that are "built up" from simpler meanings. If we knew what basic meanings there were and which words incorporated which of these basic meanings into their own meanings, then we would be able to explain a number of intuitions we have about meaning.

For example, the words *mare, stallion, hen,* and *rooster* all have the common meaning of "animal" in them. We could say that these four words share the common semantic feature ANIMAL. In addition, *mare* and *hen* share the common feature FEMALE, and similarly *stallion* and *rooster* share the feature MALE. One could add more features like HORSE and CHICKEN as more specific features of ANIMAL, so that the collection of features CHICKEN and MALE would constitute the semantic components of the word *rooster.*

Another illustration of lexical decomposition comes from causatives. Consider the following pairs of sentences, which use the intransitive verbs *boil, open, bake,* and *turn* and their transitive counterparts:

The water boiled.	*Robin boiled the water.*
The door opened.	*The wind opened the door.*
The cake baked.	*Robin baked the cake.*
The car turned.	*Robin turned the car.*

We can analyze the meaning of the transitive verbs in terms of their intransitive counterparts: in *John boiled the water*, the transitive verb *boil* can be analyzed as X CAUSE Y to BOIL, where X and Y are noun phrases (in this case, X is *Robin* and Y is *the water*) and CAUSE and BOIL are the basic components of the meaning of the transitive verb *boil*. The other intransitive-transitive verb pairs can be similarly analyzed.

In the examples of causative constructions given above, the intransitive and transitive verb pairs are morphologically indistinguishable, but this need not be the case. For example, most speakers of English would say that there is something contradictory about the sentence *The sheriff killed Jesse, but Jesse is not dead*. Without looking closely at the meaning of *kill*, however, we cannot say explicitly what is wrong. As it turns out, *kill* has several components to its meaning and might be best analyzed as X CAUSE Y to BECOME DEAD. Since it is part of the meaning of *kill* that the killed individual is dead afterwards, we can now explain why it is contradictory to say that Jesse was killed but not dead. Before decomposing the meaning of *kill* we had no direct way to explain the clear contradiction in the sentence.

It turns out that investigating semantic features can also help uncover meaning relationships of the type mentioned above. Hyponymy, especially, can be demonstrated in many cases by recourse to semantic features. For example, let us reconsider the pair of words *poodle* and *dog*. Above we reasoned that *poodle* must be a hyponym of (be more specific than) *dog* because whenever we collect all available poodles and all available dogs, the set of poodles is always contained within the set of dogs. But we can also say that one of the semantic features of being a poodle is being a dog; *poodle* is a word that conjures up an idea of "a dog with curly hair and long legs which is frequently given odd haircuts." Therefore, whenever we use the word *poodle*, the meaning of *dog* is implicitly there. It is no wonder, then, that we can never find a poodle that is not a dog.

Summary

This chapter has only scratched the surface of lexical meaning. While it may seem at first glance that a language's lexicon is little more than a mishmash of unrelated words thrown together into a big "soup," nothing could be further from the truth. The lexicon is an intricately structured system, with a dense web of relationships among its members. The lexicon is so complex, in fact, that several lines of linguistic research have adopted the assumption that basically *all* information about a language is encoded in the properties of the words in that language's lexicon and the relationships between those words. However, there must also be some principles, however general they may be, governing how words combine to form phrases and sentences. The next file takes a look at this topic, referred to as compositional semantics.

File 7.4

Compositional Semantics

An interesting question that semantics investigates is how the meanings of individual words are combined to make larger units of meaning. Note first of all that we don't just add up all the word meanings to get the meaning of the whole, as if we were making a pot of soup. If semantics worked this way, we would expect the two sentences *The cat chased the dog* and *The dog chased the cat* to mean exactly the same thing, since they are formed from exactly the same words. By this simplistic principle, we would expect to get the same meaning as well from the nonsensical string of words *The chased dog cat the,* yet this has no meaning at all. Thus, the order of words in a phrase helps determine the meaning of the phrase (although, notice that even word order does not always provide sufficient information: the sentences *The dog chased the cat* and *The dog was chased by the cat* have different meanings, although the order of the two nouns phrases is the same). But there is still more to determining the meaning of a phrase. Although the sentences *The dog chased the cat* and *The cat was chased by the dog* are not composed of exactly the same set of words and do not have the same word order, they nevertheless have the same meaning. We know, though, that the structures of these two sentences are closely related. Similarly, the two sentences *He can't stand beans* and *Beans, he can't stand* have the same meaning. From these examples we see that it is the syntactic structure as a whole, not word order alone, that, together with its word meanings, determines the meaning of a sentence. This relationship between meaning and syntactic structure is often referred to as the **Principle of Compositionality:** the meaning of a sentence is determined by the meaning of its words and by the syntactic structure in which they are combined. (This principle is also called Frege's Principle, after the mathematician and philosopher Gottlob Frege, who first stated it.)

The role of grammatical structure in semantics can also be seen from a sentence that can be formed by combining words and phrases in two different ways. Such sentences will have two different meanings depending on which way the sentence is taken to be put together, and this ambiguity is known as **structural ambiguity.** Take the sentence *They are moving sidewalks.* If we assume this is formed by combining *are* with the phrase *moving sidewalks*, then we understand the sentence to refer to sidewalks that move people along, as are found in some airports. But if we assume that the sentence is formed by combining *are moving* with *sidewalks*, then it may be describing workers who are picking up sidewalks and putting them down in another place. The meanings of the words are the same in both cases, but the syntactic structure is different, leading to different meanings. The sentence *They are visiting relatives* paraphrases as "they are relatives who are visiting" and alternatively as "they are going to visit relatives."

That word meanings normally combine by regular principles dependent on syntactic structure can be vividly seen from the exceptional cases in which they do not. Such cases are called **idioms.** The sentence *He kicked the bucket* can be used to mean "he died." We cannot determine this meaning by combining the meaning of *kick* and the meaning of *the bucket* in the normal way, but rather we must learn the special meaning of the whole phrase *kick the bucket* as if it were a new "word." Similarly, with *to pull someone's leg* or *red herring*, we can't understand the meaning simply by combining *pull* with *leg*, or *red* with *herring*. Idioms are cases where a sequence of words has a fixed meaning that is not composed of the literal meanings of its words by regular principles.

But just what are these regular principles? What does it mean in concrete terms to "combine" two meanings into a new meaning? To get a sense of how meanings are built up, we will look at two classes of examples.

Sentential Meanings

Recall that simple declarative sentences in English normally consist of a noun phrase (NP) that serves as the subject, followed by a verb phrase (VP) that serves as the predicate.

```
        S
       / \
      NP  VP
```

As an example, consider the sentence *Sandy runs.*

```
        S
       / \
      NP  VP
      |    |
    Sandy runs
```

What would be the process of computing the meaning of the whole sentence from the meanings of these two syntactic parts? Before we answer that, we need to decide what the meanings of the NP and the VP will be.

For purposes of simplifying discussion, we will consider here only the denotations and truth values of expressions with respect to a single situation or scenario and ignore the rest of their meanings; we can still clearly illustrate how compositional rules work with this simplification. We will say that the word *Sandy* has as its denotation the (real-life) individual Sandy.

What, then, could the denotation of the VP be? Earlier we took the denotation of common nouns like *dog* to be sets; the word *dog* has as its denotation the set containing all individual dogs. We can do something similar with VP meanings: a VP has as its denotation the set of individuals who "do" that VP. In our example, then, the denotation of the word *runs* is the set of individuals who run.

As for the meaning of the sentence, we want to know two things: (1) whether it is in fact true or false given what we know about the world (its truth value), and (2) the minimal conditions under which it would be true (its truth conditions). We get the first of these directly and the second indirectly. To compute the truth value we simply check to see whether the individual that is the denotation of the NP is a member of the set that is the denotation of the VP. If it is, then the sentence is true. The sentence is false if the individual is not a member. The following are two possible arrangements for our sentence, where the material after the colon (:) at each node in the tree represents the meaning of that portion of the tree:

(a)
```
        S : false (since Sandy is not a member of the set {Robin, Lee, Kim})
       /        \
   NP : Sandy   VP : {Robin, Lee, Kim}
      |             |
    Sandy         runs
```

(b)

```
        S : true (since Sandy is a member of the set {Robin, Sandy})
      /        \
  NP : Sandy   VP : {Robin, Sandy}
     |            |
   Sandy        runs
```

In tree (a), the set of people who run does not include Sandy, and so the sentence *Sandy runs* is false. In tree (b), Sandy is a member of the set of runners, so *Sandy runs* is true.

Now we have a system for computing the truth value of a (simple declarative) sentence: simply check to see whether the meaning of the subject is a member of the set that is the predicate's meaning. But how do we arrive at the truth conditions? In effect, we already have: it was implicit in the way we computed the truth value. To arrive at a truth value of "true," it must be the case that the individual Sandy is a member of the set of runners. This seems like a simple paraphrase, but it is in fact precisely the truth conditions of this sentence.

Adjective Meanings

Computing truth values for simple sentences was a fairly straightforward demonstration of semantic composition. We find a more complex sort of composition when we turn our attention to adjective-noun combinations. While there is presumably only one syntactic configuration for all three of the phrases *green screen, good food,* and *fake money,* we shall see that each of these involves a different sort of semantic combination.

Which sort is used depends primarily on the particular adjective involved. We'll start out with the simplest form of adjectival combination, **pure intersection**. In the phrase *green screen* we have two words, *green* and *screen*, each of which can be given as denoting a set of entities (individuals or objects). The denotation of *green* is the set of green entities, and that of *screen* is the set of entities that are screens. To compute the meaning of the phrase, then, we need only collect all the entities that are in the set both of green things and of screens. This is illustrated in the following Venn diagram; here, the intersection (or overlapping portions of the two circles) contains the set of entities that are both in the set of green things and of screens:

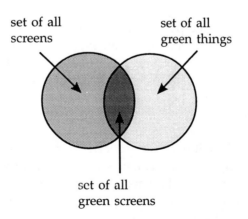

set of all
screens

set of all
green things

set of all
green screens

Other phrases that work in the same way are *Chinese screen, blue suit,* and *working woman.* An important point about these cases of pure intersection is that the two sets can be identified independently. For example, we can decide what is green and what isn't before we even know that we're going to look for screens.

Other nouns and adjectives do not combine according to this pattern, for example, *big whale* or *good beer.* In the case of *big whale,* the problem is that it is not possible to identify a set of big things in absolute terms. Size is always relative: what is big for whales is tiny for mountains; what is short for a giraffe is tall for a chicken. While it is possible to find a set of whales independently, the set represented by the adjective can't be just "big" but "big-for-a-whale." Similarly, *tall giraffe* will involve a set of things that are tall-for-a-giraffe, and *loud explosion,* a set of things that are loud-for-an-explosion (compare this with *loud whisper,* which would use a completely different norm for loudness). Cases like this we call **relative intersection,** since the members of the set denoted by the adjective are determined relative to the type of thing denoted by the noun.

Good beer is another case of relative intersection. But *good* is even more relative than tall or loud. Tall, for example, always refers to a scale of vertical distance, and loud refers to a scale of volume of sound. We might say that good refers to a scale of quality, but what kind of quality? A good beer is probably judged on its taste, but a good ladder on how sturdy and useful it is, and a good record on how pleasurable the music is. Good beer could even be a beer that removes dirt well if we said *That's good beer to wash the walls with.* So *good* apparently refers to anything that fits our purposes well, and these purposes vary with the object and with how that object is used in a given case. In order to use and understand phrases of the form *good* + N correctly, we must have more knowledge about the context than in other cases of relative intersection.

Both types of intersection, pure and relative, have in common that these combinations actually refer to some of the objects denoted by the nouns themselves. For *green screen, tall giraffe,* and *good beer,* we are necessarily talking about screens, giraffes, and beer, respectively. But in phrases like *possible solution* and *alleged thief,* this is not the case: a possible solution does not necessarily refer to a real solution, and an alleged thief does not necessarily refer to a thief. These are both examples of **non-intersection.** Logically, we can say that the use of intersection-type adjectives entails (or requires) reference to the objects denoted by the nouns, while the use of non-intersection adjectives does not.

Finally, there is a second type of non-intersection adjective that does not entail the reference to objects denoted by the nouns; the use of such an adjective with a noun in fact entails that the adjective does *not* refer to that noun. A *fake Picasso* by definition cannot refer to a Picasso. Of course, a fake thing must have some characteristics of the real thing, or the word would not be used at all; in fact a good fake may be like the N in every respect except actually being the genuine thing. Adjectives like *fake* we call **anti-intersection adjectives.**

As if this were not complicated enough, there are many other types of Adjective + Noun combinations besides the four just discussed. To give an example, the adjectives in *An occasional sailor walked by* and *I do a daily six-mile run* function very much like adverbs, as seen by the paraphrases *Occasionally, a sailor walked by* and *Every day I do a six-mile run.* These combinations do not follow the same rule of combination as the above four types. Consider yet another case: in *a hot cup of coffee,* what is hot is the coffee and not necessarily the cup. Here, the adjective combines with cup, which comes to denote its contents.

Researchers in compositional semantics concern themselves, among other things, with discovering the sorts of differences examined here and with writing precise rules to describe exactly how different types of expressions combine. It becomes obvious that these rules must actually exist in our minds once one considers that there are an infinite number of sentences in any language and hence an infinite number of meanings to understand and produce. Just as the concepts of generativity and recursion (and hence rules) were crucial in explaining how we can process sentences we have never heard before, they are also crucial in explaining how we can understand the meaning of those sentences.

Suggested Reading

Lyons, John. 1995. *Linguistic Semantics: An Introduction.* Cambridge: Cambridge University Press. (This is an excellent, nontechnical introductory text that presupposes no specialized knowledge of semantics or linguistics.)

Exercises

1. Using the example of compositional analysis of the sentence *Sandy runs* as a guide, provide an analysis for the sentence *Kim sleeps*. Draw trees as in the example in the text, with one tree showing the case where the sentence's truth value is "true," and one to show a case where the sentence's truth value is "false."

2. Think about a sentence such as *Kim doesn't sleep*. What is the meaning of *doesn't*? (Hint: consider the condition under which the sentence's truth value is "true.")

8

Pragmatics

To fully understand the meaning of a sentence we must understand the context in which it is uttered. Pragmatics concerns itself with how people use language within a context and why they use language in particular ways. This unit examines how factors such as time, place, and social relationship between speaker and hearer affect the ways in which language is used to perform various functions.

File 8.1 Meaning and Context

We have defined semantics as the study of meaning. Given this definition, we may be tempted to think that once we understand the semantics of a language, we completely understand that language. Meaning, however, involves more than just the semantic interpretation of an utterance. To fully understand the meaning of a sentence, we must also understand the context in which it was uttered. Consider the word *ball*. In a sentence such as *He kicked the ball into the net*, we may visualize a round, black and white soccer ball about nine inches in diameter. In a sentence such as *She dribbled the ball down the court and shot a basket*, we would visualize a basketball. Given yet another sentence, *She putted the ball in from two feet away*, we would visualize another ball, a golf ball. In these examples, the word *ball* is understood in different ways depending on what type of action is associated with it. Whatever understood meaning is common to *ball* in all of these contexts will be part of the word's core meaning. If we think of enough types of balls, we can come up with an invariant core meaning of *ball* that will allow speakers to refer to any ball in any context. Nevertheless, even though we can discover a word's "invariant core," we normally understand more than that. It is the **context** that fills in the details and allows full understanding—such as the usual color of a soccer ball, the size of a basketball, or the weight of a golf ball. The study of the contribution of context to meaning is often called **pragmatics**.

We must ask ourselves, then, what is context: is it simply the reality that fills in meaningful details missed by a theory, such as the invariant core theory? No, it is not. Context can be divided into four subparts, of which reality is but the first. We call this aspect of context the **physical** context; that is, where the conversation takes place, what objects are present, and what actions are taking place. Second, we have an **epistemic** context, background knowledge shared by the speakers and hearers. Third, we have a **linguistic** context, utterances previous to the utterance under consideration. Finally, we have a **social** context, the social relationship and setting of the speakers and hearers. As stated, this division of context may seem abstract, so let's consider how context helps people interpret a sarcastic remark. Suppose that two people, talking loudly, walk into an individual study section of the library (physical context). They sit down, still talking loudly, but no one says anything to them. After about five minutes, a person across the table from them says sarcastically, "Talk a little louder, won't you? I missed what you just said." The hearers will interpret this utterance as a request for them to be quiet, despite the fact that literally the speaker is requesting them to talk louder. Certain contextual facts help to signal that this is a request for silence: the utterance interrupts their conversation and breaks the silence between them and others (linguistic context); the request is made in sarcastic tone (linguistic context); people don't usually talk to strangers (epistemic context); libraries are quiet places (epistemic context); and they are in the library (physical context). From these observations, the hearers must conclude that the utterance is a request for silence.

Given this expanded definition of context, we can see that pragmatics does more than just "fill in the details." Pragmatics concerns itself with how people use language within a context and why they use language in particular ways.

File 8.2   Speech Acts

Just as people can perform physical acts, such as hitting a baseball, they can also perform mental acts, such as imagining hitting a baseball. People can also perform another kind of act simply by using language; these are called **speech acts**.

We use language to do an extraordinarily wide range of activities. We use it to convey information, request information, give orders, make requests, make threats, give warnings, make bets, give advice, etc., as the following sentences suggest:

(1) John Jones has bad breath.
(2) Who ate my porridge?
(3) Shut up.
(4) Please scratch my nose.
(5) Do that again, and I'll punch your lights out.
(6) There is a gremlin in the back seat of your car.
(7) Five bucks says that the Buckeyes will beat the Wolverines this year.
(8) You ought to go to class at least once a quarter.

There can be little doubt that it is our ability to do things with language—to perform speech acts—that makes language useful to us. In fact, with language we can do things that would otherwise be impossible. Consider (4), a request for a hearer to scratch the speaker's nose. If we did not have language (including sign language), how would this request be made? We could imagine the speaker taking the hearer's hand and rubbing his nose with it, but would this action have the same force as a spoken request? Probably not. How would the hearer know that the speaker meant "scratch," not "rub"? How would the hearer know that this action was a request and not an order? The action itself could not convey the politeness of the word *please*, a major difference between requests and orders. In (6), we could warn the speaker that a gremlin is in the back seat of his car by pointing at it, but how could we give the advice in (8) without words? It would certainly be difficult.

Although we use language for all sorts of things, many more than were just listed, three of these uses seem to be of greater linguistic importance than the others because the language makes available special syntactic structures for marking them. For direct speech acts we have a declarative sentence type, which is dedicated to assertions; an interrogative sentence type, which is dedicated to questions; and an imperative sentence type, which is dedicated to orders and requests. See the table below.

Sentence Type	*Speech Act*	*Function*	*Example*
Declarative	assertion	conveys information, is true or false	"John Jones has bad breath."
Interrogative	question	elicits information	"Who is he talking to?"
Imperative	orders and requests	causes others to behave in certain ways	"Please leave me alone." "Leave me alone."

Performative Verbs

A special kind of speech act, known as a performative speech act, shows that we consider "speech action" just as legitimate as any other physical action. This is made clear by the large number of verbs that perform purely linguistic actions. Compare (9)–(16) with (1)–(8):

(9)   I assert that John Jones has bad breath.
(10)   I ask who ate my porridge.
(11)   I order you to shut up.
(12)   I request that you scratch my nose.
(13)   I threaten you that if you do that again, I'll punch your lights out.
(14)   I warn you that there is a gremlin in the back of your car.
(15)   I bet you five bucks that the Buckeyes will beat the Wolverines this year.
(16)   I advise you to go to class at least once a quarter.

As these sentences illustrate, the speech acts performed by sentences (1)–(8) can also be performed by embedding these sentences as complements of verbs that state the speech act. The usual name for these verbs is **performative verbs**, which can be defined as verbs that can be used to perform the acts they name. In (11), for example, we have an order, with the performative verb *order*, followed by the specific command, (3) *Shut up*. Interestingly, not every speech act has its own performative verb, as is illustrated by (13). We would have to substitute *warn* for *threaten* if we wanted to use a performative verb to make a threat. Although the fact that we do not have a performative verb *threaten* might be an accident, we may not have such a verb because we find no need for a step between a warning and the threatened action.

Identifying Direct Speech Acts

The type of speech acts that we have been considering are called direct speech acts, since they perform their functions in a direct and literal manner. In the first set, (1)–(8), the sentences are statements of various actions. In the second set, (9)–(16), the sentences contain performative verbs, which actually name the speech act. The only difference between sentences (8) and (16), for example, is the fact that (16) has the performative verb *advise*, which introduces (8). When trying to identify the type of speech act, we should consider its literal meaning by considering its form. With the speech acts of questioning, asserting, requesting, and ordering, we have seen that each has a particular form associated with it—interrogative, declarative, imperative, and imperative, respectively.

When identifying direct speech acts containing performative verbs, we may want to conclude that the utterance is the action named by the verb. While our conclusion may be correct, we must look at more than the verb. Consider the following sentences:

(17)   I promise to take him to a bar tonight.
(18)   John promises to take me to a bar tonight.
(19)   I will promise to take him to a bar tonight.

Although all of these sentences use the verb *promise*, only (17) uses it as a performative verb. Sentence (18) is a report on a promise, and (19) is a promise to make a promise sometime in the future, without actually using the verb *promise* performatively. Why? Sentence (18) is not a promise because the subject of the sentence is John. When we use a performative verb, the subject must be *I*, since these speech acts concern the interaction between speakers and hearers. Sentence (19) is not a performative use of the verb *promise* because it is in the future tense using the helping verb *will*. Performative speech acts, like all actions, take place in the present, so must use the present tense. (Note that these grammatical constraints are constraints on direct performative verb speech acts, not all speech acts.) Sentence (18) is still a direct speech act, an assertion, though it does not have a first person singular subject, and (19) is a promise though it is not in the present tense.

One test to see whether a verb is used performatively or not is the hereby test. We take the word *hereby* and insert it before the alleged performative verb:

(20) I hereby promise to take him to a bar tonight.
(21) John hereby promises to take me to a bar tonight.
(22) I will hereby promise to take him to a bar tonight.

If the sentence sounds fine with *hereby*, then the verb is being used performatively. If the sentence sounds bad, then the verb is not being used performatively. Sometimes, this test is difficult to use because many sentences sound awkward with a performative verb, with or without *hereby*. This awkwardness may arise because people tend not to utter speech acts using performative verbs.

A further complication arises in identifying speech acts when a performative verb does not match the speech acts. Consider (23):

(23) I promise to tell Mom if you touch my toys one more time.

Sentence (23), though it has the verb *promise*, uses *I* as its subject, and is in the present tense, is not a promise. Instead it is a threat. When we make a promise, we offer to do something that we believe is beneficial to the hearer. When we make a threat, we offer to do something that hearers will not like. Since "telling Mom" is something that hearers generally do not appreciate, we must construe (23) as a threat. In identifying speech acts, then, we must consider what it means to perform an action. This consideration leads us to the topic of felicity conditions.

Felicity Conditions

Sentences can go wrong in a number of ways: words might be mispronounced (e.g., we might say "fog dight" instead of "dog fight"), or we might make an irregular verb regular even though we do not normally do so (e.g., we might say "he swimmed" instead of "he swam"), or we might make an ungrammatical sentence (saying "The boy who that I saw was Bill," instead of "The boy who I saw was Bill") or a sentence might not make any sense (as in the case of "I know Bush's still President, but I'm wrong"). Speech acts can go wrong too—by being situationally inappropriate.

Suppose that two drunks in a bar decide to get married and go up to the bartender and ask him to marry them. Suppose that the bartender used to be a court clerk and remembered exactly what must be said and done to marry people. Suppose finally that they go through the whole ceremony in front of witnesses, and that the bartender concludes by saying, "I hereby pronounce you husband and wife." Saying this, in this context, would not effect a marrying of these two people, and not necessarily because they are drunk or they are in a bar, but simply because the bartender does not have the official social and legal status required to marry people. The marriage pronouncement is therefore situationally inappropriate, and we say in such cases that the speech act in question is **infelicitous**—has gone awry.

Associated with each speech act is a set of **felicity conditions** that must be satisfied if that speech act is to be correctly (including honestly) performed. Here are some felicity conditions on the acts of questioning and requesting (where "S" stands for the speaker, "H" for the hearer, "P" for some state of affairs, and "A" for some action):

A.   S questions H about P:

  1. S does not know the truth about P.
  2. S wants to know the truth about P.
  3. S believes that H may be able to supply the information about P that S wants.

B.   S requests H to do A:

  1. S believes A has not yet been done.
  2. S believes that H is able to do A.
  3. S believes that H is willing to do A-type things for S.
  4. S wants A to be done.

When we think about what it means to ask a question or make a request, then, what we think about are the felicity conditions associated with each of these speech acts.

Notice that we would regard as peculiar anyone who seriously asks his or her pet dog questions about some upcoming election. The problem is that we know that dogs cannot answer serious (or any other) questions (see A.3). And in normal conversation we do not ask people questions that we already know the answers to. There are, of course, exceptions—people playing trivia or other games, lawyers questioning witnesses, teachers giving exams, but we recognize these situations to be socially exceptional in one way or another. Playing trivia violates A.2, for in trivia games people don't seriously want the information they seem to request; interrogating witnesses violates A.1, for a good lawyer tries to avoid any real surprises; and asking exam questions violates A.1 and A.2, for the teacher does know the answers. The fact is that we ask questions for a number of different purposes in different social contexts, and to reflect these differences, we can modify the particular felicity conditions. For trivia players and teachers we could eliminate felicity condition A.2, and for lawyers, we could eliminate condition A.1.

The felicity conditions for requests are less variable in the sense that we make requests for a single purpose: to get something done. Normally, we do not ask people to do things that have already been done. Indeed, doing so would make one extremely unpopular. And asking people to do things they cannot do would normally be regarded as a cruelty or a joke, depending on the nature of the request. If we do not want to get into trouble socially, we will be careful not to ask people who have higher social standing to do things for us unless the circumstances are quite special. Finally, we do not usually request things that we do not want done.

Indirect Speech Acts

Perhaps the most interesting single fact about speech acts is that we very commonly, in some cases almost invariably, perform speech acts indirectly. So far, we have discussed direct speech acts which can be performed in two ways: (1) by making a direct, literal utterance, or (2) by using a performative verb that names the speech act. In addition to these direct speech acts, we can use the felicity conditions to make indirect speech acts. Consider the speech acts question and request once again:

C. Questions

  1. Direct
       a. Did John marry Helen?
       b. I ask you whether or not John married Helen.

2. Indirect
    a.   I don't know if John married Helen. (A.1)
    b.   I would like to know if John married Helen. (A.2)
    c.   Do you know if John married Helen? (A.3)

D. Requests

1. Direct
    a.   Please take out the garbage.
    b.   I request that you take out the garbage.

2. Indirect
    a.   The garbage isn't out yet. (B.2)
    b.   Could you take out the garbage? (B.2)
    c.   Would you mind taking out the garbage? (B.3)
    d.   I would like for you to take out the garbage. (B.4)

There is something up front about the (C.1) questions and the (D.1) requests. Sentence (C.1.a) taken literally is a request for information about John's marrying Helen. The same is true of (C.1.b). Notice, however, that (C.2.a) taken literally is not a question at all. It is an assertion about the speaker's knowledge. (C.2.b) is also an assertion. (C.2.c), in contrast, is a question, but a question that literally asks whether the hearer knows something. (We sometimes say things like *It literally scared me to death*, but this is not, of course, a literal use of the word *literal*.)

As the notes given in connection with the sentences (C.2) and (D.2) suggest, indirect speech acts enjoy a very close connection with the felicity conditions on speech acts. Indeed, it can be argued that to perform a particular speech act indirectly, one need only formulate a question, assertion, request, or order that evokes a felicity condition on that speech act. In general, if the felicity condition concerns the best interests of the speaker, an assertion or request or order is used. If it concerns the best interests of the hearer, a question is used. So instead of assuming that felicity condition B.3 on requests holds, the speaker might ask if it does, as in "Would you mind taking me to work?" by way of making a polite request. This type of knowledge makes it easy to create indirect speech acts.

Identifying Indirect Speech Acts

Sentences that perform indirect speech acts are not direct, literal statements of various acts to be performed. Typically, with an indirect speech act, what the speaker actually means is different from what she or he literally says.

There are several ways to determine if an utterance is an indirect speech act. First check to see whether there is a performative verb in the sentence, since only direct speech acts are accomplished using performative verbs, never indirect speech acts. If the utterance contains a performative verb, it must be a direct speech act. If it doesn't, it might be indirect. For example, (C.1.b) and (D.1.b) both contain performative verbs, and therefore neither performs an indirect speech act.

If there is no performative verb in the sentence, check the sentence type to see if it corresponds to the sentence type typically used to perform a certain speech act. For example, an assertion is typically performed with a declarative sentence, a question is typically performed with an interrogative, and a request or command is typically performed with an imperative. In (C.2.a) and (C.2.b), however, a declarative sentence is used to ask a question. Thus, these sentences perform indirect speech acts.

We can also check to see whether any felicity conditions are violated for the literal meaning but not for its intended meaning. If there are violations for the literal but not the intended meaning, then the sentence must be an indirect speech act. For example, the literal meaning of (D.2.b) is a *question* asking whether or not the hearer can (i.e., is able to) take out the garbage. For this sentence to be a felicitous question, felicity conditions A.1 through A.3 must be satisfied. But in many situations (i.e., assuming the hearer is not disabled), A.1 is violated because the speaker clearly knows the answer to this question. On the other hand, for the intended meaning of the speaker *requesting* the hearer to take out the garbage, felicity conditions B.1 through B.4 are all satisfied. Therefore, this sentence is not a direct speech act of questioning, but an indirect speech act of making a request.

Finally, we can imagine a context in which the utterance is used and consider the way people normally respond to it. Different speech acts arouse different responses. Listeners respond to an assertion by a signal of acknowledgment, such as a nod or a verbal response like *Oh, I see*. People respond to a question by a confirmation or denial, or by supplying the information being solicited. People respond to a request or command by either carrying out the action accordingly or refusing with some explanation. If the response to an utterance is different from what its literal meaning would arouse, then it is used to perform an indirect speech act. For example, (D.2.b) is literally a question. But compare it with something like "Could you lift 200 pounds?" You can respond to this question by simply saying "Yes, I could," or "No, I couldn't," but it is not appropriate to respond to (D.2.b) this way. Instead, people normally respond to (D.2.b) by actually carrying out the requested action—taking out the garbage. This shows that while "Could you lift 200 pounds?" is a direct speech act of questioning, (D.2.b) is an indirect speech act of requesting—it has the same effect as (D.1.a). As another example, compare (C.2.c) with "Do you know John Jones?" While you just say, "Yes, I do," or "No, I don't," to answer the second question, you must provide information about whether or not John married Helen in responding to (C.2.c). The effect of (C.2.c) is the same as that of (C.1.a). Therefore, (C.2.c) performs an indirect speech act of asking a question about John's marrying Helen.

Exercises

1. Identify the speech act in each of the following sentences and state whether it is direct or indirect. Consider the contexts in which these sentences could be uttered. How does context affect their function?

    a. Don't smoke.
    b. Can you pass the salt?
    c. The washing machine is broken, dear.

2. A father tells his child: "I promise to take you to the zoo tomorrow."

    a. What is the speech act?
    b. Is it direct or indirect? Why?

3. For each of the following sentence types, write direct speech act sentences, one using a performative verb and one without. Then write an indirect speech act sentence for each.

    a. question
    b. request
    c. promise

4. The speech act of promising has the following felicity conditions:

S promises H to do A

1. S believes H wants A done.
2. S is able to do A.
3. S is willing to do A.
4. A has not already been done.

The speech act *threat* is very similar to *promise*. Because of this similarity, we can expect their felicity conditions to also be similar. Modify the *promise* felicity conditions to create the felicity conditions for a *threat*.

File 8.3

Rules of Conversation

The use of language, like most other forms of social behavior, is governed by social rules. Some rules are designed to protect people's feelings by showing respect (e.g., rules governing whether or not you can use a first name in addressing someone or must use a title and last name). Rather more important are rules designed to protect the integrity of our language. It is reasonably clear that if people were to decide to tell lies in some random way, so that listeners would have no way of determining when speakers were lying and when they were telling the truth, language would cease to be of any value to us. In response to this, we have settled on a set of conventions governing language use that preserves its integrity by requiring us, among other things, to be honest in its use, to have evidence for what we say, and to make what we say relevant to the speech context. What is interesting about these conventions is that they were never officially proposed and voted on by anybody, but instead have emerged naturally. And we learn them in much the same way we learn most social rules—by trial and error.

The philosopher H. P. Grice formulated a **Cooperative Principle**, which he believed underlies language use, according to which we are enjoined to make sure that what we say in conversation furthers the purposes of these conversations. Obviously, the requirements of different types of conversations will be different. In a business meeting, one is normally expected to keep one's remarks confined to the topic at hand unless it is changed in some approved way. Some close friends having a few beers at a bar would not be governed by tight rules of this sort. Nevertheless, even in a casual conversation, the conversation will normally have one or more purposes, and each of the parties to it can be expected by the rest to behave in ways that further these purposes. Thus, even the most casual conversation is unlikely to consist of such random sentences as:

(1) Kim: How are you today?
    Sandy: Oh, Harrisburg is the capital of Pennsylvania.
    Gail: Really? I thought the weather would be warmer.
    Mickey: Well, in my opinion, the soup could have used a little more salt.

Grice argued that there are a number of conversational rules, or **maxims**, that regulate conversation by way of enforcing compliance with the cooperative principle. At the heart of the system of maxims are the **Maxims of Quality**.

A. *Maxims of Quality:*

1. Do not say what you believe to be false.
2. Do not say that for which you lack adequate evidence.

The first Maxim of Quality is self-evident. Without regular compliance with this maxim, language would be useless to us. The second is more interesting, for it is only when we believe we have adequate evidence for some claim that we can have much confidence that we are observing the first Maxim of Quality. Nevertheless, people differ strikingly in what they think is good evidence for their views, especially in the areas of religion and politics (which is why these topics are so often off-limits as topics of conversation).

Because we may normally assume that speakers are obeying the Cooperative Principle, we sometimes draw inferences from what people say that are based on this assumption. Consider the following conversation:

(2) Sandy: We need someone to make some sort of fruit salad for the picnic.
    Tom: I can make my family's favorite fruit salad.

Sandy would likely draw the inference that Tom has actually made this fruit salad before, for the best evidence that Tom can make this salad is the fact that he has indeed made it. However, this is not a valid inference. Tom could legitimately say this was based on the fact that he had watched it being made many times and thought he knew all that needed to be known to make it. People sometimes say that the word *can* in a sentence like this is very weak (because they think it means merely 'is possible') and would therefore say that Sandy's drawing this inference is wrongheaded. However, this literalist view is out of touch with how we use the language. Suppose Tom were to make the salad and it were to come out very badly. Something like the following conversation might take place.

(3) Sandy: I thought you said you could make this salad!
    Tom: Well, I thought I could.

As Sandy's challenge illustrates, we take claims involving the word *can* quite seriously—because we assume that speakers using it are obeying the second Maxim of Quality.

A second class of maxims consists of the **Maxim of Relation** (often called the **Maxim of Relevance**).

B. Maxim of Relation/Relevance:

1. Be relevant.

This maxim is sometimes called the supermaxim because it is central to the orderliness of conversation—it limits random topic shifts like those of (1) above—but also because it is very important to understanding how we draw **conversational inferences** of the sort we talked about in connection with examples (2) and (3). Consider the following conversation:

(4) Sandy: Is Gail dating anyone these days?
    Tom: Well, she goes to Cleveland every weekend.

In this case, Sandy will likely draw the inference that Gail is dating someone because she will assume that what Tom has said is relevant to what she had said. In fact, if Tom knew that Gail goes to Cleveland every weekend because she has a job there, what he said would have been very misleading. The next pair of maxims are the **Maxims of Quantity**.

C. Maxims of Quantity:

1. Make your contribution as informative as is required.
2. Do not make your contribution more informative than is required.

The first maxim is intended to ensure that we make as strong a claim as is warranted (see the second Maxim of Quality) in any given circumstance, and the second is meant to ensure that we not make a *stronger* claim than is warranted in that circumstance. The following conversation illustrates an inference that might be drawn on the assumption that the speaker is obeying the first Maxim of Quantity.

(5) Gail: How far can you run without stopping?
    Kim: Twenty-four miles.
    Gail: I guess you can't run a whole marathon without stopping.
    Kim: Nonsense, I've done it a number of times.

Notice that what Kim says first must be true if what she says next is true. Certainly, if someone can run over twenty-six miles without stopping, then they can run twenty-four miles without stopping. However, Gail quite naturally was assuming that Kim was obeying the first Maxim of Quantity.

The final group of maxims we will discuss are the **Maxims of Manner**.

D. *Maxims of Manner:*

1. Avoid obscurity of expression.
2. Avoid ambiguity.
3. Be brief.
4. Be orderly.

These maxims are reasonably self-explanatory. The first enjoins us to avoid use of jargon or other terms our listeners cannot be expected to know. The second maxim requires us to avoid saying things that have two or more meanings (e.g., *He promised to phone at noon*) unless our listeners can be expected to know which meaning is intended. The third maxim tells us not to expound at length on a topic when a few words will do. The fourth comes down to saying that we should organize what we say in some intelligible way.

In discussing Grice's Conversational Maxims we pointed out that we commonly draw inferences from what people say based on the assumption that they are obeying the Cooperative Principle. This system of inference drawing is a kind of side effect of the maxims, maxims whose primary reason for being is to regulate conversation. One major reason for exploiting the maxims in this way is to make conversation easier. (Notice that "How far can you run without stopping?" is shorter than "What is the greatest distance you can run without stopping?") If we were to be forced in conversation to speak only in logically impeccable ways (e.g., to draw only logical inferences), conversation would proceed at a very slow pace, even assuming counterfactually that most of us have the logical capacities to do this. In conversation (4) above, Tom might have said "I believe that she may be dating someone because she goes to Cleveland every weekend, and that's not her hometown, and she doesn't have a job there." Given our set of maxims, Tom can say what he says and rely on the listener to figure out what he means.

There are two other reasons we use these maxims to communicate indirectly: (a) we sometimes need to avoid telling the truth because our frankness may hurt us; and (b) we sometimes need to avoid telling the truth because the truth may hurt someone else. Grice gave an example of a professor who was asked to write a letter of recommendation for a recent Ph.D. who was applying for a teaching position. Suppose that the letter went like this:

Dear Colleague:

Mr. John J. Jones has asked me to write a letter on his behalf. Let me say that Mr. Jones is unfailingly polite, is neatly dressed at all times, and is always on time for his classes.

Sincerely yours,

Harry H. Homer

Do you think Mr. Jones would get the job? This is an example of flouting a maxim—in this case, the Maxim of Quantity. Professor Homer has wanted to convey his negative impression of the candidate without actually saying anything negative about him. The receiver of this letter will assume that although Professor Homer has appeared to be violating the Maxim of Quantity, he is nevertheless not actually intending to be uncooperative and thus has said all of the relevant positive things he can think of—which is the essence of damning with faint praise.

Conventions of politeness (as well as a desire not to get punched in the nose) often keep us from insulting people overtly. By exploiting the maxims, we can insult people and (usually) get away with it. So, if someone does some bragging and another says, "I'm totally awed," the first will probably take this as an insult, but not one that he or she can legitimately take exception to. This conversational inference arises out of the recognition that the insulter is violating the first Maxim of Quality—the recognition that the claim is too strong (see the Maxims of Quantity) to likely be true. Such indirect communication is very important to us. If a teacher believes that his or her students are cheating on a quiz, he or she might say, "I see a lot of roving eyes!" The students will doubtless take this as an indirect charge that someone appears to be cheating. The Maxim of Relation/Relevance plays a role here because a claim about roving eyes is relevant just in case the eyes are roving to the wrong place. However, this way of trying to stop the cheating, since it falls short of an overt accusation, would probably not poison the atmosphere in the class.

The needs of social harmony and linguistic integrity are not always consistent with each other. It is said that there are societies in which the failure to answer a stranger's question is considered very impolite and therefore people in this society will give a stranger a wrong answer to a question rather than give no answer. Which is to say that Grice's maxims, being conventions, are very different from natural laws.

Exercises

1. Grice's actual statement of the third Maxim of Manner was "Be brief (avoid unnecessary prolixity)." What two Maxims of Manner does this statement violate?

2. Suppose you ask a friend what he thought of the new movie in town, and he replies, "Well, the costumes were authentic." Which rule guides you to the inference that your friend probably did not like the movie? Why?

3. Advertisements for over-the-counter drugs often make claims like "contains the most effective ingredient" or "contains the ingredient that doctors recommend most." These claims imply that the drugs are effective. What maxim is involved here? Is the inference a logically sound one? Why?

4. Jokes often rely on the hearer's knowledge of rules of conversation for their humorous effect. In the following joke by Henny Youngman, identify the rule that is being blatantly violated:

   I come home last night, and there's a car in the dining room. I said to my wife, "How did you get the car in the dining room?" She said, "It was easy. I made a left turn when I came out of the kitchen."

File 8.4

Language in Advertising

Advertising is a business in which language is used to persuade people to do things, for example, to buy a certain product, or vote for someone, or believe things, such as that a corporation is trustworthy or that a political philosophy is a good one. In the case of advertisements that make or imply substantive claims, the consumer might reasonably require that these claims be true, which brings up the age-old question of what the standards of truth in advertising ought to be. Linguists have a great deal to contribute to the answering of this question.

The focus of concern in this file will be to consider whether advertisers should be responsible only for what their claims entail or also for what they imply. The term **entail** is used here in a technical sense; File 7.4 introduced entailment relationships with respect to words, but the relationship may hold for sentences as well. (This will be explained shortly.) We will contrast the entailment relationship, that can be characterized as **logically valid** inference, with another relationship, which has been characterized as inference that is *not* logically valid but is nevertheless warranted. This relationship we will call implicature, and we will be using it in a technical sense.

Let's look first at **entailment**. If a sentence X entails another sentence Y, then whenever X is true Y must also be true. Stated in another way, there is no situation where X is true and Y is false. For example, sentence (1a) entails (1b):

(1) a. Ian drives a Corvette.
    b. Ian drives a car.

However, (1b) does not entail (1a). We can demonstrate this by citing a situation in which (1b) is true and (1a) is false. If Ian doesn't drive a Corvette, but rather a Nova, then (1b) is true and (1a) is false. The entailment relations here follow obviously from the meanings of the words *car* and *Corvette*, since all Corvettes are cars, but not all cars are Corvettes. But as we will see below, identifying entailment relationships is not always so easy.

Now consider implicature. There are two parts to the definition of **implicature**: a sentence X implicates a sentence Y if (i) X does not entail Y and (ii) the speaker is warranted in believing Y that is true based on the meaning of X and Grice's Maxims of Conversation (see File 8.3). Sentence (2a) implicates (2b):

(2) a. Not everyone is going to come.
    b. Someone is going to come.

In order to demonstrate that (2a) implicates (2b), we need to show first that (2a) does not entail (2b). We can do this by pointing out that (a) would still be true for the possible situation in which no one is going to come. In this situation, (2a) is true but (2b) is false. Next we need to show that upon hearing (2a) a speaker is warranted in believing sentence (2b). The first part of Grice's Maxim of Quantity states: make your contribution as informative as is required. Assuming that the speaker of (2a) is following this maxim, the more informative claim "no one is going to come" was not used because it was not known to be true. Thus, the hearer of (2a) is justified in believing that (2b) is true.

It can sometimes be rather difficult to distinguish what is entailed from what is implicated. Consider the following sentences. Does (3a) entail (3b)? Does (4a) entail (4b)?

3. a. ABC filters remove bacteria from your drinking water.
   b. If you use ABC filters, your drinking water will be free of bacteria.

4. a. I left because I wanted to.
   b. If I hadn't wanted to, I wouldn't have left.

In fact, neither of the (a) sentences entails its (b) counterpart. However, many people mistakenly believe that the (b) sentences are entailed. Actually, the sentences above are from an experiment that was conducted at Ohio State University. Of the subjects questioned, 60 percent thought (3a) entailed (3b), and 75 percent thought that (4a) entailed (4b). Why do these sentences not entail the others? Example (3) is the easier of the two to explain. Consider the situation in which ABC filters remove only a tiny bit of bacteria from your drinking water. Sentence (3a) is then true and (3b) is false. For the entailment relation to hold, (3a) would have to be changed to "remove *all* bacteria." Sentence (4a) appears to entail (4b), but actually it doesn't. Here's a possible situation where (4a) is true, but (4b) could very well be false: right after the speaker of (4a) decided to leave, someone came along and ordered him to leave.

The (a) sentences in (3) and (4) do, of course, *implicate* the (b) sentences. Sentence (3a) is a typical **generic** sentence (one with a possible general reading). Generic sentences are generally taken to be very strong claims, as they are often used to express significant inductive generalizations, as in "gold is heavier than water," "dogs bark," or "mass equals force times acceleration." In (3a) *bacteria* can be interpreted as either "some bacteria" (literal reading) or "all bacteria" (generic reading). In making a decision between the two, the Maxim of Relevance comes into play. If the claim in (3a) is to be relevant to your having significantly healthier drinking water—significant enough to cause you to buy the filters—then only the generic reading is relevant.

Sentence (4a) implicates (4b) through the Gricean maxims as well. If there were two reasons for the speaker's leaving—he wanted to *and* someone forced him to—and the speaker only gave one, then he would not be giving as much information as required. Assuming then that he *is* adhering to the Maxim of Quantity, we are led to believe that his wanting to leave was the *only* reason for his leaving. Thus we believe (4b), given (4a).

Before moving on to some real advertisements, let's consider the question raised at the beginning of this file. Should advertisers be responsible only for what their claims entail or should they also be responsible for what they implicate? In File 8.3 we saw that making implicatures based on the Gricean maxims is a critical part of linguistic communication. The results of the OSU survey discussed above demonstrate that implicatures are so much a part of language that most of us do not (and sometimes cannot) distinguish implicatures from logical entailments. If that is the case, then it's only right that advertisers be responsible for both the entailments and the implicatures of their claims. Unfortunately, this is usually not the case: advertisers are usually responsible for only the entailments. Much of the art of advertising, then, revolves around formulating claims that implicate a lot but entail little. Below we will investigate some of the more common techniques for accomplishing this goal.

One of the favorite ways to implicate a lot while entailing little is to leave out the *than* clause or prepositional phrase in the comparative construction. For example, Campbell's Soup recently advertised that its soups had "one-third less salt." The appropriate question to ask here is "One-third less salt than *what?*" Nowhere in the commercial is this question answered; the claim is always just "one-third less salt." By the Maxim of Relevance, the audience is inclined to fill out the comparative with the most likely choices, such as "one-third less salt than it used to have" or "one-third less salt than its competitors' soups." However, neither of these claims is entailed by Campbell's claim. All that is entailed is that their soup has one-third less salt than *something*. That something could be anything, including the Great Salt Lake.

If you think that bringing up the Great Salt Lake is going overboard just a bit, this should change your mind:

> When the Ford Motor Company advertised that the Ford LTD was 700 per cent quieter, one might have presumed that the model was 700 per cent quieter than some competing car or, at least, 700 per cent quieter than some other model of Ford. But when the Federal Trade Commission demanded substantiation of the claim, the Ford Company "revealed that they meant the inside of the Ford was 700 per cent quieter than the outside." (Bolinger 1980)

These open-ended comparatives are plentiful in the world of advertising. Here are a few recent examples.

    a.   More people sleep on Sealy Posturpedic.
    b.   Maytags are built to last longer and need fewer repairs.
    c.   Do you want better food? Better service? How about better prices? Then you'd better be at Big Bear's Carriage Place grand opening this Saturday at seven A.M.
    d.   The cars more Americans depend on. (Chevrolet)
    e.   Get the facts. Buick is better.

Another common advertising ploy is the use of "fine print" restrictions. This device is especially effective on TV because it's difficult to read very small print quickly and listen at the same time. In a McDonald's contest, if you win, you can "fly anywhere in the world Delta Airlines goes." At the bottom of the screen is written "Some restrictions apply." While "anywhere in the world" may conjure up images of island paradises, the restrictions might just limit you to Cleveland in January. UPS has a similar commercial. The narrator explains, "Our UPS Next Day Air Letter. Guaranteed overnight delivery to any address coast to coast." The fine print at the bottom of the screen reads "See Air Service Guide for Guarantee Details." This message appears as the narrator says the word *air* and disappears by the time he says the word *any*. That's a total of three seconds, and the written message is gone from the screen before the claim it restricts has been completed. Buick claims that its Le Sabre is "the most trouble-free American car," but the fine print states that this is based on a survey of "owner-related problems [whatever those might be] during the first 90 days of ownership." So, if you plan to buy a new car every three months, you're better off buying a Le Sabre (maybe).

Another favorite technique of advertisers is to make use of idiomatic language. An idiom is ambiguous between its literal and idiomatic readings, and the audience tends to lean toward the stronger of the two, that is, the reading that makes the stronger claim, because the weaker claim (the literal meaning) would be totally irrelevant given that the advertiser is attempting to persuade the listener to buy something. For example, Mercedes-Benz claims that its cars are "engineered like no other car in the world." On the idiomatic reading Mercedes are engineered *better* than any other car in the world, but on the literal meaning they're only engineered differently from any other car in the world. *Every* car can make that claim. Kenmore claims, "In one out of two American homes you'll find Kenmore appliances." The most natural reading is that 50 percent of American homes have Kenmore appliances. But there is another, more literal reading, where there are two American homes, one with Kenmore appliances and another without.

Still another way to implicate a lot and entail little is to qualify very strong claims with modal auxiliaries (e.g., *can, could, might*, etc.) or adverbs. One car manufacturer claims that its newest model "may be one of the most powerful cars in the world." But then again, of course, it may not be; it may be one of the least powerful. Here's one from Allstate: "There's another way for new homeowners to save money: the Allstate New House Discount. It could save you up to 15% on Allstate homeowners insurance." It *could* do a lot of things, but *will* it? A GMAC commercial states, "If you choose to finance or lease your new GMAC vehicle someplace other than GMAC, you might find yourself waiting in line instead of coming out hugging one." This claim not only fails to entail that you *will* wait in line elsewhere (or even have a good chance of having to do so), but also fails to entail that you *won't* wait in line if you go to GMAC. Another product "leaves clothes virtually static-free." Not static-free—*virtually* static free.

There are many other methods advertisers employ to achieve similar results; the reader can now probably extend our list considerably. We will simply reiterate the main point: making implicatures is a crucial part of linguistic communication. Language users do not easily distinguish between the logical entailments of utterances and the implicatures drawn from these utterances. Because advertisers are usually responsible only for the logical entailments of their claims, they often craft their ads so that their audience makes favorable, but false, implicatures.

Exercises

1. Comment on the entailments and implicatures of the following claims.

    a. "Interesting fact about what he took. Its decongestant lasts only 4 hours per dose, and it contains aspirin, which can upset your stomach. Contac lasts up to twelve hours per dose and does not contain aspirin." (What is entailed/implied about how long Contac lasts and whether or not it upsets your stomach?)

    b. "I used to have dandruff, so I tried Head and Shoulders. Then I tried Selsun Blue. Blue is better."

    c. "STP reduced engine lifter wear up to 68%." (Fine print at bottom of screen: "Results vary by type of car, oil, and driving.")

    d. "People from Ford [County] prefer Chevy trucks."

    e. "Isn't it time you got your health on the right course? Now you can cut back on cholesterol, cut back on sodium, cut back on fat, and still love the food you eat because now there's new Right Course from Stouffer's."

Reference

Bolinger, Dwight Le Merton. 1980. *Language, the Loaded Weapon: The Use and Abuse of Language Today.* London, New York: Longman.

File 8.5   Discourse Analysis

One of the things we do most frequently with language is to tell stories about ourselves. Children tell about what happened at Uncle Henry's or about what they did at school; adults tell about their day at the office, about what the birth of their child was like, or about what happened when they got stopped by the police. People tell stories around the dinner table, at bars, in dorm rooms—any time they are engaged in informal talk. We tell personal experience stories to instruct, to persuade, or to amuse. Perhaps most important, we tell stories in order to reenvision our own experiences so we can evaluate them, reformulate them, and fit them to our images of ourselves and our lives. In the past fifteen or twenty years, linguists have become interested in personal experience stories for what they can tell us generally about the structure of discourse and about how meaning is created as people talk, and for what they can tell us specifically about such things as tense choices and the use of words like well and so. And while personal experience stories are interesting in their own right, they are also complete, easily observable units of talk that provide examples of many of the things discourse analysts and sociolinguists are interested in.

The Structure of Personal Experience Stories

Before we proceed, we should clarify what we mean by a personal experience story. All stories involve some **narration** or chronological reporting of events in the past. Narration is characterized by *narrative clauses*: clauses that occur in the temporal order of the events they describe. Consider, for example, this narrative:

(1) a. I went to pick up some groceries,
    b. and the car died,
    c. and I had to wait for the tow truck.

Even though there are no explicit sequence words like *before*, *after*, or *then*, clauses (a)–(c) are interpreted as being in chronological order. If clause (a) came after (b) and (c), we would interpret the sequence of events differently.

The requirement that stories include some narrative clauses explains why an utterance of a single clause, like

(2) We ate at the new Chinese restaurant

is not a story. But we would not be likely to call example (1) a story, either. One way to convince yourself of this point is to imagine what would happen if a person were to say, "Listen, I've got a great story," and then give you example (1). Your response would probably be "Well?" or "So what?" or something similar. People often talk about things that happened to them for practical reasons, for example in answer to questions like "Why were you late?" or "Where were you when the theft occurred?" Reports like (1) are appropriate in such contexts, when stories would clearly be inappropriate.

The stories we will be discussing are not traditional. They are stories a teller tells about his or her own experiences. While some personal experience stories are told again and again and may in time become legends, most are only told once, and their telling is so tied to the immediate context that they simply would not work in another context. By studying personal experience stories, as opposed to traditional folklore (myths, legends, fairy tales, etc.), we can be sure that the structure of the stories reflects general linguistic and cultural knowledge about what makes a story, rather than specific conventions associated with particular legends or tales.

All complete, well-developed personal experience stories have been found to include six elements:

1. an abstract
2. orientation
3. complicating action
4. evaluation
5. result or resolution
6. coda

In discussing these elements, we will refer to example (3) below.

(3)

1	had a hell of a camping trip one weekend
2	been . . . two or three years ago now
3	went out into this woods
4	was a million miles from nowhere
5	and . . . we cleared a campspot . . . campsite . . . John and I
6	and uh . . . set our tents up
7	and gathered up some rocks
8	and made a firepit
9	had a good-looking camp when we were done
10	gathered up a bunch of brush
11	and made a big windbreak
12	by late Friday afternoon . . . we were . . . pretty well settled in
13	uh . . . like I said
14	had a good looking camp . . .
15	the Saturday that followed
16	the Saturday of that weekend
17	we just did a lot of shooting
18	and actually just lounging around camp a lot (laughter)
19	did a little bit of hunting
20	really just . . . took it good and easy that day . . .
21	but it was Sunday morning
22	when we got up
23	that was the high point of the whole camp
24	we . . . uh . . . got up that morning and
25	wearing our camouflage . . . uh to . . .
26	basically didn't want to be seen by anybody else
27	and preferred to see them before w–
28	them before they saw us
29	we were fixing coffee over the campfire
30	and I happen to look up
31	out across this field
32	at the edge of the woods
33	about three hundred yards out

34	this . . . six buck deer
35	beautiful
36	just majestic as hell
37	they stood out there for about a half hour
38	noses in the wind
39	trying to catch our scent
40	never really did
41	we finally decided to show them what we were
42	and so we both stood up
43	and (small laugh) . . . all you saw was six white tails
44	headed the opposite direction
45	but it was a truly fantastic sight
46	we closed up camp that day
47	and came back to civilization
48	never really been able to forget that day
49	or that campout
50	as a result of it (long pause)
51	its th-
52	that's the sort of thing I guess that makes life worth living

The teller of a story often begins with one or more clauses that summarize the story. In (3), the abstract is in lines 1–2. Examples of abstracts from other stories are these:

(4) You want to know how I met this guy?

(5) Well, this is the story of how I found my first cat, named Tom.

Sometimes, another participant in a conversation may provide a story's abstract, by saying something like:

(6) Tell the one about when your nephew almost drowned.

In other cases, the abstract function may be served by the conversational context as a whole. If a group of people are telling stories about high-school pranks, for example, the third or fourth teller may not need to announce that that is what he or she is going to do, too.

Orientation

After the abstract and before the narrative part of a story, there are usually a number of free (non-narrative) clauses in which the teller sets the stage for the action. In these orientation clauses, we find relevant details about the background of the story: the time, the place, who was involved and what they were doing. Lines 3–23 in example (3) provide orientation. Orientation clauses can also appear in other parts of a story to provide descriptive information that becomes relevant as the story emerges, as the teller, reacting with his or her listeners, creates it. One example in (3) is line 29. In addition to giving background details, orientation clauses can also serve as evaluations, as we will see. Orientation clauses are often in the past progressive (was V-ing) tense.

Complicating Action: Result or Resolution

The complicating action and the result or resolution form the narrative core of the story. The complicating action part of a story answers the question "Then what happened?" and the result or resolution tells "What finally happened." In (3), the complicating action begins in line 24, and the result or resolution ends at line 44. Read through this part of the story to get a feel for how the dramatic tension rises (up to line 39) and then falls. You will note that while many of the clauses are narrative clauses in the simple past or historical present tense, some are not; they would not have to be in the position they are in. We will examine the function of clauses like these shortly; see if you can form a hypothesis.

Coda

At the end of a story, the teller often summarizes it or provides a kind of moral, relating the story to the surrounding conversation and bringing the hearers back out of the world of the story and into the present. There is a clear coda in (3), in lines 45–52. Here are examples of codas from other personal experience stories:

(7) a.   and that's the honest-to-God truth
     b.   all that happened; he's still alive and well and believe it or not he's in Paris becoming a gourmet chef.
     c.   and that's how Tom found a home

Evaluation

In normal conversation, the alternation of speakers (or turn-taking) proceeds fairly regularly. While some speakers may talk more than others, all are following linguistic and cultural rules about when it is permissible to take over the conversational floor (for example, when the current speaker pauses or reaches a syntactic break), and about what sorts of simultaneous back-channeling (*uh-huh*s, *right*s, *oh yeah*s, and nonverbal cues) are required to show that a listener is attending to a speaker. When one speaker is telling a story, however, some of these rules are suspended. The storyteller takes an unusually long turn in the conversation and is generally not interrupted, except for brief requests for clarification and for back-channeling, until he or she announces, by means of a coda, that the story is over. Clearly, a person who wants others to allow him or her to take up a large block of conversational time with a story had better have something worthwhile to say. The story had better have a *point*. Pointless stories are unacceptable in conversation, and a person who tells a story without a point will be greeted with an unpleasant response like, "So what?"

What makes a story worth telling? What sorts of things can count as the point of a story? The answer depends on the context, both general (what is unusual enough, funny enough, or scary enough to tell a story about in one culture may not be in another) and specific (a person's best story may fall flat if it's told to the wrong person or in the wrong situation). In very broad terms, a story has to be about something unusual: a situation that resulted in something different than one would expect, a dangerous situation, or a situation in which the teller demonstrated special courage, intelligence, civic responsibility, or humor. The point of a story may in fact change as the story is being told, as a result of listeners' questions and comments; if it becomes clear that the teller's original claim about what makes the story tellable will not satisfy the audience, the teller may try to recast the story with a new point.

There is a wide variety of linguistic strategies a storyteller can use to underscore the fact that his or her story has a point. These strategies are referred to as **evaluation**. Evaluation occurs throughout a story—an effective storyteller constantly reminds the audience that the story is worth telling—but tends to be especially prominent immediately before the result or resolution part of the story, when the tension needs to be especially high.

Evaluative devices fall into two main categories: **external** and **internal**. External evaluation is provided by phrases and clauses that interrupt the narrative, thereby creating suspense. In story (3), the teller stops for an evaluative comment in line 23 ("that was the high point of the whole camp"). External evaluative commentary can also be placed in the mouth of another character besides the teller, as in the following example:

(8) Oh, man, he felt bad as hell about that for a long time.

Internal evaluative devices are special features of clauses that serve other functions in the story. Internal evaluation is provided by intensifiers, comparators, and modifiers. **Intensifiers** are verbal or nonverbal elements, or structural choices, that highlight a phrase or clause. These include gestures, expressive phonology (loudness or drawn-out syllables), repetition (as in the description of the "good-looking camp" in [3]), or the series of prepositional phrases in lines 31–33, and phrases like "by God" or "you know."

Since stories are about events in the past, one might ask why there should be any clauses in a story that are not in the past tense. One answer is that clauses that are not simple, positive, past-tense narrative clauses provide internal evaluation by comparing what did happen with what could have, should have, will, or didn't happen. Such clauses are called **comparators**.

Modifiers of various kinds also serve as evaluation devices. The teller can slow down the action with extra descriptions of what people were doing. Appositive (i.e., parenthetical) nouns, adjectives, and adverbial clauses can also create suspense. In (3) for example, the teller creates interest in the physical setting and in the deer by providing details about them.

If (3) had been a simple narrative report, of the kind one might be required to deliver in court for example, it would only have been necessary for the teller to say something like, "I saw six deer in the woods one weekend." The fact that he has instead evaluated his narrative is what gives the report a point and makes it a story. Evaluation, then, is the key to what makes a group of chronologically ordered clauses into a story.

Broader Perspectives

Most of us are aware that groups of written sentences (paragraphs, term papers, novels) are highly structured, because we have undergone the often agonizing conscious process of learning how to structure them, in freshman composition, creative writing, and introductory literature classes. We tend to be much less aware that groups of spoken utterances are structured, and are often surprised to find that something as casual and spontaneous as a personal experience story has the kind of elaborate organization that we have seen. The functional, content-based approach to discourse structure examined here is not the only model linguists have used. Some discourse analysts use models of the internal structure of discourse that are analogous to models of the structure of sentences, making use of such notions as story or text grammars. Others look at discourse cohesion, or what makes a group of sentences function as a single unit of discourse at all. Still others start from the assumption that the meaning of a story, or any other kind of text, is more than the sum total of the meanings of its words or sentences; they examine the cognitive schemas, cultural models, or previous knowledge that hearers use to construct the meaning of a text as they hear it.

One thing that becomes clear through any of these approaches, though, is that lexical and grammatical choices are as much the result of discourse-level requirements as they are the result of sentence-level syntactic or semantic requirements. Think, for example, about the alternation in personal experience stories between simple past and historical present tenses. In isolated sentences, the present tense ("I get out of the car") and the simple past tense ("I got out of the car") do not refer to the same time (if the simple present tense can really be said to refer to any time at all). In a story, these two sentences *could* be used to refer to the same time. But they cannot always be used interchangeably. At the beginning of a story, the teller must use the past tense to establish that he or she is talking about the past. Later in the story, the teller can switch tenses but will only do so if it is relevant for purposes of evaluation. A complete explanation of these two tenses in English (and none exists yet) would have to make reference to their functions and contexts in discourse.

A topic that we have barely touched on in this file is the relationship of stories to the conversations they are part of. We have alluded to the requirements imposed on a storyteller by the rules of conversation. (If you want to take up a large chunk of conversation you need to have something worthwhile to say, and you need to use evaluative devices to show that it's worth saying.) There are many other questions we could have asked: What do listeners contribute to the telling of a story? What kinds of conversations can include stories? How is conversation structured, in general; what are the rules? Sociologists and linguists have provided partial answers to some of these questions, particularly the last. Another interesting topic, which we have not touched on at all, is how oral stories differ from written ones, or oral language use from written language use in general. Linguists are beginning to explore this topic, too.

Perhaps the most interesting question raised in the study of personal experience narratives concerns the ways in which speakers and hearers cooperate in the reconstruction, reevaluation, and re-creation of the past through the process of talking about it. Nobody ever talks about everything; we select things to tell stories about, and we choose ways to give them a point and to make them memorable and pleasing to the ear. In doing this, we create language as we talk, and we create the world as we talk about it.

References

Labov, William. 1972. "The Transformation of Experience in Narrative Syntax." In *Language in the Inner City*. Philadelphia: University of Pennsylvania Press, 354–96.
(Uses Labov and Waletzky's framework in analyzing fight stories told by inner-city black adolescents.)

Labov, William, and Joshua Waletzky. 1967. "Narrative Analysis: Oral Versions of Personal Experience." In June Helm, ed., *Essays on the Verbal and Visual Arts*. Seattle: University of Washington Press, 12–44.
(This study describes, in more detail, the kind of analysis that has been examined in this file.)

Linde, Charlotte. 1984. *The Creation of Coherence in Life Stories*. Norwood, NJ: Ablex.
(The creation of self in personal experience stories.)

Polanyi, Livia. 1983. *The American Story: From the Structure of Linguistics Texts to the Grammar of a Culture*. Norwood, NJ: Ablex.
(What can count as the point of a story?)

Sachs, H., E. Schegloff, and G. Jefferson. 1974. "A Simplest Systematics for the Organization of Turn-Taking for Conversation." *Language* 50: 696–735.
(An analysis of how conversations are structured.)

Tannen, Deborah, ed. 1981. *Spoken and Written Language: Exploring Literacy and Orality*. Norwood, NJ: Ablex.
(A collection of essays comparing speaking and writing, many having to do with narrative.)

Wolfson, Nessa. 1982. *CHP: The Conversational Historical Present in American English Narrative*. Dordrecht: Foris.
(A detailed study of tense choices in personal experience stories.)

9

Psycholinguistics

The field of psycholinguistics attempts to answer questions about how language is represented and processed in the brain and what areas of the brain are used for language processing. Psycholinguistics is an experimental discipline that tests assumptions about the processing and the learning of language.

File 9.1

Language and the Brain

Linguists analyze the structure of language and propose models that can account for the linguistic phenomena they observe—sets of phonemes, collections of phonological or morphological rules, guidelines for building syntactic structures, and so on. However, this level of linguistic pursuit is quite abstract and often removed from considerations of the physiology of language: How is language actually stored in and processed by the brain? This question draws us into two of the newer areas of linguistic investigation: **neurolinguistics**, the study of the neural and electrochemical bases of language development and use; and **psycholinguistics**, the study of the acquisition, storage, comprehension, and production of language.

This file will introduce you to some of the regions and properties of the human brain that are thought to be essential to understanding and using language. Keep in mind as you read that the human brain is extremely complex and our knowledge of its inner workings still very limited. There are many aspects of brain function that are only poorly or not at all understood. We present you here with the facts that have been reliably established at this point and time, facts discovered through numerous elaborate psychological studies and linguistic experiments.

Physical Features of the Brain

The brain is divided into two nearly symmetrical halves, the right and left **hemispheres**, each of which is responsible for processing certain kinds of information concerning the world around us. These hemispheres are connected by a bundle of nerve fibers called the **corpus callosum**. These nerve fibers make it possible for the two hemispheres to communicate with each other and build a single, coherent picture of our environment from the many different kinds of stimuli—visual, tactile, oral, auditory, and olfactory—that we receive.

The brain is covered by a one-quarter-inch thick membrane called the **cortex**. It has been suggested that it is this membrane that makes human beings capable of higher cognitive functions, such as the ability to do math or use language, and that its development was one of the primary evolutionary changes that separated us from other animals. In fact, most of the language centers of the brain that we will be discussing later in this chapter are contained in the cortex. This is why even minor damage to the surface of the brain, e.g., that caused by a strong blow to the head, can result in language impairment.

As you can see from the drawing on the following page, the cortex is not flat but covered with bumps and indentations. The bumps on the surface of the brain are called **gyri** (sg. *gyrus*) and the depressions are called **fissures**. Scientists use certain fissures to demarcate particular areas of the brain. One of the most prominent of these is the **Sylvian Fissure**, the large horizontal fold located in the middle of each hemisphere separating the temporal lobe from the frontal lobe of the brain.

Several portions of the cortex are specialized to perform particular functions that play a role in language use. The first that we will introduce is the **auditory cortex** (in the figure referred to as "Primary Auditory Area"), located next to the Sylvian Fissure. The auditory cortex is responsible for receiving and identifying auditory signals and converting them into a form that can be interpreted by other areas of the brain. A second special area is the **visual cortex** (in the figure referred to as "Primary Visual Area"), located in the lower back of each hemisphere. This area receives and interprets visual stimuli and is thought to be the storage site for pictoral images. A third is the **motor cortex**, which is found in the upper middle of each hemisphere, perpendicular to the Sylvian Fissure. The fissure between the motor cortex and the somatic sensory cortex also separates the frontal lobe from the parietal lobe. This part of the brain is responsible for sending signals to your muscles, including those of your face, jaw, and tongue, to make them move.

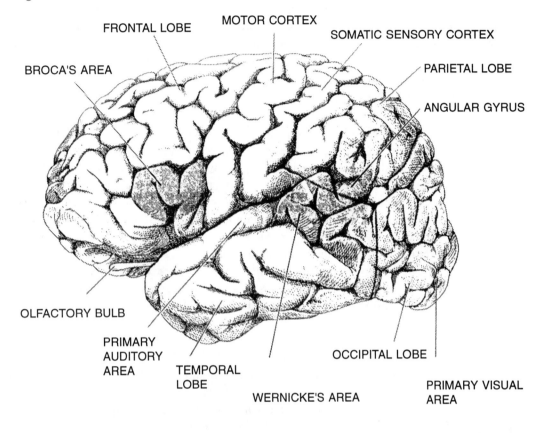

Figure 1.   The left hemisphere of the human brain. "Map of the Human Cortex," figure by Carol Donner from "Specializations of the Human Brain," by Norman Geschwind. Copyright © 1979 by Scientific American, Inc. All rights reserved.

Then there are the **language centers** of the brain—parts of the cortex that, as far as we know, are used only for the production and comprehension of language. In contrast to the other areas we have introduced here, these centers are found only in the hemisphere that is specialized for language: for approximately 90 percent of the right-handed people and 90 percent of the left-handed people, this is the left hemisphere. The opposing hemisphere does not have these language centers. The first of these language centers that we will introduce is **Broca's area**. Located at the base of the motor cortex, this language center appears to be responsible for organizing the articulatory patterns of language and directing the motor cortex when we want to talk. (This involves the face, jaw, and tongue in the case of spoken language, and the hands, arms, and body in the case of signed language.) Broca's area also seems to control the use of inflectional morphemes, like the plural and past tense markers, as well as function morphemes, like determiners and prepositions; this is a very important function with respect to the formation of words and sentences. Next, there is **Wernicke's area**. Located near the back section of the auditory cortex, this section of the brain is involved in the comprehension of words and the selection of words when producing sentences. Wernicke's area and Broca's area are connected by a bundle of nerve fibers called the **arcuate fasciculus**. Like the corpus callosum, these nerve fibers allow the two areas of the brain that they connect to share information; without them, we would not be able to look up words in our "mental lexicon" (via Wernicke's area) and then say them (via Broca's area). (Think of the mental lexicon as a dictionary, located in the brain, containing all the words an individual knows, including what each word means and how to pronounce it. Recognize, however, that this dictionary is not tangible but rather some abstract network of information scattered throughout the brain. We cannot point to it, but we have strong reasons to believe that it exists.) The final language center we will introduce is the **angular gyrus**. This area, located between Wernicke's area and the visual cortex, converts visual stimuli into auditory stimuli (and vice versa), allowing us to match the spoken form of a word with the object it describes; this ability is crucial to the human capacity to read and write.

The Flow of Linguistic Information

Now, how do all these areas of the brain work together to process language? As far as we know, that depends on what type of stimulus (auditory, visual, etc.) is involved and what type of linguistic result (speaking, reading, understanding, etc.) is desired. To produce a spoken word, for example, a person first chooses a word from the mental dictionary. This process activates Wernicke's area, which then interprets the dictionary entry, identifying the meaning of the word, how to pronounce it, and so on. The phonetic information for the entry is sent via the arcuate fasciculus to Broca's area. Then Broca's area determines what combination of the various articulators is necessary to produce each sound in the word and instructs the motor cortex which muscles to move.

To read a word, one first takes the stimulus into the visual cortex via the eyes. The angular gyrus then associates the written form of the word with an entry in the mental dictionary, which releases information about the word into Wernicke's area. Wernicke's area then interprets the entry and gives one the meaning of the word.

Before reading ahead, can you figure out how you understand and repeat a word just said to you? First, the stimulus is brought into the auditory cortex through the ears. That auditory stimulus is matched to a word in your mental dictionary. If you have an image or written form associated with the word, the angular gyrus will activate the visual cortex and you will have a picture of the item and its spelling available to you. In the meanwhile, Wernicke's area is activated, interprets the entry from the dictionary, and sends the phonetic information about the word to Broca's area, which coordinates the necessary articulatory commands and gives them to the motor cortex.

Lateralization and Contralateralization

As alluded to earlier, each of the brain's hemispheres is responsible for different cognitive functions. This specialization is referred to as **lateralization**. For most individuals, the left hemisphere is dominant in the areas of analytic reasoning, temporal ordering, arithmetic, and language processing. The right hemisphere is in charge of processing music, perceiving nonlinguistic sounds, and performing tasks that require visual and spatial skills or pattern recognition. Lateralization happens in early childhood and can be reversed in its initial stages if there is damage to a part of the brain that is crucially involved in an important function. For example, if a very young child whose brain was originally lateralized so that language functions were in the left hemisphere receives severe damage to the language centers, the right hemisphere can develop language centers to compensate for the loss. After a certain period, however, lateralization is permanent and cannot be reversed, no matter how severely the brain is damaged.

The connections between the brain and the body are almost completely **contralateral**. This means that the right side of the body is controlled by the left hemisphere, while the left side of the body is controlled by the right hemisphere. It is also important to realize that this contralateral connection means that sensory information from the right side of the body is received by the left hemisphere, while sensory information from the left side of the body is received by the right hemisphere. Sensory information can be any data one gathers through hearing, seeing, touching, tasting, or smelling.

Many different experiments have provided evidence for contralateralization. One example of this type of experiment is the **dichotic listening test.** In this test, two sounds are presented at the same time to a person with normal hearing, one in the left ear and one in the right. The sounds may be linguistic (a person saying a word) or nonlinguistic (a door slamming). The subject is asked what sound he or she heard in one ear or another. These tests show that responses to the right-ear stimuli are quicker and more accurate when the stimuli are verbal, while responses to the left-ear stimuli are quicker and more accurate when the stimuli are nonverbal. To understand why this is so, recall that the theory of contralateralization predicts that in order for a linguistic signal presented to the left ear to reach the left hemisphere (where language is processed) it must go first to the right hemisphere and then across the corpus callosum to the left hemisphere. However, a linguistic signal presented to the right ear has a more direct connection with the left hemisphere and can therefore be recognized more readily. We find just the opposite effect with nonlinguistic sounds, where a stimulus presented to the left ear is recognized faster and better than one presented to the right ear, because the right hemisphere is where nonverbal sounds are processed.

Further evidence for contralateralization comes from so-called **split-brain patients.** Normally, the two hemispheres are connected by the **corpus callosum,** but for certain kinds of severe epilepsy, the corpus callosum used to be surgically severed, preventing the two hemispheres from transmitting information to each other. (Since epileptic seizures are caused in part by a patient's motor cortices "overloading" on information sent back and forth between the two hemispheres, this procedure greatly reduced the number and danger of such seizures. This kind of treatment, however, is abandoned nowadays). Since the connections from the brain to the rest of the body are contralateral, various experiments can be performed on these split-brain patients in order to identify the cognitive characteristics of the two hemispheres. In one experiment, a patient is blindfolded and an object is placed in his or her right hand. The patient can say the name of the object. However, if an object is placed in the same patient's *left* hand, he or she usually cannot identify the object verbally. Can you explain why? When the object is in the subject's right hand, the left hemisphere is experiencing the heightened sensory activity associated with holding the object. But without a fully functioning corpus callosum, the two hemispheres cannot share information, and the right hemisphere is effectively "blind" to any input concerning the object. Conversely, when the object is placed in the subject's left hand, only the right hemisphere experiences the sensory feedback associated with holding the object. Because the subject receiving input in the left hand is unable to state the name of the object, we infer that the mental abilities and memory store needed to name the object are not available to the right hemisphere.

Hemispherectomies, operations in which one hemisphere or part of one hemisphere is removed from the brain, also provide evidence for lateralization. This operation, performed on people who experience severe seizures, affects the patient's behavior and ability to think. It has been found that hemispherectomies involving the left hemisphere result in aphasia much more frequently than those involving the right hemisphere. This indicates that the left side of the brain is used to process language in most people, while the right side has much less to do with language processing.

Language Disorders

In the 1860s, the physician Paul Broca observed that damage to the left side of the brain resulted in impaired language ability while damage to the right side of the brain did not. Since that time researchers have observed that approximately 70 percent of the people with damage to the left hemisphere experience **aphasia,** an inability to perceive, process, or produce language because of physical damage to the brain. Aphasia is found in only approximately 1 percent of people suffering from damage to the right hemisphere. This provides additional support for the view that language is localized in the left side of the brain.

As you might guess, the linguistic skills that are affected as a result of aphasia depend on where the brain damage is suffered. Individuals with **Broca's aphasia**, a damage to Broca's area, suffer from an inability to plan the motor sequences used in speech or sign. When they attempt to produce language, they speak haltingly and have a hard time forming complete words. They also display a tendency for telegraphic speech, or speech without inflections and function words such as *to* and *the*, although the basic word order is correct. Below is a sample of speech produced by someone with Broca's aphasia:

Example 1: *Broca's Aphasia*

Examiner:	Tell me, what did you do before you retired?
Aphasic:	Uh, uh, uh, pub, par, partender, no.
Examiner:	Carpenter?
Aphasic:	(shaking head yes) Carpenter, tuh, tuh, tenty year.

Broca's aphasia seems to result in primarily *expressive* disorders. Accordingly, comprehension of the speech of others is not too much of a problem for Broca's aphasics, although they may have some difficulty matching the correct semantic interpretation to the syntactic order of the sentence. For instance, comprehension is likely to break down when the sequence of words is extremely important to the understanding of their message, as in reversible passives such as *the lion was killed by the tiger*. A Broca's aphasic is quite likely to understand this as identical to the active sentence *the lion killed the tiger*.

Wernicke's aphasia, on the other hand, results in primarily *receptive* disorders: it is very difficult for a patient with this problem to understand the speech of others. As you might expect, this often results in the Wernicke's aphasic misinterpreting what others say and responding in an unexpected way. Moreover, because the Wernicke's patient has trouble interpreting words from his or her mental dictionary, he or she has a tendency to produce semantically incoherent speech. These two effects result in the type of speech you see in Example 2. Wernicke's patients also often speak in circumlocutions, or expressions that people use when they are unable to name the word they want. For example, the patient may say *what you drink* for *water* and *what we smell with* for *nose*. The syntactic order of words is also altered. *I know I can say* may become *I know can I say*. That patients with Wernicke's aphasia are unable to comprehend the speech of others is demonstrated by the fact that they often cannot follow simple instructions, such as *stand up, turn to your right*, and so on.

Example 2: *Wernicke's Aphasia*

Examiner:	Do you like it here in Kansas City?
Aphasic:	Yes, I am.
Examiner:	I'd like to have you tell me something about your problem.
Aphasic:	Yes, I, ugh, can't hill all of my way. I can't talk all of the things I do, and part of the part I can go alright, but I can't tell from the other people. I usually most of my things. I know what can I talk and know what they are, but I can't always come back even though I know they should be in, and I know should something eely I should know what I'm doing. . . .

A third type of language disorder, called **conduction aphasia**, results from damage to the arcuate fasciculus. A patient suffering from conduction aphasia sounds something like a Wernicke's aphasic (fluent but meaningless speech) but shows signs of being able to comprehend the speech of others. Like a Broca's aphasic, the patient will be able to understand utterances but will not be able to repeat them. This pattern of symptoms makes sense if you consider what the arcuate fasciculus does: it transmits information from Wernicke's area to Broca's area. If these two language centers are unable to communicate, the patient with damage to the arcuate fasciculus may be able to understand speech and correctly interpret words from the mental lexicon, but not be able to transmit information to Broca's area so that words can be articulated.

The last two language disorders we will mention are **alexia** and **agraphia**, which are both caused by damage to the angular gyrus. Alexia is defined as the inability to read and comprehend written words. This occurs when the angular gyrus cannot accurately match the visual form of a word with a phonetic form in Wernicke's area. Occasionally, this problem is accompanied by the inability to write words, known as agraphia. This disorder is often attributed to the inability of the angular gyrus to relate the phonetic form of a stimulus with a written form in the visual cortex. Note that alexia is not the same thing as dyslexia. Alexia is the result of damage to the angular gyrus caused by an accident, stroke, or lesion. Dyslexia, as current research indicates, is caused by a *structural difference* in a portion of the brain called the temporal lobe; people with dyslexia can almost always read and write normally with special training. Someone with alexia cannot ever regain his or her previous reading skill.

Although a detailed understanding of exactly how the brain stores and uses language is not possible at this time, there are some aspects of the brain's involvement in language which are understood. We have seen that language is a left hemisphere phenomenon. Evidence for this comes from patterns of aphasia, the effects of hemispherectomies, the language abilities of split-brain patients, and the results of dichotic listening experiments. We have seen that through the study of aphasia the location of specific types of linguistic abilities in the brain is possible.

References

Bayles, Kathryn. 1981. *Linguistics: An Introduction to Language and Communication*. Edited by Adrian Akmajian, Richard A. Demers, and Robert M. Harnish. Cambridge: MIT Press.

Springer, Sally, and George Deutsch. 1981. *Left Brain, Right Brain*. San Francisco: W. H. Freeman.

Exercises

1. Modify each blank diagram of the left hemisphere of the brain according to the instructions:

   a. Shade and label Broca's area, Wernicke's area, the arcuate fasciculus, and the angular gyrus.

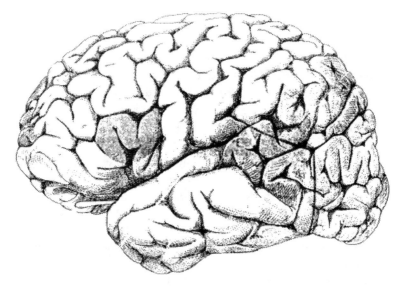

   b. Shade and label the three areas of the cortex involved in the production and comprehension of language.

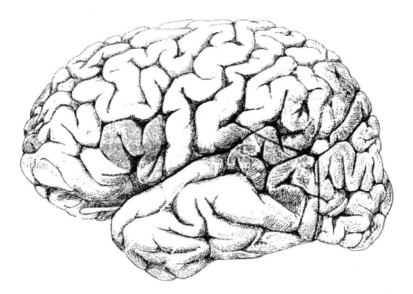

c. Using arrows, show the flow of linguistic information when one is reading a word. Label all of the areas of the brain that are directly involved in this activity.

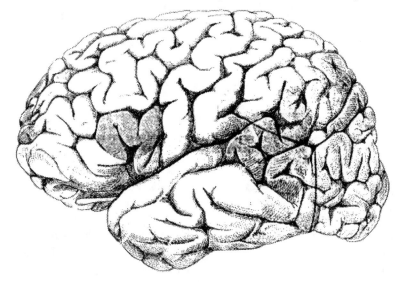

d. Do the same as in (c), but show what happens if you then say out loud the word you just read. Describe how (c) and (d) are different.

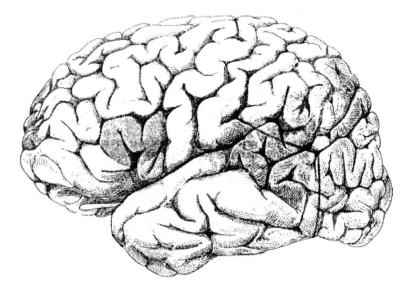

2. Indicate by putting an "X" in the appropriate box which symptoms patients with each type of aphasia have.

	Expressive disorder	Receptive disorder	Articulatory problems
Broca's aphasia	_____	_____	_____
Wernicke's aphasia	_____	_____	_____
Conduction aphasia	_____	_____	_____
Alexia	_____	_____	_____
Agraphia	_____	_____	_____

3. Assume that your brain functions are lateralized as most people's are. Assume you are a subject in a dichotic listening test where you are presented with the following combinations of stimuli. Which stimulus would you most likely hear most clearly? Explain why you think so.

a. Left ear: a man saying *cat*
   Right ear: a man saying *dog*

b. Left ear: a woman coughing
   Right ear: a woman sneezing

c. Left ear: a door hinge squeaking
   Right ear: a woman saying *horse*

4. Identify which language disorder a patient with each of the following symptoms may have.

a. the inability to follow simple verbal instructions, like *Sit down* or *Close the door*

b. slow and inaccurate pronunciation

c. loss of the ability to understand written material

File 9.2

The Innateness Hypothesis

How is it that a child does not, in its desire to communicate, merely imitate the sounds and words around it but actually seeks out patterns and hypothesizes and tests rules? No adult teaches the child that language is systematic and rule-governed; most adults are not consciously aware of this fact themselves. The Active Construction of a Grammar Theory asserts that language ability is innate in humans. That is, humans are genetically predisposed to learn and use language (though not any particular language, of course). Babies are born with the knowledge that languages are patterned and with the ability to seek out those patterns. Humans may have even have innate knowledge of some core of characteristics common to all languages, such as the concepts of "noun" and "verb." These basic features are called *linguistic universals*, and the (probably inborn) set of characteristics shared by all languages is known as **universal grammar**. No one knows exactly what the contents of universal grammar are, though this is currently an active area of research in linguistics.

The claim that linguistic ability is innate in humans is supported by the work of the biologist Eric Lenneberg. He has studied animal behavior and has developed a list of characteristics that are typical of innately determined behaviors. Such behaviors will be present in all normal individuals of a species, whereas learned behaviors will not be. Walking, for instance, is a behavior for which humans are genetically predisposed, but playing the piano or riding a bicycle must be specifically learned. Is talking like walking, or is it like playing the piano?

To answer this, let's examine Lenneberg's characteristics of biologically controlled behaviors. If language acquisition has each of these characteristics, we can safely assume that it is a genetically triggered behavior.

1. The behavior emerges before it is necessary.
2. Its appearance is not the result of a conscious decision.
3. Its emergence is not triggered by external events (though the surrounding environment must be sufficiently "rich" for it to develop adequately).
4. Direct teaching and intensive practice have relatively little effect.
5. There is a regular sequence of "milestones" as the behavior develops, and these can usually be correlated with age and other aspects of development.
6. There is likely to be a "critical period" for the acquisition of the behavior.

[from Aitchinson 1976, adapted from Lenneberg 1967]

Consider the first criterion. In what sense is language necessary? From a biological standpoint, language is a behavior that has encouraged the survival and predominance of the human species. Each individual needs the ability to use language to enable it to take care of other basic needs. But children ordinarily begin to speak a language between the ages of twelve and twenty-four months, long before their parents have stopped providing them with the necessities of life. So language is a behavior that emerges, like walking, well before a child has to fend for itself.

Language is likewise neither the result of a conscious decision nor triggered by external events. Children decide whether or not they want to learn to play baseball or checkers, but they never make a choice about acquiring a language; it's just something that all children do. Before a child can acquire a behavior such as playing the piano, certain external events must occur. The child must see and hear a piano, and typically must be taught fingering techniques, how to read music, and so on. Language, on the other hand, is not learned because something special has happened to trigger this learning. The child is spoken to by its caretakers and hears the conversations of others, but needs no other external stimulus to begin the process of analyzing language and constructing a grammar.

Doesn't intensive teaching help children learn language? Surprisingly, it has no positive effect at all. In the first place, children don't necessarily perceive their mistakes just because an adult points them out. Second, there is evidence that "coaching" by adults can have a relatively detrimental effect on children's language skills. Consider two possible types of responses that an adult might have to a child's utterances. On the one hand, the adult might correct the child's errors or expand upon what the child said; for instance, if a child says *Red ball!* the response might be *Yes, that's a red ball*. On the other hand, the child could receive normal, conversational feedback. Thus *Red ball!* might bring the response *Do you want to play with it, Mitch?* Studies have shown that children who primarily received corrections or expansions as responses were slower in the acquisition of language skills than children who received novel utterances as responses to their own speech.

Language acquisition also exhibits the characteristic of having a sequence of "milestones" or identifiable stages associated with its development. You will read in more detail about these stages in subsequent files.

Finally, innate behaviors have a **critical period** associated with their emergence. Unfortunately, this term is not very well defined in the literature. It has been commonly described as a period of time in an individual's life during which a behavior—in this case *language*—must be acquired. It seems that we need to differentiate between two *critical periods*. One lasts from birth to about age two, during which time a child needs exposure to language in order to develop the brain structures necessary for language acquisition and acquiring native speaker competence. The second "critical period" is said to last from about the age of ten years to sixteen years, during which time individuals can still easily acquire a language, but not with native competence. How can we tell whether there really are such critical periods associated with language acquisition? To prove this we would have to show that language skills could not be acquired normally if the learning began after the first period had ended. This could be accomplished by depriving a child of any linguistic input for the first years of its life, but obviously it would be highly unethical to submit any child to such treatment. However, there are least two sources of information available to linguists which support the claims that there are these critical periods for language acquisition.

The first sort of support for the **critical-age hypothesis** comes from children who, due to unfortunate circumstances, were exposed to little or no language in their early life. When these children were discovered, researchers attempted to help them acquire language. The success of these attempts depended largely on the age at which the children were discovered.

The second involves comparing the acquisition of a second language by children and by adults. Adults find it much more difficult to learn languages than children do. People who have learned a language as an adult almost always have an "accent," indicating that they have not acquired the phonological rules of the second language perfectly. They may also find the syntactic and other rules difficult to master completely. Children, however, can acquire a second (or third) language easily and completely as long as they have enough input from those languages. This ability tapers off somewhere between ten and sixteen years of age. We will consider two such cases.

1. Genie was found in 1970 when she was nearly fourteen years old. She had been abused and isolated since the age of twenty months. When first discovered, Genie was completely silent. Thereafter her language acquisition was extremely slow, and although she did learn to speak, her speech was quite abnormal. She was able to memorize many vocabulary items, but her expressions were formulaic and of a type such as *what is X* and *give me X*.

2. Isabelle was discovered in 1937 at the age of six and a half. Her mother, who was deaf and could not speak, had kept her isolated but had not otherwise mistreated her. Isabelle then began lessons at Ohio State University, and although her progress was at first slow, it soon accelerated. In two years her intelligence and her language use were completely normal for a child her age.

The linguistic abilities of these children suggest that humans can learn language normally only if they are exposed to a language by a certain age. This evidence is corroborated by the evidence from second language acquisition, which also indicates that there is a critical period for language acquisition; this critical period appears to extend from birth to approximately puberty.

To conclude, children are apparently "preprogrammed" to learn language. This innate linguistic ability enables children to analyze the language of their environment and to create and refine their own grammars until they can understand and produce the full range of utterances that adults can produce.

Reference

Aitchinson, Jean. 1976. *The Articulate Mammal: An Introduction to Psycholinguistics*. London: Hutchison and Co.

Lenneberg, Eric. 1967. *Biological Foundations of Language*. New York: John Wiley & Sons.

File 9.3

Theories of Language Acquisition

As we have seen throughout this book, language is both complex and systematic. It is composed of many layers such as phonology, or morphology, and so on, each of which contains sets of rules, and elements manipulated by those rules. It should be clear by now that a speaker's linguistic competence consists of much more than just knowing a list (however long) of words. A speaker's knowledge of language is made up not only words but also of elements of other "sizes" (sounds and morphemes, for instance), and rules for combining all of these. This knowledge enables him or her to understand and produce sentences he or she may never have heard or uttered before. Thus, given that a speaker's grammar consists of linguistic elements and rules, we can understand the infinite productivity of language. How does a child learn a language? If knowing a language were simply a matter of knowing a lot of words, language acquisition would just be a process of figuring out what the words are and memorizing them. Instead, children must acquire a grammar with all its components and rules. How do children learn these rules? For instance, how do they learn to make the plural of some nouns by adding [-s] as in *cats*, others by adding [-z] as in *dogs*, and still others by adding [-əz] as in *houses*? How do they learn that the morpheme *un-* (meaning *not*) attaches to adjectives to form other adjectives having the opposite meanings? How do they learn to compose a sentence from a noun phrase and a verb phrase? Rules, unlike words, are never explicitly stated, so the child cannot just memorize them. They must somehow figure them out on their own—a remarkable intellectual feat.

Various theories have arisen which attempt to account for how children acquire language. We will consider three of these: the *Imitation Theory*, the *Reinforcement Theory*, and a third which has no standard name but which we will call the *Active Construction of a Grammar Theory*. The **Imitation Theory** claims that children learn language by listening to the speech around them and reproducing what they hear. According to this theory, language acquisition consists of memorizing the words and sentences of some language. The idea that acquiring a language is a process of learning to imitate the speech of others is at least partly true. Because of the largely arbitrary nature of the connection between the way a word sounds and what it means, children cannot guess what the words of their target language are. They must hear those words used by other speakers and then reproduce or "imitate" them. Furthermore, this theory helps explain the fact that children learn the language that is spoken around them by parents, caretakers, and others, no matter what the language of their ancestors may have been. Thus a Korean child (for instance) will speak Korean if raised in a Korean-speaking environment, but Arabic if raised in an Arabic-speaking environment, or Swahili if raised in a Swahili-speaking environment, and so on. In other words, a child's genetic makeup has nothing to do with which language the child will acquire.

Unfortunately, however, the Imitation Theory explains little else of what we know about language acquisition. Consider that children's speech differs from adult norms: it is full of "errors" of many types. A two year old might say [nænə] for adult [bənænə] *banana* or a three year old might say "*Mommy tie shoe.*" Proponents of the theory could account for this by claiming that language is difficult to master, and so a child's first attempt at reproducing various words or sentence structures will not be perfect. This is not surprising since learning to speak needs much practice. Learning to speak is like learning to walk. A child has to learn how to coordinate the movements of the legs, to know when it will be safe to lift one foot off the ground without falling down, and so on. A child's speech is very different from an adult's speech because children are still in the process of learning how to coordinate the different articulatory movements to produce a certain sound or sequence of sounds that they aim at producing. For example, stressed syllables are easier to hear and imitate, whereas the consonant cluster [ts] in a word like *puts* is difficult to produce.

But the theory cannot account for the fact that the mistakes children make are largely predictable and consistent from child to child. For example, four-year-old English speakers often say *hitted* or *goed* rather than *hit* or *went*, even though they have never heard an adult use these forms. Moreover, no child will produce such random mistakes as forming the past tense of a verb by adding a /-z/ in one instance, prefixing an /l-/ in another or cutting off the final segment whenever in the third instance. As we shall see, the mistakes children make reveal a great deal about the grammatical system underlying their speech. However, the Imitation Theory does not recognize the existence of such a system, since it claims that children are simply imitating what they have heard in the speech of others.

The Imitation Theory alone also cannot account for the fact that even when a child attempts to repeat an adult's utterance, it is often unable to do so accurately. Consider the following exchanges, which are typical of young children trying to imitate an adult:

> Adult: He doesn't want a drink.
> Child: He no want drink.

and

> Adult: That's the dog's toy.
> Child: That dog toy.

In fact, the child's imperfect imitations exhibit regular patterns because they reflect the child's internal grammar. For a child at a particular stage of linguistic development, *He no want drink* is the grammatical way of expressing *He doesn't want a drink*. However, the Imitation Theory fails to acknowledge that a child has any sort of grammar that includes rules for combining words and other elements in systematic ways.

The most serious fault of the Imitation Theory is that it cannot account for how children and adults are able to produce and understand new sentences. If a child learned only by imitation, the only way it could understand a sentence is if it had heard it before. However, we know that there is an infinite number of possible sentences in any language, and speakers (even children) are able to understand and produce completely novel utterances. Speakers do not store whole sentences in memory; they store words and syntactic rules. The Imitation Theory cannot explain the fact that children acquire these rules even though they are never explicitly expressed by other speakers.

The **Reinforcement Theory** asserts that children learn to speak like adults because they are praised, rewarded, or otherwise reinforced when they use the right forms and are corrected when they use wrong forms. The claim that parents and other caretakers frequently correct their children's grammatical mistakes and praise their correct forms is unfounded. Such corrections seldom happen, for although parents often do correct their children, their corrections generally have more to do with the accuracy or truth of a statement and not its grammatical form. Adults also correct children's grammatical sentences if they are not true. Thus, *The dog wants to eat* may receive the response *No, the dog doesn't want to eat* if the dog has just finished its dinner, whereas the sentence *Robin goed to school today* may receive the response *Yes, he did* if Robin did go to school that day.

The Reinforcement Theory is also contradicted by the fact that even on the rare occasions when adults do try to correct a child's grammar, the attempts usually fail entirely. Consider the following conversation:

Child: Nobody don't like me.
Mother: No, say "nobody likes me."
Child: Nobody don't like me.

(repeated 8 times)

Mother (now exasperated):   Now listen carefully! Say, "Nobody likes me."
Child: Oh! Nobody don't likes me.

Notice that although the child does not form negative sentences in the same way the adult does, the child's utterances follow a pattern just as the adult's do. The child's way of forming negative sentences involving *nobody* is completely regular: every such sentence contains *nobody* + a negative auxiliary verb for example, *Nobody can't spell that* or *Nobody won't listen*. The child must possess a rule that defines this pattern, but the rule is not the same as that in the grammar of an adult. Note, though, that in the last repetition the child imitates the adult correctly by saying *likes* instead of *like*. The Reinforcement Theory cannot explain where the child's rule came from or why the child seems impervious to correction.

The **Active Construction of a Grammar Theory** holds that children actually invent the rules of grammar themselves. Of course, their inventions are based on the speech they hear around them; this is their input or data for analysis. Children listen to the language around them and analyze it to determine the patterns that exist. When they think they have discovered a pattern, they hypothesize a rule to account for it. They add this rule to their growing grammar and use it in constructing utterances. For example, a child's early hypothesis about how to form the past tense of verbs will be to add /ed/. All past tense verbs will then be constructed with this rule, producing forms such as *holded* and *eated* alongside *needed* and *walked*. When children discover that there are forms in the language that do not match those produced by this rule, they modify the rule or add another one to produce the additional forms. Eventually, the child has created and edited his or her own grammar to the point where it matches that of an adult's. At this point there are no significant discrepancies between the forms produced by the child and those produced by the adults around him or her. However, the child has a complete working grammar all along, even before it is essentially adultlike. The child uses this grammar to produce utterances; when those utterances differ from adult speech, they are reflecting the differences in the grammar underlying them.

This theory explains what the Imitation and Reinforcement Theories cannot explain alone. Within this framework children's mistakes are expected to occur and to follow nonrandom patterns, because the child is forming utterances according to grammatical rules, although the rules are often different from those adults use. For the same reasons, this theory predicts that children will fail to imitate adult forms accurately even when they are reinforced by adults when the rules for producing such forms are different from the rules the child has devised.

File 9.4

Phonetic Acquisition

Physiological Prerequisites of Sound Production

When children start to acquire a language, there are various things they have to learn first: they have to be able to identify the sounds (phonemes) of their language; they have to learn how to produce each of these phonemes and also its allophones (the variants of a sound that depend on the context in which this particular sound occurs); they have to learn how to combine sounds into larger strings, that is, syllables or words; and also how to decode larger strings of sounds into syllables and words when being talked to. Children's first vocalizations are present at the very beginning of life. (Everyone knows how adept babies are at crying!) Within a few weeks after birth a child begins to coo, producing sequences of vowel-like sounds. The child uses these cooing and gurgling noises to indicate contentment and pleasure, or at least this is how most parents or family members interpret these sounds.

Perception studies have shown that infants at the age of four months can already distinguish between the vowels [a] and [i]. In this experimental paradigm, the mouths of two adult faces are shown to an infant, one saying [a], the other one saying [i]. Simultaneously, a tape plays either one of the two sounds, either [a] or [i]. When the infants hear an [a], they have a preference to look at the face saying [a]. When the infants hear an [i], they show a preference to look at the face producing the [i]. These findings suggest that infants of about four months of age can already distinguish different vowel qualities and use visual cues to determine the kind of articulation involved in producing them. In fact, the infant's coos differ in these two contexts; they are more [a]-like (or [i]-like, respectively) to match the sound heard and the mouth watched.

Since the infant's tongue is relatively large compared to the size of the vocal tract, the front of the tongue easily makes contact with the roof of the mouth, and a baby is very likely to produce coos that sound vaguely palatal, like the adult phonemes /y/ or /ñ/. However, one needs to be aware that it is extremely difficult to transcribe infants' vocalizations, since they are very variable. Therefore, one needs to distinguish between the limits of the transcribing observer's capacities and the limits of the infant's productive capacities. Many people, especially proud parents and grandparents, report that their babies or grandchildren produced words like *mom* or *ma* very early. From very early on, the baby "practices" sounds of various kinds. What the baby has to learn are the articulatory **gestures** involved in producing a particular sound (e.g., bringing both lips together to produce a bilabial sound), as well as the timing relationships between these gestures, i.e., starting vocal fold vibration for voicing a sound; opening the mouth; lowering the velum to allow air passage through the nasal cavity; raising the tongue for an alveolar closure, and so on. The young child has to practice the execution of the motor programs that underlie speech production. This might seem to be a very easy task , but, in analogy, if you were to try patting your right hand on your left knee and rubbing your left hand in circles on your right knee, it would probably take a bit of practice to get the different movements coordinated. That is because these are fairly unusual and new tasks to you. Learning to speak is just as hard for an infant, since infants have to learn to gain control over the muscles in their speech organs and to coordinate the execution of articulatory movements. Since the task of learning to coordinate the necessary articulatory movements is not simple, a child's production of speech will generally be slower and also more variable than the speech of adults.

Babbling

At the age of four to six months or so, children in all cultures begin to babble, producing sequences of vowels and consonants. Some linguists assume that babies babble to practice the opening and closing movement of the jaw. As mentioned before, the baby's tongue is relatively big compared to the size of the oral cavity. Since the tongue is attached to the lower jaw, as the lower jaw moves up, the tongue moves up with it. For this reason, it is very likely that the infant will produce vaguely palatal sounds like [ñ] or [y]. Since the lower lip is also attached to the jaw, labials such as [b] and [m] occur frequently, too. When the jaw wags down and the tongue lies on the jaw, the infant is very likely to produce the vowel sound [a]. These are, of course, not the only sounds that an infant produces, but they are likely sounds in the very beginning. Also, keep in mind that babbling a certain sequence of sounds is not a conscious process. It is sort of an accident if the infant produces a syllable like [ti], since the tongue tip has to contact the alveolar ridge while the mouth is open. Repeated or canonical babbling starts around the age of seven to ten months. The continuous repetition of syllables like [mamama] helps the infant to practice the sequence of a bilabial nasal consonant followed by a low vowel that requires an opening of the vocal tract. Since babies breathe mostly through their noses, the velum is open already, and producing an [m] "just" involves closing the lips. However, practicing a sequence consisting of a nasal and a vowel also helps practicing the timing relationship of when the velum has to lower and open relative to when the mouth opens for the production of the vowel. Between about ten and twelve months of age, children begin to produce a variety of speech sounds, even sounds that are not part of the language the child is acquiring natively.

Though babbling is far from being language, it resembles adult language in a number of important respects. For one thing, babbled sequences are not linked to immediate biological needs like food or physical comfort and are thus frequently uttered in isolation for sheer pleasure. Moreover, babbled sequences have many physical characteristics of adult speech. Syllables can be identified in a sequence like [gɔŋggɔŋg]. Often there is a clear alternation between consonants and vowels. In longer sequences, intonation patterns that might be interpreted as questions in some languages can be discerned. However, the resemblance to adult speech stops here, since there is no evidence for the existence of more abstract structures like sentences or even single words. Only later does the child come to associate word meanings with vocal noises.

Just how babbling relates to later speech is not clearly understood. Yet psychologists and linguists have suggested that babbling has at least two functions: First, babbling serves primarily as practice for later speech. This is intuitively plausible because the fine motor movements necessary for accurate articulation are exercised extensively during babbling. Indeed, babbling children of about one year of age produce a great variety of sounds, mainly practicing sequences of consonants and vowels. The observed variety in infant's speech was taken as evidence for the **Discontinuity Hypothesis,** which is a theory that was proposed by the linguist Roman Jakobson. He claimed that there will be an abrupt change in the child's sound system (the sounds a child uses in their babbling) once he or she has acquired a system of contrasts and produces meaningful words. In other words, this theory says that in babbling, infants produce a variety of speech sounds but as soon as the child produces meaningful speech and starts pairing sounds with meanings, the infant abruptly stops producing all kinds of different sounds. Experimental evidence and long-term observations of babies between the ages of nine and fifteen months strongly suggest, though, that the transition from babbling to speech is continuous. Babbling by ten-month-old and younger infants is already beginning to reflect characteristics of the language in the child's environment. These studies have shown that words slowly emerge from the child's sound system which he or she develops while practicing babbling. Second, children babble for social reward. When children talk, parents often encourage them to continue talking by responding to the child's babbling with smiles or talk or nonsense "babbling" of their own, giving them important experience with the social aspects and rewards of speech. Evidence for the importance of the social factor in babbling comes from the study of severely neglected children, who may begin to babble at approximately the same age as children reared in normal settings but stop if not encouraged by their parents or caretakers.

It remains to be explained why babbling occurs at more or less the same time in all children, since children must certainly practice for later speech or receive encouragement for their efforts in unequal doses. According to one hypothesis, children babble because language development involves a process of biological maturation. Thus babbling occurs automatically when the relevant structures in the brain reach a critical level of development. If all children have brains that develop at comparable rates, the universality of babbling is no longer surprising.

Dramatic evidence for this hypothesis comes from some children studied by the biologist Eric Lenneberg. These children had vocal passages that had become so narrow because of swelling caused by various diseases that they were in danger of choking to death. Breathing could be restored only by constructing an alternative route that bypassed the mouth; this was accomplished by inserting tubes in the trachea (air pipe) through an opening in the neck. Under such conditions, babbling and any other vocalizations are prevented, since air never reaches the vocal cords. Yet Lenneberg observed that when children of babbling age underwent this operation, they produced the babbling sounds typical of their age as soon as the tubing was removed. The behavior of these children demonstrates that babbling is possible when the brain is ready even if physical limitations prevent any real practice.

File 9.5

Phonological Acquisition

When an eighteen-month-old child attempts to pronounce the word *water*, he or she might say [wawa], a pronunciation that is quite different from the adult's model. A child's pronunciation of the word *that* may sound like [dæt]. Differences in pronunciations like this may persist for some time, despite drilling by the child's parents or caretakers and even despite the child's own realization that his or her pronunciation does not quite match the adult's pronunciation. All children, regardless of what language they are acquiring natively, make mistakes like these before they have mastered the phonological system of their native language. Yet, such errors reveal that they have already learned a great deal, and in roughly another two-and-a-half years their speech will resemble that of their parents in all important respects. It is important to note that although children tend to go through the same developmental steps at the same time, this is only a tendency. There is much variation in the age range during which children acquire words or fundamental cognitive concepts. Just because a child is slower or faster than average, that child is not necessarily more or less intelligent or well-developed than average. It is normal for there to be quite a lot of variation among children. The ages associated with the different "stages" of language acquisition discussed here are only averages, therefore. They are not specific to children learning English, because all children tend to go through the same "stages" no matter what language they are acquiring.

Note that throughout this and other files on language acquisition, the word *stage* will appear over and over, giving you the impression that there is a fixed time frame during which a child shows a particular language behavior. It is closer to reality not to describe the appearance of a particular behavior in terms of *stages*, since there is a tremendous amount of variability from child to child in terms of displaying a particular kind of behavior. More important, this term implies categorical or abrupt changes in the behavior from one stage to the next. This, however, is not true either. There is a great deal of co-occurrence of behavior that is said to take place during different stages.

First Words

A major task in the acquisition of phonology involves understanding the word as a link between sound and meaning. It has been claimed that around the age of eighteen months, children learn and ask for many new names for objects in their environment. When children first acquire the concept of a word, these first words show tremendous variability in pronunciation. Some may be perfect adult productions; others may be so distorted that they are comprehensible only to the child's closest companions. Still other children vary considerably in their pronunciations from one occasion to the next or consistently use a "wrong" sound relative to the adult speech's model, for example, substituting a [t] with an [w] in *water*. This of course might be the child's closest approximation of the sound it intends to produce. Because of this instability, linguists have come to believe that children do not show an understanding of phonemes in their first words. Consider the one-year-old child who pronounces the words *bottle* as [ba] and *daddy* as [da]. We might conclude that [b] and [d] belong to separate phonemes because [ba] and [da] constitute a **minimal pair** just as they would if these words existed in adult English. But [b] and [d] may not be members of separate phonemes in the speech of one-year-old children if they are not used consistently to distinguish among words. Thus the same child may pronounce *bottle* either as [ba] or [da] on different occasions and do the same with *daddy*. What seems to be going on is that children first learn entire words as single units and pay little attention to parts of the word. Therefore, they are unaware of meaning distinctions induced by changes in single sounds.

Acquisition of Phonological Structures

Children initially appear to regard the entire word as if it were a single sound (a sound that can vary somewhat). However, as their vocabulary expands between fifteen and twenty-one months of age, this becomes very difficult for them to manage. So in order to learn more words, children must begin to break words into a small number of simpler units, which are sounds that can be used in different combinations to make up many other words. That is, they arrive at the idea of a word as a sequence of phonemes whose pronunciation is systematic and predictable. Children must, in the course of learning a language natively, acquire the complete set of phonemes as well as the set of phonological processes found in the language of the adults in their surroundings.

When children learn the phonemes of their native language, they first master sounds that differ maximally from one another. Thus it is no accident that the first meaningful word learned in many languages is often [ma] or [pa]. When a bilabial stop or nasal is pronounced, the passage of air in the mouth is completely blocked; but the vocal tract is wide open in the low back vowel [a]. Thus, the maximal distinction between these two sounds can be captured by the generalization that one is a consonant (C) and the other one is a vowel (V). This kind of CV-syllable structure or template appears to be the preferred structure in young children's productions. Only later will they produce consonant clusters such as [sp] in words like *spill* or [tr] as in *tree*, and syllable final consonants such as [t] in *cat*. This last consonant is often omitted in children's productions. And even later, a child will learn to produce longer words or utterances that consist of more than one syllable. However, we might still observe a child saying [paskɛɾi] instead of *spaghetti*. Very often, consonants like [l] and [r], which share many properties of vowels, are mastered last.

Speech of young children is often distinguished from that of adults because the phonological processes are used in different ways. Adult speech is full of assimilations, deletions, metatheses, and so on. A child's speech is full of variation, too. Because much of this variation resembles rules used in adult phonologies, due to the fact that the child is still observing the language and learning the structures necessary to use it, it has been claimed that the speech of a two-year-old child exhibits more processes than adult speech. However, this would only be true if we were to assume that the child has already acquired the relevant structures and rules. In other words, saying that a child has and uses more rules presupposes that he or she has already acquired these. And since, according to this assumption, there appear to be more rules active in a child's speech, the consequence is that the child has learned more of these rules than adults have. This is certainly not what we want to claim. Rather, children's speech is quite different from that of adults because the language-learning child is still observing the language being used by adults and is also figuring out what kind of processes the language he or she will be learning natively employs.

In a child's speech you can frequently observe deletion of consonant and vowel sequences. In the speech sample below, at least one syllable is omitted from every word.

> *banana* [__næna]   *granola* [__owə]   *potato*   [__dedo]

We might wonder why children leave out the first syllable in these examples and if this first syllable is in any way different from the other syllables in the word. An answer to this question is that since all of these first syllables are unstressed, they are perceptually not very salient or prominent. Syllables are mainly structures consisting of a consonant or a consonant cluster followed by a vowel (that is sometimes followed by a consonant or consonant cluster). In English or German, for example, there usually is one syllable (or vowel for that matter) within a word that is somewhat louder and more prominent in relation to the other vowels in that word. This is the primary stressed vowel. Consider the word [bə.**næ**.nə] again. The period between the phonetic symbols represents the boundary between the three different syllables of that word. Here, the second syllable is stressed, which means it is the most prominent syllable in comparison to the other two adjacent syllables. When young, linguistically inexperienced children listen to speech being produced around them, there is a good chance that they will not attend to those unstressed syllables. This makes sense if we think about the problem that an inexperienced language learner has: imagine, for example, that you are a traveler going on vacation to a place where you don't know the language. You hear all the people around you producing speech, they talk to you, but how do you know where one word starts and where it ends so that you can look it up in your dictionary? A baby has the very same problem: where, in a continuous string of speech that a caretaker addresses to the infant, does each word begin and end? For the infants, this is a big problem to solve because, just like you in the foreign country, babies have only a very limited knowledge of the structure of the vocabulary of the language that they are learning.

Just recently, linguists and other researchers have begun to understand by what strategies listeners dissect a continuous string of speech into individual components (i.e., words). A computer search of a large corpus of English words has shown that many of the words in the English vocabulary begin with a stressed syllable, like *mommy, baby, telephone, newspaper, speaker, garbage*, etc., or consist of only one syllable that is stressed, e.g., *light, desk, plane*, or *ring*. Listeners might soon notice that the beginning of a new word is very likely to occur right before a stressed syllable. A subconscious strategy of listeners might be to look for the stressed syllables within an utterance to segment a continuous string of sounds and find the beginning of new words. Of course, this generalization does not always hold true, and there are many more factors that help listeners decide where a word starts and where it ends; however, in English at least, it is not a bad strategy to begin to segment a continuous string of speech.

Babies and small children might master the difficult task of finding the boundaries between words by looking for the most stressed syllable or the most prominent part of the word. But how do babies know which syllable is most stressed? Syllables that are stressed are usually louder, longer, and more prominent in comparison to unstressed syllables. Once infants have figured out how to identify these more prominent syllables, they are able to dissect the continuous string of speech a little easier. (Note that there also appears to be a tendency to pick up the first syllable in a word when that first syllable is stressed, so a child is likely to produce [dada] for *daddy* or [baba] for *bottle*.) However, this strategy does not always guarantee the correct result or the correct analysis of where one word begins and where it ends. Consider the word *banana* again. This word consists of three syllables: [bə.**næ**.nə]. The first and the third syllable are not stressed but the second one is. That is, the second syllable is louder and longer in duration relative to the first and the third syllables. In this case, a child might unconsciously look for the most stressed syllable and overgeneralize this one to be the beginning of a word. If the child has already learned that a word can consist of more than one syllable and generalizes that the most stressed syllable is the beginning of the word *banana*, then it makes sense that he or she will overgeneralize that the word is actually [næ.na]. This kind of rhythm of speech, a sequence of two syllables, the first one stressed, the second unstressed, is called a **trochee**. For English at least, there is assumed to be a trochaic bias in children's speech.

It is important to keep in mind that adults analyze the speech of children with reference to their own adult system. What this implies is that child speech will always be analyzed as imperfect and full of errors according to the adult's model of grammar. If you listen to a child speak, you will notice that many sounds that very young children produce do not really seem to fit any of the categories that adults have established in their sound system. In other words, a sound or a sequence of sounds may sound close to that produced by an adult, but it does not quite match the adult form. It appears that children try to approximate the forms and pronunciations that they hear being used around them. Since it takes a long time to gain absolute control over the individual movements of the articulators and the timing of these gestures, we might hear something that sounds somewhat close to what an adult says but that is still rather different. For example, it will be difficult for a young child to produce a consonant sequence like [dr] as it occurs in the word *drum*. The child may say something like [duam], which sounds close enough to make an adult understand what is meant, especially if the child is pointing to a drum at the same time. Many studies in the area of child language acquisition are based on adults' transcriptions of child speech. However, since it is extremely difficult to transcribe child speech, it is likely that there is much variation from transcriber to transcriber. Very often there is no right or wrong.

Conclusion

When children acquire the phonological system of their native language, they must master the fine muscle coordination necessary for producing a rich variety of sounds, learn that combinations of sounds are associated with particular meanings, and eventually realize that their pronunciations of words must consistently match that of adults. Learning a language natively does not result from a conscious learning strategy spontaneously invented by children, or from a teaching method devised by their adult model, but is instead a consequence of the human brain's innate capacity for learning language. Children of all backgrounds will learn a language and master the phonological system of their native language provided they have enough input. The acquisition of phonology appears to involve a process of biological maturation and is in many aspects like motor development: first the child babbles to practice for later speech, then the articulatory sequences become longer and more complex and the child is able to pronounce "difficult" consonant clusters. Nevertheless, the adult phonological system is achieved only when children are given models to imitate and are provided with encouragement to continue in their linguistic development.

Exercises

The data below are from Paul at the age of two; they were collected by his father, Timothy Shopen. Consider the examples section by section, and answer the questions at the end of each section.

1.

	Adult word	*Paul*		*Adult word*	*Paul*
a.	sun	[sən]	d.	snake	[nek]
b.	see	[si]	e.	sky	[kay]
c.	spoon	[pun]	f.	stop	[tap]

State a principle that describes Paul's pronunciation of these words.

2.

	Adult word	*Paul*		*Adult word*	*Paul*
g.	bed	[bɛt]	m.	bus	[bəs]
h.	wet	[wɛt]	n.	buzz	[bəs]
i.	egg	[ɛk]	o.	man	[mæn]
j.	rake	[rek]	p.	door	[dɔr]
k.	tub	[təp]	q.	some	[səm]
l.	soap	[sop]	r.	boy	[bɔy]

State another principle describing Paul's pronunciations here. Be sure to word your statement so that (o)–(r) are not affected.

3.   *Adult word*   *Paul*

s.   laugh   [læp]
t.   off   [ɔp]
u.   coffee   [kɔfi]

State a third principle describing Paul's pronunciation in this section.

Based on the principles you have seen so far, suggest how Paul would pronounce *love*.

4.   *Adult word*   *Paul*   *Adult word*   *Paul*

v.   truck   [tək]   aa.   clay   [ke]
w.   brownie   [bawni]   bb.   cute   [kut]
x.   plane   [pen]   cc.   beautiful   [butəpəl]
y.   broken   [bokən]   dd.   twig   [tɪk]
z.   crack   [kæk]

State a fourth principle describing the new aspects of Paul's pronunciation in these examples.

5.   *Adult word*   *Paul*

ee.   quick   [kwɪk]
ff.   quack   [kwæk]

Do these two words illustrate an exception to the fourth principle? If so, how?

File 9.6 The Acquisition of Morphology and Syntax

It is not until about the age of twelve months that a child will begin to consistently produce words of the language it is learning. It is at this "stage" that we can begin to examine the development of syntax and morphology in children's speech.

The One-Word Stage

The first words uttered by a one-year-old child typically name people, objects, pets, and other familiar and important parts of its environment. The child's vocabulary soon comes to include verbs and other useful words as well as nouns (including *no, gimme,* and *mine)*. Often a phrase used by adults will become a single word in the speech of a child, such as *allgone* and *whasat?* The single words produced at this stage are used as more than just labels for objects or events; they may be used for naming, commenting, requesting, inquiring, and so on. In fact, this level of development has been called the **holophrastic** stage (a holophrase being a one-word sentence). Children at this phase are limited to a word at a time in their production, but they understand and probably intend the meaning of more than a single word. Certainly children can understand the utterances of other people even when they consist of much more than one word. The intonation children use on their one-word utterances may be that of a question, an ordinary or emphatic statement or an imperative. If children do consistently use these adultlike intonation patterns (and researchers disagree about whether they do or not), it would seem even more likely that "holophrastic" is an appropriate name for this phase.

The Two-Word Stage

Between approximately eighteen and twenty-four months of age, children begin to use two-word utterances. At first they may seem to be simply two one-word sentences produced one right after the other. There may be a pause between them, and each word may bear a separate intonation contour. Before long, however, the two words are produced without pausing and with a single intonational pattern.

Children at this stage do not just produce any two words in any order; rather, they adopt a consistent set of word orders which convey an important part of the meaning of their utterances. At this level of development, the structure of utterances is determined by semantic relationships, rather than adult syntactic ones. Only word order is used to express these semantic relations; it is not until later that additional syntactic devices are added to the basic word order rules. Most of the utterances produced by a child at this stage will express a semantic relation like one of the following:

agent + action	*baby sleep*
action + object	*kick ball*
action + locative	*sit chair*
entity + locative	*teddy bed*

possessor + possession	*Mommy book*
entity + attribute	*block red*
demonstrative + entity	*this shoe*

Words such as *more* and *'nother* may be used as modifiers of nouns (*more juice, 'nother cup*) to indicate or request recurrence. *Here* and *there* may be used as demonstratives or locatives. Some children at this stage of development also use pronouns. For the most part, however, their speech lacks function morphemes and words. Function morphemes include prepositions, auxiliary verbs, articles, and inflectional affixes.

Function morphemes are omitted during this stage and even after the child begins to produce more than two words at a time. Because of this omission, the speech of young children is often called **telegraphic**. When you send a telegram or run a classified ad, every word you include costs you money. Therefore, you only put in the words you really need, and not the ones that carry no new information. Children follow the same principle of economy. The words they use and the order in which they use them convey the relevant information; function morphemes would be redundant. Of course, pronouns, *more, 'nother,* and the other words mentioned earlier carry independent meanings and can fill one of the positions in the semantic relations listed above. Eventually, of course, children do acquire the full set of function morphemes of their language—the "syntactic devices" mentioned above that supplement the expression of semantic relations through word order rules.

Later Stages of Development

Three-word utterances are originally formed by combining or expanding two-word utterances. Two two-word strings with a common element may be combined; for example, *Daddy cookie* and *cookie eat* may be combined to form *Daddy eat cookie.* A two-word utterance may also be expanded from within, when (for example) *throw ball* becomes *throw red ball.* That is, one of the elements of a two-term relation itself becomes a two-term relation.

There is no strictly three-word stage of language acquisition, however. Once children are capable of combining more than two words into an utterance, they may use three, four, five or even more words at a time. These longer utterances are syntactically organized; that is, they possess hierarchical syntactic structure rather than being flat sequences of words like those produced in the two-word stage.

Children's speech at this stage is still telegraphic, including only morphemes and words that carry important semantic content. Gradually a child will begin to include function morphemes in his or her utterances, but these function morphemes are not acquired randomly. Instead, children acquire them in a remarkably consistent order. For example, the present progressive verbal suffix *-ing (she walking)* appears in children's speech before the third person present marker *-s (she walks)*, which in turn is acquired well before the past tense marker *-ed (she walked).* Around the time *-ing* appears, so do the prepositions *in* and *on.* Three homophonous morphemes, all phonologically /-z/, are acquired at different times. First children use the plural morpheme *-s* (for example, *shoes*); later they acquire the possessive *-'s (Mommy's);* then the present tense morpheme mentioned above is added to verbs. Articles (*a* and *the*) are acquired fairly early, but forms of the (highly irregular) verb *be* only appear at a relatively late stage.

Plurals

Recall that the plural morpheme *-s* is acquired quite early by children—in fact, it is usually one of the very first function morphemes to appear, along with *in, on,* and *-ing.* That does not mean, however, that very young children have complete mastery over the plural system of English.

At first, no plural marker is used at all. Nouns only appear in their singular forms (for example, *man*). Next, irregular plural forms may appear for a while—that is, a child may say *men* instead of *man*, using the same form adults do. Then the child discovers the morpheme *-s*, and suddenly applies it to plural nouns. In some cases this involves overgeneralization of the rule of plural formation; for example, the plural of *man* becomes *mans*. During this stage the child often leaves nouns ending in sibilants (e.g., *nose, house, church,* etc.) in their singular forms. Once children discover the generalization about how the plural of these nouns are formed, they may go through a brief period during which [-əz] is added to *all* nouns. This soon passes, however, and the child produces all plurals correctly, except for irregular ones. These are learned gradually and may not be fully acquired by the time the child is five years old. When irregular plurals first appear in a young child's speech, they are simply isolated forms that fit into no pattern. Once they are learned, however, they are exceptions to the child's regular process of plural formation.

Negatives

Children also go through a series of stages in learning to produce negative sentences. At first they simply put the word *no* in front of a sentence to negate it, for example, *no baby sleep* or *no I drink milk*. As a matter of fact, this word shows a fairly high occurrence in children's speech even if children might not initially understand what the word means. Next, they insert a negative word, especially *no, not, can't* or *don't*, between the subject and the verb of a sentence, resulting in *baby no sleep* or *I no drink milk*. It is interesting to note that at this stage, *can't, won't* and *don't* are unanalyzable negative words. The auxiliaries *can, will,* and *do* are not acquired until later; three year olds still tend to have trouble with them. Furthermore, children often omit forms of the verb *be* in their negated sentences, producing sentences such as *I not break car* and *I not thirsty*. Recall that *be* is a difficult verb. The full set of its forms takes children quite a while to acquire.

The child's system of negation continues to become more adult-like, but for a while it will use words such as *something* and *somebody* in negated sentences, producing results such as *I don't see something*. Later these are replaced by *nothing* and *nobody*. Finally, if the adult grammar possesses the forms *anything* and *anybody*, the child acquires these words.

Interrogatives

Very young children can produce questions using only a rising intonation, rather than a particular syntactic structure. The meaning of *Mommy cup?* or *more ride?* would be quite clear when produced with the same question intonation that adults use. Later, at around three years, children begin to use *can, will* and other auxiliary verbs in yes-no questions, using the appropriate word order. That is, the auxiliary precedes the subject in these questions, as, for example, in *Are you sad?* At this point, however, children still fail to use adult word order in wh- questions. They follow a question word with a sentence in normal declarative order: *Why you are sad?* Finally, they learn to invert the subject and the verb in these constructions, as the adult speakers do.

The fact that children produce words and sentences like *foots* or *I don't want something* or *Where he is going?* provides clear evidence that they are not merely imitating the adult speakers around them. What we as adults perceive and interpret as "mistaken" is not random but reflects the system that children are in the process of constructing for themselves.

File 9.7   The Acquisition of Word Meaning

When children hear a word for the first time, they have no way of knowing what makes the use of the word appropriate. Consider the case of the nursery-school pupil who played softball in school one day. The teacher chose teams by dividing the class in half, asking each team to sit on a blanket until the game started. At home later that day, one of the students got annoyed because her younger brother kept crawling onto her blanket while she was watching television. "He won't stay away from my team," she complained. With a single exposure to the word *team*, this child formed a definition something like 'a group of people on a blanket'—a reasonable, but wrong, guess.

Though this trial-and-error process may seem laborious from an adult perspective, consider what every normal child is able to accomplish: children produce their first words at age one, and by age six they have a vocabulary approaching 14,000 words. Simple arithmetic will reveal that children master almost ten words a day starting from their first birthday. This feat might suggest that children learn the vocabulary of their native language in a more systematic fashion than is apparent from a single example. While it is not possible to speak of stages like those identified in the acquisition of phonology and syntax, linguists have determined that the acquisition of word meaning is made systematic in two familiar ways. For one thing, children's first definitions do not deviate randomly from those of adults but exhibit their own structure. Second, the order in which words are learned reflects the intrinsic complexity of the concepts involved. We will explore these sources of regularity below.

Initial definitions of words adopted by children fall into three major categories. To some extent, they are present in a child's speech at the same time, though they probably result from different psychological processes.

Complexive Concepts

Many nouns are used to single out classes of objects with something in common. For example, the adult word *chair* is used appropriately with desk chairs, rocking chairs, easy chairs, and so on because all of these things can be sat on. But this apparently elementary fact about our semantic knowledge must be learned by children. Many early definitions of words shift unpredictably from one occasion to the next, with the result that the word fails to identify a class of objects with a single common property. A word with such a definition is said to represent a complexive concept.

For example, a child might learn that the word *doggie* refers to dogs and then use it to name other furry things, like soft slippers; on later occasions, she may use *doggie* to refer to things that move by themselves, like birds, toads, and small toy cars. The linguist William Labov reports a more exaggerated complexive concept. His one-year-old son used the word *oo* to refer to the music produced by his brother's rock and roll band; and on later occasions the same word was applied to the group's jackets, their musical instruments, their cigarettes, and other people's cigarettes. Note that in both examples, any two successive uses of the word pick out objects with similar properties, but that the class of objects as a whole has little in common. Complexive concepts serve to form a loose bond between items associated in the child's experience and are thought to represent the most primitive conception of word meaning.

Overgeneralizations

Overgeneralizations result when the range of a word is extended beyond that of normal adults. For example, one American English–speaking child called specks of dirt, dust, small insects, and bread crumbs *fly*; another gave *moon* as the name for cakes, round marks, postmarks, and the letter *o*. A third child overgeneralized the word *ticktock*, using it to refer to clocks, watches, parking meters, and a dial on a set of scales.

At first glance, the set of objects named in overgeneralizations may look as varied and random as those in complexive concepts. In fact, children of age two or so frequently have overextensions and complexive concepts in their speech at the same time. But closer inspection reveals that the concept defined in an overextension does not shift from one occasion to the next. In the above examples, the child's definition of *moon* is applied consistently to pick out any round thing. Likewise, *fly* refers to any small, possibly mobile object. The concept underlying the use of *ticktock* is perhaps more complex, but all of the objects in the child's list contain a dial with small marks.

In general, the common properties of objects included in the overgeneralization of a word are perceptual features like shape, size, color, or taste. And in this respect, the child's strategy for defining a word resembles that of adults, since adults also define words in terms of perceptual features. For example, most English-speaking people insist that only sweet things can be fruits; thus tomatoes are excluded from the definition of fruit, though they do possess all of the necessary botanical properties. But if the child's definitions of words now resemble those of adults, what misunderstanding is responsible for the overgeneralizations?

The linguist Eve Clark offers one plausible explanation. In her view, the child who uses overgeneralizations has only an incomplete definition of the adult word. The child who calls dogs, cats, slippers, fur coats, and rugs *doggie* has recognized the significance of being furry, but the adult definition mentions more properties; for example, dogs are four-legged. Once the child grasps this property as part of the definition of dog, it will no longer overextend the word *doggie* to slippers, rugs, and fur coats. Eventually the child becomes aware of all properties in a definition, which enables it to narrow down the class of objects named by *doggie* to just those observed in adult usage.

Underextensions

An underextension is the application of a word to a *smaller* set of objects than is appropriate for mature adult speech. Though less commonly observed than overextensions, careful study reveals that underextensions are at least equally frequent in the language of children.

The psychologist Katherine Nelson has observed that children before the age of two years form underextensions because they have trouble distinguishing the essential features of common objects from the accidental. For example, a child may call a ball *ball* only when it happens to be under the sofa. The child who underextends the word *ball* in this fashion must eventually realize that the word can be used with the appropriate object, regardless of its location.

Underextensions also occur among older, school-age children when they encounter category names like *fruit* or *mammal*. Since most people are unsure of the properties that constitute the definitions of these words, they prefer to think of them in terms of their most ordinary members; thus dogs are the most ordinary mammals for many Americans, and apples are the most ordinary fruits. But children are surprised to learn that whales are mammals, or that olives are fruits because they deviate so profoundly from the ordinary members of these categories. As a result, children underextend the words *mammal* and *fruit*, failing to apply these labels to the unusual members.

Why do children's first definitions fall into the three classes we have discussed? It might be possible to limit the answer to this question somewhat, since complexive concepts are clearly more primitive than overgeneralizations and underextensions and are present in a child's speech for a shorter period of time. Psychologists have determined that a child who overgeneralizes a word tries to make the most out of a limited vocabulary. Accordingly, overgeneralizations decrease dramatically after age two, when children experience a rapid vocabulary expansion. The opposite strategy underlies the formation of underextensions: children attempt to be as conservative as possible in their use of language, with the result that they perceive restrictions on the use of words not observed by adults. By systematically over- and underextending the range of a concept, the child eventually arrives at the adult definition.

The Intrinsic Complexity of Concepts

The words discussed so far have been limited to one type: those whose meaning identifies the members of a class. For example, the word *chair* is used correctly when it is applied to the class that includes objects as different as straight chairs, folding chairs, and rocking chairs. The same skill in identifying instances of the same class is required for understanding some types of verbs. For example, all people walk differently, but native speakers of English use the word *walk* correctly when they realize that these minor differences are irrelevant.

But not all words in a language involve the identification of classes. In fact, the mastery of a working vocabulary in any human language appeals to a wide range of intellectual skills, some easier and some more difficult than those required for grasping the meaning of common nouns and verbs. As an example of a relatively easy concept, consider what is required for understanding proper nouns: one must simply point out a single individual and attach a label, like *John* or *Daddy*. Because it is easier to associate a label with a single individual than to name a class with common properties, children master proper nouns first, sometimes when they are as young as six to nine months old.

In contrast, a relational term like *large* or *small* constitutes a relatively complex concept. The correct use of words like these requires that two things be kept in mind: the absolute size of the object in question, and its position on a scale of similar objects. For example, an elephant that is six feet tall at the shoulders may be small as far as elephants go, but a dog of the same height would be huge. Five- and six-year-old children are unable to make the shift in perspective necessary for using relational words appropriately. In one well-known experiment documenting this conclusion, children were engaged in a pretend tea party with dolls and an adult observer. The adult gave the child an ordinary juice glass and asked the child if it was large or small. Though all of the children in the study agreed that the glass was small from their own perspective, it appeared ridiculously large when placed on the toy table around which the dolls were seated. Nevertheless, the youngest children were still inclined to say that the glass was small when asked about its size with respect to its new context.

Another complex concept underlies **deictic** expressions, which are words used to point to objects and indicate their distance from the speaker. For example, the speaker may use *here* or *this* to point out objects that may be close to him, while *there* and *that* are appropriate only when the objects are relatively far away. But since there are no absolute distances involved in the correct use of a deictic expression, children have difficulty determining when the 'close' terms are to be preferred over the 'far' terms. As with relational terms, it is necessary to take into account the size of the object pointed to. Thus a thirty-story building six feet in front of us is close enough to be called *this building*, but an ant removed from us by the same distance is far enough away to be called *that ant*.

Common and proper nouns, relational terms, and deictic expressions do not exhaust the range of concepts mastered by children, but they do illustrate the variety of tasks involved in acquiring the vocabulary of a first language. Linguists can examine the evidence from the acquisition of word meaning and find support for two fundamental hypotheses: that some concepts are more complex than others, and that the acquisition of language requires a considerable exercise of intelligence.

File 9.8 Milestones in Motor and Language Development

Chart adapted from Eric H. Lenneberg, *Biological Foundations of Language* (New York: John Wiley & Sons, 1967).

Approximate Age at Onset of Behavior	Motor Development	Vocalizations and Language
12 weeks	Supports head when in prone position; weight is on elbows; hands mostly open; no grasp reflex.	Markedly less crying than at 8 weeks; when talked to and nodded at, smiles, followed by squealing-gurgling sounds usually called cooing; sustains cooing for 15 to 20 seconds; produces vaguely palatal sounds like [y] and [n].
16 weeks	Plays with rattle when placed in hands (by shaking it and staring at it); head self-supported; tonic neck reflex subsiding.	Responds to human sounds more definitely; turns head; eyes seem to search for speaker; occasionally some chuckling sounds; can distinguish between vowels [i] and [a] and the corresponding adult mouth producing these sounds.
20 weeks	Sits with props.	The vowel-like cooing sounds begin to be interspersed with more consonantal sounds.
6 months	Sitting: bends forward and uses hands for support; can bear weight when put into a standing position, but cannot yet stand without holding on. Reaching: unilateral. Grasp: no thumb opposition yet; releases cube when given another.	Cooing changing into babbling resembling one-syllable utterances; neither vowels nor consonants have very fixed recurrences; most common utterances sound somewhat like [ma], [mu], [da], or [di].
8 months	Stands holding on; grasps with thumb opposition; picks up pellet with thumb and fingertips.	Reduplication (or more continuous repetitions) becomes frequent; intonation patterns become distinct; utterances can signal emphasis and emotions.

10 months	Creeps efficiently; takes side-steps, holding on; pulls to standing position.	Vocalizations are mixed with sound-play such as gurgling or bubble-blowing; appears to wish to imitate sounds, but the imitations are never quite successful; beginning to differentiate between sounds heard by making differential adjustment.
12 months	Walks when held by one hand; walks on feet and hands—knees in air; mouthing of objects almost stopped; seats self on floor.	Identical sound sequences are replicated with higher relative frequency of occurrence, and words (*mamma* or *dadda*) are emerging; definite signs of understanding some words and simple commands (*Show me your eyes*).
18 months	Grasp, prehension, and release fully developed; gait stiff, propulsive and precipitated; sits on child's chair with only fair aim; creeps down stairs backward, has difficulty building tower of three cubes.	Has a definite repertoire of words—more than three, but less than fifty; still much babbling but now of several syllables, with intricate intonation pattern; no attempt at communicating information and no frustration at not being understood; words may include items such as *thank you* or *come here*, but there is little ability to join any of the lexical items into spontaneous two-item phrases; understanding progressing rapidly.
24 months	Runs, but fails in sudden turns; can quickly alternate between sitting and stance; walks stairs up or down, one foot forward only.	Vocabulary of more than fifty items (some children seem to be able to name everything in environment); begins spontaneously to join vocabulary items into two-word phrases; all phrases appear to be own creations; definite increase in communicative behavior and interest in language.
30 months	Jumps up into air with both feet; stands on one foot for about two seconds; takes a few steps on tiptoe; jumps from chair; good hand and finger coordination; can move digits independently; manipulation of objects much improved; builds tower of six cubes.	Fastest increase in vocabulary, with many new additions every day; no babbling at all; frustrated if not under-stood by adults; utterances consist of at least two words—many have three or even five words; sentences and phrases have characteristic child grammar—that is, are rarely verbatim repetitions of an adult utterance; intelligibility not yet very good, though there is great variation among children; seems to understand everything within hearing and directed to self.

3 years	Tiptoes three yards; runs smoothly with acceleration and deceleration; negotiates sharp and fast curves without difficulty; walks stairs by alternating feet; jumps 12 inches; can operate tricycle.	Vocabulary of some one thousand words; about 80 percent of utterances intelligible even to strangers; grammatical complexity of utterances roughly that of colloquial adult language although mistakes still occur.
4 years	Jumps over rope; hops on right foot; catches ball in arms; walks line.	Language well established; deviations from the adult norm tend to be more in style than in grammar.

File 9.9   How Adults Talk to Young Children

When people talk to one another, their general goal is to get listeners to understand what they are saying. This applies just as much when listeners are young children as when they are adults. The problem is that young children know very little about the structure and function of the language adults use to communicate with each other. As a result, adult speakers often modify their speech to help children understand them.

How adults talk to children is influenced by three things. First, adults have to make sure that children realize an utterance is being addressed to them and not to someone else. To do this, adults can use a name, speak in a special tone of voice, or even get their attention by touching them. Second, once they have a child's attention, they must choose the right words and the right sentences so the child is likely to understand what is said. For example, they are unlikely to discuss philosophy but very likely to talk about what the child is doing, looking at, or playing with at that moment. Third, they can say what they have to say in many different ways. They can talk quickly or slowly, use short sentences or long ones, and so on. How adults talk also has certain incidental consequences: children are presented with a specially tailored model of language use, adjusted to fit, as far as possible, what they appear to understand.

How Adults Get Children to Attend

Speakers depend on their listeners being cooperative and listening when they are spoken to. But when the listeners are children, adult speakers normally have to work a bit harder. They use attention getters to tell children which utterances are addressed to them rather than to someone else, and hence which utterances they ought to be listening to. And they use attention holders whenever they have more than one thing to say, for example, when telling a story.

Attention getters and **attention holders** fall into two broad classes. The first consists of names and exclamations. For example, adults often use the child's name at the beginning of an utterance, as in *Ned, there's a car.* Even four year olds know that this is an effective way to make two year olds attend. Or, instead of the child's name, adults use exclamations like *Look!* or *Hey!* as a preface to each utterance. The second class of attention getters consists of modulations that adults use to distinguish utterances addressed to young children from utterances addressed to other listeners. One of the most noticeable is the high-pitched voice adults use for talking to small children. When the linguist O. Garnica compared recordings of adults talking to two year olds, five year olds, and adults in the same setting, she found that when talking to children, adults use a wider pitch range: the pitch of the adult's voices was highest to the youngest children, next highest to the five year olds, and lowest to other adults. These results are consistent with the findings of the psychologist Anne Fernald who found that in various cultures speech directed to children is usually higher pitched and shows more pitch excursion (variation) compared to speech addressing adults.

Another modulation adults use is whispering. If children are sitting on their laps or standing right next to them, adults will speak directly into their ears so it is clear they are intended to listen. Garnica observed that all the mothers in her study on occasion whispered to two year olds, a few whispered to five year olds, but none whispered to adults. Not all attention getters and attention holders are linguistic. Speakers often rely on gestures as well, and may touch a child's shoulder or cheek, for example, as they begin talking. They also use gestures to hold a child's attention and frequently look at and point to objects they name or describe.

What Adults Say to Young Children

Adults both observe and impose the cooperative principle when they talk to young children. They make what they say relevant, talking about the "here and now" of the child's world. They encourage children to take their turns and make their contributions to the conversation. And they make sure that children make their contributions truthful by correcting them.

The "Here and Now"

Adults talk to young children mainly about the "*here* and *now.*" They make running commentaries on what children do, either anticipating their actions—for example, *Build me a tower now* said just as a child picks up a box of building blocks—or describing what has just happened: *That's right, pick up the blocks,* said just after a child has done so. Adults talk about the objects children show interest in. They name them (*That's a puppy*), describe their properties (*He's very soft and furry*), and talk about relations between objects (*The puppy's in the basket*). In talking about the "*here* and *now,*" usually whatever is directly under the child's eyes, adults are usually very selective about the words they use. They seem to be guided by the following assumptions:

1. Some words are easier for children to pronounce than others.
2. Some words are more useful for children than others.
3. Some words are hard to understand and best avoided.

Most languages contain *baby talk,* words that are considered appropriate in talking to very young children. For example, adult speakers of English often replace the words for animals by words for their sounds like *meow, woofwoof,* or by a diminutive form of the adult word like *kitty(-cat)* or *doggie.* As one would expect, the domains in which baby talk words are found overlap considerably with the domains young children first talk about. They include kinship terms and nicknames, such as *mommy, daddy*; the child's bodily functions and routines, *wee-wee, night-night*; names of animals; games and the occasional toy, *peek-a-boo, choo-choo*; and a few general qualities, *uh-oh!* (disapproval). Adults appear to use baby-talk words because they seem to be easier for children to pronounce. This assumption may well have some basis in fact, since in many languages baby talk words seem to be modeled on the sounds and combinations of sounds that young children tend to produce when trying their first words. At the same time, baby talk words provide yet another signal that a particular utterance is addressed to a child rather than someone else.

The psychologist Roger Brown has argued that the words parents use in speaking to young children anticipate the nature of the child's world. This seems to be true not only of baby talk words but also of the other words used in speaking to young children. Adults select the words that seem to have the most immediate relevance to what their children might want to talk about. For instance, they would not point to an Irish wolfhound and say to a one or two year old, *That's an Irish wolfhound.* They would be much more likely to say *That's a dog.* They supply words for different kinds of fruit the child might eat, such as *apple* or *orange,* but not the word *fruit.* They likewise supply the names of animals, but not the word *animal.* In other domains, though, they provide more general words like *tree* and do not use the more specific words for different kinds of tree like *oak, ash,* or *birch.* Some of the words adults select are very frequent in adult-to-adult speech; others are not. The criterion adults seem to use can be characterized by what Brown called *level of utility*: the judgment that one word is more likely to be useful than another in the child's own utterances.

Adults are selective in another way too: they omit some words and word endings and avoid other words. Adults tend to use fewer word endings (e.g., plural *-s* or possessive *-'s*) and articles like *the* or *a* when speaking to two year olds than to ten year olds, and fewer to ten-year-olds than to adults. Adults seem to leave out function words and word endings because they think this simplifies what they are saying. In fact, they do the same thing when talking to foreigners. Adults also try to avoid certain words. Instead of using pronouns like *he*, *she*, or *they*, they often repeat the antecedent noun phrase instead, as in *The boy was running, The boy climbed the tree*, where the second instance of *the boy* would normally be changed to *he*. Where *I* and *you* would be used in adult-to-adult speech, adults often use names instead, as in *Mommy's going to lift Tommy up* for *I'm going to lift you up*, or *Daddy wants to tie Julie's shoe* for *I want to tie your shoe*. Adults often use names in questions addressed to children too, for example, *Does Jennie want to play in the sand today?* addressed to Jennie herself. Adults seem to realize that pronouns are complicated for young children and so they try to avoid them.

Taking Turns

From very early on, adults encourage children to take their turns as speaker and listener in conversation. Even when adults talk to very small infants, they thrust "conversational turns" upon them. During the first months of life, adults respond to small infants as if their burps, yawns, and blinks count as turns in conversations. This is illustrated in the following proto-dialogue:

Mother:	Hello. Give me a smile then [gently pokes infant in the ribs].
Infant:	[yawns]
Mother:	Sleepy, are you? You woke up too early today.
Infant:	[opens fist]
Mother:	[touching infant's hand] What are you looking at? Can you see something?
Infant:	[grasps mother's finger]
Mother:	Oh, that's what you wanted. In a friendly mood, then. Come on, give us a smile.

Whatever the infant does is treated as a conversational turn, even though at this stage the adult carries the entire conversation alone. As infants develop, adults become more demanding about what "counts" as a turn. Yawning or stretching may be enough at three months, but by eight months babbling is what really counts. And by the age of one year or so only words will do.

Once children begin to use one- and two-word utterances, adults begin to provide both implicit and explicit information about conversational turns. For example, they may provide model dialogues in which the same speaker asks a question and then supplies a possible answer to it.

Adult:	Where's the ball?
	[picks up ball] THERE'S the ball.
Adult:	[looking at picture book with child]
	What's the little boy doing?
	he's CLIMBING up the TREE.

These model dialogues also give the adult speaker the opportunity to show how new information can be combined with given information in the answers to questions. New information tends to be signaled by a higher pitch of voice and by being louder relative to the other parts of the utterance. On other occasions, adults expatiate on whatever topic the child introduces:

> Child: Dere rabbit.
> Adult: The rabbit likes eating lettuce.
>   Do you want to give him some?

By ending with a question, the adult offers the child another turn and in this way deliberately prolongs the conversation. In fact, when necessary they also use "prompt" questions to get the child to make a contribution and so take his turn as speaker:

> Adult: What did you see?
> Child: [silence]
> Adult: You saw WHAT?

Prompt questions like *You saw what?* or *He went where?* are often more successful in eliciting speech from a child than questions with normal word order.

Making Corrections

Adults seldom correct what children have to say, but when they do, they only seem to do it to make sure the child's contribution is true. They may correct children explicitly, as in examples 1 and 2 below, or implicitly, as in 3. In example 4 the child is being corrected with regard to the truth value of the utterances, but the adult also uses the correct form of the verb:

> 1.   Child: [points] doggie.
>   Adult: No, that's a HORSIE.
>
> 2.   Child: That's the animal farmhouse.
>   Adult: No, that's the LIGHTHOUSE.
>
> 3.   Child: [pointing to a picture of bird on nest] Bird house.
>   Adult: Yes, the bird's sitting on a NEST.
>
> 4.   Child: Robin goed to school yesterday.
>   Adult: No, Robin went to a BIRTHDAY PARTY yesterday.

In each instance, the adult speakers are concerned with the truth of what the children have said, with whether they have used the right words for their listeners to be able to work out what they are talking about. The other corrections adults make are of how children pronounce certain words. If a child's version of a word sounds quite different from the adult version, a listener may have a hard time understanding what the child is trying to say. Getting children to pronounce recognizable words is a prerequisite for carrying on conversations. What is striking, though, is that adults do not consistently and persistently correct any other "mistakes" that children make when they talk. Even grammatical errors go uncorrected as long as what the child says is true. In correcting children's language, adults seem to be concerned primarily with the ability to communicate with a listener.

How Adults Talk to Children

Just as adults select what they say to young children by restricting it to the "here and now," so they alter the way they say what they say when talking to children. They do this in four ways: they slow down; they use short, simple sentences; they use a higher pitch of voice; and they repeat themselves frequently. Each of these modifications seems to be geared to making sure young children attend to and understand what adults say.

Speech addressed to two year olds is only half the speed of speech addressed to other adults. When adults talk to children aged four to six, they go a little faster but still speak more slowly than they do to adults. To achieve a slower rate, adults put in more pauses between words rather than stretch out each word. Adults also use very short sentences when talking to young children. The psychologist J. Phillips found that adult utterances to two year olds averaged less than four words each, while adult utterances to other adults averaged over eight words. These short sentences are generally very simple ones. There is a great deal of repetition in adult speech to children. One reason for this is the adults' use of "sentence frames" like those in the left-hand column.

$$
\left\{
\begin{array}{l}
\text{Where's} \\
\text{Let's play with} \\
\text{Look at} \\
\text{Here's} \\
\text{That's (a)} \\
\text{Here comes}
\end{array}
\right\}
\quad + \quad
\left\{
\begin{array}{l}
\text{Mommy} \\
\text{Daddy} \\
\text{(the) birdie} \\
\ldots \\
\qquad \ldots \\
\text{etc.}
\end{array}
\right\}
$$

These frames mark off the beginnings of new words by placing them in familiar slots within a sentence, and one of their main uses besides attention getting seems to be to introduce new vocabulary. Often, these kinds of sentence frames are used by the children too, and we might hear utterances like *Mommy tie shoe* or *Robin want cookie*, where we have a subject followed by a verb followed by an object. Adults also repeat themselves when giving instructions. Repetitions like those below are three times more frequent in speech to two year olds than in speech to ten year olds:

> Adult: Pick up the red one. Find the red one. Not the GREEN one. I
>   want the RED one. Can you find the red one?

These repetitions provide structural information about the kinds of frame the repeated unit (here the red one) can be used in. Also, these contrasts are often highlighted by emphasizing the difference in color (this is indicated by the capitalization). Repetitions also allow children more time to interpret adult utterances, because they don't have to try to remember the whole sentence.

When all these modifications are put together, it is clear that adults adjust what they say and modify how they say it to make themselves better understood. They first get children to attend, then select the appropriate words and the way to say them. This suggests that young children are able to understand only short sentences and need to have the beginnings and ends of sentences clearly identified. In addition, the sentences used are about the "here and now," since children rely heavily on the context to guess whenever they don't understand. But as children show signs of understanding more, adults modify the way they talk less and less. The shortest sentences and the slowest rate are reserved for the youngest children; both sentence length and rate of speech increase when adults talk to older children.

How Necessary Is Adult Speech?

The fact that adults systematically modify the speech they address to very young children forces us to ask two questions. First, are the modifications adults make necessary for acquisition? Second, even if they are not necessary, are they at least helpful? Some exposure to language is obviously necessary before children can start to acquire it. But it is quite possible that any kind of spoken language might do. We need to know, for example, whether children could learn language if their only information came from speech they overheard between adults, or from what they heard on the radio or television. If they could, it would be clear that adult modifications are not necessary, even though they might be helpful. On the other hand, if children could not, it would be clear that some adult modifications are not only helpful but necessary.

Experiments on these topics are difficult if not impossible to devise, but occasionally a real-life situation presents itself in a way that provides a glimpse of the answers to these questions. For example, the hearing children of deaf parents who only use sign language sometimes have little spoken language addressed to them by adults until they enter nursery school. The parents' solution for teaching their children to speak rather than use sign language is to turn on the radio or television as much as possible. The psychologists J. Sachs and M. Johnson reported on one such child. When Jim was approximately three and a half years old, he had only a small vocabulary that he had probably picked up from playmates plus a few words from television jingles. His language was far behind that of other children his age. Although he had overheard a great deal of adult-to-adult speech on television, no adults had spoken to him directly on any regular basis. Once Jim was exposed to an adult who talked to him, his language improved rapidly. Sachs and Johnson concluded that exposure to adult speech intended for other adults does not necessarily help children acquire language.

Exposure to a second language on television constitutes another naturalistic situation in which children regularly hear adults talking to each other. However, the psychologist C. Snow and her colleagues reported that young Dutch children who watched German television every day did not acquire any German. There are probably at least two reasons why children seem not to acquire language from radio or television. First, none of the speech on the radio can be matched to a situation visible to the child, and even on television people rarely talk about things immediately accessible to view for the audience. Children therefore receive no clues about how to map their own ideas onto words and sentences. Second, the stream of speech must be very hard to segment: they hear rapid speech that cannot easily be linked to familiar situations. All this suggests that one ingredient that might prove necessary for acquisition is the "here and now" nature of adult speech to children.

File 9.10   Adult Language Processing

There are three major areas of study in the domain of psycholinguistics; so far we have considered how language is represented in the mind and how language is acquired. But another major area is how people use their knowledge of language. How do they understand what they hear? How do they produce messages that others can understand in turn?

Much of the research on adult normal processes of the last twenty or thirty years has focused on three areas: word recognition, syntactic analysis and interpretation. This file will introduce only the first two aspects of comprehension, though many parallel issues arise in the study of language production.

Word Recognition

An initial step in understanding any message is the recognition of words. As we have seen, the meaning of a sentence is determined in part from the meanings of the words in it. Additionally, the recognition of a word provides information that determines the syntactic structure of the rest of the sentence. For instance, identifying a word also identifies what category it is, thus determining what range of phrase structures it can occur in. And when we recognize a verb like *put*, as well as accessing its meaning, we also expect certain types of complements to follow it; that is, it subcategorizes for an object noun phrase and a locative phrase. When we hear the word *arrive*, we know that it does not take an object. This kind of information is made available to speakers by recognizing a word and accessing the information that they have in their memory concerning it. Identifying words is such an effortless task under most conditions that we don't realize how difficult it really is; designing a computer system to accomplish this task, for instance, has proven virtually impossible. First recall the sheer number of words that any given person knows: the average six year old knows already about 14,000 words. A different kind of difficulty is presented by ambiguity, where two words with different meanings sound the same. Despite these difficulties, people are able to identify what they hear quite quickly. One source of evidence that this is the case comes from **shadowing experiments** in which people repeat aloud what they have just heard over a tape recorder. People can fluently and accurately repeat what they have heard with a lag of considerably less than a second. They cannot do this if what they hear is nonsense or a foreign language.

How do we go about recognizing words then? One common sense view that receives a lot of support from experimental evidence is that as soon as people hear speech, they start narrowing down the possible words that they may be hearing. If the first sound that they hear is /s/, that eliminates all words beginning with other sounds; if the next sound is /p/, many other possibilities are eliminated. A word is identified as soon as there is only one possibility left. This account is referred to as the **cohort theory** and hypothesizes that auditory word recognition begins with the formation of a group of words at the perception of the initial sound and proceeds sound by sound with the cohort of words decreasing as more sounds are perceived. This theory can be expanded to deal with written materials as well. Several experiments have supported this view of word recognition. One obvious prediction of this model is that if the beginning sound or letter of a word is missing, recognition will be much more difficult, perhaps even impossible. As early as 1900, experiments showed that word recognition is much more impaired by the mispronunciation of the initial letter of a word than by the mispronunciation of the final letter. This suggests that the cohort theory is correct; if the end of the word is missing, it can be predicted based on the initial portion, while it is much more difficult to use the end to predict the early part of the word. A recent version of this experiment looks at the accuracy and time to identify a word from the first or last half. For both of the words chosen, either half should be sufficient to unambiguously identify the word: for example, there is only one word in English that begins with *aard* and only one word which ends with *vark*. Nevertheless, people were much quicker and a good deal more accurate in identifying the word *aardvark* from the beginning than from the end.

Although this model is common-sensical and has experimental support, it leaves several questions unanswered. One problem is that people sometimes can't identify where a word starts. In written English boundaries are fairly clearly marked, but this is not the case for spoken language; there is usually no pause between one word and the next. So, for example, when someone hears the sequence [papəpozd], it is not at all obvious whether it should be understood as *Papa posed* or as *Pop opposed*. If people need to know the first sound to identify the word *opposed*, they might not even recognize it as a possibility. More examples are:

grey tie	great eye
a name	an aim
an ice man	a nice man
I scream	ice cream
see Mable	seem able

One of the most important factors that affects word recognition is how frequently the word is used in a given discourse or context. This **frequency effect** describes the additional ease with which a word is accessed due to its more frequent usage in the language. For example, words like *better* or *TV* occur more often than *debtor* or *mortgage*. This effect is not easy to explain assuming the beginning-to-end word recognition approach sketched above. One possible explanation of the frequency effect is that the lexicon is partially organized by frequency rather than simply in terms of the sounds in beginning-to-end order.

People also recognize a word faster when they have just heard it or read it than when they have not recently encountered it. Frequent words are likely to have been encountered more recently than infrequent words, so it is possible to explain the frequency effect as a **recency effect** and reduce the number of separate effects that have to be explained. Recency effects describe the additional ease with which a word is accessed due to its repeated occurrence in the discourse or context. However, again, the recency effect does not gibe with the simple beginning-to-end identification algorithm sketched above.

Another factor that is involved in word recognition is **context**. People recognize a word more readily when the preceding words provide an appropriate context for it. For example, in the sentence *This is the aorta*, people are not given any context that helps identify the word *aorta*. But in the sentence *The heart surgeon carefully cut into the wall of the right aorta*, many people would find that the cue of the heart surgeon helps them to identify the word more quickly. One mechanism that has been proposed to account for this kind of **context effect** is a **semantic association network**. This network represents the relationships between various semantically related words. Word recognition is thought to be faster when other members of the association network are provided in the discourse. It is obvious that the meaning of a word is tied to our understanding and general knowledge of the concept to which it refers. Thus, it is not unreasonable to suppose that hearing the words *heart surgeon* not only activates the direct meaning of the words *heart surgeon*, but also makes a number of associated concepts that are more available to the hearer, such as those involved in the physiology of the heart, modern surgical procedures, and so on. These concepts are in turn linked to the words that are used to refer to them.

Ambiguity

Much research has centered on how ambiguous words such as *bug* or *rose* are understood. There are two main theories: (1) *all* the meanings associated with the word are accessed, and (2) only *one* meaning is accessed initially. Support for the first position comes from experiments such as the following. When people are asked to finish a sentence, they take longer when the fragment to be finished contains an ambiguous word than when the ambiguous word is replaced by an unambiguous term, as in the following sentences:

After taking the right turn at the intersection ...	(*right* is ambiguous: *correct* vs. *rightward*)
After taking the left turn at the intersection ...	(*left* is unambiguous)

What this delay suggests is that all meanings of ambiguous words are accessed and that time has to be taken to decide among them.

However, other experiments suggest that under some circumstances, only one meaning is initially accessed. Two of the effects mentioned above have been shown to be important here: the frequency and context effects. First, if one of the meanings is much more frequent than the other, people tend to assume that the word has the more frequent meaning. The word *chair*, for example, has at least two meanings—an object to sit on and the head of a department or committee—but the former occurs much more often in speech than the latter, and people often appear to recognize only the more frequent meaning soon after the word *chair* is presented to them. This seems to suggest that only one meaning is initially considered, at least for words whose various meanings differ markedly in frequency of occurrence.

The semantic context effect also plays a significant part in deciding which meaning is the most appropriate. When a word like *bug* is seen in the context of *spy*, it is reliably identified as meaning "a listening device"; but in the context of *spiders and roaches* it is identified as meaning "an insect."

Syntactic Processing

Once a word has been identified, it is used to construct a syntactic structure. In some cases this is quite straightforward. Psycholinguists generally assume that the syntactic structure is built as soon as possible rather than waiting to see what the whole string of words is before deciding what structure it has. The reason for this assumption is that people normally already know what the beginning of the sentence means before they hear the whole thing; this must be the case given the common experience we all have of being able to fill in a word that someone else we have been listening to is groping for. The shadowing task mentioned earlier proves the same point. Sometimes when people are shadowing, they mistake what they hear and say a word that is not on the script that they are repeating aloud. This word is generally syntactically and semantically reasonable given the context. If all the words in a sentence are unambiguous or have only one possible category and those categories fit only one phrase structure, it is not hard to understand how people can build the correct structure and interpret it so quickly. For example, in *the jealous woman went away*, the word *the* can only be a determiner, *woman* is a noun, and the combination forms a noun phrase; *went* is a past tense verb, *away* is a particle, and the combination of the two makes a verb phrase; finally, the combination of a noun phrase and a verb phrase makes a sentence. From this example there is no reason to think that the process of determining the structure of a sentence is difficult.

However, as always, there are complications due to the ambiguity of individual words and to the different possible ways that words can be fit into phrases. Sometimes there is no way to determine which structure and meaning a sentence has. For example, there are two possible structures associated with the sentence *The cop saw the spy with the binoculars*. The ambiguity lies in how the prepositional phrase *with the binoculars* fits into the rest of the sentence; it can be a complement of the verb *see*, in which case it means that the cop employed binoculars in order to see the spy, or it can be part of the noun phrase, in which case it specifies that the spy has binoculars.

Some ambiguities are due to the ambiguous category of some of the words in the sentence. In *the desert trains . . .*, should *desert* be taken as the subject of the verb *trains*, or is *desert* a modifier of the noun *trains*? If the sentence continues *men to be hardy*, the first structure is correct, but if it continues *seldom run on time*, the latter is appropriate.

One interesting phenomenon concerning certain ambiguous sentences is called the **garden path**. Garden path sentences are sentences that are initially interpreted with a different structure than they actually have. It typically takes quite a long time to figure out what the other structure is if the first choice turns out to be incorrect. Sometimes people never do figure it out. They have been "led up the garden path," fooled into thinking the sentence has a different structure than it has. Reduced relative clauses quite frequently cause this feeling of having been garden-pathed. For example, *The horse raced past the barn fell* means "the horse that was raced past the barn fell," but even when this is explained, many people have trouble figuring out how it fits together. Here are some more examples of garden path sentences. Can you figure out what the structure of these sentences is?

> The boat floated downstream sank.
> While Mary was mending the sock fell off her lap.
> The daughter of the king's son admires himself.
> The florist sent the flowers was pleased.
> The cotton clothing is made from grows in Mississippi.
> They told the boy that the girl met the story.

As with lexical ambiguity, an important question in sentence processing is how people decide which structure an ambiguous sentence has. The alternatives are that people either consider all possibilities and decide which is the best, or else they use some strategy to decide which structure to consider first. If that structure does not work out, they may reconsider. This garden path phenomenon suggests that for at least some ambiguities, people try one analysis of an ambiguous sequence of words first, and only become aware of the other possibility when the one tried first does not work out. In the example above, people realize that there is something wrong with their initial analysis of the sentence because *fell* cannot be fit into the structure that they have settled on initially.

Several suggestions have been made about how people decide which analysis to try first. One guess is that there is a strong tendency to build as little structure as possible. For example, if the first word in sentence is *the*, an infinite number of structures could potentially follow; *the* is a determiner and unambiguously initiates a noun phrase, but that noun phrase can serve as a subject of a sentence, as a possessive phrase modifying the subject noun, as a possessive phrase modifying a possessive noun, etc. Because of **recursion**, there are an infinite number of possibilities.

It would be inefficient for people to assume all these infinite structures until they get some positive evidence for one of them. And if they arbitrarily choose one of the possibilities, they are most likely to choose the simplest. The idea is that people initially construct the simplest (or least complex) syntactic structure when interpreting the structure of sentences. This is called the **Minimal Attachment Theory.**

There are other types of information that people can use to choose the appropriate analysis for an ambiguous sentence as well. As with words, the semantic interpretation sometimes determines which is the most likely interpretation. Returning to the ambiguity above, it is equally likely that someone can employ binoculars to see a spy or that a spy should have binoculars. But if the word *binoculars* is replaced with the word *revolver*, the situation changes. A spy with a revolver is likely enough to be seen, but it isn't possible to see using a revolver. Therefore, the choice between the possibilities can be made based on the pragmatic plausibility of the two interpretations.

File 9.11

Errors in Speech Production and Perception

When we investigate the nature of language carefully, we sometimes make some surprising discoveries. For example, acoustic analysis of the speech signal reveals that it is for the most part continuous; i.e., in most cases, it is not possible to divide words, or even a series of words, into a sequence of discrete sounds or phonetic segments. This fact is at odds with our common sense; we feel that words and sentences *are* composed of discrete parts. It could well be that our common sense is simply wrong here (for, after all, common sense also tells us that the earth is flat and stationary), but in fact there is good evidence that, although the speech signal is physically continuous, it is also, from the perspective of how our brains process this signal, composed of discrete units. Mental (or psychological) aspects of language such as this are clearly of great interest, and a number of different areas have provided evidence to support or refute what common sense tells us about these aspects of language. One such area that has been particularly helpful in this respect is the study of errors in speech production and perception (also known as **performance errors**).

Slips of the Tongue (Production Errors)

By "slips of the tongue" we mean any inadvertent flaws in a speaker's use of his or her language. These mistakes can provide evidence for many of the linguistic constructs we have been discussing throughout this course. First and foremost, of course, is the evidence they supply for the psychological reality of discrete units in the continuous speech we hear. These units can be of various sizes—some, surprisingly, even smaller than a single sound! Evidence to support these claims is provided by the fact that the units can be moved, added, or omitted during a speech error. For example, in the errors illustrated below, individual sounds are being manipulated in various ways. This is only possible if the speaker does indeed organize the speech wave in terms of these units.

Anticipations

This type of error involves the substitution or addition of one sound which comes later in an utterance for one which comes earlier:

Intended utterance	*Actual utterance*
spl*i*cing from one *t*ape	spl*a*cing from one *t*ape
M.*U*. *v*alues	M. *v*iew values

Preservations

These involve the substitution or addition of a sound which has occurred earlier in the phrase being uttered:

Intended utterance	Actual utterance
pale sky	pale skay
John praised the *man*	John praised the *pan*

Metathesis

Metathesis is the switching of two sounds, each taking the place of the other. When a metathesis involves the first sounds of two separate words, the error is called a **spoonerism**, named after the Reverend Spooner, a renowned chronic sufferer of this type of slip of the tongue:

Intended utterance	Actual utterance
*d*ear old *q*ueen	*q*ueer old *d*ean
*f*ill the *p*ool	*f*ool the *p*ill
a *h*eap of *j*unk	a *h*unk of *j*eep

Additions and Omissions

These errors involve the addition of extra sounds (out of the blue, so to speak) and the omission of sounds, respectively:

Intended utterance	Actual utterance
spic and s*p*an	spic and s*pl*an
chrysanthemum p*l*ants	chrysanthemum p*a*nts

In order to move a sound, the speaker must think of it as a separable unit. So the speaker is imposing a structure on the speech signal in his or her mind, even though this structure does not exist physically. This is why we say that the sound unit is psychologically real.

Other Speech Units

As we mentioned above, the same is true for units of speech smaller than the sound as well. For example, in the following speech errors note that it is phonetic features, not whole sounds, which are being moved from one sound to another:

Intended utterance	Actual utterance
*c*lear *b*lue sky	*g*lear *p*lue sky
Cedars of Le*b*a*n*on	Cedars of Le*m*a*d*on

In the first case the vibration of the vocal folds is moving from the [b] in blue to the [k] in clear resulting in the phrase *glear plue* instead of *clear blue*. In the second example, air is allowed to resonate in the nasal cavity during the [b] rather than during the [n], resulting in *Lemadon* rather than *Lebanon*. The fact that individual articulatory movements can move from one sound to another shows that they too are psychologically real units to the speaker, i.e., that speakers do mentally organize sounds as being made up of a set of articulatory movements.

Units of speech larger than the single sound can be identified as well. In the following examples, morphemes have undergone metathesis. Thus, these too must be part of our mental organization of the speech wave:

Intended utterance	*Actual utterance*
a *floor* full of *holes*	a *hole* full of *floors*
a language *learn*er *need*s	a language *need*er *learn*s
I *turn*ed in a *change* of address	I *chang*ed in a *turn* of address

Language, of course, involves more than just units of speech. In particular, linguists maintain that there is a complex set of rules which the language user follows when making use of these units. The existence of these rules is much less compatible with our common sense than, say, the existence of phonetic segments—especially when we find that we cannot, without fairly extensive study, say exactly what these rules are. Nevertheless, there is considerable evidence for their existence, including much that can be obtained by examining speech errors.

One type of rule whose psychological reality can be confirmed by studying speech errors are phonotactic constraints. These rules tell us which sequences of sounds are possible in a given language. For example, the sequence of sounds [sr] cannot occur at the beginning of a word in English. That speakers of English follow this rule is clear from the following slip:

Intended utterance	*Actual utterance*
Freudian *sl*ip	fleudian *shr*ip

Notice that this looks similar to the metatheses illustrated in the first section in that the [l] and [r] were interchanged. But the [s] of *slip* has also been converted to [š]. If we recall that [sr], which would have resulted from a simple metathesis, does not occur word-initially (see File 4.5 for more on phonotactic constraints), then we can see why this further change was made—to avoid violating this phonotactic rule. Thus, speakers unconsciously follow these rules, even when making mistakes.

The rules that tell us how morphemes are to be pronounced are also obeyed when making speech errors. For example, recall that the morpheme that is used most often to indicate past tense has three different pronunciations, [d], [t], and [əd], depending on the nature of the preceding sound. The reality of the rule governing the distribution of these pronunciations is indicated by the fact that it is followed even when the past tense morpheme is attached to a different word as the result of a slip:

Intended utterance	*Actual utterance*
going to get them *clean*ed ([d])	going to get them *teeth*ed ([tiθt])
*cook*ed a *roast* ([kʊkt])	*roast*ed a *cook* ([rostəd])
likes to have his *team rest*ed ([əd])	likes to have his *rest team*ed ([d])

Since these rules are always followed, they must be part of our mental organization of the language.

These examples also demonstrate the reality of the rules for combining morphemes, since even during a speech error we find only past tense morphemes combined with verbs, plural morphemes combined with nouns, etc. Because we rarely get nonsensical combinations like "noun + past tense," the rules which tell us how words are built must also be part of our mental organization of language.

Finally, speech errors can also give us insights into the organization of words in the lexicon. For example, many errors in the production of speech involve the substitution of one word for another because of some semantic relationship between the words. The errors which follow, and many more like them, reveal that the intended word and the substituted word share some common semantic property, and that the retrieval process mistakes one word for another. Thus, these semantic similarities must be recognized and the lexical entries in the brain organized accordingly.

Intended utterance	*Actual utterance*
My thesis is too long	My thesis is too short
. . . before the place opens	. . . before the place closes
He got hot under the collar	He got hot under the belt
. . . when my gums bleed	. . . when my tongue bleeds

A similar type of speech error involves a substitution of one word for another based on phonological, rather than semantic, similarities. What happens in these cases is that the speaker's retrieval process inadvertently pulls out a word that sounds like the one they intended to use but is semantically distinct. Examples include:

Intended utterance	*Actual utterance*
spreading like wildfire	spreading like wildflowers
equivalent	equivocal
marinade	serenade

This type of error, called a **malapropism**, must be distinguished from cases where the word the speaker used is the one they intended to use, though it is semantically incorrect. This latter type of mistake, called a **classical malapropism**, does not involve a performance error per se, since the speakers are saying what they meant to say; rather it is a competence error since the speakers have incorrect beliefs about the meaning of a particular word. Mrs. Malaprop, a character from Richard B. Sheridan's eighteenth-century play *The Rivals* (and after whom this kind of error is named), was particularly prone to this kind of error, as was the television character Archie Bunker. Such errors reveal more about how words are learned than how they are organized, because the retrieval process is functioning perfectly in these cases. Some examples:

Intended utterance	*Actual utterance*
I hereby *deputize* you	I hereby *jeopardize* you
obscure	obtuse
express appreciation	. . . express depreciation

It is significant that word substitution errors can be based both on semantic similarity and on phonological similarity. The primary point of importance to a speaker searching the lexicon for a word to produce is the meaning of the word. There is a certain message that must be expressed, and words are chosen accordingly. It is not surprising that under these circumstances semantic substitution errors occur. However, the speaker is not concerned with how words sound until the word has been chosen.

Why Should Phonological Substitution Errors and Malapropisms Occur?

The most convincing explanation of malapropisms is that the two types of errors occur at different points in the word planning operation. We use concepts to help us choose the most appropriate word, and if we don't use the concept appropriately, the word chosen will be semantically the wrong word. Once the word is chosen, however, phonological information must be used to organize the pronunciation of the word, and things can go wrong at this point as well. Consider the analogy of the library. First you go to the card catalog. Using information about the topic that you want to cover, you are able to select a book, but then you have to get it off the shelf. Apparently, the shelves of words in our minds are organized in terms of their phonological structure; therefore, even after we have located the place where the word is stored, we can end up pulling out the wrong word because, although it is the wrong word, it is similar in sound. This does not tell us exactly how the mental lexicon works, but it does tell us that some possible models of the lexicon are wrong. It may help to recognize that it is not at all silly for the lexicon to be organized in terms of sound as well as meaning; it is not only speakers but listeners who must use the lexicon, and we are listeners before we are speakers.

Perception Errors

Perception errors can be viewed as "slips of the ear" and provide evidence for the same sorts of linguistic phenomena as do slips of the tongue. They do this, however, from the point of view of the listener rather than the speaker. For example, the fact that many slips of the ear involve the misperception of a single segment or phonetic feature, or a metathesis of a pair of these, shows that the speech stream is divided into units as it is perceived, not just when spoken. In addition, since such slips always result in possible (though not always actual) words, this kind of slip indicates that listeners know what to expect in the way of sequences of sounds. That is, they have unconscious knowledge of phonotactic rules; if they did not, we would expect to find slips in which impossible words were perceived as having been said. Also, since many slips of the ear involve the misperception of word boundaries, we have evidence that the listener also divides the speech stream into morphemes, just as the speaker does.

The simplest slips of the ear involve only the misperception of one or more sounds or the mishearing of a word boundary, as in the following examples:

Said	*Heard as*
death in Venice	deaf in Venice
what are those sticks?	what are those ticks?
give them an ice bucket	give them a nice bucket
of thee I sing	of the icing
the stuffy nose	the stuff he knows
the biggest hurdle	the biggest turtle
some others	some mothers

Other perception errors are more drastic in nature; for example, the phrase that is heard is significantly different from the intended phrase. This occurs because the listener is trying to edit what is heard into a meaningful utterance, as we do whenever we listen to speech. If part of the speech signal is not heard, then the listener unconsciously reconstructs what was said, often filling in the gaps with sounds or words that were never there in the first place and changing other words to make sense out of the whole phrase. Examples of this type include:

Said	*Heard as*
kill germs where they grow	kill germs with eggroll
a Coke and a Danish	a coconut Danish
pledge allegiance to the flag	play jelly dance to the flag

Conclusion

Performance errors such as slips of the tongue and slips of the ear provide us with a great deal of valuable information concerning language and how it is processed and produced. We have seen that the speech wave, despite its physical continuity, is mentally organized into discrete units and that these units follow specific rules and patterns of formation. Moreover, these constraints are the same for both speaker and listener. The fact that they are never violated, not even by mistake, shows that the constraints are an intrinsic part of language itself; that is, they *define* for us what the language is like. Thus, by studying cases in which an individual's linguistic performance is less than perfect, we can gain more insight into the nature of linguistic **competence**, the unconscious knowledge that speakers of a language possess. Linguists can then formulate hypotheses about the mental constructs that represent this knowledge.

10

Historical Linguistics

All languages change through time. But how they change, what drives these changes, and what kinds of changes we can expect are not obvious. By comparing between languages and within a language, the history of a group of languages can be discovered. We can make hypotheses about the form and sound of a language long dead. Historical linguistics considers the ways languages change through time and some of the factors that influence those changes.

File 10.1   Language Change

When linguists describe the current phonological processes of a particular language, isolate that language's morphemes, or discover that language's syntactic rules, they analyze that language **synchronically;** that is, they analyze that language at a particular point in time. Languages, however, are not static; they are constantly changing entities. Linguists can study language development through time, providing **diachronic** analyses.

Historical linguistics is concerned with language change. It is interested in what kinds of changes occur (and why), and equally important, what kinds of changes don't occur (and why not). Historical linguists attempt to determine the changes that have occurred in a language's history, and the relationship of languages historically.

To see how English has changed over time, compare the following versions of the Lord's Prayer from the three major periods in the history of English. A contemporary version is also included. (Note: the symbol Þ, called *thorn*, is an Old English symbol for the voiceless interdental fricative [θ], as in *th*ree; ð, called *edh* (or *eth*), is the symbol for the voiced interdental fricative [ð], as in *th*en.)

Old English (text ca. 1100)

Fæder ure þu þe eart on heofonum, si þin nama gehalgod. Tobecume þin rice. Gewurþe þin willa on eorðan swa swa on heofonum. Urne gedœghwamlican hlaf syle us to dæg. And forgyf us ure gyltas, swa swa we forgyfað urum gyltedum. And ne gelæd þu us on costnungen ac alys us of yfele. Soðlice.

Middle English (text ca. 1400)

Oure fadir that art in heuenes halowid be thi name, thi kyngdom come to, be thi wille don in erthe es in heuene, yeue to us this day oure bread ouir other substance, & foryeue to us oure dettis, as we forgeuen to oure dettouris, & lede us not in to temptacion: but delyuer us from yuel, amen.

Early Modern English (text 1611)

Our father which art in heaven, hallowed be thy Name. Thy kingdome come. Thy will be done, in earth, as it is in heaven. Giue vs this day our dayly bread. And forgiue vs our debts, as we forgiue our debters. And leade vs not into temptation, but deliuer vs from euill: For thine is the kingdome, and the power, and the glory, for euer, Amen.

Contemporary English

Our Father, who is in heaven, may your name be kept holy. May your kingdom come into being. May your will be followed on earth, just as it is in heaven. Give us this day our food for the day. And forgive us our offenses, just as we forgive those who have offended us. And do not bring us to the test. But free us from evil. For the kingdom, the power, and the glory are yours forever. Amen.

Languages change in all aspects of the grammar: the phonology, morphology, syntax, and semantics, as these passages illustrate. Subsequent files will describe the various types of language change in detail.

Historical linguistics as we know it began in the late eighteenth century, when Western European scholars began to notice that modern European languages shared similar linguistic characteristics with ancient languages, such as Sanskrit, Latin, and Greek. These similarities led linguists to believe that today's European languages and those ancient languages must have evolved from a single ancestor, or "mother," language called **Proto-Indo-European** (PIE).

If these languages did in fact share a common ancestor, a reasonable question to ask is, what caused them to change into the different languages that they are today? One of the causes for language change is geographical division. As groups of people spread out through Europe, they lost communication with each other, so that the language of each group went its own way, underwent its own changes, and thus came to differ from the others. Another cause for language change is language contact, with the effect that languages become more alike. English, for example, has borrowed many Spanish words from contact with Mexican and Cuban immigrants. Language contact does not, of course, explain why Proto-Indo-European subdivided as it did, but it does help to explain a number of shared characteristics—especially lexical items—among the world's languages. Language contact, like any other explanation for language change, does not provide a complete explanation, only a partial one. At times, linguists cannot find any particular cause that would motivate a language to change in a particular direction. Language change, then, may simply just happen.

Often people view such change as a bad thing, so they try to resist it. Jonathan Swift, the late seventeenth century satirist who wrote *Gulliver's Travels*, felt that if the language changed, people would no longer be able to read his essays, so he supported the movement among English grammarians to stipulate prescriptive rules that would have the effect of regulating current language usage as well as change. These grammarians based their rules on classical Latin from the first century B.C., viewing it as the perfect, model language, since it did not change. Even today when we don't look to a language such as Latin as a model, some people consciously resist linguistic change. Consider the word *comprise*. Traditionally, the "whole" *comprises* its "parts" as in:

> *A chess set comprises thirty-two pieces.*

Increasingly, however, people say:

> *Thirty-two pieces comprise a chess set.*

in which the "parts" now *comprise* the "whole." Strict prescriptive grammarians regard this second utterance as ungrammatical. Despite these social views toward change, linguists regard change as neither good nor bad; it is simply a fact of life and a fact of language.

File 10.2   The Family Tree and Wave Models

The notion that similar languages are related and descended from an earlier, common language (a protolanguage) goes back to the late eighteenth century when Sir William Jones suggested that the linguistic similarities of Sanskrit to ancient Greek and Latin could best be accounted for by assuming that all three were descended from a common ancestral language. This language was called Proto-Indo-European.

Jones's suggestion was developed in the nineteenth century and gradually came under the influence of Darwin's theory of the evolution of species. Scholars at the time considered language and linguistic development to be analogous in many ways to biological phenomena. Thus, it was suggested that languages, like other living organisms, had "family trees" and "ancestors." A sample "genealogical tree" for the Indo-European (I-E) family of languages appears at the end of this file.

The **family tree theory**, as formulated by August Schleicher in 1871, assumes that languages change in regular, recognizable ways (the **regularity hypothesis**) and that because of this, similarities among languages are due to a "genetic" relationship among those languages (the **relatedness hypothesis**). In order to fill in the particulars of such a relationship, it is necessary to *reconstruct* the hypothetical parent from which the related languages are derived. The principal technique for reconstructing the common ancestor (the protolanguage) of related languages is known as the **comparative method**.

In keeping with the analogy of language relationships to human families, the theory makes use of the terms **mother** (or **parent**), **daughter**, and **sister** languages. In the family tree of I-E, French and Spanish are sisters, both are daughters of Latin; Germanic is the mother of English, and so on. The model clearly shows the direction of change and the relations among languages, the older stages of the languages being located higher in the tree and direct descendents being linked to their ancestors through the straight lines or "branches."

However, a disadvantage exists in that the structure of the family tree may lead people to develop faulty views of two aspects of language change: (1) that each language forms a uniform speech community without internal variation and without contact with its neighbor languages, so that all speakers of Latin, for example, are assumed to have spoken exactly the same way at the time French and Spanish split off; and (2) that the split of a parent language into its daughter languages is a sudden or abrupt occurrence, happening without intermediate stages.

These two views are not supported by the linguistic evidence we have from modern languages. No language is uniform or isolated from others but is always made up of dialects that are still recognized as belonging to the same language, and always shares similarities with other languages in its family, even those belonging to a different subgroup. And as studies of modern language change show, languages do not split apart abruptly but rather drift apart indiscernibly, starting as dialects and ending up as separate languages only after years of gradual change. In fact, the dividing point between two "dialects" and two "languages" is often impossible to locate exactly and is often obscured by nonlinguistic (e.g., political) factors.

To supplement the family tree model and overcome these difficulties, Johannes Schmidt proposed the **wave theory** in 1872. This theory recognizes the gradual spread of change throughout a dialect, language, or a group of languages, much as a wave expands on the surface of a pond from the point where a pebble (i.e., the source of the change) has been tossed in. Dialects are formed by the spread of different changes from different starting points and at different rates; some changes reinforce each other while others only partially overlap or affect only a certain area, much as the waves formed by a scattering of pebbles thrown into a pond may partially overlap. In the wave diagram for

I-E below, the same basic subgroups shown in the family tree are indicated; in addition, however, similarities between various subgroups are also indicated by circles enclosing those languages that share some linguistic feature or set of features, thus cutting across the traditional categories of the family tree. By looking at ever smaller linguistic changes, one can also show the languages within each group and the dialects within each language, indicating clearly how variable languages can be, even though distinct from others. In this way the wave diagram avoids the two faults of the family tree model, though it in turn suffers from disadvantages relating to problems in analyzing the genetic history of the languages displayed.

In fact, neither the family tree model nor the wave model presents entirely adequate or accurate accounts of language change or the relatedness of languages. For example, it is now known that languages can exhibit linguistic similarities without necessarily being related. The similarities may be the result of borrowing from language contact, language drift (that is, independent but identical changes in distinct dialects or languages), similarities in types of morphological structures, syntactic similarities, or other reasons. Nonetheless, the family tree model and wave model do provide useful frameworks for the discussion of language change.

Indo-European Wave Diagram

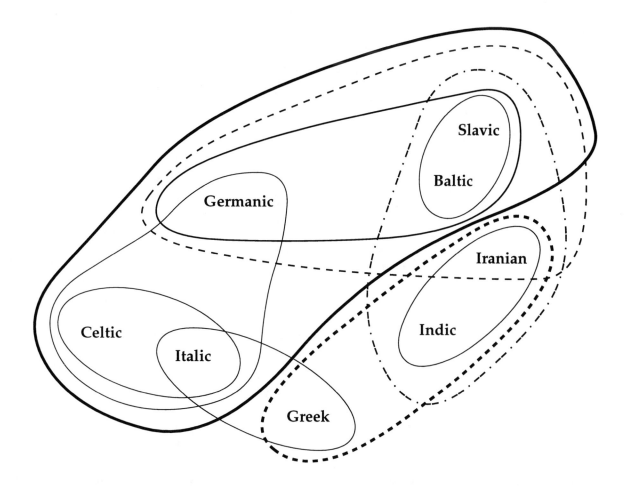

Indo-European Family Tree

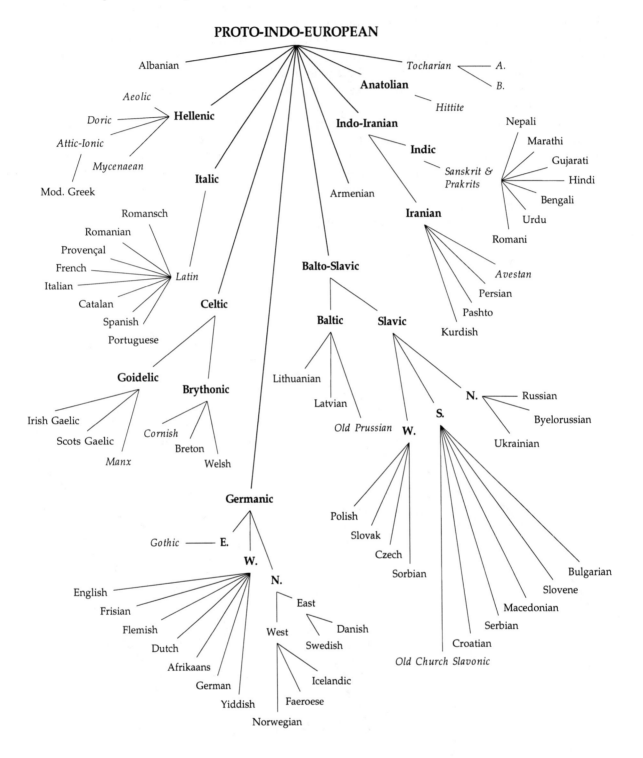

Languages that are no longer spoken are italicized (*Cornish*), and language families are in boldface (**Baltic**). Indo-European Family Tree adapted from Jeffers and Lehiste, *Principles and Methods for Historical Linguistics* (1979), p. 302. © 1979 MIT Press. All rights reserved.

File 10.3   Sound Change

Sound change is the most widely studied aspect of language change. There are a number of reasons why this is so. First, the study of how the sounds of languages change has a long tradition behind it, more so than any other area of linguistics. As a result we are more informed about this particular area of language change than others. Second, it is often impossible to understand changes in other areas of the language system without studying sound change, for sound change does not affect just the system of sounds of a language but may also affect a language's morphology, syntax, and semantics. Third, the study of sound change provides the basis for the study of language relationships and the reconstruction of parent (proto-) languages. Finally, sound change provides a very good introduction to the basic aims and goals of those who study language change: to describe the types of changes possible in language systems and to determine the causes of those changes.

What Is Sound Change?

Sound change is an alteration in the phonetic shape of a sound as a result of a phonological process. If a phonological process is introduced into a language where it did not formerly occur, it may result in a sound change. For example, at an early period in the history of English the voiceless velar stop [k] occurred before the long front vowel [ī] (also transcribed as [i:]) in words like 'chide' *cidan* [kīdan]. Later in the Old English period the velar consonant [k] was palatalized to a [č] before the front vowel [ī]. The introduction of the phonological process of palatalization resulted in the sound change k > č before [ī] in Old English. The phonetic shape of [k] (the voiceless velar stop) was altered to [č] (a voiceless palatal affricate) as a result of the phonological process of palatalization.

    At this point, it is necessary to make the distinction between the introduction of a phonological process and sound change clearly understood. The introduction of a phonological process into a language alone cannot be considered sound change. While it is a necessary first step in the process of sound change, the introduction of a phonological process at first changes the structure of a word in certain specific speech contexts. For example, the basic pronunciation of the word *interesting* is [ɪntərɛstɪŋ], and this pronunciation occurs most often in formal speech situations, e.g., when talking with business associates. When we speak with close friends in a casual situation, however, we may allow the phonological process that deletes schwa [ə] before liquids [r] and [l] to apply and pronounce the word [ɪntrɛstɪŋ]. But we cannot assume that there has been a sound change of ə > Ø before liquids on the basis that a phonological process has been applied in casual speech. For sound change to occur, the basic form of a word must be permanently altered in all contexts. In the example above, speakers would have to choose the variant pronunciation of *interesting* [ɪntrɛstɪŋ] in *all* speech situations and abandon the pronunciation [ɪntərɛstɪŋ] altogether.

    Obviously this has not happened (yet!) in the case of *interesting*, though it did happen in the Old English example discussed above. Recall that the introduction of palatalization resulted in alternate pronunciations for the word 'chide' *cidan* [kīdan] and [čīdan]. When the pronunciation [čīdan] was first introduced into Old English, it was no doubt tied to certain speech situations, much as the pronunciation [ɪntrɛstɪŋ] is in Modern English. Gradually, however, over a considerable period of time, the pronunciation [čīdan] was adopted by Old English speakers and the pronunciation [kīdan] was abandoned. In this way the basic form of the word was permanently altered in Old English to [čīdan]. Thus the introduction of the palatalization process resulted ultimately in the sound change k > č before [ī].

The Regularity of Sound Change

One of the most fascinating aspects of sound change is that if a particular sound change is studied over a long enough period of time it will be completely regular, i.e., every instance of the sound in question will undergo the change. Thus, in our Old English example we would say that the sound change k > č before [ī] is regular because every Old English word that contained [k] before [ī] changed to [č]; the change was not isolated to the word 'chide'. Sound change does not affect all possible words instantaneously, nor does every speaker in a community pick up a sound change overnight. Sound change is a very gradual process, spreading from one word to the next, and from one speaker to the next until all possible words and speakers are affected.

Though sound change takes place gradually, the ultimate regularity of sound change can be verified quite easily. In Old English, for example, the ancestor of our Modern English word *house* was spelled *hus* and pronounced [hūs]. If we compare these two words, we observe a change in the quality of the vowel. In Old English, the vowel was the long high back rounded vowel [ū], while in Modern English the vowel is a diphthong, [aw]. What is important is that this is not the only example of the sound change ū > aw in the history of English. In fact we can find any number of Old English words with [ū] that are pronounced with the diphthong [aw] in Modern English, e.g., Old English *mus* [mūs: Modern English *mouse* [maws]; Old English *lus* [lūs] : Modern English *louse* [laws]; Old English *ut* [ūt]: Modern English *out* [awt], etc.

Types of Sound Change

The development of Old English [ū] is what is known as **unconditioned sound change**. That is, every instance of [ū], no matter where it occurred in a word or what sounds were next to it, became [aw]. More often than not, it is the case that sounds are influenced by the sounds that occur around them. When a sound changes because of the influence of a neighboring sound, the change is called a **conditioned sound change**. We have already considered a good example of a conditioned sound change from the history of English, namely, the palatalization of [k] before the front vowel [ī]. Notice that the only voiceless velar stops that were palatalized were those occurring before the vowel [ī]; all other velar stops remain nonpalatal. Evidence of this is Old English *ku* [kū], corresponding to Modern English *cow* [kaw].

Conditioned and unconditioned sound changes are often subcategorized as follows: conditioned sound changes according to what type of conditioning is involved; unconditioned sound changes according to changes in articulation, e.g., according to changes in tongue position, lip rounding, etc. We will list only some of the more common types of sound changes, followed by an example or two.

Conditioned Sound Changes

1. **Assimilation.** Assimilation refers to a situation in which one sound becomes more like another sound. In Old English voiceless fricatives became voiced when they occurred between voiced sounds, e.g., Old English *wolves* [wulfas] became [wulvas].

2. **Dissimilation.** Dissimilation refers to a situation in which two similar sounds become less like one another. In some varieties of English the word *fifth* [fɪfθ] has undergone a sound change whereby the final fricative has dissimilated to a stop [fɪft].

3. **Deletion.** At the end of the Middle English period unstressed word-final [ə] was deleted, e.g., Middle English *nose* [nɔzə] : Modern English *nose* [noz].

4. **Insertion.** In a considerable number of Modern English varieties the basic form of the word

athlete is pronounced [æθəlɪt]. In this word a sound change has taken place inserting [ə] between consonants of a cluster that was perceived to be difficult to pronounce. The older, basic form of the word is [æθlɪt].

Unconditioned Sound Changes

1. **Monophthongization**. Monophthongization refers to a change from a diphthong (a complex vowel sound consisting of a vowel followed by a glide) to a simple vowel sound, a monophthong. A good example of monophthongization occurred at the beginning of the Modern English period. In Middle English the diphthong [ɪw] occurred in words such as *rude* [rɪwdə], *rule* [rɪwlə], *new* [nɪwə], *due* [dɪwə], and so forth. In Modern English this diphthong became a simple vowel [u]; witness the modern pronunciations for these words: *rude* [rud], *rule* [rul], *new* [nu], *due* [du].

2. **Diphthongization**. Diphthongization refers to the change of a simple vowel sound to a complex one. The history of English once again provides us with a very good example. In the Middle English period the high back rounded vowel [ū] became a diphthong [aw], e.g., Middle English *house* [hūs] became Modern English *house* [haws].

3. **Metathesis**. Metathesis refers to a change in the order of sounds. Some English dialects have reversed the order of the velar stop and the alveolar fricative in the word *ask* so that the word is pronounced [æks] instead of Standard English [æsk].

4. **Raising/Lowering**. The terms *raising* and *lowering* refer to changes in the height of the tongue in the production of sounds. At the beginning of the Middle English period the word *noon* was pronounced [nōn], with a mid-back round vowel. By the end of the Middle English period, however, the word was pronounced [nūn], the tongue height being raised from mid to high. Thus the sound change ō > ū is called raising.

5. **Backing/Fronting**. The terms backing and fronting refer to alterations in the frontness or backness of the tongue in the production of sounds. At the beginning of the Modern English period there was a sound change whereby the back vowel [a] became the front vowel [æ], for example in words like *calf, path, glass, past, ask*.

Phonetic versus Phonemic Change

When we speak of sound change, it is possible to make a distinction between **phonetic** and **phonemic change**. Phonetic change refers to a change in pronunciation of allophones that has no effect on the phonemic system of the language. For example, over the course of time the English phoneme /r/ has undergone several changes. Early in the history of English the unrestricted allophone of the phoneme /r/ was pronounced as a trill, [r̃] (and still is in Scottish English). At present, however, the unrestricted allophone of /r/ is pronounced as a retroflex liquid.

Similarly, in the Middle English period voiceless stops were not aspirated in initial position. There was only one allophone for the three stop phonemes: /p/-[p], /t/-[t], /k/-[k]. Then these sounds underwent a sound change whereby stop consonants became aspirated initially before an accented vowel. This sound change altered the pronunciation of the stop phonemes by adding one allophone to each phoneme: /p/-[p] and [pʰ], /t/-[t] and [tʰ], /k/-[k] and [kʰ]. Still, the phonemic system of English has remained unaffected. This, then, was a phonetic change. Phonetic changes do not affect the phonemic system at all but rather add or delete an allophone of a phoneme, or substitute one allophone for another.

Phonemic change, on the other hand, refers to sound change that changes the phonemic system of a language in some way, usually by the addition or loss of a phoneme. In Old English the phoneme /f/ had one allophone, [f], until about A.D. 700. At this time a change occurred whereby [f] was voiced when it occurred between voiced sounds, e.g., Old English *wives* [wīvas]. At this time the sound change had no effect on the phonemic system; it merely created an additional allophone for the phoneme /f/, namely [v]. Later borrowings from French into English, however, created situations in which the two sounds came into contrast with one another, e.g., *safe* [sef] and *save* [sev]. As a result, we must now consider these two sounds members of *separate* phonemes—/f/-[f] and /v/-[v] respectively. Thus, the sound change f > v ultimately led to a phonemic change, since it resulted in the creation of a new phoneme, /v/.

Exercises

1. For each word specify the sound change(s) between Proto-Quechua and Tena. Then say whether each sound change is conditioned or unconditioned, and further, what type of conditioned or unconditioned change each sound change is.

Proto-Quechua	*Tena*	*gloss*
čumpi	čumbi	*belt*
timpu	timbu	*boil*
nutku	nuktu	*brains*
akla	agla	*choose*
wakli	wagli	*damage*
utka	ukta	*fast*
kunka	kunga	*neck*
lyantu	lyandu	*shade*
mutki	mukti	*smell*
pukyu	pugyu	*spring*
inti	indi	*sun*
sanku	sangu	*thick*
hampatu	hambatu	*toad*

2. Specify the changes between Proto-Slavic and Bulgarian. Classify the changes as conditioned or unconditioned. Then say what type of conditioned or unconditioned change each sound change is. Finally, note that these changes have to occur in a particular chronological order. What is the order of the changes? Why do they have to be in this particular order?

Proto-Slavic	*Bulgarian*	*gloss*
gladuka	glatkə	*smooth*
kratuka	kratkə	*short*
blizuka	bliskə	*near*
žežika	žeškə	*scorching*
lovuka	lofkə	*adroit*

3. Determine the sound changes that took place in the development of the Maharastri Prakrit from Old Indic. Classify the sound changes as conditioned or unconditioned. Then specify what type of conditioned or unconditioned change each sound change is.

Old Indic	*Maharastri Prakrit*	*gloss*
aŋka	aŋka	*hook*
arka	akka	*sun*
bʰakti	bʰatti	*devotion*
catwāri	cattāri	*four*
kalpa	kappa	*rule*
kardama	kaddama	*mud*
kaṭaka	kaḍā	*bracelet*
kāka	kāa	*crow*
mudgara	muggara	*mallet*
pitā	piā	*father*
rudra	rudda	*terrible*
sapatnī	savattī	*co-wife*
supta	sutta	*asleep*
šabda	sadda	*sound*
šata	sā	*hundred*
utkaṇṭʰā	ukkaṇṭʰā	*desire*
vikrama	vikkama	*strength*
viṭapa	viḍava	*branch*

([bʰ] represents a murmured bilabial stop; [ṭ, ḍ, ṭʰ, ṇ] represent retroflex stops.)

4. Determine the changes which have taken place between Middle English and Modern English. What sound changes are conditioned? What sound changes are unconditioned? Further classify the unconditioned sound changes. Finally, is it possible to find a pattern to the vowel changes in these words? If so, what is it?

Middle English	*Modern English*	*spelling*
hūs	haws	*house*
wīf	wayf	*wife*
stɔ̄n	ston	*stone*
hē	hi	*he*
hrōf	ruf	*roof*
sōn	sun	*soon*
hwīt	wayt	*white*
kwēn	kwin	*queen*
nām	nem	*name*
bɔ̄n	bon	*bone*
bāk	bek	*bake*
hlud	lawd	*loud*

File 10.4 The Comparative Method

One of the major reasons for the systematic comparison of languages is the desire to establish language relationships; i.e., we want to determine what languages have descended from a common protolanguage, and we want to determine how closely these languages are related. Two tendencies make it possible to determine language relationships.

First, the relationship between the form of a word and the meaning of a word is *arbitrary*. This means that it is reasonable to assume that two (or more) languages which share words of similar form and meaning are *related*, that is, descended from a common protolanguage. Notice how important the fact is that this relationship is an arbitrary one. If the relationship were a *natural* one then we would expect languages that were unrelated to share many words with similar form and meaning. In fact it would be impossible to determine which languages were related and which were not.

Second, sounds do not change in random ways; rather, sounds change *regularly*. When a language undergoes a certain sound change, that change will (eventually) be reflected systematically throughout the vocabulary of that language. For example, a language might undergo an **unconditioned sound change** of [p] to [f], in which every [p] in every word is replaced by [f]. Or, for example, a language might undergo a **conditioned sound change** of [p] to [f] in some specific phonetic environment, such as between vowels, in which case every word with a [p] between two vowels would acquire a [f] in place of the intervocalic [p]. A sound change may be conditioned by phonetic environment (e.g., it occurs only when the sound in question is between two vowels, or before a certain other sound, or after a certain sound, or at the beginning of a word, or at the end of a word, etc.), but nothing *other* than the phonetic environment ever limits a sound change. A sound change never randomly affects some words but not other phonetically similar words, never occurs just in words with a certain kind of meaning, etc. That is what is meant by the *regularity* of sound change.

These then are the two tendencies that make it possible for linguists to establish language relationships. The arbitrary relationship between a word's form and meaning is important because it makes it highly unlikely that unrelated languages will share large numbers of words of similar form and meaning. The regularity of sound change is important because it means that two (or more) languages that are related will show **regular sound correspondences**. Let us consider an example to illustrate what we mean. Consider the following forms:

English	German	Dutch	Swedish	gloss
[mæn]	[man]	[man]	[man]	*man*
[hænd]	[hant]	[hant]	[hand]	*hand*

If we compare the vowel sounds in all four languages, we can establish the following sound correspondence in the word meaning 'man': [æ] in English corresponds to [a] in German, Swedish, and Dutch. In order for this sound correspondence to be regular, it must occur in other words that have similar form and meaning. And of course it does, as a comparison of the words meaning *hand* confirms. Note that since this correspondence (æ—a—a—a) occurs regularly (is not unique), we have eliminated the possibility of being misled by chance similarity between words with similar form and meaning in unrelated languages.

318

The task of the comparative linguist does not end with the discussion of similarities between languages or with the assumption that these similarities indicate that the languages in question are related. The linguist is also interested in discovering how languages which are related developed from the protolanguage into their present forms; in other words, the linguist is interested in linguistic history.

In order to discover how languages have developed from a protolanguage, the protolanguage itself must be recoverable. And in some cases it is. For the Romance languages (French, Spanish, Portuguese, Romanian, etc.) the protolanguage (Vulgar Latin) is attested by numerous written records, for example, manuscripts, public inscriptions, funeral inscriptions, graffiti, etc. As a result it is possible to trace the development of the various Romance languages from their parent with considerable accuracy.

In other cases, however, written records for the protolanguage do not exist. But this does not mean that we cannot gather any information about the protolanguage; in these cases it is possible to infer what the protolanguage looked like by comparing the forms and grammar of the related languages. For example some words in Proto-Indo-European can be reconstructed on the basis of words in the daughter languages. The following lists contain sets of words having the same meaning from six Indo-European languages. The asterisk (*) means that the word is a reconstructed form, or a *protoform*. The transcription is phonetic.

	father	*mother*	*brother*
Proto-Indo-European	*pətɛ:r	*ma:tɛ:r	*bhra:tɛ:r
English	faðr	mʌðr	brʌðr
Greek	patɛ:r	mɛ:tɛ:r	pʰra:tɛ:r
Latin	patɛr	ma:tɛr	fra:tɛr
Old Church Slavonic		mati	bratrə
Old Irish	aθɪr	ma:θɪr	bra:θɪr
Sanskrit	pɪtər-	ma:tər-	bʰra:tər-

	mead	*is*	*to bear*
Proto-Indo-European	*mɛdhu	*ɛsti	*bhɛr-
English	mid	ɪz	bɛr
Greek	mɛtʰu	ɛsti	pʰɛrɔ:
Latin	—	ɛst	fɛro:
Old Church Slavonic	mɪd	yɛstə	bɛrõ
Old Irish	mið	—	bɛrɪ (*bears*)
Sanskrit	mədʰu	əstɪ	bʰəra:mɪ

Since inferences are made by comparing words of similar form and meaning in the languages we assume to be related, the method is called the **comparative method**. Please note that the comparative method is itself possible because of the regularity of sound change. If two or more languages show regular correspondences between themselves in words where the meanings are the same or similar, it means that these words have descended from a common source.

As a small preliminary example of how the comparative method works, let us return to our English-German-Dutch-Swedish example. We note that the first consonant in the word in question is an [m] and that the final consonant is an [n] in all four languages. Thus we can safely assume that the protolanguage had an initial *[m] and a final *[n] in the word meaning 'man', so that at this point we can reconstruct *[m_n] in our protolanguage. With respect to the vowel sound there is some uncertainty because there is variation in the sound: English has [æ], while German, Dutch, and Swedish have

[a]. However, since there is numerical superiority on the side of [a], it is best to assume that this is the sound the protolanguage possessed, and that English alone has changed *[a] to [æ]. Thus we reconstruct the protoform for 'man' as *[man], and the sound change *a > æ ("*[a] changes to [æ]") in English.

Comparative Method Procedure

The goal of the comparative method is to reconstruct the protoforms of the protolanguage from cognates of languages that are assumed to be related. Once the protolanguage forms have been reconstructed, it is possible to determine the changes by which the daughter languages have become distinct by comparing the protoforms with the forms present in the daughter languages.

1. **Compile Cognate Sets, Eliminating Borrowings.** The first step is to gather and organize data from the languages in question, forming *cognate sets*. A **cognate** of a word is another word that has descended from the same source; consequently, cognates are very similar in form and are usually identical or similar in meaning. As an example of a cognate set, imagine three languages, A, B, and C, and the word meaning 'strawberry' pronounced as follows in each:

A	*B*	*C*	*gloss*
[siza]	[sesa]	[siza]	'strawberry'

   Because of their semantic identity and phonetic similarity, these three words form a cognate set.

   While gathering cognates you should make sure that "suspicious-looking" forms are eliminated. Sometimes among the cognate sets you are compiling for some group of languages, there will be a cognate set with an "oddball," a form that is phonetically so different from the other members of the cognate set that it is improbable that it derived from the same source. The "oddball" was probably borrowed from some other genetically unrelated language. The original form, which fit the cognate set, was probably dropped in favor of the borrowed form. When you come across one of these borrowed forms, simply ignore it.

2. **Determine Sound Correspondences.** Next determine the **sound correspondences** that exist between sounds in the same positions in the words in each cognate set. The sound correspondences for our cognate set in step (1) are:

position	*A*	*B*	*C*
1.	[s]	[s]	[s]
2.	[i]	[e]	[i]
3.	[z]	[s]	[z]
4.	[a]	[a]	[a]

3. **Reconstruct a Sound for Each Position.** Given these sound correspondences, you must try to determine the earlier protoform from which the cognates have descended, following these steps *in this order.*

(a) *Total Correspondence.* If all the languages exhibit the same sound in some position in a cognate set, reconstruct that sound. In our example, in positions 1 and 4, each of the languages has the same sound, so we can reconstruct [s] for position 1 and [a] for position 4. Leaving blanks for positions 2 and 3, we can collapse and notate this information as *[s__a].

(b) *Most Natural Development.* For each of the remaining positions, if possible, reconstruct the sound that would have undergone the most *natural* sound change. Years of study in phonetics and historical linguistics have shown that certain types of sound changes are very common, while others almost never happen. For example, in a position between vowels, the change of a stop to a fricative at the same point of articulation is a very common change, while the reverse is much less common. Thus, if one cognate contains a stop between vowels and the other contains a fricative, the stop should be reconstructed. For each of the common sound changes listed below, it should be understood that the reverse direction of change is rare, or "unnatural."

Common sound changes:

- voiceless sounds become voiced between vowels and before voiced consonants
- stops become fricatives between vowels
- consonants become palatalized before front vowels
- consonants become voiceless at the ends of words
- difficult consonants clusters are simplified
- difficult consonants are made easier
- oral vowels become nasalized before nasals
- (other) fricatives become [h]
- [h] deletes between vowels

In our example, in position 2 we have a choice between [i] and [e]. Neither direction of change is favored by our list of common sound changes, so we cannot make a choice for position 2 at this point.

In position 3, which is a position between vowels, we have a choice between [s] and [z]. Because we know that "voiceless sounds become voiced between vowels," we reconstruct [s] (so that *[s] becomes [z] in B and C; *[z] becoming [s] in A would be unnatural). At this point we have reconstructed *[s_sa] for our cognate set.

(c) *Majority Rules.* Reconstruct the sound which occurs in the greatest number of languages being compared. Having determined in (b) that no direction of change is more natural, we must resort to "majority rules." So, for position 2 in our example we reconstruct *[i]. Using the comparative method, we have determined that the pronunciation of the word meaning 'strawberry' in the protolanguage from which A, B and C descended was *[sisa]. For the problems in this book, if there is no sound in the majority when you reach this point, step (4) will probably be crucial in determining the correct sound for reconstruction.

4. **Check for Regularity of Sound Change.** Although the procedure outlined in steps (1) through (3) can be used to reconstruct a protoform for each cognate set individually, you must check to see whether your results are *consistent* across the whole collection of cognate sets. We know that sound change is regular, and therefore we should be able to give for each daughter language (A, B, and C in our example) a list of sound changes that applied regularly to all words in the protolanguage, resulting in the respective daughter languages. If you cannot formulate the sound changes, you must minimally modify the choices you made in step (3) so that your results conform to the regularity hypothesis.

In order to demonstrate this situation, we need to add another cognate set to our data:

A	B	C	gloss	protolanguage
[siza]	[sesa]	[siza]	'strawberry'	*[sisa]
[sizu]	[sisu]	[sizu]	'pitchfork'	*[sisu]

Confirm that steps (1) through (3) produce *[sisu] for the word meaning 'pitchfork'. We will see now that we run into trouble formulating the sound change for the [e] that occurs in position 2 for the word meaning 'strawberry' in language B. If we posit the sound change *i > e for language B, then we predict that the *[i] in *[sisu] should also have become [e] in B. And because both instances of *[i] occur in identical phonetic environments (between [s] and [s]), adding a condition to the rule—that is, limiting the environments in which the sound change applies—does not help.

The solution to this problem is to reverse the decision we made in step (3c) for the 'strawberry' cognate set, making our reconstruction for 'strawberry' *[sesa]. Now, the sound changes listed below can apply regularly to both reconstructed forms, giving the correct results in A, B, and C.

A	B	C
*s > z / between vowels	none	*s > z / between vowels
*e > i		*e > i

Note that the condition "between vowels" on the rule *s > z in A and C is necessary to avoid the prediction that the word-initial *[s]s also become [z]s.

File 10.5

Reconstruction Problems

We have tried to order the reconstruction problems according to their degree of difficulty, but the first few problems are no doubt of comparable difficulty. The following directions pertain to all of the reconstruction problems contained in this file.

(A) Set up the sound correspondences for each cognate set and reconstruct the earlier form for the word from which the cognates have descended.

(B) Establish the sound changes that have affected each language.

0. Middle Chinese

For this exercise, we have simplified the Chinese data.
(Answers to all zero problems can be found in Appendix A.)

	Mandarin (Beijing)	Hakka (Huizhou)	gloss
1.	[čin]	[kim]	zither
2.	[la]	[lat]	spicy hot
3.	[mɔ]	[mɔk]	lonesome
4.	[lan]	[lam]	basket
5.	[ji]	[gip]	worry
6.	[lan]	[lan]	lazy
7.	[pa]	[pa]	fear

1. Proto-Peninsular Spanish

	Castilian	Andalusian	gloss
1.	[mayo]	[mayo]	May
2.	[kaʎe]	[kaye]	street
3.	[poʎo]	[poyo]	chicken
4.	[poyo]	[poyo]	stone bench
5.	[dos]	[dos]	two
6.	[dieθ]	[dies]	ten
7.	[θiŋko]	[siŋko]	five
8.	[si]	[si]	yes
9.	[kasa]	[kasa]	house
10.	[kaθa]	[kasa]	a hunt
11.	[θiβiliθaθion]	[siβilisasion]	civilization

[ʎ] represents a palatal liquid.
[β] represents a voiced bilabial fricative.

2.   **Proto-Numic**

Yerington Paviotso	Northfork Monachi	gloss
1. [mupi]	[mupi]	*nose*
2. [tama]	[tawa]	*tooth*
3. [pɪwɪ]	[pɪwɪ]	*heart*
4. [soŋo]	[sono]	*lungs*
5. [sawaʔpono]	[sawaʔpono]	*proper name (female)*
6. [nɪwɪ]	[nɪwɪ]	*liver*
7. [tamano]	[tawano]	*springtime*
8. [pahwa]	[pahwa]	*aunt*
9. [kuma]	[kuwa]	*husband*
10. [wowaʔa]	[wowaʔa]	*Indians living to the West*
11. [mɪhɪ]	[mɪhɪ]	*porcupine*
12. [noto]	[noto]	*throat*
13. [tapa]	[tape]	*sun*
14. [ʔatapɪ]	[ʔatapɪ]	*jaw*
15. [papiʔi]	[papiʔi]	*older brother*
16. [patɪ]	[petɪ]	*daughter*
17. [nana]	[nana]	*man*
18. [ʔati]	[ʔeti]	*bow, gun*

3.   **Proto-Uto-Aztecan**

Shoshone	Ute	Northern Paiute	gloss
1. [tuhu]	[tuu]	[tuhu]	*black*
2. [nika]	[nika]	[nika]	*dance*
3. [kasa]	[kąsi]	[kasa]	*feather*
4. [tuku]	[t̥uku]	[tuku]	*flesh*
5. [yuhu]	[yuu]	[yuhu]	*grease*
6. [pida]	[pida]	[pita]	*arm*
7. [kadi]	[kadi]	[kati]	*sit*
8. [kwasi]	[kwąsi]	[kwasi]	*tail*
9. [kwida]	——	[kwita]	*excrement*

4. Proto-Romance

Spanish	Sardinian	Rumanian	gloss
1. [ilo]	[filu]	[fir]	thread
2. [viða]	[bita]	[vita]	life
3. [vino]	[binu]	[vin]	wine
4. [riva]	[riba]	[ripa]	bank
5. [rio]	[riu]	[riu]	river
6. [riso]	[rizu]	[ris]	laugh
7. [muða]	[muta]	[muta]	change

5. Proto-Tupi-Guarani

Guarani	Tupinamba	Siriono	Guarayo	gloss
1. [kičĩ]	[kitiŋ]	[kišĩ]	[kičĩ]	cut
2. [čĩ]	[tiŋ]	[šĩ]	[čĩ]	white
3. [meʔẽ]	[meʔeŋ]	[meẽ]	[meẽ]	give
4. [kwa]	[pwar]	[kwa]	[kwa]	tie
5. [ki]	[kib]	[ki]	[ki]	louse
6. [kiʔa]	[kiʔa]	[kia]	[kia]	dirty
7. [abači]	[abati]	[abaši]	[abači]	corn

6. Proto-Middle Indic

Magadhi Prakrit	Pali	Maharastri Prakrit	gloss
1. [abala]	[apara]	[avara]	other
2. [dība]	[dīpa]	[dīva]	lamp
3. [hasta]	[hattʰa]	[hattʰa]	hand
4. [loga]	[loka]	[loa]	world
5. [ṇala]	[ṇara]	[ṇara]	man
6. [ṇispʰala]	[ṇippʰala]	[ṇippʰala]	fruitless
7. [paskʰaladi]	[pakkʰalati]	[pakkʰalai]	(he) stumbles
8. [pidā]	[pitā]	[pia:]	father
9. [puspa]	[puppʰa]	[puppʰa]	flower
10. [šuska]	[sukkʰa]	[sukkʰa]	dry

[ṇ] is a retroflex nasal stop.

7. Proto-Central Pacific

	Maori	*Hawaiian*	*Samoan*	*Fijian*	*gloss*
1.	[pou]	[pou]	[pou]	[bou]	*post*
2.	[tapu]	[kapu]	[tapu]	[tabu]	*forbidden*
3.	[taŋi]	[kani]	[taŋi]	[taŋi]	*cry*
4.	[takere]	[kaʔele]	[taʔele]	[takele]	*keel*
5.	[noho]	[noho]	[nofo]	[novo]	*sit*
6.	[marama]	[malama]	[malama]	[malama]	*moon*
7.	[kaho]	[ʔaho]	[ʔaso]	[kaso]	*thatch*

8. Proto-Western Turkic

	Turkish	*Azerbaijani*	*Crimean Tartar*	*Kazan Tartar*	*gloss*
1.	[burun]	[burun]	[burun]	[bɯrɯn]	*nose*
2.	[kabuk]	[gabɯx]	[joŋga]	[kabɯk]	*bark*
3.	[boyun]	[boyun]	[moyun]	[muyɯn]	*neck*
4.	[toprak]	[torpax]	[toprak]	[tufrak]	*earth*
5.	[kuyruk]	[guyruk]	[kuyruk]	[kɯyrɯk]	*tail*
6.	[yaprak]	[yarpak]	[japrak]	[yafrak]	*leaf*

File 10.6   Morphological Change

We have now seen that change in the sounds of language can occur over periods of time. Language change is not restricted to changes in the phonology, however; all components of a language—phonology, morphology, syntax, and semantics—can and do change. In what follows, we examine change in the morphological subsystem of a language.

Proportional Analogy and Paradigm Leveling

As a first example of morphological change, which will serve to introduce the topic, let us consider the early Modern English past tense of the verb *climb*. As recently as several hundred years ago, the usual past tense of this verb was *clomb* (phonetically [kʰlom]). In Modern English, on the other hand, the past tense is *climbed* ([kʰlaymd]). Thus, over the course of the past few centuries *climbed* has replaced *clomb* as the past tense of *climb*.

It should not have escaped your notice that in this example, the new form of the past tense of *climb* is exactly what would be expected as the regular past tense of an English verb, i.e., [-d] after a voiced consonant (compare *rhyme* [raym] / *rhymed* [raym-d]). In terms of the formation of the past tense, *clomb* is an irregularity because past tense in English is not generally formed by altering the vowel of the base. Thus, it appears that the irregular past tense form *(clomb)* has given way to a past tense form made with the productive, regular past tense morpheme, *-ed*. In a sense, then, we can talk about the change as being one that brought *climb* more in line with a majority of verbs of English, and that these verbs—and in particular the productive pattern of forming the past tense with these verbs—exerted some influence on *climb*. This led to the replacement of *clomb* by the more expected and usual (by the rules of English past tense formation) *climbed*.

This account also provides us with some insight into the nature of morphological change: it often involves the influence of one form or group of forms over another. In the case of *clomb → climbed*, the influence of the regular past tense forms led to the change; this type of morphological change can often be schematized as a four-part proportion, as in:

$$a \quad : \quad a' \qquad :: \qquad b \quad : \quad X = b'$$

This four-part proportion applied to the past tense of *climb* gives the following:

$$\text{rhyme} \quad : \quad \text{rhym} + \text{ed} \qquad :: \qquad \text{climb} \quad : \quad X = \text{climb} + \text{ed}$$

You don't have to be a mathematician to solve for X and get *climbed*. The word *rhyme* was chosen here only as an example; it is perhaps more accurate to state the proportion in terms of a general pattern that is extended to another verb, i.e.,

VERB	:	VERB + *ed*	::	climb	:	climb + ed
(present)		(past)		(present)		(past)

Since this type of morphological change can be schematized as a four-part proportion, it is generally known as **proportional analogy.**

In general, morphological change involving the influence of one form or set of forms over another is called **analogy** (or **analogical change**). As with *clomb → climbed*, analogical change generally introduces regularity into a system. For example, in the early stages of Latin, the paradigm (a set of closely, inflectionally related forms) for the word 'honor' was as follows.

Nominative	honos
Genitive	honos-is
Accusative	honos-em (etc.)

This paradigm was perfectly regular in that there was just a single form of the stem (*honos-*) to which the inflectional endings were added. Somewhat later in the development of Latin, a sound change took place by which intervocalic *s* became *r*; this was quite general and affected all instances of intervocalic *s* in that language. The effect on the paradigm of 'honor' was to create two different forms of the stem, *honos-* in the nominative and *honor-* in the other cases (because the *s* was intervocalic in them but final in the nominative):

Nominative	honos
Genitive	honor-is
Accusative	honor-em

The resulting paradigm was thus irregular in having two stem shapes. Later on in Latin, a further change took place creating a regular paradigm once more: the nominative took the form *honor*, giving:

Nominative	honor
Genitive	honor-is
Accusative	honor-em

This last change was not a widespread one, and there are many instances of final *s* in Latin that did not change to *r* (e.g., *genus* 'kind', *navis* 'ship', etc.).

Note that this morphological change has a result similar to that in the first example, namely, introducing regularity. This change introduced regularity into a paradigm that had been disturbed by the workings of sound change. This type of analogical change that takes place within a paradigm is often called **paradigm leveling**; the motivation though is the same as with the form-class type of analogy (proportional analogy) seen with *clomb → climbed*.

The two analogical changes discussed above involve the elimination of irregularities in the morphological subsystem of a language. While the striving toward regularity is perhaps the most notable result of analogical change, regularity is not, however, the only outcome. There are other analogical changes that have little if anything to do with regularization. We turn now to a brief discussion of these changes.

Back Formation and Folk Etymology

The process of **back formation** can be illustrated by the following schemata:

a.	work + er (agent noun)	:	work (verb)	::	burglar (agent noun)	:	X = burgle (verb)
b.	operat + ion (noun)	:	operate (verb)	::	orientation (noun)	:	X = orientate (verb)

As you may have noticed, the process of back formation appears to be similar to the process of proportional analogy. However, the fundamental difference becomes apparent upon closer inspection. Back formation involves the creation of a new base form (e.g., *burgle*), whereas proportional analogy involves the creation of a *new derived form.*

One of the more important differences between back formation and proportional analogy has to do with the fact that back formation is often preceded by misanalysis. The example of back formation cited above is a case in point. English speakers borrowed *burglar* from Norman French speakers as a monomorphemic word; at this time there was no word *burgle* in English. But *burglar* was misanalyzed by English speakers as consisting of a verb *burgle* plus an affix *-er* because its phonological structure and its meaning resembled the set of English words that *had* been formed by such a process, e.g., *worker, runner,* etc. As a result, the identification of *burglar* with this pattern of word formation, namely *verb + -er → agent noun,* has resulted in the creation of a new verb, *burgle.*

As we saw from the preceding discussion, the primary motivation for the back formation of *burgle* from *burglar* was the common derivational process *verb + -er → agent noun.* Interestingly, the influence of productive inflectional processes can also result in back formations. Consider the case of Modern English *cherry—cherries.* This word was borrowed from Norman French *cherise.* Note, however, that this word was a singular, not a plural, noun for French speakers. But to English speakers this noun sounded like a plural since it appeared to follow the regular pattern for the formation of plural nouns. As a result, the word *cherise* was misanalyzed as a plural, and a new singular noun was back-formed, namely, *cherry.*

As a final example of analogical change we consider the process known as **folk** or **popular etymology**. As we saw from the example of back formation discussed above, misanalysis played an important role as a motivating factor for the creation of the verb *burgle.* Similarly, the driving force behind the process of folk etymology is also misanalysis. In the case of folk etymology, however, obscure morphemes are misanalyzed in terms of more familiar morphemes. As an example of folk etymology consider the following case taken from an article in the Ohio State University student newspaper (*The Lantern,* May 1984). In this article the author referred to a variety of snake known as the "garter" snake as a "garden" snake. In this example, the morpheme *garden* has been substituted for the morpheme *garter.* There were probably a number of reasons for the misanalysis of *garter* as *garden.* Foremost among them was undoubtedly the fact that the two morphemes are very similar phonologically, differing only in the point and manner of articulation of the final consonant. Moreover, from the point of view of semantics it is not very clear to most English speakers why the morpheme *garter* should be used to describe the latitudinal stripes that are found on most varieties of garter snakes, particularly since the noun *garter* refers most commonly to an elasticized band worn around the leg to support hose. The final factor contributing to this misanalysis was undoubtedly the fact that, at least in urban areas, garter snakes are commonly found in and around gardens.

The case of folk etymology just discussed illustrates an important point about this analogical process: it occurs most often in cases where the morphological makeup of a word is obscure to speakers. There are a variety of reasons for morphological obscurity. One variety is illustrated by the Old English *samblind* 'half blind' to Modern English *sandblind.* The morphological makeup of this word was obscured by the fact that *sam* 'half' ceased to exist as an independent word in English. In order to make this word more accessible in terms of its structure, English speakers substituted the word *sand.* Note again that, as was the case with the substitution of *garden* for *garter,* the substitution of *sand* is motivated by phonological similarity (*sam* and *sand* sound a lot alike) and a semantic relationship (blowing sand can cause temporary blindness). Here are some other examples of folk etymology:

Folk Etymology		*Souce Phrase or Word*
sick-as-hell anemia	<	sickle-cell anemia
old-timer's disease	<	Alzheimer's Disease
nephew-tism	<	nepotism

Summary

Proportional analogy and paradigm leveling are characterized by the elimination of irregularities from the morphological subsystem of a language. Back formation and folk etymology do not involve the elimination of irregularities per se. Rather, they involve the misanalysis of unfamiliar morphemes in ways that make them more accessible to speakers. Nevertheless, the four varieties of analogical change that we have discussed are characterized by the fact that they involve the influence of one particular form or set of forms over another.

As with sound change, the new forms introduced by morphological changes do not necessarily take hold instantaneously. Most often, there is a period of competition between the old form and the new one. This helps to explain some of the fluctuation evident in Modern English past tense formations, for example, in which some people say *fit* and others say *fitted*, or some say *lit* and others say *lighted*, etc. Thus the processes of morphological change are often at the heart of synchronic variation, which is evident in all languages.

Exercises

1. Historically, the past tense of the verb *dive* is formed by the regular pattern of past tense word formation, i.e., *verb + -ed → past tense (dived)*. However, in a number of American English dialects *dived* has been replaced by *dove*. It is normally assumed that *dove* replaced *dived* as the result of the pattern *drive* [present tense] :: *drove* [past tense]. Would you consider the replacement of *dived* by *dove* as an example of proportional analogy? What does this tell us about the notions of *productivity/regularity* and analogical change?

2. We have seen that the regularity of sound change provides one of the bases for the comparative method. How might the workings of analogical change pose problems for the comparative method?

3. Try to come up with other aspects of English morphology that currently show some degree of fluctuation and variation (e.g., *saw* vs. *seen* as the past tense of *see*). To what extent are analogical processes at work in causing these fluctuations?

4. We have seen that natural phonological processes were at the heart of most sound changes. As a result, when an unnatural change is encountered, e.g., the addition of final [-d] as part of the change of *clomb* to *climbed*, we should suspect that morphological change is at work. What is the unnatural aspect of the change of final *s* to *r* that we saw in the Latin example of paradigm leveling? We have a good indication from the lack of regularity of this change that it is the result of morphological change, but is there any phonetic reason for being suspicious of this as a sound change?

File 10.7　Adding New Words to a Language

One of the ways languages change is by the addition of new words to their vocabularies. Of course, words are often borrowed from other languages, but there are also other ways in which new words come into a language, and many of these processes occur not only in English but in many of the world's languages. Some of these, such as folk etymology and back formation were discussed in File 10.6. This file describes some of the other types of new-word formation processes.

Acronyms　These words are formed by taking the initial sounds (or letters) of the words of a phrase and uniting them into a combination that is itself pronounceable as a separate word. Thus *NATO* is an acronym for *North Atlantic Treaty Organization*, *laser* for *light amplification through the stimulated emission of radiation*, and *radar* for *radio detection and ranging*.

Blending　A blend is a combination of the parts of two words, usually the beginning of one word and the end of another: *smog* from *smoke* and *fog*, *brunch* from *breakfast* and *lunch*, and *chortle* from *chuckle* and *snort*. (Lewis Carroll invented this blend, and his poem "Jabberwocky" contains several other examples of interesting blends.)

Clipping　Frequently we shorten words without paying attention to the derivational morphology of the word (or related words). *Exam* has been clipped from *examination*, *dorm* from *dormitory*, and either *taxi* or *cab* from *taxi cab* (itself a clipping from *taximeter cabriolet*).

Coinage　Words may also be created without using any of the methods described above and without employing any other word or word parts already in existence; that is, they may be created out of thin air. Such brand names as *Kodak* and *Exxon* were made up without reference to any other word, as were the words *pooch* and *snob*.

Functional Shift　A new word may be created simply by shifting the part of speech to another part without changing the form of the word. *Laugh, run, buy, steal* are used as nouns as well as verbs, while *position, process*, and *contrast* are nouns from which verbs have been formed.

Eponymy　Many places, inventions, activities, etc., are named for persons somehow connected with them; for instance, *Washington, D.C.* (for *George Washington*, and *District of Columbia* for *Christopher Columbus)*, German *Kaiser* and Russian *tsar* (for *Julius Caesar*), and *ohm* and *watt* (for *George Simon Ohm* and *James Watt*).

File 10.8   Syntactic Change

As we have noted in File 10.1, linguistic change is not restricted to one particular component of a language. Thus, in the same way that the sounds and words and meanings of a language are subject to change, so too are the patterns into which meaningful elements—words and morphemes—fit in order to form sentences. That is to say, change can be found in the syntactic component of a language, that domain of a grammar concerned with the organization of words and morphemes into phrases and sentences.

In syntactic change, therefore, the primary data that historical linguists deal with are changes in the variety of elements that go into the syntactic structuring of a sentence. These include (but are not restricted to) changes in word order, changes in the use of morphemes that indicate relations among words in a sentence (e.g., agreement markings on a verb caused by the occurrence of a particular noun or on an adjective caused by the noun it modifies), and changes in the type of elements that one word "selects" as being able to occur with it (e.g., the adjective *worthy* requires the preposition *of*, as in *worthy of consideration*; the verb *believe* can occur with a *that*-clause following it; etc.). All of these aspects of sentence structure are subject to change through time (diachronically).

For example, in earlier stages of English, it was quite usual (though not obligatory) for a possessive pronoun to follow the noun it modified, in the opposite order from what is the rule today. Thus, where currently we say *our father*, in Old English the phrase was *fæder ūre*. One way of describing this change is to say that the generalization about the placement of words in such a noun phrase has changed. Thus whereas one of the expansions for a noun phrase in Old English was (where DET$_{possp}$ is the subcategory of DET(erminers) that includes the possessive pronouns):

$$NP \rightarrow N + DET_{possp},$$

that expansion is not a part of the grammar of Modern English; instead, the phrase structure rule for a noun phrase has as one of its possibilities:

$$NP \rightarrow DET_{possp} + N.$$

Similarly, in earlier stages of English, in an imperative (command) sentence, the pronoun *you*, if expressed at all, could appear either before or after the verb, while today, such a pronoun regularly precedes the verb (so that *You go!* is acceptable while *Go you!* is not).

The change of *fæder ūre* to *our father* shows another type of syntactic change as well. In Modern English, a noun phrase such as *our father* has the same form regardless of whether it is a subject or an object, as in

| (subject) | Our father drinks a lot of coffee. |
| (object) | We love our father. |

In Old English, however, such a difference in grammatical function of a noun phrase was signaled by changes in the form of a noun phrase:

| (subject) | fæder ūre |
| (object) | fæder ūrne |

Thus the passage from Old English to Modern English has seen a change in the way that grammatical function—a matter of sentence structure—is marked (from a "case-marking" system to a system based on word order).

Similarly, adjectives in Old English regularly agreed with the noun they modified in gender (masculine/feminine/neuter), number (singular/plural), and case (e.g., subject/object, etc.); in Modern English, only remnants of number agreement can be found, and only with the demonstrative adjectives *this/that* (with singular nouns) and *these/those* (with plural nouns).

Finally, as an example of a syntactic change involving selectional facts, we can consider the adjective *worthy*. In earlier stages of English, this adjective regularly occurred with a *that*-clause following it, as in:

ic	ne	eom	wyrðe	θæt	ic	in	sunu	beo	genemned
I	*not*	*am*	*worthy*	*that*	*I*	*your*	*son*	*be*	*called*

which literally is 'I am not worthy that I be called your son'; the Modern English equivalent of this sentence, though, is *I am not worthy to be called your son*, indicating that the selection properties of *worthy* have changed from permitting a following *that*-clause to requiring only infinitival clauses (clauses with *to* plus a verb).

The examples given here have been drawn from the history of English, but they can be taken as illustrative of change in the syntactic component of any language. Moreover, they are representative of the nature of syntactic change in general and show ways in which syntactic change differs from sound change (discussed in File 10.3), for example. Perhaps the most striking characteristic of sound change is that it is regular, in that it affects all possible candidates for a particular change; for example, all instances of Old English [ū] became Modern (American) English [aw], and no examples of the older pronunciation remain. With syntactic change, however, while new patterns are produced that the language generally adheres to, exceptions nonetheless can occur; for example, even though word order in commands changed, the interjectional commands *mind you* and *believe you me* retain the older order with the pronoun after the verb, and so does the (consciously) archaic expression *hear ye, hear ye*. Also, as noted above, number agreement is still found, but only with the demonstrative adjectives. Moreover, unlike sound change and more like morphological change, syntactic changes are often specific to the syntactic properties of particular words; thus the change in the syntax of a clause following *worthy* mentioned above is one that is specific to that word, and not, for instance, generally true for all adjectives that occur in such a construction (e.g., *hopeful* can still occur with a *that*-clause).

A few words on the causes of syntactic change are in order. As with all other language change, there is both a language-internal and a language-external dimension to the causation of change. Thus, word-order changes in specific constructions, e.g., the noun + possessive pronoun construction, are often linked (correlated) with other changes in word order (e.g., involving the placement of an object with respect to the verb, a relative clause with respect to the noun it modifies, a noun with respect to a prepositional element, etc. See File 6.7). That is, there is often a system-wide change in the ordering of elements that is realized in different ways in different constructions. At the same time, though, such system-internal factors are only one side of the story. Innovative syntactic patterns often compete with older patterns for some time, and external, i.e., social factors, often play a role in deciding the competition. An example is the case-marking distinction involving *who* versus *whom* in Modern English, where the use of one as opposed to the other in a sentence such as *I like the man who/whom I met yesterday* is tied to such socially relevant factors as speakers' educational level, their attitudes toward education, the impression they wish to convey, and the like. On the matter of causation, then, syntactic change follows much the same pattern as other types of linguistic change.

File 10.9 Semantic Change

The semantic system of a language, like all other aspects of its grammar, is subject to change over time. As a result, the meanings of words do not always remain constant from one period of the language to the next. If we think of the meaning of a word as being determined by the set of contexts in which the word can be used, we can characterize semantic change as a shift in the set of appropriate contexts for that word. Alternatively, we could view semantic change as a change in the set of **referents** for a word, i.e., as a change in the set of objects the word refers to. Since context and reference are simply two aspects of what we call meaning, these two characterizations of semantic change are more or less equivalent.

The motivating factors behind semantic change are not well understood. Such changes sometimes result from language contact or accompany technological innovations or migrations to new geographic regions. In each of these cases the introduction of a new object or concept into the culture may initiate a change in the meaning of a word for a related object or concept, though this does not always occur. Semantic changes can also result from changes in the relative status of the group referred to by the word; that is, the word will take on new aspects of meaning to reflect this difference in social status. Sometimes changes result from a change in the status of the word itself, as is often the case with taboo words. It is, however, frequently the case that the sources of particular changes are not at all obvious; they appear to be spontaneous and unmotivated (though this may simply be due to our own lack of understanding).

Whatever the underlying source, only certain types of changes seem to occur with any frequency. Some of the most common types include:

1. extensions
2. reductions
3. elevations
4. degradations

Semantic Extensions

Extensions in meaning occur when the set of appropriate contexts or referents for a word increases. These are frequently the result of generalizing from the specific case to the class of which the specific case is a member. An example of this type would be the change in meaning undergone by the Old English (OE) word *docga*, modern day *dog*. In OE *docga* referred to a particular *breed* of dog, while in modern usage it refers to the class of dogs as a whole. Thus the set of contexts in which the word may be used has been *extended* from the specific case (a particular breed of dog) to the general class (all dogs, dogs in general). A similar type of change has affected modern English *bird*. Though it once referred to a particular species of bird, it now is used for the general class.

A contemporary example of this type of change would be the shift in meaning undergone by the recently formed verb *nuke*. This verb was based on the noun *nuke*, a shortening of *nuclear weapon* (as in "no nukes"), and originally meant to drop a nuclear bomb on something. In the speech of some this verb has been extended to mean simply to *damage* or to *destroy*, as in *Robin nuked his Porsche last night*. Thus the meaning of *nuke*, for these speakers at least, has gone from referring to a particular *type* of damage or destruction to damage or destruction in general. Semantic extensions are particularly common with proper names and brand names. Thus the name *Benedict Arnold* has come to be synonymous with the word *traitor*. Similarly, the name of the fictional character *Scrooge* can be used to refer to anyone with miserly traits. Examples of the semantic extension of brand names are equally easy to find: *Jell-O* is often used to refer to any flavored gelatin, regardless of brand. *Kleenex* is used for facial tissues and *Xerox* for photocopies. In some parts of the United States *Coke* can be used for any carbonated beverage, not just one particular brand. In each of these cases the meaning of the word has been generalized to include related items in its set of referents.

In the examples discussed thus far the relationship between the original meaning of the word and the extended meaning of the word has been quite straightforward: the name of a particular traitor has been generalized to any traitor, the name of a particular type of photocopy has been generalized to any photocopy, and so on. This needn't always be the case, however. The meanings of words often become less narrow as a result of what is referred to as **metaphorical extension**. Thus, the meaning of a word is extended to include an object or concept that is like the original referent in some metaphorical sense rather than a literal sense. A classic example of this type is the word *broadcast*, which originally meant to scatter seed over a field. In its most common present-day usage, however, *broadcast* refers to the diffusion of radio waves through space—a metaphorical extension of its original sense. Another classic example of metaphorical extension is the application of preexisting nautical terms (such as *ship, navigate, dock, hull, hatch, crew,* etc.) to the relatively new realm of space exploration. Again, notice that space exploration is not like ocean navigation in a *literal* sense, since very different actions and physical properties are involved. Rather, the comparison between the two realms is a metaphorical one.

We can also find cases of metaphorical extension in progress in the language around us, particularly if we consider creative uses of slang terms. For example, the dictionary definition of the noun *load* is something like 'unit or quantity that can be carried' or 'burden of responsibility'. In some circles the meaning of this word has been extended to refer to people who are lazy or unproductive, presumably because these people do not do their fair share and therefore place a burden on others. Literally speaking, however, it is not people themselves who are the burden, rather it is the result of their actions that is the burden. Thus this use of the word is an abstraction from its original sense, i.e., a metaphorical extension. Another example of this type of change in progress is the use of the verb *nuke*, discussed above, to refer to microwave cooking. In this case, the metaphor hinges on the idea that microwave radiation is released during nuclear explosions. Thus, a parallel is being drawn between cooking in a microwave and bombing your food, though literally the two actions are quite different. Notice that these uses of *load* and *nuke* are not accepted by all speakers. However, if enough people adopt these meanings, we may eventually have a full-fledged semantic change in the language.

Semantic Reductions

Reductions occur when the set of appropriate contexts or referents for a word decreases. Historically speaking, this is relatively less common than extensions of meaning, though it still occurs fairly frequently. An example of a semantic reduction would be the Old English word *hund*, modern day *hound*. While this word originally referred to dogs in general, its meaning has now been restricted, for the most part, to one particular breed of dog. Thus its usage has become less general over time. Similarly, the word *worm* once was used for any crawling creature but is now restricted to a particular type of crawling creature.

Additional examples of this type of change include the modern English words *skyline* and *girl*. *Skyline* originally referred to the horizon in general. It has since been restricted to particular types of horizons—ones in which the outlines of hills, buildings, or other structures appear. In Middle English the word corresponding to modern day *girl* referred to young people of either sex. A semantic reduction has resulted in its current, less general, meaning.

Semantic Elevations

Semantic elevations occur when a word takes on somewhat grander connotations over time. For example, the word *knight* (OE *cniht* or *cneoht*) originally meant 'youth' or 'military follower'—relatively powerless and unimportant people. The meaning of *knight* has since been elevated to refer to people of a somewhat more romantic and impressive status. Similarly, the word *chivalrous* was at one time synonymous with *warlike*; it now refers to more refined properties such as fairness, generosity, and honor. A particularly good example of this type is the shift in meaning undergone by the word *squire*. The Middle English (ME) equivalent of *squire* was used to refer to a knight's attendant, the person who held his shield and armor for him. In Modern English, however, a *squire* is a country gentleman or large landowner. Thus the meaning of *squire* has changed rather drastically over time, acquiring a socially more positive meaning.

Semantic Degradations

Semantic degradations are the opposite of semantic elevations; they occur when a word acquires a more pejorative meaning over time. Examples of words whose meanings have been degraded include *lust*, *wench* and *silly*. In OE *lust* simply meant 'pleasure', making its current association with sinfulness a degradation of the original meaning. Similarly, the ME word *wenche(l)* meant 'female child' and later 'female servant'. It then came to mean 'lewd female' or 'woman of a low social class'. The word *silly* is a particularly interesting example of semantic degradation because the social force of the word has almost completely reversed. Whereas in ME *silly* meant something akin to 'happy, blessed, innocent', it now is more on a par with 'foolish, inane, absurd'. Thus the connotations of *silly* have gone from strongly positive to strongly negative in a matter of a few centuries.

Discussion

In conclusion, it is interesting to note that semantic changes in one word of a language are often accompanied by (or result in) semantic changes in another word. Note, for instance, the parallel changes undergone by OE *hund* and *docga*, discussed above. As *hund* became more specific in meaning, *docga* became more general. Thus, the semantic system as a whole remains in balance despite changes to individual elements within the system.

A somewhat more elaborate example of the same principle involves the OE words *mete*, *flæsc* and *foda*. In OE, *mete*, modern day *meat*, referred to food in general while *flæsc*, now *flesh*, referred to any type of animal tissue. Since then, the meaning of meat has been restricted to the flesh of animals and the meaning of flesh to human tissue. *Foda*, which was the OE word for 'animal fodder', became modern day *food*, and its meaning was generalized to include all forms of nourishment. Thus the semantic hole left by the change in referent for meat has been filled by the word food.

Exercises

1. Particularly interesting cases of semantic change are ones in which the meaning of a word appears to have been reversed through time. For example, the English word *black* is closely related to Slavic words meaning 'white'. *Black* is actually derived from a Germanic past participle meaning 'to have blazed' or 'to have burned'. Given these facts, can you think of a plausible explanation for the present-day meaning of *black*? Using a good etymological dictionary (such as the *Oxford English Dictionary* [*OED*]) for reference, list some Modern English words that are related to *black*. Try to determine the types of semantic change these words must have undergone to arrive at their present-day meanings.

2. The following paragraph is logically incoherent if all the words are understood in their current meanings. But, if we take each of the italicized words in a sense it once had at an earlier stage of English, the paragraph has no inconsistencies at all. Your job is to determine an earlier meaning for each of the italicized words that will remove the logical contradictions created by the current meaning. The earlier meanings need not be contemporary with one another. They can be found in the *OED* or in a comparably complete dictionary.

> He was a happy and *sad girl* who lived in a *town* 40 miles from the closest neighbor. His unmarried sister, a *wife* who was a vegetarian member of the Women's Christian Temperance Union, ate *meat* and drank *liquor* three times a day. She was so fond of oatmeal bread made from *corn* her brother grew, that one night, when it was dark and *wan* out, she *starved* from overeating. He fed nuts to the *deer* who lived in the branches of an *apple* tree that bore pears. He was a *silly* and wise *boor*, a *knave* and a *villain*, and everyone liked him. Moreover, he was a *lewd* man whom the general *censure* held to be a model of chastity.

What types of semantic change are illustrated here? Give examples for each type.

File 10.10

Problems in Language Change

One of the major topics of interest to historical linguists is why languages change. Unfortunately, this topic is not very easy to discuss coherently because there are so many different and seemingly independent reasons. Speaking very broadly, however, we may recognize three large categories of causation: (1) *social* reasons (e.g., change via imitation of forms that are considered prestigious); (2) *psychological* reasons (e.g., misanalysis of unfamiliar morphemes in terms of familiar ones; replacement of forms that have become taboo); (3) *physiological* reasons (e.g., the assimilation of one sound to another for ease of articulation; the elimination of consonant clusters that are difficult to pronounce). Note that each large category may cover a great number of different reasons for change, and that each large category is not entirely independent of the others.

The following problems are designed to get you to think about some of the reasons for language change (as well as some of the ways language can change). Do not consider this file exhaustive, because it is not. Nevertheless, it does provide a reasonable introduction to possible sources of language change.

Read each problem carefully and then answer the question(s) that follow the problem.

1. English has borrowed the word *memorandum* from Latin. The plural is *memoranda*. Some English speakers have replaced *memoranda* with *memorandums*. Suggest a reason for this change.

2. Middle English borrowed the word *penne* 'feather, quill' from Old French. The modern word *pen* 'writing instrument using ink' is a descendent of this word. Suggest a reason for this change.

3. Until the nineteenth century, the male chicken was referred to (on both sides of the Atlantic) by the word *cock*. In America, *rooster* has gradually replaced this word; it is now the only term used by many Americans. Why has the word *cock* been replaced by the word *rooster*?

4. English speaking tourists in Finland are often introduced to an after-dinner drink called *jaloviina* [yalovi:na]. This drink is not yellow and it is not wine, but most of the tourists call it "yellow wine." Why?

5. In Trinidad English the suffixes indicating present and past tense have been lost. Present tense is indicated by use of the auxiliary *do*, so that Trinidad English *he does give* equals Standard English *he gives*, and Trinidad English *he roll* equals Standard English *he rolled*. Why is the use of the auxiliary *do* to indicate present tense understandable?

6. Beginning in the seventeenth century, *kine* as plural of *cow* was gradually replaced by *cows*. Suggest a reason for the replacement of *kine* by *cows*.

7. During World War I in the United States, *sauerkraut*, 'fermented cabbage used for food', was abandoned in favor of *liberty cabbage*. Why?

8. In Old English the word *bead* meant 'prayer'. In the religious practice of the time it was very important to keep track of the number of prayers. The instrument that was used to do this was the rosary with its small balls. When one prayed and used this device to count the prayers it was called 'counting one's beads', that is, 'prayers'. Now the word *bead* means `small ball'. Suggest a reason for this meaning change.

9. In Finnish the word *kutsua* means 'to invite', but it may also mean 'to call' in some contexts. In a Finnish dialect spoken in Sweden *kuhrua* retains the meaning 'to invite', but the Finnish-speaking Swedes have borrowed the Swedish word *kalla* meaning 'to call'. Why do you think this Finnish dialect borrowed a different word for the second meaning?

10. In the fifteenth and sixteenth centuries most central and southern British English dialects lost the consonant /r/ when it occurred at the end of a word before a pause, or when it occurred before a consonant. As a result, a word like *better* was pronounced [bɛtə] before words beginning with a consonant but [bɛtər] before words beginning with a vowel. What is interesting is that at the present time British speakers pronounce such phrases as *the idea of it* and *America and England* as [ði aydiɾ əv ɪt] and [əmɛrɪkɾ n̩ ɪŋglənd]. How might you account for such pronunciation?

11. Between Proto-Slavic and Old Church Slavonic (a language related to, but not identical with, Old Russian) a number of interesting sound changes took place. (1) There was a metathesis of vowel-liquid (VL) sequences, so that a Proto-Slavic structure CVLCV became CLVCV in Old Church Slavonic. (2) Proto-Slavic diphthongs became monophthongs, e.g., CeyCV became CiCV. (3) Consonant clusters were simplified. (4) Word-final consonants were lost. So, for example, Proto-Slavic **supnos* became Old Church Slavonic *sŭnŭ* 'sleep'. Note that though all of these changes are quite different from one another, they are all responsible for creating the same type of syllable structure in Old Church Slavonic. What do you think this syllable structure is, and how did these changes work together to create it? Moreover, what is significant about this type of syllable structure in the first place?

12. Middle English borrowed the word *naperon* from Old French. The modern descendent of this word is *apron*. What reason can you give for the disappearance of the initial *n*?

13. The fourteenth century compound *ekename* (from *eke* 'to increase' and *name* 'name') was, by the sixteenth century, replaced by *nekename*, modern *nickname*. What reason can you give for the appearance of the *n* initially?

File 10.11 — A Chronological Table of the History of English

The English language has changed dramatically over its history. As one can tell from the versions of the Lord's Prayer in File 10.1, a speaker of Modern English would not understand Old English at all and would have to work hard to figure out the Middle English text. Even the Early Modern English of Shakespeare is different enough from Modern English to warrant annotated versions of his plays.

While all languages naturally change over time, and English is no exception, some dramatic changes have been induced or encouraged by major historical events as well. The following tables present some of the major influences and developments in the history of English. The first section mentions some of the major landmarks in the internal history of English—that is, the actual changes in the language itself that have been influenced by outside events. The second section presents major landmarks in the external history of English—that is, factors such as conquest of English speakers by speakers of other languages; intellectual attitudes toward languages; social, religious, and political changes, and so on, which affect how a language changes. English has been influenced by other languages throughout its development and has borrowed a great many vocabulary items, samples of which are presented in the chart.

Internal History

1.	Proto-European to Germanic	Grimm's Law
2.	OE to ME	Loss of /x/
		Adoption of /ž/
		Allophonic variants [f]/[v], [ð]/[θ], [s]/[z], [ŋ]/[n] become phonemic.
		Vowel reduction and subsequent loss of final [ə] in unstressed syllables lead to loss of case endings, more rigid word order, greater use of prepositions.
3.	Middle English to Early Mod English (1300–1600)	The Great Vowel Shift Simplification of some initial consonant sequences: [kn] >[n] (*knee*); [hl] > [l] (*hlaf > loaf*); [hr] > [r] (*hring > ring*); [wr] > [r] (*wrong*).

External History

Dates	Events	Language Influence	Stages
700–900? B.C.	Settlement of British Isles by Celts	Celtic—in London, Dover, Avon, Cornwall	**Pre-English**
55 B.C.	Beginning of Roman raids	Latin—preserved in a few forms: *-chester < castra* 'camp'	
43 A.D.	Roman occupation of "Brittania"		
Early 5th c.	Romans leave British Isles		
449 A.D.	Germanic tribes defeat the Celts	Germanic—Anglo-Saxon	**Old English (450–1100)**
ca. 600 A.D.	England converted to Christianity (Borrowings: *abbot, altar, cap, chalice, hymn, relic, sock, beet, pear, cook, rue, school, verse*)	Latin, via the Christian Church	
ca. 750 A.D.	*Beowulf* writings are composed (only extant manuscript written ca. 1000 A.D.)		
9–11th c.	Invasions by Scandinavians (Borrowings: *birth, sky, trust, take, skirt, disk, dike*; simplified pronoun system)	Scandinavian	
1066 A.D.	Battle of Hastings—Norman Conquest (Borrowings: *court, enemy, battle, nation, crime, justice, beef, pork, veal, mutton, charity, miracle*)	Norman French, Latin via Norman French for learned vocabulary	
ca. 1200 A.D.	Normandy and England are separated		**Middle English (1100-1450)**
13th–14th c.	Growing sense of Englishness		
1337–1450	Hundred Years' War		
1340–1450	Chaucer		
1476	First English book is published; spelling standardized		**Early Modern English (1450–1700)**
1564–1616	Shakespeare (Greek & Latin borrowings: *anachronism, allusion, atmosphere, capsule, dexterity, halo, agile, external, insane, adapt, erupt, exist, extinguish*)	Latin and Greek, via the influence of printing and the Renaissance in Europe	
16th–19th c.	Imperialism (Borrowings: *mogul, rajah, safari, loot, bandana, pajama*)	Swahili, Hindi, Tamil, Chinese, etc., via the various colonies	**Modern English (1700–present)**
19th–20th c.	Development of North American, Australian, African, Caribbean, South Asian varieties of English; Scientific and Industrial Revolution	Technical and regional vocabularies	

File 10.12

English Borrowings

In a survey of the 1,000 most frequently used words in English, it was found that only 61.7 percent had Old English origins. The other 38.3 percent were borrowed from a variety of other languages: 30.9 percent French, 2.9 percent Latin, 1.7 percent Scandinavian, 1.3 percent mixed, and .3 percent Low German and Dutch. The following list provides a sample set of words that we have incorporated into English. While some of these words will sound foreign, those that were borrowed early in the history of our language will sound amazingly English.

French: aisle, apparel, arch, art, assault, assets, bail, bailiff, barber, barricade, beauty, bisque, boil, brassiere, broil, butcher, campaign, captain, carpenter, cartoon, catch, cattle, cell, chancellor, chaplain, charity, chase, chattel, chemise, chivalry, color, column, commandant, company, corps, corpse, county, court, design, dinner, dragoon, dress, embezzle, enemy, evangelist, exchequer, fork, format, garment, govern, grace, grocer, hors d'oeuvres, jail, judge, jury, lance, lease, lieutenant, lingerie, mason, mercy, minister, miracle, napkin, nativity, navy, painter, paradise, passion, perjury, pillar, plaintiff, plate, plead, porch, power, reign, sacrament, saint, sergeant, soldier, suit, supper, table, tailor, tapestry, transept, troops

Latin: abbot, affidavit, agenda, alibi, alms, animal, bonus, clerk, coaxial, deficit, diet, exit, extra, fiat, fission, geography, interstellar, item, logic, maximum, memento, memorandum, monk, neutron, omnibus, penicillin, physic, pope, posse, priest, propaganda, quorum, radium, rhetoric, spectrum, sponsor, sulfur, surgeon, synod, terminus, theology, verbatim, veto, via

Greek: adenoids, bacteriology, botany, catastrophe, climax, comedy, dialogue, drama, dynatron, epilogue, episode, histology, kenatron, melodrama, osteopathy, pediatrics, physics, physiology, prologue, psychiatry, psychoanalysis, scene, telegraph, theater, tragedy, zoology

Native American Languages: caucus, chinook, chipmunk, hickory, hogan, hominy, igloo, kayak, mackinaw, manitou, moccasin, moose, muskrat, opossum, papoose, pecan, persimmon, podunk, pow-wow, quahog, raccoon, sequoia, skunk, squash (a clipped borrowing from [æskutɛskwæš]), succotash, teepee, terrapin, tomahawk, totem, wampum, wigwam, woodchuck

Spanish: adobe, alfalfa, armada, burro, bronco, cafeteria, canyon, cargo, castanet, cockroach, coyote, cigar, desperado, guerilla, marijuana, matador, mosquito, mustang, plaza, poncho, pueblo, punctilio, quadroon, renegade, rodeo, sombrero, tequilla, tornado, tuna, vanilla, vigilante

German: angst, bockbeer, bratwurst, bub, delicatessen, dunk, frankfurter, hausfrau, hex, hum, kindergarten, lager, liverwurst, loafer, noodle, ouch, pinochle, poke, pretzel, pumpernickel, rathskeller, sauerbraten, sauerkraut, schnitzel, spiel, spieler, stein, stube, wunderkind, zwieback

Scandinavian Languages: batten, billow, blight, by-law, clumsy, doze, fiord, floe, geyser, law, maelstrom, nag, outlaw, riding, saga, scamp, ski, them, their, they

Italian: alto, attitude, balcony, fiasco, fresco, isolate, motto, opera, piano, soprano, stanza, studio, tempo, torso, umbrella

South Asian Languages (India, Pakistan, Bangladesh, Sri Lanka): bandanna, brahmin, bungalow, calico, chutney, curry, indigo, juggernaut, jungle, loot, pajama, pundit, rajah, sandal, thug

Yiddish: challah, chutzpah, gefilte fish, goy, klutz, knish, latke, matzah (ball), mazeltov, nebbish, oy vey, schlemiel, schlep, schmuck, schnook

Dutch: avast, bow, bowsprit, buoy, commodore, cruise, curl, dock, freight, hops, keel, keelhaul, leak, lighter, pump, scour, scum, spool, stripe, yacht, yawl

Arabic: algorithm, bedouin, emir, fakir, gazelle, ghoul, giraffe, harem, hashish, lute, minaret, mosque, myrrh, salaam, sirocco, sultan, vizier

Chinese: mandarin, pongee, serge, tea, yen

Japanese: anime, bonsai, hara-kiri, hibachi, karaoke, jujitsu, kimono, tycoon, typhoon

Russian: balalaika, czar, glasnost, perestroika, sputnik, vodka

File 10.13   Germanic Consonant Shifts

Proto-Indo-European had three series of stop consonants: a voiceless series, *p, *t, *k; a voiced series, *b, *d, *g; and a series of (so-called) voiced aspirates written *bʰ, *dʰ, *gʰ. In the transition from Proto-Indo-European to Proto-Germanic, these series of consonants underwent an organized set of changes, or **shifts**, as follows:

Proto-Indo-European:	*p	*t	*k	*b	*d	*g	*bʰ	*dʰ	*gʰ
	⇓	⇓	⇓	⇓	⇓	⇓	⇓	⇓	⇓
Germanic:	f	θ	x	p	t	k	b	d	g

This change is known as **Grimm's Law** and is one of the changes that distinguishes the languages of the Germanic subgroup from all other Indo-European language groups. That is to say, every Germanic language will show a different set of developments in the Proto-Indo-European (PIE) sounds. Examples of words affected by Grimm's Law are listed below.

PIE	*Non-Germanic*	*Germanic (English)*
*pəter	pater (Latin)	father
*trei-	tres (Latin)	three
*kerd	kardia (Greek)	heart
*leb-	labium (Latin)	lip
*dekm	decem (Latin)	ten
*gʷena	gyne (Greek)	queen
*bhratēr	bhratar (Sanskrit)	brother
*dhe	facere (Latin)	do
*ghos-ti	hostis (Latin)	guest

Modern High German has undergone a second consonant shift similar to the first in nature; this **second Germanic consonant shift** differentiates the High German dialects from other Germanic dialects and languages. Thus, only High German will exhibit evidence of the shift.

The second consonant shift was a rather complicated change. The figures below captures the major changes but omits certain details.

Proto-German		High German	
		After Vowels	Elsewhere
*p	>	f	pf
*t	>	s	ts
*k	>	x	k (but kx in some dialects)
*d	>	t	t

Consider the following examples of the correspondence between Modern English, which did not undergo the second shift, and Modern German, which, of course, did undergo the shift.

Modern English	Modern German
o*p*en	o*ff*en
*p*ath	*pf*ad
bi*t*e	bei*ss*en
*t*o	*z*u (z = [ts])
boo*k*	Bu*ch* (ch = [x])
*c*ome	*k*ommen
ri*d*e	rei*t*en
*d*oor	*T*ür

Based on the statement of the changes and the examples cited above, what sound in Modern German would correspond to the italicized Modern English sounds?

Modern English	Modern German
floo*d*	Flu____
shi*p*	Schi____
ea*t*	e____en
re*ck*on	re____nen
ha*t*e	Ha____

Now, given the italicized Modern German sounds, what would the corresponding sound be in Modern English?

Modern German	Modern English
Gri*ff*	gri____
Her*z*	hear____
Fu*ss*	foo____
ma*ch*en (ch = [x])	ma____e
wa*ff*enlos	wea____onless
*Pf*lug	____low

File 10.14

Major Sound Changes in Old, Middle, and Modern English

This file describes some of the major sound changes that have occurred in the history of English. To give you the chronology of these sound changes, we have arranged them according to the three periods of historical development: Old, Middle, and Modern. **Old English** covers the period from the invasion of Britain by the Angles and Saxons in A.D. 449 to A.D. 1050. Written records are not extant for Old English, however, until around 700. The **Middle English** period extends from 1050 to 1450, approximately fifty years after the death of the poet Chaucer. The period from 1450 to the present is usually considered the **Modern English** period, although there are some scholars who prefer to divide this period into two sections and recognize an **Early Modern English** period, from roughly 1450 to 1700, and a **Modern English** period, from 1700 to the present.

The Old and Middle English words are in broad transcription. The Modern English forms are in current orthography.

Old English

A. One of the most important changes to occur during the Old English period was *i-umlaut.* **Umlaut** is a type of assimilation whereby one vowel sound becomes more like some other vowel sound that follows it. In Old English the back vowels [a, ā, ɔ, ō, ʊ, ū] became [ɛ, æ, ɛ̄, ē, ɪ, ī] when an [ɪ] or [i], that is, a high front vowel, occurred in the following syllable. Later, [ɪ] was lost if the preceding syllable ended with a consonant or contained a long vowel:

Change in Old English	*Modern English*	
fōtɪ > fēt	*feet*	[fit]
lūsɪ > līs	*lice*	[lays]
mannɪ > mɛnn	*men*	[mɛn]
dālɪ > dæl	*deal*	[dil]
fʊllɪan > fɪllan	*fill*	[fɪl]
brūdɪ > brīd	*bride*	[brayd]

B. The velar consonants [g] and [k] were palatalized when they occurred before the front vowel sounds [æ, ǣ, ɛ, e, ɪ, ī] or before the diphthongs beginning with a front vowel (a vowel plus [ə] represents a diphthong):

Old English	Modern English	
kınn	*chin*	[čın]
gıə̯dan	*yield*	[yild]
kıə̯l	*chill*	[čıl]
gæə̯r	*year*	[yir]

C. The consonant cluster [sk] was palatalized to [š] before front vowels:

Old English	Modern English	
skē̯ə̯p	*sheep*	[šip]
skīr	*shire*	[šayr]
skıə̯ld	*shield*	[šild]
skɛə̯kan	*shake*	[šek]

D. Fricative consonants became voiced when they stood between voiced sounds:

Old English	Modern English	
nɔsʊ	*nose*	[noz]
wʊlfas	*wolves*	[wʊɫvz], [wʊɫfs]
baθıan	*bathe*	[beð]
knafa	*knave*	[nev]

Middle English

A. Two changes occurred early in the development of Middle English that affected the quantity of vowels.

(i) Long vowels were shortened when they were followed by two or more consonants:

Old English	Middle English	Modern English	
sōftɛ	sɔftə	*soft*	[sɔft]
fīfta	fıftə	*fifth*	[fıfθ], [fıft]
kēptɛ	kɛptə	*kept*	[kɛpt]
wīzdɔm	wızdəm	*wisdom*	[wızdm̩]

(ii) The short vowels [a, e, ɔ] became long when they occurred in open syllables (i.e., in syllables that don't end in a consonant):

Old English	Middle English	Modern English	
nama	nāmɛ	*name*	[nem]
stɔlɛn	stɔ̄lən	*stolen*	[stoln̩]
——	mētɛ	*meat*	[mit]
nɔsʊ	nɔ̄zə	*nose*	[noz]
knafa	knāvə	*knave*	[nev]

B. Between the beginning and end of the Middle English period, two important changes occurred in the final syllables of words.

   (i) When the vowels [a, ɛ, ɔ, ʊ] occurred in the final syllable of a word and were unaccented, they became schwa [ə]. (Note however that the vowel [ɪ] did not become schwa but remained as [ɪ].) Word-final schwa was lost by the end of the Middle English period. For the development of syllable-final schwa followed by a consonant, see Modern English (D).

Old English	*Middle English*	*Modern English*	
krabba	krabə	*crab*	[kræb]
hɛlpan	hɛlpən	*help*	[hɛlp]
sʊnʊ	sʊnə	*son*	[sʌn]
klǣnɛ	klǣnə	*clean*	[klin]
nakɔd	nākəd	*naked*	[nekɪd]

   (ii) Word-final [m] and [n] were lost very frequently in unstressed syllables:

Old English	*Middle English*	*Modern English*	
sɪŋgan	sɪŋgə	*sing*	[sɪŋ]
ɛndʊm	ɛndə	*end*	[ɛnd]

C. The sound [h] was lost when it began a word and occurred before the sounds [l, r, n, w]:

Old English	*Middle English*	*Modern English*	
hrɪŋg	rɪŋg	*ring*	[rɪŋ]
hnɛkka	nɛkkə	*neck*	[nɛk]
hlāf	lɔ̄f	*loaf*	[lof]
hwætɛ	wǣtə	*wheat*	[wit]

Modern English

A. In the first two periods of the development of the English language the vowel sounds underwent very few changes. But the development of the Middle English vowels into Modern English is quite a different story indeed. Between 1400 and 1600 almost all of the English vowels (and diphthongs) underwent some sort of change. In fact only two vowels [ɪ] and [ɛ] were unaffected. So great was the alteration of the English vowel system that these changes are often collectively referred to as the Great Vowel Shift.

If we focus on the development of the back vowels, the appropriateness of the term "vowel shift" can easily be illustrated. The Middle English long vowel [ɔ̄] was raised to [ō]; but [ō] in turn was raised to [ū]. The high back rounded vowel was diphthongized, becoming [aw]. Notice that the first element is a low back vowel. Finally, to complete the shift the Middle English diphthong [aw] was monophthongized to [ɔ] (or [a]). The shift can be characterized with the following diagram:

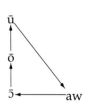

			Middle English	Modern English	

High long vowels become diphthongs:

(i)	ī	>	ay	līk	*like*	[layk]
				wīd	*wide*	[wayd]
(ii)	ū	>	aw	ūr	*our*	[awr̩]
				θūsɛnd	*thousand*	[θawzn̩d]

Nonhigh long vowels are raised:

(iii)	ē	>	i	bēə	*bee*	[bi]
				bētə	*beet*	[bit]
(iv)	ō	>	u	mōnə	*moon*	[mun]
				dō	*do*	[du]
(v)	ǣ	>	i via ē	dǣd	*deed*	[did]
				tǣčən	*teach*	[tič]
(vi)	ɔ̄	>	o	hɔ̄l	*whole*	[hol]
				ɔ̄k	*oak*	[ok]
(vii)	ā	>	e via ǣ	nāmə	*name*	[nem]
				mādə	*made*	[med]

Short vowels become unrounded and centralized:

(viii)	ʊ	>	ʌ	sʊnə	*son*	[sʌn]
(ix)	ɔ	>	a	ɔks	*ox*	[aks]

Diphthongs become monophthongs:

(x)	aw	>	ɔ/a	fawxt	*fought*	[fat]
(xi)	æy	>	ɛ	sæyd	*said*	[sɛd]
(xii)	ɪw	>	u	rɪwdə	*rude*	[rud]
(xiii)	ɔ̄w	>	o	sɔ̄wlɛ	*soul*	[sol]
(xiv)	ɔw	>	a	θɔwxt	*thought*	[θat]

B. The velar fricative [x] was lost when it occurred before a word-final [t]:

Middle English	Modern English	
fawxt	*fought*	[fat]
nīxt	*night*	[nayt]
θɔwxt	*thought*	[θat]
brīxt	*bright*	[brayt]

C. Word-initial and word-final consonant clusters have undergone considerable simplification between the Middle English and Modern English period.

    (i) Word-initial velar stop consonants [k] and [g] were lost when they occurred before the nasal [n]:

Middle English	*Modern English*	
gnawən	*gnaw*	[na]
knɪxt	*knight*	[nayt]

    (ii) Initial [w] was lost when it occurred before [r]:

Middle English	*Modern English*	
wrītan	*write*	[rayt]
wrɛkkən	*wreck*	[rɛk]

    (iii) Word final [mb] was reduced to [m]:

Middle English	*Modern English*	
dʊmb	*dumb*	[dʌm]

    (iv) Word final [ŋg] was reduced to [ŋ]:

Middle English	*Modern English*	
θɪŋg	*thing*	[θɪŋ]

D. As we mentioned earlier in Middle English (B), the Old English vowels [ā, ɛ, ɔ, ʊ] became [ə] in Middle English when they occurred in an unaccented final syllable. Subsequently [ə] was lost when it occurred word-finally, e.g., [nɔsʊ > nōzə > noz]. But [ə] remained in the final syllable of a word throughout the Middle English period if it was followed by a consonant, e.g., in the Middle English plural ending [əz], things [θɪŋgəz], and in the Middle English past tense ending [əd], *loved* [lʊvəd]. At the beginning of the Modern English period this [ə] was lost in the plural inflectional ending except after [s, z, š, č, ǰ], e.g., Middle English *fishes* [fɪšəz], Modern English *fishes* [fɪšəz], and in the past tense ending except after [t, d], e.g., Middle English *hunted* [hʊntəd], Modern English *hunted* [hʌntəd]. After the loss of [ə] in these inflectional endings, the final consonant of the ending was assimilated to the voicing of the final sound of the stem, e.g., *books* [bōkəz] > [bʊkz] > [bʊks].

Middle English	*Modern English*	
θɪŋgəz	*things*	[θɪŋz]
fɪšəz	*fishes*	[fɪšəz]
wīvəz	*wives*	[wayvz]
trēəz	*trees*	[triz]
sunəz	*sons*	[sʌnz]
čɪṛčəs	*churches*	[čṛčəz]
mūðəz	*mouths*	[mawθs]

lōkəd	*looked*	[lʊkt]
hʊntəd	*hunted*	[hʌntəd]
stɪrəd	*stirred*	[str̩d]
lʊvəd	*loved*	[lʌvd]

Morphological Alternations

As we have seen from our survey of sound changes that have occurred in the history of English, one of the effects of conditioned sound change is the creation of alternate pronunciations for the same morpheme, what is usually called morphological alternation. For example, early in the history of English fricatives became voiced intervocalically. As a result, the plural form of the word *wife* changed from [wifas] to [wīvas]. In the singular form [wīf], however, the fricative [f] did not become voiced because it did not occur before vowels. The net result of this sound change was to create alternate pronunciations for the morpheme 'wife', [wīf] in the singular but [wīv] in the plural. The alteration is still evident in Modern English today, as the forms *wife/wives* bear witness.

When morphological alternations are created by sound change, we can often examine the phonetic context of the alternate pronunciations and infer what sound change(s) caused the alternations in the first place. This type of analysis, whereby the linguist examines data available from one language and one language only and makes hypotheses about that language's history, is known as internal reconstruction. It is distinct from comparative reconstruction, which compares related languages in order to hypothesize about sound changes. Using the internal reconstruction method, a linguist may learn much about a language's history, even if for some reason there are no known related languages to compare it with.

English can provide us with a very straightforward example of the recovery of an earlier sound change via morphological alternation. In English the voiced velar stop [g] is not pronounced when it precedes a word-final nasal, e.g., *sign* [sayn], but it is pronounced if this nasal is not word-final, e.g., *signal* [sɪgnəl]. As a result, morphological alternations occur between morphemes with and without the voiced velar stop, e.g., *dignity* [dɪgnəti], *deign* [deyn]; *paradigmatic* [perədɪgmætɪk], *paradigm* [perədaym]. On the basis of these alternations we can make some inferences about the history of English. Specifically, we can assume that at an earlier period the morphological alternation did not exist—that there was only one pronunciation for morphemes that had the sound sequence [gn] or [gm], and that at some point there was a sound change whereby voiced velar stops were lost when they occurred before a word-final nasal.

Sometimes, however, it is impossible to detect the sound change(s) that have created the morphological alternations which exist in a language. This is usually the case when later sound changes take place which obscure the original cause of the alternate pronunciations. Consider the following example for the history of English. At present in English the past tense of the verb *sleep* is [slɛpt] and not [slipt] as we might expect. It is only natural to wonder why the morpheme 'sleep' has alternate pronunciations [slɛp] and [slip]. Unfortunately we can arrive at no satisfactory answer just by considering the evidence that exists in Modern English. We cannot say that the alternation is due to the fact that the vowel is followed by two consonants in the past tense form, because other verbs that form the past tense in a similar manner do not have alternate pronunciations, e.g., *freak* [frik], *freaked* [frikt] and *peak* [pik], *peaked* [pikt]. Since we have morphemes that form the past tense regularly and morphemes that have an alternate pronunciation in the past tense and we can determine nothing from the phonetic contexts, it is impossible to attempt internal reconstruction in the way we did with *sign* and *signal*. In cases such as this we must consider evidence from the Middle English period in the form of written records to find out how the alternate pronunciation came into existence.

Exercises

1. Refer to the sound changes discussed above and indicate how the following Old English words are pronounced today.

dǽl	nōn	līf	mūs
knīf	stān	swētə	lūd
alʊ	kēsɪ	tōθɪ	kɪnn
knafa	gnæt	mūθas	knēɔ

2. Given what you know about the sound changes that occurred between Old English and Modern English, how do you think the following words were pronounced in Old English? Give the processes responsible for the various changes that occurred in each word. Transcribe each phonetically and figure out what a sound might have been in Old English, assuming the regular processes discussed above. Remember to consider both conditioned and unconditioned sound change.

house	ship	shell	child
keep	road	right	noon
whale	writhe		

3. Is it possible to reconstruct the sound change which caused the morphological alternation [na] in knowledge and [kna] in acknowledge? If so, state the sound change. Can you find any other pairs of words which exhibit this particular type of alternation?

4. The Modern English words goose [gus] and gosling [gazlɪŋ] both have, historically, the same root morpheme: [gōs] (note Old English [gōs]). What is the source of this morphological alternation?

5. In Modern English the plural of house is houses [hawzəz]. The morpheme 'house' thus has two pronunciations: [haws] and [hawz]. Let's assume that you had no written records for the history of English. Could you suggest a plausible sound change to account for this alternation? Is it possible to suggest more than one plausible sound change to account for this alternation?

11

Language Contact

In language contact situations, two or more distinct languages come in contact with one another either through the direct social interaction of the speakers or through written form. This unit looks at the social relationships of speakers in contact, the influences of language contact on linguistic systems, and the nature of pidgin and creole languages.

File 11.1

Language Contact

Linguistic contact entails contact between distinct languages either through written form or through direct social contact between speakers. An example of the former is the contact between Latin and contemporary English. Language contact of this type, however, is more the exception than the rule. The more common type of contact is that involving direct social contact between speakers, since languages and their speakers do not exist in isolation but in social settings. The recruiting of foreign workers from Turkey by German companies, for example, has resulted in the contact of German with Turkish in many large cities in Germany. And the arrival of immigrants from Mexico and Cuba to the United States has resulted in close contact between Spanish and American English. Sometimes contact situations are established in the history of a language but later exist to a much lesser extent. For example, English was in very close contact with French after the Norman French invasion of England in 1066, but today the contact between these two languages in England (and in the United States) is much less intense. Contact situations can be described in terms of their influence on the linguistic systems (i.e., the grammars), the social relationships of the speakers in contact, and the linguistic outcome of the contact.

In language contact situations, the linguistic systems involved are often influenced by **borrowing,** the adoption by one language of linguistic elements from another language. Borrowing can be **lexical** (i.e., the borrowing of words) or **structural** (i.e., the borrowing of phonological, morphological, or syntactic items). Lexical borrowing is the adoption of individual words into one language from another language. These words are commonly referred to as **loans** or **loanwords.** Examples in American English include the words *ballet* and *chaise* from French, *macho* and *taco* from Spanish, *pizza* and *spaghetti* from Italian, *realpolitik* and *sauerkraut* from German, and *skunk* and *wigwam* from Algonquian.

In addition to single lexical items, whole phrases and idiomatic expressions can also be borrowed. Examples include English *it goes without saying* from French *il va sans dire,* German *Kettenraucher* from English *chain smoker,* and English *worldview* from German *Weltanschauung.* Phrases such as these, acquired through a word-for-word translation into native morphemes, are called **loan translations** or **calques.**

Phonological borrowing occurs when a language adopts new sounds or phonological rules from a language with which it is in contact. In many cases, this comes about through the borrowing of words. For example, New York English has borrowed the sound [x] (a voiceless velar fricative) in words like *yecch* [yex] from Yiddish, and word-final [ž] has been introduced into English from French in French loanwords like *rouge* and *prestige.* Educated Moslem speakers of Urdu have borrowed the Arabic sounds [z] and [ʔ]. Phonological rules that convert root-final [k] to [s] in word pairs like *electric/electricity* and [t] to [š] in word pairs like *nominate/nomination* were borrowed into English from French.

Morphological borrowing is the adoption of morphological features by one language under the influence of another language. English adopted its productive derivational suffixes *-able/-ible* from French (as in *readable, incredible*) and the productive agentive suffix *-er* from Latin *-arius* as in *reader, writer.*

In syntactic borrowing, ordering requirements of surface elements in one language may be borrowed into another language, replacing the native word order. For example, Romansch, spoken in Switzerland, adopted an adjective-noun ordering under the influence of German, replacing its original noun-adjective ordering. Syntactic borrowing also occurs in Wutun (which belongs to the Chinese language family) from Tibetan. Wutun has borrowed rigid verb-final word order from Tibetan, as well as the use of postpositions instead of prepositions. Asia Minor Greek dialects have adopted subject-object-verb word order under the influence of Turkish.

Linguistic borrowing is related to certain nonlinguistic characteristics such as **intensity of contact**, which is determined by the duration of the linguistic contact as well as by the level of interaction between the speakers. Intensity of contact is best seen as a continuum ranging from high intensity to low intensity (high intensity◄————►low intensity). A long-term contact with a high level of social interaction is considered to be an intense contact situation, whereas contact that has not existed for a long time and that can be described as allowing only limited social interaction of the speakers in contact is characterized as a low-intensity contact situation.

Intensity of contact affects the influence of the contact on the linguistic system. Lexical borrowing only requires a low-intensity contact situation, since single words can be adopted without an in-depth knowledge of the grammatical system of the donor language. However, the adoption of elements, rules, or structures embedded in the phonology, morphology, or syntax of one language into another requires the existence of at least some speakers who are knowledgeable in both languages. In other words, structural borrowing requires the existence of **bilingualism,** which requires a relatively intense degree of contact between the groups in order to develop.

Another social factor that influences the effect of contact on the linguistic systems is the **prestige** (or power) of the speakers. If the speakers in the contact situation consider themselves to be equally prestigious, their respective languages are said to be in an **adstratal** relationship. For example, English and Norse in contact in early England were **adstratum languages.** If the speakers consider themselves to be unequal in terms of prestige, the language of the dominant group is called the **superstratum language**, while the language of the less dominant group is called the **substratum language.** In the contact between English and Native American languages, English is the superstratum language and Native American languages are the substratum languages, because of an imbalance in power and prestige. In Germany, the various languages of the foreign workers (e.g., Turkish, Serbo-Croatian, Greek and Italian) are considered to be substratum languages, and German is considered to be the superstratum language.

In both adstratal and substratal/superstratal contact situations, lexical borrowing usually occurs first. However, the direction of the borrowing process usually differs. If the languages are adstratal, the borrowing takes place in both directions. Adstratum languages function as donor and recipient at the same time. However, in a situation of unequal prestige or power, the superstratum language is typically the donor language and accepts only a few loanwords from the substratum language(s). To put it simply, adstratal borrowing is primarily bidirectional, while substratal/superstratal borrowing is unidirectional.

If speakers of different adstratal languages enter into an extensive, long-term contact, **language convergence** may result. Convergence is the development of an increasingly mutual agreement of the language systems in contact. Languages which enter into such a linguistic alliance form a so-called *Sprachbund* (i.e., union of languages). An example is the Balkan Sprachbund area of Southeastern Europe where Albanian, Macedonian, Greek, Romanian, Bulgarian, and Serbo-Croatian show signs of linguistic convergence as a result of a long-standing linguistic contact.

If there is extensive, long-term contact between languages that have an unequal prestige relationship, **language shift** may result. This is defined as the shift by a group of speakers toward another language, while abandoning the native language. If the shifting group is the only group of speakers who used their original language, that language will die once the shift is completed. This is called **language death.** Many Native American languages in the United States have undergone the process of language death through language shift. In Oberwart, a village at the border between Austria and Hungary, language shift can be observed. After the Second World War, German came to be associated with the prestigious industrial economy, while Hungarian was felt to represent unprestigious "peasantness." The long-standing bilingualism of German and Hungarian, therefore, is giving way to a preference for German monolingualism, especially in the younger generation of Oberwart. Once the shift has been completed, Hungarian will no longer be used in Oberwart. However, this is not language death, because Hungarian is, of course, still widely used in Hungary.

Finally, two distinct outcomes of language contact are the creation of **pidgin languages** and **creole languages.** A pidgin language typically arises in a setting where two or more peoples come together for the purposes of trade. If the traders do not share a common language for communication, they might create a simplified, yet distinct language, a pidgin, to help facilitate trading. An example of such a trade pidgin is Chinook Jargon, a pidgin spoken by Native American, British, and French traders in the Pacific Northwest in the nineteenth century. Whereas pidgins are not the primary languages of their users, creole languages arise in situations where the speakers in contact are in need of a common, primary means of communication. This characterizes plantation settings on the Caribbean islands and in the southern United States. Here, a large number of Africans speaking a multitude of mutually unintelligible native languages came together with a small number of Europeans. This situation created the need for a common means of communication among the Africans as well as between the Africans and the Europeans. Since the common language that was created was used for a wide range of communicative purposes, not just for the facilitation of trade as in the case of pidgins, this contact situation led to the development of creole languages. Examples of creoles include English-based Jamaican Creole, Trinidadian Creole, and Gullah (a creole spoken in the coastal and island regions of South Carolina and Georgia), as well as French-based Haitian Creole.

Summary

The main points of this file are summarized below.
1. Linguistic contact arising through the social interaction of speakers is more the rule than the exception.
2. Lexical borrowing does not require an intense contact, whereas structural borrowing (i.e., phonological, morphological, syntactic borrowing) usually does.
3. Social characteristics of the contact situation, such as power and prestige, and intensity and duration of contact strongly influence the effects of contact on the linguistic systems.
4. In intense contact situations and depending on the prestige and power relationships, language convergence, language shift, and language death may arise.
5. In certain social settings, pidgin and creole languages may arise as a result of contact. Pidgins typically arise as trade languages, whereas creoles are languages typically developed in plantation settings where the need for a common primary language arises.

References

Conklin, Nancy F., and Margaret A. Lourie. 1983. *A Host of Tongues.* London: Collier Macmillan.
Gal, Susan. 1978. "Variation and Change in Patterns of Speaking: Language Shift in Austria." In David Sankoff, ed., *Linguistic Variation: Models and Methods.* New York: Academic Press, 227–38.
Hock, Hans H. 1991. *Principles of Historical Linguistics.* 2nd edition. New York: Mouton de Gruyter.
Lehiste, Ilse. 1988. *Lectures on Language Contact.* Cambridge: MIT Press.
Thomason, Sarah G., and Terrence Kaufman. 1988. *Language Contact, Creolization, and Genetic Linguistics.* Berkeley and Los Angeles: University of California Press.
Weinreich, Uriel. 1968. *Languages in Contact.* The Hague: Mouton.

File 11.2

Pidgin Languages

Speakers of mutually unintelligible languages who are brought together (perhaps by social, economic, or political forces) and have the need to communicate with one another, develop various ways of overcoming the barriers to communication. In situations in which a group of speakers absorbs relatively small numbers of people from outside their group, speaking different languages from their own, it is often the case that the new members will adopt the language spoken natively by the larger group. Over the years, such has taken place in the United States, as immigrants from all parts of the globe have entered the country and learned the language of the majority, in this case, American English. Alternatively, groups of speakers in contact may make use of a language that none speaks natively. During the Middle Ages, for example, scholars from all parts of Europe used Latin to communicate. And in many North American universities today, international students from many different countries, who are native speakers of many different languages other than English, interact with one another using English.

A third type of solution to overcoming the barriers to communication is the creation of **pidgin languages.** Pidgins are languages developed by speakers of distinct languages who come into contact with one another and share no common language among them. Pidgins typically spring up in trading centers or in areas under industrialization, where the opportunities for trade and work attract large numbers of people with different native tongues.

Pidgin languages are usually made up of mixtures of elements from all of the languages in contact. Quite often most of the vocabulary of pidgin languages is derived from the socially and/or economically dominant language in the contact situation (called the **superstrate** language). This is because speakers of the nondominant languages (called **substrate** languages) have higher economic or social motivation to learn the superstrate language than vice versa. Furthermore, in the contact between cultures where pidgin languages are formed, there is neither adequate instruction nor adequate time for complete mastery of the superstrate language. Hence, it is often the case that substratum speakers learn only the vocabulary of the superstrate. An instance of this phenomenon can be seen in Tok Pisin, a pidgin language spoken in Papua New Guinea, some examples of which are given below with their glosses (meanings) in English. Most of the words of Tok Pisin are clearly derived from English:

Tok Pisin	English source	Gloss
dok	dog	dog
pik	pig	pig
fis	fish	fish
painim	find	to find
hukim	hook	to hook
nogut	no good	bad
man	man	man
baimbai	by and by	soon
sekan	shake hands	to make peace

357

Notice that most of the words in the above list have undergone some phonological changes from English to Tok Pisin. For example, the word *find* shows [f] changing to [p], and the deletion of [d] in the [nd] cluster. There are also morphological differences between English and Tok Pisin, as evidenced by the *-im* ending on verbs in Tok Pisin. Semantic changes are also evident, as in the extension of *shake hands* to the much more general meaning *to make peace*.

These changes from English to Tok Pisin are at least due in part to contributions from the grammar(s) of the substrate language(s). Pidgin languages usually resemble their substratal inputs in everything from features of pronunciation to the organization of sentences and beyond. We will look at a few examples from diverse pidgin languages to show the universality of this characteristic of pidgins.

Chinook Jargon was a pidgin language spoken during the second half of the nineteenth century in Canada and the northwestern United States. There are still a few speakers of Chinook Jargon, but the language is nearly extinct. It was used as a trade language among several Native American groups and was also learned by Europeans who began to settle in the Northwest. It is presumed that Chinook Jargon predates European settlement. It certainly shows little or no European influence. Chinook Jargon's main source of vocabulary was Lower Chinook, and many of the features of Chinook Jargon grammar clearly are derived from other Native American languages that played a role in its formation. One of the most interesting aspects of Chinook Jargon grammar is its rich and complex consonant inventory, a feature found frequently among the input languages but rarely among the languages of the world and not at all among other pidgins. Examples of the complexity of Chinook Jargon phonology include its numerous secondary articulations, such as glottalized stops and labialized back consonants; its clusters consisting of two stop consonants; and its rare phonemes, such as lateral obstruents, a velar and post-velar series of stops, and a glottal stop phoneme. These examples provide strong evidence of the substratum influence on pidgin formation.

Disentangling the sources of grammatical features in pidgin languages can be extraordinarily complex. As an illustration of this, let us consider Solomon Islands Pidgin, spoken (as you might guess) on the Solomon Islands. This language is a near relative of Tok Pisin. The **lexifier** (=**superstrate**) language that gave Solomon Islands Pidgin its vocabulary was English; the substrate languages were all Oceanic languages. Recent research has shown that many of the grammatical rules of Solomon Islands Pidgin come from the Oceanic substrate languages. One of the most interesting examples of a substrate-derived construction is the transitive marker that is suffixed to verbal stems.

The transitive marker is pronounced [im]. Most linguists have associated this marker with the English words *him* or *them*. This makes sense, especially if one looks at the sorts of places where *-im* occurs:

Solomons Pidgin	*Gloss*
luk	*look*
luk-im	*see something*
hamar	*pound, hammer*
hamar-im	*pound, hammer something*
sut	*shoot*
sut-im	*shoot something*

As a speaker of English, one might easily imagine that a sentence like *mi hamar-im* (*I pounded it/him/ them*) is based on English *I hammered (h)im* or *I hammered (th)em*. In fact this analysis may be partially correct, but the facts are actually more complex. If we look at Kwaio (an Oceanic language) and compare some transitive and intransitive verbs, such as *look* and *see*, we notice an interesting similarity to the Solomons Pidgin data:

Kwaio	*Gloss*
aga	*look*
aga-si-	*see something*
gumu	*pound, hammer*
gumu-ri-	*pound, hammer something*
fana	*shoot*
fana-si-	*shoot something*

These data are strikingly similar to the Solomons Pidgin examples above: both languages have intransitive verbs that also serve as verbal stems that can take a transitive suffix (TRS). There are numerous reasons to believe that this grammatical rule derives from Oceanic substrate languages rather than from English. First of all, we can see immediately that Solomons Pidgin does not exactly follow English in every use of *-im*. In English one can either *look at 'em* or *see 'em*, but never *look 'em*. In Solomons Pidgin, however, one can *luk-im*. Second, in English it is ungrammatical to use *(h)im* or *(th)em* as an object of a transitive verb if there is another explicit object of the verb. For example, one can say,

       I shot the burglar

or,

       I shot 'im

but not,

       *I shot 'im the burglar.

In Solomons Pidgin it is not only possible to use *-im* if there is an object present but necessary to do so.

       mi no luk-im   pikipiki bulong iu
       I   not see-*TRS* pig   belong you
       I didn't see your pig(s)

Without *-im* the sentence is ungrammatical:

       *mi no luk pikipiki bulong iu.

      Third, and perhaps most persuasive, researchers have noted that very few European speakers of Solomons Pidgin ever master this detail of the grammar. Had this grammatical feature come from English, one would expect English speakers to have no trouble in mastering it. It seems clear, therefore, that the substrate languages have contributed this rule of grammar to Solomons Pidgin.
      However, there is yet another source of pidgin grammar formation that may have come into play in this example. It is often the case that speakers "simplify" and modify their language in contact situations. These modification strategies are referred to as **foreigner talk**. Some aspects of foreigner talk are probably universal, such as the elimination of complicated constructions and inflectional mor-

phology; others are culture-specific. For example, there is a long tradition of English speakers using -*um* as a suffix when talking to people who don't speak English (be they Native American, Oceanic, or whatever). We have all heard lines something like the following in old Western movies, *You want-um firewater, I want-um furs. We trade-um.* Whatever their origins, it is clear that English speakers use modification strategies such as this in certain contact situations.

Many researchers believe that these foreigner-talk features are a significant ingredient in the creation of pidgins. In the example given above, Oceanic peoples may have focused on this aspect of English foreigner-talk and interpreted it in terms of their own grammars. It is unlikely, however, that the foreigner talk explanation can account for everything, since foreigner talk is notoriously unsystematic. The -*um* strategy was probably never used consistently enough by English speakers to form the basis for a grammatical rule in the developing pidgin. Nonetheless, the accidental conspiracy of factors present in this example—the English contractions '*im* and '*em*, foreigner-talk -*um*, and substrate transitive suffixes—probably all contributed to the rule ultimately found in Solomons Pidgin.

It has been suggested that another driving force in the formation of pidgins may well be universal strategies of second-language learning. Currently debated by researchers is the question of whether errors people make when learning a foreign language are a result of the strategies adults use in learning second languages or of some innate language learning device. It seems likely that a full account of pidgin formation will have to include an appeal to some sort of language universals.

There is one last characteristic of pidgins that should be mentioned here. Pidgins have often been considered "grammarless," "broken" versions of other languages. This is most certainly not true, as anyone who has ever really learned a pidgin language can tell you. It is true, however, that pidgin languages grow and develop through time. In the initial stage of pidgin formation, often called the **prepidgin jargon** stage, there is little or no grammar and rampant speaker-to-speaker variation. For this reason pidginists talk about pidgins becoming *crystallized*, or establishing grammatical conventions. This is an essential characteristic of pidgins—if there is no established grammar, there is no pidgin.

Some Features of Pidgins

Many pidgin languages, regardless of their source languages, share certain characteristics. Some typical features are described in this section. Examples are taken from Cameroonian Pidgin and Korean Bamboo English, two pidgins for which English supplied much of the vocabulary. Cameroonian Pidgin is used in Cameroon, in West Africa. Korean Bamboo English developed among Koreans and Americans during the Korean War. For reference, an excerpt from Loreto Todd's *Some Day Been Dey*, a folktale about a tortoise and a hawk told in Cameroonian Pidgin is given below, with a free translation into English.

We join the tale after the hawk meets the tortoise, explains that she needs food for her children, and invites the tortoise to visit them.

1. [a datwan go gud pas mak, trɔki. yu go kam, e]
   "Oh, that would be great, tortoise. You will come, won't you?

2. [a go glad dat dey we yu go kam fɔ ma haws]
   "I'll be glad the day when you come to my house."

3. [i tɔk so, i tɔn i bak, i go]
   She said this, turned her back, and left.

4. [i di laf fɔ i bele. i tɔk sey:]
   She was laughing inside and said:

5. [ha so trɔki tiŋk sey i tu fit go flay ɔp stik. i go si]
   "Ha! So Tortoise thinks he too can fly up trees. We'll see."

   [The tortoise notices the hawk's disdain and tricks her into carrying him to her nest, where he eats the hawk's young. She tries to kill him by dropping him from the sky.]

6. [bɔt trɔki gɛt trɔŋ nkanda. nɔtiŋ no fit du i.]
   But the tortoise has strong skin. Nothing could hurt him.

7. [i wikɔp. i šek i skin, muf ɔl dɔs fɔ i skin]
   He got up, shook himself, removed all the dust from his body,

8. [i go, i sey: a! a dɔn du yu wɛl!]
   and left, saying: "Oh! I have taught you a good lesson!"

9. [ɔl dis pipul we dem di prawd!]
   "All these people who are proud!

10. [dem tiŋk sey fɔseka sey]
    "They think that because

11. [a no gɛt wiŋ a no fit du as dem tu di du]
    "I don't have wings I can't do as they do.

12. [a no fit flay, bɔt mi a dɔn šo yu sey sens pas ɔl]
    "I can't fly, but I've shown you that intelligence beats everything."

Phonology

Consonant clusters are usually reduced in pidgins (see *strong* [trɔŋ] in line (6) and *dust* [dɔs] in (7)). Consonant cluster reduction is an indication that pidgins have a preference for syllable types closer to the CV type.

Morphology

A common feature of pidgin morphology is the absence of affixal marking. Notice from the Cameroonian example that *wings* is [wiŋ] (11), *thinks* is [tiŋk] (5), and *passes* is [pas] (12).

Note that [i] is the only third person pronoun in Cameroonian, replacing *he, she, him,* and *her* (objective), and *his* and *her* (possessive). This simplification avoids the use of case and gender marking.

Finally, it should be noted that reduplication is often used in pidgins as a simple word formation process (a) to avoid homonymy, as in Korean Bamboo English [san] *sun* and [sansan] *sand,* or (b) for emphasis, as in Korean Bamboo English [takitaki] *very talkative.*

Semantics

Pidgins usually have very small vocabularies. To compensate for lack of variety, meanings are extended. Thus [stik] means not only *stick* but also *tree* (5) and [wikɔp] means not only *wake up* but also *get up* (7).

In Korean Bamboo English, the meaning of *grass* is extended, so that *gras bilong head* means *hair* and *gras bilong mouth* means *mustache*.

Because there are not many words in the vocabulary of the typical pidgin, compounds are more frequent. For example, *dog baby* and *cow baby* can be used for *puppy* and *calf*.

Syntax

The basic word order for pidgins tends to be subject-verb-object (SVO). Like other SVO languages, pidgins generally use prepositions rather than postpositions and auxiliaries are usually ordered before main verbs and nouns before relative clauses.

Pidgins show a preference for compound sentences (sentences connected by conjunctions like *and, or,* etc.) over subordinate clauses, though subordinate structures do sometimes exist.

Articles are generally not used in pidgins, as illustrated by [ɔl dɔs] *all the dust*, in line (7).

Aspectual distinctions are often marked by auxiliaries in pidgins. Cameroonian, for example, classifies actions as to whether they are *ongoing, completed,* or *repeated* as shown below:

ongoing	di	[di laf]	*was laughing*	(4)
completed	dɔn	[dɔn du]	*have done*	(8)
repeated	di	[di du]	*do (always)*	(11)

References

Holm, John. 1988. *Pidgins and Creoles*. Vol. 1. Cambridge Language Surveys. Cambridge: Cambridge University Press.

Keesing, Roger. 1988. *Melanesian Pidgin and the Oceanic Substrate*. Stanford, CA: Stanford University Press.

Mühlhäusler, Peter. 1986. *Pidgin and Creole Linguistics*. Oxford and New York: Basil Blackwell.

Thomason, Sarah G., and Terrence Kaufman. 1988. *Language Contact, Creolization, and Genetic Linguistics*. Berkeley and Los Angeles: University of California Press.

Todd, Loreto. 1971. *Some Day Been Dey: West African Pidgin Folktales*. London: Routledge and Kegan Paul.

File 11.3

Creole Languages

Imagine yourself as the son or daughter of first-generation slaves in the New World. Your parents and others like them were kidnapped from their homes, corralled together with other slaves, shipped across vast oceans under inhuman conditions, and forced to work and live in a strange country surrounded by people who didn't speak their language. Slave owners were known to divide slaves into linguistically diverse groups so that no one slave was likely to be with very many other slaves who spoke the same language. This tactic kept slaves from organizing any sort of resistance. Of course it also meant that if slaves wished to communicate with either the slaveholders or each other, they had to adopt some new form of communication. It is in plantation settings of this sort that the classic **creole** languages came into being.

File 11.2, on pidgin languages, covers some of the ways in which new languages come into being in the sort of social context found on slave-labor plantations. There are some differences, however, between pidgin and creole languages. Traditionally, creole languages were defined as pidgin languages that had been adopted as the first, or native, language of a group of speakers. There is an element of truth in this definition, but recent research has suggested it is not entirely accurate.

The kernel of truth in the traditional definition of creolization is that all creoles *do* seem to be languages that were initially not native to any group of speakers but were adopted as first languages by some speech community. The problem with the traditional definition is that it presumes a predecessor pidgin language for every creole language. However, in most of the classic creole languages there is no attested evidence for a prior pidgin. In fact, among the creole languages spoken in the Caribbean, which are the traditional prototype creoles, there is reason to suspect that the predecessor languages were not pidgins but **prepidgin jargons.** A jargon is an extremely rudimentary and variable type of language formed in contact situations. If the conditions are right, jargons can settle and crystallize into pidgin languages.

Various researchers have suggested that the social context found in multilingual plantation settings is unique in human history. On plantations there was a radical break in linguistic tradition. Children rarely learned the native language of their parents because it was of little or no value to them on the plantation. The only accessible variety of language of significant usefulness in plantation settings was the unstable, highly variable jargon used by their parents and the other slaves.

Furthermore, these prepidgin jargons were the primary language of the adults as well, since they were the best means of communicating with others from such varied linguistic backgrounds. Thus these greatly simplified, extremely rudimentary, shifting jargons became the primary language of the adult slaves and their children. There was no time for leisurely crystallization and development of these jargons *before* they became the native language of the entire plantation community. This common social context is shared by nearly all of the Caribbean creole communities and a few others besides (e.g., Hawaiian Creole). All of the classic creoles (i.e., those that developed under the conditions described above) have structural features in common. In fact the features that these creole languages share are so numerous and so specific, that they suggest that the shared social background of these languages has somehow led to their structural similarity.

Before discussing these shared features in more detail, let us compare the traditional view of creolization with the slightly different definition employed here. The traditional view groups together languages that all have **nativization** in common. Nativization is the process by which some variety of speech that was no one's native language is learned by children in a speech community as their first language. This variety of speech could be a jargon, as described above, or a pidgin, or what is referred to as an **expanded pidgin** (a later stage in the development of pidgins). Peter Mühlhäusler, a pidginist, gives the following diagram showing the different types of creolization in the traditional view:

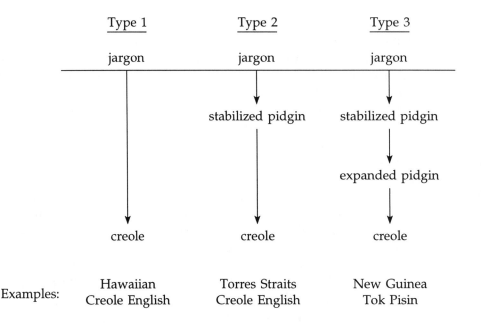

Figure 1.   "Three Types of Creoles." Adapted by permission of Basil Blackwell Publishers from Mühlhäusler, *Pidgin and Creole Linguistics* (1986), p. 8.

These situations all have nativization in common, but the difference among the three lies in the degree of maturity that the precreole language attained before it became the native language of some speech community. In Hawaiian Creole English and Caribbean creoles the predecessor language was an unstable, rudimentary jargon. In Torres Straits Creole there was a crystallized pidgin that had not yet expanded into a full-fledged language. In Tok Pisin, the precreole language was a quite sophisticated language that was already used for such subtle and sophisticated purposes as parliamentary debate in the Papua New Guinea parliament and television and radio broadcasting.

The structural outcomes of these different types of nativization (or *creolization*, in the traditional view) are quite different. Where the precreole language is a crystallized or expanded pidgin (i.e., a Type 3 pidgin), the creole bears many of the same features as its predecessor language. For example, Gillian Sankoff and others have shown that the differences between nativized and nonnativized varieties of Tok Pisin are quite subtle. Often native speakers of Tok Pisin will employ the same grammatical devices as second-language speakers of Tok Pisin, but on a more frequent or consistent basis. Also, native speakers of Tok Pisin phonologically reduce various linguistic elements more than nonnative speakers do. On the whole, though, the differences between nativized and nonnativized Tok Pisin are rather small.

Type 1 creoles bear relatively less imprint from their predecessor jargons. However, the structural similarities among all the Type 1 creoles (classic creoles) are quite striking, especially given the diversity of their sources. Derek Bickerton and other scholars have catalogued many of the similarities among the Type 1 creoles. One of the most striking of these similarities is verb conjugation. In a recent article, Bickerton gives the following table (slightly modified), which illustrates the similarities in verb conjugation among Type 1 creoles. (Note: *anterior, irreal,* and *nonpunctual* refer to **aspects** that verbs can assume. The *anterior* is similar to the English past tense; *irreal* refers to the *future, conditional,* and *subjunctive; nonpunctual* refers to ongoing action.)

	Hawaiian Creole	*Haitian Creole*	*Sranan*
BASE FORM *(he walked/s)*	He walk	Li maché	A waka
ANT(erior) *(he had walked)*	He bin walk	Li té maché	A ben waka
IRR(eal) *(he would/will walk)*	He go walk	L'av(a) maché	A sa waka
NON(punctual) *(he is/was walking)*	He stay walk	L'ap maché	A e waka
ANT + IRR *(he would have walked)*	He bin go walk	Li t'av(a) maché	A ben sa waka
ANT + NON *(he was/had been walking)*	He bin stay walk	Li t'ap maché	a ben e
IRR + NON *(he will/would be walking)*	He go stay walk	L'av ap maché	A sa e waka
ANT + IRR + NON *(he would've been walking)*	He bin go stay walk	Li t'av ap maché	a ben sa e

The examples above include two English-based creoles (Hawaiian Creole and Sranan) and one French-based creole (Haitian Creole). But the patterns of verb conjugation are the same nonetheless. Note in each of these creoles that the anterior always precedes the irreal and nonpunctual, and the irreal always precedes the nonpunctual. It should also be noted that the substrate languages that contributed to the three languages represented in the table above are quite different. In Sranan (spoken in Surinam) and Haitian Creole, the substrate was composed of African languages. In Hawaiian Creole the substrate was composed of various Asian languages, notably several Philippine languages and Japanese.

What is the source of these shared features among such diverse Type 1 creoles? Bickerton attributes the similarities among Type 1 creoles to innate properties of human minds. He claims that the similarities among widely scattered Type 1 creoles provide support for the claim that human beings are linguistically preprogrammed. Bickerton would say that the shared verb conjugation pattern shown above follows from a very specific "bioprogram" in the human mind. Part of this bioprogram includes the verb conjugation that human beings will always use automatically unless the patterns of whatever language they are learning are different.

In plantation contexts, where there is only a relatively grammarless jargon available to children who are trying to acquire a native language, children will force the jargon into the bioprogram mold. For example, if the jargon has no verb conjugation, the children who are learning it will create one with the bioprogram conjugation. This, according to Bickerton and his followers, is the primary mechanism of creolization, and it fully accounts for all of the similarities among Type 1 creoles.

It should be noted, however, that other scholars have been critical of this approach and have suggested other possible sources to account for the similarities among Type 1 creoles, including the common social context of Type 1 creolization, universal strategies of language learning, universal strategies for reducing language in contact situations, and structural similarities among the substrate and/or superstrate languages that were historically present in Type 1 creole contact situations.

References

Bickerton, Derek. 1983. "Creole Languages." *Scientific American* 249.1 (July 1983): 116–22.

Mühlhäusler, Peter. 1986. *Pidgin and Creole Linguistics.* Oxford and New York: Basil Blackwell.

Romaine, Suzanne. 1988. *Pidgin and Creole Languages.* London and New York: Longman.

Winford, Donald. 1989. "Pidgin and Creole Languages." Unpublished manuscript, The Ohio State University, Department of Linguistics.

12

Language Variation

No two speakers of a language speak exactly the same way; nor does any individual speaker speak the same way all the time. Variation is a natural part of human language, and it is influenced by such factors as socio-economic status, region, and ethnicity.

File 12.1   Introduction to Language Variation

Most people are aware of the fact that systematic differences exist among languages—for example, that English is different from Spanish, which is different from Arabic, which is different from Russian, and so on. However, many people are probably not aware of the extent to which systematic differences exist *within* languages. **Internal variation** refers to the property of languages of having different ways of expressing the same meaning. This is a property that is inherent to all human languages and to all speakers of a language. Thus, no two speakers of a language speak exactly the same way; nor does any individual speaker speak the same way all the time. The purpose of this unit is to introduce to you the ways in which languages vary internally and the factors that contribute to language variation. For purposes of familiarity, these files will focus primarily on variation in English, but you should keep in mind that variation exists in all languages.

Varieties, Dialects, and Idiolects

The term **language variety** is used among linguists as a cover term to refer to many different types of language variation. The term may be used in reference to a distinct language such as French or Italian, or in reference to a particular form of a language spoken by a specific group of people such as Appalachian English, or even in reference to the speech of a single person. In addition to this cover term, there are more specific terms that are used to talk about these different types of language varieties.

When a group of speakers of a particular language differs noticeably in its speech from another group we say that they are speaking different **dialects**. In English, the term *dialect* often carries negative connotations associated with nonstandard varieties. However, a dialect is any variety of a language spoken by a group of people that is characterized by systematic differences from other varieties of the same language in terms of structural or lexical features. In this sense, every person speaks a dialect of his or her native language. The term *dialect* is also misused by laypeople to refer strictly to differences in pronunciation. Such a mistake is easy to understand since differences in pronunciation are usually accompanied by variation in other areas of the grammar as well and thus correspond to dialectal differences. However, the appropriate term for systematic phonological variation is **accent**. In layperson's terminology, *accent* is often used in reference to "foreign accents" or regionally defined accents such as southern or northern accents. However, here again it must be noted that every person speaks with an accent. Also, as mentioned above, there is variation from speaker to speaker within any given language. The form of a language spoken by one person is known as an **idiolect**.

While these terms may seem simple and convenient here, when we consider actual languages, it becomes immediately obvious how difficult it is to make certain distinctions. How do we know, for example, if two or more language varieties are different dialects of the same language or if in fact they are separate, distinct languages? One criterion used to distinguish dialects from languages is **mutual intelligibility**. If speakers of one language variety can understand speakers of another language variety and vice versa, we say that these varieties are mutually intelligible. Suppose you are a native of Brooklyn, New York, and you go to visit some friends in Beaumont, Texas. You may notice some differences in the speech of your Beaumont friends (and they in yours), but essentially you will be able to understand each other. Your variety of speech and theirs are mutually intelligible but differ systematically, and are therefore dialects of the same language.

It is not always this easy, however, to decide whether two language varieties are different dialects of the same language or different languages just on the basis of mutual intelligibility. Other factors, such as cultural or historical considerations, may cloud the issue. In China, for example, Mandarin is spoken in the northern provinces and Cantonese in the southern province of Kwang Tung. Even though in spoken form these language varieties are not mutually intelligible, they are considered by the speakers of these varieties themselves to be dialects of the same language. Why? One reason is that these two varieties share a common writing system and are thus mutually intelligible in written form.

The opposite situation exists in the American Southwest between Papago and Pima, two Native American languages. These two language varieties are indeed mutually intelligible, having less linguistic difference between them than exists between Standard American English and Standard British English. However, because these two tribes regard themselves as politically and culturally distinct, they consider their respective languages to be distinct as well.

Another complication for the criterion of mutual intelligibility is found in a phenomenon known as a **dialect continuum**. This is a situation where, in a large number of contiguous dialects, each dialect is closely related to the next, but the dialects at either end of the continuum (scale) are mutually unintelligible. Thus, dialect A is intelligible to dialect B, which is intelligible to dialect C, which is intelligible to dialect D; but D and A are not mutually intelligible. A situation such as this is found near the border between Holland and Germany, where the dialects on either side of the national border are mutually intelligible. Because of international boundaries, however (and probably political and cultural considerations as well), speakers of these varieties regard them as distinct languages.

At what point is the line drawn? Clearly, the criterion of mutual intelligibility does not account for all the facts. Indeed, there may be no clear-cut, black-and-white answer to such a question in every case. From the Family Tree Model, discussed in the unit on historical linguistics, we saw that a parent language may split and form daughter languages—e.g., Germanic split off into English, Dutch, and German (among others). This type of split may also occur when dialect differences become so great that the dialects are no longer mutually intelligible to the speakers of these language varieties.

Speech Communities

A group of people speaking the same dialect is known as a **speech community**. Speech communities may be defined in terms of a number of **extralinguistic factors**, including region, socioeconomic status, and ethnicity. However, it is rarely, if ever, the case that there exists a speech community in which a "pure" **dialect**—i.e., purely regional, purely ethnic, etc.—is spoken, because the identification of any speech variety as a pure dialect requires the assumption of **communicative isolation**. Communicative isolation results when a group of speakers forms a coherent speech community relatively isolated from speakers outside of that community. This type of isolation was perhaps once a possibility but is becoming increasingly rare these days owing to social and geographic mobility, mass media, etc. What is more likely the case today is that a particular dialect of a speech community is influenced by regional, social, and cultural factors. Thus, in most instances the varieties spoken among members of a speech community are not pure dialects but instead are influenced by the interaction of many different factors. Consider, for example, the following utterances:

(a)   I <u>used to could</u> read.
(b)   I <u>ain't no</u> girl now.
(c)   He had a broken back ____was never set.
(d)   Put some bakin' <u>sody</u> on it.
(e)   I fell <u>upside of</u> the building.

Note the underlined parts of each sentence: (a) a double modal, (b) multiple negation, (c) relative pronoun deletion, (d) substitution of unstressed [a] in *soda* [soda] by [i] [sodi], and (e) lexical substitution of *up against the side of* by *upside of*.

All of these features have been identified as characteristic of Appalachian English (AE), a variety that, from its name, appears to be regional. However, to label this variety of English as regional tells only part of the story. The speaker of these utterances was a sixty-eight-year-old male, belonging to a lower socioeconomic status group. He was a native of a southeastern Ohio county that borders several Appalachian counties and that experienced a post–World War II influx of Appalachian blue-collar workers. Clearly, where this person lives has something to do with his variety of speech. But there are other relevant factors as well. For example, it has been determined that the pronunciation of *soda* in (d) represents a dying feature of AE and seems to be limited to older speakers. This feature, then, is not only geographically related but seems age related as well. Moreover, studies indicate that in careful speech men tend to use more nonstandard forms than women. So the fact that this speaker is male may also be relevant to his dialect. Finally, AE is a dialect spoken primarily by low-income, rural speakers, a group to which our southeastern Ohio speaker belongs.

So while it is true that AE is a dialect generally restricted to that area designated as Appalachian by the Appalachian Regional Commission, it can also be seen that geographic region overlaps with at least three other factors—age, gender, and socioeconomic status. This sort of interaction among extralinguistic factors seems to be true of most, if not all, speech communities and their corresponding dialects.

File 12.2 Variation at Different Levels of Linguistic Structure

While we are probably most consciously aware of differences in vocabulary choice or pronunciation, internal variation exists at all levels of linguistic structure. The examples below illustrate different types of variation in English at each level of linguistic structure.

Phonetic Level

1. In most American dialects, the sounds [t, d, n, s, z] are produced with alveolar articulation, but some New York City dialects have dental articulation whereby the tongue tip touches the top teeth.

2. Some British and Scottish dialects of English produce a trilled *r*, [r̄], while most American dialects have either a retroflex [r] or a "bunched" [ɹ].

Phonological Level

1. Most American dialects have one vowel in *caught, dawn,* and *hawk* (something close to [ɔ] but a little lower) and another in *cot, Don,* and *hock* [a]. However, some dialects have the same vowel in all of these words, so that in these particular dialects *Don* and *dawn* would be homophonous.

2. In southern England, words like *flood, but, cup* have the vowel [ʌ] and words like *full, good, put* have the vowel [ʊ]. In northern English dialects, however, both sets of words have the vowel [ʊ].

3. Standard British English does not permit sequences of V–r–C or V–r–#. This is similar to Bostonian English, where the sentence *Park the car* would be pronounced [pak ðə ka].

4. Some African-American English dialects do not permit sequences of C–r or C-l, especially in unstressed syllables, so that the word *professor* would be pronounced [pʌfɛsə].

Morphological Level

1. Some rural British English dialects use the possessive morpheme with pronouns but not with nouns, e.g., *my life, his dog* but *Tom egg, the old lady purse.*

2. In parts of northern England and southern Wales *-s* is not just a third singular present tense marker, but a general present tense marker. These speakers say sentences like *I likes him, We goes,* etc.

3. Many dialects of English have *hisself* and *theirselves* where Standard English has *himself* and *themselves.*

4. Appalachian English has past tense forms for various verbs that are different from the past tense forms found in other American dialects, e.g., Appalachian English has [klʌm], [ɛt], and [hɛt] where other dialects have *climbed, ate,* and *heated,* respectively.

Syntactic Level

1. For many southern speakers *done* can function as an auxiliary, as in *She done already told you* rather than *She has already told you.*

2. For many Appalachian speakers *right* can function adverbially, e.g., *a right good meal.*

3. In some dialects combinations of auxiliaries like *might could, might would, may can,* and *useta could* are permitted and form a single constituent.

4. Many midwestern dialects have the construction *The crops need watered* as a variant of *The crops need to be watered.*

Semantic Level (Vocabulary Choice)

1. *Knock up* means 'rouse from sleep by knocking' in British English but 'make pregnant' in American English.

2. Words for carbonated beverages differ from place to place. *Soft drink, soda, pop, soda pop* are all different ways of expressing the same meaning.

Exercises

For each example below, identify the level of linguistic structure at which the variation exists.

P = Phonetic
Ph = Phonological
M = Morphological
S = Syntactic
Sm = Semantic

_____ Some Caribbean English dialects do not have the sounds [θ] or [ð]; instead the sounds [t] and [d], respectively, are substituted, e.g., *both* [bot], *there* [dɛr].

_____ Many dialects of English have multiple negation, as in *I didn't see nobody take no pictures.*

_____ Many American dialects have the mid back lax vowel [ɔ]. However, this vowel is produced very differently in different dialects—some are more rounded, some less so; some are higher or lower than others (but not as high as [u] or as low as [a]).

_____ Names differ from place to place to refer to an insect that glows in the dark, including *firefly, lightning bug, glowworm,* and *fire bug.*

_____ Some African-American English dialects do not mark the third person singular present tense with a suffix, e.g., *he kiss, she see, it jump.*

_____ In some southern and midwestern dialects of American English there is no distinction between [ɪ] and [ɛ] before nasals; only [ɪ] occurs. So in the words *pen* and *pin,* which are pronounced [pɛn] and [pɪn], respectively, by SAE speakers, the pronunciation is [pɪn] for both words.

File 12.3

Language and Socioeconomic Status

Standard vs. Nonstandard Varieties

The popular notion persists that every language consists of one "correct" dialect from which all other "inferior" or "substandard" dialects emerge. This misconception has arisen from social stereotypes and biases. It is not a linguistic fact. It is important to realize that a person's use of any particular dialect is not a reflection of his or her intelligence or judgment. *Linguistically speaking, no one dialect or language is better, more correct, or more logical than any other.* Rather, every language variety is a rule-governed system and an effective means of communication. The aim of this file is to provide you with an understanding of how the terms **standard dialect** and **nonstandard dialect** are defined linguistically, and to dispel some of the myths associated with these terms.

Standard Dialects

The notion of standard dialect is really a complex one and in many ways an idealization. Descriptively speaking, the standard dialect is the variety used by political leaders, the media, and speakers from higher socioeconomic classes. It is also the variety taught in schools and to nonnative speakers in language classes. Every language has at least one standard dialect, which serves as the primary means of communication across dialects.

In actuality, there is no one standard dialect but instead many different varieties of what people consider to be the standard. What ties these different notions together is **prestige.** Socially speaking, the standard dialect is the dialect of prestige and power. However, the prestige of any speech variety is wholly dependent upon the prestige of the speakers who use it. In the United States, the prestige group usually corresponds to those in society who enjoy positions of power, wealth, and education. It is the speech of this group, therefore, that becomes the standard, but there is nothing about the variety itself that makes it prestigious.

For proof of this claim, consider a case in which the status of a particular linguistic feature has changed over time from standard to nonstandard. Recall from the file on *Prescriptive vs. Descriptive Rules of Grammar* that multiple negatives were once commonly used by speakers of standard Old English and Middle English. Take, for example, this multiple-negative construction from Geoffrey Chaucer's description of the Knight in the General Prologue to the Canterbury Tales (from Millward 1989: 158):

> He nevere yet no vileynye ne sayde
> *He never yet no villainy not said*

> In al his lyf unto no maner wight
> *In all his life to no kind of creature*

Today, however, speakers who most commonly employ multiple-negative constructions are not members of the higher socioeconomic (i.e., prestige) group. Such constructions are rarely used in public spheres by political leaders or media spokespeople, and English grammar instructors discourage use of these forms in writing or in speech. Thus multiple negation is today considered a nonstandard feature. This example illustrates a change over time in the **prescriptive standard**, the standard by which we make judgments of "right" and "wrong." This example proves that such judgments are not linguistically founded but are instead governed by societal opinion, and most often by societal evaluation of speakers.

To consider another example of how linguistically arbitrary notions of the standard are, let us look at the following case. Few standard English speakers use object pronouns in subject position, as in (1) below:

1. Kim and me went to the store.

Yet media spokespeople, political leaders, and others of higher socioeconomic status are more and more frequently observed using subject pronouns in object position as in (2) and (3):

2. This is a matter between Kim and I.
3. Give the books to Kim and I.

According to the prescriptive standard, sentences (1), (2), and (3) should all be "corrected" as follows:

4. Kim and I went to the mall.
5. This is a matter between Kim and me.
6. Give the money to Kim and me.

However, not only would many standard English speakers not recognize (2) and (3) as violations of prescriptive rule, many would argue that intuitively sentences (2) and (3) seem "correct" while (5) and (6) seem "incorrect." This is known as **hypercorrection**, the act of producing nonstandard forms by way of false analogy. This example shows us that even violations of prescriptive rule (such as sentences 2 and 3 above) can be perceived as standard if they are used by members of the prestige group.

Standard American English (SAE)

The standard dialect in the United States is called **Standard American English** (SAE). As with any standard dialect, SAE is not a well-defined variety but rather an idealization, which even now defies definition because agreement on what exactly constitutes this variety is lacking. SAE is not a single, unitary, homogeneous dialect but instead comprises a number of varieties. When we speak of SAE, we usually have in mind features of grammar more than pronunciation. In the United States, where class consciousness is minimal, pronunciation is not terribly important. Thus, there are varieties of SAE that are spoken with northern accents, southern accents, coastal New England accents, etc., but that are still considered standard. This is not to say that we do not make evaluations of speech based on accent, because we do. But we seem to be far more "tolerant" of variation in accent than we are of grammatical variation. Compare, for example, the varieties of English spoken by Connecticut native George Bush, Arkansan Bill Clinton, and Texan Ross Perot in the 1992 presidential debates. Most would agree that all three are speakers of SAE. And yet they all speak with distinctly different accents.

In Britain, on the other hand, where class divisions are more clearly defined and social mobility is more restricted, standard pronunciation or Received Pronunciation (RP), also known as BBC English or the "Queen's English," takes on the importance of standard grammar and vocabulary. Thus in Britain both pronunciation and grammar are markers of social status.

Nonstandard Dialects

All dialects that are not perceived as varieties of the standard are called **nonstandard**. It is important to understand that nonstandard does not mean "substandard" or "inferior," although this is the perception held by many. Just as standard dialects are associated with the language of the "powerful" and "prestigious," nonstandard dialects are usually associated with the language of the lower socioeconomic classes.

Most nonstandard varieties are stigmatized in the wider community as illogical and unsystematic. It is on this basis that many justify labeling nonstandard varieties as "bad" or "improper" ways of speaking, as opposed to standard varieties, which are said to be "good" or "proper." Again, it must be emphasized that such evaluations are linguistically unfounded. Consider the following paradigms illustrating the use of reflexive pronouns in two varieties of English—one standard, the other nonstandard.

Standard	*Nonstandard*
I like myself	I like myself
You like yourself	You like yourself
He likes himself	He likes hisself
She likes herself	She likes herself
We like ourselves	We like ourselves
You like yourselves	You like yourselves
They like themselves	They like theirselves

Given these two paradigms, we can develop descriptive rules for the construction of reflexives in these two varieties.

Standard: Add the reflexive suffix -*self* to possessive pronouns in the 1st and 2nd person singular and -*selves* to possessive pronouns in the 1st and 2nd person plural.

Add the reflexive suffix -*self* to object pronouns in the 3rd person singular and -*selves* to object pronouns in the 3rd person plural.

Nonstandard: Add the reflexive suffix -*self* to possessive pronouns in the 1st–3rd person singular and -*selves* to possessive pronouns in the 1st–3rd person plural.

Given these rules, what about the nonstandard variety makes it any less systematic or less logical than the standard variety? Nothing. Both varieties are systematic and both are logically constructed. In fact, some may argue that the nonstandard variety is more systematic than the standard variety because it has a leveled paradigm, which, consequently, would be much easier to teach to nonnative speakers of English or children learning a first language.

Overt vs. Covert Prestige and Acts of Identity

Often, speakers who do not adapt to the standard are considered "lazy," "uneducated," and "unambitious." Speakers of nonstandard varieties are told that the varieties they speak are "wrong" and "inferior" and that they must learn to speak the varieties taught in school in order to become successful. As a result, children who come from homes where nonstandard varieties are spoken are at an immediate disadvantage in school, where they are forced to make adjustments from the language of their home communities to the standard varieties of the schools (an adjustment unnecessary for children from homes where standard varieties are spoken). Some make these adjustments and become **bidialectal speakers**, having a mastery of two dialects—one a standard variety, the other a nonstandard variety. Others become only marginally fluent in the standard but gain a mastery of the nonstandard dialect. And yet others master the standard and reject the nonstandard dialect altogether.

Which adjustments are made depends on a number of different factors. One factor returns us to the notion of prestige, specifically to the distinction between **overt prestige** and **covert prestige**. Overt prestige is the type of prestige discussed in the section above entitled "Standard Dialects." This is the prestige that is attached to a particular variety by the community-at-large, which defines how people should speak in order to gain status in the wider community. But there is another type of prestige that exists among members of nonstandard speaking communities and defines how people should speak in order to be considered members of those particular communities. The desire to "belong" to a particular group often becomes the overriding factor. Thus, in many ways nonstandard varieties persist, despite their stigmatized status, because of covert prestige. In this sense, language becomes a marker of group identification.

Another way of looking at this is in terms of what researchers R. B. Le Page and Andrée Tabouret-Keller refer to as "acts of identity." In their book, *Acts of Identity: Creole-Based Approaches to Language and Ethnicity*, these two researchers investigate the relationship between language and social identity, working from the following hypothesis:

> The individual creates for himself the patterns of his linguistic behaviour so as to resemble those of the group or groups with which from time to time he wishes to be identified, or so as to be unlike those from whom he wishes to be distinguished. (181)

Their theory is that we choose to speak the way we do based on how we identify ourselves and how we want to be identified. The extent to which we are able to make certain linguistic choices as acts of identity is dependent upon the following conditions being met:

1. We can identify the groups
2. We have both adequate access to the groups and ability to analyse their behavioural patterns
3. The motivation to join the groups is sufficiently powerful, and is either reinforced or reversed by feedback from the groups
4. We have the ability to modify our behaviour. (182)

Thus to the extent that we are able to make certain linguistic choices, social identity plays a major role. Teenagers who wish to distinguish themselves from adults, members of rural communities who wish to be distinguished from members of urban communities, members of certain ethnic groups who wish to be identified as distinct from other ethnic groups, etc., may do so through language.

In this sense, language is more than just a means of communication; it is a type of "social badge." Of course, how we speak is not totally up to us; linguistic exposure is also a major factor, as discussed in the files on language acquisition. However, what this shows is that variation does not degrade a language or make it in some way imperfect. It is a natural part of every language to have different ways of expressing the same meanings. And linguistically speaking, the relationship between standard and nonstandard varieties is not one of good vs. bad, right vs. wrong. They are simply different ways of speaking, defined and determined by social structure and function.

For Discussion

1. Consider the following:

    At the turn of the century, the form *ain't* was prestigious among many upper middle class English speakers in southern England. Today, however, its use is considered nonstandard or at best appropriate only for casual conversation.

    In the United States "dropped *r*'s" in words like *car, father,* and *bark* are perceived as features of nonstandard speech. In Britain, however, "dropped *r*'s" are characteristic of Received Pronunciation and are thus considered part of the prestige dialect.

    What do these two examples tell us about standard and nonstandard features? Are they defined on linguistic or social grounds? Explain your answer.

2. What is the significance of having a standard dialect in every language?

3. How might evaluations we make about language as "good" or "bad" help to preserve and perpetuate social stereotypes and biases?

References

Benson, Larry D., ed. *The Riverside Chaucer.* 3rd edition. Boston: Houghton Mifflin.

LePage, R. B., and Andrée Tabouret-Keller. 1985. *Acts of Identity: Creole-Based Approaches to Language and Ethnicity.* Cambridge: Cambridge University Press.

Millward, C. M. 1989. *A Biography of the English Language.* Orlando, FL: Holt, Rinehart and Winston.

Moss, Beverly J., and Keith Walters. 1993. "Rethinking Diversity: Axes of Difference in the Writing Classroom." In Lee Odell, ed., *Theory and Practice in the Teaching of Writing: Rethinking the Discipline.* Carbondale: Southern Illinois University Press.

File 12.4   Language and Region

The Study of Regional Dialects

Language varieties that are defined in terms of geographical boundaries are called **regional dialects**. The study of regional dialects, known formally as **dialectology**, got its start in the United States around 1889 with the formation of the American Dialect Society (ADS). In 1929, Hans Kurath was designated director of a project aimed at compiling a comprehensive atlas known as the *Linguistic Atlas of the United States and Canada*. The first research on this project focused on the New England states, where data were collected by fieldworkers who traveled around the region eliciting linguistic forms, to determine their geographical distributions. Early methods of data collection consisted of using questionnaires to elicit and manually record items from each level of linguistic structure. These methods were later enhanced by the use of audio recording equipment and a shift to more conversational-style interviews. The initial project led by Kurath resulted in the *Linguistic Atlas of New England*, published in 1939. In 1949, Kurath summarized a field survey of the Atlantic States in *A Word Geography of the Eastern United States*. Additional volumes of this nature have since followed, covering other regions of the United States, including the Middle and South Atlantic and Gulf states.

These volumes contain linguistic maps showing the geographical distributions of various linguistic forms. The boundaries of areas where a particular linguistic form is used are marked by lines called **isoglosses**. When many isoglosses surround the same region or separate the same group of speakers, there is said to be a **bundle of isoglosses**, which indicates that the speech of that particular group is different in a number of ways from other groups around it. In this sense, a bundle of isoglosses may correspond to a dialect boundary.

This relationship between isoglosses, bundles, and boundaries is illustrated in Figures 1–3 below. In Figure 1, the solid black line is an isogloss that marks the boundaries for areas in which speakers use *pail* as opposed to *bucket* to refer to the same object.

Figure 1.   "The Isoglosses for Bucket/Pail."
Reproduced by permission from The University of Michigan Press from Carver, *American Regional Dialects* (1987), p. 11 (original source *A Word Geography of the Eastern United States* (1949), fig. 66).

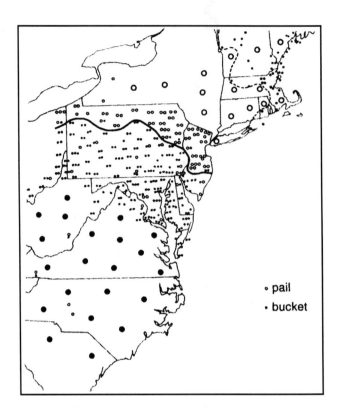

Figure 2 shows a bundle of isoglosses demarcating the area where the words *pail, whiffletree* (or *whippletree*) and *darning needle* are used most commonly. Note that this bundle includes the isogloss illustrated in Figure 1 above for *pail* and *bucket*.

Figure 2.   "Bundling of Three Northern Isoglosses."
Reproduced by permission from The University of Michigan Press from Carver, *American Regional Dialects* (1987), p. 12 (original source *A Word Geography of the Eastern United States* (1949), fig. 5a).

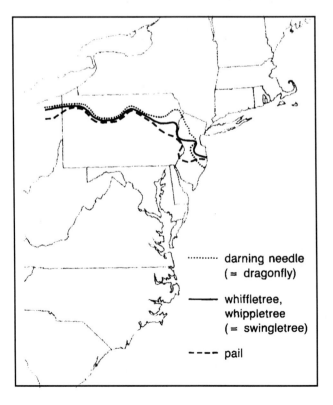

And in Figure 3, we see that the bundle of isoglosses shown in Figure 2 corresponds to the northern dialect boundary.

Figure 3. "Dialect Regions of the Eastern United States by Kurath." Reproduced by permission from The University of Michigan Press from Carver, *American Regional Dialects* (1987), p. 13 (original source *A Word Geography of the Eastern United States* (1949), fig. 3).

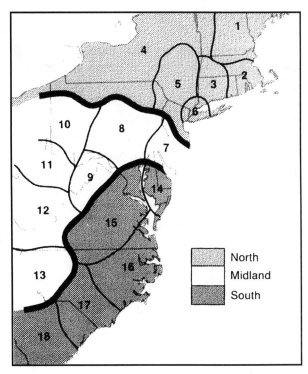

Regional Variation in the United States

The formation of U.S. regional dialects in part had its beginnings in England as speakers from various regions of England journeyed across the Atlantic and settled the Eastern seaboard of the United States. Dialectal boundaries still present today are reflected in these earliest settlement patterns. Settlers from the eastern regions of central and southern England settled in eastern New England and the Virginia Tidewater area. From northern and western parts of England came settlers to the New Jersey and Delaware areas. And Scots-Irish from Ulster settled in parts of western New England, New York, and Appalachia. In time, certain colonial cities such as Boston, Philadelphia, and Charleston acquired prestige as centers of trade and culture. As a result, the dialects spoken in these cities became prestigious as well and began to exert influence on nearby settlements.

Migration westward to a large extent reflected the settlement patterns of the Atlantic states. Yankees from western New England and upstate New York, in moving west, fanned out, settling chiefly in the Great Lakes area; settlers from the Middle Atlantic region (primarily Pennsylvania and Maryland) journeyed west to Ohio, West Virginia, and the Mississippi Valley. Influence from the southern Atlantic colonies was felt as speakers from this area settled in the Gulf states. The lines are never clearly drawn, however, because the streams of migration often mingled. Sometimes, New Englanders and speakers from the Middle Atlantic region would form compact communities outside of their usual area of settlement—e.g., the Yankee enclave of Worthington, Ohio, or the North Carolina Quaker settlement of Richmond, Indiana. The spread of migration continued to the Rocky Mountain states, essentially following previously established patterns but with greater mingling, and finally reached the West Coast, resulting in even greater crossing of dialect lines.

These patterns of Anglo settlement and migration tell only part of the story, however. Contact between English and Native American languages in the seventeenth century contributed significantly to the development of English and English dialectal regions in the United States. The later arrival of other European immigrants resulted in some very distinct regional dialect areas in the United States, including the major influences of French in New Orleans, German in southern Pennsylvania, and Spanish in the southwest. The arrival of African slaves along the southeast Atlantic seaboard contributed significantly to the development of southern varieties of English. And the later migration of African Americans from rural areas such as Mississippi, Alabama, Georgia, and South Carolina to northern cities such as Chicago, Detroit, New York, Philadelphia, and Washington, D.C., also had a major impact on the development of American English dialects.

Finally, geographic barriers also play a role in the formation of regional dialects; that is, regional dialect boundaries often coincide with natural barriers such as rivers, mountains, or swamps. Tangier Island off the coast of Virginia has preserved a very distinctive dialect owing in part to its geographic isolation, as have speakers of Gullah along the Sea Islands of South Carolina. And the distinctive dialect known as Appalachian English can be attributed at least in part to the isolation imposed by the Appalachian mountain range.

Figure 4 below shows the boundaries of the major dialect regions in the United States. The boundary lines on this map do not represent sharp demarcations but compromises between bundles of isoglosses that roughly come together along these lines.

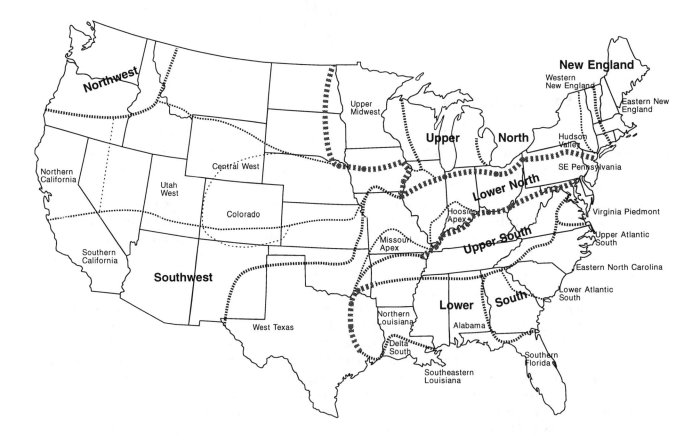

Figure 4.   "Regional Dialects in the United States." Adapted by permission from The University of Michigan Press from Carver, *American Regional Dialects* (1987), p. 248.

Appalachian English

The term Appalachian English is used primarily to refer to nonstandard varieties of English spoken in the southern Appalachian mountain range, including mid and southern regions of West Virginia, western North Carolina and Virginia, eastern Tennessee and Kentucky, northwest Arkansas and southern Missouri. Settlers to this region included English, Scots-Irish, Pennsylvania Dutch, and French Huguenots, all of whom contributed to the language varieties that developed in this area.

Because of the mountainous barriers, speakers in these areas were for many years severely restricted in their travel outside of the Appalachian region. Out of this isolation developed a culture and language that is today still noticeably distinct from those of its surrounding areas, and one that appears to have preserved several linguistic features that no longer exist in surrounding dialects. While linguists disagree on the extent to which Appalachian English can be considered a single dialect, it is clear that the varieties spoken in these areas share certain features that set them apart from other varieties of English. As a result, Appalachian English is considered to be a regional dialect of American English.

The following description (adapted from Brandes and Brewer 1977) is intended to give you a sense of some of the features that are said to be characteristic of Appalachian English, but it is not in any way an exhaustive description. For point of reference, some of the features below are discussed relative to their Standard English counterparts. However, such comparisons are not to be interpreted as instances of "correct" vs. "incorrect" but instead as a descriptive analysis of certain features in two different English varieties.

It is important to stress that not everyone who lives in the Appalachian region is a speaker of Appalachian English. As with any region, there are also standard varieties of English spoken in these areas. And consequently, many speakers who are native to the Appalachian region are either bidialectal or strictly speakers of standard varieties.

A. Phonological Features

1. **Vowel Correspondences:** The following list illustrates some of the differences in vowel distributions between Appalachian English varieties and varieties of Standard English.

	Appalachian English (AE)	*Standard English (SE)*
pinch	[pi̯nč]	[pɪnč]
ten	[tɪn]	[tɛn]
think	[θæŋk]	[θɪŋk]
rather	[ru̯ðr̩]	[ræðr̩]
push	[pṳš]	[pṳš]

2. **Metathesis:** Instances of **metathesis** (i.e., sound reversals) are found in AE varieties as in other varieties of English.

asked	[ækst]
prevail	[pʌrvel]
album	[æbləm]

3. **Syllable-initial stress**: AE places primary stress (´) on the first syllable of certain words where SE varieties place the primary stress elsewhere.

	Appalachian English (AE)	*Standard English (SE)*
Detroit	Détroit	Detróit
cigar	cígar	cigár
directly	dírectly	diréctly
November	Nóvember	Novémber

B. Morphological Features

1. **a-prefix**: Appalachian English has preserved the prefix *a-* (used commonly in the twelfth to seventeenth centuries) in certain verbal constructions.

   He come a-running
   I knew he was a-telling the truth
   I was a-washing one day

2. **Retention of irregular verb conjugations**: AE has preserved certain irregular verb conjugations in constructing the past tense where SE varieties now use the regular past tense suffix *-ed*.

Present Tense	*AE Past Tense*	*SE Past Tense*
climb	*clumb*	*climbed*
heat	*het*	*heated*
rake	*ruck*	*raked*
drag	*drug*	*dragged*

C. Syntactic Features

1. Double modals

   He <u>musta didn't</u> hear me.
   I <u>might could</u> make one up.
   I <u>useta couldn't</u> count.

2. Multiple negation

   He <u>ain't never</u> done <u>no</u> work to speak of.
   There <u>ain't never none</u> on that shelf.
   I <u>can't hardly</u> read it.

References

Brandes, Paul D., and Jeutonne Brewer. 1977. *Dialect Clash in America: Issues and Answers.* Metuchen, NJ : Scarecrow Press.

Carver, Craig M. 1989. *American Regional Dialects: A Word Geography.* Ann Arbor: University of Michigan Press.

Kurath, Hans. 1949. *A Word Geography of the Eastern United States.* Ann Arbor: University of Michigan Press.

Wolfram, Walt. 1991. *Dialects and American English.* Englewood Cliffs, NJ: Prentice Hall.

File 12.5 Language and Ethnicity: The Case of African-American English

Interest in African-American English (AAE) was rekindled in December 1996 following an announcement by the Oakland, California, school board that they planned to implement instructional methods based on a recognition and respect for "Ebonics" (their label for AAE). The announcement sparked a national debate that quickly moved beyond discussion of the proposal's intent—which was to utilize knowledge of African-American English to aid students in their acquisition of Standard American English—and into angry warnings against legitimizing "broken English" and ill-conceived parodies of the imagined detrimental effects of the word *be* and other stereotyped features of AAE.

Neither the proposal nor the debate is new. In 1977 a lawsuit brought by African-American parents against the school board in Ann Arbor, Michigan, resulted in the implementation of a similar measure to provide teachers with a background in what was then called Black English, so as to help them improve their ability to teach Standard American English. That proposal, too, was met with skepticism and outrage by blacks and non-blacks alike.

There are at least two questions raised by these debates:

1. Are AAE varieties systematic and rule-governed just like all other language varieties?
2. Can an understanding and appreciation for AAE varieties help students whose home language is AAE acquire Standard American English?

The answer to the first question is an unqualified *yes*. Some of the systematic features of AAE will be illustrated later in this file. The answer to the second question is also *yes*, although we will not explore the pedagogical issues it raises here.

There are also larger questions of interest to students of language and society. How does ethnicity shape one's language? What ethnic varieties exist in the United States?

While the list of varieties of English that have become associated with particular ethnic groups in the United States (such as Navajo English, Appalachian English, or Puerto Rican English) is extensive and certainly growing, it is AAE that has been of primary interest to linguists for a number of years. The unique experience of African Americans in the United States is reflected in the development of a language that is equally unique in many ways.

> The Afro-American experience in the USA has been different from that of any other group, and the language situation of Black Americans is correspondingly different. Unlike other groups who came to America, almost all Africans were brought over as slaves, and up until the Emancipation Proclamation, the overwhelming majority of Blacks in the USA were still slaves. During the period of slavery, as well as in the modern period, the patterns of communication between Blacks and other Americans reflected the social distance between them. (Whatley 1981: 92)

This file provides an introduction to some of the major issues concerning African-American English, as one example of the interrelationship of language variation and ethnicity.

African-American English

African-American English (AAE) is a cover term used by linguists to refer to a continuum of varieties whose features (depending on which end of the continuum you consider) may be very similar or very different from those of Standard American English (SAE). The name African-American English is used in acknowledgment of the fact that these varieties are spoken primarily by and among African Americans. However, it is very important to note that not all African Americans are speakers of African-American English and not only African Americans speak African-American English. Remember from the files on child language acquisition that the language a person speaks is not in any way predestined but is instead determined by the language she or he is exposed to. So just as someone born in Boston does not automatically become a speaker of Bostonian English, an African American is not predestined to become a speaker of AAE. And similarly, a member of a different ethnic group who is exposed to AAE as her or his first language will likely become a speaker of AAE.

While these varieties are defined in terms of ethnicity, other factors such as age, socioeconomic status, gender, and style influence African-American English varieties, as they do other language varieties. A speaker of African-American English who is eighty years old will speak differently from a thirteen-year-old AAE speaker. Male AAE speakers will likely have different features in their speech than female AAE speakers. AAE speakers from New York will speak differently from AAE speakers from Alabama. And it is likely that you will observe different features in the speech of middle-class AAE speakers compared to working-class AAE speakers. Furthermore, no individual speaker of AAE speaks the same way all the time. Rather, one varies her or his speech depending on style and context.

The Study of AAE

Linguists' interest in AAE may have first been sparked by a desire to reeducate society about the nature of AAE and other nonstandard varieties of English that have been stigmatized as "bad English" or "broken English." Prior to linguistic research on AAE, some laypeople made attempts to link the characteristic (often stereotypical) speech of African Americans to certain physical features or to some sort of "linguistic deprivation" that caused various impediments in the production of the sounds and grammatical features of Standard English. However, such ridiculous notions were easily dismissed by examples of African Americans who grew up with no exposure to AAE and consequently were not AAE speakers, as well as examples of members of other ethnic groups who grew up in AAE–speaking environments and were speakers of AAE.

By researching varieties of African-American English, linguists are able to prove that AAE is not a collection of random deviations from Standard English, as many have said it is. Instead it is both systematic and rule-governed, just like all language varieties, standard or nonstandard.

The Origin of AAE

The origin of African-American English has been and, to some extent still is, an issue of great debate among sociolinguists. There are two main theories:

1. *Dialectologist View:* AAE traces its roots back to the varieties of English spoken in the British Isles, just like other regional varieties of American English.

2. *Creolist View:* AAE developed out of a creole language used during the times of slavery, which ultimately traces its origins back to the various West African languages of the slaves who were transported to the New World.

These two theories are described in more detail below.

The Dialectologist View

Beginning around the 1920s and continuing into the 1940s, dialectologists presented the first scholarly analyses of African-American English, arguing that AAE should be analyzed in terms of regional differences just like any other variety of English. Essentially, it was believed that blacks spoke the language of the whites with whom they shared comparable socioeconomic and regional backgrounds. AAE was believed to have originated as a southern variety of English, which spread northward during the 1920s migration of blacks out of the South and into northern cities, because of the decline of the cotton industry and the growing job opportunities in the industrial North. Varieties of southern English spoken by African Americans in areas such as Mississippi, Alabama, Georgia, and South Carolina were thus spread northward into Chicago, Detroit, New York, Philadelphia, and Washington, D.C. This migration was said to account for the fact that, unlike other regional varieties of English, certain features of AAE exhibited a sort of "supraregional homogeneity."

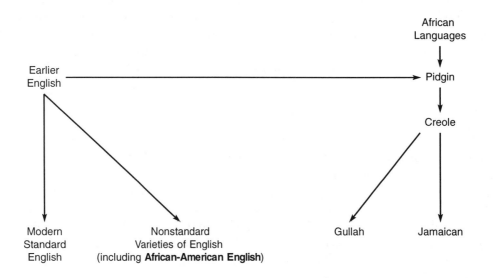

Figure 1.   "The Dialectologist Hypothesis." Adapted by permission of Holt, Rinehart, and Winston, Inc., from Burling, *English in Black and White* (1973), p. 114.

The Creolist View

The dialectologist view was later challenged by creolists, who argued that AAE derived from creole and ultimately West African origins. This theory traced AAE origins back to the times of the slave trade when West Africans from regions such as Sierra Leone, Nigeria, Ghana, and the Ivory Coast were forced together on slave ships with no common language among them. They were exposed to many different African languages such as Hausa, Wolof, Bulu, and Twi, as well as the English of the ship's sailors. And in most instances, slaves were isolated from speakers of their own native languages in order to avoid possible uprisings. As a result, slaves were forced to develop some common form of communication.

Out of this language contact developed a **pidgin language**—a speech system that is formed to provide a means of communication between people who have no common language. As the slaves formed communities on the slave plantations of the southeast Atlantic seaboard, this pidgin became the primary means of communication for many slaves. When a pidgin becomes the principal language of a speech community, it is known as a **creole language.** According to creolists, increased contact between speakers of this creole and speakers of other English varieties resulted in the **decreolization** of this language, which has led to the development of present-day AAE.

For proof of this theory, creolists analyze features found in AAE that resemble English-based creoles of the Caribbean such as Jamaican Creole or creoles of Africa such as Krio (spoken along the coast of West Africa in Sierra Leone). The only surviving English-based creole in the United States is Gullah, which is spoken primarily in the southeastern regions of South Carolina. Many creolists today consider Gullah to be a direct link to the origins of AAE, believing it to resemble the creole ancestor of AAE.

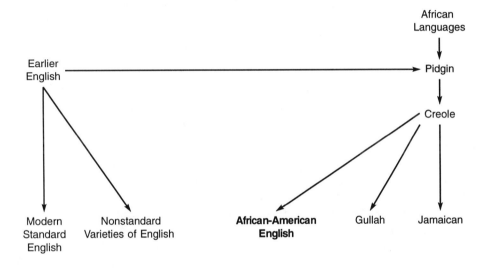

Figure 2.   "The Creolist Hypothesis." Adapted by permission of Holt, Rinehart, and Winston, Inc., from Burling, *English in Black and White* (1973), p. 115.

A Unified View

For many years, sociolinguists were radically divided between these two opposing theories concerning AAE's origins. Today it is still an issue that has not been fully resolved. However, it appears that sociolinguists are moving toward an understanding of AAE that accepts some reasoning from both points of view. In other words, the dialectologist and creolist positions may not be mutually exclusive but may instead both contribute to our understanding of the origins, history, and development of African-American English in the United States.

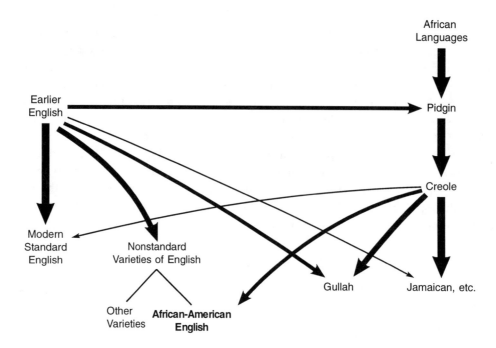

Figure 3.   "A Unified Approach." Adapted by permission of Holt, Rinehart, and Winston, Inc., from Burling, *English in Black and White* (1973), p. 122.

Structural Features of AAE

To illustrate the systematic nature of AAE as a rule-governed system, the following features are presented as characteristic of AAE varieties. However, this list is not in any way comprehensive. Keep in mind that not all varieties of AAE or even all speakers of AAE will exhibit all of these features at all times. For point of reference, many of the features or processes presented below are discussed in relation to their SAE counterparts, not as examples of "right" vs. "wrong" but as descriptive comparisons of the two systems.

1. Monophthongization

In AAE there is a phonological process by which diphthongs get reduced to monophthongs word-finally or before voiced consonants.

now	[na]
side	[sad]
time	[tʰam]

Monophthongization before voiceless consonants is found much less frequently in AAE, although it may be characteristic of some southern varieties.

kite	[kʰayt] or [kʰat]
like	[layk] or [lak]

2. Word-Final Consonant Cluster Reduction

In AAE there is a process of word-final consonant cluster reduction when the following word begins with a consonant. This same process is found in varieties of SAE.

| *cold cuts* | [kʰol kʰəts] |
| *best kind* | [bɛs kʰaynd] |

AAE differs from SAE here, however, in that it is also possible to reduce word-final consonant clusters when the following word begins with a vowel.

| *cold eggs* | [kʰol ɛgz] |
| *best apple* | [bɛs æpl̩] |

In English, the past tense is formed by the addition of a suffix, [t], [d], or [əd], depending on the final sound of the verb base. If the base ends in a consonant, the addition of the past tense suffix may create a consonant cluster. Word-final consonant clusters that are created by the addition of the past tense suffix are also subject to deletion in AAE, as illustrated below:

burned my hand	[br̩n may hæn]
burned up	[br̩n ʌp]
messed up	[mɛs ʌp]

The fact that word-final past tense suffixes can be deleted in these environments may give AAE the appearance of lacking a past tense suffix. However, past tense suffixes that do not form consonant clusters are not deleted by this phonological process.

| *hated* | [hetɛd] |
| *shouted* | [šawtɛd] |

3. Absence of 3rd Singular -s

In many AAE varieties, there is an absence of the 3rd singular suffix -s, as shown in the following sentences:

> He <u>need</u> to get a book from the shelf.
> She <u>want</u> us to pass the papers to the front.

4. Multiple Negation

In SAE a sentence such as (a) below can be negated as either (b) or (c).

> (a) I had some lunch.
> (b) I didn't have any lunch.
> (c) I had no lunch.

While sentences (b) and (c) may not be exact equivalents stylistically, they have the same basic meaning. The main point is that in SAE this sentence is negated by performing one of these two operations, but not both. In AAE on the other hand, it is possible to do both in the same sentence. The result is **multiple negation**, as in (d):

> (d) I didn't have no lunch.

In fact in AAE this operation may be performed any number of times in one sentence.

> (e) I don't never have no lunch.

5. *Habitual* be

Where SAE varieties use adverbials such as *always* or *usually* to express habituality, AAE can employ habitual *be*.

SAE	AAE
The coffee is always cold.	*The coffee always be cold.*
Sometimes she is angry.	*Sometimes she be angry.*
She is late everyday.	*She be late everyday.*

The use of uninflected *be* in the AAE sentences above indicates that a state or activity is habitual or repeatable. Thus, *The coffee be cold* means that this is a recurring property of the coffee, as opposed to *The coffee is cold,* which means that the coffee has the property of being cold at that particular moment. The sentence *The coffee be cold right now* is, therefore, ungrammatical in AAE since *be* indicates habituality, while *right now* indicates a punctual, momentary state.

Notice in SAE that if the adverbial is missing the sentence generally loses its habitual interpretation. Compare the following two sentences:

The coffee is always cold. (habitual state)
The coffee is cold. (momentary state)

In AAE, however, uninflected *be* is itself sufficient for marking habituality, as in *The coffee be cold* (=*The coffee is always cold*).

References

Burling, Robbins. 1973. *English in Black and White*. Orlando, FL: Holt, Rinehart and Winston.

McCrum, Robert,William Cran, and Robert MacNeil. 1986. *The Story of English*. New York, NY: Viking Penguin.

Pullum, Geoffrey K. 1997. "Language That Dare Not Speak Its Name." *Nature*, March 27.

Rickford, John R. 1997. "Suite for Ebony *and* Phonics." *Discover*, December, 82–87.

Whatley, Elizabeth. 1981. "Language Among Black Americans." *Language in the USA*. Cambridge: Cambridge University Press, 92–107.

File 12.6

Language and Gender

Research in language and gender seeks to elucidate the role of language in defining, constructing, and reproducing gendered identities, as well as the role of gender in the perception and production of language. Our framework for approaching these questions has shifted from anatomically and biologically based ideas about sex to more fluid notions about psychosocially and culturally defined gender identities (Giddens 1989:58). Thus, we have also come to understand gender not so much as a dichotomous category, with all people being defined as males on the one hand or females on the other, but instead as a *practice*. Because we will henceforth be talking about cultural patterns and not about biological questions, we will be using the term *gender*, not *sex*, in the rest of this file.

Gender then is not a system for sorting people and making generalizations based on the classification "men do X," or "women do Y." Instead, gender can be thought of a set of ongoing behaviors, so that in a sense we are always already *doing gender*. To quote West and Zimmerman, "'Doing gender' involves a complex of socially guided perceptual, interactional, and micropolitical activities that cast particular pursuits as expressions of masculine and feminine natures" (1991:13–14).

The linking of cultural norms for behavior—including linguistic behavior—with sex is arbitrary. This is evidenced by the fact that stereotypes involving language use (i.e., talkativeness, loudness, silence) are, in different cultures, associated with different genders. For instance, in Malagasy culture (located on Madagascar and other islands in the Indian Ocean), indirect, deferential speech is valued. Malagasy men are often silent in public confrontations, while Malagasy women express anger and criticism through direct, confrontational speech, often to the benefit of their husbands or other male family members (Keenan 1974:137–39). But there is clearly no direct link between silence and maleness in all cultures. Many western cultures value direct, public speech. A number of studies of conversation (see Coates 1993:115 for a brief overview) have shown that in western societies public speech tends to be dominated by men. Although the speech behaviors typical of Malagasy males and females are very different from those of much of western society, note that in both instances it is the male norms that are more highly valued by the community.

These examples raise the question of the role of *power* in shaping gendered norms for language use, specifically, the asymmetrical allocation of power through which men generally occupy a more powerful position than women. Another factor that researchers have explored in trying to explain language variation across genders is that of *subcultural differences* thought to exist between women and men. We will explore both of these factors in more detail later.

The field of language and gender as a whole has primarily employed two methodologies of linguistic inquiry: investigation of phonetic and morphosyntactic variation on the one hand, and discourse/conversation analysis (DA/CA) on the other. We will begin our discussion with the variationist tradition, and continue with studies of DA/CA later in the file.

Phonetic and Morphosyntactic Variation

As sociolinguistic inquiry began in earnest in the 1960s and 1970s, many researchers noted that the use of particular linguistic forms in a given speech community correlated not only with measures of socioeconomic status, age, and ethnicity but also with gender. For example, a study in Norwich, England (Trudgill 1974), showed that members of the middle class and women were more likely to use standard verb forms like *running* (with word-final [ɪŋ]), as opposed to nonstandard forms like *runnin'* (with word-final [ən]). This is not to say that the use of forms like *running* was limited only to women, or only to the middle class, but rather that Norwich women, on average, used these forms more frequently than men. This difference in usage of [ɪŋ] vs. [ən] reveals a gendered pattern of phonetic realizations of the same phoneme (see Figure 1).

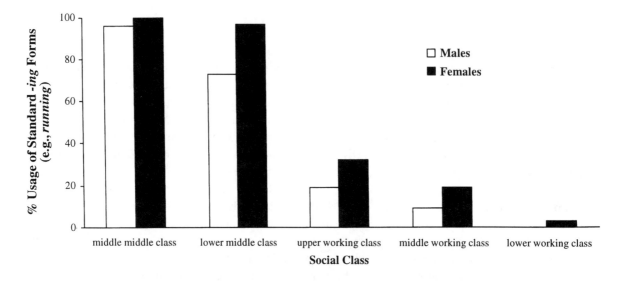

Figure 1.   % (ɪŋ) usage in formal speech in Norwich by social class and gender (based on Trudgill 1974, p. 94).

A similar pattern occurred in the speech of working-class adolescents in Sydney, Australia. Boys were more likely than girls to use nonstandard syntactic features such as multiple negation, e.g., *they don't say nothing,* and nonstandard past tense forms, e.g., *he woke up an' seen something* (Eisikovits 1988:37–40).

Not only did these earliest studies indicate that women used more prestige variants (i.e., standard variants) than men, but in addition, it appeared that listeners actually expected female speech to be more like that of the middle class and male speech to be more like that of the working class. John Edwards (1979) demonstrated this in a study conducted in Dublin, Ireland, in which adults were asked to listen to recordings of preadolescent children, some of whom were from working-class families and some of whom were from middle-class families. The adults were then asked to identify the sex of each child. The adults had few problems identifying the working-class boys as boys and the middle-class girls as girls, but they did much worse identifying the middle-class boys and the working-class girls, more than doubling their number of errors. To these listeners, the speech of middle-class boys was perceived as girl-like, and the speech of working-class girls was perceived as boy-like.

These and other studies have reported similar findings of phonetic and morphosyntactic variation carried out mainly in European and Euro-American contexts: the generalization would appear to be that women are more likely to use standard, prestige linguistic forms than are men of the same social class. This was the first puzzle confronting the newly emerging field of language and gender: how do we explain women's lead in the use of prestige forms, as well as male use of nonstandard, stigmatized variants? Even if one speculated that women were somehow more sensitive to prestige norms, why would they act on this in the first place? Three kinds of explanations have been offered to account for this phenomenon: (1) so-called linguistic insecurity, (2) women's role in child rearing, and (3) labor market dynamics. We will explore the first two explanations here and look at the third in the following section.

The "linguistic insecurity" explanation claimed that women imitate the prestigious and more standardized language of the social classes immediately above their own in order to become more prestigious and powerful themselves. This explanation was initially advanced as a way of explaining not only women's usage patterns but also the usage patterns in these same studies of the lower middle class, which "hypercorrected" its language, emulating linguistic features (and actually overshooting the targets) of the middle class in order to gain social prestige (Labov 1966, Trudgill 1972). In this way the language of men was linked to a working-class orientation seeking covert prestige and local affiliation, while the language of women, reaching upward across sociolinguistic class strata, was held to reflect their social and linguistic insecurity. One problem with this account is that it takes our social stereotypes and reifies them into scientific explanation. We might easily understand the situation as working in the opposite direction, with local, vernacular solidarity and pressure to sound like "one of the guys" as a kind of linguistic insecurity.

A related explanation emphasized women's role in child rearing. Since in most societies women are responsible for taking care of children, researchers theorized that women would try to improve their children's prospects by exposing them to the most prestigious language possible, and that children would in turn perceive this input as the normal distribution for their social class and carry those changes further. Each succeeding generation of girls would co-opt higher and higher strata of linguistic behavior, and thus would slowly but surely propel language change (Labov 1990). This explanation has difficulty accounting for the speech of the many women who are not involved in or oriented toward child rearing in any significant way.

Neither of the above explanations is wholly satisfactory. One reason is that they both try to forge a simple link between language use and gender across a wide variety of situations, while ignoring the possibility that other social factors, such as ethnic identity and workplace interactions, might play a crucial role in shaping the language use of women and men in a given speech community. Some researchers have responded to this criticism by conducting detailed ethnographic studies of women and/or men in specific communities. Their results force us to question the validity of our earlier generalizations that women conform to standard norms, and that men conform to vernacular norms.

Two Ethnographic Studies

Labor Market Dynamics in a South Carolina Community

One such study was undertaken by Patricia Nichols (1983) in an African-American community in Georgetown County, South Carolina, on the Atlantic coast. Nichols spent several months on an island community volunteering as a teacher, an experience that allowed her to come to a detailed understanding of the lives of its 200 residents. She describes the language shared by this community as "a speech continuum which ranges from an English creole known as *Gullah* or *Geechee* on the one end, to a variety of Black English [AAVE] in the center, to a regionally standard variety of English at the other end" (p. 56). Of the three varieties on the continuum, the most local and least prestigious variety, Gullah, is being used less as speakers favor the other two.

Nichols investigated how frequently speakers incorporated the following Gullah forms in their speech (pp. 59–60):

- the pronoun *ee*, e.g., *Miss Hassell had—ee had all kinds of flowers.*
- the word *fuh* used to mean 'to', e.g., *I come fuh get my coat.*
- the preposition *to* used to mean 'at', e.g., *Can we stay to the table?*

She discovered that older women and men used more Gullah forms generally, but among the younger women and men there was a sharp difference. Beginning at about age ten, males used much more Gullah than females. Clearly it is not possible to generalize that women on the island use more standard language forms than men, because it is only the younger women who do so.

An analysis of the social networks of the island residents helps to explain their linguistic behavior. The men, both young and old, generally take construction jobs, which require little education but pay well. On the job the men interact a great deal with each other—their coworkers are their friends, family, and neighbors—and this reinforces both Gullah language norms and their group identity as Gullah speakers. Older women have primarily worked as farm day laborers or maids, jobs in which interaction is also primarily with coworkers. The younger women, on the other hand, are taking up less lucrative, service-related jobs associated with the tourist industry. As sales clerks, mail carriers, and elementary school teachers, young women need to have a higher level of education, and they have a great deal of interaction with speakers of standard English.

Nichols's study makes it clear that we cannot isolate gender as the only factor leading to differences in standard language use. In Georgetown County, it is also the economic opportunities afforded women and men that shape their language usage.

Jocks and Burnouts in Suburban Detroit

Penny Eckert and Sally McConnell-Ginet (1995) studied the interaction between gender and peer group identity in a suburban Detroit high school. They studied two groups, the "jocks" and the "burnouts." Jocks included students who gained power and status through school-sponsored activities. As might be guessed, boy jocks typically attained status through athletic achievement, although excellence in academics and other areas was also significant (e.g., one could be a "choir jock"). Status as a girl jock depended primarily on the subjective notions of popularity and personality. Burnouts were oriented toward the local community and toward work and entertainment in the "real world" rather than at school. For boy burnouts, the quality of "toughness" was valued and established through use of controlled substances, encounters with the law, and physical fights. Status as a girl burnout involved cultivation of verbal and emotional, but not physical, toughness.

Eckert and McConnell-Ginet studied two phonological changes in the vowel systems of these high school students. The innovations, part of a larger set of changes currently taking place in the speech of Euro-Americans in Detroit and other cities in the northern United States, are exemplified in the pronunciation of the word *fun* as *fawn* [fɔn], and the word *file* as *foil* [foyl] (ibid., p. 500). Both of these changes correlated most strongly with burnouts and with females. It is impossible to say that the use of one of these innovative forms, as in *we'd . . . pull an all-noiter*, "means" only female-ness—or only burnout-ness—and that speakers then use it as a tool to convey that attribute. Again, we cannot isolate gender as a factor in structuring language use, because the categories female and burnout are both being constructed in part by the use of these vowel changes (p. 503).

It is particularly interesting to note that the linguistic differences between boys belonging to the two peer groups were less than the differences between girls. That is, girl jocks and girl burnouts diverged more sharply from each other in their speech than boy jocks did from boy burnouts. This reflects the fact that, in this community, boys are able to attain social status via personal (often physical) achievement, whereas girls, especially girl jocks, are denied equivalent status through achievement and must instead develop associations with the "right" people (popularity). So there are fewer social ramifications for a jock boy who says *we had fawn* than there are for a jock girl who sounds "like a burnout" (pp. 496, 499).

Ethnographic studies like Eckert and McConnell-Ginet's and Nichols's show us that in order to understand gender-correlated differences in phonetics and morphosyntax we cannot isolate gender from other social attributes. The behaviors—including language—"that help constitute a particular person as a woman may, for example, also help constitute her as 'African-American' and 'middle-class' and 'a mother' and 'a sister' and 'a neighbor' and so on" (Eckert and McConnell-Ginet 1992:463).

Studies in Discourse Analysis and Conversation Analysis

Robin Lakoff's 1975 book, *Language and a Woman's Place,* has served as the catalyst for a great deal of research in language and gender, much of which falls in the domain of discourse analysis and conversation analysis (DA/CA). In her book, Lakoff contended that women are denied means of strong self-expression. On the one hand, women are ridiculed if they don't "talk like a lady," but on the other hand, "women's language" is interpreted as weak and concerned with the trivial.

Among the features Lakoff described as "women's language" are the use of precise color terms (e.g., *mauve* instead of *purple*), weak expletives (e.g., *oh dear* vs. *shit*), "empty" adjectives (e.g., *darling, adorable*), the use of tag questions (e.g., *it's late, isn't it?*), and the use of polite speech (e.g., *would you please close the door?* vs. *close the door*). The expression of power and access to power are central to this conception of gender-differentiated language use.

Language and Power

Lakoff did not, however, gather quantitative data to support her claims. As a result, language and gender research through much of the 1970s and 1980s was bent on substantiating or refuting her hypotheses. In the wake of this research, most of Lakoff's specific claims about "women's language" have been modified or discarded. Many studies have shown, for example, that men and women both make frequent use of tag questions, though not necessarily the same kind of tag questions (see Cameron et al. 1989 for an overview). It is clear that Lakoff's interpretation of tag questions was simplistic: not all tag questions communicate uncertainty or inability to express oneself strongly. Some tag questions simply encourage further conversation (e.g., *nice day, isn't it?*), while others can be quite powerful and even threatening (e.g., prosecutor to defendant: *You shot Chris, didn't you?*).

Similar questions have been raised with regard to other DA/CA studies on, e.g., the amount of interruptions in conversation. Some studies have suggested that in cross-sex conversations men interrupt women more frequently than women interrupt men. However, the majority of studies have found no significant difference between genders in the number of interruptions (James and Clark 1992:287). Nevertheless, the crucial difficulty in studying interruptions is determining when they occur and what they mean. Like tag questions, interruptions can have several functions. Not all interruptions are attempts to dominate the floor of discussion. For example, some interruptions are simply overlaps in speakers' turns and some interruptions are perceived by both speaker and interrupter to be collaborative and supportive of the conversation. Since there is no precise way to determine when an interruption is, in fact, a violation of a speaker's turn, it is difficult to reach any conclusions about this particular potential manifestation of power in conversational interaction.

But despite the difficulty in designing effective research and despite the lack of evidence corroborating her specific claims, Lakoff's general thesis that linguistic differences stem from and reproduce power differences has been supported by a steady stream of research in DA/CA. One such study has demonstrated that silence can be interpreted as a measure of power in conversation. In an analysis of the October 1991 congressional hearings of Supreme Court nominee Clarence Thomas, Mendoza-Denton (1995) paid special attention to the contexts in which silence was used in the testimony of Thomas and Anita Hill, who accused Thomas of sexual harassment. The average length of the silent gaps following statements by Thomas was 33% longer than the average length of the silent gaps following statements by Hill. According to Mendoza-Denton, this difference produced the effect of giving more weight and credibility to Thomas's statements.

Other studies have shown that American men tend to be more likely to give direct commands, while American women are more likely to ask questions to further a conversation, give verbal responses to their interlocutor's statements, and give compliments. The combination of these behaviors appears to place men in the position of controlling conversation, while women do the "interactional housework" to keep conversation going (see Coates 1993:114-29 for an overview).

William O'Barr and Bowman Atkins's (1980) study of speech in a North Carolina courtroom gives further support to the view that so-called women's language is equated with relative powerlessness. They observed the use of hedges (e.g., *It's sort of hot; I'd kind of like to go*), polite speech, and other putative features of "women's language" and found that their use did not correlate most strongly with women but rather with people who had relatively little power in the courtroom—people of low socioeconomic status or people with no previous courtroom experience, whether male or female. That this "powerless language" also appears to be linked, though less directly, to women's usage suggests a difference in power between men and women.

Language and Cultural Difference

Some researchers have suggested that power inequities cannot account for all gender-related differences in speech. Daniel Maltz and Ruth Borker (1982) note that some difficulties in cross-sex communication parallel difficulties in cross-cultural communication. The basic idea is that interlocutors have good intentions but do not always operate on the same assumptions. As an example, they cite the use of minimal responses (e.g., *mmhmm, yes*, etc., in response to an interlocutor's statement), which women generally use more than men. Women, they claim, interpret minimal responses as an indication that the interlocutor is listening. Men, on the other hand, interpret them as an indication of agreement. The result is an unintentional misunderstanding in which women think men aren't listening and men think women are agreeing with everything they say.

Linguist Deborah Tannen has popularized the different-subcultures approach in several best-selling books. She accounts for stereotypical cross-sex communication scenarios—e.g., the man who is lost but won't ask for directions; the woman who wants to talk about, but not solve, her problems—by characterizing American male culture as oriented toward independence and speech as report-giving, while characterizing female culture in America as oriented toward intimacy and speech as rapport-building.

Maltz and Borker propose that we acquire these different assumptions about language use as school-age children, roughly ages 5–15, when interactions are focused in same-sex peer groups. In these play groups, gender differences are exaggerated. Girls learn to use language to establish emotional intimacy, and boys learn to use language to establish status in a social hierarchy. There are other ways, however, in which girls and boys might acquire gender-differentiated language. They can be told explicitly how to speak (e.g., *girls don't say that!*), they can observe adults interacting with each other, they can observe how adults talk to girls and boys differently (e.g., adults tend to interrupt girls more), and they can observe how adults respond differently to boys and girls (e.g., assertive boys tend to receive positive responses).

One problem with the different-subcultures approach is that it does not allow for the possibility that individuals might, in fact, be aware of communicative behaviors and interpretations other than their own, and that they might then choose to use those behaviors and interpretations in certain settings. For example, a man involved in a romantic relationship may "sweet talk" his partner, that is, he may employ expressive, "rapport-building" conversational strategies such as minimal responses and frequent questions. By doing so he demonstrates competency in the linguistic behavior of the so-called women's subculture, when it is to his advantage to do so (Freed 1992:149, Eckert and McConnell-Ginet 1992:466–67). Another problem is that power differences, in fact, do exist between men and women (and between other social groups as well), and often cultural differences are summoned to maintain these power differences. For example, American women tend to use more dynamic intonation patterns than men, a difference that may be linked to their respective "subcultures." However, when this difference is interpreted to mean that a woman is "emotional" and thus, e.g., not capable of rational leadership, we have entered into the arena of power politics.

Current Directions in Language and Gender Research

It is difficult to precisely determine the roles of power and (sub)cultural difference in shaping the language of women and men. Eckert and McConnell-Ginet (1992) suggest that limiting the scope of inquiry to just these two factors will prove unfruitful. They propose centering language and gender research on *communities of practice*. By their definition, a community of practice is "an aggregate of people who come together around mutual engagement in an endeavor" (p. 464). So a community of practice may be a softball team, a family sharing a meal, participants in a linguistics classroom, an election campaign team, the office staff in a workplace, and so on. An individual belongs to any number of overlapping communities of practice, and in each of them she or he will construct a gendered identity differently. For example, an outspoken leader of the local labor union may be quite docile as a student in night school. Morgan's (1996) analysis of conversational indirectness as a "resource for mediating and realigning social relationships" (p. 405) among African-American women in the context of a family visit is another example of this microcommunity approach. Focusing on local communities of practice may allow researchers to better understand the complex nature of gender as it is continually being redefined by individual and group behaviors. This, in turn, can enlighten our understanding of the role of gender in the construction of language in the community and the role of language in the construction of gender in the community.

References

Cameron, Deborah, Fiona McAlinden, and Kathy O'Leary. 1989. "Lakoff in context: The social and linguistic functions of tag questions." Pp. 74–93 in Jennifer Coates and Deborah Cameron, eds., *Women in Their Speech Communities: New Perspectives on Language and Sex*. New York: Longman.

Coates, Jennifer. 1993. *Women, Men and Language*. New York: Longman.

Eckert, Penelope, and Sally McConnell-Ginet. 1992. "Think practically and look locally: Language and gender as community based practice." *Annual Review of Anthropology* 21:461–90.

———. 1995. "Constructing meaning, constructing selves." Pp. 469–507 in Kira Hall and Mary Bucholtz, eds., *Gender Articulated: Language and the Socially Constructed Self*. New York: Routledge.

Edwards, John R. 1979. *Language and Disadvantage*. London: Edward Arnold.

Eisikovits, Edina. 1988. "Girl-talk/boy-talk: Sex differences in adolescent speech." Pp. 35–54 in Peter Collins and David Blair, eds., *Australian English*. St. Lucia: University of Queensland Press.

Freed, Alice. 1992. "We understand perfectly: A critique of Tannen's view of cross-sex communication." Pp. 144–52 in Kira Hall, Mary Bucholtz, and Birch Moonwomon, eds., *Locating Power: Proceedings of the 2nd Berkeley Women and Language Conference*. Vol. 1. Berkeley: Berkeley Women and Language Group.

Giddens, Anthony. 1989. *Sociology*. Cambridge: Polity.

James, Deborah, and Sandra Clarke. 1992. "Interruptions, gender, and power: A critical review of the literature." Pp. 286–99 in Kira Hall, Mary Bucholtz, and Birch Moonwomon, eds., *Locating Power: Proceedings of the 2nd Berkeley Women and Language Conference*. Vol. 1. Berkeley: Berkeley Women and Language Group.

Keenan, Elinor. 1974. "Norm-makers and norm-breakers: Uses of speech by men and women in a Malagasy community." Pp. 125–43 in R. Bauman and J. Sherzer, eds., *Explorations in the Ethnography of Speaking*. New York: Cambridge University Press.

Labov, William. 1966. *The Social Stratification of English in New York City*. Washington D.C.: Center for Applied Linguistics.

———. 1990. "The intersection of sex and social class in the course of linguistic change." *Language Variation and Change* 2:205–54.

Lakoff, Robin. 1975. *Language and a Woman's Place.* New York: Harper & Row.

Maltz, Daniel N., and Ruth A. Borker. 1982. "A cultural approach to male-female miscommunication." Pp. 195–216 in John Gumperz, ed., *Language and Social Identity.* Cambridge: Cambridge University Press.

Mendoza-Denton, Norma. 1995. "Pregnant pauses: Silence and authority in the Anita Hill–Clarence Thomas hearings." Pp. 51–66 in Kira Hall and Mary Bucholtz, eds., *Gender Articulated: Language and the Socially Constructed Self.* New York: Routledge.

Morgan, Marcyliena. 1996. "Conversational signifying: Grammar and indirectness among African American women." Pp. 405–34 in Elinor Ochs, Emanuel A. Schegloff, and Sandra Thompson, eds., *Interaction and Grammar.* New York: Cambridge University Press.

Nichols, Patricia. 1983. "Linguistic options and choices for black women in the rural south." Pp. 54–68 in Barrie Thorne, Cheris Kramarae, and Nancy Henley, eds., *Language, Gender and Society.* Rowley, MA: Newbury House.

O'Barr, William, and Bowman Atkins. 1980. "'Women's language' or 'powerless language'?" Pp. 93–110 in Sally McConnell-Ginet, Ruth Borker, and Nelly Furman, eds., *Women and Language in Literature and Society.* New York: Praeger.

Tannen, Deborah. 1991. *You Just Don't Understand: Women and Men in Conversation.* London: Virago.

Trudgill, Peter. 1972. "Sex, covert prestige and linguistic change in the urban British English of Norwich." *Language in Society* 1:179–95.

———. 1974. *The Social Differentiation of English in Norwich.* Cambridge: Cambridge University Press.

West, Candance, and Don Zimmerman. 1991. "Doing Gender." Pp. 13–37 in Judith Lorber and Susan Farrell, eds., *The Social Construction of Gender.* London: Sage.

Further Readings

Bonvillain, Nancy. 1997. "Cross-Cultural Studies of Language and Gender." Chap. 8, pp. 194–216 in her *Language, Culture, and Communication: The Meaning of Messages.* Upper Saddle River, NJ: Prentice Hall.

Goodwin, Marjorie Harness. 1990. *He-said-she-said: Talk as Social Organization among Black Children.* Bloomington: Indiana University Press.

Graddol, David, and Joan Swann. 1989. *Gender Voices.* Oxford: Basil Blackwell.

McConnell-Ginet, Sally, Ruth Borker, and Nelly Furman, eds. 1980. *Women and Language in Literature and Society.* New York: Praeger.

Thorne, Barrie, Cheris Kramarae, and Nancy Henley, eds. 1983. *Language, Gender and Society.* Rowley, MA: Newbury House.

File 12.7

Variation in Speech Style

You probably don't speak to your grandmother exactly as you do to the neighbor's two year old; nor do you speak to your minister as you do to your roommate. In fact, no speaker speaks the same way all the time. Instead we all make use of a number of different **speech styles** depending on the context in which we are speaking. Speech styles may be thought of as variations in speech based on factors such as topic, setting, and addressee, and they are normally described in terms of degrees of formality. Thus a speech style may be described as "formal" or "informal," "casual" or "careful." While we may be aware of making a special effort to produce our best language along with our best manners for certain people or in certain situations, the changes that we make are usually performed effortlessly. Automatically adjusting from one speech style to another is known as **style shifting**.

Many people deny even having different speech styles, on the grounds that it would be insincere, a form of play acting, to speak differently to different people. However, "putting on airs" is not the only way to change speech style. It isn't even one of the most common. In reality, adapting one's spoken style to one's audience is like choosing the right tool for a particular task. You can't eat bouillon with a fork or sirloin steak with a spoon. And you may have eaten your peas with a spoon when you were three years old, but you wouldn't feel comfortable doing it at a dinner party now. If you were questioned by your four-year-old cousin about why your begonia needs light, you probably wouldn't explain it in terms of "photosynthesis." On the other hand, you probably would include that word in your answer to the same sort of question on a botany exam. You may tell your mechanics that one of the wires seems to have come loose from "that funny looking black thing," and they may respect the depths of your ignorance by replying to you in similar terms. However, if they talk that way to each other, you may begin to doubt their competence. Thus common sense makes you choose simple words to speak to a small child and appropriate technical words, if you know them, to speak to an expert about his or her field. Speech styles differ in at least three major ways—in pronunciation, in syntax, and in vocabulary.

Pronunciation

A number of studies have been done concerning "casual" or "fast speech" phonology. For people who are not linguists, the most obvious feature of casual speech is probably "dropping *g*s" in words that end in *–ing*. (Quotation marks are used around this phrase because what actually happens phonetically is a change from [ŋ] to [n], with no [g] involved in either pronunciation.) We all know about "dropping *g*s" because most of us have had teachers who told us not to do it. But even people who spend their lives telling other people not to, at least occasionally "drop their *g*s" in expressions like *going fishing*. If you listen very carefully, you will find that people you think never "drop their *g*s" do so sometimes, and others who you think always "drop their *g*s" actually use them sometimes.

People often disapprove officially of casual speech patterns and "sloppy" or "careless" speech, but features of casual speech can be economical and efficient. You may have been taught, for example, that it is inappropriate to use contractions in formal writing. In speech, however, it is extremely formal, even stilted, not to use contractions. Contractions like *he'll, she'd, won't*, and *can't* are relatively neutral in style. But in tag questions like *Herbert could do that, **couldn't he?***, the contraction of *not* is almost obligatory. And a sentence like *You are studying English, **are you not?*** could only be spoken by a nonnative speaker or an extremely highbrow native speaker. In fairly careful style we might say *he'd* for *he would* or *he had*. In casual speech, we might say *he'd've* for *he would have*. And in the most informal style, that might become *he'd'a*. Thus a sentence like *It would have been funny* can come out as [ɪdəvbɪnfəni], with *it would* reduced to *it'd* and then *id*, and *have* reduced to something that sounds just like *of*. Children often write *of* for *have* in these contexts because they sound the same in casual speech.

Syntax

In casual speech we may use syntactic constructions that we would avoid in writing or in speaking to an audience. *There's sandwiches in the fridge* is normal in casual speech for many people who would write *There are sandwiches in the refrigerator*. The sentence *Where's it at?* is good casual style for many who would say *Where is it?* if they were speaking carefully.

There may be a number of constructions that we save for writing or for very formal speech that don't fit our everyday usage. One of these is the subjunctive. The subjunctive is technically a verbal **mood** contrasted with the indicative. The indicative is prescribed for statements of fact, and the subjunctive for wishes, suppositions, and other nonfactive uses. Many people today don't use the English subjunctive at all, or if they do, it is reserved for their most formal style. Only the "contrary-to-fact" subjunctive in clauses like *If I were rich* occurs at all regularly in speech or informal writing, and even that seems to be getting rarer. Forms of the subjunctive other than *were* in if-clauses usually occur only in fixed phrases of extreme formality, such as a lawyer's *if it please the Court* or a written petition's *we hereby request that this be done*. Sentences that begin with a subjunctive element—*Be he live or be he dead, I'll grind his bones to make my bread!*—are almost never heard in modern speech and are only rarely seen in writing.

Finally, the use of passive rather than active constructions is generally formal. For example, the previous sentence would sound less formal written this way: *When you use passive constructions rather than active ones, you usually sound formal.*

Vocabulary

Probably the most obvious style shifts involve changes in vocabulary. Two types of style shifts involving distinctive changes in vocabulary are what we will refer to as *bad language* and *best language*. Almost everybody learns "bad words" at an early age. Four-year-olds come home proudly from preschool with brand new words like *son-of-a-bitch*. And even if they can be persuaded not to use their store of adult shockers, they seem endlessly fascinated by their own taboo words like *wee-wee* and *poopoo*. Although nearly everybody outgrows this stage, most of us do occasionally use some kind of bad language—some words or expressions we wouldn't want to say in front of the primmest person we know. Because of the forbidden aura around words that have to do with sex and excretion on the one hand and God and religion on the other, we are particularly aware of this part of our vocabulary. We sometimes talk as if it were the whole of speech, when in fact, *Watch your language!* usually just means *Cut out the naughty words.*

In addition to bad language we often have a set of words or phrases that belongs to best language, a set we keep for our most formal and impressive occasions, just as we might keep the best china. Not everybody has best china, of course, but most of us do have best language. You may find that you save your best for formal writing. Look for it in term papers or English compositions or the kind of description of your aims and ambitions you often have to write on college or graduate school applications. Poetic words like *myriad* or scholarly sounding ones like *multiplicity* might belong to this section of vocabulary.

In between these two levels, nearly everybody uses some technical language, or **jargon**. Many of us are more or less fluent in a number of different jargons. Every job and every field of study has some technical terms of its own, as does every hobby and sport. Within its own area, technical jargon is clear, expressive, and economical; for outsiders, much of it usually remains incomprehensible. Professional jargons are often used to impress people outside the profession. *Rhinitis* sounds a great deal more impressive than "a runny nose." *Rhinoplasty* sounds a lot more complicated and serious than "nose job." When the dermatologist says you have *dermatitis* it sounds like a real diagnosis by an expert; if he calls it a "rash" you might not be so sure that he knows more about it than you do. Occasionally a word or expression that has a jargonistic origin escapes from that context into general use. In recent years we have seen this happen with *bottom line* (originally a technical term used in reference to business reports), with *hardware, software,* and *system* (all from computer usage), and less recently with words like *cool* (originally used to refer to a type of jazz). The space program has given us all *countdown, A-OK* and *blast off,* and even people with no interest in baseball know how it feels to *strike out.*

Besides technical language, most people make occasional use of a very informal, colloquial language, often marked by highly colorful usage, known formally as **slang**. There are two basic types of slang. The nearly neutral everyday language that is just a little too informal for letters of application and the like is known as **common slang**. This includes words like *fridge* for *refrigerator* or *TV* for *television*. The more specialized, "slangier" slang of a particular group at a particular time is known as **in-group slang**. In-group slang, like technical language, can be used to keep insiders together and to exclude outsiders. Learning the appropriate slang can thus be a key to entrance into a particular group. In order for the group to preserve its closed status, however, there is often a fairly high turnover and renewal of slang expressions. Some slang is very short-lived, like *Twenty-three skidoo!* but some lasts long enough to become accepted in the stuffiest circles. *Fan* appeared as a slangy shortening of *fanatic* in the late sixteenth century, and today we have *fan letters, fan clubs,* and *fan magazines* for all kinds of things from baseball stars to rock groups. Similarly, the fact that slang often injects a bit of color into otherwise ordinary language means that as the color fades, so to speak, new expressions will be needed. In this way, we see that slang in a sense is the linguistic counterpart of fad behavior; just as hula hoops came and went (and perhaps are coming back again), certain slang expressions have come and gone over the years, some to return again, but others not.

The very word *slang* summons up images of four-letter words, of sloppy speech, of admonitions from parents and teachers not to say certain things, of words and expressions you might use with your friends but not with your parents, in your dorm but not in a job interview, etc. These images give us a good first approximation of what slang is, for they all revolve around language used in particular contexts, as defined by the speakers participating in a conversation (e.g., you and your parents vs. you and your friends), or by the general situation in which the conversation takes place (e.g., in your room with friends vs. in a job interview with someone you have never met before). In a similar way, most speakers of English would agree that *Can it!* is a slang way of telling someone to be quiet, or that *Beat it!* is a slang expression for telling someone to leave, but at the same time, these expressions have perfectly ordinary and nonslangy uses in different contexts (e.g., *Can it* in the context of talking about what to do with a salmon or tuna you have just caught, or *Beat it* in a recipe telling you what to do with the egg you have just cracked into a bowl). Thus context is a key to understanding what constitutes slang usage.

Slang responds to a need in people to be creative in their language use and to show group membership (often unconsciously) through their language use. These observations liken slang to some feature in the nature of being human and of interacting with humans. For these reasons, slang is found in all languages and has been found at all times (even in Ancient Greek of 2,500 years ago, for instance). Slang is thus a legitimate sociolinguistic phenomenon and is studied by linguists as such.

Exercises

1. Have a friend read the series of numbers 15—70—21. Then have your friend count from 69 to 80. Use a sheet of paper with columns headed "unassimilated" and "assimilated." For each time your friend says a clear *seventy* with three syllables, a *v*, and an *n*, make a check in the first column; for each time your friend says something different make a check in the second column. Try to describe or transcribe the pronunciation you actually hear.

2. Suppose that you have a very close relationship with someone that you plan to marry. How would you introduce your fiancé(e) to the following people under the following circumstances:

    a. your grandmother, at a family dinner;
    b. your best friend from high school, at a picnic;
    c. the dean of your college, at a reception for a visiting scholar;
    d. a group of eight-year-olds in a Saturday morning class you've been working with?

    See how many differences you can find in the forms of introduction you can come up with. Then compare your list with a friend's to determine if they differ significantly.

3. Make up your own list of jargon by examining the terms and expressions that are associated with your major (or hobby or whatever). Compare your list with that of someone else in your major (or hobby or whatever) and with someone not in that group. Does the in-group/out-group designation applied to slang hold here?

4. The following are some popular myths about slang. See if you can explain what about them is misconceived, especially from the viewpoint established in the above discussion on slang.

    a. Slang is bad and degrades the user and the language itself.
    b. Only young people use slang.
    c. There are languages that have no slang.

5. To give you some idea of the richness and variety of slang we give below a collection of terms for two popular activities at many universities: drinking and throwing up. As you look through these lists, compare your own current slang usage with that reported here. Which terms are new to you? Can you see how they may have originated? Why do you suppose there are so many different terms for these activities?

Throwing Up		*Getting Drunk*	
puke	talk to Ralph	get wasted	loose
barf	talk to Earl	get stiff	fried
harf	pray to the porcelain god	snockered	zoned
yack	kiss the porcelain god	crocked	ripped
blow chunks	drive the porcelain bus	slushed	buzzed
blow lunch	drive the Buick	stoned	tanked
blow chow	sell the Buick	shit-faced	lubered
chunk cookies	sell the Porsche	plowed	rimmed
fumble	yawn in technicolor	hazed	aced
boot it	eat backwards	z'd	pound a few
double fault		blasted	catch a cold
play tag		plastered	wear the leash
lose your luggage		loaded	

File 12.8

Case Studies

The following two case studies, conducted by sociolinguist William Labov, illustrate how different factors, such as region, age, style, etc., interact with language within a given speech community. Both studies were conducted in the early 1960s and are considered to be classic studies of language variation and the interaction of linguistic behavior and society.

Martha's Vineyard

In 1961, William Labov conducted a sociolinguistic study on the island of Martha's Vineyard in Dukes County, Massachusetts, to investigate the impact of social patterns on linguistic variation and change. The linguistic feature chosen for analysis was centralization of the diphthongs /ay/ and /aw/, as in *why* and *wow,* to [əy] and [əw], respectively. In a preliminary investigation Labov discovered that after all phonetic, prosodic, and stylistic motivation had been accounted for, there was still variation in speakers' use of centralized diphthongs. His subsequent study was designed to discover the motivation underlying this residual variation.

Toward this end, Labov set out to test a number of different variables. Was centralization related to *geography?* The island was, by universal consensus, divided into up-island (strictly rural) and down-island (consisting of the three small towns where 75 percent of the population lived). United States Census reports were consulted for information on the population distribution of the island.

Was *ethnic group* a factor in centralization? Native Vineyarders fell into four ethnic groups: (1) descendents of old English families, (2) descendents of Portuguese immigrants, (3) a small Native American population, and (4) a miscellaneous group from a number of origins. Another group, not considered in the study, was the summer population.

Was the *economic background* and current economic situation of the island in any way correlated with linguistic behavior? In comparison to the rest of the state, the Vineyard had higher unemployment, lower average income, no industry, and thus was heavily dependent on the summer tourist trade. This heavy reliance on tourism was viewed by some islanders as a threat to independence. As a result many islanders displayed resistance to the summer mainlanders and took pride in being different from the tourists, the greatest resistance being felt in the rural up-island areas.

The results of the study revealed that, first of all, centralization was a linguistic feature of Martha's Vineyard, thus *regional* in character. That is, residents of the island pronounced /ay/ and /aw/ as [əy] and [əw], while summer tourists and mainland residents did not centralize the diphthongs. But within the island population, some residents centralized, while some did not.

Analysis of centralization by *age* indicated an increase of centralized diphthong use with age, peaking between thirty-one and forty-five years and then decreasing. It was also interesting to note the economic situation of this particular group. Members of this age group seemed to suffer the greatest degree of economic pressure, having chosen to remain on the island while supporting their families, even though employment opportunities were not abundant. Additionally, high school students planning to go to college and then return to the island exhibited greater centralization than those going to college but not planning to return to the island.

With respect to ethnic group, the Portuguese population, which for years had been attempting to enter the mainstream of island life, showed a high degree of centralization. And those of Native

American descent, having battled discrimination from the other groups for more than 150 years and also desiring acceptance, also displayed a high incidence of centralization.

One way to summarize the effects of these different factors on centralization is in terms of *group identification*. How closely speakers identified with the island, wanted to remain, wanted to enter into the mainstream, saw themselves as Vineyarders and were proud of it, was positively correlated with degree of centralization.

New York City: *R*-Lessness

New York City speech is famous for its *r*-lessness, i.e., lack of [r] in words such as *four, card, papers, here, there*, etc. A common misconception holds that there is a total lack of [r] in such words for speakers of the dialect. Another study, also conducted by William Labov, looks at variation in the use of [r] as influenced by certain social factors.

Labov began his study, on the basis of preliminary investigations, with the assumption that speakers vary in their use of [r] according to their social status. The use of [r] is associated with high prestige, while the lack of [r] is associated with low prestige. He set out to interview salespersons from large New York department stores, on the further assumption that salespeople tend to reflect the prestige of their customers. If the customers ranked high in prestige, salespeople would "borrow prestige from their customers" (Labov 1972: 45). Similarly, if customers ranked low in prestige, salespeople would reflect this too. Labov's hypothesis, then, was this: salespeople from the highest prestige store would exhibit the highest incidence of [r] in their speech, while those from the lowest prestige store would exhibit the lowest incidence of [r].

Labov selected for his study three department stores: Saks 5th Avenue (high prestige), Macy's (moderate prestige), and S. Klein (low prestige). Then, in spontaneous interviews, salesclerks were asked a question that elicited the answer *fourth floor*, this first elicitation representing casual speech. The interviewer then, pretending not to hear the answer, would lean forward asking the clerk to repeat the answer. The clerk repeated the answer, but this time in careful speech under emphatic stress.

The results of the study, summarized in the table below, showed a clear stratification of [r] among the salespeople in support of Labov's hypothesis.

Percentage of [r]s in *floor*

	Casual	Careful
Saks	63	64
Macy's	44	61
S. Klein	8	18

Looking at the effects of style, we notice that for each department store, there is a correlation between the increase in the percentage of [r]s produced and the shift from casual to careful style. Interestingly, the biggest difference between styles is found at Macy's, where there is a difference of 17 percent between casual and careful styles (compared with a 10 percent difference at S. Klein and only a 1 percent difference at Saks). The researchers in this study attribute this difference to notions of *linguistic security*. The [r] for Macy's employees is apparently the norm or target at which they aim, yet not the one they reach most of the time. Thus, while [r] may disappear in casual speech it reappears in careful pronunciation. In contrast, "in Saks we see a shift between casual and emphatic pronunciation, but it is nunciation. In contrast, "in Saks we see a shift between casual and emphatic pronunciation, but it is much less marked. In other words, Saks employees have more *security* in a linguistic sense" (1972: 52). Note that the difference in careful speech between Saks and Macy's (3 percent) is very slight.

In terms of the prestige factor, we notice a consistent decrease in the percentage of [r]s correlated with a decrease in the prestige associated with the department stores. The overall totals for this study, provided below, show that in Saks 62 percent of the employees interviewed used all or some [r], in Macy's 51 percent, and in S. Klein 20 percent. Thus, the highest incidence of some or all [r] was, predictably, in the high-prestige store, supporting the original hypothesis.

Total percentage of [r]s produced

Saks	62
Macy's	51
S. Klein	20

Summary

What do these studies show? Essentially they illustrate how regional and social factors interact with language to create linguistic variation. These studies by Labov have sparked a great deal more research in social and regional variation.

Reference

Labov, William. 1972. *Sociolinguistic Patterns*. Philadelphia: University of Pennsylvania Press.

File 12.9 Language Variation Exercises

Pronunciation

Below is a list of words that have different pronunciations in different dialects. Circle the letter corresponding to the pronunciation you use in *relaxed, casual conversation*. If you use more than one, circle all the appropriate letters. If you use an entirely different pronunciation, indicate your pronunciation in the blank at the right. Finally, if you think there is a distinction among the choices between a standard and a nonstandard pronunciation, X out the letter corresponding to the one you consider to be *standard*.

1. nucleus: (a) [nukyələs] (b) [nukliəs]   a   b   _____

2. washing: (a) [woršɪŋ] (b) [wašɪŋ]   a   b   _____

3. fire: the vowel is (a) [ay] (b) [a]   a   b   _____

4. tomato: the second vowel is (a) [e] (b) [a]   a   b   _____

5. where: begins with (a) [w̥] (b) [w]   a   b   _____

6. often: (a) [ɔfn̩] (b) [ɔftn̩]   a   b   _____

7. greasy: (a) [grisi] (b) [grizi]   a   b   _____

8. bottle: (a) [baɾl̩] (b) [baʔl̩]   a   b   _____

9. Columbus: (a) [kəlʌmbəs] (b) [klʌmbəs]   a   b   _____

10. police: stressed on (a) 1st syllable (b) 2nd syllable   a   b   _____

Vocabulary

Here are some sentences containing words and idioms that differ from dialect to dialect. Circle the letter corresponding to the expression you use. If you ordinarily use more than one, circle all the appropriate letters. If you use an entirely different word or idiom, write it in the blank at the right.

1. A large open metal container for water is a (a) bucket (b) pail. _____

2. To carry groceries, you put them in a paper (a) bag (b) sack (c) poke. _____

3. Window coverings on rollers are (a) blinds (b) shades (c) roller shades (d) window shades (f) curtains. _____

4. Pepsi-Cola, Coca-Cola, and Seven-Up are all kinds of (a) soda (b) pop (c) coke (d) soft drinks (e) soda pop. _____

5. On summer nights when we were kids we used to try to catch (a) fireflies (b) lightning bugs (c) fire bugs. _____

6. If it's a popular film, you may have to stand (a) on line (b) in line. _____

7. If your living room is messy, before company comes you (a) straighten it up (b) red it up (c) ret it up (d) clean it up. _____

8. If you're talking to a group of friends, you call them (a) you guys (b) you all (c) y'all (d) youse guys. _____

9. It's now (a) a quarter of 5 (b) a quarter to 5 (c) a quarter till 5. _____

10. Last night she (a) dove (b) dived into an empty swimming pool. _____

Syntax

The sentences below, based on a questionnaire used by W. Labov, were all produced by some speaker of English. Go through the list of sentences and check, for each sentence, whether you think it is:

    a.   natural for you to use in casual conversation;
    b.   something that some people would use but others wouldn't;
    c.   something that only a nonnative speaker would say.

This exercise is intended to be **descriptive** not **prescriptive**. The point is not whether you think the sentences are "correct" or "incorrect," "good" or "bad."

	(a) natural	(b) some	(c) nonnative
1. The dog is falled asleep.	_____	_____	_____
2. Everyone opened their books.	_____	_____	_____
3. My shirt needs cleaned.	_____	_____	_____
4. Ever since he lost his job, he be sleepin' all day long.	_____	_____	_____
5. You shouldn't ought to put salt in your coffee.	_____	_____	_____

6. You usually go to the
    one you want, but me never.   _____   _____   _____

7. You can see the cops like they're
    grabbing kids left and right.   _____   _____   _____

8. He didn't have no book.   _____   _____   _____

9. I want for you to go home.   _____   _____   _____

10. Me and Sally played all afternoon.   _____   _____   _____

11. Noodles, I can't stand in chicken soup.   _____   _____   _____

12. There's nobody can beat her at telling stories. _____   _____   _____

13. Of whom are you speaking?   _____   _____   _____

14. Them tomato plants won't live.   _____   _____   _____

15. So don't I.   _____   _____   _____

For Discussion

1. Compare your responses in the exercise above with others in the class. What are some of the factors that may influence the choice of one form over another. (For example, *My shirt needs cleaned* is more typical of midwestern speech. It is, therefore, influenced by region).

2. Hopefully this unit on language variation has given you a better understanding of how regional and social influences affect the way we speak. Given this knowledge you've acquired, explain why it is inappropriate to talk about linguistic forms in terms of being "good" or "bad."

13

Visual Languages

It has long been believed that visual-gestural languages are not "true languages." Only recently has this view come under scrutiny in scholarly circles and among the public. We now realize that all of the complexities that can be communicated in any of the world's languages can be communicated in visual languages, including American Sign Language (ASL).

File 13.1   True Language?

Speech vs. Language

It has been a commonly held (though incorrect) view throughout history that language and speech are inseparable. The terms are often used interchangeably by both academics and the general public. As a result, the view that visual-gestural (signed) languages are not true languages has permeated our society. Only in the past twenty-five years has this view come under scrutiny in scholarly circles, and only in the past decade has the public begun developing an awareness of signed languages' status as true languages.

Recall from previous files that **language** is an abstract cognitive system, which uniquely allows humans to produce and comprehend meaningful utterances (regardless of the mode of communication of those utterances). **Speech**, on the other hand, is an action: the use of the vocal apparatus to produce strings of sounds, encoded with linguistic information for the purpose of communication. Thus speech uses the vocal-auditory mode (sound) to convey linguistic information. As a tool for the transmission of language, speech is distinct from the cognitive system of language.

Similarly, signed languages utilize the visual mode to convey linguistic information. The hands, body, eyes, lips, and tongue are used in production (analogous to the vocal apparatus for spoken languages), and the eyes are the instruments of reception (analogous to the ears for a spoken language). All of the complexities that can be communicated in any of the world's spoken languages can be communicated in visual languages. The design features that distinguish human language from other animal communication systems (refer to File 2.1) describe signed language as well as spoken language. There is nothing in the structure of language that necessitates the vocal-auditory mode as opposed to the visual.

How do we distinguish the universal qualities of language from features that are restrictions due to a language's mode of transmission? This is one important question that sign investigators address in their research. From this research we have gleaned invaluable insight into the nature of the cognitive system of language itself.

The Relevance of a Writing System

One source of confusion surrounding this question concerns the importance of a language having a writing system. Those who would refuse true language status to signed languages point to the lack of a writing system or any written literature as evidence that such languages are qualitatively different from spoken languages. This unfortunate confusion between writing and language arises perhaps because writing is such a large part of the cultures we are familiar with. However, there are thousands of modern-day spoken languages which also have no writing system or written literature (See File 1.3). The existence of an accompanying writing system is irrelevant to the question of whether or not signed languages are true languages.

Signed Languages vs. Pantomime

Signed languages are considered by some people merely to use the hands to draw pictures in the air; they are considered to be completely iconic and devoid of any internal structure. As a result, signed languages have been relegated to sublanguage status by many disciplines, more on a par with panto-

414

mime than with true language. But pantomime must confine its subject to iconic, concrete representations. In contrast, signed languages can convey abstract concepts as well; neither signed languages nor spoken languages are restricted to iconic representations. Signed language is predominantly arbitrary in its form-meaning relationship. There is a certain universality of pantomime (due to **iconicity**), but signed languages are not universal; they are not intelligible to people who haven't learned them. To illustrate, look at the ASL sign below (Figure 1). If it's iconic, as pantomime is, you ought to be able to guess fairly easily what its meaning is. The answer is at the end of this file. Did you guess correctly?

Figure 1.   What does this ASL sign mean?
From *Signing: How to Speak with Your Hands* by Elaine Costello. Copyright 1983 by Elaine Costello. Used by permission of Bantam Books, a division of Bantam Doubleday Dell Publishing Group, Inc., p. 67.

A greater number of signs in signed languages represent some aspect of the referent, because we can imitate more things visually than vocally (more physical objects can be uniquely distinguished by shape than by sound). However, the vast majority of the signs of a given language are not interpretable to the outside observer. Any feature of a referent might be represented by the shape of the sign, leading some to call it iconic, but it is only one feature out of many possible. Some linguists have differentiated three levels of iconicity for signs: **transparent, translucent,** and **opaque.** Transparent signs have the highest degree of iconicity, being easily understandable by the untrained observer. Translucent signs are less iconic but retain some recognizable relationship to their referent (these signs are not understandable by the untrained observer; however, the features of the referent that are represented by the sign are easy to recognize once they are explained by a knowledgeable user). Opaque signs have no recognizable relationship to their referent. It is interesting to note that in research on the degree of iconicity of signs, very few signs are understandable to the untrained observer, and diachronic processes tend to lessen the iconicity of even these signs.

Signed Language vs. Manual Codes

There is also a common myth that signed languages are inferior versions of spoken languages or at least are somehow based on them. Signed languages, for example, are thought to be no more than conventions for spelling out each word from a spoken language. These notions are the result of confusion between true signed **languages** and manually signed **codes**. Codes and languages are radically different systems in several ways. A code is an artificially contrived system for representing a natural language; it has no syntax or structure of its own, but instead borrows any structure it may use from the natural language it represents. Morse Code is a well-known example of a code. Signed languages evolve naturally and are not based on the spoken languages that surround the "speakers" of the signed language. Thus the structure of signed languages is quite distinct from that of surrounding spoken languages. Note, in addition, that since they are artificial systems, codes do not have native speakers (people who learn them as children, as their primary form of communication). Languages, of course, do have native speakers. Signed languages are learned natively by people all over the world. However, both codes and signed languages have been used by members of the deaf community.

Manually Coded English (MCE) systems are communication systems created by hearing people for the deaf. They are based on spoken language, and their main focus is an attempt to teach English to deaf people. Examples include Seeing Essential English (SEE I), Signing Exact English (SEE II), and Linguistics of Visual English (LOVE). MCE transliterates English words morpheme-by-morpheme into a manual code, a process that also encodes bound morphemes, such as *-ing, -ed, -able*, and *in-* (Figure 2). Such transliteration is unnatural, as true translation between languages focuses on conveying meaning, not form.

in-   -divis-   -ible
                            (literally: in-divide-able)

SEE II: 'indivisible'

American Sign Language: INDIVISIBLE

Figure 2.   SEE II 'in-divis-ible' vs. ASL INDIVISIBLE

An indication of this unnaturalness is the striking difference between MCE and language in the rate of transmission of propositions (semantic information). Proposition rates can be measured by rendering the same proposition into different languages or codes, then measuring the time it takes for someone to produce the proposition in each language or code. A comparison of these rates showed an average seconds-per-proposition rate of 1.5 for both English and American Sign Language, a signed language used by the deaf in the United States and Canada, whereas SEE II scored at a distant 2.8. This suggests that true language, be it spoken or signed, is a much more efficient means of communicating than signed codes such as MCE.

Research has shown that when deaf children are given such a slow system in lieu of a natural language, they quickly pare off many of the artificial structures of the code and create their own grammatical system. This removal of artificial forms and substitution of more natural forms suggests the existence of an innate language acquisition device of the sort posited by generative linguists, which all humans (deaf or hearing) use for first language learning. It is also interesting that the instructors who are teaching these codes to the deaf omit a great deal of the coded information that is simple in spoken English but awkward in the visual mode. If the educators whose task it is to teach the codes find them too cumbersome to use accurately, how much more so for the children who are attempting to learn them for the first time?

Another manual system for learning English is called the **Rochester Method**. This system uses a fingerspelled alphabet to manually spell out every word in English sentences, simultaneously with speech. It is perhaps even more removed from true language than MCE; whereas MCE is a code based on a language, the Rochester Method is a code based on the English writing system, which itself is a code based on the units of spoken English. Fingerspelling requires many more difficult articulations per word than signing does, and fast spelling introduces comprehension problems; therefore the fingerspeller must omit a certain amount to keep conversation at a normal pace. One study showed that the more fluent users of the Rochester Method produced only 56 percent of the letters of an English utterance clearly! Needless to say, this is not a very efficient communication system.

It should be pointed out that signed languages employ "fingerspelling systems" to spell out words that have been borrowed from spoken languages. (The Rochester Method uses the ASL fingerspelling alphabet.) These systems are based on the alphabetic orthographies of spoken languages, with a specific handshape assigned to each letter of the alphabet. However, fingerspelled words constitute a very small portion of the vocabularies of signed languages.

We have examined some claims suggesting that signed languages are not true language, and we have shown that these claims are quite inaccurate. First, the terms *speech* and *language* are not interchangeable. It is our innate ability to use abstract symbols to communicate meaning which defines language, not the medium in which we choose to create our symbols. Second, writing and language are also not equivalent terms, since many spoken languages have no written form. Finally, signed languages are very different from pantomime and codes. To defend this view, we have claimed that signed languages do have internal structure, just as all human languages do. In other words, signed languages are organized in much the same way as spoken ones, with syntactic, morphological, semantic, and "phonological" components, although there are some fascinating twists in signed languages owing to the uniqueness of the visual mode. Although this internal structure is just beginning to be explored by linguists, some interesting things have been uncovered, and they will be discussed in the next file.

(Answer to the question in Figure 1 is the ASL sign SOME.)

File 13.2 American Sign Language

Background

American Sign Language (ASL) is a signed language used by the deaf in the United States and Canada. The origin of ASL dates back to 1815 when Thomas Hopkins Gallaudet was commissioned to investigate methods being employed in Europe to educate deaf children. Not finding success in England, Gallaudet visited the school for the deaf that had been established in Paris by the Abbé Charles Michel de l'Epée, who is famous for having promoted and standardized French Sign Language (SLF). Returning to America, Gallaudet was accompanied by a young deaf instructor, Laurent Clerc, who was instrumental in establishing SLF as the base for ASL.

In the United States, this early form of SLF began a separate development, merging with the signs in use by deaf Americans at that time; in its isolation from Europe, ASL evolved differently from SLF. ASL also exhibits influence from written and spoken English in its split from SLF. SLF is the source for other signed languages as well. For example, Brazilian Sign Language is thought to be derived from it. There is a limited degree of similarity among ASL, SLF, Brazilian, and certain other, mostly European, signed languages.

On the other hand, ASL is *not* mutually intelligible with British Sign Language. Similarly, Chinese SL and Russian SL are distinct languages from all of the signed languages discussed so far. As an example of signed languages' differences, the sign POSSIBLE in ASL means WEIGH in Finnish Sign Language (Figure 1). (Note: because of the absence of a generally accepted writing system for ASL, it is common practice to use uppercase English letters when transcribing ASL.)

repeat movement

Figure 1.   POSSIBLE (ASL) and WEIGH (Finnish SL).
From *Signing: How to Speak with Your Hands* by Elaine Costello. Copyright 1983 by Elaine Costello. Used by permission of Bantam Books, a division of Bantam Doubleday Dell Publishing Group, Inc., p. 196.

Structure of ASL

Parameters and Primes

Probably the greatest contributor to the study of ASL was the linguist William Stokoe, who went against the prevailing mood of scholarship in the 1950s and 1960s to attempt the first serious structural description of a signed language. His *Dictionary of American Sign Language* (*DASL*) was the flagship publication in sign linguistics. Stokoe developed a transcription system for signs, noting that sign structure can be analyzed into three categories of formational elements (or **parameters**):

1. the shape of the hand used in the sign (i.e., which fingers are used, whether fingers are extended or bent, and the general configuration of the hand);

2. the place of articulation of the sign in space or on the signer's body (e.g., temple, ear, chest, etc.);

3. the particular movement associated with the sign (e.g., repeated circular motion, slow elliptical motion, and so forth).

At least three additional parameters, listed below, have since been posited by other linguists. But until more is known about the nature of signed language, and we can arrive at a typology for its study, it will be difficult to reach an agreement about the exact number of parameters (Klima and Bellugi, 1979: ch. 2):

4. the region of the hand that contacts the body;

5. the orientation of the hand with respect to the body;

6. the orientation of the hands with respect to each other.

Each of the above parameters contains values (known as **primes** or **cheremes**) that are used distinctively, much as phonemes are in spoken languages. Stokoe lists twenty-four movement primes, nineteen handshape primes, and twelve place of articulation primes. Primes also have nondistinctive variants (called **allochers**). Primes, like phonemes, are mental representations and not physical constructs, while allochers, like allophones, are the physical representations of the mental representations. In fact, some linguists now refer to primes as "phonemes." This terminology is somewhat misleading, since primes have nothing to do with sounds as the word "phoneme" implies, but merely represent a parallel level of organization to the phonemes of a spoken language.

While both phonemes and primes are used distinctively, there are formational differences between the two: primes cannot exist in isolation, as phonemes can. One fascinating difference between ASL and English (or for that matter, a comparison of any signed and spoken language) is the manner in which their fundamental elements (phonemes/primes) are combined into utterances. In spoken languages, owing to the nature of the speech mechanism, phonemes are organized in linear temporal order; several phones cannot be produced at the same time. (Imagine trying to produce all the phones of a word at the same time!) In contrast, a prime in ASL always occurs simultaneously with other primes. Primes cannot stand alone but must co-occur with primes from the other parameters. For example, one could not simply have a hand movement without also having the hand in a particular handshape or location.

Note that signs, which serve the same function as whole words in spoken languages, have internal structure. Thus it can be seen that signs in ASL involve discrete components, just as words in spoken language do. These elements in spoken language are studied as phonology; since the internal structure of signs parallels the internal structure of words, the term phonology is used (albeit not quite so literally) when studying signed languages as well.

If primes are used distinctively, we should find minimal pairs involving these primes, and we do. ASL has minimal pairs for all three of the parameters Stokoe classified. For example, the signs APPLE and CANDY contrast in handshape (Figure 2). The signs APPLE and ONION contrast in place of articulation (Figure 3). The signs THINK and WONDER differ only in movement (Figure 4). Changing only one prime in each group causes the semantic distinctions; this is exemplary of the contrastive (or phonemic) status each prime holds.

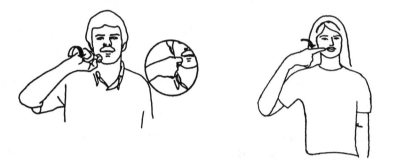

Figure 2.   APPLE vs. CANDY. APPLE.
From *Signing: How to Speak with Your Hands* by Elaine Costello. Copyright 1983 by Elaine Costello. Used by permission of Bantam Books, a division of Bantam Doubleday Dell Publishing Group, Inc., p. 67.

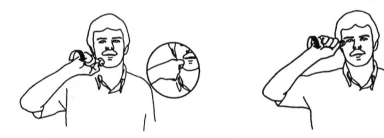

Figure 3.   APPLE vs. ONION.
From *Signing: How to Speak with Your Hands* by Elaine Costello. Copyright 1983 by Elaine Costello. Used by permission of Bantam Books, a division of Bantam Doubleday Dell Publishing Group, Inc., pp. 67 & 222.

Figure 4.   THINK vs. WONDER.
From *Signing: How to Speak with Your Hands* by Elaine Costello. Copyright 1983 by Elaine Costello. Used by permission of Bantam Books, a division of Bantam Doubleday Dell Publishing Group, Inc., pp. 200–01.

Morphology and Syntax

ASL morpho-syntax is a fascinating example of grammar applied to the spatial realm. Many languages form pronouns to eliminate the need to repeat a noun phrase every time a speaker wants to refer to it in a conversation. Instead, the speaker states the noun phrase once and then uses language-specific conventions to replace it through the rest of the conversation. For example, English uses pronouns such as *I, she, he,* and *they*. ASL, on the other hand, makes use of discrete locations in space to show pronominal relationships. The speaker first signs the person or object noun being discussed, then either points or gazes to a particular point in space in front of the body. This sets that location as a representation of the original noun. From that point on in the conversation, the signer need only point to that location as a pronominal reference to the original noun. (In signs where the hands do not actually make contact with the body, the signer may initially just articulate the sign in a particular location, without a point or gaze, and subsequently refer to the sign by pointing to that location.)

This pronominalization convention is used in combination with another process: directional verb formation. Certain verbs in ASL exhibit directionality, where the location(s) and direction of the verb's movement in space are tied to any pronouns that may have been previously established. Using this process with the verb GIVE, the signer begins the sign at the location of the agent of the action and ends the sign at the location of the person receiving the action (Figure 5).

'She/he give to you.'   'I give to you.'   'You give to her/him/it.'

'She/he give to you.'   'I give to him/her/it.'   'You give to her/him/it.'

Figure 5.   GIVE.

Reduplication is an interesting morphological process used in ASL, as well as in many spoken languages (not so much in English, however). This occurs when a morpheme is repeated one or many times in succession as a regular morphological process. The distributive aspect of many verbs is one example of this process in ASL. Using reduplication, distributive verbs show that a verb acts on many individual verbal objects (as in *give to <u>each and every</u> person*; see Figure 6).

Figure 6.   GIVE in the distributive aspect.

Also, some verbs that consist of a single movement can be made into nouns using a derivational process of reduplication. As an example, the verb EAT, when reduplicated, becomes FOOD (Figure 7). Likewise, SIT becomes CHAIR through the same process.

Figure 7.   EAT vs. FOOD.
From *Signing: How to Speak with Your Hands* by Elaine Costello. Copyright 1983 by Elaine Costello. Used by permission of Bantam Books, a division of Bantam Doubleday Dell Publishing Group, Inc., p. 181.

Compounding

The formation of compound signs in ASL bears a
striking resemblance to spoken language compounding. In English, compound words are detected by their differences in stress and timing from two-word strings. For example, the phrase *black bird* has approximately equal stress and timing on both words; in contrast, the compound *blackbird* bears primary stress on the first syllable, while the second syllable has reduced stress. The unstressed syllable is also articulated faster and takes less time to produce than the stressed syllable. Similarly, ASL compounds exhibit altered timing and reduction in form. An example is the sign BRUISE; it is a compound of the signs BLUE + SPOT. ASL, in contrast to English, reduces timing and emphasis on the first word in a nominal compound. As a result, in the compound BLUE-SPOT, BLUE is shorter and less clear in form than SPOT.

Historical Changes

All languages are in a state of flux, undergoing rule-governed changes through time. As expected, ASL has also undergone historical changes in the relatively short period in which it has been studied. At the turn of the century, the National Association of the Deaf rushed to film as many movies of the great orators of deaf culture as they could afford to make. The catalyst for this was the 1880 International Council on the Education of the Deaf, held in Milan, Italy. At this infamous meeting, where all deaf educators were barred from voting, the hearing teachers of the deaf voted to ban the use of sign language in deaf education. Instead, they decided to emphasize lipreading and oral production of spoken language. Ironically, the council that attempted to eradicate the use of sign language and deny its validity as language actually gave us reels upon reels of evidence for the historical change of ASL.

Evidence can also be found in older manuscripts that discussed "digital" communication, in interviewing older generations of ASL signers, and in applying the comparative method to ASL and SLF. One tendency that has been observed in the evolution of ASL is commonly referred to as the rule of bilateral symmetry. In Old ASL signs, all of the body as well as the space around it was used in signing. Today's signing space is more restricted, occurring mainly in front of the body within reach of the arms when they are bent at the elbow. Signs that were formerly made outside this space have moved toward the center, toward the sagittal axis that bisects the body from head to feet.

A second historical change that is evident in modern ASL has to do with the involvement of both hands in particular signs. Signs that used both hands on the head (e.g., COW in Figure 8) in Old ASL have been reduced to one hand. Signs that formerly used one hand on the periphery of the signing space (e.g., DIE, Figure 9) now use two.

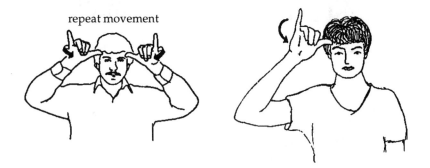

Figure 8.   COW (older) and COW (newer).
From *Signing: How to Speak with Your Hands* by Elaine Costello. Copyright 1983 by Elaine Costello. Used by permission of Bantam Books, a division of Bantam Doubleday Dell Publishing Group, Inc., p. 29.

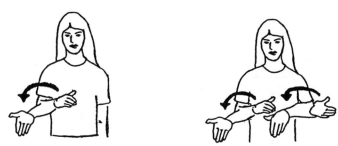

Figure 9.   DIE (older) and DIE (newer).

Sociolinguistics

There are actually many dialects of ASL, as there are of many of the world's languages. Several factors have led to the great amount of diversity among speakers of ASL. Because of the generally unpredictable occurrence of hearing loss and the resultant scattering of the hearing impaired throughout the general population, deaf people are often geographically isolated from one another. Contact among deaf people does occur, of course. Residential schools for the deaf bring hearing-impaired children from wide areas to live together through the period of their education. These children come from very diverse linguistic backgrounds and are a sort of "melting pot" of the deaf. For those hearing-impaired adults fortunate enough to live in areas with many other deaf people, deaf clubs are a gathering place for social functions, sports, and conversations with others. The sociolinguistic picture that emerges is one of many relatively small groups of language users, without a great amount of contact between groups. This has led to much linguistic diversity among areas.

Some of the diversity is minor and is analogous to differences in pronunciation in spoken language (i.e., accents). Look at the small articulatory differences in the sign for ABOUT in Figure 10. Other differences are more striking. Consider FOOTBALL in Figure 11.

(CA, ME, MA, MI, NM, NY, ND, PA, VA)   (AL, LA, NC)

Figure 10.   ABOUT variants. Reproduced by permission of Gallaudet College Press, from Shroyer and Shroyer, *Signs across America* (1984), p. 3.

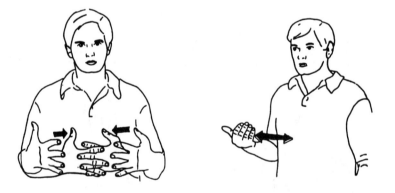

Figure 11.   FOOTBALL (widespread) and FOOTBALL (Ohio). Reproduced by permission of Gallaudet College Press, from Shroyer and Shroyer, *Signs Across America* (1984), pp. 96, 97.

One social factor that contributes to ASL's linguistic diversity is the close contact with and strong pressure from the English language. Many signs have been borrowed from English for a variety of reasons, among them:

1. Bilingualism. Many people lose their hearing after having acquired English as their native language. Upon learning ASL, these people tend to be influenced by English syntactic structures and use a lot of fingerspelled English borrowings in their vocabulary. Many teachers and interpreters for the deaf are native speakers of English as well, and their bilingualism influences the way they sign in ASL. In addition, not all ASL signers are completely deaf; some are only partially hearing impaired and have access to both English and ASL. Some deaf people lip-read and are also bilingual in ASL and English.

2. The extremely large specialized vocabulary of English, combined with the correspondingly small specialized vocabulary of ASL. For example, ASL has different signs corresponding to English *car* and *truck*, but to describe something more specific (such as *semitrailer*), the speaker may choose to fingerspell the English borrowing for *semitrailer*. Also, terms from more specialized fields such as finance (e.g., *mortgage, certificate of deposit, interest rate*) are often fingerspelled borrowings from English. It should be pointed out that deaf people who work in such specialized fields (e.g., truckers or bank tellers) have often created specialized signs for such concepts which may not be known by the deaf community at large.

3. Linguistic oppression against the deaf by the predominantly hearing educational establishment for the deaf. Since that infamous meeting of teachers in Milan, Italy, the world's deaf education systems have been dominated by the philosophy that signed languages are inferior to spoken language, that the deaf should be taught speech only, and that signed languages should be prohibited in schools for the deaf. Some educators are of the opinion that it is to a deaf person's advantage to learn coded English rather than ASL, since English is the dominant language in North American culture. (See File 13.1 for more information on coded English and the difficulties in its usage.) Other educators do not accept that ASL is a legitimate human language, often labeling it "animalistic gesturing" or an inferior form of English. Fortunately, the current trend in deaf education is toward true bilingual approaches (using both ASL and English).

4. The struggle between pro-English and pro-ASL factions among the deaf has resulted in very strong, often negative connotations for the use of signs that are markedly English in origin. A common process known as *initialization* has caused the hand configuration in some signs to change. Many handshapes in signs are arbitrary forms needed only for contrast. Influence from English has made handshapes come to resemble particular letter handshapes. For example, there are two variants of the sign DECIDE—both use the same point of articulation and movement primes, but they differ in hand configuration. One variant has the F-letter configuration (Figure 12, next page); the other has a D-configuration. The former is historically older and bears no relation to the meaning. The D-handshape clearly comes from the English *d* in *decide*. For deaf people who identify strongly with deaf culture and feel ASL is a means of showing their membership in deaf society, English signs (and signs with English influences) are a symbol of outsiders' attempts to anglicize ASL. Thus, usage of such markedly English constructions can be perceived as a declaration of antagonism toward ASL and toward deaf culture in general.

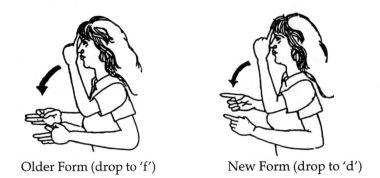

Older Form (drop to 'f')   New Form (drop to 'd')

Figure 12.   ASL DECIDE (older) and DECIDE (newer).

Conclusion

ASL is a viable visual-gestural language, unrelated to English. It has a structure quite distinct from English, using a spatial grammar with directional verbs, spatial pronoun formation, and morphological reduplication. It has a different mode of transmission; however, this does not limit its capacity to completely serve the communicative requirements of its users. It is as capable of expanding to meet the growing needs of its users as any spoken language is.

All aspects of language can be explored for ASL: its structure—phonology, morphology, syntax, semantics—its interaction with social factors, its change over time, and so on. While ASL shares with spoken languages certain universal features, some interesting differences, which are due to the unique modality in which the linguistic information is conveyed, have emerged. Only in the last twenty years have linguists begun to examine ASL in this way, so we expect to learn much more about this language in the future.

For Further Reading

There are about a dozen ASL dictionaries on the market.

Baker, C., and R. Battison. 1980. *Sign Language and the Deaf Community: Essays in Honor of William C. Stokoe*. Silver Spring, MD: National Association of the Deaf.

Baker, C., and D. Cokely. 1980. *American Sign Language: A Teacher's Resource Text on Grammar and Culture*. Silver Spring, MD: T. J. Publishers.

Battison, Robbin. 1978. *Lexical Borrowing in American Sign Language*. Silver Spring, MD: Linstok Press.

Fromkin, V. 1988. "Sign Languages: Evidence for Language Universals and the Linguistic Capacity of the Human Brain," *Sign Language Studies* (Summer): 115–27.

Gannon, J. 1981. *Deaf Heritage: A Narrative History of Deaf America*. Silver Spring, MD: National Association of the Deaf.

Klima, E. S., and U. Bellugi. 1979. *The Signs of Language*. Cambridge, MA: Harvard University Press.

Kyle, Jim, and Vivian Edwards, eds. 1982. *Language in Sign: An International Perspective on Sign Language*. London: Croom Helm.

Lane, Harlan. 1984. *When the Mind Hears*. New York: Random House.

Sacks, Oliver. 1989. *Seeing Voices*. Berkeley: University of California Press.

Wilbur, Ronnie B. 1979. *American Sign Language and Sign Systems*. Baltimore: University Park Press.

Woodward, James. 1982. *How You Gonna Get to Heaven If You Can't Talk with Jesus: On Depathologizing Deafness*. Silver Spring, MD: T. J. Publishers.

14

Language in a Wider Context

The study of language and linguistics encompasses many areas, as can be seen in this text. Even here, however, we could not cover all these areas. These files are a sampling of some other aspects and areas of language study.

File 14.1

The Whorf Hypothesis

It is commonly assumed that language simply reflects culture. The hectic pace of American life, for instance, is shown in the numerous metaphors involving verbs of action, such as catch a train and grab a bite to eat. The Whorf Hypothesis, or the hypothesis of linguistic relativism, is the contrary proposition; namely, that the worldview of a culture is subtly conditioned by the structure of its language. Westerners, for example, tend to divide reality into things and actions (or events). If we look closely at these two categories, we note that what we classify as "things" are nouns in our language, and "actions" or "events" turn out to be verbs. An example is lightning, which many of us unconsciously consider a thing, although physically it is closer to an action or an event.

In the early twentieth century, Franz Boas and his student Edward Sapir did extensive research on American Indian languages. They both stressed the unconscious connections between language and culture and the great diversity of linguistic structure in New World languages.

Benjamin Lee Whorf was professionally neither an anthropologist nor a linguist. He was born in 1897, studied chemical engineering at the Massachusetts Institute of Technology, and worked as a fire prevention expert for the Hartford Fire Insurance Company. His interest in linguistics stemmed from problems in interpreting the Bible. His work in fire prevention made him keenly aware of the consequences of unconsidered action. Workers tended to be cautious around full gasoline drums but might smoke or throw cigarette stubs around apparently empty gasoline drums, which were even more dangerous because they were full of explosive vapor. In another case, a workman threw a lighted match into a partially covered pool of wastewater. Evolving gases over the pool ignited, and the fire spread to an adjoining building. Perhaps these workers associated emptiness with inertness, and water with noncombustibility.

Whorf suspected that the relationship between language and worldview went far beyond word association and involved the structure of the language. He made contact with a Hopi Indian living in New York City and started eliciting data on the language spoken by Pueblo Indians living in Arizona.

Whorf's great contribution to the hypothesis of linguistic relativism was his attempt to work out the interrelationship between language and worldview of a non-Western group, and to compare it with the "Standard Average European" (SAE) worldview and linguistic categories. For example, in English, an SAE language, we apply plurality and cardinal numbers to both spatial and temporal entities. We say ten days and ten men. Yet physically they are quite different. It is possible to place ten men in an objective group, but not ten days, ten steps forward, or ten strokes on a bell. Physically, such events are cyclical rather than spatial, but our language predisposes us to place them in an imaginary mental group.

A Hopi could not say *they stayed ten days* because time is expressed by adverbs rather than count nouns in Hopi. A Hopi would say *they left after the tenth day*. Ten days is not viewed as a collection of different days but as successive appearances of the same day. The same is true of years and other temporal units.

The fact that days and other time periods are count nouns in SAE languages predisposes us to regard time as linear and segmentable. This attitude is reinforced by our tense system, in which past, present, and future are obligatory categories. We think of ourselves as on a point, the present, moving on the line of time, which extends indefinitely into the past and future. The past is irrevocably behind us, whether an event occurred ten minutes or ten million years ago. In addition, each of us carries his or her own "imaginary space," the realm of dreams, hopes, and wishes, which are assumed to have no direct effect on the external world.

The Hopi recognize no "imaginary space." If one holds a mental image of a corn plant, it will have a direct effect on that plant. If the thought is wholesome, its growth will be helped. If the thought is destructive, the plant might wither. Consequently, the Hopi emphasize preparing for an event, whether it is a rabbit hunt or a ceremonial rain dance.

Hopi verbs lack the tense system so common in SAE languages. The primary distinction indicated by Hopi verbs concerns whether the action takes place in the Objective (Manifested) Realm or the Subjective (Unmanifest) Realm. The Manifested Realm includes everything that is concretely in existence. This comprises the recent past (no suffix on Hopi verbs) and the edge of the present that has just emerged, for which Hopi verbs take the inceptive suffix *-va*. The Realm of the Unmanifest includes everything mental (thoughts, wishes, striving, dreams, possibilities) as well as events remote in space and time, the mythological past, the edge of the present about to emerge, and the whole of the future. Corresponding Hopi verbs take the expective suffix (*-ni* and variants). Examples include the following:

wari	*is running, ran*
wárik-ni	*will run*
wárik-ní-qa	*a possible runner*
tewá̧-ni	*(I) will see, would have seen*

If we contrast the Hopi system with SAE, we note that in the SAE, "present" is split between the Manifested and the Unmanifest Realms. Only a portion of the SAE past, the recent past of "real space," occupies the Hopi Manifested Realm. All the rest is in the Unmanifest, which is not thought of as unreal but as intensely real and potent, the source of all change in the Manifested Realm. The following schematic diagrams illustrate the differences between the SAE and the Hopi treatment of space and time, according to Whorf.

Standard Average European

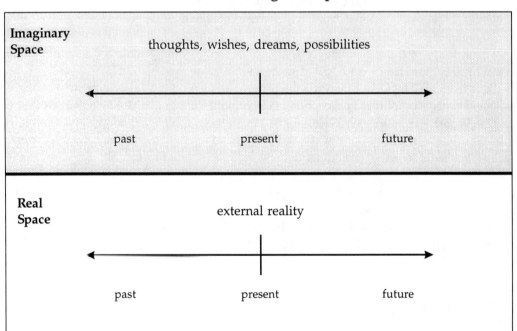

Hopi

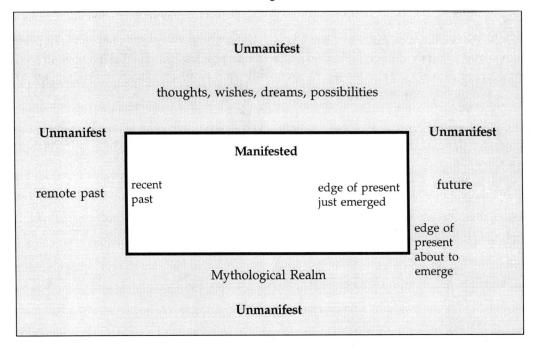

The Hopi do not have a concept of time as linear progression. They substitute the notion of "becoming later" ("latering"), through which items in the Manifested Realm undergo growth, development, and change. The source of this change, the Unmanifest, is thought to be already vibrantly present among us, working out its effects. An analogy not used by Whorf would be a supersaturated solution (corresponding to the Unmanifest) precipitating crystals (corresponding to the Manifested). The Hopi tend to be unconcerned with exact dates and records, which are so important in Western society. Whatever has happened still is, but in an altered form. We should not record the present, but treat it as "preparing."

Whorf wrote articles on such diverse groups as the Shawnee, the Chinese, and the Mayan. His early death in 1941 prevented him from synthesizing his ideas on language and culture into a textbook.

The validity of the Whorf Hypothesis remains in question. Some scholars have questioned Whorf's analysis of the Hopi worldview of space and time, suggesting that Whorf was simply projecting his ideas from the Hopi grammatical structure, which would make his statements circular. Other scholars have stated that Whorf's perception of the general Pueblo worldview was highly accurate.

The Whorf Hypothesis is difficult to test. In one study E. H. Lenneberg and J. M. Roberts describe an experiment in which a group of English speakers and a group of monolingual Zuñi speakers were presented with diverse colors ranging between yellow and orange. The English speakers, who have two basic color terms for this range, were highly consistent in naming the colors, whereas the Zuñi, who have a single term encompassing yellow and orange, made no consistent choice of names. These results support the Whorf Hypothesis.

A similar experiment with Quechi subjects on the blue–green area of the spectrum (for which Quechi has a single term) showed that speakers tended to perform groupings based on criteria apart from their lexicon. These findings would tend to negate the Whorf Hypothesis.

A strong view of linguistic relativism (one not espoused by Whorf) would claim that world-view is almost totally dependent upon language, and that it is possible to greatly modify public attitudes by forcing changes in language. The error of this assumption becomes apparent when one examines the results of past substitutions, such as *underprivileged* or *disadvantaged* for *poor* and *retarded* for *dull* or *stupid*. In time, the substitutions acquire most of the unpleasant connotations of the original term.

There are additional ways to test weaker forms of the hypothesis of linguistic relativism. One would be an investigation of non-Western cultures speaking languages with elaborate tense systems. In what ways are speakers preoccupied with time? Another avenue of research is comparison of the Hopi with another Pueblo culture speaking an unrelated language. There has been too much speculation concerning the Whorf Hypothesis and not enough data gathering to test it.

References

Von Wattenwyl, Andre, and Heinrich Zollinger. 1978. "The Color Lexica of Two American Indian Languages, Quechi and Misquito: A Critical Contribution to the Application of the Whorf Thesis to Color Naming." *International Journal of American Linguistics* 44.1:56–68.

Whorf, Benjamin Lee. 1935. "The Hopi Language." Unpublished manuscript.

———. 1956. *Language, Thought, and Reality: Selected Writings of Benjamin Lee Whorf.* Cambridge, MA: MIT Press.

File 14.2　　　Color Terms

The color words of languages have long been used as examples of how each language imposes its own categorization on the world and how these categorizations can differ. Here is a typical quotation, from H. A. Gleason's *Introduction to Descriptive Linguistics* (p. 4–5):

> Consider a rainbow or a spectrum from a prism. There is a continuous gradation of color from one end to the other. That is, at any point there is only a small difference in the colors immediately adjacent on either side. Yet an American describing it will list the colors as *red, orange, yellow, green, blue, purple*, or something of the kind. The continuous gradation of color which exists in nature is represented in language by a series of discrete categories. . . . There is nothing inherent either in the spectrum or the human perception of it which would compel its division in this way. The specific method of division is part of the structure of English.
>
> By contrast, speakers of other languages classify colors in much different ways. In the accompanying diagram, a rough indication is given of the way in which the spectral colors are divided by speakers of English, Shona (a language of Rhodesia [now referred to as Zimbabwe]), and Bassa (a language of Liberia).

English:

purple	blue	green	yellow	orange	red

Shona:

cipswuka	citema	cicena	cipswuka

Bassa:

hui	ziza

> . . . In addition to these three terms [in Shona], there are, of course, a large number of terms for more specific colors. These terms are comparable to English *crimson, scarlet, vermilion*, which are all varieties of *red*. The convention of dividing the spectrum into three parts instead of six does not indicate any difference in visual ability to perceive colors, but only a difference in the way they are classified or structured by the language.

The suggestion in passages like this is that languages could divide the spectrum in innumerable ways (and, in general, that "languages can differ without limit as to either extent or direction," as the linguist Martin Joos has put it). More recent work suggests that the extent of variation from language to language is much less than people had supposed.

Berlin and Kay experimentally investigated the color terms of twenty languages. For each language, they listed the basic color words—color words that every speaker knows and that have essentially the same reference for all speakers; such words tend to be offered at the beginning of lists of color terms, they are not used only for certain objects (as English *blond* is), they are not included in the range of another color word (as English *magenta* is), and they do not have meanings predictable from the meanings of their parts (as English *bluish* does). Then they gave speakers of each language a chart of 329 chips of different colors and asked them to perform two tasks: (a) for each basic color word, to circle all those chips that could be called by that word, and (b) for each basic color word, to select the best, most typical example of that color. They then calculated the focus of each color word in each language—the best and most central chips for each color.

Berlin and Kay found that:

1. About 70 percent of the chips did not fall within the range of any color word in any language.

2. The foci of the color terms for different languages were quite close.

3. Universally, every language has at least two color words: *black* (covering also most dark hues) and *white* (covering also most light hues).

4. If a language has more than two basic color terms, then it follows a hierarchy of color terms:

   a. Languages with three color terms have *black*, *white*, and *red* (with focus close to English *red*);

   b. Languages with four terms have *black*, *white*, *red*, and either *green* or *yellow*;

   c. Languages with five terms have *black*, *white*, *red*, and both *green* and *yellow*;

   d. Language with six terms have these five plus *blue*;

   e. Languages with seven terms have these six plus *brown*;

   f. Languages with more than seven terms have these seven plus some of *purple*, *pink*, *orange*, or *gray*.

English (contrary to what Gleason says above) is an eleven-term language, as are Japanese, Zuñi, and Hebrew. Hungarian and Russian have twelve basic terms—Hungarian has the standard eleven with a distinction between *vörös* 'dark red' and *piros* 'light red', while Russian has the standard eleven with a distinction between *siniy* 'dark blue' and *goluboy* 'light blue'. Shona is a typical three-term language: *citema* covers black, *cicena* white, and *cipswuka* red. Bassa is a typical two-term language in the Berlin-Kay color scheme.

Though controversial, the Berlin-Kay findings provide a relatively clear case in which similar physical stimuli are categorized differently by speakers of different languages.

References

Berlin, Brent, and Paul Kay. 1969. *Basic Color Terms: Their Universality and Evolution*. Berkeley and Los Angeles: University of California Press.
Gleason, H. A. 1961. *Introduction to Descriptive Linguistics*. Orlando, FL: Holt, Rinehart and Winston.

File 14.3

An Official Language for the United States?

Many people think that English is the official language of the United States, but it is not. The United States does not have an official language. When a country declares an official language it simply means that all official government business must be done in that language. All official government business in the United States is done in English, but no law requires this. English can nevertheless be considered the national language of the country, insofar as it is most widely used in the country.

In 1986, the Senate held hearings to debate whether or not the United States should add an amendment to the Constitution declaring English to be the official language of the country. The amendment never made it out of the hearings. Since then, a similar amendment has been introduced each year, but none has yet been successful. However, as of early 1998, twenty-two states have declared English to be their official language: Alabama, Arkansas, Arizona, California, Colorado, Florida, Georgia, Illinois, Indiana, Kentucky, Louisiana, Mississippi, Montana, Nebraska, New Hampshire, North Carolina, North Dakota, South Carolina, South Dakota, Tennessee, Virginia, and Wyoming. On the other hand, some states and cities have recognized other languages as well as English: Hawaii has declared English and Hawaiian as co-official languages; New Mexico has passed a referendum supporting language rights in the United States; and several cities, including Cleveland, have declared themselves multicultural, multilingual, bilingual, or multiracial.

When governments make policies or laws that deal with language, as they often must, it is referred to as language planning. Language planning can range from merely encouraging citizens to learn the languages of other countries to declaring official languages. Why is there so much political activity concerning language in the United States? Why should the United States declare an official language?

There are many reasons for nations to declare an official language. Many developing nations have so many languages spoken within their borders that they must pick one or two to be the official language to avoid trying to deal with five, ten, or more languages on an official level. Some countries declare an indigenous language to be official in order to preserve the language's heritage. In Ireland, for example, the indigenous language was Irish, but it is in the process of being replaced by English. Declaring Irish the official language of the country is a way of recognizing the place and importance of this language in the country's past. A world language, a language such as English or French, used over wide areas of the globe, is often chosen as the official language of developing countries, even though it may not be the native language of any speakers in that country. Making a world language official in a country makes it easier for that country to participate in the world economy.

However, there are also good political and social reasons against declaring an official language in some places. What is the situation in the United States compared to other nations? What implications might declaring an official language have for us?

Some nations are monolingual, some are bilingual, while others are multilingual. Each situation poses its own problems and can be complicated by various social factors. Monolingual nations, where the majority speaks only one language, are rare. Language planning might not seem to be much of a problem in such countries, but it is. Korea, for example, is an example of a monolingual nation, the world economy. Bilingual nations such as Canada have two large separate language speaking groups. Quebec has a French-speaking majority, while the rest of the country has an English-speaking majority. Multilingual nations, where many different languages are spoken, are most common. In Switzerland, for example, French, German, Italian, and Romansch are spoken. Over three hundred languages are spoken in India. Often in these cases, one or more languages are recognized and promoted as national or official languages to allow the government to efficiently conduct its business. So, for example, Hindi and English are the official languages of India (and various states have additional official languages).

The United States is hard to characterize as either monolingual or multilingual. We could, in a way, be considered either. The majority of citizens speak English, but there are hundreds of different languages spoken within our borders. Over thirty languages have more than a thousand speakers each. In New Mexico, nearly half the population speaks a non-English language, but the majority of these people speak English as well. One out of seven people in the United States speaks a language other than English at home or lives with other family members who do. Almost three out of five of those people who speak languages other than English at home are American-born (and thus are citizens of the United States). However, English is not being overtaken by any other language in the United States. In fact, English is probably one of the most widespread languages in the world. We already have one of the strongest world languages as our national language, and all official governmental business is already done exclusively in English. So is there really any need for an official language in the United States ?

Proponents of official English claim that making English official will force immigrants to learn English. Opponents contend, however, that most immigrants who come to the United States know that learning English is essential and that a law is not required to tell them this, nor will it make them learn English faster. Opponents fear that declaring English the official language could tell newcomers that the United States is not tolerant of differences. People sometimes have the impression that immigrant groups do not make progress in learning English. However, this is certainly not the case. It may seem this way since there is usually a gradual flow of immigrants to one area, and as one group masters English, another group arrives and begins to learn it.

Many people feel very strongly that making English official will imply that other languages don't deserve a noteworthy place in our history. English is not the only language that has played a special role in the development of our country. The modern United States was built by immigrants from many different countries, many speaking different languages, such as Spanish, Polish, and German. In the late eighteenth century, for example, there was a large German-speaking population in the United States. And of course, before the Europeans ever came to the "New World," there were hundreds of languages spoken by Native Americans in the area of what is now the United States. These languages have played important roles in our national history and enriched the English language itself.

Proponents have claimed that making English the official language of the United States is only a symbolic act. But opponents counter that symbolic acts can carry a lot of weight, both politically and socially. On the political side, they contend that making English the official language sets a precedent of placing English above all other languages. This opens the door for laws abolishing bilingual ballots, which might prevent citizens who are not comfortable with English from participating in the political process. It could also lead to laws prohibiting the use of public funds for printing materials in non-English languages, including safety messages on insecticides and other products, which, if used improperly, could be dangerous for the users as well as others around them.

On the social side, opponents of official English argue that making English the official language degrades all non-English languages and gives people the feeling that their prejudices are justified. They worry that some individuals who might dislike a non-English speaking group could feel that making English the official language validates their feelings, thus allowing them to be more open in their contempt of non-English speaking groups.

We must analyze the motivations of the official English movement carefully. Are the proposed threats real? Are the supposed advantages needed? First and foremost we must recognize the potentially destructive consequences of declaring one language the official language in a multicultural, democratic nation.

References

Conklin, Nancy Faires, and Margaret A. Lourie. 1983. *A Host of Tongues: Language Communities in the United States.* New York: Free Press.

McKay, Sandra Lee, and Sau-ling Cynthia Wong, eds. 1988. *Language Diversity: Problem or Resource?* New York: Newbury House.

File 14.4

Language and Computers

Computational linguists use computers to deal with language in some way. In particular, there are a number of things that humans do with language that can be automated to some degree on a computer—translating from one language to another, recognizing the words in speech, pronouncing these words, understanding sentences and larger texts, and producing text that conveys meaning or information. The fact that programming a computer requires that all details of an operation be explicitly specified makes computers an ideal environment for linguists (including theoretical linguists, psycholinguists, and sociolinguists) to test their theories and models.

Machine translation is the use of computers to translate one language to another. Some machine translation programs rely on a "dictionary look-up" method combined with some simple rules of syntax which switch and modify words. For example, *white house* in English would first be translated into the Spanish phrase *blanco casa*. Then, syntactic rules would add gender agreement and switch the words in order to translate it into the correct Spanish phrase *casa blanca*. The translated text is somewhat awkward, but the results are good enough that the text is intelligible and useful for most technical applications. As for translating literary texts, such as novels or textbooks, machine translation still cannot come close to human translators.

Speech recognition involves the use of computers to transform spoken language into written language. There are obvious uses for such a device—e.g., voice-controlled computers, games, and other machines. You may have already used a speech recognition system if you have been polled by a computer over the telephone or if you have a home computer with such capabilities. One system of speech recognition uses sound templates (or sound patterns) of individual words, which are matched to the incoming words through a microphone. This process is slow and limited, however, requiring the speaker to teach the computer the words before any translations can be performed. A more linguistic approach to speech recognition involves combining all the levels of linguistic knowledge (e.g., phonology, syntax, semantics, and pragmatics) in order to allow speaker-independent understanding of continuous speech. Speech recognition of this type has been the focus of a lot of time, money, and research, yet the results are still less than satisfying. Today's commercial speech recognition systems still use some sort of template matching, can only recognize words in isolation (spoken separately one at a time), and have a vocabulary of about 100 to 5,000 words. The most ambitious effort to date using template-matching techniques is the Kurzweil VoiceWriter, which can have a user-specific vocabulary of 7,000 to 20,000 words and can translate words spoken one at a time by using many powerful microchips working at the same time.

Speech generation (or speech synthesis) is the use of computers to produce humanlike speech. Today, telephones, cars, elevators, and even soft drink machines talk to us, in varying degrees of naturalness. This variation in naturalness stems from the fact that speech generation ranges from the use of simple "recordings" of actual human speech that have been digitized by a computer, to the use of phonemes and phonological rules to produce speech. Speech generators that use phonemes and phonological rules can "pronounce" most words and phrases by rule, thus enabling computers to read free text aloud. Such machines are now in use for reading to the blind. Speech generators that use linguistic rules of pronunciation are flexible and understandable, yet they still lack naturalness.

Text understanding involves the use of computers that can be programmed to analyze sentences syntactically, that is, to parse sentences. There are, however, two problems with automated parsing. First, parsing is extremely slow even with modest-sized grammars. Second, syntactic rules alone are not sufficient to guide the parsing process. Semantics, pragmatics, context, and world knowledge must play a role as well. The applications for this research are numerous: programs that allow users to communicate with computers using natural language, programs that take text and create databases of information, programs that summarize and index, and programs that correct grammar.

Text generation involves the use of computers to create sentences from abstract knowledge and to respond to humans using human language (whether it be spoken or written). Just as with text understanding, syntactic rules alone are not sufficient to generate meaningful text. A text-generation program must first know what real world knowledge is relevant for a specific text before it decides on such things as the type of sentence it wants to generate (e.g., question, statement), or what tenses, order, and types of words it wants to use. Applications in text generation include answering questions about a database, summarizing text, creating fluid, natural language from outlines, generating stories, and generating translations of foreign languages.

File 14.5

Machine Translation

The existence of a large number of diverse languages and cultures makes for a much more interesting world, but at the same time it poses a problem when texts in one language need to be read in another. The task of converting the contents of a text written in a given language (source language, or SL) into a text in another language (target language, or TL) is referred to as **translation.**

The need for translation may arise not only in the case of literary works but also in the world of international business, where all kinds of reports, legal documents, instruction manuals, technical documents, and correspondence must be routinely, rapidly, and accurately translated. **Machine Translation** (MT)—the use of computers to carry out translation—has recently emerged as a viable alternative to human translators for such business and technical translating needs. Two main factors make MT an attractive alternative. First, with increasing globalization, the volume of business-oriented translation has increased so much in recent years that often there aren't enough full-time or freelance translators to meet the demand. Second, and perhaps more pressing, human translators can be extremely expensive. For example, a translation into English of a Japanese technical document of moderate difficulty could cost up to 30 cents a word, so that a standard double-spaced page containing 300 words would cost $90.

From the user's point of view, speed, accuracy, and cost of translation are the main issues, and MT's goal is to optimize these elements: to provide accurate translations at high speed and a very low cost. This goal is far from being achieved, however. Although many commercial MT systems exist today—some of them fairly successful—the fact remains that not enough is known about language and the process of translation to enable a computer to duplicate the efforts of a human being. In this file, we consider what the process of translation involves, and how machines (computers) are made to approximate this process. (We will not consider automated **interpreting**—the translation by a computer of a spoken text—which is quite a different problem from translating.)

The Translation Problem

Suppose that you are a translator, and that you work with Japanese and English as your SL and TL, respectively. Given a sentence in Japanese, how would you proceed to translate it? First, you must understand the content of the SL text. To do this, you would have to consult a physical or mental dictionary and parse the sentence correctly. Your decisions about the meanings you assign to each word and the correct parse will depend on "common sense" and on several syntactic, semantic, and pragmatic factors. Having understood the SL sentence, your next step would be to create a sentence in English that is equivalent in meaning to the SL sentence. Again, you would look up English equivalents of the Japanese words in a physical or mental dictionary and then construct a grammatical English sentence using those words. This process sounds so deceptively simple that many scientists and philosophers were fooled into believing it could be easily mechanized.

To appreciate the difficulty involved in translation, let us consider a simple example: your job is to translate into English a sentence from a car repair manual written in Japanese. Suppose that the Japanese text is instructing the reader to remove the front wheels for carrying out a particular procedure. As it happens, Japanese does not have a plural marker to refer to more than one wheel, like -s as in *wheels.* The Japanese text may say either something like "remove both front wheel," or it may just say something like "remove front wheel." In the former case, there will be no problem in translating the sentence into English with the plural *wheels* because the word "both" is present in the Japanese version. But in the latter case, only the context can tell the translator whether the instruction is to remove a single front wheel or both front wheels. This would involve extralinguistic knowledge about the particular procedure: does it require the removal of both the front wheels or not? This sort of knowledge is extremely difficult, some say impossible, to encode in an MT system. Another simple example is the problem of lexical ambiguity. In German, there are two words that correspond to English "wall," with *Mauer* referring to an external wall and *Wand* referring to an internal wall. A human translator translating from English to German would know which one to use from the context, but encoding this information into an MT system is not an easy task. In a real translation, such problems (and many others) appear so frequently that mechanizing translation appears to require simulating general human intelligence in addition to knowledge of language.

Perhaps the first person to try to automate the translation process was a Russian named Petr Smirnov-Troyanskii. In 1933 he thought of a three-step process: (1) analysis of the SL, (2) the conversion of SL sequences into TL sequences, and (3) the synthesis of these TL sequences into a normal TL form. These three stages form the conceptual basis of most MT systems today, with conversion, the second stage, receiving the focus of attention.

In the United States, the first steps toward building MT systems culminated in a public demonstration at Georgetown University in 1954. Although this MT system was very modest in scope, it sparked a great deal of interest, and large-scale funding became available for MT research. Over the following decade, however, it soon became apparent that the main aim of achieving **fully automatic high-quality translation** (FAHQT) was far from being achieved. Growing criticism of the MT effort resulted in government sponsors of MT research forming the Automatic Language Processing Advisory Committee (ALPAC) in 1964. This committee came to the strong conclusion that useful MT had no "immediate or predictable prospect." The ALPAC report turned out to be very influential, and funding for MT research in the United States was effectively cut off for subsequent years, although research continued in other countries. It wasn't until 1985 that MT was revived in the United States, this revival being due largely to successful efforts in Japan and Europe, improvements in computer technology and developments in linguistics, and more realistic expectations about the goals of MT: instead of aiming for FAHQT, the emphasis shifted to machine-aided human translation, and human-aided machine translation.

MT System Design

In developing an MT system, several design decisions need to be made at the start that will determine the details of the final working system. The design decisions discussed below do not constitute a complete list; other factors, like the choice of a linguistic theory and certain computational decisions too complex to outline here, also play an important role (see the additional reading suggested at the end of this file).

First, the designers need to decide whether the system will be fully or partly automatic. A fully automatic system would, in principle, not require any human intervention in the translation process: given an SL text, the MT system would output an accurate translation in the TL. However, as the discussion above shows, this is rarely a realistic goal. Partial automation is a more practical approach, and one that most systems use. In partial automation, the SL text can first be **pre-edited,** so as to "prime" it, as it were, for the MT system. Typically, this involves rewriting the SL text into a **controlled language,** which has fewer ambiguities and simpler syntactic patterns, or marking the SL text to indicate word boundaries, proper names, plurals, etc. Further, the system can be designed to be **interactive,** so that it turns to a person to resolve ambiguities (such as the singular-plural problem discussed above). Finally, the output of the system can be **post-edited.** Here, a person revises the machine's output, either correcting errors due to ambiguities in the SL text (e.g., converting wrong instances of singular nouns to plurals), or converting the translated text into an idiomatic version of the TL.

Another major consideration is the proposed application of the system. Will the system serve to translate texts in a particular technical or business field, or will it be for general use? Generally, the more limited the type of document, the easier it is to design the system, since a more restricted field allows the use of a smaller lexicon and less variation in syntactic patterns.

A third consideration is whether to build a **multilingual** system, involving more than one language pair, or a **bilingual** one, which deals with only one language pair. Bilingual systems may be bidirectional, carrying out translation in either direction for the language pair chosen (e.g., Japanese to English, or English to Japanese), or unidirectional, in which case the SL and TL will be invariant (e.g., Japanese to English only). A real-life example of a multilingual system is the European Commission's Eurotra project, which aims to translate nine languages in all directions—that is, 72 language pairs.

Another consideration is which translation approach to adopt. MT systems in operation today use one of three strategies. The oldest one (1950s to early 1960s) is known as **direct translation.** In this approach, the MT system is designed for bilingual, unidirectional translation; every word is translated, and then some reordering is done to produce the TL text. No attempt is made at parsing or semantic analysis. The result is, predictably, unsatisfactory, as shown in the Russian to English examples below.

(1) Vcera my tselyi cas katalis' na lodke.
    Yesterday we the entire hour rolled themselves on a boat.
    Intended: Yesterday we went out boating for a whole hour.

(2) Ona navarila scei na nescol' ko dnei.
    It welded on cabbage soups on several days.
    Intended: She cooked enough cabbage soup for several days.

As computer science and linguistic theory developed, an improved method was proposed whereby the SL text is first translated into an intermediate abstract representation that contains sufficient information in it to allow the creation of a TL text. This is referred to as the **interlingua** method. This method is an improvement over the direct method, since it allows the creation of multilingual systems with relative ease: for every language, we only need to have a method for analyzing the language into an intermediate representation, and a way to generate the language from this intermediate representation; the intermediate representation is common to all the language pairs. However, with this method the problem is that creating a common intermediate representation, or interlingua, is a very difficult task, even for closely related languages like English and French. In spite of the emergence of sophisticated syntactic and semantic theories of natural language over the last 40 years or so, we simply do not know enough yet about language to create an interlingua for MT systems.

In response to the difficulties encountered in attempts to create language-independent intermediate representations, one solution is to have language-*dependent* ones. Such a strategy is called the **transfer** method. In this case, the SL text is analyzed to produce an SL intermediate representation, which is then transferred to a TL intermediate representation, and then the TL text is generated. Although the transfer method involves more steps, it is more effective than the interlingua method because language-dependent intermediate representations are easier to create.

MT systems still have a long way to go, but there have been some success stories. One such case is the Canadian METEO system for translating English-language weather reports into French. In Canada, a bilingual country, weather bulletins must be produced in both languages, but translating weather bulletins is an extremely boring and repetitive job. The METEO system was installed in 1976 and has been producing accurate translations ever since; today (in 1997), METEO translates some 30 million words a year with 93% accuracy. It succeeds precisely because the range of expressions found in weather reports is very limited; this illustrates the fact, mentioned earlier, that restricted types of documents are easier for designing MT systems.

A central issue in designing MT systems has been the lack of an adequate theory of translation, which in turn rests on the development of satisfactory linguistics theories. But some MT researchers dispute the central role of linguistics in MT systems, and alternative strategies range from example-based MT (the use of large amounts of pre-translated parallel texts of the SL and the TL) to statistics-based MT (for example, using probability to determine the likelihood that a word in the SL corresponds to a word or words in the TL). The trend in the 1990s, however, has been toward hybrid or mixed systems, that is, systems that are based on more than one principle (linguistics, examples, statistics).

Suggested Reading

A comprehensive introduction to machine translation, with additional references, can be found in W. John Hutchins and Harold Somers, *An Introduction to Machine Translation* (San Diego: Academic Press, 1992).

File 14.6

Language and Computers: Speech Synthesis

Not too many years ago talking machines were found only in science fiction stories. Computers like HAL in *2001: A Space Odyssey* were far removed from normal life. Now they are found in cars and other daily items such as elevators, automatic lottery machines, and some answering machines. In fact, you may have grown up playing with toys that talk. Making machines that talk is especially interesting to linguists because, besides producing something with obvious practical uses, it provides an opportunity to test the knowledge gained by linguistic investigation. Comparing speech produced by a computer to that produced by people is a very rigorous test of how thorough our knowledge of language and speech is.

Speech Synthesis

At first glance, making talking machines may seem to be very simple. One might simply make a recording of all the sentences that a machine needs to use, and store them in the machine. Many simple talking machines do exactly this (such as toys that play back animal sounds or words beginning with a certain letter, when a string is pulled). Besides being linguistically uninteresting, these machines have very real shortcomings. First and foremost, they are very limited as to the number of things they can say—even with extremely large storage devices—for two reasons. First, recall that the number of sentences in a language is not finite. If one recorded complete sentences, one could never even closely approach the number of things a person could produce. Second, speech can be stored either on tape or it can be digitized—information about the speech wave is converted to numbers ("digits") which the computer stores and can use to reproduce the waveform—and both storage types take up a lot of "space," either on the tape or in the computer's memory. To overcome this difficulty, machines have been programmed to take smaller units—such as words or phonemes—and put them together to make utterances. This process of generating speech from various pieces is speech synthesis.

One possible method of synthesis might be to record all of the words a machine might need, and then make sentences from them. This general approach has been used in some commercially available talking machines, such Texas Instruments' Speak 'n Spell toy. This method greatly increases the amount of things the machine can say (indeed it increases the possibilities infinitely—as File 6.5 points out), but it also requires that a syntactic grammar, or rule set, be programmed as well, so well-formed sentences can be produced. Although this approach is a step in the right direction, there are still two problems: (1) sentences produced in this fashion will not sound at all natural, since there is considerable variation in the way a word sounds in different sentences or in different positions in a sentence, because of differences in rhythm and intonation; and (2) while the number of words in a language (like the number of sentences) is in principle unlimited, the number of utterances such a machine could produce would be artificially limited by the amount of available storage space for words.

Phonemes to Speech Conversion

A more recent approach is to have machines "talk" by combining phonemes. This enables the machine to produce as many words as humans produce, since any number of words could be created from a finite set of phonemes, eliminating the second problem mentioned above. It also greatly reduces the amount of storage that a machine must use, since the number of phonemes in a language is finite and relatively quite small. The biggest problem with this approach is that the sounds associated with phonemic units are dependent on the context in which the phoneme appears. For example, the sound of a /g/ before /i/ is quite different from of a /g/ before /u/. The sound /s/ before a high front vowel is acoustically identical to an /š/ before a non-high front vowel. Ignoring these allophonic differences produces not only unnatural but totally unintelligible speech. Since around the time of World War II, linguists and electrical engineers have set about tackling this problem and have achieved a considerable amount of success.

The other contextual problem discussed above must also be dealt with when speech is reconstructed from phonemes; namely, different sentences can have different intonation patterns or contours, so that a given word, depending upon what sort of sentence it occurs in and where it falls in the sentence, can have a completely different pitch. Think of the pitch on the word *Tom* in the following:

> Hi, I'm Tom.
> Are you Tom?
> Tom! Please stop crying!
> Tom went to the store.
> Sam, Tom, and Sue went to the store.

Furthermore, the length of words depends on where they fall in a sentence, among other things. For example, consider the duration of the word *car* in the following:

> The car crashed into the tree.
> It's my car.
> Cars, trucks, and bikes are vehicles.

One example of a solution to the problem of synthesizing speech from phonemes is a synthesis program called Klattalk. This program takes a string of typed-in text as its input, converts the string first into phonemes, and then finds the appropriate allophone of each phoneme by looking at its position in the utterance. Then the program figures out what duration the sound should have in that environment by using a very complicated algorithm (series of equations) derived from large amounts of human speech.

Synthesizing Speech Sounds

Klattalk and Speak 'n Spell do not, however, simply access recordings of the units they use and then play them in the right context. The reason for this is simple—high-quality sound recordings, whether stored on tape or digitally, are extremely bulky (even if only allophones are stored). So Speak 'n Spell actually stores a simplified mathematical representation of each word. From these representations, the machine generates, or synthesizes, the actual waveform that is played out. Similarly, the Klattalk synthesizer stores a mathematical representation of what each allophone is likely to sound like, rather than a recording of it.

A crucial step, then, for a state-of-the-art synthesizer is converting the allophonic representations to actual sounds. Crucial to the implementation of this process is the source-filter theory of speech production, which claims that there are two independent stages in the production of speech sounds in the vocal tract. The first stage is called the source, which involves the production of a certain sound wave, either by the vibration of the vocal folds in voiced sounds, or the generation of noise in fricatives, affricates and stops. The second is the filter, which enhances certain frequencies in the source wave and damps others by altering the shape of the vocal tract (see Files 3.9 and 3.10).

Klattalk takes the string of allophones it has assigned to a given string of text and generates a pitch contour according to the sentence structure. Then the program determines where the sound should be voiced and where there might be frication noise according to the string of allophones—thus synthesizing the source. Then it again looks at the string of allophones and goes through the complicated process of generating appropriate formant patterns, imitating the function of the filter (see File 3.9).

Of course, Klattalk is not the only synthesis program available; nor is the approach it uses the only one that achieves any success. There have been many synthesizers over the years, each with different approaches to the problems of mimicking human linguistic and speech behavior.

Early Synthesis Machines

The earliest electronic speech synthesizer seems to have been made in the early 1920s by J.Q. Stewart, who put together circuitry that gave vowel-like formants to the sound generated by a buzzer. The 1930s saw the appearance of the "Voder," a device something like an electronic organ. An operator could change the pitch of the voice-source by pushing a pedal while turning various frequencies on and off with the buttons on a keyboard. The output of this machine, if the operator was a virtuoso, was marginally intelligible.

The 1950s saw the advent and extensive use of the "Pattern Playback" machine in research on speech perception. Literally hundreds of experiments were performed, forming the basis of much of the present research on speech perception. This machine takes as its input spectrograms (see File 3.10), which a researcher can paint on a clear piece of plastic. The machine "reads" these spectrograms by shining light through the plastic. The ghostly sounds that this machine emits are estimated to be between 85 and 95 percent intelligible, depending on how good the painted spectrograms are.

Later speech synthesizers differed crucially from these early ones in one respect. The early ones took as input a tremendously rich and complicated description of the sound to be produced. Therefore these machines could mimic not only speech sounds but any sound. Later machines were designed to take into account only the types of sounds humans emit as speech, thus greatly limiting the types of sounds the machine has to be able to produce, and therefore limiting the amount of information the machine needs to produce the appropriate sound.

The OVE (Orator Verbis Electris) and the PAT (Parametric Artificial Talker), developed in the 1950s and 1960s, were made of circuitry that imitates various aspects of sounds produced in the vocal tract. Both machines have some method of producing voicing and noise (the source), similar to that produced in the larynx and oral cavity during fricative closures, and some method of manipulating the value of the formants shaping the sounds (the filter). In addition, the OVE had circuitry that mimicked sounds produced with a nasal opening. After a long series of manipulating the settings for various routines in the OVE II, J. N. Holmes finally generated an utterance by a male speaker that was indistinguishable from that of a real speaker.

This basic method of producing speech sounds has remained essentially the same to the present day. Klattalk, for example, generates speech sounds using some methods pioneered in the OVE and some pioneered in the PAT. The major difference between these pioneering synthesizers and those made today is that the electronic circuitry used in the earlier machines has been replaced with programmable digital computers.

Some Remaining Problems

Though the basic approach to synthesizing speech has already been laid out, and speech perceptually identical to human speech has been generated from scratch, a problem remains in making the output of these synthesizers sound natural. Most approaches to the problem of contextual variability have been plagued with an inability to implement differences because of intonation, sentence stress, and timing. The general sentential context of the sounds being produced has subtle effects on every aspect of speech sounds, from formant frequencies to the loudness of frication to the characteristics of the voice source. The perception of all sounds seems be tied not just to the type of sound a person produces but also to how the sound changes over time, i.e., the timing of the changes. Today, work is still being done on the encoding of intonational and rhythmic structure in speech synthesis. These areas are the most recently addressed ones, with much work being done since the late 1970s in understanding how stress and intonation and dynamic (changing over time) information should be encoded in synthesizers.

Another problem, which has proved to be extremely difficult, is the synthesis of female speakers. It is only very recently that convincing female voices have been synthesized. They have been generated from synthesized male voices by (1) raising all of the formant frequencies to simulate the effect of females having shorter vocal tracts, (2) raising the fundamental frequency of the voice source, since women typically have higher voices than men, (3) changing the shape of the waveform coming out of the glottis and adding a low amplitude noise at the larynx, to compensate for an effect due at least to culturally defined differences in what is considered a masculine or feminine voice (and perhaps also due to physiological differences in the larynx).

The most problematic of these three processes is the third. The problem, which has also plagued the synthesis of male voices, is that of generating a voice source that closely resembles the human voice. Besides being extremely complex at any given time, the characteristics of voicing are continuously changing, depending on the thickness and consistency of the vocal folds, how close the speaker places the vocal folds to one another during voicing, and how much air is being pumped through the larynx. Earlier speech synthesizers used unchanging buzzers to initiate the sound, producing the highly unnatural speech which has come out of numerous robot mouths in science fiction movies. Well-defined mathematical descriptions of the actual shape of the waveform coming out of the larynx have very recently contributed to the consistent generation of convincing voices of different kinds, which change in the same manner as human voices do. Yet much remains to be sorted out.

Articulatory Synthesis

In the early 1960s it was often thought that if one could come up with the perfect set of rules to convert basic units into sound patterns, one might be able to make a synthesizer produce speech that is more intelligible than speech produced by humans, because the synthesizer would not produce extraneous lip smacking, etc. However, various lines of research in perception have suggested that any sound that a human emits consistently when producing speech sounds is used by the hearer to figure out what the speaker said. This, along with research into the timing of speech sounds, suggests that a slightly different approach to synthesizing speech should be taken.

Whereas almost all of the commercially available speech synthesizers generate speech by manipulating mathematical descriptions of the sound that the synthesizer is to produce according to a stored phoneme, a separate line of research has suggested that an intermediate step might be useful. Work at the Massachusetts Institute of Technology in the 1950s showed that one could economically describe the shape of a person's vocal tract during the production of vowel sounds and from that description generate electronically the sound the person was making.

Along this line, several synthesizers have been designed that do not directly manipulate the sound produced according to a particular phoneme or allophone, but rather manipulate the shape of an abstract vocal tract. Implementations of articulatory synthesis have been able to imitate not only the sounds coming out of the mouth but also the actual way in which the sounds were generated in the vocal tract. At the present time, these kinds of simulations of the vocal folds themselves offer a promising way of solving the voice-source problems. In addition to solving some of the naturalness problems for the voice source, this approach offers promise for solving problems of timing.

Applications

One research application has already been mentioned, that of testing our knowledge of language and speech. As a research tool in linguistics, the value of synthesis programs has only begun to be tapped. While synthesis machines have been extensively used to sort out people's perception of certain languages, such as English and Swedish and German, which were spoken by the designers of the synthesis machines, their application to other languages has had but a small start. When a researcher is faced with some phonemic contrast that is peculiar, or unlike the contrasts linguists have seen before, synthesizing the contrast and then testing how native speakers perceive the synthesized speech is one of the best ways to test hypotheses as to what that contrast might be.

Commercial applications are numerous, such as in educational toys, like Speak 'n Spell, discussed above, as well as some implementations on personal computers. Systems designed especially to help in teaching children with reading disorders are available today and are easily extendable to teaching anyone to read. Various manufacturers have given voices to their products. The simple recordings used today could soon be replaced with synthesis machines to increase flexibility and simplify the machinery needed to produce the speech. Telecommunications companies, among others, are very interested in developing synthesis for such things as the distribution of telephone numbers and interactive bank or credit card information. Interactive registration systems are already in use at many universities. Computer companies also find attractive the enhanced appeal of home and business computers that can "talk."

Perhaps more important, though not as well funded, are uses of synthesis in various aids for the physically handicapped. One such use is for the vocally handicapped. The American Speech and Hearing Association estimates that there are around 1.5 million nonspeaking people in this country alone (not including the deaf), people who have lost the use of their larynx through injury or disease, for instance. Modern speaking aids allow anyone who can spot a position on a keyboard to be able to communicate vocally.

A similar application is in reading aids. The number of people in this country who cannot, even with corrective glasses, read normal newspaper print is about as high as the number of vocally impaired. For this segment of the population, machines that read print out loud prove to be invaluable, if expensive. A good part of the cost in these machines is involved in producing a machine that picks up the text from the printed page. Of course, the availability of newspapers and books in digital form on computers eliminates the need for such expensive items and makes reading aids considerably more affordable.

Suggested Reading

For additional information, we suggest the excellent article by Dennis Klatt in *Journal of the Acoustical Society of America* 82: 737–93.

File 14.7

Writing Systems

Many different writing systems have been devised to render human language into a form that allows messages to be preserved over time. But these writing systems differ greatly from one another with respect to the appearance of the graphic symbols (or "characters") they utilize. In fact, only three basic ways of using characters have been employed in any of the writing systems that people have adopted.

The system of writing used to render English is, as you know, called an alphabet. But not all languages are written in alphabets. *Alphabet* has come to be used as a technical term which refers to only one of the three basic types of writing systems. The other two types are called logographic systems and syllabaries. It is easiest to talk about the three basic types of writing by first defining these terms.

The Basic Types of Writing Systems

Logographic Writing

In **logographic writing systems** each character represents a separate morpheme. (For this reason, these systems are also called ideographic.) The term *logographic* is derived from the Greek word *logos*, meaning 'word'. Since the words of any language are structural elements that represent concepts, the written symbols of a logographic system are equivalent to words. Thus each character used stands for a word as a whole, and not for any of the sounds that make up the word.

Logographic writing systems have been developed independently in separate parts of the world and are the oldest type of writing. The "hieroglyphic" writing of ancient Egypt, the "cuneiform" writing of ancient Mesopotamia, and the Chinese writing system were all logographic in their earliest form, although they each became modified as they were utilized by succeeding generations. All three of these writing systems were invented at least five thousand years ago and survived for thousands of years. The Chinese logographic system is still in use wherever Chinese is spoken.

An example from Chinese will suffice to demonstrate how a logographic system works. In the following sentence, each symbol stands for a word.

Figure 1.

he   be   center-country -person.
'He is Chinese.'

A logographic system has the great disadvantage that an enormous number of symbols must be memorized, since each word has its own equivalent symbol. It has been estimated, for example, that a person must learn approximately 5,000 characters in order to read a newspaper printed in Chinese and as many as twice that number to read a college-level textbook. China has a highly literate population; thus it is not beyond the capacity of most people to learn such a large number of characters, although the task requires years of schooling.

448

On the other hand, a logographic system has the great advantage that it is not necessary for a person to know how to pronounce the language represented by the writing system in order to learn to read the messages written in it. This is because the characters represent concepts and have little or nothing to do with their pronunciation. Persons who speak different dialects of Chinese—like Mandarin and Cantonese—which are so different that they can be considered different languages, can still read the same books and newspapers.

Syllabic Writing

A second type of writing system is one in which each symbol represents a syllable used in composing words. This is called a **syllabic writing system**. The total set of characters that are used for a given language is referred to as a **syllabary**. Syllabaries have been used for several languages, including Ancient Persian, Sanskrit, Japanese, and Cherokee.

The following Japanese example illustrates the way in which words are represented in the syllabary and characters used in Japanese.

これは本です。

ko   re   wa   hon   de   su   .

これはほんです。

ko   re   wa   ho   -n   de   su   .

Kore   wa   hon   desu.
this   TOP   book   is.

Figure 2.   The sentence *This is a book* written in Japanese.

Each unique syllable of the language is represented by a unique character in a syllabary. In the sample in Figure 2, the symbols spell out the sentence *This is a book*. The difference between the first and the second examples is this: the first uses the syllabic symbols mixed with the ideographic symbol for the word *book*, [hon]. These ideographic symbols are used in Japanese for content morphemes, like nouns, verbs, and adjectives. The second example in Figure 2 uses only the syllabic characters. Notice how the word *book*, [hon], is spelled with two symbols. One stands for the syllable [ho-] and the other for the final nasal [-n]. Remember from File 4.5 that Japanese allows [n] in syllable final position. Japanese writing normally uses a combination of syllabic symbols for function morphemes and ideographs for content morphemes. These ideographs are called *kanji* and were borrowed and adapted from Chinese ideographic writing.

Each syllable in a language is either a vowel sound or a combination of consonants with a vowel sound. Since the pronunciation of each word in a language is composed of a single syllable or a sequence of syllables, you can see that a syllabic writing system requires far fewer symbols than a logographic writing system. Therefore, a syllabary has the advantage that it is more economical, in the sense that it requires far less memorization and learning time. Any word in the Japanese language, for example, can be written with a combination of the characters in the following syllabary, called *hiragana*:

449

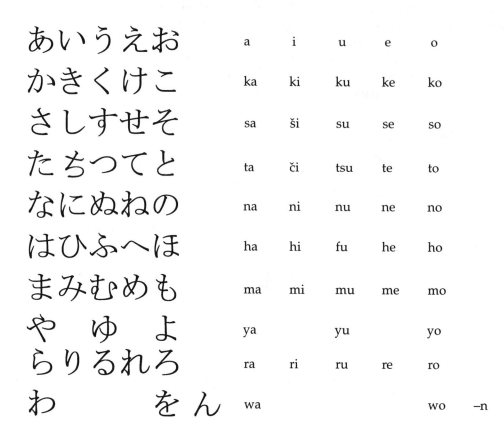

あいうえお	a	i	u	e	o
かきくけこ	ka	ki	ku	ke	ko
さしすせそ	sa	ši	su	se	so
たちってと	ta	či	tsu	te	to
なにぬねの	na	ni	nu	ne	no
はひふへほ	ha	hi	fu	he	ho
まみむめも	ma	mi	mu	me	mo
や　ゆ　よ	ya		yu		yo
らりるれろ	ra	ri	ru	re	ro
わ　　をん	wa			wo	–n

Figure 3.   The Japanese *hiragana* syllabary.

Alphabetic Systems

The third major type of writing system is the type we use to write English, called an alphabetic writing system. An **alphabetic writing system** employs a character or combination of characters to represent the speech sounds used by that language. Each of the syllables that make up the words of a language is, in turn, composed of one or more speech sounds. Since there are just a limited number of speech sounds used by any given language, there are fewer unique speech sounds than unique syllables in a language. Therefore, it stands to reason that an alphabetic writing system requires even fewer characters than a syllabic writing system. Figure 4 provides a list of the symbols of the Cyrillic alphabet used to write Russian. Slightly different versions of the Cyrillic alphabet are used to write other Slavic languages like Serbian, Bulgarian or Ukrainian (some Slavic languages, like Polish and Czech, use the Roman alphabet). The Cyrillic alphabet is also used to write some non-Slavic languages of the former Soviet Union (for example, Moldovan, a Romance language, or Uzbek, a Turkic language).

Аа	[a]	Кк	[k]	Хх	[x]
Бб	[b]	Лл	[l]	Цц	[ts]
Вв	[v]	Мм	[m]	Чч	[č]
Гг	[g]	Нн	[n]	Шш	[š]
Дд	[d]	Оо	[o]	Щщ	[šʸ]
Ее	[ye]	Пп	[p]	Ъъ	'hard sign'
Ёё	[yo]	Рр	[r]	Ыы	[ɨ]
Жж	[ž]	Сс	[s]	Ьь	'soft sign'
Зз	[z]	Тт	[t]	Ээ	[ɛ]
Ии	[i]	Уу	[u]	Юю	[yu]
Йй	[y]	Фф	[f]	Яя	[ya]

Figure 4.   The Cyrillic alphabet used for Russian.

In the Cyrillic alphabet, the "hard sign" and the "soft sign" usually have no pronunciation of their own: they indicate something about the preceding consonant. The "soft sign" indicates that the preceding consonant is palatalized and it generally appears only at the ends of words or between consonants. When a consonant is followed by a vowel, palatalization is represented by using a different vowel sign. All the vowels that are of the form [yV], where V is any vowel, are the symbols used after a palatalized consonant. Finally, the symbol "ё" isn't usually used in writing, instead "e" is written. Native speakers of Russian know that when the main stress of a word falls on the vowel sound whose symbol is "e," the pronunciation may change from [ye] to [yo], so they do not usually indicate the pronunciation difference (in phonological terms, "ё" is *predictable*). This is the reason a former leader of the Soviet Union's name is sometimes spelled "Gorbachev" and sometimes "Gorbachov." The final "e" of his name could be spelled using the letter "ё" or the letter "e," but it is always pronounced [gorbačóf] (Russian also has final devoicing).

There are two types of alphabetic writing systems that have been developed. One is the **consonantal alphabet**, in which only the consonants in words are written, with the vowels left out. Both the Hebrew and Arabic alphabets are of this type. An example of this type of writing is shown in the following Hebrew words. (Note: Hebrew is written from right to left.)

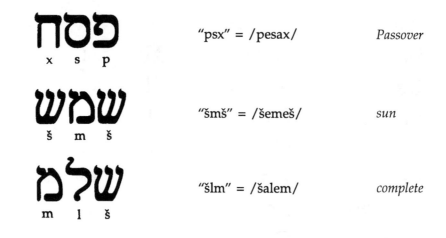

פֶּסַח	"psx" = /pesax/	*Passover*
שֶׁמֶשׁ	"šmš" = /šemeš/	*sun*
שָׁלֵם	"šlm" = /šalem/	*complete*

Figure 5.   Hebrew

Notes: [š] represents a voiceless palato-alveolar fricative.
[dž] represents a voiced palato-alveolar fricative.
[tš] represents a voiceless palato-alveolar fricative.
[ç] represents a voiceless palatal fricative
[β] represents a voiceless bilabial fricative.

It might at first seem such writing would be very difficult to read. But the fact that one's knowledge of the language allows one to "fill in" the vowels by observing the overall context of a sentence is illustrated by using this example from English, in which only the consonants are written: *Ths sntnc s wrttn wth th vwl smbls lft t.* The second type of alphabetic system, in which the vowels are represented as well as the consonants, is referred to as a true alphabet.

Another writing system that is somewhere between the consonantal alphabet of Hebrew and the alphabetic system of the Cyrillic or Roman alphabets is one in which all symbols automatically have a vowel sound (usually short [a] or [ə]), unless another vowel symbol is used. Many of the languages of South Asia make use of such a system. Sanskrit, Hindi, Marathi, Nepali and others use a writing system called *Devanāgarī*. Figure 6 gives some Sanskrit words in Devanāgarī and their transcriptions.

अति	əti	*across*
अतीव	ətīvə	*very*
तत	tətə	*father, dad*
तत्र	tətrə	*herein*
कुल	kulə	*herd*
उद	udə	*water*
धनम्	dʰənəm	*wealth*
बुद्ध	buddʰə	*enlightened, Buddha*

Figure 6.   Sanskrit words in Devanāgarī.

अ [ə]   ी [ī]   त्र [trə]   द [də]

ि [i]   व [və]   क [kə]   ध [dʰə]

त [tə]   उ [u]   कु [ku]   द्ध [ddʰə]

Figure 7.   How to write some syllables in Devanāgarī.

Compare Figure 6 with the symbols in Figure 7. When the sound [ə] appears at the beginning of a word, it has its own symbol, as in [əti]. But when it appears after a consonant, it is not written, as in [tətə] or [udə]. This vowel is called the *inherent vowel*: it is inherent in any consonant. Now look at the words for 'across' and 'very': the first has a short [i] sound, the second has a long [ī] sound. However, you might notice something odd: the short [i] *precedes* the consonant it is pronounced with. On the other hand, the long [ī] follows the consonant. (Look at the word for 'father' if you want to see the symbol for [t].) Now compare the symbols for [d] and [dʰ] in the words 'water' and 'wealth'. Notice that to combine them in the word 'enlightened' they are stacked. As you can see from these examples, there are several different ways sound symbols combine with each other. As an exercise, compare the words 'herd', 'water', and 'enlightened' and figure out how the sound [u] is represented in different positions.

The Historical Evolution of Writing Systems

As stated above, logographic writing systems were the first type developed. The first characters developed for such systems were simple pictograms. **Pictograms** are merely stylized drawings of concrete objects. The Ancient Egyptian, Ancient Mesopotamian, and Ancient Chinese writing systems used the following pictograms.

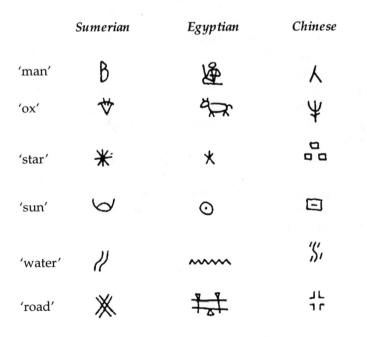

Figure 8.   Comparison of some pictograms.

A refinement that was soon made in each of these ancient writing systems was the semantic extension of the original pictograms. This means that the original pictograms came to be used not just to refer to concrete objects but also to refer to activities and abstract concepts associated with the objects originally pictured. For instance, the following Ancient Egyptian hieroglyphs were used to refer to activities or concepts that were not directly picturable.

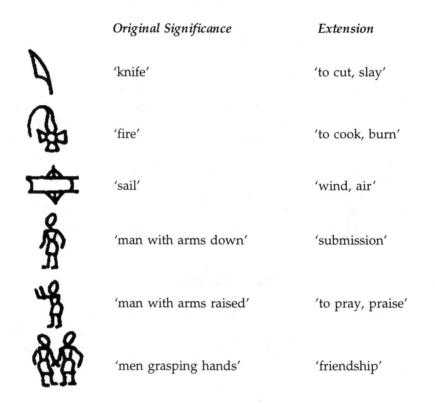

Original Significance	*Extension*
'knife'	'to cut, slay'
'fire'	'to cook, burn'
'sail'	'wind, air'
'man with arms down'	'submission'
'man with arms raised'	'to pray, praise'
'men grasping hands'	'friendship'

Figure 9.   Semantic extension of some Egyptian hieroglyphs.

At the point where such semantic extension has taken place, the characters of a writing system are considered logograms, rather than pictograms, because they are used to represent all types of words—abstract nouns, verbs, adjectives, etc., as well as concrete nouns.

It is thought that syllabic writing systems and alphabetic writing systems were developed from logographic writing systems. Although at first logographic characters symbolized entire words, as time went on the conventional symbols used as logograms came to be associated more closely with the pronunciations of the words they represented. This meant that in the minds of their users the symbols began to represent sequences of sounds. Consequently, the people used the symbols as characters to write sequences of sounds, or syllables, rather than whole words. For example, the Egyptians used the following hieroglyphs to represent syllables.

Figure 10.   Sound associations of some Egyptian hieroglyphs.

Also, some logographic characters were used to refer to sequences of sounds in an abbreviated fashion. That is, they came to represent the first sound in the pronunciation of the word to which they originally referred. For example, the Egyptians originally used the symbol,

to represent an owl, the word for which was pronounced something like [mulok]. Eventually this hieroglyphic character came to indicate the sound [m].

There were similar developments in other originally logographic writing systems, including the Mesopotamian cuneiform system and the Chinese systems, to a limited extent.

The Semitic tribes living in the Sinai developed a system of writing based on the Egyptian usage of symbols to represent the first sound in the pronunciation of the word represented by the character. This eventually gave rise to the consonantal alphabets used by the Hebrews and the Arabs. For example, in the Semitic writing system, the character in Figure 11 represented an ox's head, and the character in Figure 12 represented a house. The Semitic words for these objects were pronounced something like [ʔalef] and [bet], respectively. Therefore, the Semites used the first symbol to write the glottal stop consonant [ʔ], which began the word for 'ox', and the second to write the bilabial stop consonant [b], which began the word for 'house'. (All the characters in this alphabet were called by the names of the objects which they originally represented.)

Figure 11.    ⨯

Figure 12.    ⌐

The Phoenicians who used the Semitic consonantal alphabet taught it to the Greeks, who adapted it for use in writing the words of their own language. Since Ancient Greek did not possess some of the consonants used in the pronunciation of Semitic languages, the Greeks began employing some of the borrowed characters to write vowel sounds of their language. For example, since the glottal stop [ʔ] was not used in the pronunciation of any Greek words, the symbol came to represent the vowel [a] at the beginning of the borrowed word [ʔalef], which the Greeks pronounced [alpʰa] (which later became [alfa]). The Greeks borrowed all the names for the Phoenician characters along with the characters, pronouncing them each with a Greek accent. They referred to the whole list of symbols by the Greek version of the names of the first two symbols in the list, namely, [alfa] and [beta], which is the source of the term alphabet.

The Greek alphabet was adapted by the Romans. Thus, the alphabet we use today is referred to as the "Roman" alphabet. The Cyrillic alphabet seen above in Figure 4 was based on the Greek alphabet (see if you can figure out which characters correspond to the Greek letters). In fact, nearly all the alphabetic writing systems of the world can be traced directly or indirectly to the original writing system of the Phoenicians.

Appendix A

Answers to Practice Problems

Exercise 4.4.0 (Mokilese)

Since there are no minimal pairs where [i] and [i̥] are the only different sounds between the pair, and none where [u] and [ṳ] are the only different sounds, we proceed to look for complementary distribution. To examine the environments more easily, we can list the sounds which surround the sounds in question.

[i̥]	[i]	[ṳ]	[u]
p_s	t_#	p_k	#_d
k_s	p_l	s_p	l_ǰ
k_t	p_d		d_k
	k_#		d_p
			ǰ_k

If these allophones are in complementary distribution, the environment that precedes them does not appear to be the conditioning environment. For the pair [i̥] and [i], there is overlapping distribution, since they both can appear after [p] and [k]. Therefore, we cannot use the environment that precedes [i̥] and [i] to predict which allophone will occur. For the pair [ṳ] and [u], the distribution is not overlapping. However, the sounds that precede [u] do not form a natural class, and although the sounds that precede [ṳ] are all voiceless consonants, we should not assume that we have found the conditioning environment for [ṳ]. This would mean that the conditioning environments for the two pairs of vowels ([u]-[ṳ] and [i]-[i̥]) were different. This could happen, of course, but it is more likely that both are conditioned by the same environment, so we should continue to check out others.

    The environment that follows the sounds in question also does not appear to be the conditioning environment. The sounds [ṳ] and [u] are in overlapping distribution. Both precede [k], and the enviroments which follow [i̥] form a natural class but present us with the same problem as the sounds following [ṳ] (i.e., having to pose different conditioning environments for the two pairs). Before we give up the hypothesis that these pairs of sounds are in complementary distribution, we must examine another possibility: that the environment that surrounds the sounds in question is the conditioning environment.

    The sounds that surround [i̥] are voiceless, as are the sounds that surround [ṳ]. In addition, the sounds that surround [i] and [u] are voiced. These two sets do not overlap; therefore, we have complementary distribution. This means that [i̥] and [i] are allophones of a single phoneme, as are [ṳ] and [u]. We can state a rule that accounts for the distribution of these sounds:

    [i] and [u] become voiceless between voiceless consonants

Note that we cannot say that all vowels become voiceless between voiceless consonants as the word [kaskas] illustrates. However, we could make our rule more general by noting that [i] and [u] are both high vowels. Thus our rule becomes:

High vowels become voiceless between voiceless consonants.

Exercise 5.3.0

Draw a tree for the word *disappearance*.

The tree diagram is a representation of the structure of the word, so before you can draw a tree, you must determine what this structure is. That is, you must determine how many morphemes there are in this word and in what order they attach to one another. The word disappearance can be broken down into three morphemes, *dis-* (meaning roughly 'not'), *appear* and *-ance* (functioning to change a verb into a noun).

We must next determine whether *dis-* or *-ance* attaches first to *appear*. This can be done by listing words which have the prefix *dis-* and other words which have the suffix *-ance*. For example,

disconnect	appearance
disembark	endurance
disbelieve	grievance
disappear	acceptance
disassociate	interference

When drawing up such lists, it is important to keep a couple of things in mind. First of all, choose words with only two morphemes (the one in question and another). Secondly, the other morpheme should belong unambiguously to one part of speech. For example, words such as *discombine* might be excluded since *combine* could be either a noun (farm machinery) or a verb. Third, make sure that the words you include have the morpheme in question. For example, the word *distant* has *dis* in it, but this *dis* is not the same as that in *disappearance* since it cannot be analyzed as being a separate morpheme in this word.

Now, we can determine the types of words that *dis-* and *-ance* attach to. *Connect, embark, believe, appear,* and *associate* are all verbs, so *dis-* must attach to verbs. Furthermore, since *disconnect, disembark,* etc. are all verbs as well, *dis-* does not change the part of speech. *Endure, grieve, accept,* and *interfere* are all verbs, so *-ance* attaches to verbs as well. But *appearance, endurance,* etc., are all nouns, so *-ance* changes verbs into nouns.

Let's see how we can use these facts to determine the structure of *disappearance*. Let's consider all possible combinations (there are two in this case):

(1)	appear + ance	(2)	dis + appear
	dis + appearance		disappear + ance

In (1), *-ance* connects first to *appear*, then *dis-* connects to *appearance* But this arrangement would violate the rules that govern how the affixes may attach. When *-ance* attaches to *appear*, it forms a noun. To say that *dis-* then connects to *appearance* violates the rule that *dis-* connects only to verbs. The arrangement in (2), on the other hand, involves no violations of these rules. Therefore, we know that *dis-* must first attach to *appear*, and that then *-ance* attaches to *disappear*.

The tree representing this stucture is given below.

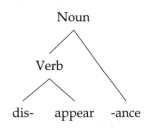

Exercise 5.6.0 (Isthmus Zapotec)

a. The morpheme indicating possession is [s], for 3rd person singular is [be] and for 2nd person is [lu].

b. The allomorphs for 'tortilla' are [geta] and [keta], for 'chicken' are [bere] and [pere], and for 'rope' are [doʔo] and [toʔo].

c. The allomorphs are conditioned by the devoicing of consonants when they follow a voiceless consonant, which is an assimilatory process.

Exercise 6.1.0

Use constituency tests to determine if the following underlined groups of words are constituents or not.

a. <u>Many retired workers</u> spend their time on relaxing hobbies.
b. Many retired workers spend their time <u>on relaxing hobbies</u>.
c. Many retired workers <u>spend their time</u> on relaxing hobbies.

a. ✔*Ability to stand alone*: Who spends their time on relaxing hobbies? <u>Many retired workers</u>. (Sounds good)
    ✔*Substitution*: <u>They</u> spend their time on relaxing hobbies. (Sounds good)
    ✘*Movement*: Can't be applied since the group of words is already at the beginning of the sentence.
    YES, it's a constituent. Even though it only passes two out of three tests, it can still be a constituent. Remember that the tests are not absolute. Also, remember that the Movement test does not always apply to every constituent.

b. ✔*Ability to stand alone*: How do they spend their time? <u>On relaxing hobbies</u>. (Sounds good)
    ✔*Substitution*: Many retired workers spend their time <u>so</u>. (Sounds good)
    ✔*Movement*: <u>On relaxing hobbies</u> many retired workers spend their time. (Sounds o.k.)
    YES, it's a constituent.

c. ✘*Ability to stand alone*: What do they do? <u>spend their time</u>. (Sounds bad—what do they spend their time on?)

✗*Substitution*: Many retired workers <u>do</u> on relaxing hobbies. (Sounds bad)
✗*Movement*: <u>Spend their time</u> many retired workers on relaxing hobbies. (Sounds bad)
NO, it's not a constituent.

Exercise 6.3.0

Draw a tree for the following sentence:

Many retired workers spend their time on relaxing hobbies.

In order to draw the tree we must know the structure; that it, we must know what all of the constituents in the sentence are and what syntactic categories, both lexical and phrasal, each belongs to. In order to determine constituency, you must apply the constituency tests. (Some constituents in this particular sentence were already determined in Exercise 6.1.0.) The phrasal constituents for this sentence and their phrasal categories, are given below:

a.   many retired workers (NP)
b.   spend their time on relaxing hobbies (VP)
c.   their time (NP)
d.   on relaxing hobbies (PP)
e.   relaxing hobbies (NP)

Each of these can be shown to be constituents with the constituency tests.
    When drawing the tree, you might begin by labelling the lexical category of each word:

DET	ADJ	N	V	DET	N	P	ADJ	N
many	retired	workers	spend	their	time	on	relaxing	hobbies

Now indicate the smallest phrasal constituents by drawing lines from each word of a constituent to a point above and label the category to which it belongs:

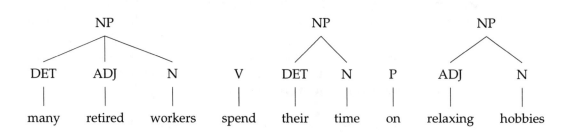

Then indicate which of these constituents form larger constituents by drawing lines from the labels to a point and indicating the category to which they belong:

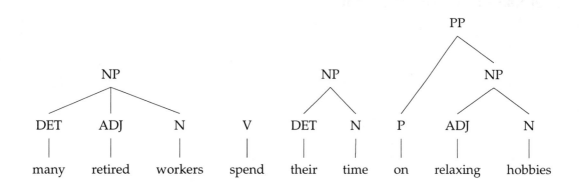

Continue until the constituents which form the sentence (S) have been represented:

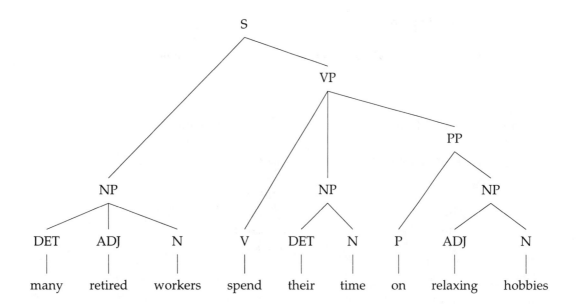

Note that there is a line from every lexical item to some constituent node.

Exercise 10.5.0 (Middle Chinese)

(A) Protoforms:

Proto-language	Gloss
*[kim]	*zither*
*[lat]	*spicy hot*
*[mɔk]	*lonesome*
*[lam]	*basket*
*[gip]	*worry*
*[lan]	*lazy*
*[pa]	*fear*

(B)

Mandarin	*Hakka*
*velar stops > palatal affricates / before [i]	none
*m >n / at the ends of words	none
*voiceless stops > Ø / at the ends of words	none

Explanation:

Total correspondence allows us to reconstruct the following sounds:

Proto-language	Gloss
*[_i_]	*zither*
*[la_]	*spicy hot*
*[mɔ_]	*lonesome*
*[la_]	*basket*
*[_i_]	*worry*
*[lan]	*lazy*
*[pa]	*fear*

Position 1 in the 'zither' cognate set exhibits a [č]-[k] alternation. Since [č] is palatal and "consonants become palatalized before front vowels," we need to know if there is a front vowel in position 2. There is, so we reconstruct *[k] because doing so results in the most natural development. In the cognate set for 'worry', we have a very similar choice. By the same reasoning we reconstruct *[g]. *[č,ǰ] and *[k,g] are the natural classes of palatal affricates and velar stops, respectively. Therefore we can group these two sound changes together and use a single rule—making use of natural classes—to describe the change for both alternations.

In position 3 in the 'zither' cognate set, there is an [m]-[n] alternation. Neither direction of change is more natural, and the "majority rule" is of no help. In such a case, we need to look at the other cognates sets. In the cognate set for 'lazy,' both languages have a word-final [n]. This information resolves the [m]-[n] alternation dilemma because sound change is regular. We must reconstruct *[m], because if we reconstructed *[n], then in Hakka we cannot account for a word-final [n] in [lan] 'lazy' and a word-final [m] in [kim] 'zither' with a regular sound change. Of course, the change of *[m] to [n] in Mandarin only occurs word finally (because [mɔ] 'lonesome' begins with a [m]). We also need to put that condition on the rule.

In cognate sets 2, 3, and 5, there are [t]-Ø, [k]-Ø, and [p]-Ø alternations, respectively. [t,k,p] is a natural class (voiceless stops). Once again, we must reconstruct the voiceless stops and delete them in Mandarin in order to be able to posit regular sound changes. If we chose not to reconstruct the stops, we would have trouble predicting which stop would be added to the end of a word in Hakka. Worse yet, there would be no explanation for why there is no [k] at the end of [pa] 'fear' in Hakka. This sound change too is limited to the ends of words, as the word-initial [p] in Mandarin [pa] 'fear' does not delete.

Appendix B   Taking Exams

In the examinations you will be taking in this course, you will encounter several different types of questions. While some may be quite familiar types to you and thus pose no real difficulties in terms of your strategy for completing the exam successfully (for example, true-false or multiple choice questions), others may prove somewhat more difficult. Two types of questions that prove especially troublesome for students are *definitions* and *essay questions*. Below are some hints regarding each of these types as well as some pointers on exam taking in general.

Definitions

Most people have a hard time giving good, concise, and informative definitions for the technical terms that come up in a beginning linguistics class. The reason for this is not just that the terms are quite new, but also that the act of defining is actually not something one is commonly called upon to perform in ordinary everyday language use. As an exercise in what constitutes a good definition, consider the following task: define what an *orange* is (notice that this is parallel to tasks on linguistics exams, such as "Define *dissimilation*").

Let's see what a good answer to this question would be—that is, what a good definition of an orange would be. Consider the following possible definitions:

1. An orange is when you have a fruit that is colored orange and you squeeze it to make juice; it comes from a tree.
2. An orange is a round, orange-colored citrus fruit that yields a sweet or bitter acidic juice.

Clearly the second definition is preferable to the first. Why? Both definitions give information about oranges and how one might identify such a fruit, but the second is structured in a much better way than the first. The second definition starts out by classifying *orange*, i.e., identifying as narrowly as possible that class of objects to which it belongs, thereby reducing the range of possible fields a reader has to consider when trying to determine what an orange is. Then it gives some salient characteristics of an orange that help to differentiate it from other members of its class, in this case other citrus fruits like the grapefruit or tangerine. By contrast, the first definition does none of that, and moreover, by using the construction "an orange is when . . . ," it is considering an orange to be an event, something that *happens*, rather than an object, or something that *is*.

Let's apply this strategy of defining terms to a linguistic example now, namely, *dissimilation*. A definition parallel to the first for *orange* would be:

3. Dissimilation is when there are two sounds in a word that become less like one another.

Compare that with a definition parallel to the second one for *orange*:

4. Dissimilation is a type of phonological process in which one sound in a word becomes less like another sound in the same word with respect to one or more phonological features.

The second definition again is to be preferred, in part because it locates dissimilation in its proper class, namely, that of phonological processes, and then goes on to specify the features that distinguish it from other members of that class. In contrast, the first definition (3) does not give this "genus and species" information, and a teacher grading such an answer would have to ask himself or herself whether the student understood just what sort of thing *dissimilation* actually is.

Finally, it is often a good idea to give an appropriate example, real if possible, or made-up if necessary, to indicate that you really do understand just what it is you are defining; thus a fully complete answer to the task "Define dissimilation" would be:

5. Dissimilation is a phonological process in which one sound in a word becomes less like another sound in the same word with respect to one or more phonological features; for example, the Latin word *peregrinus* turned into French *pelerin* 'pilgrim' and the *–r–* changing to *–l–* is a case of dissimilation.

Essay Questions

The purpose of essay questions is to allow an instructor to find out whether the student understands the course material well enough to see the relationships among the data and to create some synthesis in his or her own mind, rather than to just regurgitate a more or less random collection of ideas. Thus essay questions test the depth of a student's knowledge. In order to answer them properly, you must be able to present the required information in an organized, logical way. The following are some suggestions to aid you in this endeavor.

1. *Know* the material. For instance, a typical essay question on a linguistics exam might be "Is language more iconic than arbitrary? Support your answer with illustrations from human language." To study for questions such as this, you should not simply memorize all the terms you have heard your instructor mention in class. Rather you should understand what the terms mean in relation to language and why the distinctions they make are important. For this particular example you should discuss both the iconic and the arbitrary features of language. Be prepared to give specific examples of each type of feature. Based on your observations you should determine which type of feature seems to be dominant in characterizing the system of language as a whole.

2. *Read* the questions. This may sound trivial, but it's amazing how many people do poorly on exams simply because they don't make sure they know what they're being asked to do. If you can't understand the question after reading it carefully, don't hesitate to ask the instructor what he or she is asking you to do. For example, failing to take note of the crucial words *more . . . than* in the example given above, you may give examples of arbitrariness and iconicity in language without ever addressing the question of which term more obviously characterizes language—an oversight on your part which will probably result in the loss of most of the points for the question.

3. *Plan* your answer. Once you know what the instructor wants, take a little time to figure out how to give the answer. What are the main points you are trying to make? How can you support them? For instance, if you decide that language is more arbitrary than iconic, you've done the easy part and answered the first part of the question. However, now comes the hard part, backing up your claim with actual facts from English or other languages. The main point you want to make is that language is mostly arbitrary. Before you start writing your answer, you should think of and jot down data that support this claim. For example:

   • The same object in nature is referred to with different sequences of sounds in different languages. For instance, in English we call paper, bound together with writing on it, a *book*; in French it is a *livre*, and in Russian *kniga*.

- The fact that there is no intrinsic reason for calling a dog in English *dog*. It just so happens that at one time speakers agreed upon a sequence of sounds to represent such an object, and we have inherited, in a somewhat changed phonetic form, this verbal label.

4. *Write in essay format.* Write in complete sentences and paragraphs; don't use sentence fragments and don't just list ideas or examples. Start with a topic sentence that shows that you are responding to the question being asked and that states clearly what your position is. Then utilize relevant paragraph breaks and transition sentences. State your conclusion explicitly. Do not expect your instructor to read between the lines to figure out what your conclusion is. It is *your* job to make what you mean clear.

5. *Don't pad your answer.* You don't have the time to wander off into irrelevance, and your instructor doesn't have the time to read it. So, all other things being equal (accuracy, clarity, completeness), the shorter answer is better than the longer answer. If your points are substantial and relevant, extra words are unnecessary and potentially confusing.

6. *Pace* yourself. Remember that you're working against the clock, and don't spend half your time on a question worth ten percent of your grade. If the exam allows you to choose questions, don't spend a lot of time deciding; if one is clearly easier for you, answer it, and if two are of about the same difficulty, pick the first one. If the questions are worth different numbers of points, spend proportionally more time on the more heavily weighted ones. If you get stuck, go on to the next question and come back later.

7. *Proofread your answer.* If you have a few extra minutes, use them to make sure that you (a) said what you meant to say and (b) said it clearly (most teachers will take points off if you make it difficult for them to figure out what you're talking about). Proofreading may prove even more valuable in the question above if, for instance, you inadvertently confused the terms *iconic* and *arbitrary* and have them completely backwards.

Sample Essay

The following provides you with a sample essay based on the question above. Read the essay carefully and note how it addresses the question with clear and concise details. Immediately after the essay is a sample outline that shows the organization of the essay. You will probably not have enough time to make an outline quite as complete as this one in an actual test situation, but even a rough sketch of the points you want to make (written as you think of them) will be of great use when organizing your answer.

Although natural language contains elements of both arbitrariness and iconicity, it is beyond a doubt more arbitrary than iconic.

The term *arbitrariness* refers to the fact that in human language there is not a natural connection between the sound symbol (word) that stands for an object and the object itself. *Iconicity*, on the other hand, refers to a very close relationship between the verbal label for an object and the object itself. Onomatopoetic words (words that sound like what they name, such as *hiss* for the sound a snake makes) illustrate iconicity in language. The arbitrary nature of language can be more easily illustrated. For example, in the word *stereo* there is no clue as to the nature of the object referred to. The same object could just as easily have been called a *frimble*. Nor in the case of the word *sincerity* is there any clue as to the nature of the concept.

One reason why language is more arbitrary than iconic is somewhat obvious: there are many, many more examples of words which are arbitrarily related to the thing they name than there are examples of iconic words.

A second reason for arguing that language is mostly arbitrary is that we use different sequences of sounds to name the same object in different languages. For example, the word *book* in English names a particular kind of object, but in French, a different word labels this object, namely *livre*, and in Russian the word is *kniga*. If the choice of word to name 'paper bound together with writing on it' were not arbitrary, we would not expect different languages to use different words.

For these two reasons, then, it is clear that language is a predominantly arbitrary system of communication. The connections between the sounds of words and their meanings are usually arbitrary, not iconic.

Outline

A. Introduction
   1. Introducing the terms *arbitrary* and *iconic*
   2. Language is more arbitrary than iconic
B. Defining arbitrariness and iconicity
   1. Example of iconicity in English
   2. Examples of arbitrariness in English
C. Why language is more arbitrary than iconic
   1. There are more examples of arbitrary words
   2. Cross-linguistic evidence
D. Conclusion: restating evidence
   1. Most of language is arbitrary
   2. Sound-meaning connections are usually arbitrary, not iconic

Additional Information

Unfortunately, knowing *how* to apply the techniques discussed above is not enough; you must also know *when* each type of answer is appropriate. For example, the clearest definition in the world is not going to help you much if the question is really asking you to do something else. This mistake is particularly common when students are asked to compare and contrast terms. First impulse tells us to simply define the two terms and go on, but if we think a minute about what "compare" and "contrast" *mean* we see that this really isn't sufficient. Compare-and-contrast questions are asking you to go beyond definitions, to *synthesize* what you know about the material. To satisfactorily answer a compare-and-contrast question you must make *explicit* the properties or features that the two items share and the properties or features that distinguish them. Simply defining the two terms achieves neither of these goals.

A similar point can be made about essay writing. It is a waste of time and effort (especially time) to develop an elaborate response for a simple short answer question. On the other hand, you do want to be certain that your answer is complete enough. One important clue to the degree of depth expected is the relative point value of the question. The more the question is worth, the more detailed your answer should be. Another indication is the amount of time spent on the topic. If the issue was not addressed in detail in class or in the readings, then your instructor probably won't expect a very detailed answer either. Finally, the phrasing of the question itself can be a clue. General, open-ended questions, such as *Discuss the phenomenon of dissimilation* or *Argue for or against the view that language is more arbitrary than iconic*, require more detailed answers than questions like *What is dissimilation?* or

Give an example of arbitrariness in human language. The latter pair explicitly ask for a particular piece of information, the former merely supply the topic to be expanded upon. It is up to you to determine what or how much needs to be said. All of these factors—point value, degree of emphasis, and phrasing—should be taken into consideration *before* you begin your answer so that you can budget your time wisely. If you have any doubts at all as to how much is expected of you be sure to ask your instructor. After all, he or she is the one who will be judging your work.

In closing, let us emphasize again an important general strategy mentioned above in regard to taking an examination (and this holds, by the way, for any exam, not just those in linguistics classes and for any type of exam question, not just essays): allot your time according to the relative importance of the questions. Thus, if one question is worth only 10 points out of 100, don't spend 20 minutes on it in an hour-long exam. Since many universities' class "hours" are 48 or 50 minutes in length and exams are often calculated on a scale of 100 points, it is a good rule of thumb to allow yourself no more than one-half as many minutes as the points the question is worth. For example, a ten-point question should at first occupy you no more than five minutes, a twenty-pointer no more than ten minutes. Once you have made an attempt to answer all the questions, you can go back (time permitting) to work on ones you were not able to complete at first.

Appendix C

Symbol Guide

Consonants

The following guide lists the phonetic symbols used in this book. Our choice of phonetic symbols has been guided by pragmatism and the desire to make the symbols as accessible as possible to the greatest number of students. We generally use the conventions of the subfield under investigation, with the exception of the files on phonetics (phoneticians follow International Phonetic Alphabet [IPA] conventions). Many of the symbols listed below are taken from the American tradition of phonetic transcription. Where this departs from IPA conventions, we list both in parallel, with the IPA symbol shaded.

Obstruents

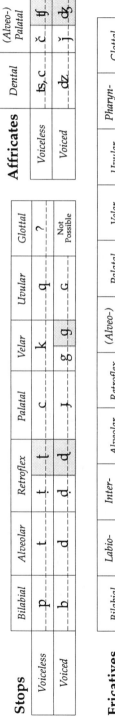

Stops

	Bilabial	Alveolar	Retroflex	Palatal	Velar	Uvular	Glottal
Voiceless	p	t	ṭ/ʈ	c	k	q	ʔ
Voiced	b	d	ḍ/ɖ	ɟ	g	ɢ	Not Possible

Fricatives

	Bilabial	Labio-Dental	Inter-Dental	Alveolar	Retroflex	Palatal	(Alveo-)Palatal	Velar	Uvular	Pharyngeal	Glottal
Voiceless	ɸ/φ	f	θ	s	ṣ/ʂ	ç	š/ʃ	x	χ	ħ	h
Voiced	β	v	ð	z	ẓ/ʐ	j	ž/ʒ	ɣ	ʁ	ʕ	ɦ

Affricates

	Dental	(Alveo-)Palatal
Voiceless	ts, c	č/ʧ
Voiced	dz	ǰ/ʤ

Special Symbols

	'C' = any consonant
Devoiced	C̥
Dental	C̪
Retroflex	C̣
Palatalized	Cʸ C'
Velarized	Cˠ
Glottalized	Cʔ
Syllabic	C̩
Unreleased	C˺
Aspirated	Cʰ

Sonorants

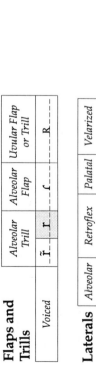

Flaps and Trills

	Alveolar Trill	Alveolar Flap	Uvular Flap or Trill
Voiced	r̃/r	ɾ	ʀ

Laterals

	Alveolar	Retroflex	Palatal	Velarized
Voiced	l	ḷ	ʎ	ł/ɫ

Nasals

	Bilabial	Alveolar	Retroflex	Palatal	Velar	Uvular
Voiced	m	n	ṇ	ñ/ɲ	ŋ	ɴ

Glides and Approximates

	Labio-Velar	Palatal	Labial-Palatal	Retroflex	Bunched
Voiced	w	y/j	ɥ	r̠/ɹ	ɻ

Vowels

Vowels	Round	Front		Central		Back	
High — Tense	+	ü	y			u	
	–	i				ɨ	ɯ
High — Lax	+	ü	ʏ			ʊ	
	–	ɪ					
Mid — Tense	+	ö	ø			o	
	–	e					
Mid — Lax	+	ɔ̈	œ			ɔ	
	–	ɛ		ʌ	ə		
Low — Lax	+	æ				a	ɑ

Special Symbols — 'V' = any vowel

Special Symbols	'V' = any vowel
Voiceless	V̥
Long	V: V̄
Nasalized	Ṽ
High Tone	V́
Low Tone	V̀
Falling Tone	V̂
Rising Tone	V̌
Short	V̆

Tone Letters

Tone Letters	
High Tone	˥
Low Tone	˩
Mid Tone	˧
Rising Tone	˦
Falling Tone	˨

Glossary

A

ABSTRACT NOUNS. Nouns that denote a mental object, an idea, or concept (e.g., *love, truth, honesty, hate*).

ACCENT. Characteristics of pronunciation inherent in every person's speech.

ACOUSTIC PHONETICS. Subfield of **phonetics** that is concerned with the physical characteristics of the sounds of speech.

ACRONYMS. Abbreviations formed by taking the initial sounds (or letters) of the words of a phrase and uniting them to form a pronounceable word (e.g., RADAR: RAdio Detecting And Ranging; SCUBA: *Self-Contained Underwater Breathing Apparatus*).

ACTIVE CONSTRUCTION OF A GRAMMAR THEORY. Theory of child language which says that children acquire a language by inventing rules of grammar based on the speech around them. (See also **Reinforcement Theory** and **Imitation Theory**.)

ADSTRATE LANGUAGES. Two or more languages in contact that mutually influence one another, owing to relatively equal degrees of power and prestige associated with the groups of speakers. (See also **Substrate Languages** and **Superstrate Language**.)

ADSTRATUM INFLUENCE. Mutual influence of two or more languages in contact through **borrowing** (e.g., English and French in Canada).

AFFIXATION. Process of forming words by adding **affixes** to **morphemes**.

AFFIXES. **Bound morphemes** that change the meaning or syntactic function of the words to which they attach. **Prefixes, infixes**, and **suffixes** are the three types of affixes.

AFFRICATE. Sound produced by complete obstruction of airflow followed by slight release of the articulators, allowing frication. An affricate can be thought of as a combination of a **stop** and a **fricative** (e.g., [č] and [ǰ]).

AGGLUTINATING LANGUAGE. A type of language in which the relationships between words in a sentence are indicated primarily by **bound morphemes**. In agglutinating languages, morphemes are joined together loosely so that it is easy to determine where the boundaries between morphemes are (e.g., Swahili: *tulimpenda* = "We loved him": *tu* = 'we', *li* = 'past,' *m* = 'him', *pend* = 'love', *a* = verbal suffix).

AGRAPHIA. Language disorder caused by damage to the angular gyrus; characterized by an inability to write words. Often accompanied by **alexia**.

ALEXIA. Language disorder caused by damage to angular gyrus; characterized by an inability to read and comprehend written words. Often accompanied by **agraphia**.

ALLO-. Prefix meaning *same*. (See **Allochers, Allomorphs, Allophones**.)

ALLOCHERS. Nondistinctive realizations of the same **chereme**.

ALLOMORPHS. Nondistinctive realizations of a particular morpheme that have the same function and are phonetically similar (e.g., English past tense *-ed* can appear as [-əd], [-t], or [-d] as in *started* [startəd], *picked* [pɪkt], *loved* [lʌvd]).

ALLOPHONES. Nondistinctive realizations of the same phoneme (e.g. Spanish /b/ appears as [b] when adjacent to a consonant or word-initially, but as [β] when between vowels. So [b] and [β] are allophones of the phoneme /b/.

ALPHABETIC WRITING SYSTEM. A system of consonant and vowel symbols that, either individually or in combinations, represent the speech sounds of a written language (e.g., English, Cyrillic, Hindi).

ALVEOLAR. Description of sounds produced by making contact between the tongue and the **alveolar ridge**.

ALVEOLAR RIDGE. Small bony ridge located just behind the upper front teeth.

AMBIGUITY. Property of words or sentences of having two or more meanings. Words with more than one meaning are said to be **lexically ambiguous** (e.g. *bank, crane*). Phrases with more than one meaning because of the structure of the phrase are referred to as **structurally ambiguous** (e.g., *Flying planes can be dangerous*).

ANALOGICAL CHANGE. A type of historical change in the grammar that involves the influence of one form or group of forms on another, causing one group of forms to become more like the other.

ANALYTIC LANGUAGES. Types of languages in which words consist mainly of one morpheme, and sentences are composed of sequences of these free morphemes. Grammatical relationships are often indicated by word order (e.g., Chinese, Vietnamese). (Also known as **isolating languages**.)

ANGULAR GYRUS. Language center of the brain located between **Wernicke's area** and the **visual cortex**, responsible for converting visual stimuli to auditory stimuli (and vice-versa).

ANTHROPOLOGICAL LINGUISTICS. The study of the relationship between language and culture.

ANTONYMS. Words that are in some sense opposite in meaning. See **gradable pairs** (also known as **scalar antonyms**), **relational opposites**, and **contradictory pairs** (also known as **complementary pairs**).

APHASIA. Inability to perceive, process, or produce language because of physical damage to the brain. See **Broca's Aphasia**, **Wernicke's Aphasia**, and **Conduction Aphasia**.

APPLIED LINGUISTICS. The application of the methods and results of linguistic research to such areas as language teaching; national language policies; lexicography; translation; and language in politics, advertising, classrooms, and courts.

ARBITRARINESS. In relation to language, this term is used to refer to the fact that a word's meaning is not predictable from its linguistic form, nor is its form dictated by its meaning. In other words, form and meaning in language are arbitrarily related.

ARGUMENT. (1) A reason put forth in support of or against a particular theory or belief. (2) The required elements of a sentence that combine with other elements to form larger syntactic units (e.g., in the sentence *Take a break!* the direct object *a break* is an argument of the verb *take*.)

ARTICULATORS. The parts of the **vocal tract** that are used to produce speech sounds (e.g., lips, tongue, **velum**, etc.)

ARTICULATORY GESTURES. Individual movements of the articulators to perform a particular articulation.

ARTICULATORY PHONETICS. Subfield of **phonetics** concerned with the production of speech sounds.

ASPECT. A grammatical category (usually of verbs) related to the notions of completeness or incompleteness of an action (e.g., in the sentence *We are working*, the aspect is "progressive" indicating that the action of working is still in progress [i.e., not complete]).

ASPIRATION. A puff of air that follows the release of a consonant when there is a delay in the onset of voicing. Symbolized by a superscript *h* (e.g., [p^h]).

ASSIMILATION. A process by which a sound becomes more like a nearby sound in terms of some feature(s) (e.g., nasals may assimilate to a following consonant's place of articulation: *phone book* /fonbʊk/ becomes [fombʊk] by assimilation.

ATTENTION GETTERS. Words used by parents to initiate an address to children (e.g., *Robin! Hey! Look!*).

ATTENTION HOLDERS. Tactics used to maintain children's attention for extended amounts of time (e.g., using whispering or a higher pitch).

AUDITORY CORTEX. Language center of the brain located next to the **Sylvian fissure**, responsible for receiving or identifying auditory signals and converting them into a form interpretable by other language centers of the brain.

AUDITORY PHONETICS. Subfield of **phonetics** concerned with the perception of speech sounds.

AUXILIARY VERBS. Verbs whose function is primarily to add grammatical information to an utterance, usually indicating tense, **aspect**, or other grammatical information that is not conveyed by the main verbs of the sentence.

B

BABBLING. A phase in the course of child language acquisition during which time the child produces nonmeaningful sequences of consonants and vowels. Generally begins around the age of six months.

BACK FORMATION. Word formation process in which a new base form is created from an apparently similar form (e.g., *to burgle* is a back formation from *burglar*).

BACKING. A type of sound change (either **diachronic** or **synchronic**) in which a front sound (usually a vowel) becomes a back sound.

BASIC ALLOPHONE. The allophone of a phoneme that is used when none of the change-inducing conditions are fulfilled. It is generally *least* limited in where it can occur. Also termed the *elsewhere allophone*.

BILABIAL. Sound produced by bringing both lips together (*bi* = 'two'; *labial* = 'lips').

BILINGUAL(ISM). State of commanding two languages; having linguistic **competence** in two languages.

BLENDING. Process of creating a new word by combining the parts of two different words, usually the beginning of one word and the end of another (e.g., *smoke* + *fog* > *smog*; *breakfast* + *lunch* > *brunch*).

BORROWING. Process by which one language adopts words and phrases from another language.

BOUND MORPHEMES. Morphemes that always attach to other morphemes, never existing as words themselves. (See also **Affixes**.)

BROAD PHONETIC TRANSCRIPTIONS. Phonetic transcriptions that show little or no phonetic detail.

BROCA'S APHASIA. Inability to plan the motor sequences used in speech or sign, owing to damage to **Broca's area** of the brain.

BROCA'S AREA. The region of the brain located at the base of the motor cortex in the left hemisphere of the brain. (See also **Broca's Aphasia**.)

C

CALQUES. See **Loan Translations**.

CAUSATIVE. A form of the verb indicating that the actor is making or causing an action on the part of someone or something else.

CENTRALIZATION. Process by which a speaker's pronunciation of a vowel approaches that of the central vowels [ə] or [ʌ].

CHEREMES. The smallest gestural units in sign languages. The gestural equivalent of the **phoneme**. Also termed *primes*. (See also **Allochers**.)

CLIPPING. Process of creating new words by shortening parts of a longer word (e.g., *phone* from *telephone*; *exam* from *examination*).

COGNATES. Words that descend from the same source. Usually similar in form and meaning.

COHORT THEORY. Theory of auditory word recognition hypothesizing that word recognition begins with the formation of a cohort (i.e., group) of words at the perception of the intial sound of a word and proceeds sound by sound with the cohort of words decreasing as more sounds are received.

COINAGE. Process of creating new words without employing any other word or word part already in existence. Words created "out of thin air" (e.g., *Kodak* or *Pepsi*).

COMMUNICATIVE ISOLATION. Situation in which a group of speakers forms a coherent speech community relatively isolated from speakers outside of that community.

COMPARATIVE METHOD. A technique that compares words of similar form and meaning in languages that are assumed to be related, in order to establish historical relationships among them. (Also known as *comparative reconstruction*.) (See also **Internal Reconstruction**.)

COMPETENCE. What we know when we know a language; the unconscious knowledge that a speaker of a language has about her or his native language.

COMPLEMENTARY DISTRIBUTION. The occurrence of sounds in a language such that they are never found in the same phonetic **environment**. Sounds that are in complementary distribution are **allophones** of the same **phoneme**.

COMPLEMENTARY PAIRS. See **Contradictory Pairs**.

COMPOUNDING. Word formation process by which new words are formed by combining two or more independent words (e.g., *basketball*).

COMPRESSION. Physical phenomenon resulting in a higher concentration of air molecules within a given space. (See also **Rarefaction**.)

CONDITIONED SOUND CHANGE. Sound change that occurs under the influence of nearby sounds.

CONDITIONING ENVIRONMENTS. Neighboring sounds of a given sound that cause it to undergo a change (e.g., the conditioning environment for the devoicing of a liquid is a preceding voiceless **obstruent** in syllable-initial position).

CONDUCTION APHASIA. A speech disorder caused by damage to the arcuate fasciculus, a nerve pathway that connects **Broca's area** to **Wernicke's area**. The speaker shows signs of **Wernicke's aphasia** but still appears able to understand the speech of others.

CONJUNCTIONS. Function words (belonging to the class of closed lexical categories) that join words and phrases of the same category (e.g., *and*, *or*, *but*).

CONSONANTAL ALPHABET. Alphabetic writing systems in which only the consonants in words are written, and the vowels are left out (e.g., Hebrew and Arabic use consonantal alphabets).

Constituent. Groupings of words that form a coherent syntactic or semantic unit.

Constituent Structure. The relationship between constituents in a sentence. (See also **Phrase Structure Rules**.)

Constriction. A narrowing in the **vocal tract** caused by articulator movement.

Contact Situations. Social situations in which speakers of distinct language varieties are brought together by social and/or economic factors such as settlement, trade, or relocation.

Content Morphemes. Morphemes that carry a semantic content as opposed to performing a grammatical function. (See also **Function Morphemes**.)

Context. The real-world facts that fill in the details not necessarily present in the discourse but useful or necessary in interpreting what is said. (See also **Epistemic Context, Linguistic Context, Physical Context, Social Context**.)

Context Effects. See **Semantic Association Network**.

Contour Tone Languages. Tone languages that have gliding tones, in which a transition is made from one tone to an adjacent tone (e.g., a rise from low to high), as well as level (or register) tones (in which no transition is made) (e.g., Chinese, Vietnamese, and Thai). (See also **Register Tone Languages**.)

Contradictory Pairs. Pairs of words that are opposites such that when one is applicable the other is not (e.g., *alive* and *dead*). (Also known as **complementary pairs**.)

Contralaterality. Property of the brain such that one side of the body is controlled by the opposite **hemisphere** of the brain. The **left hemisphere** controls the right side of the body, and the **right hemisphere** controls the left side of the body.

Contrastive Distribution. The occurrence of sounds in a language such that their use distinguishes between the meanings of the words in which they appear, indicating that those sounds are **phonemes** of the language in question. (See also **Overlapping Distribution**.)

Conversational Inferences. Conclusions drawn based on understood "rules" of conversation. (See also **Implicatures** and **Entailment**.)

Cooperative Principle. Principle formulated by philosopher H. P. Grice that says that underlying a conversation is the understanding that what one says is intended to contribute to the purposes of the conversation. Certain rules of maxims of conversation are said to enforce compliance with this principle.

Corpus Callosum. Bundle of nerve fibers connecting the two hemispheres of the brain for the purpose of exchanging information between the two halves.

Cortex. Outer surface of the brain responsible for many of the cognitive abilities or functions of the brain.

Count Nouns. Nouns denoting objects that are discrete, countable units (e.g., *cat, house, human, tree*). (See also **Mass Nouns** and **Abstract Nouns**.)

Covert Prestige. Type of prestige that exists among members of nonstandard-speaking communities that defines how people should speak in order to be considered members of those particular communities.

Creole Language. A language that develops from contact between speakers of different languages and serves as the primary means of communication for a particular group of speakers.

Critical Period. (1) Age span during which children must have exposure to language and must built the critical brain structures to be able to gain native speaker **competence**, usually between birth and approximately two years of age. (2) Age span during which individuals can easily acquire a second language; said to be between the ages of about ten to sixteen years.

D

Deep Structure. The form of a sound, word, or sentence before any **transformations** or **rules** have been applied to it.

Degradations. Semantic change by which a word acquires a more pejorative meaning over time (e.g., *hussy* used to mean 'housewife' but now means 'lewd or brazen woman').

Deictic Expressions. Words or expressions that are relative to the time and place of the utterance; may be used to point to objects and indicate their distance from the speaker (e.g., *go!, come!, here, there, now, then, this,* or *that*).

Deletion. Process by which a sound present in the phonemic form (=underlying form) is removed from the phonetic form in certain environments (e.g., *Columbus* /kəlʌmbəs/ → [klʌmbəs]). (See also **Insertion**.)

Derivation. Process by which an underlying form is changed as phonological, morphological, or syntactic rules act upon it.

DERIVATIONAL MORPHEMES. Morphemes that change the meaning or lexical category of the words to which they attach. (See also **Inflectional Morphemes**.)

DESCRIPTIVE GRAMMAR. Objective description of a speaker's knowledge of a language (**Competence**) based on their use of the language (**Performance**).

DETERMINERS. A closed set of **morphemes**; semantically, often indicating definiteness or indefiniteness (e.g., *a, an, the, those, many, most, some,* etc.).

DIACHRONIC ANALYSIS. Analysis of language change through time (*dia* = 'across'; *chronos* = 'time').

DIALECT. A variety of a language defined by both geographical factors and social factors, such as class, religion, and ethnicity.

DIALECT CONTINUUM. Situation in which a large number of contiguous dialects exist, each mutually intelligible with the next, but with the dialects at either end of the continuum not being mutually intelligible.

DIALECTOLOGY. Study of regional dialects.

DICHOTIC LISTENING TESTS. Experiments that present two different sounds (speech and/or nonspeech) simultaneously, one in each ear.

DIGLOSSIA. Situation in which two varieties of a language are used for clearly defined functions. One variety is used for more prestigious functions, as for example in education, politics, and literature; the other is used for less prestigious functions and predominantly for everyday conversation.

DIPHTHONG. Two-part vowel sounds consisting of a vowel and a **glide** in the same syllable (e.g., [ay], as in *fly* [flay], is a diphthong of English).

DIPHTHONGIZATION. Change of a simple vowel sound to a complex one. Process by which a **monophthong** becomes a **diphthong**.

DIRECT SPEECH ACTS. Utterances that perform their functions in a direct and literal manner. (See also **Performative Verbs** and **Indirect Speech Acts**.)

DISCOURSE. A continuous stretch of speech or written text, going beyond the size of a sentence.

DISCOURSE ANALYSIS. The study of the use of language at a level usually above the sentence. Discourse analysts examine the structure of the information flow of speech, the interdependencies of sentences in speech, and other aspects of language use.

DISCRETENESS. Term used to refer to the property of languages to have complex messages built up out of smaller, separable units.

DISPLACEMENT. Term used to refer to the ability to communicate about things that are not physically or temporally present.

DISSIMILATION. Process by which two nearby sounds become less alike with respect to some feature.

DISTINCTIVE SOUNDS. Sounds that distinguish meanings of words in a language (e.g., in the words [fil] *feel* and [ful] *fool*, the vowels [i] and [u] are the distinctive sounds). (Also known as *contrastive sounds*.) (See also **Phoneme**.)

DISTRIBUTION. The set of phonetic environments in which a sound occurs. (See also **Overlapping Distribution, Complementary Distribution,** and **Contrastive Distribution**.)

DITRANSITIVE VERBS. Verbs that take both a direct object and an indirect object (e.g., *gave* in the sentence *Robin gave Pat a book* is a ditransitive verb that takes the direct object *a book* and the indirect object *Pat*).

DYNAMIC PALATOGRAPHY. Experimental method that tracks the contacts and contact patterns between the tongue and the hard palate over time.

E

ELEVATION. Semantic change by which words take on a grander or more positive connotation over time (e.g., the word *knight* once meant 'youth or military follower' but now has a more romantic and impressive connotation).

ENTAILMENT. A relationship between two words or sentences such that if the first is true, the second must be true (e.g., if something is a couch, then it is also a piece of furniture; therefore, *couch* entails *furniture*.)

ENVIRONMENT. The preceding and following contexts of a sound.

EPISTEMIC CONTEXT. Background knowledge shared by speakers and hearers.

EPONYMY. Process of naming places, inventions, activities, etc., based on the names of persons somehow connected with them (e.g., the word *watt* is named after James Watt, a Scottish inventor).

EXPANDED PIDGIN. A later stage in the development of a **pidgin**, which has most of the structural features of a primary language (also known as *crystallized pidgin*).

EXTENSIONS. Diachronic semantic change by which the set of appropriate contexts or referents for a word increases (e.g., the word *Coke* used to refer to a particular brand but now can be used for any carbonated beverage).

F

FAMILY TREE THEORY. Theory formulated by August Schleicher that says that languages change in regular, recognizable ways, and similarities among languages are due to a "genetic" relationship among them.

FEATURE MODEL. Model of the **lexicon** assuming that information about words is locally stored with the lexical entry in terms of semantic features.

FEATURE NETWORK MODEL. Model of the **lexicon** assuming that information about words is stored in terms of semantic features that are distributed to the lexical entries.

FELICITY CONDITIONS. A set of conditions that must be satisfied if a speech act is to be correctly and honestly performed.

FISSURES. Depressions in the cortex of the brain's hemispheres that serve as physical boundaries for the identification of different sections of the brain. (See also **Gyri**.)

FLAP. Sound produced by the tongue tip hitting the **alveolar ridge** at a high speed. In English, the voiced alveolar flap can function as an allophone of the phoneme /t/ or /d/ as in the words *writer* [rayɾr̩] or *rider* [rayɾr̩].

FOLK ETYMOLOGY. The reanalysis of a word or phrase (usually an unfamiliar one) into a word or phrase composed of more commonly known words (e.g., Alzheimer's disease > oldtimer's disease; nepotism > nephew-tism; sickle-cell anemia > sick-as-hell anemia). Also known as *popular etymology.*

FOREIGNER TALK. Modification strategies used by native speakers to communicate with second-language learners.

FORMANTS. Resonant frequencies that amplify some groups of harmonics above others; appearing as dark bands on a **spectrogram**.

FREE MORPHEMES. Morphemes that can stand alone as words.

FREE VARIATION. Term used to refer to two sounds that occur in overlapping environments but cause no distinction in the meaning of their respective words (e.g., the sounds [p] and [pʰ] are in free variation in the two pronunciations [lip] and [lipʰ] *leap*).

FREGE'S PRINCIPLE. Principle stating that the meaning of a sentence is determined by the meaning of its words and by the syntactic structure in which they are combined. Also known as the *Principle of Compositionality.*

FREQUENCY EFFECTS. Additional ease with which a word is accessed owing to its repeated occurrence in the discourse or context.

FRICATIVES. Sounds made by forming a nearly complete obstruction of the airstream so that when air passes through the small passage, turbulent airflow (i.e., frication) is produced.

FRONTING. A type of sound change (either **diachronic** or **synchronic**) in which a back sound (usually a vowel) becomes a front sound.

FUNCTION MORPHEMES. Morphemes that provide information about the grammatical relationships between words in a sentence.

FUNCTION WORDS. Words that relate phrases of various types to other phrases, but have little meaning outside of their grammatical purposes.

FUNCTIONAL SHIFT. Process of creating a new word by shifting from one part of speech to another without changing the form of the word.

FUNDAMENTAL FREQUENCY. The rate at which the vocal folds vibrate during voicing. The frequency of repetition of a periodic wave. Closely related to pitch.

FUSIONAL LANGUAGE. A type of language in which the relationships between the words in a sentence are indicated by **bound morphemes** that are difficult to separate from the stem. In fusional languages it is difficult to tell where one morpheme ends and the next begins (e.g., Spanish: cantó: cant = 'sing', -ó = third person, singular, past).

G

GARDEN PATH. Phenomenon by which people are fooled into thinking a sentence has a different structure than it actually does because of an apparent ambiguity (e.g., *The horse raced past the barn fell* where you expect the sentence to end on *barn*, but it can end on *fell* if you interpret *raced past the barn* as a passive participial phrase modifying *horse*).

GENERATIVITY. Property of human languages to use a finite set of rules and elements to produce an infinite set of grammatical sentences.

GLIDES. Sounds produced with a closure in the vocal tract that is only slightly more constricted than that for vowels (e.g., in English the glides are [y], [w] and [w]).

GLOTTAL. Produced at the **glottis**.

GLOTTIS. The space between the **vocal folds**. (See also **Voicing**.)

GRADABLE PAIRS. Words that have opposing meanings because they represent opposite ends of a scale (e.g., *bright* and *dark; light* and *heavy*). Also known as *scalar antonyms*.

GRAMMAR. A system of linguistic elements and rules. (See also **Prescriptive Grammar** and **Descriptive Grammar**.)

GREAT VOWEL SHIFT. A change that occurred in the English vowel system wherein the long high vowels diphthongized and the other long vowels rise to fill in the empty spaces created.

GRICEAN MAXIMS. Conversational rules that regulate conversation by enforcing compliance with the **Cooperative Principle**.

GYRI. Bumps in the cortex of the brain's hemispheres. (Sing. *gyrus*) (See also **Fissures**.)

H

HARMONICS. Overtones of the fundamental frequency of the vocal tract; multiples of the fundamental frequency (e.g., if the fundamental is 150 Hz, it will have harmonics at 300 Hz, 450 Hz, 600 Hz, and so on).

HEAD. The constituent from which a phrase is named (e.g., in a verb phrase, the head is the verb; in a noun phrase, the head is the noun).

HEAD-FINAL LANGUAGES. A syntactic type of language in which the **head** word of a phrase appears at the end of the phrase.

HEAD-INITIAL LANGUAGES. A syntactic type of language in which the **head** word of a phrase appears at the beginning of the phrase.

HEMISPHERECTOMIES. Operations in which one hemisphere or part of one hemisphere is surgically removed from the brain.

HEMISPHERES. The two nearly symmetrical halves of the brain. (See also **Left Hemisphere** and **Right Hemisphere**.)

HIERARCHICAL STRUCTURE. Term used to describe the dominance relationship among elements in a word, phrase, or sentence. (See also **Constituent Structure**.)

HISTORICAL LINGUISTICS. The study of how languages change through time; the study of how languages are historically related to one another.

HOLOPHRASTIC PHASE. Phase in child language acquisition in which children are limited to one word at a time in their production.

HOMONYMS. Two or more distinct words with the same pronunciation and spelling but different meanings (e.g., *pool table* and *swimming pool*).

HOMOPHONES. Two or more distinct words with the same pronunciation but different meanings and spellings (e.g., *two, too, to*).

I

ICONICITY. Relationship between form and meaning in which the form is dictated by the meaning (e.g., a sign with a picture of a crossed-out cigarette, forbidding smoking in public areas).

IDEOGRAPHIC WRITING SYSTEMS. See **Logographic Writing Systems**.

IDIOLECT. The language variety of an individual speaker.

IDIOMS. Fixed sequences of words with a fixed meaning that is not composed of the literal meanings of the individual words (e.g., *to kick the bucket* means 'to die', but this meaning cannot be obtained from the literal meanings of the individual words).

IMITATION THEORY. Child language acquisition theory that claims that children acquire language by listening to the speech around them and reproducing what they hear. (See also **Reinforcement Theory** and **Active Construction of a Grammar Theory**.)

IMPLICATIONAL LAWS. Observations about language universals that take the form of an implication (e.g., if *A* then *B*, meaning that if a language has feature *A*, then we can expect it to have feature *B* or if a language has the sound [ŋ] then it probably has the sound [n]).

IMPLICATURES. A conclusion drawn in conversation based on warranted evidence, though not necessarily logically valid. (See also **Conversational Inferences** and **Entailment**.)

INDIRECT SPEECH ACTS. Utterances that perform their functions in an indirect and nonliteral manner (e.g., asking the question *Does anyone have the time?* as a request for the time is an indirect speech act, since a literal interpretation of this question would yield the answer *yes* or *no*).

INFIX. A type of **bound morpheme** that is inserted into the root (See also **Affixes**, **Prefixes**, and **Suffixes**.)

INFLECTION. Modification of a word to express grammatical relationships to other words in the sentence.

INFLECTIONAL MORPHEMES. Morphemes that serve a purely grammatical function, never creating a new word but only a different form of the same word. (See also **Function Morphemes, Content Morphemes,** and **Derivational Morphemes**.)

INNATENESS HYPOTHESIS. A hypothesis that humans are genetically predisposed to learn and use language.

INSERTION. Phonological process by which a segment not present in the phonemic (or underlying) form is added in the phonetic form (e.g., the insertion of a vowel into a consonant cluster in the word *athlete* /æθlit/ → [æθəlit]. (See also **Deletion**.)

INTERDENTAL. Term used to refer to sounds produced by positioning the tongue tip between the upper and lower teeth.

INTERNAL RECONSTRUCTION. Method of analysis that makes hypotheses about a language's history by comparing forms that are assumed to be related within a single language. (See also **Comparative Method**.)

INTERNAL VARIATION. Property of languages of having more than one way of expressing the same meaning.

INTRANSITIVE VERBS. Verbs that only take subject noun phrases and no object noun phrases (e.g., *fall, die, exist*).

ISOGLOSS. A line drawn on a dialect map marking the boundary of an area where a particular linguistic feature is found.

ISOLATING LANGUAGES. See **Analytic Languages**.

J

JARGON. Speech usually associated with or used within a particular occupation, hobby, or sport. Also known as *technical language.*

L

LABIODENTAL. Term used to refer to sounds produced by making contact between the lower lip and the upper teeth.

LANGUAGE CONTACT. Situation in which groups of speakers of different languages come into contact with one another.

LANGUAGE CONVERGENCE. The development of an increasingly mutual agreement of two or more languages in contact.

LANGUAGE DEATH. The complete demise of a language; a dead language is no longer being acquired as a first language by speakers.

LANGUAGE PLANNING. Process by which governments make policies or laws concerning language.

LANGUAGE SHIFT. Transfer by a group of speakers to another language, while abandoning their native language.

LARYNX. Cartilage and muscle located at the top of the **trachea**, containing the **vocal folds**; commonly referred to as the *voicebox.* (See also **Glottis**.)

LATERALIZATION. Specialization of the brain hemispheres for different cognitive functions.

LAX VOWELS. Vowel sounds that have less peripheral positions in the vowel space; vowels that involve small changes from the mid-central position of the tongue. (See also **Tense Vowels**.)

LEFT HEMISPHERE. The left side of the brain; generally thought to be the location of many language-controlling parts of the brain.

LENGTH. Increased duration of segments. (See also **Suprasegmental Features**.)

LEXICAL AMBIGUITY. A situation in which a lexical item has two or more meanings (e.g., *pen* meaning writing instrument or place where pigs live). (See also **Structural Ambiguity**.)

LEXICAL CATEGORIES. Classes of words grouped together based on their morphological and syntactic properties. Traditionally known as *parts of speech* (e.g., nouns, verbs, adjectives, etc.).

LEXICON. Mental listing of the words in a language, including information about their meaning, grammatical function, pronunciation, etc.

LEXIFIER LANGUAGE. See **Superstrate Language**.

LINEAR ORDER. Sequence of words in sentence.

LINGUIST. Someone who studies the structure of language and its use.

LINGUISTIC CONTEXT. The preceding and following utterances surrounding a given discourse.

LINGUISTIC SIGN. The combination of linguistic form and meaning.

LINKING VERBS. Verbs that indicate a relationship of identity between the subject and the predicate of the verb, or of a quality possessed by the subject and found in the predicate (e.g., *be, smell, look, seem; The pudding looks delicious*).

Liquids. Consonant sounds produced by an obstruction of airflow that is less narrow than that of stops or fricatives, but more narrow than that of glides.

Loan Translations. Phrases borrowed into a language by way of a word-for-word translation into native morphemes. (Also termed **calques**.)

Loanwords. Words that are borrowed from one language into another. (Also known as *loans*.)

Logographic Writing Systems. Systems of writing in which each character represents a separate morpheme. Also known as *ideographic writing systems*.

Lowering. A type of sound change (either **diachronic** or **synchronic**) in which a high or mid sound (usually a vowel) becomes a lower sound.

M

Machine Translation. Use of computers to translate from one language to another.

Malapropism. Type of production error by which a speaker uses a semantically incorrect word in place of a phonetically similar word without having an awareness of his or her mistake (e.g., saying that a person who can function equally well with both hands is *ambivalent*, when the intended word is *ambidextrous*).

Manner of articulation. Term used to refer to how the airstream is modified by the articulators in the **vocal tract** to produce a sound.

Mass Nouns. Nouns denoting objects that are not countable or divisible into discrete units (e.g., *clay, sand, water, air*).

Metathesis. Switching of the order of two sounds, each taking the place of the other.

Minimal Attachment Theory. Idea that people initially construct the least complex structure in interpreting sentences.

Minimal Pair. Two words that differ only by a single sound in the same position and have different meanings but are otherwise identical (e.g., *pin* and *bin*).

Monophthong. A simple vowel sound. (See also **Diphthong.**)

Monophthongization. Vowel change from a complex vowel sound to a simple vowel sound; vowel change from a diphthong to a monophthong.

Mood. A category realized by inflecting the verb or by modifying it by means of auxiliaries; usually indicating the speaker's attitude toward the information being conveyed. *Declarative, interrogative,* and *subjunctive* are three types of mood.

Morpheme-Internal Change. A type of word formation process wherein a word changes internally to indicate grammatical information (e.g., some English plurals: *mouse-mice; goose-geese* and past tense: *give-gave*, etc.).

Morphemes. Smallest linguistic unit that has a meaning or grammatical function.

Morphological Alternation. A **diachronic** change that results in the creation of an alternative pronunciation for a given morpheme.

Morphological Frames. Position of a word with respect to the bound morphemes that can attach to it (e.g., '___-s' is a morphological frame for nouns that can be marked by plural -s).

Morphology. The study of the construction of words out of **morphemes**.

Motor Cortex. Language center of the brain located in the upper middle of each hemisphere, perpendicular to the **Sylvian fissure**, responsible for sending impulses to the muscles.

Mutual Entailment. A logical relationship between two propositions such that each one entails the other; only true if both propositions are true (e.g., *couch* and *sofa* represent mutual entailments; if something is a *couch*, then it is also a *sofa*, and vice-versa). Also known as *complete synonymy*.

Mutual Intelligibility. Situation in which speakers of different language varieties are able to understand and communicate with one another.

N

Narrow Phonetic Transcriptions. Transcriptions that record the fine details of the articulation of phones.

Nasals. Sounds produced by making a complete obstruction of the airflow in the oral cavity and by lowering the **velum** to allow air to pass through the nasal cavity. Also known as *nasal stops*.

Nativization. Process by which some variety of speech that was no one's native language is learned by children in a speech community as their first language.

NATURAL CLASSES. Groups of sounds in a language that satisfy a given description to the exclusion of other sounds in that language (e.g., *nasal* describes the natural class of sounds produced with a nasal airflow: [n, m, ŋ] in English).

NEUROLINGUISTICS. The study of the brain and how it functions in the production, perception, and acquisition of language.

NONSTANDARD VARIETY. Any variety of a language not considered to be representative of the **prestige** or **standard variety**.

NONSTATIVE ADJECTIVES. Adjectives denoting temporary or changeable qualities (e.g., *happy, loud, impatient*).

NOUN. See **Count Nouns, Mass Nouns**, and **Abstract Nouns**.

O

OBLIGATORY RULES. Rules that apply in the speech of all speakers of a language or dialect, regardless of style or rate of speech.

OBSTRUENTS. A natural class of sounds produced with an obstruction of the airflow in the oral cavity while the nasal cavity is closed off. Includes oral stops, fricatives, and affricates. (See also **Sonorants**.)

ONOMATOPOEIA. Use of words that are imitative of sounds occurring in nature or that have meanings that are associated with such sounds (e.g., *moo, meow,* and *bow wow*).

OPAQUE SIGNS. Signs used in sign language that have no recognizable relationship to their **referents**. (See also **Transparent Signs** and **Translucent Signs**.)

OPTIONAL RULES. Phonological, morphological, and syntactic rules that may or may not apply in an individual's speech.

ORAL STOPS. Sounds produced by completely obstructing the airstream in the oral cavity and then quickly releasing the constriction to allow the air to escape from the oral cavity.

OVERLAPPING DISTRIBUTION. The occurrence of sounds in the same phonetic environments. (See also **Complemetary Distribution**.)

OVERT PRESTIGE. Type of prestige attached to a particular variety by the community at large that defines how people should speak in order to gain status in the wider community.

P

PALATALS. Refers to sounds made with the tongue approximating the hard part of the roof of the mouth (i.e., the hard **palate**).

PALATALIZATION. A process wherein a sound takes on a palatal place of articulation, usually in **assimilation** to high or mid front vowels like [i] or [e].

PALATE. Bony roof of the mouth (also known as the *hard palate*), extending from the **alveolar ridge** to the **velum**.

PALATO-ALVEOLAR. Refers to sounds made in the area between the **alveolar ridge** and the hard **palate**.

PARADIGM. A set of grammatically related (i.e., **inflectional**) forms all stemming from a common root.

PARADIGM LEVELING. A type of morphological change in which irregular members of a **paradigm** become regularized through **analogy**.

PASSIVE. A form of the verb in which the grammatical subject is the semantic object of the action of the verb (e.g.,*The test was given yesterday* is a passive sentence).

PERFORMANCE. The observable use of language. The actualization of one's linguistic **competence**.

PERFORMATIVE VERBS. Verbs that can be used to perform the acts they name (e.g., in the sentence *I promise not to lie,* the verb *promise* is performative because it performs the action of promising).

PERIODIC WAVES. Sound waves that repeat themselves at regular intervals.

PHARYNX. The part of the oral tract above the **larynx** but behind the uvula. Commonly referred to as the *throat*.

PHONE. Speech sound.

PHONEME. A class of speech sounds identified by a native speaker as the same sound; a mental entity (or category) related to various **allophones** by phonological rules: "/t/ → [tʰ] / ___ stressed vowel," where /t/ is the **phoneme** and [tʰ] is an **allophone** of /t/.

PHONEMIC SOUND CHANGE. Sound change that results in the addition or loss of a phoneme in the phonological inventory of a language.

PHONETIC SOUND CHANGE. Change in the pronunciation of **allophones** which has no effect on the phonological inventory of the language.

PHONETICS. The study of speech sounds; how they are produced in the **vocal tract (articulatory phonetics)**, their physical properties (**acoustic phonetics**), and how they are perceived (**auditory phonetics**).

PHONOLOGICAL RULE. The description of a relationship between a **phoneme** and its **allophones** and the **conditioning environment** in which the **allophone** appears. (See also **Rule.**)

PHONOLOGY. The study of the sound system of a language; how the particular sounds contrast in each language to form an integrated system for encoding information and how such systems differ from one language to another.

PHONOTACTIC CONSTRAINTS. Restrictions on possible combinations of sounds (e.g., [pt] is not a possible English initial consonant cluster). (See also **Sound Substitution.**)

PHRASAL CATEGORY. A syntactic category whose members are composed of one or more words that form a phrase. One type of phrase is usually interchangeable with another phrase of the same category.

PHRASE STRUCTURE RULES. Rules that show the possible (i.e., grammatical) relationships between phrasal categories and the words or phrasal categories that they dominate (e.g., 'NP → Det N' says that the phrasal category *noun phrase* is composed of a **determiner** and a **noun**).

PHYSICAL CONTEXT. The type of **context** concerned with where the conversation takes place, what objects are present, and what actions are taking place.

PICTOGRAMS. Stylized drawings of concrete objects used as characters in certain writing systems to represent the idea of the object directly.

PIDGIN. A language developed by speakers in contact who otherwise share no common language.

PLACE OF ARTICULATION. Place in the **vocal tract** where the constriction for the production of a speech sound is made by the articulators (e.g., **alveolar**, where the tip of the tongue touches or approaches the **alveolar ridge**).

POLYGLOT. Refers to a person who speaks many languages.

POLYSYNTHETIC LANGUAGE. A type of language that attaches several affixes to a stem to indicate grammatical relationships. (See also **Analytic Languages.**)

POPULAR ETYMOLOGY. See **Folk Etymology.**

POSTPOSITION. A grammatical function word that follows the phrase with which it is associated in order to give information about grammatical relations. (See also **Prepositions.**)

PRAGMATICS. The study of how the meaning conveyed by a word or sentence depends on the context in which it is used (such as time, place, social relationship between speaker and hearer, and speaker's assumptions about the hearer's beliefs).

PREDICTABLE SOUNDS. Sounds that are in **complementary distribution** and thus predictable by **phonological rule**; allophones.

PREFIX. An affix that attaches to the beginning of a word.

PREPIDGIN JARGON. An extremely rudimentary and variable type of language formed in the earlier stages of **contact situations**. Under the appropriate conditions, a prepidgin jargon can crystallize into a **creole.**

PREPOSITIONS. A grammatical function word that precedes the phrase with which it is associated in order to give information about grammatical relations. (See also **Postposition.**)

PRESCRIPTIVE GRAMMAR. A set of rules designed to give instructions regarding the "correct" or "proper" way to speak or write.

PRESTIGE VARIETY. See **Standard Variety.**

PRINCIPLE OF COMPOSITIONALITY. See **Frege's Principle.**

PRODUCTIVE. Characteristic of a morpheme such that it is used to form new words.

PRODUCTIVITY. The ability to produce and understand an infinite number of linguistic terms that have never been expressed before and that may express novel ideas.

PRONOUNS. A closed lexical class of words that may stand in for a noun phrase or refer to some **noun** previously mentioned or assumed in the **discourse.**

PROPORTIONAL ANALOGY. A type of morphological change caused by the influence of one pair of morphologically related words on another. (See also **Analogical Change.**)

PSYCHOLINGUISTICS. The study of the interrelationship of language and the brain (i.e., cognitive structures) which encompasses the acquisition of language.

PULMONIC EGRESSIVE AIRSTREAM MECHANISM. Airstream mechanism that produces speech sounds by modifying the stream of air forced out of the lungs and passed through the oral and/or nasal cavities.

R

RAISING. A description of a type of sound change in which the vowel sounds become higher.

RAREFACTION. Physical phenomenon by which air molecules become less concentrated within a given space (i.e., pressure decreases).

RECENCY EFFECTS. A psycholinguistic phenomenon whereby word recognition or production occurs faster owing to recent exposure to that word.

RECURSION. Property of languages allowing for the repeated application of a rule, yielding infinitely long sentences or an infinite number of sentences (e.g., the sentence *I saw the dog that bit the cat that bit the mouse that bit the cheese*, etc.).

REDUCTIONS. Semantic change though time by which the set of appropriate contexts or referents for a word decreases (e.g., the word *hound* once referred to all breeds of dogs but now only refers to a specific breed).

REDUPLICATION. Process of forming new words either by doubling an entire word (total reduplication) or part of a word (partial reduplication).

REFERENT. The entity (idea, object, etc.) to which a word or linguistic expression relates. The referent to the word *table* is the actual table existing in the physical world.

REGIONAL DIALECT. Variety of a language defined by geography.

REGISTER TONE LANGUAGES. Tone languages having only register, or level, tones such as high, mid, and low.

REGULARITY HYPOTHESIS. Assumption that languages change in regular, recognizable ways.

REINFORCEMENT THEORY. Theory of child language acquisition saying that children learn to speak like adults because they are praised, rewarded, or otherwise reinforced when they use the right forms and are corrected when they use the wrong forms. (See also **Imitation Theory** and **Active Construction of a Grammar Theory**.)

RELATEDNESS HYPOTHESIS. Assumption that similarities among languages are due to a genetic relationship among them.

RELATIONAL OPPOSITES. Pairs of words that are opposites because they represent a symmetrical relationship (e.g., *doctor-patient, student-teacher*).

RESTRICTED ALLOPHONE. The **allophone** of a **phoneme** that appears in a more limited set of phonetic environments. (See also **Basic Allophones**.)

RETROFLEX. Sound produced by curling the tip of the tongue back behind the **alveolar ridge** usually to the top of the mouth, found in many languages of India.

RIGHT HEMISPHERE. The right half of the brain, which receives and controls nerve input from the left half of the body.

RIGHT-EAR ADVANTAGE. The phenomenon wherein a language stimulus received through the right ear is processed more quickly than if it were received through the left ear. Right-ear advantage is evidence that the brain's language centers are located in the **left hemisphere**.

ROOT MORPHEME. A content morpheme in a given word. Also called a *stem* or *base*.

RULE. A formal statement of an observed generalization about patterns in language, usually stating the input, output, and conditioning environment. (See also **Phonological Rules** and **Phrase Structure Rules**.)

S

SCALAR ANTONYMS. See **Gradable Pairs**.

SEMANTIC ASSOCIATION NETWORK. The relationships between various related words. Word recognition is thought to be faster when other members of an association network (i.e., semantically related words: *surgeon, artery*) are also provided in the **discourse**.

SEMANTICS. The study of meaning in language.

SHADOWING EXPERIMENTS. A type of language processing experiment used in psycholinguistics in which subjects are given the task of repeating aloud a text as soon as it is heard.

SHIFTS. A series of organized **diachronic** sound changes that occur when a group of similar sounds undergoes a phonological change that conditions further changes in another group of sounds.

SIBILANTS. Natural class of sounds marked by a high-pitched hissing sound quality. In English, the sibilants are [s], [z], [š], [ž], [č], [ǰ].

Signed Languages. Languages that use a visual mode to convey linguistic information, usually encoding this information in handshapes, directions of movement and orientation to the body, facial expression, etc.

Slang. Words or expressions used in informal settings, often to indicate membership in a particular social group (common vs. in-group).

Social Context. Context that involves the social relationship among speakers and hearers.

Social Dialect. Variety of a language defined by social factors such as age, religion, ethnicity, or socioeconomic status.

Sociolinguistics. The study of the interrelationships of language and social structure, of linguistic variation, and of attitudes toward language.

Sonorants. Sounds (usually voiced) produced with a relatively open passage of air flow. **Nasals, liquids, glides**, and vowels are all sonorants.

Sound Substitution. A process whereby sounds that already exist in a language are used to replace sounds that do not exist in the language when borrowing or trying to pronounce a foreign word (e.g., in English the final consonant sound in the last name of the composer Johann Sebastian Bach is commonly pronounced as a voiceless velar stop [k] as a substitute for the voiceless velar fricative [x]). (See also **Phonotactic Constraints**.)

Sound Symbolism. Phenomenon by which certain sounds are evocative of a particular meaning (e.g., the sound [fl-] in *flee, fly, flit* is supposed to be indicative of a quick, flying motion).

Source-Filter Theory. Theory of speech production claiming that there are two elements in the production of speech sounds. The first, the source, involves the production of a sound wave caused by vibration of the **vocal folds** or noise caused by air passing through the open **glottis**. The second, the filter, enhances certain frequencies in the source wave and damps (deemphasizes) others by altering the shape of the **vocal tract**.

Spectrogram. A three-dimensional representation in which the vertical axis represents frequency, the horizontal axis represents time, and the darkness of shading represents amplitude.

Spectrograph. Equipment that generates **spectrograms** from speech input.

Speech. The use of the vocal apparatus to produce strings of sounds, encoded with linguistic information, for the purpose of communication.

Speech Act. A term describing the use of speech with a focus upon the speakers' intentions and the possible or intended effects upon the hearers.

Speech Community. A group of people speaking the same dialect, usually defined by factors such as geographical distribution, age, gender, and socioeconomic class.

Speech Recognition. Use of computers to transform spoken language into written language through an analysis of the acoustic signal and comparison with the expected acoustic form of words in the **lexicon**.

Speech Styles. The various ways of speaking marked by degrees of formality (i.e., formal vs. informal, casual vs. careful).

Speech synthesis. The use of computers and sound-generating devices for the creation of speech sounds that approximate or duplicate the acoustic characteristics of actual speech.

Split-brain Patients. Individuals whose **corpus callosum** has been surgically disconnected (a procedure once commonly used in the treatment of severe epilepsy). (See also **Left Hemisphere** and **Right-Ear Advantage**).

Standard Variety. The variety of a language used by political leaders, the media, and speakers of higher socioeconomic classes. The variety taught in schools. The variety of a language associated with prestige.

Static Palatography. Experimental method that displays the contact resulting from a single **articulatory gesture** between the tongue and the hard palate at the moment of contact.

Stative Adjectives. Adjectives denoting more or less permanent qualities (e.g., *blue, plastic, tall*).

Stops. See **Oral stops** and **Nasals**.

Stress. Property of syllables; the increased duration and loudness of a syllable compared to other syllables in the same word. (See **Suprasegmental Features**.)

Structural Ambiguity. A characteristic of phrases that have more than one possible constituent structure and therefore more than one semantic interpretation (e.g., *Kim likes chocolate pie and cake* means either that Kim likes chocolate pie and chocolate cake or that Kim likes chocolate pie and any type of cake). (See also **Lexical Ambiguity**.)

Style Shifting. Process of automatically adjusting from one speech style to another.

SUBJUNCTIVE. A verbal mood indicating vagueness, tentativeness, or uncertainty on the part of the speaker or actor.

SUBSTRATAL INFLUENCE. A type of **transfer** from the native language of a speaker or group of speakers learning a new language, that typically compensates for those features not acquired in the **target language** in language acquisition/language contact situations (e.g., Celtic influence on English in Scotland and Ireland).

SUBSTRATE LANGUAGES. The native languages of speakers in a **contact situation**; associated with the politically and economically subordinate group. (See also **Adstrate Languages** and **Superstrate Language**.)

SUFFIX. An **affix** that attaches to the end of a stem. In English suffixes may be **inflectional** or **derivational**.

SUPERSTRATAL INFLUENCE. A type of **transfer** from the **target language** into the native language of speakers in a contact situation (e.g., Turkish influence on Greek in Asia Minor).

SUPERSTRATE LANGUAGE. The **target language** in a language contact situation; the language associated with the politically and economically dominant group. (See also **Adstrate Languages** and **Substrate Languages**.)

SUPPLETION. A relationship between forms of a word wherein one form cannot be phonologically or morphologically derived from the other (e.g., most English past tenses are formed by suffixing [-əd], but some words have an irregular form (a *suppletive* form) (e.g., the past tense of *go* is not *goed* but *went*).

SUPRASEGMENTAL FEATURES. Phonetic (and phonological) features of words and sounds that can range over several segments (e.g., **tone**, **length**, and **stress** are all types of suprasegmentals).

SURFACE STRUCTURE. The form that a sound, word, or sentence has after one or more transformations has been applied.

SYLLABARY. The total set of characters representing the syllables of a **syllabic writing system**.

SYLLABIC CONSONANT. A consonant that is a **syllable nucleus** and takes on the function of the vowel in that particular syllable (e.g., in the word *bottle* [baɾl̩], the sound [l̩] is syllabic and constitutes the second syllable).

SYLLABIC WRITING SYSTEMS. Writing systems in which each symbol represents a syllable. (See also **Syllabary**.)

SYLLABLE NUCLEUS. The core element of the syllable, carrying **stress**, **length**, and pitch information (**tone**). It usually consists of a vowel sound or **syllabic consonant**.

SYLVIAN FISSURE. The fissure in the brain separating the temporal lobe from the frontal lobe.

SYNCHRONIC ANALYSIS. Analysis of a language at a particular point in time. (See also **Diachronic Analysis**.)

SYNONYMS. Two or more words with the same **referent** or semantic interpretation (e.g., *sofa* and *couch* both refer to the same real-world object).

SYNTACTIC FRAMES. Position in which a word occurs relative to other classes of words in the same phrase (e.g., 'Determiner _____' is a syntactic frame for nouns indicating that nouns follow **determiners**). (See also **Morphological Frames**).

SYNTAX. The study of the way in which sentences are constructed from smaller units called **constituents**; how sentences are related to each other. (See also **Phrase Structure Rules**.)

SYNTHETIC LANGUAGES. Languages in which affixes are attached to other morphemes, so that a word may be made up of several meaningful elements.

T

TARGET LANGUAGE. See **Superstrate Language**.

TECHNICAL JARGON. Language specialized to a particular job, hobby, sport, etc. (e.g., words like *phoneme, allophone,* and *syllable nucleus* are all technical jargon).

TELEGRAPHIC STAGE. A phase during child language acquisition in which children use utterances composed primarily of content words (e.g., *give bear, Daddy read,* etc.).

TENSE VOWELS. Vowels whose positions are farthest from the mid-central position of the vowel space. They are usually located at the outer edges (peripherals) of the **vowel space** (e.g., [i], [e], [o], and [u] are the tense vowels in English). (See also **Lax Vowels**.)

TEXT GENERATION. Use of computers to create sentences from abstract knowledge and to respond to humans using human language (whether spoken or written).

TEXT UNDERSTANDING. Use of computers to analyze sentences syntactically.

TONE. Pitch at which the syllables of a word are pronounced; can make a difference in meaning. (See also **Register Tone Languages, Contour Tone Languages, Suprasegmental Features**.)

TRACHEA. The windpipe; the tube between the **larynx** and the lungs through which air travels.

TRANSFER. The process of carrying over features from one language into another in language contact or second language acquisition situations.

TRANSFORMATION. An operation that takes a sequence of objects (words, phrases, etc.) and outputs them in a different sequence. A transformation shows the relationship between two levels of a **derivation**. (See also **Deep Structure** and **Surface Structure**.)

TRANSITIVE VERBS. Verbs that take a noun phrase direct object (e.g., in the sentence *Robin eats pretzels, eat* is a transitive verb that takes the direct object *pretzel*).

TRANSLUCENT SIGNS. Gestures in a sign language that have arbitrary meaning, but that may be interpreted based upon the gesture's resemblance to the **referent**. They are less **iconic** than **transparent signs**, but more iconic than **opaque signs**.

TRANSPARENT SIGNS. Gestures in a sign language whose meaning is derivable from the form of the gesture. These signs are the least **arbitrary** and the most **iconic**. (See also **Translucent Signs** and **Opaque Signs**.)

TRUE ALPHABET. Type of writing system in which both vowels and consonants are represented.

TRUTH CONDITIONS. The facts that must be true in order for a statement to be interpreted as true (e.g., *Bill Clinton is the president* is a true statement only if there is a person named Bill Clinton and he is the president).

U

UMLAUT. Type of assimilation whereby a vowel sound becomes more like the vowel in the following syllable.

UNCONDITIONED SOUND CHANGE. Sound change that occurs without influence from neighboring sounds.

UNDEREXTENSION. Application of a word to a smaller set of objects than is appropriate for mature adult speech or the usual definition of the word (e.g., using the term *mammal* to refer only to dogs and cats but not to whales).

V

VARIETY. Any form of language characterized by systematic features. Varieties can range from **idiolects** to **dialects** to distinct languages.

VELAR. Sounds produced when the back of the tongue is raised toward the **velum** as the **place of articulation**.

VELUM. Soft part of the roof of the mouth behind the hard palate (also known as the *soft palate*). When the velum is raised, the passage between the **pharynx** (throat) and the nasal cavity is closed. When it is lowered, air escapes from the nose and a **nasal** sound is produced.

VISUAL CORTEX. Area of the brain located at the lower back of each hemisphere responsible for receiving and interpreting visual stimuli and said to store pictoral images.

VOCAL FOLDS. Folds of muscle in the **larynx**. (See also **Voicing** and **Glottis**.)

VOCAL TRACT. The entire air passage above the **larynx**, consisting of the **pharynx**, oral cavity, and nasal cavity.

VOICE ONSET TIME. The amount of time (usually in milliseconds) from the release of a stop closure to the vibration of the **vocal folds** (regular **voicing**).

VOICING. Vibration of the approximated **vocal folds** caused by air passing through them. When the vocal folds vibrate, a *voiced* sound is produced; when the vocal folds do not vibrate, a *voiceless* sound is produced.

VOWEL SPACE. Range of possible vowel sounds of a language, from the high front vowel to the high back vowel. Languages and dialects choose a subset of the vowel space but do not exploit all possibilities.

W

WAVE THEORY. Theory describing the gradual spread of change throughout a dialect, language, or group of languages, similar to a wave expanding on the surface of a pond from the point where a pebble (i.e., the source of the change) has been tossed in.

WERNICKE'S APHASIA. A speech disorder, commonly associated with brain damage to **Wernicke's area**. The speech of Wernicke's aphasics is usually characterized by being apparently grammatical but lacking in meaning.

WERNICKE'S AREA. A region of the brain found in the **left hemisphere** at or around the posterior end of the **Sylvian fissure**.

WHORF HYPOTHESIS. A hypothesis that the worldview of a speech community is subtly conditioned by the structure of its language.

Language Index

Index